W9-ARK-410

Board Basics® 3

An Enhancement to MKSAP®

Your Last Stop before the Boards

For the third consecutive edition of MKSAP, we bring you Board Basics, the only publication that compiles the essential facts and strategies for passing the Internal Medicine Certification and Maintenance of Certification (MOC) Exam into one book and digital application. (You can access the app at http://mksap.acponline.org/16/apps.) We are confident that this volume will meet your needs. A total of 84% of surveyed Board Basics 2 users told us that Board Basics 2 effectively helped them prepare for the Certification or MOC exams. As many as 97% found this resource to be user-friendly and three quarters said they would recommend it to a colleague.

How to Use Board Basics 3

The goal of this enhancement to MKSAP 16 is to prepare you for the Boards after you have completed a systematic review of MKSAP 16 and its more than 1200 multiple-choice questions. Once again, we have combed through volumes to produce a concise compilation of only the information that you will most likely see in the exam.

Our intention has not been to create a concise guide to patient care but to develop an exam preparation tool to help you quickly recognize the most likely answers on a multiple-choice exam. Drug dosages are not included since they are rarely, if ever, tested. You will also see many sections where information has been omitted because the omitted material is difficult to test or is otherwise unlikely to appear on the exam.

Broad differential diagnoses are not provided for most problems. Instead, Board Basics focuses on the entities that have the highest probability of appearing on the exam as the "correct answers." Critical points that appear on the exam are often presented here in isolation, stripped of context that is not relevant to answering a multiple-choice question. If you review these points shortly before your exam, you will have the best chance of remembering what you need to know to do well. Knowing that most Board questions are prefaced with the words "most likely," we have tried to be very directive, skipping important steps in the patient evaluation. When you see the words "select" or "choose," think in terms of selecting or choosing a particular answer, not an intervention in the practice of medicine. Remember that board Basics is *not* a patient care resource.

Content Organization

Abbreviations, spelled out in a convenient list at the back of the book, are used frequently to increase reading efficiency.

Content is organized by topic and in consistent categories, such as Prevention, Screening, Diagnosis, and Therapy. Special components have been designed to enhance learning and recall. Look for:

- *Don't Be Tricked*: Incorrect answers that may masquerade as correct choices.
- *Test Yourself*: Abbreviated case histories and answers found in Board exam questions.
- *Study Tables*: Key concepts to prepare you for specific types of questions.
- *Yellow highlighting*: We applied our own "marker" to call your attention to important phrases.

Why This Text Makes Sense

For Board Basics 3, MKSAP 16 authors reviewed the latest literature and produced a concise syllabus and 1200-plus Board-like multiple-choice questions. Next, the content was turned over to 13 carefully selected chief residents, fellows, instructors, and professors of medicine who have expertise in Board preparation and the subspecialties of internal medicine. These physicians strained the essential points from MKSAP 16 and added their insights to update the content of Board Basics. Board Basics 3 editors also added information requested by readers of the second edition. Insights gleaned from ACP's Internal Medicine In-Training Examination were also added.

Board Basics includes core information to supplement MKSAP 16, information that is likely testable material for board examinations. Joining me in this effort were Associate Editors Edward R. Bollard, MD, DDS, FACP, of the Penn State College of Medicine, and Joyce E. Wipf, MD, FACP, of the University of Washington.

Patrick Alguire, MD, FACP, Senior Vice President of the Medical Education Division of the American College of Physicians and Editor-in-Chief of MKSAP 16, pulled all of the content together, eliminating overlap and excessive material to focus the text as sharply as possible. The end product is what you have in your hands—the best Board prep tool that you will find anywhere. We hope you enjoy it and benefit from your study. Best wishes on your exam.

Douglas S. Paauw, MD, MACP
Editor
Board Basics

Board Basics 3

Jennifer Wright, MD[1]
Acting Instructor
Department of Medicine
University of Washington
Seattle, Washington

Nathan J. Yeasted, MD[1]
Fellow, Division of Gastroenterology and Hepatology
Penn State College of Medicine
Milton S. Hershey Medical Center
Hershey, Pennsylvania

Board Basics ACP Editorial Staff

Linnea Donnarumma[1], Assistant Editor
Sean McKinney[1], Director, Self-Assessment Programs
Margaret Wells[1], Managing Editor
Becky Krumm[1], Senior Staff Editor
Ellen McDonald, PhD[1], Senior Staff Editor
Katie Idell[1], Senior Staff Editor
Randy Hendrickson[1], Production Administrator/Editor
Megan Zborowski[1], Staff Editor
John Haefele[1], Assistant Editor

ACP Principal Staff

Patrick C. Alguire, MD, FACP[1]
Senior Vice President, Medical Education

D. Theresa Kanya, MBA[1]
Vice President, Medical Education

Sean McKinney[1]
Director, Self-Assessment Programs

Margaret Wells[1]
Managing Editor

Valerie Dangovetsky[1]
Program Administrator

Becky Krumm[1]
Senior Staff Editor

Ellen McDonald, PhD[1]
Senior Staff Editor

Katie Idell[1]
Senior Staff Editor

Randy Hendrickson[1]
Production Administrator/Editor

Megan Zborowski[1]
Staff Editor

Linnea Donnarumma[1]
Assistant Editor

John Haefele[1]
Assistant Editor

Developed by the American College of Physicians

1. Has no relationships with any entity producing, marketing, re-selling, or distributing health care goods or services consumed by, or used on, patients.

2. Has disclosed relationships with entities producing, marketing, re-selling, or distributing health care goods or services consumed by, or used on, patients. See below.

Conflicts of Interest

The following committee members, reviewers, and ACP staff members have disclosed relationships with commercial companies:

Brian S. Porter, MD
Employment
University of Washington

Joyce E. Wipf, MD, FACP
Royalties
UpToDate

Acknowledgments

The American College of Physicians (ACP) gratefully acknowledges the special contributions to the development and production of the 16th edition of the Medical Knowledge Self-Assessment Program® (MKSAP® 16) made by the following people:

Graphic Services: Michael Ripca (Technical Administrator/Graphic Designer) and Willie-Fetchko Graphic Design (Graphic Designer).

Production/Systems: Dan Hoffmann (Director, Web Services & Systems Development), Neil Kohl (Senior Architect), and Scott Hurd (Senior Systems Analyst/Developer).

MKSAP 16 Digital: Under the direction of Steven Spadt, Vice President, ACP Digital Products & Services, the digital version of MKSAP 16 was developed within the ACP's Digital Product Development Department, led by Brian Sweigard (Director). Other members of the team included Sean O'Donnell (Senior Architect), Dan Barron (Senior Systems Analyst/Developer), Chris Forrest (Senior Software Developer/Design Lead), Jon Laing (Senior Web Application Developer), Brad Lord (Senior Web Developer), John McKnight (Senior Web Developer), and Nate Pershall (Senior Web Developer).

The College also wishes to acknowledge that many other persons, too numerous to mention, have contributed to the production of this program. Without their dedicated efforts, this program would not have been possible.

Introducing the MKSAP Resource Site (mksap.acponline.org)

The MKSAP Resource Site (mksap.acponline.org) is a continually updated site that provides links to MKSAP 16 online answer sheets for print subscribers; access to MKSAP 16 Digital, Board Basics® 3, and MKSAP 16 Updates; the latest details on Continuing Medical Education (CME) and Maintenance of Certification (MOC) in the United States, Canada, and Australia; errata; and other new information.

Disclosure Policy

It is the policy of the American College of Physicians (ACP) to ensure balance, independence, objectivity, and scientific rigor in all of its educational activities. To this end, and consistent with the policies of the ACP and the Accreditation Council for Continuing Medical Education (ACCME), contributors to all ACP continuing medical education activities are required to disclose all relevant financial relationships with any entity producing, marketing, re-selling, or distributing health care goods or services consumed by, or used on, patients. Contributors are required to use generic names in the discussion of therapeutic options and are required to identify any unapproved, off-label, or investigative use of commercial products or devices. Where a trade name is used, all available trade names for the same product type are also included. If trade-name products manufactured by companies with whom contributors have relationships are discussed, contributors are asked to provide evidence-based citations in support of the discussion. The information is reviewed by the committee responsible for producing this text. If necessary, adjustments to topics or contributors' roles in content development are made to balance the discussion. Further, all readers of this text are asked to evaluate the content for evidence of commercial bias and send any relevant comments to mksap_editors@acponline.org so that future decisions about content and contributors can be made in light of this information.

Resolution of Conflicts

To resolve all conflicts of interest and influences of vested interests, the ACP precluded members of the content-creation committee from deciding on any content issues that involved generic or trade-name products associated with proprietary entities with which these committee members had relationships. In addition, content was based on best evidence and updated clinical care guidelines, when such evidence and guidelines were available. Contributors' disclosure information can be found with the list of contributors' names and those of ACP principal staff listed in the beginning of this book.

Educational Disclaimer

The editors and publisher of MKSAP 16 recognize that the development of new material offers many opportunities for error. Despite our best efforts, some errors may persist in print. Drug dosage schedules are, we believe, accurate and in accordance with current standards. Readers are advised, however, to ensure that the recommended dosages in MKSAP 16 concur with the information provided in the product information material. This is especially important in cases of new, infrequently used, or highly toxic drugs. Application of the information in MKSAP 16 remains the professional responsibility of the practitioner.

The primary purpose of MKSAP 16 is educational. Information presented, as well as publications, technologies, products, and/or services discussed, is intended to inform subscribers about the knowledge, techniques, and experiences of the contributors. A diversity of professional opinion exists, and the views of the contributors are their own and not those of the ACP. Inclusion of any material in the program does not constitute endorsement or recommendation by the ACP. The ACP does not warrant the safety, reliability, accuracy, completeness, or usefulness of and disclaims any and all liability for damages and claims that may result from the use of information, publications, technologies, products, and/or services discussed in this program.

Publisher's Information

Copyright © 2012 American College of Physicians.
All rights reserved.

This publication is protected by copyright. No part of this publication may be reproduced, stored in a retrieval system, or transmitted in any form or by any means, electronic or mechanical, including photocopy, without the express consent of the ACP.

Unauthorized Use of This Book Is Against the Law

Unauthorized reproduction of this publication is unlawful. The ACP prohibits reproduction of this publication or any of its parts in any form either for individual use or for distribution.

The ACP will consider granting an individual permission to reproduce only limited portions of this publication for his or her own exclusive use. Send requests in writing to MKSAP® Permissions, American College of Physicians, 190 N. Independence Mall West, Philadelphia, PA 19106-1572, or email your request to mksap_editors@acponline.org.

MKSAP 16 ISBN: 978-1-938245-00-8
(Board Basics 3) ISBN: 978-1-938245-13-8

Printed in the United States of America.

For order information in the U.S. or Canada call 800-523-1546, extension 2600. All other countries call 215-351-2600. Fax inquiries to 215-351-2799 or email to custserv@acponline.org.

Errata

Errata for MKSAP 16 will be available through the MKSAP Resource Site at mksap.acponline.org as new information becomes known to the editors.

Table of Contents

Gastroenterology and Hepatology

General Internal Medicine

Hematology

Psychiatry

Pulmonary and Critical Care Medicine

Rheumatology

Women's Health

Allergy

Allergic Rhinitis

Diagnosis

Rhinitis is an inflammation of the nasal mucosal membranes that causes rhinorrhea, nasal itching, sneezing, nasal congestion, and postnasal drainage.

Allergic rhinitis can be seasonal or perennial. Diagnosis of allergic rhinitis is usually made by history and confirmed with empiric treatment. If empiric treatment fails, diagnostic allergy testing may be appropriate to guide allergen avoidance or immunotherapy. In this setting, allergy skin testing is preferred to in vitro specific IgE antibody assay (or RAST).

Other causes of rhinitis include acute viral infections, pregnancy, hypothyroidism, atrophic rhinitis (occurring in elderly patients), α-blockers, mechanical obstruction (nasal septal deviation, nasal polyps), and rhinitis medicamentosa. Chronic nonallergic rhinitis (vasomotor rhinitis) is described as a syndrome of sneezing, rhinorrhea, congestion, or postnasal discharge in the absence of an identified cause. Chronic nonallergic rhinitis generally has a later age of onset than allergic rhinitis, with perennial symptoms that are often exacerbated by weather and irritants rather than allergens.

In allergic rhinitis, the nasal mucosa is edematous and pale. Select CT for cases of persistent or refractory rhinitis.

STUDY TABLE: Mimics of Allergic Rhinitis	
Look for...	Diagnose...
Systemic illness with saddle nose deformity, nasal ulceration, or chronic sinusitis	Granulomatosis with polyarteritis (Wegener granulomatosis)
Young person, nasal polyposis, chronic sinusitis, malnourishment, infertility, and chronic or recurrent bronchitis	Cystic fibrosis
Nonseasonal rhinitis with negative skin tests	Chronic nonallergic rhinitis (vasomotor rhinitis)
Refractory congestion after chronic use of topical nasal decongestants	Rhinitis medicamentosa
Nasal congestion in the last 6 or more weeks of pregnancy	Pregnancy rhinitis
Rhinitis, nasal polyps, asthma, and aspirin intolerance (respiratory symptoms)	Aspirin sensitivity (triad asthma or Samter syndrome)

Therapy

Therapy includes the select removal of pets, animals, and carpet; allergy encasements for bedding; and small-particle filters for air conditioning. Most patients will require the addition of pharmacotherapy or immunotherapy. Intranasal corticosteroids are used as first-line therapy. The following can be used as second-line agents: intranasal antihistamines, oral combination antihistamines/decongestants, oral montelukast, or intranasal cromolyn. Ipratropium bromide is effective for severe rhinorrhea.

Choose skin testing and allergen immunotherapy if symptoms are not well controlled by intranasal corticosteroids with supplemental antihistamines or decongestants.

The most consistently effective treatments for chronic nonallergic rhinitis are topical intranasal corticosteroids, topical intranasal antihistamines, and topical ipratropium bromide. Patients with chronic rhinitis, nasal polyps, asthma, and aspirin intolerance may improve following aspirin desensitization.

◆ DON'T BE TRICKED

- Do not select antibiotics for URI-related rhinitis, because such therapy does not reduce symptoms compared with placebo but significantly increases the risk of adverse events.
- Do not refer patients with allergic rhinitis for skin testing/immunotherapy without a trial of empiric therapy.

❖ Test Yourself

For the past 2 months, a 30-year-old man has had nasal congestion that began with rhinorrhea, coughing, and sore throat. His only medication is oxymetazoline nasal spray BID.

ANSWER: The diagnosis is rhinitis medicamentosa. Stop the topical decongestant and select a short course of prednisone or intranasal corticosteroid.

Urticaria

Diagnosis

The hallmark of urticaria (hives) is the wheal, a superficial itchy swelling of the skin. Wheals involving the skin around the mouth are considered an emergency, requiring careful observation and investigation for airway obstruction. Concomitant angioedema and urticaria occur in 40% of patients, with another 40% experiencing urticaria alone and 20% developing angioedema but no urticaria.

Acute urticaria lasts less than 24 hours but may recur. β-Lactams, sulfonamides, NSAIDs, opioids, insect stings, contrast dyes, latex (including condoms), nuts, fish, and eggs are common causes. Urticaria can also be initiated by pressure, cold, heat, vibration, water, or sunlight. Chronic urticaria is defined as having symptoms most days for >6 weeks.

Evaluate most patients with chronic urticaria with a CBC, ESR or CRP, and TSH (higher incidence of hypothyroidism). Lesions persisting >24 hours with purpura/ecchymoses upon resolution are likely due to urticarial vasculitis. In this situation, definitive diagnosis is made by skin biopsy. If urticaria is associated with a travel history and prominent eosinophilia, select parasitic infection.

◆ DON'T BE TRICKED

- Do not select ANA testing for acute or chronic urticaria.

STUDY TABLE: Differential Diagnosis of Urticaria	
If you see this...	Select this...
↑ESR, ↑CRP, lesions persisting >24 hours	Vasculitic urticaria; perform skin biopsy and obtain serum complement levels, hepatitis B and C serology, cryoglobulins, and serum protein electrophoresis.
Fever, adenopathy, arthralgias, and antigen or drug exposure	Serum sickness; measure IgE level (elevated).
Features of anaphylaxis, obvious allergen exposure	Immediate hypersensitivity reaction; treat emergently with epinephrine, corticosteroids, and antihistamines.
Marked eosinophilia	Parasitic infection, possibly strongyloidiasis, filariasis, or trichinosis (especially with periorbital edema).

Therapy

Avoid aspirin and other NSAIDs. Select nonsedating antihistamines as first-line therapy. If no response is seen, add an H_2-blocker (cimetidine, ranitidine), although evidence for effectiveness is mixed. Doxepin blocks H_1, H_2, and serotonin receptors and is often effective. Short-term oral corticosteroids are indicated in very symptomatic patients with acute urticaria. Patients who have chronic autoimmune urticaria may require methotrexate, azathioprine, or cyclosporine.

◆ DON'T BE TRICKED

- Systemic and topical corticosteroids are not beneficial for patients with chronic urticaria.
- Measurement of C1 inhibitor levels is not indicated in patients with urticaria, because deficiency of C1 inhibitor is associated with angioedema, not with hives.

❖ Test Yourself

A 31-year-old man has a 2-week history of hives. Individual lesions persist for less than 24 hours and are not worsened by cold, sunlight, or pressure. He has been taking diphenhydramine without relief.

ANSWER: The diagnosis is acute urticaria. Additional diagnostic studies are not indicated. Add an H_2 blocker.

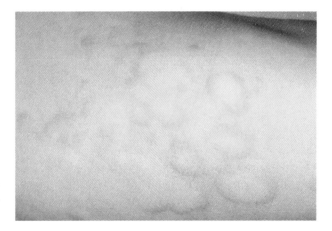

Urticaria: Urticaria is characterized by small white, pink, or flesh-colored pruritic papules.

Angioedema

Diagnosis

Angioedema is characterized by a sudden, temporary edema of a localized area of skin or mucosa, usually the lips, face, hands, feet, penis, or scrotum. Abdominal pain may be present owing to bowel wall edema.

Mast cell–mediated angioedema is often associated with urticaria, bronchospasm, or hypotension. This can be due to allergic reaction (peanuts, shrimp, latex, or insect stings) or to direct mast cell stimulation (NSAIDs, radiocontrast media, or opiates).

Bradykinin-mediated angioedema is NOT associated with urticaria. In the setting of angioedema without urticaria, consider a limited differential diagnosis.

STUDY TABLE: Differential Diagnosis of Bradykinin-Mediated Angioedema		
Condition	**Historical Clues/Disease Associations**	**Laboratory Studies**
Hereditary angioedema	Family history of angioedema	Low C1 inhibitor and C4 levels
Acquired C1 inhibitor deficiency	Lymphoma, MGUS, or SLE	Low C1q levels (in addition to low C4 and C1 inhibitor levels)
ACE inhibitor effect	Medication history	Low C1 inhibitor and C4 levels

◆ DON'T BE TRICKED

- In patients with urticaria and angioedema, diagnose food or drug allergy, food additive sensitivity, or urticarial vasculitis. Do not diagnose HAE.

Therapy

Select epinephrine, antihistamines, and corticosteroids for acute episodes of mast cell–mediated (allergic) angioedema with airway compromise or hypotension. Epinephrine is effective in racemic nebulized form or by subcutaneous or IM injections. Patients should carry an epinephrine autoinjector. Use antihistamines and corticosteroids alone in cases of allergic angioedema that is not part of an anaphylaxis syndrome (absent airway compromise or hemodynamic instability).

Select IV C1 inhibitor concentrate for acute episodes of bradykinin-mediated angioedema (hereditary or acquired angioedema); use FFP in an emergency. For long-term management of HAE, select danazol and stanozolol to elevate hepatic synthesis of C1 esterase inhibitor protein.

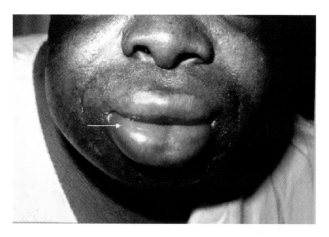

Angioedema: Angioedema differs from urticaria in that it covers a larger surface area and involves the dermis and subcutaneous tissues.

Anaphylaxis

Diagnosis

Anaphylaxis is a life-threatening syndrome caused by the release of mediators from mast cells and basophils triggered by an IgE-allergen interaction (termed an *anaphylactic reaction*) or by a non–antibody-antigen mechanism (termed an *anaphylactoid reaction*). The most common causes are peanut/nut ingestion, insect stings, latex, and medications (penicillin, NSAIDs, and aspirin). Flushing, urticaria, conjunctival pruritus, bronchospasm, nausea, and vomiting usually develop within 30 minutes to 1 hour if the antigen was injected or up to 2 hours if ingested. Anaphylactic shock is caused by severe hypovolemia (fluid shifts owing to increased vascular permeability) and vasodilatation. Shock may occur without prominent skin manifestations or a history of exposure; therefore, anaphylaxis is part of the differential diagnosis for patients who present with shock and no obvious cause. The diagnosis of anaphylaxis is made clinically, but elevated urine and serum histamine and plasma tryptase concentrations are supportive. Death occurs from refractory bronchospasm, respiratory failure with upper airway obstruction, and cardiovascular collapse.

Therapy

Epinephrine is first-line therapy even if the only presenting signs are hives or pruritus. Corticosteroid therapy prevents late-onset reactions. Use inhaled bronchodilators for bronchospasm and IV saline for shock or hypotension. Treat refractory hypotension with repeated doses of epinephrine or a continuous epinephrine infusion. Anaphylaxis may progress over 12 hours and requires observation for late recurrence (biphasic anaphylaxis). β-Blockers may blunt the effect of epinephrine, but epinephrine remains the drug of first choice; reserve glucagon for epinephrine-refractory anaphylaxis. Patients with diffuse rash or anaphylaxis from hymenoptera sting (bee, yellow jacket, and wasp) should undergo venom skin testing and immunotherapy.

◆ **DON'T BE TRICKED**

- Don't confuse SC with IV dosages of epinephrine. IM or SC epinephrine (0.3-0.5 mg of 1:1000) is first-line treatment for classic anaphylaxis. IV epinephrine (1:10,000) is reserved for anaphylactic shock or refractory symptoms.

❖ Test Yourself

A 25-year-old woman has shortness of breath and wheezing after a bee sting 1 hour ago. Her blood pressure is 80/50 mm Hg and heart rate is 110/min.

ANSWER: Treat anaphylaxis with epinephrine and IV fluids. Observe for at least 12 hours. Discharge with self-administered epinephrine.

Also look for anaphylaxis during surgery or anaphylaxis in a woman during coitus and consider latex allergy.

Food Allergy

Diagnosis

Food allergies are immunologically mediated and should be distinguished from food intolerance (e.g., lactose or monosodium glutamate intolerance, pancreatic insufficiency). Clinical effects of food allergy develop within 2 hours of ingestion and include rash, GI distress, pruritus, and edema of the oral mucosa (oral allergy syndrome), or anaphylaxis. Eight allergens are responsible for 90% of all food allergies (tree nuts, eggs, milk, peanuts, shellfish, wheat, fish, and soy).

The diagnosis of food allergy or oral allergy syndrome is made by history and elimination diet or food challenge. Skin testing or IgE immunoassays (RAST) can be useful.

Therapy

Patients should avoid culprit foods. Prescribe an epinephrine autoinjector for patients with systemic symptoms.

Drug Allergy

Diagnosis

Immediate drug reactions (type I reactions) are usually IgE-mediated hypersensitivity reactions and cause symptoms of anaphylaxis within minutes to hours. Commonly implicated drugs are β-lactams, neuromuscular blocking agents, and platinum-containing chemotherapies. Delayed drug reactions (type II-IV) typically present several days to months after treatment. Typical presentations include cytopenias (type II); vasculitis or serum sickness (type III); or rash, fever, and multiorgan involvement (type IV). Common causes include β-lactams, sulfa drugs, anticonvulsants, allopurinol, and abacavir. Radiocontrast agents, opiates, and NSAIDs cause a non–IgE-mediated degranulation of mast cells.

Penicillin is the most common self-reported medication allergy. Penicillin or one of its analogues should be avoided if the patient has a history of anaphylactic symptoms. If penicillin or one of its analogues must be used (treatment of neurosyphilis) in a patient with a penicillin allergy, choose skin testing, which identifies 95% of patients at risk for immediate reaction; do not select RAST or ELISA.

IgE-mediated cephalosporin reaction occurs in 2% of patients who are allergic to penicillin. Cephalosporins and carbapenems should be avoided in those with positive skin test for penicillin or convincing history of anaphylactic penicillin allergy.

Antibiotic therapy for syphilis may precipitate the Jarisch-Herxheimer reaction, characterized by fever, headache, myalgia, rash, and hypotension. This reaction, related to dying spirochetes releasing endotoxin, begins within 2 hours of treatment, resolves by 48 hours, and is particularly common in pregnant women. Management is supportive. Continue antibiotic therapy.

STUDY TABLE: Common Drug-Mediated Skin Eruptions

Type	Description
AGEP	Acute onset of widespread pustules, fever, leukocytosis, and possibly eosinophilia. AGEP is usually self-limiting and clears without residual skin changes approximately 2 weeks after drug cessation.
DRESS (also known as hypersensitivity syndrome)	Acute onset of generalized papular eruption, facial edema, fever, arthralgia, and generalized lymphadenopathy, elevated serum aminotransferase levels, eosinophilia, and lymphocytosis.
Erythema multiforme, Stevens-Johnson syndrome (SJS), TEN	Spectrum ranges from classic target lesions (erythema multiforme), to involvement of mucous membranes with systemic symptoms (SJS), to a life-threatening loss of epidermis (TEN). SJS involves less than 10%, SJS/TEN overlap involves 10% to 30%, and TEN involves greater than 30% detachment.

(Continued on next page)

STUDY TABLE: Common Drug-Mediated Skin Eruptions (*continued*)

Type	Description
Erythema nodosum (EN)	Tender subcutaneous nodules on lower leg. The eruption is often preceded by a prodrome of fever, malaise, and/or arthralgia. Causes of EN fall into three broad categories: infections, drugs, and systemic diseases (usually inflammatory disorders).
Exfoliative and erythrodermic	Widespread generalized redness and scaling reaction.
Fixed drug eruption	Discrete, often round or oval lesions that recur in exactly the same spot when rechallenged with the drug.
Maculopapular and morbilliform (small discrete papules)	Most common type of drug reaction. Symmetric distribution, usually truncal, hardly ever on palms or soles; associated with fever and pruritus.
Photosensitive skin reaction	Phototoxic reaction consists of severe sunburn after drug exposure (tetracycline). Photoallergic reaction presents as a rash after days or months of use (sulfonamides).
Red man syndrome	Body flushing, hypotension, and muscle pain associated with vancomycin and ciprofloxacin. This is not an allergic reaction.
Urticarial	Second most common drug-reaction type, with or without angioedema.

The most common drugs causing skin eruptions are antibiotics (penicillins and sulfa drugs) and anticonvulsants (phenytoin and carbamazepine).

The appearance of a maculopapular rash is associated with the use of ampicillin in EBV and CMV infections or underlying acute lymphoblastic leukemia. Duration of the rash is independent of whether the drug is continued. Subsequent reactions on re-exposure to the drug are not a risk after resolution of the underlying medical condition.

Hypersensitivity is the most common cause of drug fever, and fever may be the only manifestation. Fever appears several days to 3 weeks after the drug has been started and resolves 1 to 3 days after drug withdrawal. Patients with HIV infection are more susceptible to drug reactions of all types, including fever.

◆ DON'T BE TRICKED

- The absence of rash does not rule out a drug hypersensitivity reaction as a cause of fever.
- The absence of eosinophilia does not rule out drug reaction or DRESS.

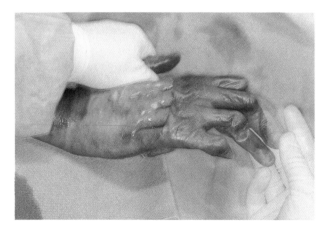

Toxic Epidermal Necrolysis: Shedding of entire sheets of skin is characteristic of TEN.

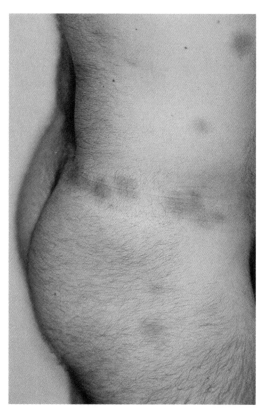

Fixed Drug Eruption: Discrete round to oval lesions characteristic of a fixed drug eruption.

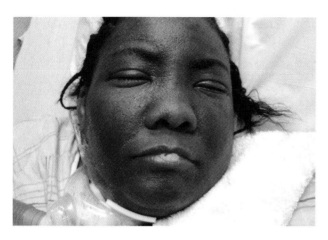

Drug Reaction with Eosinophilia and Systemic Symptoms: Acute facial edema in a patient with anticonvulsant-induced DRESS.

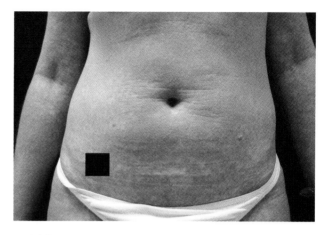

Morbilliform Drug Eruption: Morbilliform drug eruption consisting of symmetrically arranged erythematous macules and papules, some discrete and others confluent.

Therapy

Discontinue the offending medication. Treat anaphylaxis, if present, with epinephrine, antihistamines, and corticosteroids. AGEP is typically self-limited. Treat DRESS with corticosteroids or IV immune globulin. Stevens-Johnson syndrome/TEN treatment is supportive (fluid and electrolyte management, wound care); IV immune globulin may decrease mortality, but the effect of corticosteroids is uncertain.

❖ **Test Yourself**

A 37-year-old man is prescribed ceftriaxone and a macrolide for community-acquired pneumonia. Five days later, he is feeling better, coughs less, and produces less sputum, but he continues to have daily temperatures of up to 38.3 °C (101.0 °F).

ANSWER: Suspect drug fever for cause of persistent fever despite improvement in all other clinical parameters.

Immunodeficiency

Diagnosis

Consider primary immunodeficiency syndromes in the differential diagnosis of patients with multiple or recurrent infections. Primary deficiencies are most commonly found in children but are increasingly being recognized in adults. The most common primary immunodeficiency is congenital IgA deficiency. Most patients with isolated IgA deficiency are clinically normal, but symptomatic patients may present with recurrent respiratory infections and giardiasis and have an increased risk for autoimmune disorders, including rheumatoid arthritis and SLE. Patients with undetectable levels of serum IgA are at high risk for transfusion reactions because of the development of anti-IgA antibodies.

CVI is the most common symptomatic primary immunodeficiency and comprises a group of acquired disorders most often characterized by low levels of one or more immunoglobulin classes or subclasses. Findings include:

- hypogammaglobulinemia
- recurrent bacterial upper and lower respiratory infections (including bronchiectasis)
- predilection for infection with encapsulated bacteria (pneumococcus, *Haemophilus*, staphylococcus)
- infectious diarrhea, specifically *Giardia lamblia* infection
- chronic diarrhea/malabsorption

Some other considerations:

- Autoimmune manifestations are found in one third of cases (hemolytic anemia and thrombocytopenia, SLE, rheumatoid arthritis). CVI increases the risk for gastric adenocarcinoma, intestinal lymphoma, and non-Hodgkin lymphoma.
- Choose measurement of serum IgM, IgA, IgG (all low), and IgG subclasses (variably low), and measure the ability to mount an antibody response to tetanus toxoid (protein) and pneumococcal vaccine (polysaccharide) antigens. If serum immunoglobulins are very low, do not test response to vaccines, because the antibody response will be predictably absent.

Therapy

Choose IV immune globulin as first-line therapy for CVI. Most patients with selective IgA therapy do not require treatment.

◆ DON'T BE TRICKED

- Standard IV immune globulin is contraindicated in isolated IgA deficiency, because these patients may have IgG or IgE antibodies directed against the transfused IgA. Blood transfusion is also contraindicated unless washed erythrocytes are used.

❖ Test Yourself

A 37-year-old woman has had eight episodes of sinusitis annually for the past 15 years. She had a single episode of pneumonia as a child.

ANSWER: The patient has probable CVI. Choose measurement of serum immunoglobulin levels and, if low, measurement of antibody response to pneumococcal and tetanus vaccines.

Complement Deficiency

Diagnosis

Persons with deficiencies of the terminal components of the classic complement pathway (C5, C6, C7, C8, and C9) are susceptible to recurrent neisserial infections. Defects in components of the alternative complement pathway of activation and the lectin pathway may also be associated with neisserial infections. Choose CH_{50} assay. If CH_{50} is low, follow up with individual component measurements. Screen all patients with repeated episodes of disseminated gonorrhea or neisserial meningitis with CH_{50} assay. Measurement of the alternative and lectin pathway components is indicated in patients in whom complement deficiency is suspected but CH_{50} is normal. Patients with deficiencies of the early components of the complement system will have repeated bacterial infections and often SLE.

Therapy

Patients with complement deficiency respond to standard antibiotics. Patients should maintain currency of vaccinations, especially meningococcal, pneumococcal, and *Haemophilus* b conjugate vaccine.

STUDY TABLE: Pattern Recognition of Repeated Infections

Presenting Pattern	Congenital Defect	Test
Invasive skin infections	Granulocyte (chronic granulomatous disease)	Nitroblue tetrazolium dye test (respiratory burst assay)
Benign or intracellular viral or fungal infections	Cell-mediated	Skin test response to PPD, mumps, and *Candida* antigen
Repeated sinopulmonary infections with encapsulated bacteria	Immunoglobulins	Quantitative serum immunoglobulins and response to tetanus and pneumococcal vaccines
Sinopulmonary infections, malabsorption, infertility, family history of CF	*CFTR* gene (*CF*)	Sweat chloride test
Neisseria meningitidis meningitis and disseminated gonorrhea	Terminal complement components (C5, C6, C7, C8, and C9), alternative and lectin pathways	CH_{50} assay; alternative and lectin pathways

❖ **Test Yourself**

A 21-year-old male college student has meningococcal meningitis for the third time in 2 years.

ANSWER: The patient has probable terminal complement deficiency. Select serum CH_{50} assay.

Cardiovascular Medicine

Acute Coronary Syndromes

Diagnosis

Look for clinical syndromes caused by acute myocardial ischemia:

- unstable angina
- NSTEMI
- STEMI

Classic anginal symptoms include substernal chest pain, shortness of breath, and diaphoresis. Anginal equivalents are most commonly found in patients with diabetes and in women and include exertional dyspnea, fatigue, nausea, and vomiting.

Signs of cardiac ischemia include new MR and S_3 and S_4 gallops.

The 12-lead ECG and serum biomarkers distinguish three types of ACS:

- Unstable angina: Normal cardiac biomarkers (troponin and CK-MB) without characteristic ECG changes (nonspecific ECG changes or normal)
- NSTEMI: Positive biomarkers without ST elevations or ST-elevation equivalents (although ST depression and nonspecific changes can be seen)
- STEMI: Positive biomarkers and ST-segment elevation in two or more contiguous leads; ST-elevation equivalents include a new LBBB or posterior MI (tall R waves and ST depressions in V_1-V_3)

Echocardiogram may show regional wall motion abnormalities in ACS. This may be especially useful in patients with LBBB.

STUDY TABLE: ECG Localization of Acute MI		
Anatomic Location	**ST-Segment Change**	**Indicative ECG Leads**
Inferior	Elevation	II, III, aVF
Anteroseptal	Elevation	V_1-V_3
Lateral and apical	Elevation	V_4-V_6, possible elevations in I and aVL
Posterior wall*	Depression	Tall R waves in V_1-V_3
Right ventricle*	Elevation	V_4R; tall R waves in V_1-V_3
*Often associated with inferior and/or lateral ST-elevation infarctions.		

The Thrombolysis in Myocardial Infarction (TIMI) risk score is a seven-point score for estimating risk in patients with ACS and is used to guide therapy. The rate of death or MI significantly increases with a higher TIMI risk score. One point is awarded for each of the following prognostic factors:

- age ≥65 years
- ≥3 traditional CAD risk factors
- coronary obstruction ≥50%
- ST-segment deviation
- ≥2 episodes of angina in the past 24 hours
- aspirin use in the past week
- elevated biomarkers

STUDY TABLE: Unstable Angina or NSTEMI Risk Stratification

TIMI Risk Score	Strategy
5-7	Early angiography
3-4 or recurrent angina, elevated serum biomarkers, or previous revascularization	Early angiography
0-2	Stress testing and angiography if testing reveals significant myocardial ischemia

◆ DON'T BE TRICKED

- **STEMI is not the only cause of ST-segment elevations.** Consider acute pericarditis, left ventricular aneurysm, takotsubo (stress) cardiomyopathy, coronary vasospasm, or normal variant.

Therapy

In STEMI, PCI is the preferred strategy and should be performed as soon as possible, with a door-to-balloon goal of ≤90 minutes.

Stent thrombosis may occur 24 hours to 1 year after placement and often presents as recurrent angina, sudden death, or MI, usually with ST-segment elevation. To prevent stent thrombosis, start aspirin and a thienopyridine (clopidogrel or prasugrel) early, continue dual therapy for at least 1 month and ideally up to 12 months after the insertion of a bare-metal stent, with continuation of aspirin thereafter. With drug-eluting stents, treat with clopidogrel for 12 months or longer. If prompt PCI is not available, administer fibrinolytic therapy. Other indications for PCI are:

- fibrinolytic therapy is contraindicated
- STEMI >4 hours after the onset of chest pain with continued chest pain or ST-segment elevation
- history of CABG surgery
- new HF or cardiogenic shock

Administer thrombolytic agents when PCI is not available. The most commonly encountered absolute and relative contraindications include:

- previous intracranial hemorrhage
- ischemic stroke within 3 months EXCEPT acute ischemic stroke within 3 hours
- malignant intracranial neoplasm (primary or metastatic)
- significant closed-head or facial trauma within 3 months
- aortic dissection, active bleeding, or active peptic ulcer disease
- major surgery (within 3 weeks)
- recent (within 2-4 weeks) internal bleeding
- blood pressure >180/110 mm Hg on presentation
- >10 minutes of cardiopulmonary resuscitation
- pregnancy
- concurrent warfarin therapy

CABG surgery is indicated for STEMI in the presence of:

- failure of fibrinolysis or PCI
- cardiogenic shock
- left main or left main equivalent disease
- two- or three-vessel disease involving the LAD artery and a reduced LVEF

Patients with a RV/posterior MI may present with hypotension or may develop hypotension following the administration of nitroglycerin; treat these patients with IV fluids. Look for elevated CVP with clear lungs, hypotension, and tachycardia. The most predictive ECG finding is ST-segment elevation on right-sided ECG lead V_4R.

Place an intra-aortic balloon pump for patients with cardiogenic shock, acute MR or VSD, intractable ventricular tachycardia, or refractory angina.

◆ DON'T BE TRICKED

- Choose transfer for PCI instead of thrombolytic therapy for STEMI only if transfer and PCI can be done within 90 minutes.
- Do not choose thrombolytic therapy for patients with NSTEMI or for asymptomatic patients with onset of pain >24 hours ago.
- Reperfusion arrhythmias following thrombolytic therapy, typically manifested as a transient accelerated idioventricular arrhythmia, do not require additional antiarrhythmic therapy.

STUDY TABLE: Drug Therapy for ACS	
Therapy	**Considerations**
Aspirin	If contraindicated, use clopidogrel, except if CABG surgery is likely
Clopidogrel	Use for unstable angina, NSTEMI and STEMI, and for PCI with stent placement
IV β-blockers for acute care	Avoid in pulmonary edema and/or cardiogenic shock, SBP <90 mm Hg, HR <50/min, or second-degree AV block
Calcium channel blockers (except nifedipine)	Use in patients with contraindications to β-blockers and in those with continued angina despite β-blockers and nitrates
IV nitroglycerin	Use except with suspected RV infarction
LMWH or UFH	Use for all cases of ACS
Bivalirudin	Alternative to UFH/LMWH, especially in patients undergoing PCI
Fondaparinux	Alternative to UFH/LMWH
Glycoprotein IIb/IIIa antagonists	Use in STEMI and with PCI and high-risk NSTEMI, particularly for ongoing ischemia
ACE inhibitors	Use ARBs as an alternative
Statins	Use within 24-96 hours
Cardioselective β-blockers (atenolol, metoprolol)	Use within 3-21 days, continue indefinitely
Eplerenone	Use for severe LV dysfunction after MI

◆ DON'T BE TRICKED

- Do not select spironolactone, because its effectiveness in patients with acute MI is unknown.

Recommendations for temporary pacing in the setting of acute MI are:

- asystole
- symptomatic bradycardia (including complete heart block)
- alternating LBBB and RBBB
- new or indeterminate-age bifascicular block with first-degree AV block

Follow-up

Mechanical complications (VSD, papillary muscle rupture, and LV free wall rupture) may occur 2 to 7 days after an MI. Emergency echocardiography is the initial diagnostic study.

- Patients with VSD or papillary muscle rupture develop abrupt pulmonary edema or hypotension and a loud holosystolic murmur and thrill.
- LV free wall rupture causes sudden hypotension or cardiac death associated with pulseless electrical activity.

Cardiac catheterization is indicated for patients with postinfarction angina or the following post-MI stress test results:

- exercise-induced ST-segment depressions or elevations
- inability to achieve 5 METs during testing
- inability to increase systolic blood pressure by 10 to 30 mm Hg
- inability to exercise (arthritis)

ICDs are indicated in patients meeting the following criteria:

- >40 days since MI
- >3 months since PCI or CABG
- EF <30%

All post-MI patients should be screened for depression, because it is associated with increased hospitalization and death.

STUDY TABLE: Other Causes of Acute Chest Pain

Vignette	Consider	Test/Therapy
Young woman with history of migraines, acute chest pain, and ST-segment elevation	Coronary vasospasm (Prinzmetal angina, variant angina)	Calcium channel blocker
Young person with chest pain following a party	Cocaine	Calcium channel blocker (avoid β-blockers)
A tall, thin person with long arms with acute chest and back pain, a normal ECG, and an aortic diastolic murmur	Marfan syndrome and aortic dissection	MRI, contrast CT, or TEE
A patient who recently traveled or with immobility, sharp or pleuritic chest pain, and nondiagnostic ECG	PE	UFH or LMWH; CTA or V/Q scan
A tall, thin young man who smokes with sudden pleuritic chest pain and dyspnea	Spontaneous pneumothorax	Chest x-ray
A perimenopausal woman with atypical chest pain, ST depressions on exercise testing, and unremarkable coronary angiography	"Cardiac syndrome X"	β-blocker, reassurance
A postmenopausal woman with substernal chest pain following severe emotional/physical stress has ST-segment elevation in the anterior precordial leads, troponin elevation, and unremarkable coronary angiography	Stress-induced (takotsubo) cardiomyopathy	β-blocker
A young man with substernal chest pain, deep T-wave inversions in V_2-V_4, and a harsh systolic murmur that increases with Valsalva maneuver	HCM	Echocardiography, β-blocker

❖ **Test Yourself**

A 56-year-old woman has a 3-hour history of chest pain. Blood pressure is 80/60 mm Hg, respiration rate is 30/min, and pulse is 120/min. Physical examination shows jugular venous distention, inspiratory crackles, and an S_3 gallop. ECG shows ST-segment elevation in leads V_2-V_6.

ANSWER: The diagnosis is STEMI and cardiogenic shock. Choose cardiac catheterization and PCI.

A 58-year-old man with acute chest pain has ST-segment elevation in leads II, III, and aVF. Blood pressure is 82/52 mm Hg and pulse is 54/min. Physical examination shows jugular venous distention, clear lungs, and no murmur or S_3.

ANSWER: Choose IV fluids to treat RV MI. Obtain ECG lead V_4R tracing.

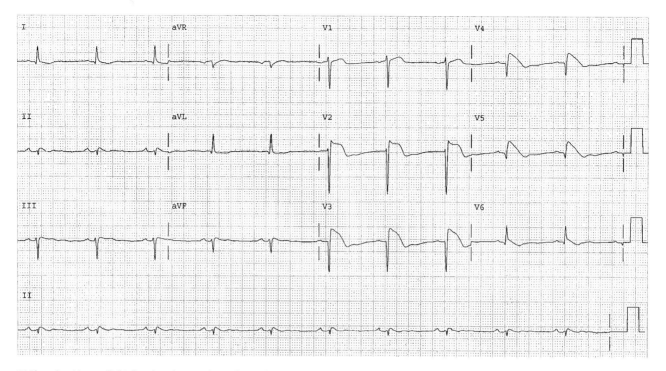

ST-Elevation Myocardial Infarction: The ECG shows abnormal Q waves in leads V_3-V_5 and ST-segment elevation in leads V_2-V_5. The T waves are beginning to invert in leads V_3-V_6. This pattern is most consistent with a recent anterolateral MI.

Chronic Stable Angina

Prevention

Lifestyle modifications (smoking cessation, regular physical activity, "heart healthy" diet) are indicated for all patients. The diet should be rich in fresh fruits, vegetables, and fiber and low in cholesterol, saturated fats, and refined sugars.

Treatment is indicated to achieve the following goals: LDL cholesterol <100 mg/dL, blood pressure <140/90 mm Hg, and hemoglobin A_{1c} <7%. Patients with moderate to high risk for CAD or with known CAD should take aspirin, including patients with a history of GI bleeding (combine with a PPI).

◆ DON'T BE TRICKED
- **Do not select hormone replacement therapy (in women), antioxidant vitamins (vitamin E), or treatment of abnormal lipoprotein(a) levels or serum homocysteine levels with folic acid or vitamin B_{12}.**

Diagnosis

Symptomatic ischemia is manifested principally as classic angina pectoris. Some patients with CAD are asymptomatic but have evidence of ischemia on ECG or imaging studies. Medical history may include:

- risk factors for CAD or previous MI
- peripheral arterial or cerebrovascular disease
- diabetes, hypertension, or HF

Consider non–coronary artery causes of angina, especially AS and HCM.

STUDY TABLE: Estimating Probability of CAD

	Pretest Probability					
	Nonanginal Chest Pain[a]		Atypical Chest Pain[b]		Typical Chest Pain[c]	
Age (y)	Men	Women	Men	Women	Men	Women
30-39	4	2	34	12	76	26
40-49	13	3	51	22	87	55
50-59	20	7	65	31	93	73
60-69	27	14	72	51	94	86

[a]Nonanginal chest pain has one or none of the components for typical chest pain.
[b]Atypical chest pain has two of the three components for typical chest pain.
[c]Typical chest pain has three components: (1) substernal chest pain or discomfort, (2) provoked by exertion or emotional stress, (3) relieved by rest and/or nitroglycerin.
Adapted with permission from Gibbons RJ, Abrams J, Chatterjee K, et al. ACC/AHA 2002 guideline update for the management of patients with chronic stable angina: a report of the American College of Cardiology/American Heart Association Task Force on Practice Guidelines (Committee to Update the 1999 Guidelines for the Management of Patients with Chronic Stable Angina). 2002:13. Available at www.cardiosource.org/~/media/Images/ACC/Science%20and%20Quality/Practice%20Guidelines/s/stable_clean.ashx. Accessed February 27, 2012. Copyright 2002 American College of Cardiology.

Choose the proper stress test for patients with intermediate probability (10%-90%) of CAD:

- exercise ECG without imaging for patients who are able to exercise and have normal or nonspecific baseline ECG changes or for those with complete RBBB
- exercise ECG with myocardial perfusion imaging or exercise echocardiography for patients who are able to exercise and have had a myocardial revascularization procedure or are at increased likelihood of having false-positive ECG changes provoked by exercise (e.g., preexcitation [WPW pattern], baseline ST-segment depression >1 mm, taking digoxin)
- vasodilator myocardial perfusion imaging for patients with LBBB
- pharmacologic stress myocardial perfusion imaging or dobutamine echocardiography for patients unable to exercise
- pharmacologic stress myocardial perfusion imaging for patients with ventricular paced rhythm

Select coronary angiography for patients with high pretest probability of disease or:

- LV dysfunction
- class III or IV angina despite therapy
- highly positive stress or imaging test
- high pretest probability of left main or three-vessel CAD (a Duke treadmill score ≤−11)
- uncertain diagnosis after noninvasive testing
- history of surviving sudden cardiac death
- suspected coronary spasm

Therapy

Intensive lifestyle modification is appropriate for all patients. Most patients also need aspirin (not clopidogrel) and a statin. β-Blockers are used to achieve a resting heart rate of 55 to 60/min. Adding a calcium channel blocker is appropriate if β-blockers are inadequate or as an alternative if β-blockers are not tolerated.

- Non-dihydropyridine agents (verapamil and diltiazem) have the greatest effect on myocardial contractility and conduction.
- Dihydropyridine agents (amlodipine, felodipine, isradipine, and long-acting nifedipine) exert relatively more effect on vasodilation.
- Short-acting calcium channel blockers are contraindicated.
- Ranolazine is reserved for patients who have not responded to standard antianginal therapy. Diltiazem and verapamil increase the level of ranolazine by as much as 50%; ranolazine dose reduction is required.

When giving nitrates, select long-acting preparations with an 8- to 12-hour nitrate-free period to avoid tolerance. Nitrates are contraindicated in patients taking phosphodiesterase type 5 (PDE-5) inhibitors such as tadalafil, vardenafil, and sildenafil. ACE inhibitors are recommended if the EF is <35% or if the patient has a history of CAD, stroke, or peripheral vascular disease or has diabetes and at least one additional CAD risk factor. Coronary revascularization with either PCI or CABG surgery is beneficial only in patients with chronic stable angina who also have:

- angina pectoris refractory to medical therapy
- a large area of ischemic myocardium and high-risk criteria on stress testing
- high-risk coronary anatomy, including left main coronary artery stenosis or three-vessel disease
- significant CAD with reduced LV systolic function

Consider CABG surgery in patients with large amounts of myocardium at risk owing to:

- severe left main disease
- three-vessel disease

◆ DON'T BE TRICKED

- Do not select PCI or CABG as a treatment for chronic stable angina in the absence of high-risk features for early mortality or unresponsiveness to medical therapy.

❖ Test Yourself

A 69-year-old man has burning retrosternal discomfort related to exertion. His father died of an acute MI at 61 years of age. Physical examination is unremarkable, and the resting ECG is normal.

ANSWER: Prescribe aspirin, sublingual nitroglycerin, and a β-blocker, and follow up with an exercise stress test.

Heart Failure

Diagnosis

Characteristic findings of HF are dyspnea, fatigue, orthopnea, edema, and cough. Physical examination shows an elevated jugular venous pressure, cardiac murmurs, an S_3, crackles, hepatomegaly, and peripheral edema.

Initial diagnostic testing includes an ECG, chest x-ray, and echocardiography. The ECG may show a previous MI, ventricular hypertrophy, arrhythmias, or conduction abnormalities. Chest x-rays may show cardiomegaly, pulmonary edema, and pleural effusion. Echocardiography may detect systolic HF (EF <50% and ventricular dilatation), valvular heart disease, and regional wall abnormalities suggesting CAD. HF with preserved EF (diastolic HF) is associated with an EF >50%.

Other studies include stress testing to detect myocardial ischemia, coronary angiography in patients with symptoms or risk factors for CAD, and measurement of serum TSH levels. In the presence of suggestive symptoms, evaluate for sleep apnea. An elevated serum BNP level is a nonspecific finding that does not establish the diagnosis of HF. However, a BNP level >500 pg/mL is compatible with HF, and a level <100 pg/mL effectively excludes HF as a cause of acute dyspnea.

◆ DON'T BE TRICKED

- Do not select endomyocardial biopsy unless hemochromatosis, sarcoidosis, or amyloidosis is suspected.
- BNP cannot be used to differentiate between systolic and diastolic HF.
- Kidney failure, older age, and female sex all increase BNP, and obesity reduces BNP.

Therapy

For making treatment decisions, disease classification systems have been developed.

STUDY TABLE: Classification of Heart Failure	
ACC/AHA Stage	**NYHA Functional Class**
A At risk; no structural disease or symptoms	—
B Structural disease but no symptoms	I Structural disease but no symptoms
C Structural disease with previous or current symptoms	II Symptomatic; slight limitation of physical activity
C–D	III Symptomatic; marked limitation of physical activity
D Refractory disease	IV Inability to perform any physical activity without symptoms

Pharmacologic agents for HF:

- ACE inhibitors for all stages of HF to reduce mortality. If a patient cannot tolerate ACE inhibitors, ARBs are an acceptable alternative.
- Hydralazine plus nitrates, in addition to standard therapy, for NYHA class III-IV to reduce mortality in black patients and in patients who cannot tolerate ACE inhibitors or ARBs.
- β-Blockers for all stages of HF to reduce mortality.
- Spironolactone for NYHA class III-IV HF to reduce mortality. If a patient cannot tolerate spironolactone, eplerenone is an alternative.
- Digitalis for NYHA class III-IV HF to reduce symptoms and length of hospitalization.
- ICD for ischemic and nonischemic cardiomyopathy with an EF ≤35%.
- Biventricular pacing for NYHA class III-IV HF, LVEF ≤35%, and QRS duration >120 msec
- Biventricular pacing for NYHA class II HF, LVEF ≤30%, and QRS duration >150 msec
- Cardiac transplantation for patients with low peak oxygen uptake ($Vo_{2\,max}$) (<14 mL/kg/min or <50% age-predicted maximum).

◆ DON'T BE TRICKED

- Do not begin β-blocker therapy in patients with decompensated HF.
- Generally, continue β-blockers during decompensated states of HF if the patient was previously stable while using β-blocker therapy.
- Use metoprolol in patients with COPD or with mild to moderate asthma.
- Do not prescribe or continue NSAIDs or thiazolidinediones because they worsen HF.
- Calcium channel blockers have no direct role in the treatment of systolic HF.
- Avoid digoxin in patients with changing kidney status or chronic kidney disease.

❖ Test Yourself

A 64-year-old woman with previously stable HF now has increasing orthopnea. Medications are lisinopril 5 mg BID and furosemide 20 mg/d. Blood pressure is 140/68 mm Hg and heart rate is 102/min. Pulmonary crackles and increased jugular venous distention are present.

ANSWER: Increase the furosemide and lisinopril dosages and add a β-blocker when the patient is stable.

Heart Failure with Preserved Ejection Fraction

Diagnosis

Diagnose HF with preserved EF (also known as diastolic HF) when signs and symptoms of systolic HF are present but the echocardiogram reveals normal LVEF (EF >50%) and significant valvular abnormalities are absent.

Therapy

Candesartan has been shown to reduce HF-related hospitalizations but not mortality. Otherwise, the primary treatment goals in diastolic HF are to treat the underlying etiology (hypertension, AF), to manage potentially exacerbating factors (e.g., tachycardia), and to optimize diastolic filling (avoid decreased effective circulating blood volume).

Dilated Cardiomyopathy

Diagnosis

Dilated cardiomyopathy is characterized by dilation and reduced function of one or both ventricles manifesting as HF, arrhythmias, and sudden death. The most common cause is idiopathic dilated cardiomyopathy (50%), but the differential diagnosis is broad.

STUDY TABLE: Differential Diagnoses of Dilated Cardiomyopathy	
Condition	**Distinguishing Characteristics**
Acute myocarditis	Associated with bacterial, viral, and parasitic infections and autoimmune disorders. Cardiac troponin levels are typically elevated; ventricular dysfunction may be global or regional. Can cause cardiogenic shock and ventricular arrhythmias. Choose supportive care in the acute phase, then standard HF therapy.
Alcoholic cardiomyopathy	Associated with chronic heavy alcohol ingestion, but other manifestations of chronic alcohol abuse may be absent. Typically, the left ventricle (and frequently both ventricles) is dilated and hypokinetic. Choose standard HF therapy and total abstinence from alcohol.
Arrhythmogenic RV dysplasia	Characterized by pathologic fibrofatty infiltration of the right ventricle evident on biopsy or by MRI. Manifests as significant RV enlargement and dysfunction out of proportion to preserved LV function or as ventricular tachycardia and sudden death.
Drug-induced cardiomyopathy	Illicit use of cocaine and amphetamines has been associated with myocarditis and dilated cardiomyopathy, as well as MI, arrhythmia, and sudden death. Choose standard HF treatment. In patients with stimulant-induced acute myocardial ischemia, β-blockers may exacerbate coronary vasoconstriction; labetalol is preferred.
Giant cell myocarditis	Rare disease characterized by biventricular enlargement, refractory ventricular arrhythmias, and rapid progression to cardiogenic shock in young to middle-aged adults. Histologic examination demonstrates the presence of multinucleated giant cells in the myocardium. Choose immunosuppressant treatment and/or cardiac transplantation.
Tachycardia-mediated cardiomyopathy	Occurs when myocardial dysfunction develops as a result of chronic tachycardia. Primary treatment is to slow or eliminate the arrhythmia.
Takotsubo (stress-induced) cardiomyopathy	Characterized by acute ventricular dysfunction in the setting of intense emotional or physiologic stress. May mimic acute MI with ST-segment elevation and elevated biomarkers. Dilation and akinesis of the LV apex occur in the absence of CAD. Resolves in days to weeks with supportive care.

Therapy

In addition to reversal of the underlying cause, if possible (alcohol, drug, and tachycardia-mediated cardiomyopathies), choose the standard medical therapy for HF.

❖ **Test Yourself**

A 35-year-old man develops abdominal discomfort and swelling in both legs. He has an 18-pack-year smoking history and drinks a six-pack of beer daily but has no other significant medical history. Physical examination shows an elevated CVP, a displaced apical impulse, distant heart sounds, a grade 2/6 apical holosystolic murmur, an enlarged and tender liver, and peripheral edema.

ANSWER: The diagnosis is alcoholic cardiomyopathy. Choose echocardiography and alcohol cessation.

Peripartum Cardiomyopathy

Diagnosis

Peripartum cardiomyopathy is the presence of HF with an LVEF <45% diagnosed between 1 month before and 5 months after delivery. Even if ventricular function improves with therapy, the risk of recurrence is very high. Subsequent pregnancies should, therefore, be discouraged.

Therapy

Management includes early delivery (when peripartum cardiomyopathy is identified before parturition) and HF treatment similar to that in nonpregnant women, except that ACE inhibitors and ARBs should be avoided because of their association with fetal renal agenesis.

Hypertrophic Cardiomyopathy

Screening

All first-degree relatives of patients with HCM should have echocardiographic screening.

Diagnosis

HCM is an uncommon primary cardiac disease characterized by diffuse or focal myocardial hypertrophy disproportionate to loading conditions. The disease is genetically inherited in an autosomal dominant pattern in approximately 50% of patients. Symptoms of HCM are caused by a combination of diastolic dysfunction, ischemia, arrhythmias, and outflow obstruction. Patients may present with syncope (often arrhythmogenic), chest pain, and sudden cardiac death.

STUDY TABLE: Distinguishing HCM from AS		
Assessment/Finding	HCM	AS
Carotid pulse	Rises briskly, then declines, followed by a second rise (pulsus bisferiens)	Rises slowly and has low volume (pulsus parvus et tardus)
Ejection sound	None	Present
Aortic regurgitation	None	May be present
Valsalva maneuver	Increased murmur intensity	Decreased murmur intensity
Squatting to standing position	Increased murmur intensity	Decreased murmur intensity
Standing to squatting position	Decreased murmur intensity	Increased murmur intensity
Carotid radiation	None	Usually present
Apex beat	"Triple ripple"	Sustained single

The ECG shows LV hypertrophy and left atrial enlargement. Deeply inverted, symmetric T waves in leads V_3-V_6 are present in the apical hypertrophic form of the disease (mimics ischemia). Echocardiography is the diagnostic technique of choice.

Therapy

Patients with HCM should avoid strenuous exercise, including competitive sports and intense isometric exercise. β-Blockers are first-line agents for patients with an EF ≥50%, dyspnea, and/or chest pain. Calcium channel blockers may be substituted for β-blockers. Disopyramide (third-line agent) may be added if symptoms and a significant gradient persist. ACE inhibitors are used only if systolic dysfunction is present. Surgery or septal ablation is indicated for patients with an outflow tract gradient of >50 mm Hg and continuing symptoms despite maximal drug therapy.

STUDY TABLE: Sudden Death Risk Factors in HCM	
Major Risk Factors	**Minor Risk Factors**
Previous cardiac arrest	Unexplained syncope
Spontaneous sustained VT	LV septal thickness >30 mm
Family history of sudden death (first-degree relative)	Blunted or hypotensive response during exercise
	Nonsustained VT
	LV outflow obstruction
	Microvascular disease on perfusion study
	High-risk genetic defect

The presence of one major risk factor or two minor risk factors is a strong predictor of sudden death. The absence of any risk factors has a high negative predictive value (>90%). For test-taking purposes, focus on major risk factors.

Patients at high risk for sudden death are candidates for an ICD.

◆ DON'T BE TRICKED

- Electrophysiologic studies are not useful in predicting sudden cardiac death.
- Do not prescribe digoxin, vasodilators, or diuretics, which increase LV outflow obstruction.

Follow-up

All patients with HCM should receive genetic counseling.

❖ Test Yourself

An 18-year-old high school basketball player is evaluated after he collapsed during practice and was resuscitated.

ANSWER: HCM is the most likely diagnosis in almost every young person who collapses during an athletic event.

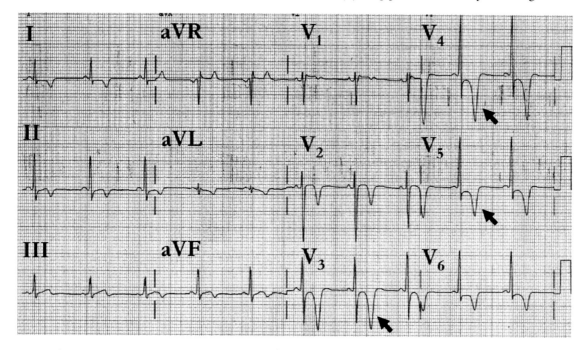

Hypertrophic Cardiomyopathy: The ECG shows ST-segment depression and deeply inverted T waves (*arrows*) in the precordial leads consistent with marked apical hypertrophy.

Restrictive Cardiomyopathy

Diagnosis

Although the cause of restrictive cardiomyopathy is often unknown, be alert for the following:

- infiltrative diseases (amyloidosis, sarcoidosis, hemochromatosis)
- glycogen storage diseases
- endomyocardial processes (endomyocardial fibrosis, hypereosinophilic syndrome, carcinoid, radiation therapy, anthracycline toxicity)
- noninfiltrative diseases (scleroderma)

In restrictive cardiomyopathy, abnormally rigid ventricular walls cause diastolic dysfunction in the absence of systolic dysfunction, manifesting as impaired ventricular filling and elevated diastolic ventricular pressures. Pulmonary venous congestion, pulmonary hypertension, and right-sided HF ensue. Jugular veins may engorge with inspiration (Kussmaul sign). Cardiac catheterization shows elevated LV and RV end-diastolic pressures and a characteristic early ventricular diastolic dip and plateau. Systolic function is normal in many patients.

STUDY TABLE: Clues to Underlying Systemic Diseases Causing Restrictive Cardiomyopathy	
Disease	**Clues**
Amyloidosis	Neuropathy, proteinuria, hepatomegaly, periorbital ecchymosis, bruising, low-voltage ECG. Diagnosis can be confirmed with abdominal fat pad aspiration.
Sarcoidosis	Bilateral hilar lymphadenopathy; possible pulmonary reticular opacities; and skin, joint, or eye lesions. Cardiac involvement is suggested by the presence of arrhythmias, conduction blocks, or HF. Diagnosis is supported by CMR imaging with gadolinium.
Hemochromatosis	Abnormal aminotransferase levels, osteoarthritis, diabetes, erectile dysfunction, and HF; elevated serum ferritin and transferrin saturation level.

Restrictive cardiomyopathy must be differentiated from constrictive pericarditis.

Therapy

Treat any underlying disease that affects diastolic function (hypertension, diabetes, ischemic heart disease, amyloidosis). Loop diuretics are used to treat dyspnea and peripheral edema. However, because ventricular volumes are normal to small, excessive volume reduction can result in reductions in stroke volume and cardiac output, predisposing to orthostatic hypotension and syncope. β-Blockers and/or nondihydropyridine calcium channel antagonists enhance diastolic function and should be considered if diuretic therapy is not effective or in the presence of atrial tachyarrhythmias. In patients with conduction abnormalities, however, β-blockers and calcium channel blockers can result in third-degree heart block. ACE inhibitors and ARBs improve diastolic filling and may be beneficial in patients with diastolic dysfunction.

❖ **Test Yourself**

A 63-year-old man develops dyspnea and fatigue. Physical examination shows jugular venous distention, a prominent jugular *a* wave, a prominent S$_4$, and a grade 2/6 holosystolic murmur at the left sternal border. The lungs are clear. Other findings include an enlarged, tender liver; petechiae over the feet; and periorbital ecchymoses.

ANSWER: The diagnosis is amyloid cardiomyopathy, indicated by the noncardiac symptoms and signs.

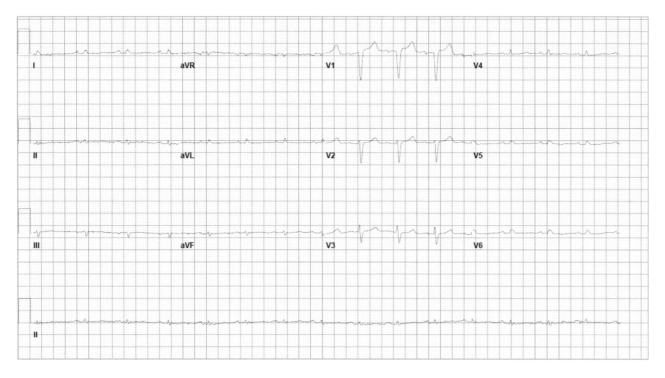

Cardiac Amyloidosis: The ECG shows low voltage, the most common ECG abnormality associated with cardiac amyloidosis.

Pericardial Tamponade and Constriction

Diagnosis

Patients with cardiac tamponade present with dyspnea, fatigue, peripheral edema, hepatomegaly, hepatic dysfunction, and ascites in the absence of pulmonary congestion. The diagnosis may be suggested by risk factors for tamponade, including patients with:

- metastatic cancer
- recent cardiac surgery
- dissecting aneurysm
- recent viral or bacterial pericarditis
- collagen vascular disease

Physical examination reveals jugular venous distention, pulsus paradoxus, tachycardia, reduced heart sounds, and/or hypotension. CVP may increase with inspiration (Kussmaul sign). Echocardiography can confirm an elevated intrapericardial pressure, which is manifested by:

- right ventricular or atrial free wall invagination or diastolic "collapse"
- accentuated respiratory variation in peak mitral and tricuspid inflow velocities
- reduction in or absence of the normal decrease in inferior vena cava diameter during inspiration.

Absence of a pericardial effusion virtually excludes a diagnosis of cardiac tamponade.

Constrictive pericarditis is characterized by thickened, fibrotic, and adherent pericardium that restrains ventricular diastolic expansion, leading to impaired filling. Constrictive pericarditis is often a sequela of acute pericarditis. Constrictive pericarditis is associated with a loud S_3 (pericardial knock), and a friction rub may be present. Echocardiogram in constrictive pericarditis shows:

- accentuated transmitral or tricuspid early filling velocity with a rapid decrease in early filling velocities
- accentuated phasic changes in filling during respiration
- abnormal diastolic septal motion

MRI or CT confirms pericardial thickening. X-ray evidence of a calcified pericardium strongly supports the diagnosis.

Therapy

Acute management of cardiac tamponade includes maintenance of systemic blood pressure with volume resuscitation and vasopressors. Pericardial fluid should be drained by percutaneous pericardiocentesis or surgery.

In patients with chronic constrictive pericarditis, cardiac output depends on a high preload; therefore, diuretics must be used cautiously, if at all. Pericardiectomy is the most effective treatment but is unnecessary in patients with early disease (NYHA functional class I) and is unwarranted in patients with advanced disease (NYHA functional class IV).

◆ DON'T BE TRICKED

- **In constrictive pericarditis, the echocardiogram will demonstrate shifting of the ventricular septum to and fro during diastole as a manifestation of the right and left ventricle competing for a confined space during filling; these findings are not seen in restrictive cardiomyopathy.**

❖ Test Yourself

A 44-year-old woman with a history of ovarian cancer presents with fatigue, dyspnea, and peripheral edema. Examination shows jugular venous distention that increases with inspiration, reduced heart sounds, blood pressure of 94/50 mm Hg, and heart rate of 132/min. A 20 mm Hg pulsus paradoxus is present.

ANSWER: The diagnosis is acute pericardial tamponade probably secondary to metastatic disease. Order echocardiography, and support blood pressure with fluids and vasopressors.

STUDY TABLE: Constrictive Pericarditis vs. Restrictive Cardiomyopathy		
Test	Constrictive Pericarditis	Restrictive Cardiomyopathy
Physical examination: pericardial knock	Supportive	Unusual
Physical examination: S_3	May be present	Supportive
ECG: LBBB or RBBB	Not helpful	Supportive
Chest x-ray: pericardial calcification	May be present	Absent
Echocardiography: LV hypertrophy and atrial enlargement	Absent	Present
Echocardiography: accentuated drop in peak LV filling during inspiration	Present	Absent
MRI: increased pericardial thickness	Usually present	Absent
Right heart catheterization: elevated and equalized diastolic LV and RV pressures (within 5 mm Hg)	Present	Absent
BNP level	Normal or slightly elevated	Significantly elevated

Acute Pericarditis

Diagnosis

The most common symptom is acute sharp or stabbing substernal chest pain that worsens with inspiration and when lying flat and is alleviated when sitting and leaning forward. Medical history may include:

- cancer (current or in the past)
- recent trauma

- arthralgia (suggesting collagen-vascular disease)
- MI
- recent thoracic surgical procedures
- use of medications, including hydralazine and minoxidil

A two- or three-component pericardial friction rub is characteristic. Pericardial tamponade (pulsus paradoxus ≥10 mm Hg) may be present. ECG findings of diffuse ST-segment elevation with an upward concave movement (without the reciprocal ST-segment depression found in MI), PR-segment depression in limb leads, PR-segment elevation in aVR, and electrical alternans (alternating high- and low-voltage QRS complexes) may be present in patients with large effusions.

Remember that evolution of ECG in acute MI and acute pericarditis are similar. However, Q waves do not develop in acute pericarditis. An echocardiogram may show evidence of an effusion or of early tamponade.

◆ DON'T BE TRICKED
- **Cardiac enzyme values may be slightly elevated in patients with isolated pericarditis.**

Therapy

First-line treatment is aspirin (preferred after MI), NSAIDs, or colchicine (choose colchicine plus aspirin for recurrent pericarditis). Choose a 2- to 3-day course of corticosteroids for pericarditis that does not respond to aspirin or NSAIDs (but increases the risk of recurrent pericarditis). Choose emergent pericardiocentesis for tamponade and hemodynamic instability, including pulsus paradoxus.

❖ Test Yourself

A 57-year-old man has a 2-day history of chest pain that worsens when he lies flat. Cardiac examination shows a three-component friction rub.

ANSWER: The diagnosis is pericarditis. Look for diffuse ST-segment elevation and PR-segment depression. Ignore an elevated serum troponin level tempting you to answer "acute MI."

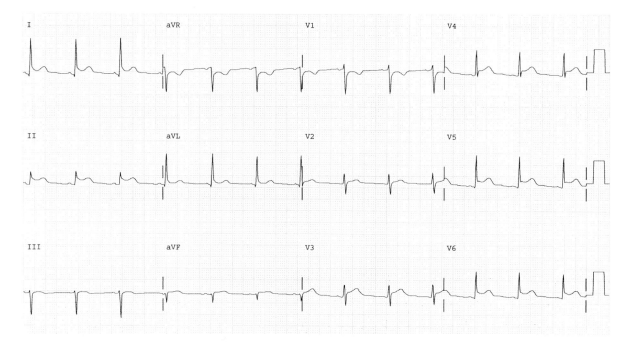

Acute Pericarditis: The ECG shows sinus rhythm with diffuse ST-segment elevation and PR-segment depression in lead II, characteristic of acute pericarditis.

Rheumatic Fever

Prevention

Give penicillin to patients with group A streptococcal infection (or erythromycin to patients with penicillin allergy). Patients with a history of rheumatic fever (RF) require long-term prophylactic penicillin, and patients with rheumatic valvular disease should continue prophylaxis for at least 10 years after the last episode of RF or until at least 40 years of age (whichever is longer).

Diagnosis

RF is the most common cause of valvular heart disease in Africa, Asia, South America, and the Middle East. Mitral stenosis and regurgitation are common consequences of RF. The aortic valve is the second most likely affected valve.

STUDY TABLE: Jones Criteria for Diagnosis of Rheumatic Fever	
Manifestations*	
Major	Carditis, polyarthritis, chorea, subcutaneous nodules, erythema marginatum
Minor	Arthralgia, fever
Minor	Elevated ESR, elevated CRP, evidence of group A streptococcal infection, prolonged PR interval on ECG

*Note: two major manifestations or one major and two minor manifestations establish the diagnosis.

Therapy

Antibiotic therapy is required even if the throat culture is negative for group A streptococci. Salicylates are the drug of choice; nonresponse to salicylates makes RF unlikely.

Heart Murmurs

Diagnosis

Right-sided heart murmurs increase in intensity during inspiration. Murmurs due to HCM increase in intensity during the Valsalva maneuver and on standing from a squatting position. The clicks due to mitral valve prolapse may move closer to S_1, and the murmur lengthens during the Valsalva maneuver.

Abnormal splitting of S_2 helps differentiate heart murmurs. Normally, a split S_2 is heard only during inspiration. Splitting during inspiration and expiration occurs in conditions that further delay RV ejection, including RBBB, pulmonic stenosis, VSD with left-to-right shunt, and ASD with left-to-right shunt. Reversed or expiratory splitting occurs in conditions that prolong LV ejection, including LBBB, AS, HCM, and ACS with LV dysfunction.

Innocent heart murmurs are typically midsystolic, located at the base of the heart, grade 1/6 to 2/6 without radiation, and associated with normal splitting of S_2. Signs of serious cardiac disease include an S_4, murmur grade ≥3/6 intensity, any diastolic murmur, and fixed splitting of S_2. TTE is indicated in symptomatic patients, in those with a systolic murmur grade 3/6 intensity or greater, and in those with any continuous murmur (a murmur that begins after S_1 and extends beyond S_2) or diastolic murmur.

◆ DON'T BE TRICKED

- An increased P_2, an S_3, and an early peaking systolic murmur over the upper left sternal border are normal findings during pregnancy.
- Innocent heart murmurs do not require echocardiographic confirmation.

A 19-year-old asymptomatic woman has a heart murmur first heard during a college sports physical examination. A nonradiating grade 2/6 midsystolic murmur is heard over the upper right sternal border. Physiologic splitting of S_2 is present, and a soft S_3 is heard at the cardiac apex.

ANSWER: The diagnosis is an innocent heart murmur.

Aortic Stenosis

Diagnosis

The most common cause of AS is progressive calcific valve disease of a normal trileaflet valve that is usually diagnosed in patients ≥60 years of age. Aortic valve sclerosis, or valve thickening without outflow obstruction, is an earlier phase of calcific aortic valve disease present in more than 20% of persons >65 years. Patients with a congenital bicuspid aortic valve usually present at a younger age (40-60 years). Patients with bicuspid aortic valves should be evaluated for dilatation of the aortic arch.

Signs and symptoms of AS are HF, angina, and syncope. Findings include:

- a midsystolic murmur at the upper right second intercostal space
- a murmur that radiates to the carotid arteries
- a delayed, low-amplitude carotid pulse (pulsus parvus et tardus)
- chest x-ray showing a boot-shaped cardiac silhouette and poststenotic aortic dilatation
- echocardiography showing left atrial enlargement and LVH, as well as calcified aortic valve leaflets with restricted motion
- severe AS associated with a valve area <1 cm² and a mean transvalvular gradient >50 mm Hg

Rarely, AS is diagnosed in the setting of GI bleeding in patients with Heyde syndrome. This disorder is associated with an acquired von Willebrand disease, and the bleeding is thought to be caused by disruption of von Willebrand multimers during turbulent passage through the diseased aortic valve.

◆ DON'T BE TRICKED

- **Echocardiography significantly underestimates the transvalvular gradient in patients with decreasing LV function. If the calculated valve area increases with dobutamine-augmented cardiac output, then diagnose pseudostenosis.**

Perform exercise stress testing for patients with documented AS with equivocal symptoms. A hypotensive response identifies candidates for immediate valve replacement. Perform right- and left-sided cardiac catheterization if noninvasive tests fail to define the severity of the stenosis or if clinical and echocardiographic findings are inconsistent. Select coronary angiography for all patients >35 years of age for whom surgical replacement of the aortic valve is considered.

◆ DON'T BE TRICKED

- **Do not select exercise stress testing for symptomatic patients with AS.**

Therapy

Treat patients with HF with diuretics, digoxin, and ACE inhibitors; those with atrial fibrillation (AF) require cardioversion. Patients with severe AS may not tolerate nitrate preparations. Select aortic valve replacement for symptomatic patients of any age with AS, patients who are undergoing CABG surgery, and patients with LV dysfunction or hypotension during exercise stress testing. Percutaneous balloon valvuloplasty is a treatment for young patients with congenital AS and no aortic valve calcification.

◆ DON'T BE TRICKED

- **Do not select balloon valvuloplasty for adults with calcific AS.**

Use serial echocardiography to evaluate the left aortic valve area, degree of ventricular hypertrophy, and LV function every year in asymptomatic patients with severe AS, every 2 years in patients with moderate AS, and every 5 years in those with mild disease.

❖ Test Yourself

A 71-year-old man is evaluated for symptoms of HF. On physical examination, the apical impulse is enlarged and displaced laterally, and a grade 2/6 midsystolic murmur is heard at the right upper sternal border that radiates to the carotid arteries. Echocardiography shows hypokinesis and an LVEF of 30%. The aortic valve cusp is calcified with diminished mobility, and the transvalvular mean gradient is 26 mm Hg.

ANSWER: The diagnosis is severe AS with cardiomyopathy despite the low transvalvular gradient (which is low because of severe LV dysfunction). Select cardiac catheterization and probable valve replacement.

Aortic Regurgitation

Diagnosis

AR is classified as chronic or acute. Chronic AR occurs most often in patients with a bicuspid aortic valve. Other causes may include aortic aneurysm and Marfan syndrome. Findings in chronic, severe AR include:

- angina, orthopnea, and exertional dyspnea
- widened pulse pressure
- de Musset sign (head bobs with each heartbeat)
- Duroziez sign (systolic murmur heard with compression of the proximal femoral artery)
- Traube sign ("pistol shot" sounds over the peripheral arteries)
- Corrigan pulse ("water-hammer" type pulse with abrupt distention and collapse)
- Quincke pulse (systolic plethora and diastolic blanching in the nail beds with nail compression)
- soft S_1, soft or absent A_2, and loud S_3
- diastolic murmur immediately after A_2 along the left sternal border (primary aortic valvular disease) or right sternal border (secondary to aortic root dilatation)
- enhanced auscultation when leaning forward and exhaling
- left axis deviation and LVH on ECG
- cardiomegaly and aortic root dilatation and calcification on chest x-ray

Causes of acute AR include aortic dissection, valve destruction from endocarditis, and, rarely, traumatic rupture. Acute AR is associated with a short, soft, and sometimes inaudible diastolic murmur and normal heart size and pulse pressure. Severe acute AR causes early mitral valve closure and diastolic aortic flow reversal on echocardiography.

Diagnostic studies in patients with chronic AR include serologic testing for syphilis and echocardiography.

Therapy

Schedule immediate aortic valve replacement for patients with acute AR. Bridging medical therapy includes sodium nitroprusside and IV diuretics. Dobutamine or milrinone are also indicated if the blood pressure is unacceptably low.

Treat patients with chronic AR with ACE inhibitors, nifedipine, or hydralazine and venodilators (to decrease LV preload). Choose aortic valve replacement for patients with chronic AR who are symptomatic (even if the EF is normal); who will undergo CABG or other valve surgery; or who have progressive LV dilatation, an EF <50%, or declining exercise performance.

◆ **DON'T BE TRICKED**

- Do not select β-blockers or intra-aortic balloon pumps for patients with acute AR, because both may worsen the AR.

Follow-up

For patients with chronic AR who have no indications for valve replacement, perform clinical evaluation and echocardiography 2 to 3 months after diagnosis to exclude a rapidly progressive process, every 6 to 12 months in asymptomatic patients with LV dilatation, and every 2 to 3 years in asymptomatic patients with a normal left ventricle.

❖ **Test Yourself**

A 36-year-old man with aortic valve endocarditis is transferred to the ICU because of the abrupt onset of hypotension and hypoxemia. Physical examination findings include a blood pressure of 80/30 mm Hg, heart rate of 120/min, bilateral crackles, and a summation gallop. No murmurs are heard.

ANSWER: The diagnosis is acute AR. Select echocardiography, IV sodium nitroprusside, and dobutamine as a bridge to urgent surgery.

Mitral Stenosis

Diagnosis

MS usually presents 20 to 40 years after an episode of RF. The most common symptoms are orthopnea and paroxysmal nocturnal dyspnea. Patients may have a history of AF or systemic thromboembolism. Physical examination findings include:

- a prominent *a* wave in the jugular pulse
- a prominent tapping apical impulse
- signs of right-sided HF
- accentuation of the P_2 and an opening snap
- a low-pitched, rumbling diastolic murmur with presystolic accentuation

A chest x-ray shows an enlarged pulmonary artery, left atrium, right ventricle, and right atrium. The ECG shows RV hypertrophy and a notched P-wave duration >0.12 sec in lead II (P mitrale).

TTE is needed to confirm MS and detect left atrial thrombus. TEE is used to evaluate a thromboembolic event.

Therapy

Choose β-blockers or calcium channel blockers for patients with sinus tachycardia. Treat new-onset AF with heparin followed by warfarin and β-blockers or calcium channel blockers for rate control. Patients with MS and risk factors for venous thromboembolism (previous embolic event, paroxysmal or chronic AF, left atrial thrombus, sinus rhythm and left atrial diameter >5.5 cm) require long-term warfarin therapy to achieve an INR of 2.0 to 3.0.

Consider electrical cardioversion to re-establish sinus rhythm in patients with MS and new-onset AF. Percutaneous valvulotomy is indicated:

- if echocardiography has excluded the presence of a left atrial appendage thrombus
- in symptomatic patients with a valve area <1 cm² or a valve area <1.5 cm² when limitations in exercise are present

Valvular characteristics that favor a successful percutaneous valvulotomy include the presence of pliable leaflets, minimal commissural fusion, and minimal valvular or subvalvular calcification. Concurrent mitral regurgitation is a contraindication to valvulotomy. In patients whose anatomy is not amenable to this procedure, surgical commissurotomy or mitral valve replacement can be performed.

❖ Test Yourself

A 28-year-old woman who is 29 weeks pregnant has progressive dyspnea. Physical examination shows tachycardia, jugular venous distention, a parasternal impulse, an opening snap, and a grade 2/6 diastolic rumble with presystolic accentuation.

ANSWER: This is the classic presentation for MS with associated increased intravascular volume in a pregnant patient. Select metoprolol to allow greater time for LV diastolic filling and relief of pulmonary hypertension.

◆ DON'T BE TRICKED
- **Treat all patients with MS and AF, regardless of CHADS$_2$ score, with warfarin.**

Mitral Regurgitation

Diagnosis

MR may be either acute or chronic. Acute MR most often occurs in patients with chordae tendineae rupture due to myxomatous valve disease or endocarditis. In the setting of an MI, consider papillary muscle dysfunction or rupture. Characteristic findings in acute MR include the abrupt onset of dyspnea, pulmonary edema, or cardiogenic shock. Physical examination shows right-sided HF associated with a holosystolic murmur at the apex that radiates to the axilla and occasionally to the base. The murmur may be short or absent in patients with acute MR.

Causes of chronic MR include:

- mitral valve prolapse
- IE
- HCM
- ischemic heart disease
- ventricular dilatation
- Marfan syndrome
- prolonged use of ergotamine, pergolide, or cabergoline

Characteristic findings include orthopnea, paroxysmal nocturnal dyspnea, and edema. Physical examination shows a holosystolic murmur that radiates to the left axilla or to the base if the posterior leaflet is involved; a displaced, hyperdynamic apical impulse; and decreased intensity of S$_1$, a widely split S$_2$, an S$_3$, and an increased P$_2$.

Therapy

Drug therapy for acute MR includes sodium nitroprusside to reduce the mean arterial pressure to ≤60 mm Hg; nitroglycerin for patients who remain symptomatic after taking arterial vasodilators and diuretics; and dobutamine, amrinone, or milrinone for patients with hypotension. Select an intra-aortic balloon pump for patients with acute MR who are hemodynamically unstable but who respond to vasodilators and inotropic agents. Acute severe MR requires surgical intervention.

Treat chronic MR with diuretics, β-blockers, ACE inhibitors, or ARBs. Add digoxin and spironolactone as needed. Associated AF requires anticoagulation and drug therapy for rate control.

Patients with symptomatic chronic MR require mitral valve surgery, even if systolic function and LV size are normal. Mitral valve surgery is also indicated for symptomatic or asymptomatic MR when the LVEF is <55% or LV dilatation is >45 mm. Mitral valve repair is preferred to mitral valve replacement when the anatomy is suitable and avoids the risks of anticoagulation. MR resulting from ischemia-induced dysfunction of the papillary muscle should improve after appropriate revascularization.

◆ DON'T BE TRICKED

- **Do not select mitral valve surgery if the LVEF is <30%.**

❖ Test Yourself

A 63-year-old man who is asymptomatic and active is found to have MR during a physical examination. LV size is 51 mm and the EF is 52%.

ANSWER: Select mitral valve replacement or repair.

Mitral Valve Prolapse

Diagnosis

MVP is the most common cause of significant MR, but most patients with prolapse have either minimal or no MR. MVP syndrome is usually asymptomatic but can cause chest pain, palpitations, syncope, dyspnea, and embolic phenomena. On physical examination, a high-pitched midsystolic click is heard followed by a late systolic murmur that is loudest at the apex. Standing from a sitting position and performing the Valsalva maneuver cause the click and murmur to occur earlier. Squatting from a standing position delays the click and murmur and decreases the intensity. The initial diagnostic study is echocardiography. Patients with symptoms of arrhythmia require ambulatory ECG monitoring.

Therapy

Treat patients with palpitations, chest pain, anxiety, or fatigue with β-blockers. Aspirin is appropriate for patients with unexplained TIA who have sinus rhythm and no atrial thrombi. Warfarin is indicated for patients with recurrent ischemic neurologic events despite aspirin; patients with a history of stroke; and patients >65 years of age with AF, hypertension, MR, or HF. Surgery is required for significant MR, a flail leaflet caused by a ruptured chorda, or marked chordal elongation.

❖ Test Yourself

A 28-year-old woman has palpitations. Cardiac examination is normal except for an isolated click. Echocardiography is also normal except for mild MR, and 24-hour ECG monitoring shows 728 isolated, unifocal, premature ventricular complexes.

ANSWER: Provide reassurance and counsel on lifestyle modification (reduction of caffeine and other stimulants).

Tricuspid Regurgitation

Diagnosis

Primary causes of TR include Marfan syndrome and congenital disorders such as Ebstein anomaly and AV canal malformations. Common secondary causes include IE, carcinoid syndrome, pulmonary hypertension, and RF. Physical examination shows prominent *v* waves in the neck, increased jugular venous pressure during inspiration, and hepatic pulsations. Patients with severe disease may have ascites and pedal edema. A holosystolic murmur is heard at the left lower sternal border, increasing in intensity during inspiration. Echocardiography is diagnostic.

Therapy

Consider tricuspid valve surgery only if other cardiac surgery is planned.

◆ DON'T BE TRICKED

- Mild or less severe TR is common, can be easily identified by echocardiography, is physiologically normal, and does not require treatment.

Prosthetic Heart Valves

Characteristics

Mechanical valves are more durable than bioprosthetic valves but require lifelong anticoagulation. Prosthetic valves in the aortic position are more durable and less prone to thromboembolism than valves in the mitral position.

Complications

Common complications include structural valve deterioration, valve thrombosis, embolism, bleeding, and endocarditis. In the immediate postoperative period, valve dehiscence or dysfunction should be suspected in patients who develop acute HF. Valve dysfunction is characterized by new cardiac symptoms, embolic phenomena, hemolytic anemia (with schistocytes on peripheral blood smear), or new murmurs. If valve dysfunction is suspected, TEE is the diagnostic procedure of choice.

◆ DON'T BE TRICKED

- Begin long-term anticoagulation only for patients with mechanical heart valves.

Anticoagulation

For patients at low risk, those with a mechanical aortic valve with no other risk factors, the INR goal is 2.0 to 3.0. In patients at high risk, those with a mechanical mitral valve or aortic valve plus an additional risk factor (AF, LV dysfunction, previous thromboembolism, or hypercoagulable condition), an INR of 2.5 to 3.5 is recommended. The addition of low-dose aspirin (81 mg/d) to warfarin further decreases the risk of thromboembolism and is recommended in all patients with prosthetic heart valves.

Keep the following in mind:

- Interrupt anticoagulation in patients with a prosthetic heart valve before they undergo noncardiac or dental surgery (but not cataract surgery).
- For aortic valve prostheses, stop warfarin 4 to 5 days before the procedure, allow the INR to fall below 1.5, and restart as soon as postprocedure control of bleeding allows.
- In patients at high risk for thrombosis (mitral prostheses, multiple prosthetic valves, AF, or previous thromboembolic events), stop warfarin 4 to 5 days before surgery and begin inpatient IV heparin after the INR falls below 2.0 and again within 24 hours after surgery. Warfarin is initiated after surgery, and heparin is discontinued when INR is therapeutic.
- Do not use vitamin K to reverse anticoagulation. If urgent reversal is needed, choose FFP.

Atrial Septal Defect

Diagnosis

Findings of ASD include fixed splitting of the S_2, a pulmonary midsystolic murmur, and tricuspid diastolic flow murmur. The CVP may be normal, or equal *a* and *v* waves may be noted. An RV impulse is present.

The most common form of ASD is the ostium secundum defect, which usually occurs as an isolated abnormality. The ECG shows right axis deviation and partial RBBB. The ostium primum ASD is often associated with a cleft in the mitral or tricuspid valve with associated valve regurgitation. A VSD may also be present. The ECG characteristically shows first-degree AV block, left axis deviation, and RBBB.

Therapy

Closure is indicated for right atrial or ventricular enlargement, large left to right shunt, or symptoms (dyspnea, paradoxical embolism). Select percutaneous device closure for ostium secundum ASD and surgical closure for ostium primum ASD and associated mitral valve defects.

◆ DON'T BE TRICKED

- **Closure of an ASD is contraindicated if shunt reversal is present.**

❖ Test Yourself

An asymptomatic 26-year-old woman who is 30 weeks pregnant has a recently discovered heart murmur. Physical examination shows a right parasternal lift, a normal S_1, fixed splitting of S_2, and a grade 2/6 early systolic ejection murmur at the upper left sternal border.

ANSWER: The diagnosis is ASD. The murmur is often first discovered during pregnancy as a result of increased intravascular volume.

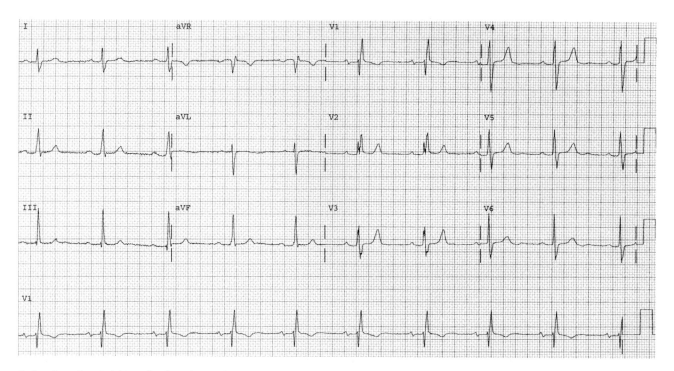

Ostium Secundum Atrial Septal Defect: The ECG shows right axis deviation, partial RBBB, and evidence of RV hypertrophy characteristic of ostium secundum ASD.

Ventricular Septal Defect

Diagnosis

A small VSD causes a loud systolic murmur that obliterates the S_2. A displaced apical LV impulse and mitral diastolic flow rumble suggest a hemodynamically important VSD. TTE demonstrates the hemodynamic impact of a VSD.

Therapy

Consider closure in adults with progressive regurgitation of the aortic or tricuspid valve, progressive LV volume overload, and recurrent endocarditis. Device closure is possible in patients with muscular VSD. Without closure, large VSDs cause pulmonary hypertension with eventual right-to-left shunt (Eisenmenger syndrome). At this stage, closure is contraindicated and pulmonary vasodilators may be used for progressive symptoms.

Arrhythmia Recording

In a patient with palpitations, dizziness, and syncope, the key diagnostic test is an ECG recorded during the clinical event. In patients with suspected structural heart disease, obtain an echocardiogram. All patients should have a resting ECG. Several approaches are available for recording an intermittent arrhythmia; the most appropriate test is based on the frequency and duration of symptoms.

STUDY TABLE: Diagnostic Studies for Arrhythmias			
Diagnostic Test	**Utility**	**Advantages**	**Limitations**
Resting ECG	Initial diagnostic test in all patients	Diagnostic if recorded during the arrhythmia	Most arrhythmias are intermittent and not recorded on a resting ECG
Ambulatory (24-hour) ECG	Indicated for frequent (at least daily) arrhythmias	Records every heart beat during a 24-hour period	Not helpful if arrhythmia is infrequent
Exercise ECG	Indicated for arrhythmias provoked by exercise	Allows diagnosis of exercise-related arrhythmias	Physician supervision required
Event monitor	Indicated for infrequent arrhythmias >1-2 min in duration	Small recorder is held to the chest when symptoms are present	Limited to symptomatic arrhythmias that persist long enough for patient to activate the device
Loop recorder	Indicated for infrequent symptomatic brief arrhythmias	Saves previous 30 sec to 2 min ECG signal when patient activates the recorder	ECG leads limit patient activities
Implanted recorder	Indicated for very infrequent arrhythmias	Long-term continuous ECG monitoring	Invasive procedure with some risk
Electrophysiology study	Indicated for treatment (e.g. catheter ablation), not for diagnosis	The origin and mechanism of an arrhythmia can be precisely defined	Invasive procedure with some risk

Atrial Fibrillation

Diagnosis

Findings of AF include an irregularly irregular ventricular rhythm at a rate of 80 to 170/min and absence of P waves in all ECG leads. The presence of deformed T waves or ST segments "hiding" P waves rules out AF. Do not confuse AF with sinus tachycardia with premature atrial beats, multifocal atrial tachycardia in patients with COPD, Mobitz type 1 second-degree AV block (Wenckebach) with characteristic group-beating, or arrhythmia due to digitalis toxicity (atrial tachycardia with block). AF can appear as irregular, wide-complex tachycardia in the setting of underlying intraventricular conduction delay (RBBB) or in the presence of an accessory pathway.

Diagnostic studies include measurement of serum TSH and digoxin levels (if appropriate), pulse oximetry, and echocardiography.

Therapy

Almost all patients with AF need chronic anticoagulation. The risk of stroke in patients who have nonvalvular AF plus one other risk factor exceeds the risk of hemorrhage from anticoagulation.

Remember the CHADS$_2$ mnemonic for stroke risk in patients with nonvalvular AF:

- Chronic HF
- Hypertension
- Age >75 years
- Diabetes mellitus
- Stroke or TIA (presence of either scores 2 points)

STUDY TABLE: Anticoagulation Goals in AF	
Condition	**Treatment Recommendation**
No heart disease or CHADS$_2$ score = 0	Aspirin
CHADS$_2$ score = 1	Individual assessment
CHADS$_2$ score ≥ 2	Warfarin; INR 2.0-3.0

Direct thrombin inhibitors such as dabigatran may be used in place of warfarin.

Because the daily risk of stroke in nonvalvular AF is low, most patients do not require bridging anticoagulation when warfarin is interrupted for procedures.

Perform emergency electrical cardioversion for patients with hemodynamically unstable AF. Before elective cardioversion, patients who have been in AF for ≥48 hours or an unknown duration should receive 3 weeks of anticoagulation with warfarin or undergo TEE to rule out a clot. All patients undergoing cardioversion should receive anticoagulation for at least 4 weeks after cardioversion (or chronically, depending on other risk factors).

No mortality benefit is evident from restoration of sinus rhythm ("rhythm control") compared with rate control. Older patients with chronic AF or AF of unknown duration should have rate control with diltiazem, verapamil, atenolol, or metoprolol. For older, asymptomatic patients, clinical outcomes are not improved with a ventricular resting rate <80/min compared with a more lenient target rate (<110/min).

Rhythm control is an appropriate management for younger patients with persistent symptomatic AF. Rhythm control may be achieved with medications, synchronized cardioversion, or both. If rhythm control is unsuccessful or not tolerated, catheter-based AF ablation is an option. A "maze" procedure may be useful for patients undergoing cardiac surgery for other reasons.

◆ DON'T BE TRICKED

- **Do not begin digoxin as a single agent for rate control.**
- **Do not use catheter ablation of the AV node before a trial of medication for rate control.**
- **Do not begin calcium channel blockers, β-blockers, or digoxin in patients with AF and WPW syndrome.**

❖ Test Yourself

A 55-year-old woman has dyspnea and chest pain of 12 hours' duration. Blood pressure is 75/44 mm Hg, and bibasilar crackles are heard. ECG shows a wide-complex tachycardia of 160/min.

ANSWER: Cardioversion is always the answer in patients with AF who are hemodynamically unstable.

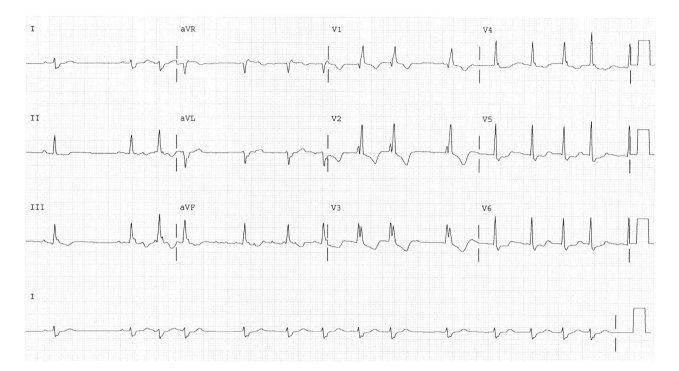

Atrial Fibrillation: ECG shows two sinus beats followed by AF. The AF rhythm is irregular, and fibrillatory waves are clearly seen. RBBB is also present.

Atrial Flutter

Diagnosis

Atrial flutter is a reentrant arrhythmia with atrial rates typically between 250 and 340/min. ECG typically shows a saw-tooth pattern on the inferior leads and a positive deflection in lead V_1. The ventricular response is often regular. Most patients have 2:1 conduction resulting in a ventricular response close to 150 beats/min. Atrial flutter may be seen interspersed with AF or may follow treatment of AF. Atrial flutter is often the result of pulmonary disease exacerbation or pericarditis, or may occur after open heart surgery.

Therapy

Atrial flutter can be successfully eliminated with radiofrequency catheter ablation, which is superior to medical therapy. Guidelines for anticoagulation for atrial flutter are similar to those for AF.

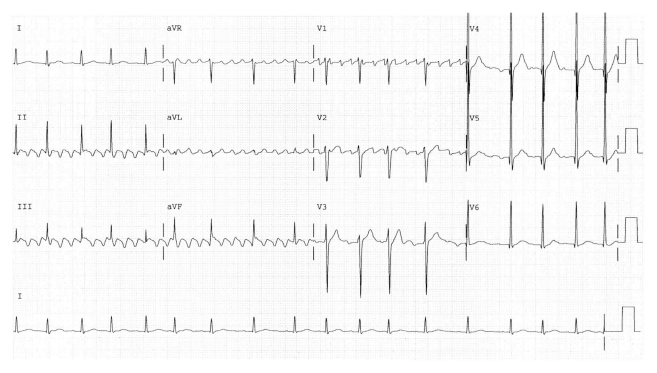

Atrial Flutter: ECG shows a "saw-tooth" pattern in leads II and III characteristic of atrial flutter.

Supraventricular Tachycardia

Diagnosis

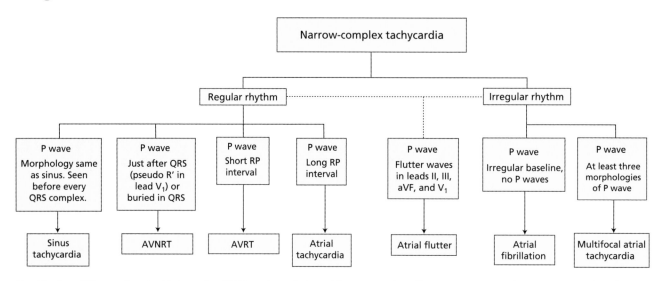

Classification of Narrow-Complex Tachycardia: AVNRT = atrioventricular nodal reentrant tachycardia; AVRT = atrioventricular reciprocating tachycardia.

Therapy

Sinus tachycardia is characterized by an accelerated sinus rate and normal ventricular conduction usually defined as >100/min. The most common causes are response to exercise, fever, exposure to stimulants and excessive catecholamine release in response to physiological challenges such as fright and anger. In most cases, treatment is not necessary or is directed to the underlying condition. Sinus tachycardia associated with mitral valve stenosis is treated with β-blocker therapy.

Treatment of multifocal atrial tachycardia is directed at correcting associated pulmonary and cardiac disease, hypokalemia, and hypomagnesemia. Drug therapy is indicated for patients who are symptomatic or experience complications such as HF or chest pain secondary to cardiac ischemia. Metoprolol is the drug of choice followed by verapamil in patients with bronchospastic disease.

The drug of choice for the acute treatment of AV-nodal reentrant tachycardia is adenosine. Adenosine may induce bronchospasm in patients with reactive airways disease. Verapamil is as effective as adenosine and has the advantage of preventing immediate recurrences; however, it takes longer to act and may cause hypotension.

Acute atrial tachycardias often terminate with administration of adenosine. If the arrhythmia does not terminate, rate control can be achieved with β-blockers or calcium channel blockers. Use oral calcium channel blockers and β-blockers to prevent recurrent AV node–dependent SVT. Teach selected patients with AV node–dependent SVT to use the Valsalva maneuver or carotid sinus massage to help terminate episodes of arrhythmia.

Adenosine can be the initial therapy in patients with hemodynamically stable wide-complex tachycardia of uncertain etiology. Patients with SVT (and aberrant conduction) typically convert; VT will not convert.

◆ DON'T BE TRICKED

- **Do not treat irregular wide-complex tachycardia or polymorphic tachycardia with adenosine.**

❖ Test Yourself

A 32-year-old woman has a 4-hour history of palpitations. Blood pressure is 80/50 mm Hg, and the heart rate is very rapid. An ECG shows regular, narrow-complex tachycardia of 180/min and normal QRS complex morphology. No P waves are seen.

ANSWER: The diagnosis is AV-nodal reentrant tachycardia. Choose the Valsalva maneuver, carotid sinus massage, verapamil, or IV adenosine.

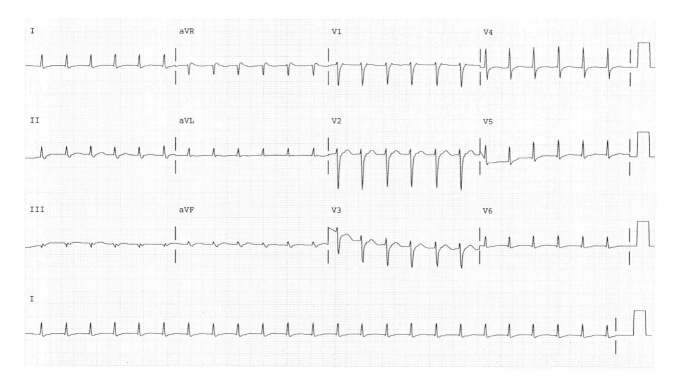

AV-Nodal Reentrant Tachycardia: The ECG shows a narrow-complex tachycardia at 144/min and no visible P waves.

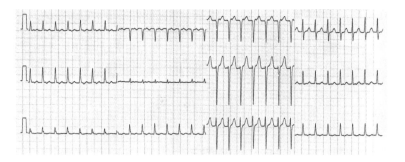

AV Reciprocating Tachycardia: ECG shows a narrow-complex tachycardia with the P wave buried in the ST segment.

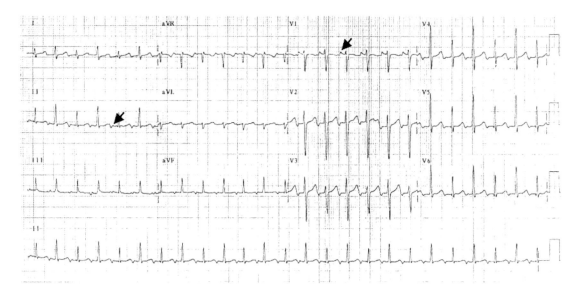

Atrial Tachycardia: The ECG shows a narrow-complex tachycardia with P waves most clearly seen in lead V₁ and at the end of the T wave in other leads.

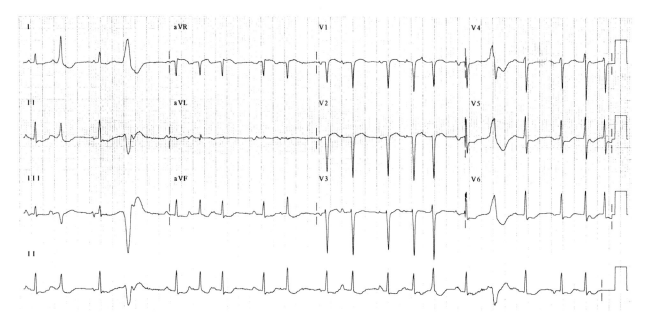

Multifocal Atrial Tachycardia: The ECG shows an irregular tachycardia with three distinct P wave morphologies characteristic of multifocal atrial tachycardia.

Wolff-Parkinson-White Syndrome

Diagnosis

Preexcitation (WPW syndrome) is caused by an accessory AV conduction pathway that is

- usually antegrade to the ventricles, resulting in the delta wave that indicates ventricular preexcitation (in this situation, WPW is described as "manifest").
- occasionally concealed or retrograde; ventricles are depolarized over the normal AV node–His-Purkinje network, resulting in a normal surface ECG (in this situation, WPW is described as "concealed").

ECG findings include a short PR interval, delta wave, and normal or prolonged QRS. Reentrant tachycardia is common. AF associated with WPW syndrome is a risk factor for sudden death caused by degeneration into VF.

◆ DON'T BE TRICKED

- **Asymptomatic WPW conduction without arrhythmia does not require investigation or treatment.**

Therapy

Begin procainamide or another class I or class III agent for patients with wide-complex tachycardia, especially when AF and preexcitation are present. Cardioversion is the preferred treatment for any unstable patient with WPW syndrome.

Ablation of the accessory bypass tract is used for patients with drug-resistant tachycardia or for those who want to avoid long-term drug therapy.

◆ DON'T BE TRICKED

- **Do not select calcium channel blockers, β-blockers, or digoxin for patients who have AF with WPW syndrome because such treatment may convert AF to VT or VF.**

❖ Test Yourself

A 28-year-old woman has a 4-hour history of palpitations. Physical examination shows a blood pressure of 132/80 mm Hg, an irregularly irregular heart rate of 140/min, and no other abnormal findings. The ECG shows AF with a ventricular rate of 180 to 270/min. QRS complexes are broad and bizarre.

ANSWER: The diagnosis is WPW syndrome. Begin IV procainamide.

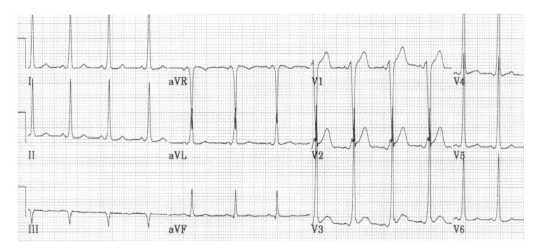

WPW Syndrome: WPW syndrome is diagnosed by a short PR interval, prolonged QRS, and a slurred onset of the QRS (delta wave).

Heart Block

Diagnosis

AV nodal block results from functional or structural abnormalities at the AV node or in the His-Purkinje system. Half the cases are due to fibrosis of the conduction system.

- First-degree block: PR interval >0.2 sec without alterations in heart rate.
- Second-degree block: Intermittent P waves not followed by a ventricular complex; further classified as Mobitz type 1 or type 2.
- Third-degree block (complete heart block): Complete absence of conducted P waves (P-wave and QRS complex rates differ, and the PR interval differs for every QRS complex) and an atrial rate that is faster than ventricular rate. It is the most common cause of ventricular rates 30 to 50/min.
- LBBB: Absent Q waves in leads I, aVL, and V_6; large, wide, and positive R waves in leads I, aVL, and V_6; QRS > 0.12 sec.
- RBBB: rsR' pattern in lead V_1 ("rabbit ears"), wide negative S wave in lead V_6, QRS >0.12 sec.
- Bifascicular block: Right bundle branch and one of the fascicles of the left bundle branch are involved.
- Trifascicular block: Characterized by bifascicular block and prolongation of the PR interval.

Quick Check Criteria for left anterior hemiblock:

- left axis usually −60°
- upright QRS complex in lead I, negative QRS complex in aVF
- normal QRS duration

Quick Check Criteria for left posterior hemiblock:

- right axis usually +120°
- negative QRS complex in lead I, positive QRS complex in lead aVF
- normal QRS duration

STUDY TABLE: Second-Degree AV Block: Mobitz Type 1 and Type 2		
Type	Characteristics	Significance
Mobitz type 1 (Wenckebach block)	Constant P-P interval with progressively increased PR interval until the dropped beat	Rarely progresses to third-degree heart block
Mobitz type 2	Usually associated with RBBB or LBBB; constant PR interval in the conducted beats; R-R interval contains the nonconducted (dropped) beat equal to two P-P intervals	May precede third-degree heart block

Therapy

Initial therapy of AV block includes correcting reversible causes of impaired conduction such as ischemia, increased vagal tone, and elimination of drugs that alter electrical conduction, including digitalis.

Guidelines for permanent pacemaker implantation include:

- persistent, advanced (Mobitz type 2) second-degree heart block
- transient second-degree heart block with bundle branch block
- third-degree heart block
- symptomatic heart block at any level

Permanent pacemaker implantation may be considered if bifascicular or trifascicular block is associated with syncope that can be attributed to transient complete heart block after exclusion of other plausible causes.

Choose IV atropine and/or transcutaneous or transvenous pacing for symptoms of hemodynamic compromise caused by bradycardia or heart block.

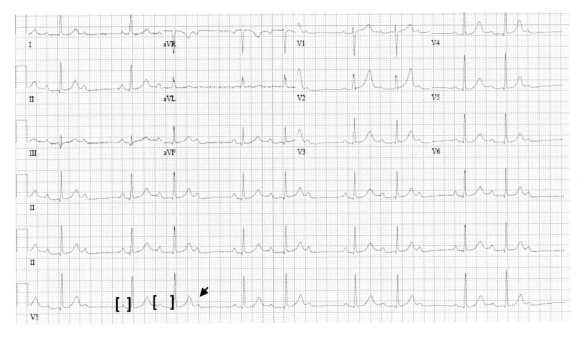

Mobitz Type 1 Heart Block: Rhythm strip shows progressive prolongation of the PR interval until the dropped beat.

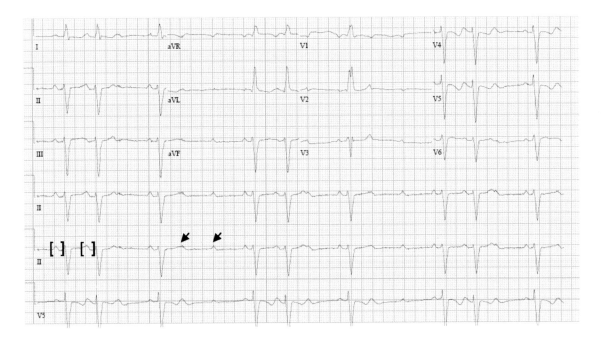

Mobitz Type 2 Heart Block: Rhythm strip shows constant PR interval. The R-R interval containing the nonconducted beat is equal to two P-P intervals.

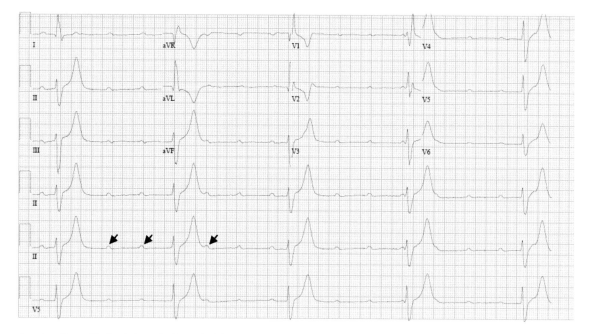

Complete Heart Block: Rhythm strip shows third-degree heart block with three nonconducted atrial impulses and a pause of 4.5 seconds.

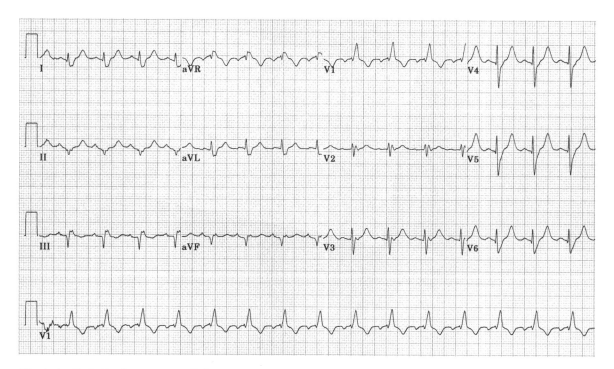

Bifascicular Block: ECG showing RBBB and left anterior hemiblock characteristic of bifascicular block.

Ventricular Tachycardia

Diagnosis

Premature ventricular complexes (PVCs) can be single, in pairs (couplets), or alternating with sinus beats. These beats are usually followed by a compensatory pause. In healthy adults, PVCs are benign.

Ventricular tachyarrhythmias consist of VT, VF, and torsades de pointes. Ventricular tachyarrhythmias are characterized by:

- QRS >0.12 sec
- AV dissociation

In VT, the ventricular rate typically ranges from 140 to 250/min, VF rate is typically >300/min, and torsades de pointes is characterized by a ventricular rate of 200 to 300/min.

VT can be further classified as sustained or nonsustained. Nonsustained VT lasts <30 sec.

VT is also categorized by the morphology of the QRS complexes:

- Monomorphic VT: QRS complexes in the same leads do not vary in contour.
- Polymorphic VT: QRS complexes in the same leads do vary in contour.

Differentiating VT from SVT with aberrant conduction is important because the treatment differs markedly. VT is more common than SVT with aberrancy, particularly in persons with structural heart disease. A key point is that any wide QRS tachycardia should be considered to be VT until proven otherwise. In the presence of known structural heart disease, especially a previous MI, the diagnosis of VT is almost certain.

Torsades de pointes is a specific form of polymorphic VT associated with long QT syndrome, which may be congenital or acquired (see Sudden Cardiac Death). Torsades de pointes episodes are typically short-lived and terminate spontaneously, but multiple successive episodes may result in syncope or VF.

◆ DON'T BE TRICKED

- **In patients with structural heart disease, therapy to suppress PVCs does not affect outcomes.**

Therapy

In otherwise healthy patients, suppression of PVCs with β-blockers is only indicated for disabling symptoms. Patients with nonsustained VT should be treated with β-blockers only if symptoms are present. The acute treatment of sustained VT depends on the degree of hemodynamic compromise:

- For unstable patients: Immediate electrical cardioversion is indicated. Pulseless VT is treated in the same way as VF.
- For hemodynamically stable patients with impaired LV function: IV lidocaine or amiodarone is preferred. Procainamide and sotalol are additional therapeutic possibilities.

An ICD reduces sudden cardiac death in patients with VF or sustained VT associated with hemodynamic compromise.

❖ Test Yourself

A 65-year-old woman with chronic stable angina and a history of an anterior MI is evaluated in the emergency department for palpitations and lightheadedness. Vital signs are stable. ECG shows a wide-complex tachycardia with an RBBB pattern. No previous ECGs are immediately available.

ANSWER: The diagnosis is most likely sustained VT. The acute treatment is IV lidocaine or amiodarone.

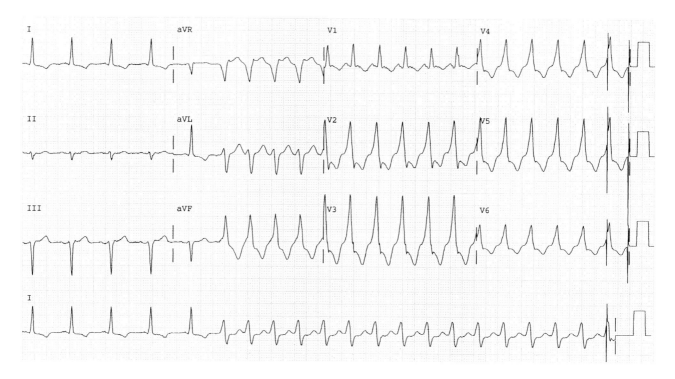

Monomorphic VT: Approximately one quarter of the way into this ECG, monomorphic VT begins; it is associated with an abrupt change in the QRS axis.

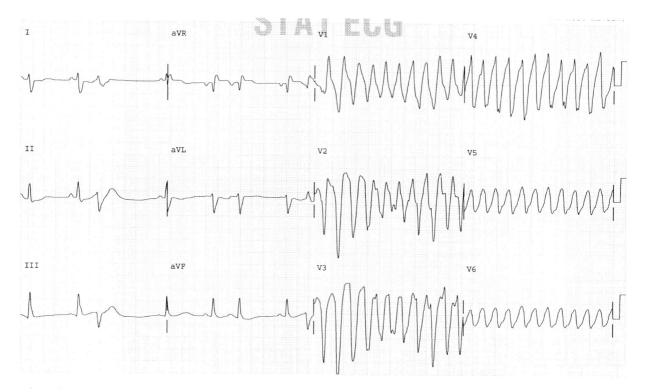

Polymorphic VT: This ECG shows degeneration of the sinus rhythm into polymorphic tachycardia.

Sudden Cardiac Death

Diagnosis

Sudden cardiac death is most often associated with structural heart disease, abnormal cardiac rhythms or conduction, HF, WPW syndrome, Brugada syndrome, and long QT syndrome.

Long QT syndrome may be inherited or acquired. Patients may experience syncope or sudden cardiac death as the result of torsades de pointes, a specific form of polymorphic VT. Risk factors for acquired long QT syndrome include female sex, hypokalemia, hypomagnesemia, structural heart disease, and medications and drug interactions (look specifically for macrolide and fluoroquinolone antibiotics, terfenadine and astemizole antihistamines, antipsychotic and antidepressant medications, methadone, antifungal medications, and class Ia and class III antiarrhythmics). Risk is greatest with QTc interval greater than 500 msec.

Brugada syndrome is an inherited condition characterized by a structurally normal heart but abnormal electrical conduction associated with sudden cardiac death. Classic Brugada syndrome is recognized as an incomplete RBBB pattern with coved ST-segment elevation in leads V_1 and V_2. Other variations of this electrical pattern exist. The risk of sudden cardiac death is also increased in patients taking antiarrhythmic agents, using alcohol excessively, and taking illicit drugs.

Select echocardiography for survivors of sudden cardiac death to identify anatomic abnormalities, impaired ventricular function, and/or myopathic processes. Electrophysiologic studies are indicated for patients with suspected ventricular arrhythmias, episodes of impaired consciousness, and structurally abnormal hearts. Patients taking antiarrhythmic agents should have a serum drug level measurement and an ECG to look for long QT syndrome.

Therapy

Therapy includes pharmacologic treatment of underlying CAD and a revascularization procedure if anatomically possible. Inherited long QT syndrome may be treated with β-blockers.

Select an ICD in the following scenarios:

- for survivors of cardiac arrest due to VF or VT not explained by a reversible cause
- after sustained VT in the presence of structural heart disease
- after syncope and sustained VT/VF on electrophysiology study
- for ischemic and nonischemic cardiomyopathy with an EF <35%
- for Brugada syndrome
- for inherited long QT syndrome not responding to β-blockers
- after MI with an EF <30%
- for high-risk HCM (familial sudden death; multiple, repetitive nonsustained VT; extreme LVH; malignant genotype; and exercise hypotension)

❖ **Test Yourself**

A 55-year-old man is evaluated 4 months after a large anterior MI. He has no symptoms, and his physical examination is normal. Follow-up echocardiography documents an LVEF of 28%.

ANSWER: This patient is at high risk for sudden cardiac death and should be considered for an ICD.

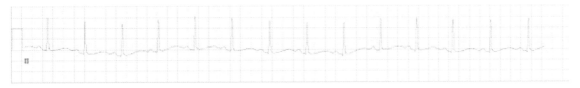

Prolonged QT syndrome: The ECG shows a prolonged QT interval of 590 msec.

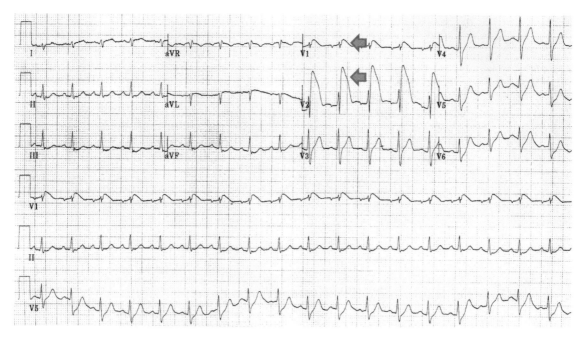

Brugada Pattern on ECG: Incomplete RBBB pattern and elevation of the ST segments that gradually descends to an inverted T wave in leads V_1 and V_2 is characteristic of the classic variety of Brugada syndrome. Image courtesy of Patrick T. Ellinor, MD, PhD, Massachusetts General Hospital.

Aortic Atheroemboli

Diagnosis

Plaque in either the ascending or descending thoracic aorta is associated with an increased risk of clinical thromboembolism, including stroke. Characteristic findings include livedo reticularis, gangrene of the digits, and transient vision loss (a golden or brightly refractile cholesterol body within a retinal artery [Hollenhorst plaque] is pathognomonic). Patients often present with stroke or acute kidney injury following recent cardiac or aortic surgery or other intravascular procedures (catheterization). Biopsy of muscle, skin, kidney, or other organs confirms the diagnosis.

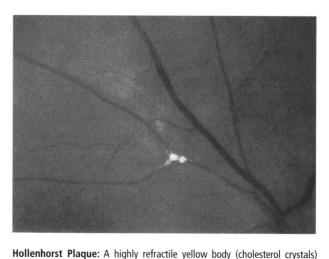

Hollenhorst Plaque: A highly refractile yellow body (cholesterol crystals) within a retinal artery. Image courtesy of Dr. Edward Jaeger, Jefferson Medical College and Wills Eye Institute.

Therapy

Treatment is control of cardiovascular risk factors.

❖ **Test Yourself**

A 67-year-old man has acute kidney injury following coronary angiography 10 days ago. Blood pressure is 168/100 mm Hg. Bruits are noted over the abdomen and femoral arteries. His legs have a lacy, purplish discoloration.

ANSWER: Look for cholesterol emboli to the skin and renal vasculature. Select skin biopsy and control of all cardiovascular risk factors.

Coarctation of the Aorta

Diagnosis

Coarctation of the aorta is a congenital disorder that may not be discovered until young adulthood. Characteristic findings include hypertension, diminished femoral pulses, radial-to-femoral pulse delay, and a murmur of AS with a continuous murmur audible over the back.

A chest x-ray shows the classic "figure 3" sign (an indented aortic wall at the site of the coarctation with dilatation above and below the coarctation) and notching on the undersides of the posterior ribs. MRA confirms the diagnosis.

Therapy

Schedule balloon dilation for patients with a discrete area of aortic narrowing, proximal hypertension, and a pressure gradient exceeding 20 mm Hg.

❖ **Test Yourself**

A 35-year-old female immigrant reports cold feet and leg cramping when walking long distances. Blood pressure is 160/90 mm Hg. Cardiac examination shows a sustained apical impulse, an early systolic ejection sound, and an early systolic murmur at the upper right sternal border.

ANSWER: The diagnosis is coarctation of the aorta with an associated bicuspid aortic valve. Be alert for congenital heart disease in questions featuring an immigrant patient.

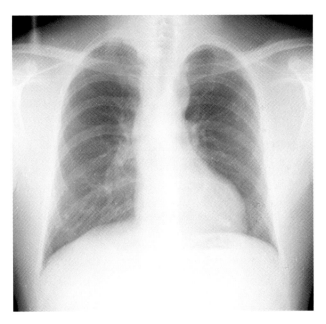

Aortic Coarctation: A chest x-ray shows rib notching and the classic "figure 3" sign (an indented aortic wall at the site of the coarctation with dilatation above and below the coarctation).

Thoracic Aortic Aneurysm and Dissection

Monitoring

Echocardiography is performed yearly for patients at risk until the aortic root reaches 4.5 cm and then every 6 months thereafter. Repair is appropriate when the aortic root measures 5.0 to 5.5 cm. Counsel against pregnancy in patients with an aortic root diameter >4 cm.

Diagnosis

Most thoracic aortic aneurysms are asymptomatic and are typically incidental findings on imaging studies. Patients present with symptoms attributable to compression or distortion of adjacent structures, such as hoarseness, dysphagia, recurrent pneumonia, and superior vena cava syndrome. Risk factors in younger patients include Marfan syndrome, cocaine abuse, and a bicuspid aortic valve. Poorly controlled hypertension is a risk factor in older patients.

Signs and symptoms include chest, flank, abdominal, and back pain. Physical examination findings may include new aortic regurgitation, HF, and a blood pressure differential between the arms. A widened mediastinum is seen on chest x-ray. Patients may also have evidence of thromboembolism, dissection of branch arteries (stroke, MI), or cardiac tamponade. Dissections involving the ascending aorta are classified as type A, and all other dissections are classified as type B.

The diagnosis is established by TEE, a CT scan with contrast, or MRA. Bedside TEE is used for critically ill patients who cannot be moved.

Therapy

For thoracic aneurysms, β-blockers reduce the rate of thoracic aortic dilation. Prophylactic surgery is recommended for the following clinical situations:

- symptoms of hoarseness, dysphagia, back pain
- ascending aorta diameter >50 to 60 mm
- descending aorta diameter >60 to 70 mm
- rapid growth >10 mm/year

For acute dissection, begin IV β-blocker therapy and nitroprusside, fenoldopam, or enalaprilat. Emergent surgery is required for type A dissection. Uncomplicated type B dissection is treated with continued medical therapy alone.

◆ DON'T BE TRICKED

- **Do not use hydralazine for acute aortic dissection because it increases shear stress.**
- **Schedule surgery for type B dissection if major aortic vessels (renal arteries) are involved.**

❖ Test Yourself

A 73-year-old man has a 1-hour history of severe, tearing substernal chest pain. Blood pressure is 90/60 mm Hg in the right arm and 130/70 mm Hg in the left arm. A chest x-ray shows a widened mediastinum.

ANSWER: The diagnosis is dissection of the aortic arch. Choose β-blockers, sodium nitroprusside, and emergent imaging studies.

Abdominal Aortic Aneurysm

Screening

One-time ultrasonographic screening is indicated to detect an asymptomatic AAA in any man between the ages of 65 and 75 years who has ever smoked.

Diagnosis

Most chronic AAAs are asymptomatic and are detected by palpating a pulsatile mass in the midabdomen. Signs and symptoms of a ruptured AAA include new abdominal, flank, or back pain; hypotension; syncope; and sudden collapse and shock. The diagnosis is confirmed by MRA or CT.

◆ DON'T BE TRICKED

- **Ultrasonography is not accurate for diagnosing a ruptured AAA.**

Therapy

Therapy includes treatment of cardiovascular risk factors. In the treatment of hypertension, no evidence supports the preferential use of β-blockers. Schedule surgical repair of an asymptomatic AAA ≥5.5 cm in diameter, those growing ≥0.5 cm per year, or a symptomatic AAA. Ruptured AAA requires emergent surgery.

Follow-up

Patients with an unrepaired AAA require ultrasonographic monitoring at 6-month intervals if the AAA measures 4.0 to 5.4 cm and every 2 to 3 years for smaller AAAs.

Peripheral Arterial Disease

Diagnosis

PAD most commonly involves the lower extremities and is the result of atherosclerosis involving the aorta and branch vessels. Clinical risk factors include:

- age
- smoking
- diabetes mellitus
- hyperlipidemia

Intermittent claudication is the classic sign of PAD. Most patients with PAD have coexisting coronary artery and cerebrovascular disease. The absence of a femoral pulse suggests in-flow disease of the aorta or iliac arteries. Patients with a good femoral pulse and no femoral bruit but an absent popliteal pulse likely have disease confined to the arteries in the leg. Differentiate claudication due to PAD from claudication due to spinal stenosis. Spinal stenosis is associated with pain that occurs when standing and resolves when sitting or lying down or flexing the spine (bending forward).

Interpret the ABI:

- ABI for each side is the ratio of the highest systolic arm blood pressure (regardless of side) compared with the highest systolic ankle blood pressure for that side.
- ABI ≤0.90 is compatible with PAD; ABI ≤0.40 is associated with ischemic rest pain.
- False-normal ABI occurs in patients with diabetes with calcified, noncompressible arteries (ABI >1.40).

Recall the "five Ps" to diagnose acute arterial ischemia:

- Pain
- Paresthesias
- Pallor
- Paralysis
- Pulselessness

Acute ischemia can be caused by in-situ thrombosis or remote embolization. Echocardiography is used to locate the embolic source of acute ischemia.

◆ DON'T BE TRICKED

- When the ABI is >1.40, a toe-brachial index will provide a better assessment of lower extremity perfusion.

Therapy

PAD is a CAD risk equivalent. The same risk factor reduction and blood pressure and LDL cholesterol goals apply. All patients with symptomatic PAD should begin a supervised exercise training program. Medications include:

- aspirin (preferred over ticlopidine or clopidogrel)
- statins to reduce the LDL cholesterol level to <100 mg/dL

- cilostazol for symptomatic PAD
- ramipril to reduce the risk of MI, stroke, or vascular death in PAD

Schedule angioplasty or surgery for patients who do not improve on medical therapy or have pain at rest or poorly healing ulcers. Patients with acute arterial ischemia require antiplatelet agents and heparin anticoagulation as well as urgent surgical consultation.

◆ DON'T BE TRICKED

- **Do not use cilostazol in patients with a low LVEF or history of HF.**
- **β-Blockers are not contraindicated in patients with PAD.**

❖ Test Yourself

A 60-year-old man has a 6-month history of claudication in both thighs and calves. ABI is 0.66 on the right side and 0.55 on the left side. He is symptomatic despite an intensive lifestyle management program.

ANSWER: Begin cilostazol.

Preoperative Cardiac Risk Assessment

Surgical Risks

Emergency surgery for life-threatening conditions should not be delayed for cardiac risk stratification.

Patients with active cardiac conditions should delay elective surgery for further evaluation or treatment:

- unstable coronary syndromes (MI <30 days ago, unstable or severe angina)
- decompensated HF
- significant arrhythmia
- severe valvular disease

Patients who can proceed with elective surgery without further cardiac evaluation:

- those undergoing low-risk surgery (endoscopic, superficial, breast, cataract, ambulatory)
- those able to climb a flight of stairs, walk up a hill, or walk on level ground at 4 miles/hour without symptoms (≥4 METs)

For those patients who do not meet any of the above criteria, the Revised Cardiac Risk Index (RCRI) factors are used to decide whether further testing is indicated.

STUDY TABLE: Revised Cardiac Risk Index
Risk Variables
High-risk surgery (emergent major surgery, aortic surgery, major vascular surgery, peripheral vascular surgery, long procedures with large fluid shifts and/or blood loss)
History of ischemic heart disease
History of HF
History of cerebrovascular disease
Insulin treatment
Serum creatinine >2.0 mg/dL

Patients at low risk (score 0) can undergo any surgery without further risk stratification. Consider noninvasive testing in patients with ≥3 risk factors or those undergoing vascular surgery (aortic or other major vascular surgery; peripheral vascular surgery) if it will change management. Guidelines vary regarding the necessity of performing preoperative noninvasive testing for patients with intermediate risk of CAD. Because of this, it is unlikely a test question will address this issue.

Preoperative cardiac risk assessment is not needed for patients at low risk who:

- are having minor surgery under local anesthesia (cataract removal) and have no major comorbidities
- are <55 years of age, have no pre-existing illnesses, and do not have a cardiac murmur
- have had recent (6 months to 1 year) normal coronary imaging studies and no new symptoms
- require emergent surgical intervention for life-threatening problems

Patients with compensated, asymptomatic HF can generally undergo surgery if other risk factors are acceptable. The risk for cardiac complications appears increased within 1 week of an episode of pulmonary edema; therefore, elective procedures should be delayed at least that long in these patients.

Isolated blood pressure ≤180/110 mm Hg does not appear to increase the risk for complications.

Patients with chronic MR, AR, or MS and asymptomatic HF generally tolerate noncardiac surgery well.

Therapy

Continue β-blockers for patients taking chronic β-blocker therapy. Otherwise, guidelines recommend restricting β-blockers to patients with inducible ischemia undergoing elective vascular surgery. In addition, consider β-blockers for patients at high risk (RCRI score ≥3) undergoing vascular or nonvascular surgery.

Patients taking statins should continue taking them perioperatively. The initiation of perioperative statin therapy in patients undergoing major vascular surgery with or without clinical risk factors is considered reasonable.

Consider valve replacement in patients with severe or symptomatic AS before elective major noncardiac surgery is performed.

Perform coronary revascularization before noncardiac surgery if the need for revascularization is independent of the upcoming surgery (left main disease, three-vessel disease) and if medical urgency allows. For patients who received angioplasty and stenting, elective surgery should be postponed for at least 4 to 6 weeks after bare-metal stent placement and 12 months after a drug-eluting stent. Patients requiring emergency surgery should take aspirin during the perioperative period and restart clopidogrel following the procedure.

Patients should continue taking β-blockers, oral nitrates, and most antihypertensive medications until the morning of surgery and resume taking them when they begin to eat after surgery. Most antiarrhythmic agents and long-acting drugs (digoxin and amiodarone) can be briefly withheld. IV forms or alternative agents can be given to patients in whom arrhythmias occur.

◆ DON'T BE TRICKED

- **The urgency of surgery may preclude risk assessment and intervention.**
- **Hypertension is not an independent predictor of postoperative cardiac complications.**
- **Whenever possible, avoid perioperative pulmonary artery catheterization to monitor hemodynamic status.**
- **Do not delay surgery in patients with traumatic hip fracture, because delay is associated with increased mortality.**

The peak incidence of postoperative MI is 24 to 48 hours after surgery. Chest pain is the presenting symptom in only 50% of patients; the remaining patients have new-onset HF, hypotension, or SVT. The ECG usually shows new Q waves, ST-segment changes, or conduction block. Monitor asymptomatic patients at high cardiac risk with ECGs and serum cardiac enzyme level measurements for up to 1 week postoperatively.

❖ Test Yourself

An 82-year-old man is evaluated before resection of a chronically expanding AAA. He has hypertension treated with lisinopril but no history of MI, angina pectoris, arrhythmias, stroke, kidney disease, or diabetes mellitus. Blood pressure is 136/86 mm Hg, and heart rate is 80/min. The examination is normal except for the AAA. Laboratory studies are normal except for a serum creatinine level of 1.2 mg/dL. ECG shows LV hypertrophy.

ANSWER: Proceed to surgery without additional preoperative testing.

Dermatology

Cellulitis and Soft Tissue Infection

Diagnosis

Impetigo, an infection of the epidermis, is characterized by crusted pustules.

Erysipelas affects the superficial skin layers, including the dermis and dermal lymphatics. It classically involves the malar region. The key clinical finding is a sharply raised border and orange-peel texture. It is usually due to streptococcal infection.

Cellulitis, an infection of the dermis and deeper subcutaneous tissue, features a well-demarcated area of warmth, swelling, tenderness, and erythema.

Deep tissue infection is indicated by violaceous bullae, necrosis, rapidly increasing extent of infection, massive swelling, and pain out of proportion to injury. Loss of sensation may indicate compartment syndrome (increased tissue pressure within a closed muscle compartment) secondary to deep tissue infection and may be present even if peripheral pulses are palpable.

Most diagnoses are based on clinical findings alone. Choose blood cultures in the presence of signs and symptoms of systemic toxicity.

STUDY TABLE: Skin and Soft Tissue Infection	
If you see...	**Think...**
Honey-colored, crusted pustules	Impetigo caused by β-hemolytic *Streptococcus* or *Staphylococcus*
Cellulitis after exposure to saltwater fish or shellfish; bullous cellulitis and cirrhosis	*Vibrio vulnificus* infection
Skin ulcer in a patient with neutropenia	Ecthyma gangrenosum from *Pseudomonas* infection
Chronic nodular infection of distal extremities with exposure to fish tanks	*Mycobacterium marinum*
Chronic nodular infection of distal extremities with exposure to plants/soil	*Sporotrichosis* and *Nocardia*
Sepsis following a dog bite in an asplenic patient	*Capnocytophaga canimorsus*
Swelling and erythema with pain out of proportion to physical examination findings	Necrotizing (deep) soft tissue infection
Acute, tender, well-delineated, purulent lesions	Abscess caused by *Staphylococcus aureus*
Follicle-centered pustules in beard and pubic areas, axillae, and thighs	*Staphylococcus aureus* folliculitis
Follicle-centered erythematous papules and pustules on the trunk, axillae, and buttocks 1-4 days after hot tub or whirlpool exposure	*Pseudomonas* folliculitis

Therapy

Cellulitis associated with purulent drainage or exudate should be treated empirically for MRSA pending culture results. Nonpurulent cellulitis should be treated empirically for β-hemolytic streptococci and MSSA. IV antibiotics are reserved for unsuccessful outpatient treatment or patients with signs of toxicity.

Prompt surgical debridement for deeper soft tissue infection is required for:

- toxicity, purple bullae, ecchymoses, or sloughing of skin
- necrotizing fasciitis or myonecrosis on CT or MRI
- infection following recent trauma, surgery, or childbirth
- evidence of compartment syndrome

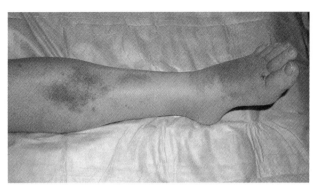

Cellulitis: Cellulitis is characterized by well-demarcated areas of tender erythema.

STUDY TABLE: Drug Therapy for Cellulitis and Soft Tissue Infection	
Diagnosis	**Treatment**
Nonpurulent cellulitis	Dicloxacillin, cephalexin, clindamycin (all oral)
Purulent cellulitis	Clindamycin, trimethoprim-sulfamethoxazole, minocycline, doxycycline, linezolid (all oral)
Purulent cellulitis with extensive disease or signs of systemic toxicity	Vancomycin (IV) or linezolid (oral or IV)
Impetigo	Extensive disease, cephalexin (oral); limited disease, mupirocin (topical)
Erysipelas	With systemic symptoms, ceftriaxone (parenteral); if mild/asymptomatic, penicillin or amoxicillin (oral)
Folliculitis (staphylococcal and pseudomonal)	Spontaneous resolution is typical
Human bites (clenched fist injury)	Ampicillin-sulbactam (IV)
Animal bites	Ampicillin-sulbactam (IV) or amoxicillin-clavulanate (oral)
Neutropenia	A fluoroquinolone (oral or IV)
Necrotizing fasciitis	Ampicillin-sulbactam (IV) and debridement

Treat risk factors for recurrent cellulitis, such as lymphedema, tinea pedis, and chronic venous insufficiency.

◆ DON'T BE TRICKED

- **Pyoderma gangrenosum is a noninfectious skin ulceration that is associated with inflammatory bowel disease, arthritis, or lymphoproliferative disorders.**
- **Skin abscesses <5 cm not associated with systemic toxicity can be treated with incision and drainage alone.**

❖ Test Yourself

A 60-year-old woman has a temperature of 38.8 °C (102.0 °F). Her right thigh is swollen and extremely tender to deep touch, with a 5-cm red patch in the middle of the tender area. She requires morphine for pain.

ANSWER: The diagnosis is myonecrosis. Select urgent MRI followed by surgical debridement.

A 20-year-old college football player has a fever, furuncles, and associated cellulitis.

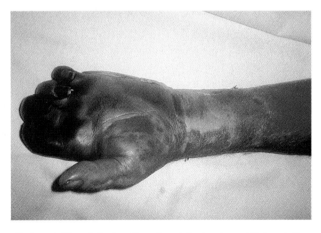

***Vibrio vulnificus* Infection:** Deep tissue infection due to *Vibrio vulnificus* in a patient with cirrhosis.

ANSWER: Likely MRSA infection; treat with trimeth-oprim-sulfamethoxazole.

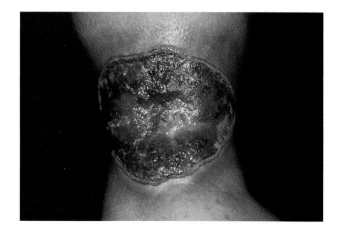

Pyoderma Gangrenosum: Pyoderma gangrenosum involves a rapidly evolving, irregular, blue-red ulcer with undermined borders and a purulent, necrotic base.

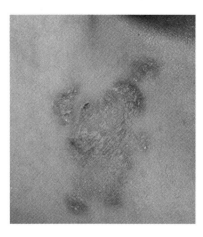

Impetigo: Erosions with golden-yellow crusts confirm the presence of impetigo.

Dermatophyte and Yeast Infections

Diagnosis

Dermatophyte fungi invade epidermal stratum corneum, hair, and nails, causing tinea infections.

- Tinea pedis presents as chronic fissuring and scaling between the toes, but some patients have a chronic "moccasin-type" form of infection with a fine, silvery scale extending from the sole to heel and sides of the feet.

- Tinea corporis most typically presents as an annual lesion with an active erythematous border of small vesicles and scales, often with central clearing.

- Tinea versicolor is characterized by hypo- or hyper-pigmented scaly macules on the trunk and proximal extremities.

- Onychomycosis is usually characterized by a thickened, yellow or white nail with scaling under the elevated distal free edge of the nail plate. Sometimes, however, the infecting organism invades the surface of the toenail.

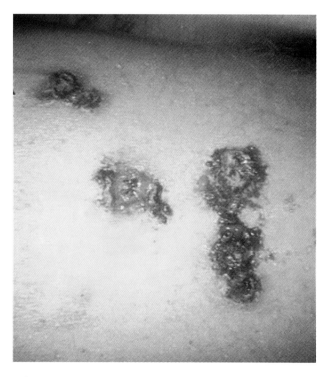

Ecthyma Gangrenosum: Ecthyma gangrenosum is characterized by single or multiple cutaneous ulcers evolving from painless nodular lesions, with surrounding erythema to central hemorrhage, ulceration, and necrosis.

Cutaneous candidiasis is characterized by red, itchy, inflamed skin. At sites of skin-to-skin contact, lesions have glazed, shiny, and at times eroded surfaces and may be characterized by burning more than pruritus. Satellite pustules (yellow, fluid-filled lesions at the edge of the confluent red eruption) are another key physical finding.

◆ DON'T BE TRICKED

- Diagnose dermatophyte and yeast infections with KOH preparation of skin scraping.
- Nail dystrophy may also be caused by psoriasis, other dermatologic conditions, aging, or peripheral vascular disease.

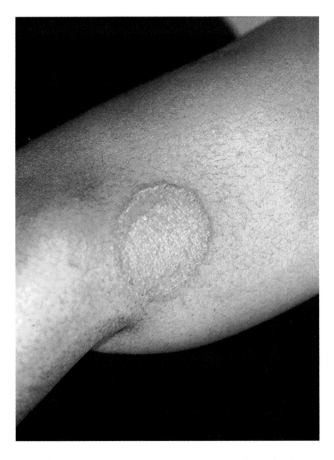

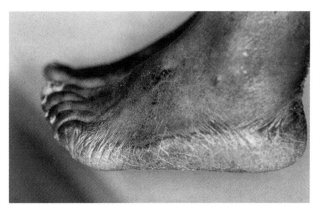

Tinea Pedis: Extension of tinea pedis onto the sole and sides of the foot ("moccasin" appearance) presents as chronic scaling.

Tinea Infection: Tinea most commonly presents as a round or oval erythematous scaling patch that spreads centrifugally with central clearing. It has an active border that is raised, consisting of tiny papules or vesicles. Image courtesy of Barbara Mathes, MD, FAAD, FACP.

***Candida* Infection:** Bright red papules, vesicles, pustules, and patches with satellite papules are characteristic of candidiasis.

Therapy

Select:

- topical antifungal creams (clotrimazole, terbinafine) for most dermatophyte infections except tinea capitis and onychomycosis
- oral terbinafine or itraconazole for confirmed onychomycosis, tinea capitis, extensive tinea corporis, or treatment-resistant dermatophytosis
- ketoconazole or fluconazole in a single dose to treat recurrent tinea versicolor
- topical nystatin, miconazole, clotrimazole, ketoconazole, and econazole for *Candida* infections

Treatment of onychomycosis is recommended for patients with peripheral vascular disease or diabetes mellitus to prevent development of cellulitis.

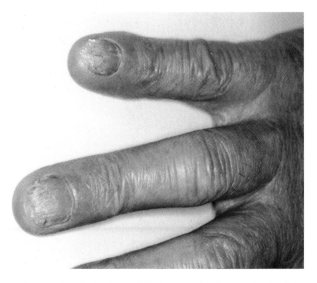

Onychomycosis: Distal subungual thickening and nail separation involving most of the nails are associated with onychomycosis.

◆ **DON'T BE TRICKED**

- Do not select antifungal treatment for thick, yellow, and crumbling toenails without KOH scraping or positive culture for dermatophytes.

- Never select a combination of a topical antifungal agent and a corticosteroid for treatment of an unknown skin rash or dermatophyte infection.

❖ **Test Yourself**

A 35-year-old man has a nonpruritic rash on his chest. He previously had a similar rash that became hypopigmented when he became suntanned. What is the diagnosis?

ANSWER: Choose tinea versicolor and KOH preparation of the scale to demonstrate a "spaghetti and meatballs" hyphae pattern.

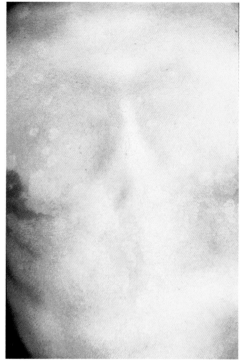

Tinea Versicolor: Hypopigmented, scaly macules are present on the chest.

Pityriasis Rosea

Diagnosis

Pityriasis rosea is an inflammatory, mildly pruritic eruption, possibly related to herpesvirus 6 or 7, that occurs in the spring and fall. It begins with a herald patch, a single, raised, bright-red, oval plaque, 2 to 5 cm in diameter with a fine scale and is followed by smaller pink papules and plaques with the distinctive ring of scale at the periphery. The lesions follow the skin cleavage lines on the trunk and chest, producing a "Christmas tree" pattern.

Therapy

The rash spontaneously resolves in 6 to 12 weeks. Oral antihistamines or topical corticosteroids can be used for itching.

◆ **DON'T BE TRICKED**

- Secondary syphilis can mimic pityriasis rosea; check rapid plasma reagin if in doubt or if the patient has risk factors for STI.

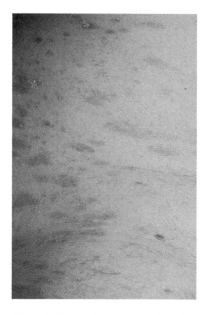

Pityriasis Rosea: Pink plaques with a fine collarette of scale, characteristic of pityriasis rosea.

Scabies

Diagnosis

Look for itching (particularly at night) and burrows appearing as wavy, threadlike, grayish-white skin elevations capped with small vesicles at the terminal ends. Scabies is the correct answer when an "itchy rash" is described between the fingers and on the penis, scrotum, areolae, and nipples. Patients with AIDS and those in institutions may develop widespread scabies with extensive scaling that may not itch.

Microscopic identification of the mite, feces, or eggs using KOH or simple mineral oil is important. A skin biopsy may also establish the diagnosis.

Therapy

Treat all family members and close contacts of the patient simultaneously. Clothing, linens, and towels must be washed in hot water and dried at high heat. Topical permethrin and malathion are preferred agents. Oral ivermectin is indicated for relapsed scabies, except when treating children and pregnant or lactating women.

◆ DON'T BE TRICKED

- **Do not re-treat scabies because of persistent itching, which can continue for 2 weeks after successful treatment.**

❖ Test Yourself

A 67-year-old woman and her 3-year-old granddaughter have a 3-week history of generalized pruritus. Both patients have widespread excoriations and a linear burrow between the thumb and index finger.

ANSWER: The diagnosis is scabies. Select topical permethrin for both patients and for close contacts.

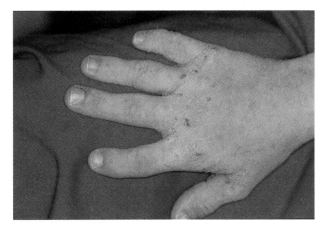

Scabies: Multiple pink papules, erosions, and excoriations with diffuse scaling are shown, predominantly in the finger webs.

Leishmaniasis

Diagnosis

Leishmaniasis is a parasitic infection caused by several species of *Leishmania* and is transmitted by the sandfly. Military personnel returning from Afghanistan and Iraq and travelers to Saudi Arabia, Brazil, and Peru are at risk. The disease begins as a small, red, painless papule on the limb or face, usually 2 to 4 weeks after the sandfly bite. The papule enlarges to approximately 2 cm over the next 2 to 4 weeks, becomes dusky red to violaceous in color, and may ulcerate. Diagnosis is based on finding parasites on biopsy of the skin.

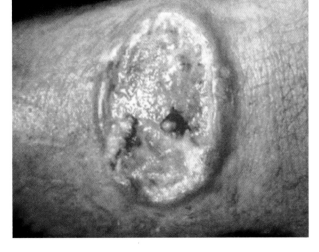

Leishmaniasis: The characteristic shallow ulcer of leishmaniasis is shown on an arm.

Herpes Zoster

Prevention

Administer varicella zoster virus vaccine to adults aged 60 years and older—regardless of previous history of varicella infection—who do not have contraindications for live vaccine (immunosuppression) to prevent or attenuate illness due to herpes zoster infection and reduce postherpetic neuralgia.

Diagnosis

Localized pain and a vesicular rash in a dermatomal distribution are characteristic features. Dermatomal neuropathic pain may develop before skin lesions occur. Be alert for two special syndromes:

- Lesions along the first division of the trigeminal nerve (zoster ophthalmicus), including the tip of the nose, may require referral to an ophthalmologist.

- Vesicles in the ears, diminished taste on the anterior two thirds of the tongue, and ipsilateral facial paralysis (Ramsay Hunt syndrome) require referral to an ENT specialist.

In patients with HIV or in those undergoing chemotherapy, the lesions may be bullous; may occur in multiple, widely separated dermatomes; may be disseminated on the skin and internally; or may produce recurrent disease. Severe, complicated, or recurrent herpes zoster should trigger testing for possible associated HIV infection.

Select a direct fluorescent antibody test on scrapings from active vesicular skin lesions that have not yet crusted or viral culture from a vesicle when the diagnosis is not clear.

Therapy

Give valacyclovir or famciclovir (7-day course) within 72 hours of lesion onset. Antiviral agents are used to treat zoster ophthalmicus even if more than 72 hours have elapsed. Gabapentin or amitriptyline is indicated for neuropathic pain.

◆ **DON'T BE TRICKED**

- **Do not select topical acyclovir or penciclovir for the treatment of herpes zoster.**

Oral corticosteroids provide symptomatic relief but do not reduce the risk of postherpetic neuralgia.

❖ **Test Yourself**

A 72-year-old man has a 4-day history of a painful vesicular rash in the distribution of the first division of the trigeminal nerve and conjunctival inflammation.

ANSWER: The diagnosis is zoster ophthalmicus. Select urgent referral to an ophthalmologist.

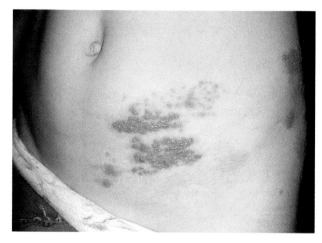

Herpes Zoster: Herpes zoster is characterized by the dermatomal distribution of painful grouped vesicles on an erythematous base.

Eczemas

Diagnosis

Vesicles are typical of acute eczema; lichenification defines chronic eczema and is an exaggeration of skin markings, with skin thickening, scaling, and abnormal pigmentation. There are several types of eczema. Three common types include atopic, asteatotic, and contact dermatitis.

Atopic dermatitis is the development of eczema in patients with an inherited atopic diathesis. Look for:

- a waxing and waning course
- pruritic, erythematous papules and plaques that may be vesicular and weeping
- chronic lesions that may be lichenified and hyperkeratotic
- involvement of the flexural surfaces

Asteatotic eczema usually occurs on the anterior shins of older persons with dry skin. Affected skin is red, dry, and cracked with multiple fine fissures that resemble cracks in porcelain. The dermatitis is more common in winter or in dry conditions.

Contact dermatitis is precipitated by local absorption of an allergen or irritant through the stratum corneum. Common allergens include nickel, topical anesthetics, neomycin, poison oak, poison ivy, and strong soaps or personal care products. Look for clues such as a neck rash caused by a necklace to identify the causative agent. For patients in whom treatment is refractory, consider patch testing for nickel, fragrance, and rubber.

The differential diagnosis of eczema includes seborrheic dermatitis, characterized by erythematous plaques with a dry or oily scale occurring in hair-bearing parts of the body. Areas include the scalp (dandruff), forehead, eyebrows, nasolabial folds, jawline (beard), and chest.

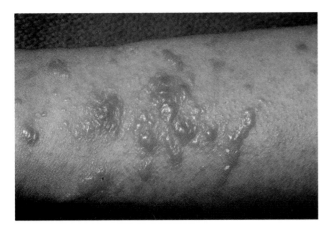

Contact Dermatitis: Discretely grouped red vesicles and bullae in a linear distribution are characteristic of contact dermatitis due to poison ivy.

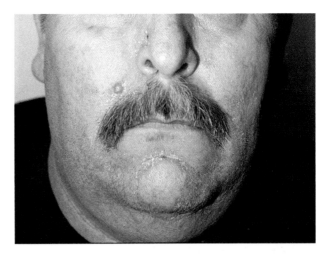

Seborrheic Dermatitis: Erythematous plaques with scale are characteristic of seborrheic dermatitis.

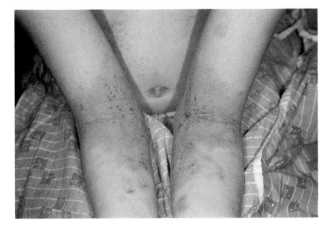

Atopic Dermatitis: The rash involves the antecubital fossae, with lichenification and surrounding excoriations.

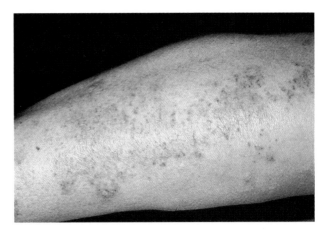

Asteatotic Dermatitis: Asteatotic dermatitis is characterized by the location on the anterior shin of red, dry, and cracked skin with multiple fine fissures.

Therapy

For atopic eczema and acute contact dermatitis, choose:

- 1% topical hydrocortisone for the face and intertriginous areas
- 0.1% triamcinolone for other body sites
- nighttime sedating antihistamines to reduce scratching
- topical tacrolimus for recalcitrant atopic eczema
- potent corticosteroids for the palms, soles, and extremely thick eruptions (atopic eczema)
- systemic corticosteroids for widespread contact dermatitis, tapered over 2-4 weeks

Treatment of asteatotic eczema consists of regular emollient use. Mid- to low-potency topical corticosteroids may minimize itching and facilitate healing.

Scalp seborrheic dermatitis is treated with selenium sulfide, coal tar, or ketoconazole shampoos. The face can be treated with 1% topical hydrocortisone and 2% ketoconazole cream.

Always select emollients as part of eczema treatment. Emollients work through various mechanisms, including by trapping water in the skin (petrolatum), introducing water into the skin (aqueous cream), or increasing the water-holding capacity of the skin (urea).

◆ DON'T BE TRICKED

- Do not select potent corticosteroids for the face because of the risk of corticosteroid-induced acne and cutaneous atrophy.

❖ Test Yourself

A healthy 40-year-old female nurse has a 1-month history of vesicular eruptions on the dorsum and distal areas of her hands.

ANSWER: The diagnosis is acute eczema. Select a topical corticosteroid.

A 28-year-old man is evaluated for severe seborrheic dermatitis of acute onset.

ANSWER: Test for HIV infection.

Acne and Rosacea

Diagnosis

Consider hyperandrogenism in women whose acne is severe, cyclical, or unresponsive to conventional therapy and is associated with menstrual irregularities, hirsutism, or rapid onset of severe disease with associated virilization.

Rosacea is a chronic inflammatory skin disorder that affects the cheeks and nose and usually occurs after the age of 30 years. Erythema with telangiectasias, pustules, and papules without comedones is typically seen. In early stages, rosacea can resemble the malar rash of SLE. However, the rash of SLE spares the nasolabial folds. The development of papules, pustules, and flushing is inconsistent with SLE and supports the diagnosis of rosacea.

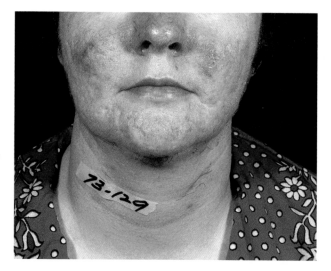

Rosacea: Papules, pustules, and dilated blood vessels involving the central face are typical of rosacea.

STUDY TABLE: Differential Diagnosis of Acne	
Description	**Diagnosis**
Onset after age 18 years with erythematous lesions involving the central face	Rosacea
Discrete papules and pustules on an erythematous base that are centered around the mouth following the use of topical or inhaled corticosteroids	Periorificial dermatitis
Acute, pustular eruption on areas other than the face and upper trunk	Bacterial folliculitis and pustular contact dermatitis
Painful, recurrent, chronic, sterile abscesses; sinus tract formation; and scarring of the axillary, inguinal, perianal, and inframammary intertriginous areas	Hidradenitis suppurativa
Comedones (the hallmark of acne), pink papules, pustules, and cysts on the face and upper trunk	Acne vulgaris

◆ DON'T BE TRICKED

- The prominent papules and pustules seen in rosacea are not typical of the malar rash seen in SLE.

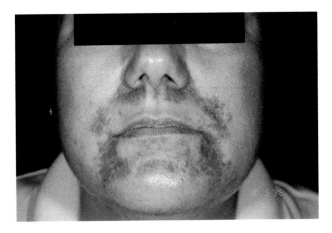

Perioral Dermatitis: Discrete papules and pustules on an erythematous base that are centered around the mouth.

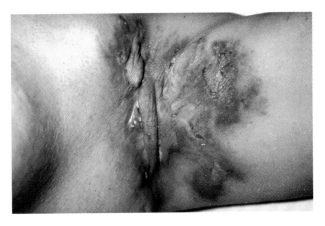

Hidradenitis Suppurativa: This chronic skin condition is characterized by painful, recurrent, chronic, sterile abscesses; sinus tract formation; and scarring.

Therapy

STUDY TABLE: Drug Therapy for Acne	
Indication	**Drug**
Mild noninflammatory acne (comedones)	Comedolytic agent (topical retinoid)
Mild inflammatory acne (papules and pustules)	Topical retinoid and topical antibiotic (erythromycin or clindamycin)
Moderate noninflammatory acne	Topical retinoid and benzoyl peroxide or azelaic acid
Moderate to severe inflammatory acne	Topical retinoid, topical antibiotic, and an oral antibiotic (tetracycline or others)
Acne in women with hyperandrogenism	Oral contraceptive
Severe recalcitrant nodular acne	Oral isotretinoin (women require two forms of birth control when taking this drug because it is teratogenic)
Rosacea	Metronidazole gel, low-dose oral tetracycline, or erythromycin
Perioral acne	Stop corticosteroid

❖ **Test Yourself**

An 18-year-old man has had nodular and cystic acne. Pustules and nodules with scarring are present on the chin, face, back, and chest.

ANSWER: The diagnosis is severe inflammatory acne. Select isotretinoin.

Psoriasis

Diagnosis

Typical findings of chronic plaque psoriasis are erythema, scaling, and induration on the extensor surfaces, scalp, ears, intertriginous folds, and genitalia. The nails may be pitted, thickened, loose, or yellow and may be the only manifestation of psoriasis. Psoriatic arthritis and spondylitis may coexist in 25% of patients.

Psoriasis is exacerbated by systemic corticosteroids, lithium, antimalarial drugs, tetracyclines, β-blockers, NSAIDs, and ACE inhibitors.

STUDY TABLE: Clinical Appearance of Common Psoriasis Subtypes	
Subtype	**Description**
Chronic plaque psoriasis	Thick, erythematous lesions with silvery, adherent scale anywhere on the body
Guttate psoriasis	Many small droplike papules and plaques on the trunk often developing after infection with β-hemolytic *Streptococcus*
Erythrodermic psoriasis	Generalized erythema and scaling involving most of the body, often occurring after abrupt discontinuation of systemic corticosteroids

Therapy

Select topical corticosteroids for limited, localized plaques. Next, rotate therapy with topical vitamin D analogues (calcipotriene, tacalcitol), retinoids, anthralin, or tar preparations.

Phototherapy is indicated for plaque or guttate psoriasis involving >5% of the body surface area, inadequate response to topical medications, or intolerance to systemic therapy. Use methotrexate, cyclosporine, sulfasalazine, or etanercept for psoriatic arthritis to improve skin and joints. Patients receiving systemic corticosteroids or cyclosporine are at risk for acute erythrodermic or pustular flares with sudden cessation of medication. Erythrodermic psoriasis is a dermatologic emergency, because patients are at high risk for infection and electrolyte abnormalities secondary to fluid loss.

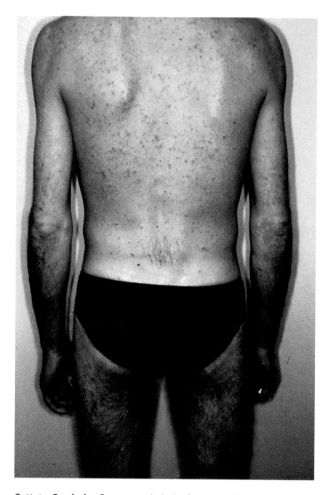

Guttate Psoriasis: Guttate psoriasis is characterized by small, droplike, scaly plaques. Image courtesy of David L. Crosby, MD, Aurora Medical Group, Waukesha, WI.

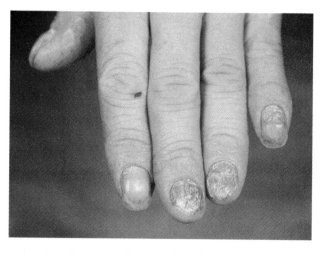

Nail Findings in Psoriasis: Psoriatic nails with characteristic discoloration, crumbling, subungual debris, and separation of the nail plate from the nail bed.

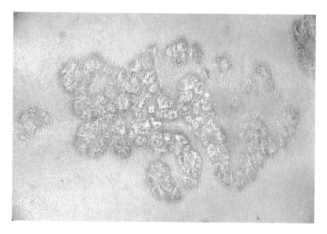

Chronic Plaque Psoriasis: Typical plaque psoriasis consists of a polymorphic red plaque covered with a thick, silvery scale.

◆ **DON'T BE TRICKED**

- Never select systemic corticosteroids for the treatment of psoriasis.

❖ **Test Yourself**

A 28-year-old woman has a chronic extensive skin rash consisting of multiple small and large plaques with an adherent, thick, silvery scale covering 25% of her body surface area.

ANSWER: The diagnosis is psoriasis.

Pemphigus Vulgaris and Pemphigoid

Diagnosis

Pemphigus vulgaris often presents initially as painful, nonhealing oral erosions. Also look for flaccid, hemorrhagic, or seropurulent bullae and denuded areas that ooze serous fluid, bleed, or are covered with crusts. The esophagus and vulva may also be involved.

Look for a positive Nikolsky sign (erosion of normal-appearing skin by application of sliding pressure) or a positive Asboe-Hansen sign (ability to laterally extend bullae by applying gentle pressure).

STUDY TABLE: Differential Diagnosis of Blisters	
Condition	**Key Features**
Pemphigus vulgaris (IgA pemphigus)	Flaccid blisters that rapidly transform to large, weeping, denuded areas and appear most commonly on the trunk and proximal extremities. Only erosions may be clinically apparent. Punch biopsy shows deposition of intercellular IgA at the epidermal surfaces on direct immunofluorescence.
Paraneoplastic pemphigus	Painful oral, conjunctival, esophageal, and laryngeal erosions. Associated with lymphoma or chronic lymphocytic leukemia.
Bullous pemphigoid	Tense blisters most commonly seen in older adults on the trunk, limbs, and flexures. Direct immunofluorescence shows linear IgG deposition at the basement membrane.
Dermatitis herpetiformis	Severely pruritic vesicles on elbows, knees, back, and buttocks associated with celiac disease. Lesions occur in crops and are symmetrically distributed.
Toxic epidermal necrolysis (TEN)	A potentially lethal disease characterized by peeling of large areas of erythematous epidermis. Immunopathologic findings are negative.
Porphyria cutanea tarda	Vesicles and bullae form in sun-exposed areas following minor trauma. Urine fluoresces dark orange with Wood lamp.

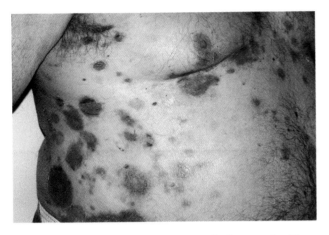

Pemphigus: This patient has multiple erosions and only an occasional intact blister.

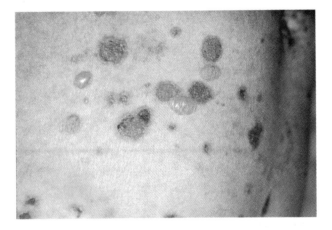

Bullous Pemphigoid: An autoimmune blistering disease characterized by multiple tense bullae and erosions.

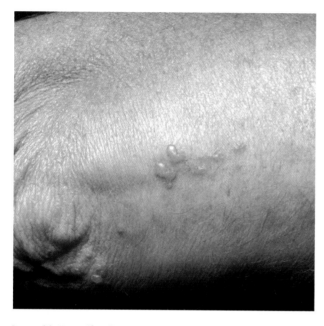

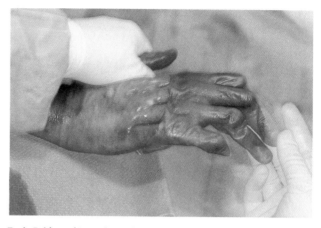

Toxic Epidermal Necrolysis: Shedding of entire sheets of skin is characteristic of TEN. Image courtesy of Barbara Mathes, MD, FAAD, FACP.

Dermatitis Herpetiformis: Dermatitis herpetiformis is characterized by pruritic papulovesicles over the external surface of the extremities and on the trunk.

Therapy

Oral corticosteroids are first-line therapy for pemphigus vulgaris and pemphigoid. Patients who do not respond to conventional drug treatment require plasmapheresis.

❖ **Test Yourself**

A 72-year-old man has a 1-week history of a rash on his trunk and upper arms. He has lost 5 kg (11 lb). Oral erosions and numerous 1.5-cm bullae are present on his trunk. Pressure applied to the edge of one of the blisters causes it to extend laterally without eruption.

ANSWER: Choose either pemphigus vulgaris or paraneoplastic pemphigus. Biopsy is required for diagnosis.

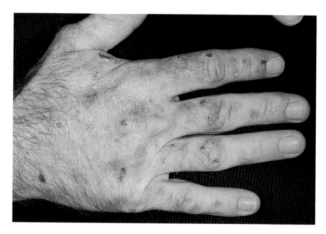

Porphyria Cutanea Tarda: Bullae and erosions on the dorsal hands may be found in a patient with hepatitis C.

Molluscum Contagiosum

Diagnosis

Molluscum contagiosum is a self-limited viral infection characterized by skin-colored, umbilicated papules that are typically found in children and sexually active adults. Associated HIV infection may cause multiple, large, disfiguring lesions.

Therapy

Treatment is generally not necessary but may include curettage and freezing; topical imiquimod may be considered second-line therapy.

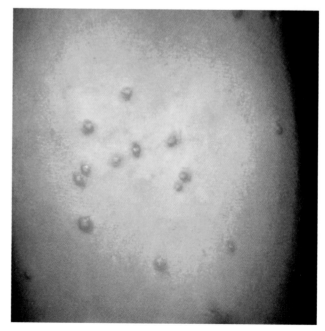

Molluscum Contagiosum: Molluscum contagiosum presents as small, flesh-colored, umbilicated papules in sexually active adults.

Warts (Verruca Vulgaris)

Diagnosis

Look for flesh-colored, exophytic, hyperkeratotic papules or nodules.

Therapy

Use salicylic acid (a keratolytic agent). Alternatives to drug therapy include duct tape or cryotherapy. "No therapy" is an acceptable answer, because spontaneous resolution is possible.

Seborrheic Keratosis

Diagnosis

Seborrheic keratosis is a painless, nonmalignant growth that appears as a "stuck-on" waxy, brownish patch or plaque. It is more common in older adult patients and does not require treatment except for cosmetic reasons. Rapid onset of pruritic seborrheic keratoses can be a sign of GI adenocarcinoma.

Therapy

Therapy is not required. A shave excision or liquid nitrogen destruction can be performed for lesions that are irritated (e.g., rubbed by clothing, jewelry).

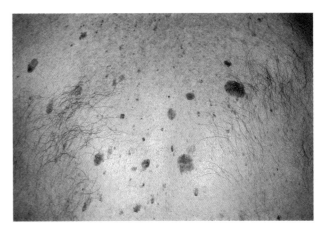

Seborrheic Keratoses: Brown to tan, sharply demarcated, waxy-like papules, plaques, and nodules are characteristic of seborrheic keratoses.

Actinic Keratosis

Diagnosis

Actinic keratosis is a precursor to squamous cell carcinoma. Lesions are located on sun-exposed sites and appear as 2- to 3-mm, elevated, flesh-colored or red papules with adherent, whitish scale or "rough spots" that may be easier to palpate than to visualize. Biopsy is indicated for larger lesions (>5 mm); thick, indurated papules; lesions that have grown rapidly; and lesions that bleed, itch, or are painful.

Therapy

Destruction by liquid nitrogen or curettage is the preferred treatment for most single lesions. Select topical 5-fluorouracil for treatment of numerous lesions. Lesions suspicious for squamous cell carcinoma require standard excision.

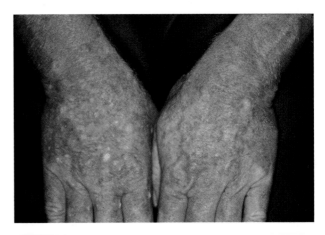

Actinic Keratoses: Multiple, white, scaly patches measuring 1-3 mm on the hands, characteristic of actinic keratoses.

Squamous Cell Carcinoma

Diagnosis

Cutaneous SCC presents as a slowly evolving, isolated, keratotic, or eroded macule, papule, or nodule that commonly appears on the scalp, neck, pinna, or lip. Bowen disease is a form of anaplastic in situ SCC that presents as circumscribed erythematous or pigmented patches that typically have a keratotic surface. Shave or punch biopsy confirms the diagnosis of SCC, and referral for definitive treatment is recommended. Keratoacanthoma is a form of rapidly growing SCC that may undergo terminal differentiation, in which the tumor "keratinizes itself to death" and involutes spontaneously within months. Early lesions present as solitary, round nodules that grow rapidly. As the lesions mature, a central keratotic plug becomes visible and the lesion becomes crater-like.

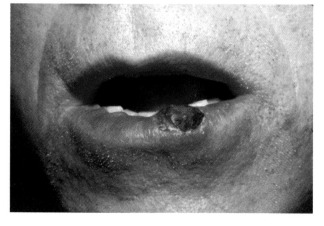

Cutaneous Squamous Cell Carcinoma: Typically presents as a slowly evolving, isolated, keratotic, or eroded macule, papule, or nodule that commonly appears on the scalp, neck, pinna, or lip. Image courtesy of Barbara Mathes, MD, FAAD, FACP.

Therapy

Although small lesions can be treated with electrodesiccation and curettage, most lesions require excision.

Basal Cell Carcinoma

Diagnosis

The most characteristic lesion is a pink, pearly, translucent papule with telangiectasias, rolled borders, and central depression with ulceration. Patients may have a history of radiation therapy, immunosuppression, or arsenic or (most commonly) excessive sun exposure. Choose biopsy for clinically suspicious lesions.

Therapy

Most basal cell carcinomas are treated with simple excision. Ill-defined lesions, high-risk histologic types, and tumors on the face and hands are often best treated with Mohs micrographic surgery, which is a staged tumor excision with mapping of specimens and preparation and interpretation of the frozen sections. Treat superficial basal cell carcinoma of the trunk and extremities with topical imiquimod or 5-fluorouracil.

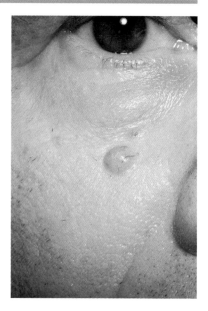

Basal Cell Carcinoma: This pink, pearly, translucent, dome-shaped papule with telangiectasias is characteristic of basal cell carcinoma.

Dysplastic Nevi

Diagnosis

Dysplastic nevi are markers for melanoma diathesis. A low percentage transform into melanoma. Dysplastic nevi have some features of melanoma, including:

- diameter ≥5 mm
- asymmetric shape with indistinct borders

- a "fried egg" appearance with a darker, elevated, central portion and tan, flat shoulders blending into surrounding skin
- pigmentation ranging from light tan to dark brown and occasionally black

Autosomal-dominant familial melanoma/dysplastic nevus syndrome is defined by the presence of melanoma in at least two relatives and dysplastic nevi in other family members.

Therapy

Only dysplastic nevi that develop increased characteristics associated with melanoma (fuzzy or ill-defined borders, multiple colors, size >5-12 mm) must be removed and sent for pathology.

Melanoma

Prevention

Select sun avoidance and sun-protective clothing.

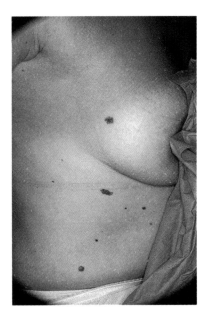

Dysplastic Nevi: Dysplastic nevi share similar characteristics with melanoma.

Diagnosis

STUDY TABLE: "ABCDE" Rule to Diagnose Melanoma	
Characteristic	**Description**
Asymmetry	Not regularly round or oval
Border irregularity	Notching, scalloping, or poorly defined margins
Color variegation	Shades of brown, tan, red, white, blue-black, or combinations
Diameter	Size >6 mm (early melanomas may be diagnosed at a smaller size)
Evolution	Lateral expansion or vertical growth

Lentigo maligna is the most common form of melanoma. It begins as a uniformly pigmented, light brown patch on the face or upper trunk that is confined to the epidermis. Over time, the lesion expands and becomes more variegated in color. Lentigo maligna melanoma is a lentigo maligna that has invaded the epidermis. Superficial spreading melanoma is the next most common variant and presents as a well-defined asymmetric patch or plaque with an irregular border, variation in color, and an expanding diameter. Most melanomas occur on exposed skin, but superficial spreading melanoma tends

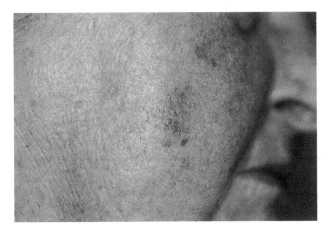

Lentigo Maligna: This carcinoma in situ appears as a brown patch on sun-exposed skin. Image courtesy of Barbara Mathes, MD, FAAD, FACP.

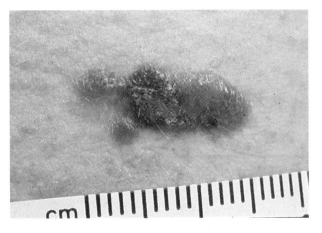

Melanoma: This asymmetric pigmented skin lesion has irregular, scalloped, notched, and indistinct borders with variegated coloration.

to occur on the back in men and the legs in women (areas that receive intermittent sun and are prone to sunburn). Nodular, acral lentiginous, and mucosal melanomas are less common but are very important because there is often a delay in diagnosis. Lentigo maligna can be diagnosed with a paper-thin shave biopsy. Complete excision is the preferred biopsy technique for all other varieties of melanoma, and sentinel lymph node biopsy is indicated for melanomas >1 mm thick.

Therapy

The extent of the surgical excision depends on the thickness of the primary melanoma. Choose interferon for melanomas >4 mm thick or for lymph node–positive disease without distant metastases.

◆ DON'T BE TRICKED

- The use of sunscreen has been shown to protect against development of nonmelanoma skin cancers.
- Early detection of asymptomatic metastatic melanoma does not improve survival. Do not select follow-up x-rays and laboratory tests.

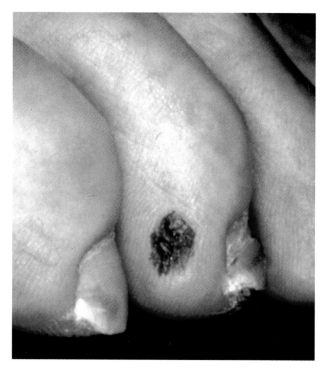

Acral Melanoma: Acral melanoma on the toe.

Erythema Multiforme

Diagnosis

Look for target-like erythematous macules or papules, each with an outer ring and a violaceous or dark center. Mucosal erosions may also be found. Recurrent HSV infection is the most common inciting factor. Drug allergy (most often to sulfonamides, penicillin, and phenytoin) is another common cause. Widespread blisters and mucosal lesions with systemic symptoms are seen in Stevens-Johnson syndrome, a severe form of erythema multiforme.

Therapy

Treat erythema multiforme by removing the offending agent and including supportive care. Systemic corticosteroids (questionable efficacy) and supportive measures are used to treat Stevens-Johnson syndrome.

◆ DON'T BE TRICKED

- Corticosteroids are ineffective and are not a choice for treating erythema multiforme.

❖ Test Yourself

A 24-year-old man is evaluated for target lesions on his hands and arms, which he says he has had twice before in recent years.

ANSWER: Diagnose recurrent erythema multiforme due to HSV.

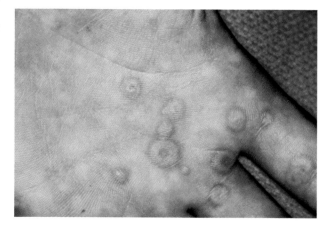

Erythema Multiforme: This flat, dull, red macule expands into a concentric ring, with the darkest part of the lesion in the center.

Dermatologic Signs of Systemic Disease

Diagnosis

Causes of generalized pruritus include hepatitis C, primary biliary cirrhosis, Hodgkin disease, lymphoma, leukemia, and polycythemia vera. Patients with generalized pruritus often do not have associated skin findings.

Specific dermatologic disorders may be associated with systemic diseases.

STUDY TABLE: Important Associations	
If you see this...	**Consider diagnosis of...**
Porphyria cutanea tarda, palpable purpura	Hepatitis C
Severe or recalcitrant seborrheic dermatitis or abrupt onset of severe psoriasis	Initial manifestation of HIV infection
Erythema nodosum (EN)	Inflammatory bowel disease, tuberculosis, sarcoidosis, coccidioidomycosis, streptococcal infection; look particularly for Löfgren syndrome (bilateral hilar lymphadenopathy, EN, and lower extremity arthralgia)
Dermatitis herpetiformis	Celiac disease
Livedo reticularis	Atheroemboli, thrombophilia, hyperviscosity syndrome, vasculitis
Pyoderma gangrenosum	Inflammatory bowel disease, inflammatory arthritis, lymphoproliferative disorders
Acanthosis nigricans (hyperpigmentation and velvety hyperkeratosis on flexural surfaces)	Diabetes
Xanthomas	Familial hypercholesterolemia

STUDY TABLE: Skin Conditions and Associated Malignancies	
Skin Condition	**Malignancy**
Acanthosis nigricans	GI cancer (i.e., gastric cancer)
Acute febrile neutrophilic dermatosis (Sweet syndrome): acute onset of erythematous plaques	Leukemia
Amyloidosis (primary systemic): pinch purpura, macroglossia, and waxy skin	Multiple myeloma
Dermatomyositis: heliotrope-violaceous periorbital eruption; scaly red papules and plaques over bony prominences	Various cell types, but ovarian cancer is overrepresented
Paraneoplastic pemphigus: polymorphous erythematous plaques, blisters, and mucosal erosions	Lymphoma, Castleman disease, and CLL
Paget disease of the breast: nipple "eczema"	Breast cancer
Necrolytic migratory erythema: eczematous or psoriasiform eruption located around orifices and flexural and acral areas	Glucagonoma
Keratoderma of the palms and soles: bilateral thickening of the epidermis	Squamous cell carcinoma of the esophagus
Explosive onset of multiple pruritic seborrheic keratoses	GI adenocarcinomas

❖ **Test Yourself**

A 36-year-old woman has a rash around the left nipple that she attributes to jogging. No discharge, mass, or other abnormality of either breast is noted.

ANSWER: Select Paget disease of the breast, biopsy of the rash, and mammography.

A 25-year-old man presents with a painful leg ulcer and new-onset diarrhea.

ANSWER: The diagnosis is pyoderma gangrenosum. Select colonoscopy to diagnose inflammatory bowel disease.

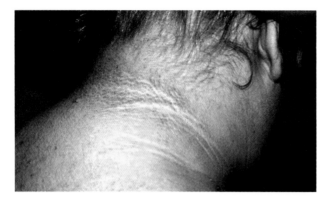

Acanthosis Nigricans: Acanthosis nigricans presents as a hyperpigmented hyperkeratosis on flexural surfaces and is most commonly associated with conditions such as diabetes mellitus and obesity.

Palpable Purpura: The hallmark of leukocyto-clastic vasculitis is palpable purpura consisting of bright red macules and papules and occasionally hemorrhagic bullae confined to the lower leg and foot.

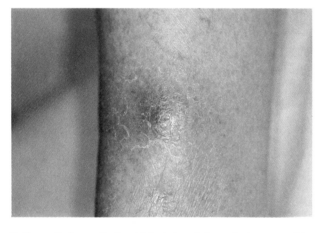

Erythema Nodosum: Tender, pink to dusky red, deep, subcutaneous nodules located on the anterior leg are characteristic of erythema nodosum.

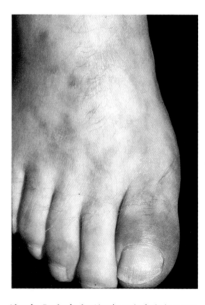

Livedo Reticularis: Livedo reticularis is a net-like red or blue rash.

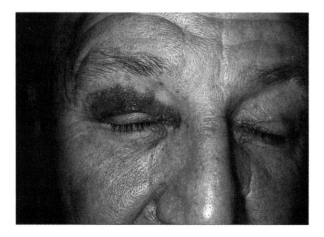

Pinch Purpura: "Pinch purpura" is characterized by purpura in the perior-bital region and is associated with amyloidosis.

Endocrinology and Metabolism

Diabetes Mellitus

Type 1 Diabetes Mellitus

Type 1 diabetes is characterized by a beta cell destructive process that is either autoimmune or idiopathic and may eventually lead to absolute insulin deficiency. The onset of type 1 diabetes is typically abrupt and severe, with marked hyperglycemia developing over several days to weeks, and may be associated with a precipitating event, such as infection, pregnancy, or myocardial infarction. Look for fatigue, polyuria, polydipsia, blurring of vision, weight loss, and dehydration.

More than 90% of cases of type 1 diabetes are autoimmune (type 1A). Several autoantibodies directed against beta cells or their products (anti–glutamic acid decarboxylase, anti–islet cell autoantigen, and anti-insulin antibodies) are usually detectable. Approximately 20% of patients with type 1 diabetes develop other organ-specific autoimmune diseases, such as celiac disease, Graves disease, hypothyroidism, Addison disease, pernicious anemia, and vitiligo.

Type 1B diabetes is idiopathic, has no autoimmune markers, and occurs more commonly in patients of Asian or African ancestry. Some older patients with diabetes have autoimmune beta-cell destruction, albeit of a more gradually progressive nature, termed latent autoimmune diabetes of adulthood.

Type 2 Diabetes Mellitus

Type 2 diabetes is characterized by a combination of insulin resistance and a beta cell secretory defect. The spectrum of type 2 diabetes ranges from predominantly insulin resistance with relative insulin deficiency to a predominantly secretory defect with or without insulin resistance. With time, progressive beta-cell dysfunction can develop, leading to absolute insulin deficiency.

In general, patients with type 2 diabetes present to medical attention less dramatically than those with type 1 diabetes. DKA is rare because patients maintain some degree of insulin secretion allowing for suppression of lipolysis. Because symptoms may be subtle, the time to diagnosis may be delayed. Consequently, approximately 20% of patients with type 2 diabetes have microvascular complications of the disease at presentation; an even higher percentage may have CAD or peripheral vascular disease. Most patients with type 2 diabetes are obese or at least have abdominal obesity. Characteristic findings include:

- polyuria, polyphagia, and polydipsia
- retinal microaneurysms, dot-blot hemorrhages, macular edema
- symmetric sensory "stocking-glove" peripheral neuropathy
- cardiovascular and kidney disease

Five percent of patients with diabetes in the United States have an autosomal dominant form of the disease known as maturity-onset diabetes of youth. Presentation is generally before age 25 years but can occur at any age. The cause is diminished insulin secretory capacity due to mutations in the gene for glucokinase, the rate-limiting enzyme in the glycolytic pathway, or in genes for transcription factors involved in regulating the insulin gene.

STUDY TABLE: Diagnosis and Classification of Type 2 Diabetes Mellitus				
Diagnosis	**Fasting Glucose**	**Random Glucose**	**2-Hour Glucose During OGTT**	**Hemoglobin A$_{1c}$**
Prediabetes	100-125 mg/dL	140-199 mg/dL	140-199 mg/dL	5.7%-6.4%
Diabetes	≥126 mg/dL	≥200 mg/dL with symptoms	≥200 mg/dL	≥6.5%

◆ DON'T BE TRICKED

- The diagnosis of type 1 diabetes is not excluded by age or obesity.

- Look for other autoimmune diseases in patients with type 1 diabetes, including hypothyroidism and adrenal insufficiency.

Therapy

Insulin options for patients with type 1 diabetes include:

- Insulin glargine or insulin detemir: A single 10 PM dose controls nocturnal plasma glucose levels and glucose levels between meals. It also counters the early morning rise in glucose level ("dawn phenomenon") caused by hepatic gluconeogenesis.

- Isophane (NPH) intermediate-acting insulin: This insulin can be used in the morning and evening to provide basal plasma insulin levels and to suppress hepatic gluconeogenesis.

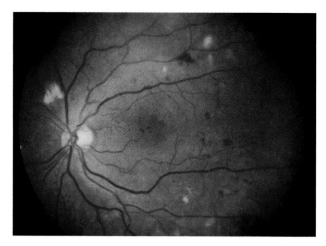

Nonproliferative Diabetic Retinopathy: Dot-and-blot hemorrhages and clusters of hard, yellowish exudates characteristic of nonproliferative diabetic retinopathy. Image courtesy of Edward Jaeger, MD.

- Insulin aspart, insulin glulisine, and insulin lispro: Rapid-acting insulin is given 5 to 15 minutes before meals to modulate the postprandial rise in glucose level.

- Regular insulin: This is given 30 minutes before meals to prevent postprandial excursions in blood glucose.

- Insulin pumps: Subcutaneous infusion of rapid-acting insulin is delivered continuously for basal insulin requirements and given in intermittent boluses for prandial needs.

STUDY TABLE: Adjusting Insulin Dose in Diabetes Mellitus

Condition	Cause
Fasting hyperglycemia	Not enough bedtime basal insulin
Prelunch hyperglycemia	Not enough rapid-acting insulin at breakfast or not enough morning NPH insulin
Predinner hyperglycemia	Not enough rapid-acting insulin at lunch or not enough morning NPH insulin
Bedtime hyperglycemia	Not enough rapid-acting insulin at dinner
Fasting or nocturnal hypoglycemia	Too much basal insulin at bedtime
Prelunch hypoglycemia	Too much rapid-acting insulin at breakfast or too much morning NPH insulin
Predinner or bedtime hypoglycemia	Too much rapid-acting insulin at lunch or dinner

Hypoglycemia unawareness describes the presence of severely low plasma glucose levels that occur without warning symptoms followed by sudden loss of consciousness. Treat immediately with rapid-acting carbohydrates or a glucagon injection followed by food. Lowering the insulin dose and allowing the average plasma glucose level to increase for several weeks restores sensitivity to hypoglycemia.

In additional to life-style modification, the American Diabetes Association recommends metformin to prevent the development of diabetes in patients with prediabetes. Initiate intensive lifestyle modification (exercise, 30 min/d, 5 d/week; weight loss; diet high in high-fiber carbohydrates and relatively low in saturated fats and proteins) at diagnosis for all patients with prediabetes or type 2 diabetes. Patients with symptomatic hyperglycemia at diagnosis require insulin initially, changing to oral hypoglycemic therapy later.

◆ DON'T BE TRICKED

- No FDA-approved drugs are available for the prevention of diabetes.

STUDY TABLE: Drug Therapy for Type 2 Diabetes Mellitus

First-Tier Validated Therapy (in suggested order)	Notes
1. Life-style changes plus metformin	Avoid metformin in patients with a creatinine level >1.5 mg/dL, heart and liver failure, or alcoholism and stop before procedures that require radiocontrast administration.
2. Add basal insulin (± preprandial insulin) or add sulfonylurea	Insulin and sulfonylureas can cause hypoglycemia.

STUDY TABLE: Adverse Effects Associated with Common Noninsulin Diabetes Medications

Class	Adverse Effect	Caution
Sulfonylureas (glyburide, glipizide, glimepiride, others)	Weight gain, hypoglycemia, skin rashes	Reduced drug clearance in kidney failure
Biguanides (metformin)	Diarrhea, abdominal discomfort, lactic acidosis	Contraindicated in progressive heart, liver, or kidney failure
		Avoid in the setting of IV iodinated contrast
α-Glucosidase inhibitors (acarbose)	Abdominal discomfort	None
Thiazolidinediones (rosiglitazone, pioglitazone)	Weight gain, edema, HF, macular edema, osteoporosis	Cardiovascular events and mortality increased with rosiglitazone
Meglitinides (repaglinide, nateglinide)	Weight gain, hypoglycemia	Reduced drug clearance in kidney failure
Amylinomimetics (pramlintide)	Nausea, vomiting	Increases hypoglycemia associated with insulin
GLP-1 mimetics (exenatide, liraglutide)	Nausea, vomiting	Possible increased risk of pancreatitis and kidney failure
DPP-4 inhibitors (sitagliptin, saxagliptin)	Nausea, skin rashes, increased risk of infections	Possible increased risk of pancreatitis

DPP-4 = dipeptidyl peptidase-4; GLP-1 = glucagon-like peptide-1.

STUDY TABLE: Treatment of Type 1 and Type 2 Diabetes Mellitus

Condition	Goal	Treatment
High plasma glucose level	Hemoglobin A_{1c} <7%	Oral antihyperglycemic medications (type 2 diabetes only) and/or multiple injections of short- and long-acting insulin
Cardiovascular disease	Reduce cardiovascular risk factors	Aspirin for patients with or at high risk for cardiovascular disease; smoking cessation
Hypertension	Blood pressure <140/90 mm Hg; consider <130/80 mm Hg for patients with diabetic nephropathy or proteinuria	ACE inhibitor or ARB
High serum total cholesterol level	If total cholesterol level is >135 mg/dL, reduce LDL-cholesterol level with a statin by 30% to 40% regardless of LDL-cholesterol level	Statin
High serum LDL-cholesterol level	<100 mg/dL	Statin
Nephropathy	Urine albumin excretion <30 mg/g of creatinine	ACE inhibitor or ARB
Diabetic retinopathy	Dilated eye examination by an ophthalmologist 3 to 5 years after initial diagnosis of type 1 diabetes or immediately after diagnosis of type 2 diabetes	Prevent with excellent blood glucose and blood pressure control, ACE inhibitors, and smoking cessation
		Laser therapy and/or intraocular injections of bevacizumab or ranibizumab for macular edema, severe nonproliferative retinopathy, or any proliferative retinal changes

◆ DON'T BE TRICKED

- Aspirin is not contraindicated in patients with diabetic retinopathy.
- Unless a compelling contraindication exists, metformin is always the first-line oral medication for type 2 diabetes.

STUDY TABLE: Complications of Type 1 and Type 2 Diabetes Mellitus	
If you see this...	**Select this...**
A history of peripheral or carotid artery disease, two or more cardiovascular risk factors (dyslipidemia, hypertension, smoking, family history of premature cardiovascular disease, microalbuminuria), sedentary lifestyle, age ≥35 years, and desire to begin a vigorous exercise program	Exercise stress test (see Cardiovascular Medicine)
Painful peripheral neuropathy	Stabilizing glycemic control; duloxetine (first line) or pregabalin (second line)
Acute mononeuropathy	No action; resolves spontaneously over several months
Gastroparesis	Small feedings; metoclopramide or erythromycin
Orthostatic hypotension	Compression stockings and/or fludrocortisone
Erectile dysfunction	Oral phosphodiesterase inhibitor (sildenafil, vardenafil, tadalafil, or intraurethral alprostadil)

Patients with type 1 or type 2 diabetes require:

- blood pressure measurement and foot inspection at every visit
- hemoglobin A_{1c} measurement every 3 (type 1 diabetes) to 6 (type 2 diabetes) months
- urinalysis for microalbuminuria yearly
- ophthalmologic examination yearly
- lipid measurement yearly
- comprehensive foot examination (with monofilament) yearly

Patients with diabetes who are at risk for ulceration and amputation can be identified by three features based on history:

- previous lower extremity amputation
- previous foot ulcer
- peripheral arterial disease

and four features based on physical examination:

- impaired sensation on monofilament testing
- major foot deformities
- absent pulses
- abnormal ABI

Patients at high risk have sensory neuropathy and one or more of the other key risk factors.

❖ **Test Yourself**

A 29-year-old woman with a 10-year history of type 1 diabetes has nocturnal hypoglycemia. Her insulin schedule includes 24 units NPH insulin/10 units regular insulin before breakfast and 14 units NPH insulin/10 units regular insulin before dinner. Her hemoglobin A_{1c} is 7.2%. What change should be made in her insulin regimen?

ANSWER: Two answers are possible: Delay the NPH insulin until bedtime or (an even better choice) stop the NPH insulin and substitute insulin glargine at bedtime.

A 58-year-old man with type 2 diabetes has a hemoglobin A_{1c} value >9%. He takes metformin 1000 mg/d and glyburide 10 mg/d. His fasting and preprandial plasma glucose levels are >130 mg/dL.

ANSWER: Add evening basal insulin to control his hyperglycemia.

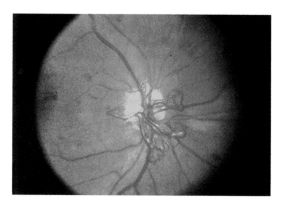

Proliferative Diabetic Retinopathy: A network of new vessels (neovascularization) is shown protruding from the optic nerve.

Hyperglycemic Hyperosmolar Syndrome

Diagnosis

Hyperglycemic hyperosmolar syndrome is defined as a plasma osmolality >320 mosm/kg H_2O, a plasma glucose level >600 mg/dL, either no or low serum levels of ketones, and a relatively normal arterial pH and bicarbonate level. The diagnosis is considered in any older adult patient with altered mental status and dehydration.

Therapy

Manage hyperglycemic hyperosmolar syndrome mainly by identifying the underlying precipitating illness and restoring the contracted plasma volume. Choose normal saline first to replenish the extracellular space. When blood pressure is restored and urine output is established, administer hypotonic solutions. Only administer IV insulin after expansion of the intravascular space has begun. After the plasma glucose level decreases to <200 mg/dL and the patient is eating, begin subcutaneous insulin injections.

Diabetic Ketoacidosis

Diagnosis

DKA is the most life-threatening acute complication of diabetes and is often the presenting manifestation of type 1 diabetes. The major manifestations of DKA (hyperglycemia, ketosis, and dehydration) are directly or indirectly related to insulin deficiency.

Laboratory findings include a plasma glucose level ≥250 mg/dL, arterial blood pH ≤7.30, bicarbonate level ≤15 meq/L, widened anion gap, and positive serum ketone levels. Evaluate patients for underlying precipitants of DKA, such as medication nonadherence, infection, and MI.

Therapy

Give normal saline solution for immediate volume replacement. Switch to 0.45% sodium chloride after the initial bolus if the serum sodium level is high or normal. Then give:

- insulin infusion (delay if serum potassium level is <3.3 meq/L)
- potassium replacement when the serum potassium level is <5.5 meq/L
- glucose infusion (5% dextrose with 0.45% normal saline) when the plasma glucose level is <250 mg/dL
- continuation of insulin infusion and glucose infusion until the serum anion gap is <12 meq/L

Treatment of severe acidosis with bicarbonate is controversial and evidence of benefit is lacking.

◆ **DON'T BE TRICKED**
- **Reducing the insulin infusion before complete clearing of ketones will cause a relapse of DKA.**

Diabetes Care for Hospitalized Patients

Therapy

STUDY TABLE: Modifying Oral Diabetes Regimens for Inpatients	
If you see this...	**Discontinue this oral agent...**
New onset kidney failure or plan for IV contrast dye administration for procedure or study	Metformin
Findings of peripheral edema, HF, or osteoporosis	Thiazolidinediones
Unpredictable food intake	Sulfonylureas and meglitinides

Intensive insulin therapy does not reduce mortality in hospitalized patients with or without diabetes. In SICU and MICU patients requiring insulin therapy, a reasonable target blood glucose level is between 140 and 200 mg/dL.

◆ DON'T BE TRICKED

- Do not use a sliding scale of regular or rapid-acting insulin in the absence of basal insulin to control the blood glucose of hospitalized patients.

Pregnancy and Diabetes Screening

Diagnosis

Untreated gestational diabetes is associated with congenital malformations and increased fetal loss. Lowering the hemoglobin A_{1c} value to within 1% of normal decreases the risk of congenital malformations and fetal loss.

Women with a decline in kidney function (serum creatinine >3 mg/dL or creatinine clearance <50 mL/min/1.73 m²) are at high risk of a permanent decline in kidney function. During pregnancy, the risk of accelerated diabetic retinopathy is also increased.

◆ DON'T BE TRICKED

- Women with a history of gestational diabetes are at very high risk for developing type 2 diabetes and require annual screening following delivery.

Therapy

Try lifestyle interventions as initial therapy, with the addition of insulin if glycemic targets are not met. Glycemic targets in pregnancy include premeal plasma glucose <90 mg/dL and 1-hour postprandial values <120 mg/dL.

Management strategies in pregnant women are different from those in other patients with diabetes:

- Insulin should replace oral hypoglycemic agents.
- NPH or short-acting prandial insulins should replace insulin glargine, exenatide, and pramlintide, because the safety of these agents is not established in pregnancy.
- ACE inhibitors, ARBs, and cholesterol-lowering drugs should be stopped before pregnancy.
- A comprehensive eye examination should be done once per trimester.

Employ aggressive control of blood pressure to avoid worsening of nephropathy and retinopathy. Antihypertensive agents that can be safely used during pregnancy include methyldopa, β-blockers (except atenolol), calcium channel blockers, and hydralazine.

Hypoglycemia in Patients Without Diabetes

Diagnosis

In persons without diabetes, hypoglycemia is defined as a plasma glucose level <50 mg/dL. Look for Whipple triad:

- symptoms of hypoglycemia
- low plasma glucose levels
- resolution of symptoms after glucose administration

Hypoglycemic disorders are classified as postprandial or fasting. A common cause of postprandial hypoglycemia is previous gastrectomy or gastric bypass surgery. Clinical manifestations include hypoglycemia approximately 30 to 60 minutes after meals due to rapid intestinal absorption of glucose triggering excessive secretion of insulin.

Fasting hypoglycemia is associated with several serious conditions.

STUDY TABLE: Diagnosis of Nondiabetic Fasting Hypoglycemia	
Condition	**Diagnosis**
Surreptitious use of oral hypoglycemic agents	Patient has access to hypoglycemic agents. Serum C-peptide levels are inappropriately elevated at time of hypoglycemia. Perform urine screen for sulfonylurea and meglitinide metabolites.
Surreptitious use of insulin	Patient has access to insulin. Serum C-peptide levels are low at time of hypoglycemia.
Insulinoma	Perform 72-hour fast and document fasting plasma glucose level <45 mg/dL and serum insulin >5-6 mU/L. If positive, schedule abdominal CT.
Substrate deficiency	Starvation, hepatic failure, or sepsis; suppressed hepatic glucose production (alcoholism, cortisol or GH deficiencies)

mU = milliunit.

Begin the evaluation of all patients with fasting hypoglycemia with screening for surreptitious use of a sulfonylurea or insulin.

MEN1 can present as hyperparathyroidism, pituitary neoplasms, or pancreatic neuroendocrine tumors (gastrinomas that can cause peptic ulcer disease and insulinomas that can cause hypoglycemia).

◆ DON'T BE TRICKED

- Home glucose meters may be inaccurate in the hypoglycemic range, so interpret their results cautiously.
- Asymptomatic hypoglycemia with a plasma glucose level <60 mg/dL is often found after fasting in patients without underlying disease and does not require evaluation.

Therapy

Treat acute hypoglycemia with oral carbohydrates, IV glucose, or IM glucagon.

For management of postprandial hypoglycemia associated with previous gastrectomy or gastric bypass surgery, choose small mixed meals containing protein, fat, and high-fiber complex carbohydrates.

❖ Test Yourself

A previously healthy 28-year-old woman is unconscious. Her plasma glucose level is 28 mg/dL. She regains consciousness following IV glucose administration. Serum insulin level is 42 milliunits/L (normal, 2-20 milliunits/L), and serum C-peptide level is 7.2 ng/mL (normal, 0.9-4.0 ng/mL). She is a registered nurse.

ANSWER: Select factitious hypoglycemia and screening for surreptitious ingestion of sulfonylureas. Demographically, women in the health professions are most likely to self-induce hypoglycemia.

Hyperlipidemia

Screening

The U.S. Preventive Services Task Force recommends screening serum total and HDL-cholesterol levels beginning in men age ≥35 years and women age ≥45 years or age 20 years in the presence of diabetes or cardiovascular risk factors. Testing is repeated every 5 years. The Adult Treatment Panel III of the National Cholesterol Education Program recommends screening beginning at age 20 years, with repeat testing every 5 years.

Diagnosis

Look for secondary causes of hyperlipidemia, which include hypothyroidism; obstructive liver disease (primary biliary cirrhosis); nephrotic syndrome; smoking; diabetes mellitus; alcoholism; and medications such as retinoic acid (isotretinoin), estrogens, corticosteroids, and protease inhibitors.

In younger patients with hyperlipidemia or patients with very high serum total cholesterol levels, think of familial combined hyperlipidemia or familial hypercholesterolemia. Both are autosomal dominant, and patients often have tendinous xanthomas.

Assess cardiac risk to determine LDL cholesterol therapeutic goals. Look for:

- Presence of CHD
- CHD risk equivalents: diabetes mellitus, aortic aneurysm, peripheral vascular disease, symptomatic carotid artery disease, or 10-year risk of MI >20% based on Framingham risk score
- CHD risk factors, outlined below

STUDY TABLE: Risk Factors for CHD

Factor	Risk Range
Patient's age	Men ≥45 years; women ≥55 years
CHD in first-degree relative	Male relative <55 years; female relative <65 years
Cigarette smoking	Current smoker
Blood pressure	>140/90 mm Hg or undergoing treatment for hypertension
HDL-cholesterol level	<40 mg/dL or subtract one risk factor if >60 mg/dL

STUDY TABLE: CHD Risk Factors and Cholesterol Goals

Risk Profile	Goals
CHD or CHD risk equivalents or 10-year risk of MI >20%	LDL cholesterol: <100 mg/dL, optional LDL-cholesterol goal <70 mg/dL Non-HDL cholesterol: <130 mg/dL
Two or more CHD risk factors and 10-year risk of MI 10%-20%	LDL cholesterol: <130 mg/dL, optional LDL-cholesterol goal <100 mg/dL Non-HDL cholesterol: <160 mg/dL
Two or more CHD risk factors and 10-year risk of MI <10%	LDL cholesterol: <130 mg/dL Non-HDL cholesterol: <160 mg/dL
One or no CHD risk factors	LDL cholesterol: <160 mg/dL Non-HDL cholesterol: <190 mg/dL

- Non–HDL-cholesterol level (total cholesterol level minus HDL-cholesterol level) is a secondary target for patients with high triglyceride levels (≥200 mg/dL).
- For patients with high triglyceride levels, the goal for non-HDL cholesterol is 30 mg/dL higher than the goal for LDL cholesterol.

◆ DON'T BE TRICKED
- Do not measure lipoprotein(a), apolipoprotein B, or homocysteine levels, which have no impact on mortality.

- Normal pregnancy is associated with increases in triglyceride and cholesterol levels by 300% and 50%, respectively.

Therapy

Initially treat patients with hyperlipidemia with intensive lifestyle modification, including weight loss, aerobic exercise, reduced carbohydrate consumption, and limited alcohol consumption. If lifestyle modification is ineffective, begin drug therapy. In patients with CHD or CHD risk equivalents, begin drug therapy at the same time as lifestyle modification if LDL target is unlikely to be met with lifestyle changes alone.

STUDY TABLE: Drug Therapy for Hypercholesterolemia	
Lipid Profile	**Medications**
High LDL-cholesterol level	Statins (first choice)
	Bile acid sequestrants (usually combined with a statin)
High triglyceride level	Statins if LDL is above goal
	Fibrates or nicotinic acid if LDL is at goal
Low HDL-cholesterol level	Nicotinic acid or fibrates (usually reserved for patients with CAD)

◆ DON'T BE TRICKED

- **Do not select a bile acid sequestrant if the serum triglyceride level is >400 mg/dL.**

Persons at high risk or moderately high risk who have lifestyle-related risk factors, such as the metabolic syndrome, are candidates for therapeutic lifestyle changes to modify these risk factors regardless of LDL-cholesterol level.

STUDY TABLE: Criteria for Metabolic Syndrome	
Any Three of the Following:	
Risk Factor	**Defining Level**
Abdominal obesity (waist circumference)	>40 in (102 cm) in men; >35 in (88 cm) in women
Triglycerides	≥150 mg/dL
HDL cholesterol	<40 mg/dL in men; <50 mg/dL in women
Blood pressure	≥130/≥85 mm Hg
Fasting glucose level	≥100 mg/dL

Drug interactions (between statins and fibrates, cyclosporine, macrolide antibiotics, calcium channel blockers, amiodarone, various antifungal drugs) may cause myalgia and rhabdomyolysis. If myalgia develops, discontinue the statin and switch to another statin or drug. Niacin may cause hyperglycemia, increased serum aminotransferase levels, and gout. Discontinue niacin or decrease the dose if any of these occur.

❖ **Test Yourself**

A 45-year-old man with CHD has been taking simvastatin and gemfibrozil for hyperlipidemia and develops myalgia and weakness.

ANSWER: Stop drugs and measure serum CK for suspected myositis and possible rhabdomyolysis.

Hyperthyroidism

Diagnosis

The term thyrotoxicosis encompasses any cause of thyroid hormone excess, including primary and secondary hyperthyroidism, excessive thyroid hormone release due to thyroid destruction, and excessive exogenous thyroid hormone ingestion. The term hyperthyroidism refers specifically to disorders of increased thyroid hormone production and release, such as destructive thyroiditis, Graves disease, autonomous thyroid nodules, and toxic multinodular goiter.

Thyrotoxicosis occurs in destructive thyroiditis because thyroid damage results in release of preformed thyroid hormone into the circulation. Forms of destructive thyroiditis include subacute (de Quervain), silent (painless), and postpartum thyroiditis. Subacute thyroiditis is a nonautoimmune inflammation that generally presents with a firm and painful thyroid gland. Postpartum thyroiditis is a painless autoimmune thyroiditis occurring within a few months of delivery. Permanent hypothyroidism may follow all forms of destructive thyroiditis.

Look for symptoms of thyrotoxicosis:

- nervousness, emotional lability
- increased sweating, heat intolerance
- palpitations
- increased defecation
- weight loss
- menstrual irregularity

Look for signs of thyrotoxicosis:

- tachycardia
- lid lag
- fine tremor
- muscle wasting, proximal muscle weakness
- hyperreflexia

Ancillary laboratory testing may reveal:

- mild hypercalcemia
- elevated alkaline phosphatase level
- low total and HDL cholesterol levels

Physical examination findings specific for Graves disease include goiter, ophthalmopathy (proptosis, chemosis, and extra-ocular muscle palsy), and pretibial myxedema.

Older adult patients with hyperthyroidism may present with depression, atrial fibrillation, and HF.

STUDY TABLE: Historical Clues to the Cause of Thyrotoxicosis	
If you see this...	**Choose this...**
Hyperthyroidism following oral or IV iodine load (radiocontrast)	Toxic multinodular goiter or toxic adenoma
Family history of autoimmune thyroid disease or personal history of another autoimmune condition	Graves disease
Neck tenderness and recent history of viral infection	Subacute (de Quervain) thyroiditis
Thyrotoxicosis after initiation of treatment for atrial fibrillation	Amiodarone-induced thyrotoxicosis
Medical professional with small thyroid gland and low radioactive iodine uptake	Surreptitious thyroid ingestion

Order serum TSH, triiodothyronine (T_3), and free thyroxine (free T_4) levels to make the diagnosis of thyrotoxicosis.

STUDY TABLE: Interpreting Thyroid Function Tests in Hyperthyroidism	
If you see this...	**Choose this...**
↓ TSH, ↑ T_3, ↑ free T_4	Primary hyperthyroidism
↓ TSH, ↑ T_3, normal free T_4	Primary hyperthyroidism with T_3 toxicosis
↓ TSH, normal T_3 and free T_4, without symptoms	Subclinical hyperthyroidism
↑ TSH, ↑ T_3, ↑ free T_4	Secondary hyperthyroidism from a pituitary tumor

A thyroid scan and radioactive iodine uptake test can differentiate thyrotoxicosis caused by increased production of thyroid hormone (high uptake) from thyroiditis or surreptitious ingestion of thyroid hormone (low uptake). Color-flow Doppler ultrasonography can also be useful to distinguish hyperthyroidism (high flow) from thyroiditis (low flow), especially in the setting of amiodarone-induced thyrotoxicosis when thyroid uptake and scan is not clinically useful.

STUDY TABLE: Radioactive Iodine Uptake and Scan Interpretation	
Result	**Diagnosis**
Diffuse homogeneous increased uptake	Graves disease
Patchy areas of increased uptake	Toxic multinodular goiter
Focal increased uptake with decreased uptake in the rest of the gland	Solitary adenoma
Decreased or no uptake	Iodine load (IV contrast or amiodarone)
	Thyroiditis (silent, subacute, postpartum, or amiodarone induced)
	Surreptitious ingestion of excessive thyroid hormone

Thyroglobulin levels can be elevated in both hyperthyroidism and thyroiditis. Intake of exogenous thyroid hormone generally suppresses thyroglobulin levels, which makes its measurement useful in patients with thyrotoxicosis due to surreptitious use of thyroid hormone.

An elevated serum ESR supports thyroiditis, whereas TSH-receptor antibodies are associated with Graves disease. However, antibodies need not be checked routinely in the evaluation of hyperthyroidism unless the diagnosis is unclear.

Thyroid storm is the development of life-threatening hyperthyroidism associated with cardiac decompensation, fever, delirium, and psychosis. It may occur following surgery, infection, or administration of an acute iodine load and may also develop in patients with untreated Graves disease. Thyroid storm is a clinical diagnosis; no level of thyroid hormone elevation is diagnostic.

◆ DON'T BE TRICKED

- Acutely ill patients with euthyroid sick syndrome have normal free T_4 and suppressed TSH levels; this is not hyperthyroidism.

Therapy

Available strategies for managing hyperthyroidism include antithyroid drugs, radioactive iodine therapy (^{131}I), and thyroid surgery. Radioactive iodine therapy is associated with few adverse effects but may lead to radiation thyroiditis and sialadenitis; it is not used during pregnancy or when breastfeeding.

STUDY TABLE: Comparison of Antithyroid Drugs		
Treatment	**Indicated for...**	**Watch for...**
Methimazole	First-line antithyroid medication for most patients	Agranulocytosis, drug rash, hepatotoxicity
Propylthiouracil	Treatment of choice in first trimester of pregnancy; preferred in thyroid storm (inhibits peripheral T_4 to T_3 conversion)	Same as methimazole, except more frequent hepatotoxicity

Graves disease can be treated effectively with any of the three major therapeutic modalities. Choice of therapy is based on patient preference and other considerations. Antithyroid drugs may lead to a drug-free remission of Graves disease in 30% to 50% of patients after treating for 1 year. Antithyroid drugs may also be used short term as a bridge to more definitive therapy (radioactive iodine or thyroidectomy).

Choose ^{131}I therapy or surgery to treat toxic multinodular goiter or toxic adenoma. With ^{131}I ablation, hyperactive nodules take up iodine preferentially, while suppressed normal tissue receives minimal radiation exposure. Treatment frequently restores euthyroidism.

STUDY TABLE: Management of Thyrotoxicosis	
If you see this...	**Choose this...**
Sympathetic nervous system symptoms	Atenolol or propranolol
Preparation for thyroidectomy	Methimazole
Severe Graves ophthalmopathy	Methimazole or thyroidectomy
	Avoid radioactive iodine (may cause worsening of ophthalmopathy unless pretreated with corticosteroids)
Pregnancy	Propylthiouracil in first trimester of pregnancy, methimazole thereafter. Radioactive iodine is contraindicated
Subclinical hyperthyroidism	Methimazole if TSH <0.1 μU/mL
Subacute thyroiditis	NSAIDs or corticosteroids
Suspicious nodule (malignancy)	FNAB followed by thyroidectomy (if malignant)
Thyroid storm	Propylthiouracil (preferred) or methimazole, iodine-potassium solutions, corticosteroids, and β-blockers
μU = microunit.	

◆ DON'T BE TRICKED

- A fever or sore throat in a patient taking methimazole or propylthiouracil should be presumed agranulocytosis until proven otherwise.

❖ Test Yourself

An asymptomatic 78-year-old woman has a serum TSH level of 0.2 microunits/mL. Serum T_3 and T_4 levels are normal.

ANSWER: The diagnosis is subclinical hyperthyroidism. Repeat the thyroid tests in 4 to 6 months, because thyroid studies will normalize in 50% of patients without intervention.

Hypothyroidism

Diagnosis

The most common causes of hypothyroidism include:

- chronic lymphocytic (Hashimoto) thyroiditis
- thyroidectomy
- previous radioactive iodine ablation
- history of external beam radiation to the neck

Hashimoto thyroiditis increases in prevalence with age and is usually associated with a goiter.

Transient mild hypothyroidism typically occurs during the second phase of destructive thyroiditis (initial phase is hyperthyroidism). Permanent hypothyroidism may follow either postpartum thyroiditis (more common) or subacute thyroiditis (less common).

Certain medications may be associated with hypothyroidism, including lithium carbonate, interferon alfa, interleukin-2, and amiodarone.

Central hypothyroidism results from pituitary disease or previous surgery or radiation therapy to the sella. TSH and free T_4 are suppressed.

Look for symptoms suggesting hypothyroidism:

- weakness, lethargy, fatigue
- depression, impaired concentration

- myalgia
- cold intolerance
- constipation
- weight gain
- menstrual irregularity or menorrhagia
- carpal tunnel syndrome

Examination findings include bradycardia, hypothermia, diastolic hypertension, husky voice, goiter, cool dry skin, brittle hair, edema, and delayed relaxation phase of deep tendon reflexes.

Hypothyroidism may be associated with hyponatremia and increased CK, AST, and cholesterol levels.

Order TSH and free T_4 to make the diagnosis. Measurement of T_3 levels is generally not necessary. An anti–thyroid peroxidase antibody assay is associated with Hashimoto thyroiditis but is not needed to make the diagnosis; high levels are associated with an increased risk of permanent hypothyroidism. A thyroid scan and radioiodine uptake test are not needed to make the diagnosis of hypothyroidism.

STUDY TABLE: Interpreting Thyroid Function Tests in Hypothyroidism	
If you see this...	**Choose this...**
↑ TSH, ↓ T_3, ↓ free T_4	Primary hypothyroidism
↑ TSH, normal T_3 and free T_4	Subclinical hypothyroidism
↓ TSH, ↓ T_3, ↓ free T_4	Secondary (central) hypothyroidism; consider hypopituitarism
↓ TSH, ↓ T_3, ↓ or normal free T_4 and critical illness	Euthyroid sick syndrome; no treatment required

Euthyroid sick syndrome occurs in patients acutely ill with a nonthyroidal illness. Testing reveals low T_3, elevated reverse T_3 (measurement not necessary for diagnosis), low or normal free T_4, and suppressed TSH (initially) followed by elevated TSH (recovery phase). Normalization of thyroid function tests occurs 4 to 8 weeks after recovery.

Myxedema coma is defined as severe hypothyroidism leading to decreased mental status, hypothermia, hypotension, bradycardia, hyponatremia, hypoglycemia, hypoxemia, and hypoventilation. It occurs in patients with severe, long-standing, untreated hypothyroidism and may be precipitated by an acute medical or surgical event or the administration of opiates.

Therapy

Levothyroxine is the only agent used to treat hypothyroidism. Therapy is indicated for subclinical hypothyroidism when the serum TSH is >10 microunits/mL.

Treat women with subclinical hypothyroidism who are pregnant or want to become pregnant, because greater maternal and fetal risk is associated with this disorder.

Check thyroid function tests frequently during pregnancy in women with a known diagnosis of hypothyroidism, because maternal thyroxine demand may increase up to 30% to 50%.

STUDY TABLE: Treatment of Hypothyroidism	
Condition	**Answer**
Age <60 years	Begin full-dose levothyroxine (about 100 µg/d).
Age >60 years	Begin levothyroxine at 25-50 µg/d. Increase by 25 µg every 6 weeks until TSH level is 1.0-2.5 µU/mL.
Heart disease	Begin levothyroxine at 12.5-25 µg/d. Increase by 12.5-25 µg every 6 weeks until TSH level is 1.0-2.5 µU/mL.
Myxedema coma	Begin levothyroxine and hydrocortisone. Hydrocortisone should be given until concomitant adrenal insufficiency has been ruled out.
µg = microgram(s); µU = microunit(s).	

Celiac disease can be associated with inadequate levothyroxine absorption and resultant increased levothyroxine dosing requirements in patients with established hypothyroidism.

Thyroid Nodules

Diagnosis

Thyroid nodules are common and are often found incidentally on imaging tests. When a nodule is discovered, assess thyroid function with a serum TSH level. A low TSH level suggests a benign, autonomously functioning thyroid adenoma. If TSH is suppressed, order a radioisotope scan to confirm the diagnosis and to rule out additional nonfunctioning nodules within a multinodular goiter. The serum TSH level is normal (and unhelpful) in most other patients with thyroid nodules. Thyroid ultrasonography allows for accurate detection and sizing of all nodules on the thyroid gland, and ultrasound characteristics can be used to further delineate cancer risk.

Look for risk factors for thyroid cancer, including family history of thyroid malignancy, personal history of radiation therapy to the head and neck, or other radiation exposure in childhood.

FNAB is indicated for:

- all thyroid nodules >1 cm associated with a normal TSH level
- nodules <1 cm in patients with risk factors for thyroid cancer or suspicious ultrasound characteristics

Evaluate patients with multinodular goiter for compressive symptoms. Ask about dysphagia, hoarseness, and dyspnea (due to tracheal compression from substernal goiter). Consider evaluation with barium swallow, direct vocal cord visualization, spirometry with flow volume loops, and/or chest CT if clinical suspicion is increased.

◆ DON'T BE TRICKED

- **Serum thyroglobulin measurement is not helpful in distinguishing benign and malignant thyroid nodules.**
- **Calcitonin measurement is only considered in patients with hypercalcemia or a family history of thyroid cancer or MEN2.**

Therapy

Follow benign nodules with periodic ultrasonography. Although benign thyroid nodules usually remain stable or decrease in size, one third may increase in size. Malignancy must be ruled out when growth exceeds 50% by volume or if a nodule develops concerning ultrasound characteristics.

Treat hyperfunctioning solitary thyroid nodules with radioactive iodine ablation or hemithyroidectomy.

Indicate surgery for patients with continued nodule growth despite normal initial FNAB results or nondiagnostic results on repeat FNAB and for patients with malignant cytology. Surgery is also indicated for large multinodular goiters associated with significant compression of nearby structures.

◆ DON'T BE TRICKED

- **Do not prescribe T_4-suppression therapy for benign thyroid nodules.**

❖ Test Yourself

An 18-year-old man has a 2-cm right-sided thyroid nodule. The serum TSH level is 1.4 microunits/mL.

ANSWER: Perform an FNAB.

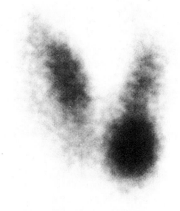

Thyroid Nodule: A hyperfunctioning nodule is shown on the lateral aspect of the left thyroid lobe on thyroid scan.

Pituitary Tumors

Diagnosis

Pituitary tumors are benign adenomas that originate from one of the different anterior pituitary cell types. They are classified based on size as microadenomas (<10 mm) or macroadenomas (≥10 mm). Pituitary adenomas become symptomatic by two different mechanisms:

- mass effect causing hypopituitarism (anterior hormone deficiencies more common than posterior), headaches, visual disturbance/visual field defects, and cranial nerve dysfunction

- endocrine hyperfunction caused by excess secretion by the tumor

STUDY TABLE: Diagnosis of Pituitary Tumors		
If you see this...	**Think this...**	**Order this...**
Galactorrhea, amenorrhea, or impotence	Prolactinoma	Serum prolactin level
Enlargement of hands, feet, nose, lips, or tongue; increased spacing of teeth	Acromegaly	Serum IGF-1
		Oral glucose tolerance test (fails to suppress GH)
Proximal muscle weakness, facial rounding, centripetal obesity, purple striae, diabetes mellitus, and hypertension	Cushing disease	24-hour urine cortisol excretion or late night salivary cortisol level (elevated), serum ACTH level (elevated)

Order MRI if testing indicates hormonal hypersecretion due to a pituitary source. If mass effect is the presenting symptom (headache, visual disturbances), obtain MRI first and endocrine testing later.

Screen patients with a family history of MEN1 and at least one component of MEN1 (usually hyperparathyroidism) for a pituitary adenoma.

Test patients with an incidentally discovered pituitary adenoma for hormone hypersecretion. Not all pituitary adenomas secrete hormones.

Psychotropic agents, tricyclic antidepressants, antiseizure medications, metoclopramide and domperidone, calcium channel blockers, methyldopa, opiates, and protease inhibitors can cause hyperprolactinemia.

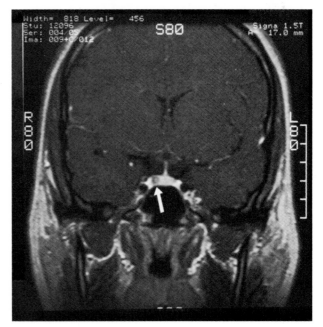

Prolactinoma: Discrete area of hypolucency (see arrow) in otherwise normal-sized pituitary gland of homogeneous density.

◆ DON'T BE TRICKED

- **Hyperprolactinemia caused by drugs and other nonprolactinoma conditions is usually <150 ng/mL.**
- **Obtain a pregnancy test in all women with hyperprolactinemia.**
- **Obtain a serum TSH level in all patients with hyperprolactinemia (hypothyroidism can cause hyperprolactinemia).**

Therapy

Choose observation for women with microprolactinoma and normal menses. Otherwise, choose a dopamine agonist (cabergoline preferred to bromocriptine) for symptomatic prolactinoma. Consider withdrawal of dopamine agonist therapy for prolactinomas no longer visible on neuroimaging if the prolactin level has normalized. Close follow-up is required because of recurrence rates of up to 50%.

Choose surgery for adenomas secreting GH, ACTH, or TSH; for adenomas associated with mass effect, visual field defects, or hypopituitarism; and for prolactinomas unresponsive to dopamine agonists.

Radiation therapy may be indicated for the management of hormonal hypersecretion that persists after surgery or to treat residual tumor after resection. It may also be given as primary therapy for patients who are not surgical candidates. Radiation therapy frequently results in hypopituitarism.

Medical therapy with somatostatin analogues or cabergoline (both first line) and pegvisomant (second line) is used to manage acromegaly not cured by surgery.

❖ **Test Yourself**

A 32-year-old woman has a 4-mm hypointense area in the pituitary gland discovered incidentally on an MRI. Medical history, including menstrual function, and physical examination are normal. The serum prolactin level and thyroid function tests are normal.

ANSWER: The patient has an incidental nonfunctioning pituitary adenoma. Repeat the MRI and recheck the prolactin level in 6 months.

Hypopituitarism

Diagnosis

Hypopituitarism may be partial or complete. Most commonly, hypopituitarism is the result of a pituitary tumor that causes progressive hypofunction by applying pressure to the normal gland. Pituitary surgery and cranial irradiation are other common causes. Pituitary apoplexy causes acute hypopituitarism, results from sudden pituitary hemorrhage or infarction, and is often associated with sudden headache, visual change, ophthalmoplegia, and altered mental status.

Postpartum pituitary necrosis (Sheehan syndrome) is due to silent pituitary infarction and is usually associated with obstetric hemorrhage and hypotension. Acutely, vascular collapse may occur, but more commonly the syndrome presents with amenorrhea, a postpartum inability to lactate, and fatigue. Lymphocytic hypophysitis causes hypopituitarism and, possibly, symptoms of a mass lesion. Most cases of lymphocytic hypophysitis occur during or after pregnancy.

Symptoms of anterior hypopituitarism are identical to primary target-organ hypofunction. However, the presence of headache and loss of peripheral vision suggest a pituitary mass effect.

Look for:

- history of cranial radiation therapy or pituitary surgery
- difficult delivery with hemorrhage or hypotension
- amenorrhea, loss of libido, or erectile dysfunction
- fatigue, nausea, vomiting, weight loss, or abdominal pain
- cold intolerance, weight gain, or constipation
- loss of muscle mass
- polydipsia, polyuria, and nocturia (DI)
- visual field diagram showing bitemporal loss of vision (mass effect)

Diagnosis is confirmed by documenting target-organ hormone deficiency and a corresponding low or "normal" serum pituitary hormone level. Stimulation testing may be needed to document hypopituitarism.

STUDY TABLE: Key Hormone Tests for Hypopituitarism	
Hormone	**Findings**
GH	Diminished response to provocative hypoglycemia or arginine and GH-releasing hormone stimulation
	Depressed IGF-1
FSH/LH	Depressed FSH, LH, and estradiol or testosterone levels
TSH	Depressed free T$_4$ and TSH
ACTH	Low cortisol level and depressed ACTH
	Depressed response of 11-deoxycortisol and cortisol to metyrapone
	Positive cortisol response to 1 μg of ACTH
Prolactin	Level may be elevated from loss of tonic inhibition

μg = microgram.

After documenting hypopituitarism or hyperprolactinemia, select MRI of the pituitary gland.

◆ DON'T BE TRICKED

- **Measurement of serum FSH/LH levels is not needed in women who have normal menstrual cycles.**

Therapy

Hydrocortisone is indicated for patients with adrenal insufficiency. Androgen replacement therapy is appropriate for men with hypogonadism, and estrogen replacement therapy is used for premenopausal women with hypogonadism. Consider GH replacement for biochemically confirmed deficiency and consistent symptoms.

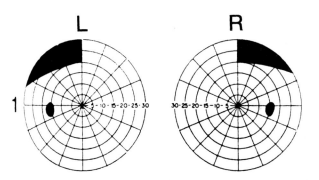

Visual Field Defects: Bitemporal quadrant visual field defects secondary to a pituitary mass.

Pituitary apoplexy requires acute administration of corticosteroids until acute adrenal insufficiency has been ruled out and may also require urgent neurosurgical decompression.

◆ DON'T BE TRICKED

- **Thyroxine dosing for central hypothyroidism is based on serum free T$_4$ rather than TSH levels.**
- **T$_4$ replacement is indicated only after hypoadrenalism has been ruled out or treated.**

❖ Test Yourself

A 65-year-old man was diagnosed with small cell lung cancer 20 years ago and received chemotherapy and chest and cranial irradiation. Physical examination shows hypotension, tachycardia, and small testes. Serum sodium is 123 meq/L.

ANSWER: The diagnosis is hypopituitarism. Select immediate replacement with stress doses of hydrocortisone followed by confirmatory testing.

Diabetes Insipidus

Diagnosis

DI is characterized by an inability to concentrate urine because of insufficient arginine vasopressin (AVP, antidiuretic hormone) release (central DI) or activity (nephrogenic DI). Signs and symptoms of central DI are cravings for water or cold liquids, urinary frequency, nocturia, visual field deficits, amenorrhea, and galactorrhea. Important clues are a history of head trauma, recent neurosurgery, pituitary mass lesion, evidence of anterior hypopituitarism (adrenal insufficiency, hypothyroidism), history of an infiltrative disorder (such as sarcoidosis), kidney disease (tubulointerstitial disease), or medications such as lithium.

Patients typically have large-volume polyuria with urine osmolality <200 mosm/kg H_2O. Measure a plasma glucose level to rule out diabetes mellitus and a serum calcium level to rule out hypercalcemia. The inability to increase the concentration of the urine during a water deprivation test confirms the diagnosis. When DI has been confirmed, a desmopressin challenge test is done to differentiate between central and nephrogenic forms. If the desmopressin challenge test is positive (urine concentrates, indicating central DI), order an MRI of the pituitary gland. If the test is negative (urine does not concentrate, indicating nephrogenic DI), order kidney ultrasonography.

Therapy

Treatment of DI depends on the cause.

STUDY TABLE: Treating Diabetes Insipidus	
If you see...	**Choose...**
DI after neurosurgery or head trauma	If unable to drink, 5% dextrose in 0.45% sodium chloride IV
	Add desmopressin if urine output is high or hypernatremia develops
Chronic central DI	Intranasal or oral desmopressin
Lithium-induced nephrogenic DI	Amiloride
Non–drug-induced nephrogenic DI	Thiazide diuretic and salt restriction

❖ **Test Yourself**

A previously healthy 27-year-old woman has a 1-month history of polydipsia and polyuria. She has had amenorrhea since giving birth 9 months ago. The plasma glucose level is 90 mg/dL, urine output is 4 L/d, and urine osmolality is 95 mosm/kg H_2O.

ANSWER: The patient has probable central DI. Select a water deprivation test.

Hyperparathyroidism and Hypercalcemia

Diagnosis

Primary hyperparathyroidism is the most common cause of hypercalcemia in outpatients. Primary hyperparathyroidism commonly presents as asymptomatic hypercalcemia. Less common presentations are kidney stones, osteoporosis, pancreatitis, and fractures (osteoporosis). Malignancy is the most common cause of hypercalcemia in hospitalized patients. Hypercalcemia may also occur with the use of lithium (PTH-mediated) or thiazide diuretics (non-PTH-mediated) and in the setting of excessive ingestion of vitamin D and calcium. Sarcoidosis may be associated with hypercalcemia (10% of patients) and hypercalciuria (50% of patients).

Measure the ionized calcium to exclude pseudo-hypercalcemia caused by an increase in plasma proteins capable of binding calcium; total calcium will be increased and ionized calcium will be normal.

If hypercalcemia is confirmed, check calcium, PTH, phosphate, creatinine, and 25-hydroxyvitamin D levels. If PTH is elevated or inappropriately normal in the setting of elevated serum calcium, the most likely cause is primary hyperparathyroidism.

◆ DON'T BE TRICKED

- **In patients with hypercalcemia and normal or elevated parathyroid hormone levels, measure urinary calcium excretion to exclude familial hypocalciuric hypercalcemia.**

If hyperparathyroidism is confirmed and surgery is indicated, do a sestamibi parathyroid scan to look for an adenoma.

STUDY TABLE: Causes of Hypercalcemia

Diagnosis	Key features include hypercalcemia and...
Primary hyperparathyroidism	PTH elevated (80%) or inappropriately normal (20%); phosphorus low. X-rays may show chondrocalcinosis or osteitis fibrosa cystica.
Humoral hypercalcemia of malignancy	PTH suppressed; phosphorus normal or low. PTH–related protein normal or elevated but not needed for diagnosis. This is the most common cause of hypercalcemia in patients with cancer.
Local osteolytic hypercalcemia	PTH suppressed, alkaline phosphatase usually elevated. Hypercalciuria without hypercalcemia is most common.
Multiple myeloma	PTH suppressed, phosphorus elevated. Look for patients presenting with new kidney injury and anemia. Diagnose with serum and urine protein immunoelectrophoresis.
Granulomatous disease (sarcoidosis and tuberculosis) and B-cell lymphoma	PTH suppressed; phosphorus elevated; calcitriol elevated (particularly in sarcoidosis)
Milk-alkali syndrome	PTH suppressed; phosphorus, creatinine, carbon dioxide elevated. Consider in healthy persons in whom primary hyperparathyroidism has been excluded. Excessive ingestion of calcium-containing antacids is a cause.
Hyperthyroidism	Hypercalcemia is a frequent incidental finding in hyperthyroidism due to direct stimulation of osteoclasts by thyroid hormone.

Primary hyperparathyroidism is the most common manifestation of MEN1.

STUDY TABLE: Multiple Endocrine Neoplasia Types 1 and 2

MEN1	MEN2
Multigland hyperparathyroidism is the most common manifestation	Medullary thyroid cancer is the most common manifestation and may be associated with a palpable neck mass.
Pituitary neoplasms associated with prolactinoma (amenorrhea and erectile dysfunction), acromegaly (enlargement of hands, feet, tongue, frontal bossing), Cushing disease (bruising, hypertension, central obesity, hirsutism)	Pheochromocytoma (hypertension and palpitations)
Pancreatic neuroendocrine tumors associated with gastrinoma (diarrhea, ulcers), insulinoma (fasting hypoglycemia), vasoactive intestinal polypeptide–secreting tumor (watery diarrhea, hypokalemia), carcinoid syndrome (diarrhea, flushing, right heart valvular lesion)	Multigland hyperparathyroidism is the least common manifestation

◆ DON'T BE TRICKED

- About 50% of patients with primary hyperparathyroidism have coexisting vitamin D deficiency, and serum and urine calcium levels may be decreased. Select measurement of serum vitamin D levels in all patients with hyperparathyroidism.

Therapy

Parathyroidectomy is indicated for patients with primary hyperparathyroidism and hypercalcemic complications, such as kidney stones, overt bone disease, or previous episodes of hypercalcemic crisis. Asymptomatic patients are surgical candidates if they have any of the following:

- serum calcium level >1 mg/dL above upper limit of normal
- estimated GFR <60 mL/min/1.73 m^2
- reduction in bone mineral density (T-score <–2.5)
- age <50 years

Watch for a precipitous fall in the serum calcium level caused by relative hypoparathyroidism after parathyroidectomy ("hungry bone" syndrome). Monitor serum calcium after surgery, and give oral calcium if mild hypocalcemia develops.

Treat patients who are not candidates for parathyroidectomy with bisphosphonates.

Hypercalcemia requiring acute intervention is most common in the setting of malignancy. Select:

- volume resuscitation with normal saline
- IV bisphosphonates
- oral corticosteroid therapy if due to multiple myeloma or a granulomatous process

◆ DON'T BE TRICKED

- **In the absence of hypervolemia, adding a loop diuretic (such as furosemide) to IV hydration is of unproven utility and has the potential for serious electrolyte complications.**

❖ Test Yourself

A 44-year-old man has a 1-year history of fatigue and poor concentration. His serum calcium level is 10.9 mg/dL, serum phosphorus level is 2.8 mg/dL, and PTH level is 75 pg/mL.

ANSWER: Diagnose primary hyperparathyroidism, measure serum vitamin D levels, and select parathyroidectomy.

Hypocalcemia

Diagnosis

Most cases of hypocalcemia are due to low serum albumin levels; the ionized calcium concentration is normal. Total calcium declines by 0.8 mg/dL for each 1 g/dL decrement in serum albumin concentration. The most common cause of acquired hypocalcemia is surgical excision of or vascular injury to the parathyroid glands. Other causes include neck irradiation, congenital hypoparathyroidism (DiGeorge syndrome), autoimmune destruction, infiltrative diseases, and as a complication of plasmapheresis. Autoimmune hypoparathyroidism occurs as an isolated defect or as part of polyglandular autoimmune syndrome type 1 in association with adrenal insufficiency and mucocutaneous candidiasis. In addition to hypoparathyroidism, hypocalcemia may result from pseudohypoparathyroidism, vitamin D deficiency, hypomagnesemia, or pancreatitis or may occur in the setting of rhabdomyolysis, kidney failure, and tumor lysis syndrome.

Look for:

- circumoral and acral paresthesias
- carpal-pedal spasm
- positive Trousseau sign
- positive Chvostek sign

Order calcium, phosphate, magnesium, creatinine, PTH, 25-hydroxyvitamin D, albumin, and/or ionized calcium tests. Order an ECG to evaluate for QTc interval prolongation.

STUDY TABLE: Differential Diagnosis of Hypocalcemia	
Diagnosis	**Key features include hypocalcemia and...**
Hypoparathyroidism	Hyperphosphatemia; low PTH and variable vitamin D levels
Pseudohypoparathyroidism (resistance to PTH)	Hyperphosphatemia; elevated PTH and normal vitamin D levels
Chronic kidney disease	Hyperphosphatemia; elevated PTH and low 1,25-dihydroxyvitamin D levels
Vitamin D deficiency	Hypophosphatemia; bone tenderness or fibromyalgia-like syndrome
Impaired PTH secretion and PTH resistance	Magnesium deficiency (small bowel bypass, diarrhea, alcoholism, diuretic therapy)
"Hungry bone" syndrome	Recent parathyroidectomy

Therapy

Treat acute symptomatic hypocalcemia with IV calcium gluconate and vitamin D. Chronic hypocalcemia is treated with oral calcium supplements and vitamin D. Choose the type of vitamin D based on the presence of underlying disease:

- kidney disease: calcitriol (1,25-dihydroxyvitamin D)
- liver disease: 25-hydroxycholecalciferol
- any other cause of hypocalcemia: cholecalciferol (D_3) or ergocalciferol (D_2)

The main side effect of therapy is hypercalciuria and nephrolithiasis. Remember to correct hypomagnesemia with magnesium supplements.

❖ **Test Yourself**

A 46-year-old woman has cramps in her hands and feet. She has pernicious anemia and Hashimoto thyroiditis. Her serum calcium level is 7.9 mg/dL, and her serum phosphorus level is 4.1 mg/dL.

ANSWER: Diagnose autoimmune hypoparathyroidism and select a serum PTH level.

Osteomalacia

Diagnosis

Osteomalacia is a metabolic bone disease resulting from failure of the organic matrix of bone to mineralize because of lack of available calcium or phosphorus. Many cases of osteomalacia are related to abnormalities in vitamin D but may also result from deficiencies of calcium or phosphate.

Look for:

- fatigability, malaise, and bone pain
- generalized bone tenderness
- proximal muscle weakness
- Looser zones—bands perpendicular to the bone surface visible on x-rays
- hypocalcemia and hypophosphatemia
- elevated serum alkaline phosphatase level

Evaluate for underlying conditions that may lead to intestinal malabsorption of vitamin D, such as celiac disease, or abnormalities in vitamin D metabolism, such as liver and kidney disease. Diagnosis is confirmed with bone biopsy when necessary.

Therapy

If osteomalacia is secondary to vitamin D deficiency, treat with oral ergocalciferol 1000 to 2000 units/d and elemental calcium 1 g/d.

◆ **DON'T BE TRICKED**

- **Not all fractures in older adult patients are due to osteoporosis. Look for osteomalacia, particularly in nursing-home residents.**

Paget Disease

Diagnosis

Paget disease is a focal disorder of bone remodeling that leads to greatly accelerated rates of bone turnover, disruption of the normal architecture of bone, and sometimes gross deformities of bone (enlargement of the skull, bowing of the femur or tibia). Most patients are asymptomatic, and the disease is suspected when an isolated elevation of alkaline phosphatase is detected.

Characteristic findings of symptomatic Paget disease include:

- bone pain, fractures
- cranial nerve compression syndromes, spinal stenosis, nerve root syndromes
- high-output cardiac failure
- angioid retinal streaks

If the serum alkaline phosphatase level is elevated in a symptomatic patient, order a bone scan and follow-up x-rays of areas that localize radionuclide.

Therapy

Indications to treat Paget disease include bone pain, radiculopathy, or involvement of a weight-bearing bone or a joint, regardless of symptoms. Bisphosphonates are the first-line agents.

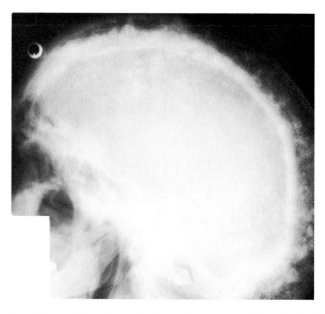

Paget Disease: X-ray showing "cotton wool" appearance of the skull typical of Paget disease.

Hypercortisolism (Cushing Syndrome)

Diagnosis

The most common cause of Cushing syndrome is the use of corticosteroids. Most endogenous cases are caused by ACTH-secreting pituitary tumors (Cushing disease). Less common causes of hypercortisolism include adrenocortical adenomas (rarely carcinoma) and ectopic ACTH-secreting malignant tumors. When the syndrome is due to an ectopic ACTH-secreting tumor, symptoms of weight loss, muscle weakness, and profound hypokalemia may predominate. ACTH-dependent forms of Cushing syndrome may result in bilateral adrenal enlargement.

Characteristic findings are:

- facial rounding
- prominent supraclavicular or dorsocervical fat pads
- centripetal obesity
- purple striae
- diabetes mellitus
- osteoporosis
- hypertension
- feminization or virilization

First-line diagnostic studies include the 1-mg dexamethasone suppression test, 24-hour urine cortisol level (elevated), and measurement of late night salivary cortisol level (elevated). The dexamethasone test is positive if failure to suppress serum cortisol to <5 micrograms/dL occurs.

Measurements of ACTH can differentiate ACTH-dependent states of hypercortisolism, in which ACTH levels are inappropriately normal or elevated (as with a pituitary adenoma), from ACTH-independent states, in which ACTH levels are low or undetectable (as with adrenal neoplasms). If ACTH is suppressed, obtain an adrenal gland CT scan to look for adrenal adenoma or hyperplasia. If ACTH is not suppressed, select a pituitary gland MRI to look for a pituitary adenoma. If a pituitary adenoma >6 mm is seen and no clinical features are suggestive of ectopic ACTH secretion, the diagnosis is consistent with Cushing disease. Only after Cushing disease has been definitively excluded should evaluation for an ectopic ACTH-secreting malignant tumor be undertaken.

The most common ACTH-secreting malignant tumors are small cell lung cancer, bronchial carcinoid, pheochromocytoma, and medullary thyroid carcinoma. Select a chest MRI or CT.

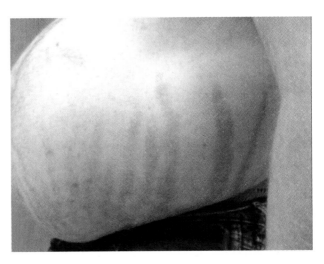

Cushing Syndrome: Wide purple striae characteristic of Cushing syndrome. Image courtesy of Rebecca L. Adochio, MD.

◆ DON'T BE TRICKED

- **False-positive results (failure to suppress cortisol) with the 1-mg dexamethasone suppression test are commonly due to alcohol use, obesity, and psychological disorders.**

Therapy

Surgical resection of the adrenal, pituitary, or ectopic tumor is the optimal therapy for Cushing syndrome. Bisphosphonates are the treatment of choice for low bone density caused by hypercortisolism.

❖ Test Yourself

A 43-year-old woman has diabetes mellitus, hypertension, hirsutism, and central obesity. The serum cortisol level is 26 micrograms/dL after administration of 1 mg of dexamethasone and 8.2 micrograms/dL after 8 mg of dexamethasone. The serum ACTH level is 50 pg/mL.

ANSWER: The diagnosis is a pituitary tumor. Select pituitary gland MRI.

Hypoadrenalism (Addison Disease)

Diagnosis

Adrenal insufficiency may be due to disease of the adrenal glands (primary) or disorders of the pituitary gland (secondary). Autoimmune adrenalitis is the most common cause of primary insufficiency. Corticosteroid use is the most common cause of secondary insufficiency (hypothalamic-pituitary suppression). Primary disease results in loss of cortisol, aldosterone, and adrenal androgens, whereas secondary insufficiency causes only cortisol and adrenal androgen deficiencies (aldosterone synthesis is not ACTH dependent).

Characteristic findings include:

- weight loss
- fatigue, anorexia, nausea, vomiting
- orthostatic hypotension
- hyperpigmentation (primary adrenal insufficiency)
- hypoglycemia, hyponatremia, and hyperkalemia (primary adrenal insufficiency)
- eosinophilia

Look for patients who recently discontinued corticosteroid therapy or did not increase their corticosteroid dose in times of stress.

Diagnostic studies include measuring the morning serum cortisol level followed by a cosyntropin stimulation test (a serum cortisol level rising to >18 micrograms/dL rules out adrenal insufficiency). Measurement of a morning serum ACTH level can help differentiate between primary and secondary causes. If the ACTH level is elevated, order a CT of the adrenal glands. If the ACTH level is normal or low, order MRI of the brain to evaluate the pituitary gland.

Approximately 50% of patients with autoimmune adrenal insufficiency have other autoimmune endocrine disorders (thyroid disease, type 1 diabetes), and screening for these disorders is an appropriate answer.

◆ DON'T BE TRICKED

- Hyperpigmentation and hyperkalemia are common in primary but not secondary adrenal insufficiency.

Therapy

If acute adrenal insufficiency is suspected, give high-dose dexamethasone (administration will not interfere with serum cortisol assay) and IV saline before obtaining cortisol and ACTH levels and without waiting for the ACTH and cortisol level results to return from the laboratory. After a diagnosis is made, hydrocortisone 10 to 30 mg/d is the standard therapy. Increase the hydrocortisone dose 2 to 10 times the standard replacement dose during periods of physiological stress, including surgery. Oral fludrocortisone is only appropriate for treatment of primary adrenal insufficiency.

◆ DON'T BE TRICKED

- Do not prescribe dexamethasone for chronic replacement therapy.

❖ Test Yourself

A 32-year-old man with hypothyroidism has a 3-month history of fatigue, weakness, nausea, and a 13.9-kg (30-lb) weight loss. He has orthostatic hypotension and increased pigment in the palmar creases. The serum sodium level is 132 meq/L, and the serum potassium level is 5 meq/L.

ANSWER: Diagnose autoimmune adrenalitis.

Adrenal Incidentaloma

Diagnosis

An adrenal incidentaloma is a mass >1 cm in diameter that is discovered incidentally. The two goals of evaluation are to determine if an adenoma is functioning and if it is malignant. All patients with adrenal incidentaloma should have a 1-mg overnight dexamethasone suppression test and measurement of plasma or urine levels of fractionated metanephrines (catecholamine metabolites). Patients with hypertension or spontaneous hypokalemia and an incidentaloma also require measurement of the plasma aldosterone/plasma renin activity ratio.

Adrenal metastases are common in patients with a known nonadrenal malignancy. Adenomas >4 cm are more likely to be malignant.

Therapy

Choose surgery for adrenal masses >6 cm in diameter or functioning tumors. Controversy exists regarding the optimal management for adrenal masses 4 to 6 cm in diameter, whereas masses <4 cm in size are monitored radiographically.

Follow-up

Repeat imaging scan in 6 to 12 months for all patients with nonfunctioning tumors that fail to meet surgical criteria. Also repeat screening for hormonal hypersecretion.

Pheochromocytoma

Diagnosis

Pheochromocytomas are rare tumors arising in the chromaffin cells of the adrenal medulla that secrete biogenic amines (norepinephrine, epinephrine or dopamine) or their metabolites.

Characteristic findings may be remembered by the 7 "H"s (hypertension, headache, hypermetabolism, hyperhidrosis, hyperglycemia, hypokalemia, hypotension [during anesthesia induction]). Pheochromocytoma is associated with MEN2, von Hippel-Lindau disease, and neurofibromatosis type 2. Suspect a familial form in patients with a family history of pheochromocytoma, those with bilateral disease or an extra-adrenal location, and younger patients with a history of MEN2 or neurofibromatosis.

Orthostatic hypotension (due to vasoconstriction-related volume depletion) is a helpful physical examination clue. First-line studies include measurement of serum metanephrine and normetanephrine levels or 24-hour urine collection for metanephrines and catecholamines. Positive biochemical tests are followed by MRI or CT of the abdomen. A ^{131}I or ^{123}I-MIBG scan may aid in localization when CT or MRI scans are negative.

Therapy

Surgery is the treatment of choice. Use phenoxybenzamine, doxazosin, or nicardipine to control blood pressure preoperatively. Give IV normal saline to maintain intravascular volume; nitroprusside or phentolamine is indicated for treating intraoperative hypertensive crisis.

◆ DON'T BE TRICKED
- Select β-adrenergic blockade only after adequate α-adrenergic blockade is achieved.

Primary Hyperaldosteronism

Diagnosis

Hyperaldosteronism is diagnosed in up to 14% of unselected patients with hypertension. Characteristic findings are difficult-to-treat hypertension and hypokalemia. Screen patients with hypertension with unprovoked hypokalemia, a family history of primary hyperaldosteronism, or resistant hypertension with simultaneous measurements of plasma aldosterone and plasma renin activity. A plasma aldosterone/plasma renin activity ratio >20, with a plasma aldosterone level >15 ng/dL, strongly suggests primary hyperaldosteronism. Testing can be done in patients receiving treatment with any antihypertensive agent except spironolactone and eplerenone, both of which antagonize the aldosterone receptor. The diagnosis is confirmed by demonstrating nonsuppressibility of elevated plasma aldosterone in response to a high salt load given intravenously or orally. In healthy patients, the plasma aldosterone level is suppressed to <5 ng/dL.

After autonomous hyperaldosteronism is diagnosed, select either CT or MRI of the adrenal glands.

Therapy

Spironolactone or eplerenone is the treatment of choice for adrenal hyperplasia, and laparoscopic adrenalectomy is indicated for an aldosterone-producing adenoma. If additional antihypertensive medications are required to control blood pressure, select a thiazide diuretic agent.

Male Hypogonadism

Diagnosis

Characteristic findings are fatigue, decreased strength, poor libido, hot flushes, erectile dysfunction, and gynecomastia.

Serum total testosterone values <200 ng/dL are diagnostic, and values >350 ng/dL are normal. If values are between 200 and 350 ng/dL, measure free (by equilibrium dialysis) or bioavailable testosterone levels or the calculated free androgen index. If the testosterone level is low, measure LH, FSH, and prolactin levels. Elevated LH and FSH values indicate primary testicular failure. Causes include Klinefelter syndrome, atrophy secondary to mumps orchitis, autoimmune destruction, and previous chemotherapy or pelvic irradiation. Low or normal LH and FSH levels indicate secondary hypogonadism. Causes include hypogonadotrophic hypogonadism, hyperprolactinemia, other hypothalamic or pituitary disorders, and use of opiates or corticosteroids. If secondary hypogonadism is confirmed, in addition to measuring prolactin, check iron studies to rule out hemochromatosis and obtain an MRI to evaluate for hypothalamic or pituitary lesions.

Men who self-administer anabolic steroids can come to medical attention because of infertility. Physical examination typically reveals irritability, acne, muscular hypertrophy, testicular atrophy, and gynecomastia (if the patient is using testosterone). Laboratory data show suppressed LH and FSH levels, variable testosterone levels, and otherwise normal pituitary function.

◆ DON'T BE TRICKED

- Severe erectile dysfunction is almost always due to coexisting vascular, neurologic, or cavernosal pathologic findings and not solely to hypogonadism.

Therapy

Testosterone can be administered as a transdermal (preferred), buccal, or IM preparation.

Before initiation of testosterone replacement and during therapy, routinely monitor hematocrit and PSA to screen for the development of erythrocytosis and prostate cancer, respectively. In patients <60 years of age, if the testosterone level is modestly reduced (150-300 ng/dL) and both LH and prolactin are normal, diagnose androgen deficiency in the aging male (ADAM) syndrome, and select testosterone replacement therapy without further investigation. Treating men >60 years of age with no identifiable pituitary or hypothalamic disease with testosterone is controversial.

Gastroenterology and Hepatology

Dysphagia

Diagnosis

Dysphagia is defined as difficulty swallowing and is classified as oropharyngeal or esophageal.

Oropharyngeal dysphagia frequently results from muscular or neurologic disorders, most commonly stroke, Parkinson disease, amyotrophic lateral sclerosis, myasthenia gravis, and muscular dystrophy. Patients with pharyngoesophageal (Zenker) diverticulum often present with regurgitation of undigested food and severe halitosis. Videofluoroscopy is the most effective study for evaluating suspected oropharyngeal dysphagia.

Patients with esophageal dysphagia report food "sticking" or discomfort in the retrosternal region. Solid-food dysphagia is most often due to a structural esophageal abnormality. Dysphagia for solids and liquids or for liquids alone suggests an esophageal motility abnormality such as achalasia. Solid-food dysphagia that occurs episodically for months to years is most characteristic of an esophageal web or a distal esophageal ring (Schatzki ring). Progressively increasing solid-food dysphagia generally indicates a peptic stricture or carcinoma. Diagnosis of esophageal dysphagia often entails an endoscopic visualization procedure.

Therapy

Therapy is dictated by the underlying cause.

❖ **Test Yourself**

A 75-year-old man with Parkinson disease has difficulty initiating a swallow.

ANSWER: The diagnosis is probably neuromuscular pharyngeal dysphagia; order oropharyngeal videofluoroscopy.

Achalasia

Diagnosis

Achalasia is caused by degeneration of the myenteric plexus with the loss of inhibitory neurons, failure of the LES to relax in response to swallowing, and absent peristalsis. This leads to the retention of food and liquids in the body of the esophagus, the characteristic findings of dysphagia with solids and liquids (regurgitation, coughing, choking), and "bird's beak" narrowing of the GE junction on barium swallow. If the patient has a history of travel to South America, suspect Chagas disease as the cause of achalasia.

Diagnostic evaluation should be done in the following order:

- barium swallow: the preferred screening test when diagnosis is suspected clinically
- esophageal manometry: confirms the diagnosis by documenting the absence of peristalsis and incomplete relaxation of the LES with swallows
- upper endoscopy: performed to rule out adenocarcinoma (pseudoachalasia) at the GE junction

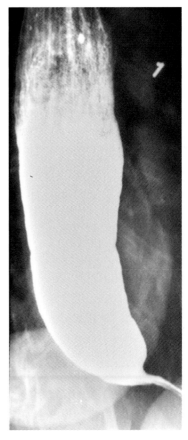

Barium Esophagogram: The "bird's beak" finding reflects narrowing of the distal esophagus and is characteristic of achalasia.

97

Therapy

Laparoscopic surgical myotomy of the LES and endoscopic pneumatic dilatation of the esophagus are first-line therapies for achalasia, although myotomy predisposes the patient to reflux and dilatation may require periodic repeating. Select calcium channel blockers, nitrates, or botulinum toxin injection if the patient cannot tolerate dilation or surgery.

GERD

Diagnosis

GERD is caused by reflux of gastric contents into the esophagus. Characteristic findings of GERD are heartburn and/or regurgitation. Extraesophageal symptoms may include wheezing, cough, hoarseness, and chest pain. Barrett esophagus results from injury to the esophagus in patients with chronic GERD. In these patients, the risk of developing esophageal cancer is increased 30-fold but the absolute risk remains small.

STUDY TABLE: GERD Diagnostic Studies	
Indication	Test
GERD symptoms refractory to empiric therapy with PPIs	Upper endoscopy; if normal, then choose ambulatory esophageal pH monitoring while taking a PPI for symptom–reflux correlation
Dysphagia, odynophagia, and weight loss	Upper endoscopy to rule out cancer
Symptoms >5 years, age >50 years, white male	Consider upper endoscopy to rule out Barrett esophagus; screening recommendations are controversial
Confirmed Barrett esophagus	Periodic upper endoscopy to monitor for dysplasia and cancer; surveillance recommendations are controversial

◆ DON'T BE TRICKED

- Treat before upper endoscopy for uncomplicated GERD.
- Perform upper endoscopy for red flags for cancer (progressive dysphagia, weight loss).

Therapy

PPIs are first-line therapy for GERD and the extraesophageal manifestations of GERD. Select antireflux surgery for patients who are refractory to medical management or those who have an excellent response to a PPI but do not want long-term medical therapy. PPI therapy is associated with an increased risk for enteric infections, pneumonia, and hip fractures. Antireflux surgery does not prevent Barrett esophagus or adenocarcinoma. Select esophagectomy for patients with high-grade dysplasia or early-stage esophageal cancer. Endoscopic eradication therapy is an alternative to esophagectomy in patients with high-grade dysplasia.

❖ Test Yourself

A 34-year-old woman has frequent heartburn. She has tried a PPI, once before breakfast and once before dinner, without improvement.

ANSWER: The probable diagnosis is GERD. Order endoscopy and, if normal, 24-hour esophageal pH monitoring while the patient is taking a PPI.

Esophagitis

Diagnosis

Infectious esophagitis is uncommon in the healthy patient (but is associated with inhaled corticosteroid use) and occurs most often in patients with an underlying immune disorder or an esophageal motility disorder. In patients who are immunosuppressed, the characteristic finding is odynophagia. *Candida albicans* is the most common infectious cause, followed by CMV and HSV. Two thirds of patients with candidal esophagitis have oral thrush. Patients with viral esophagitis rarely have associated ulcerative oropharyngeal lesions. Upper endoscopy establishes the diagnosis. In patients with odynophagia who are immunosuppressed, begin empiric therapy for esophageal candidiasis. Perform upper endoscopy if empiric therapy is unsuccessful. Pill-induced esophagitis may be caused by tetracycline, NSAIDs, potassium chloride, iron, and alendronate. Young adults with eosinophilic esophagitis present with extreme dysphagia and food impaction. Macroscopic findings at endoscopy are nonspecific but may show mucosal furrowing, stacked circular rings, white specks, and mucosal friability. Endoscopic biopsies show marked infiltration with eosinophils. Treat with topical corticosteroids.

❖ Test Yourself

A 30-year-old man has frequent heartburn and recurrent episodes of food impaction.

ANSWER: Diagnose eosinophilic esophagitis.

◆ **DON'T BE TRICKED**
- **Do not select barium esophagography to evaluate suspected esophagitis.**
- **Absence of oral *Candida* lesions does not rule out esophageal candidiasis.**

Therapy

Choose fluconazole or itraconazole for esophageal candidiasis. Select oral acyclovir or famciclovir for HSV esophagitis (select IV treatment if patient cannot swallow). If initial therapy is ineffective, begin IV foscarnet. IV ganciclovir or foscarnet is indicated for CMV esophagitis.

❖ Test Yourself

A 28-year-old man with HIV infection has a 2-month history of odynophagia. On physical examination, oral thrush is present.

ANSWER: Choose empiric treatment with fluconazole.

Nonulcer Dyspepsia

Diagnosis

Nonulcer dyspepsia is defined as nonspecific upper abdominal discomfort or nausea not attributable to peptic ulcer disease or GERD. Various drugs may cause dyspepsia, including NSAIDs, antibiotics, bisphosphonates, and potassium supplements. Diagnosis is based on satisfying one or more of the following criteria:

- bothersome postprandial fullness
- early satiety
- epigastric pain
- epigastric burning

Patients aged >55 years or patients with alarm features require investigation with upper endoscopy. Alarm features include unexplained iron-deficiency anemia, heme-positive stools, progressive dysphagia, weight loss, new-onset dyspepsia, vomiting, and family history of GI malignancy.

Therapy

For patients ≤55 years without alarm features, a test-and-treat approach for *Helicobacter pylori* is reasonable. For those who test negative for *H. pylori*, an empiric trial of acid suppression using a PPI for 4 to 6 weeks is recommended.

◆ DON'T BE TRICKED

- Do not order upper GI x-ray, ultrasonography, or gastric emptying as initial studies for patients with dyspepsia and alarm features.

Peptic Ulcer Disease

Diagnosis

Most PUD is caused by *H. pylori* infection or NSAID use. Upper endoscopy is the best way to diagnose PUD. Gastric ulcers should be biopsied to rule out malignancy. Duodenal ulcers carry little risk of malignancy and do not require biopsy unless they are refractory or suspicion for malignancy exists. All patients with PUD should be tested for *H. pylori* infection regardless of NSAID use. In patients undergoing endoscopy, select biopsy and histologic assessment for *H. pylori* or rapid urease testing for *H. pylori*.

In young patients without alarm symptoms, most guidelines advocate "testing and treating" for *H. pylori* without endoscopy. Noninvasive strategies for diagnosing *H. pylori* include serum antibody tests, urea breath tests, and stool test for *H. pylori* antigens.

Look for complications of PUD by remembering the mnemonic *POB*:

- *P*erforation characterized by severe, sudden abdominal pain that is often associated with shock and peritoneal signs
- *O*utlet obstruction characterized by nausea, vomiting, and/or early satiety and a succussion splash
- *B*leeding characterized by hematemesis, melena, or hematochezia (see Upper GI Bleeding)

◆ DON'T BE TRICKED

- False-negative rapid urease tests, urea breath tests, and stool antigen results for *H. pylori* may occur in patients who recently took antibiotics, bismuth-containing compounds, or PPIs; these drugs should be stopped at least 2 weeks before testing or histologic assessment should be performed.

Therapy

STUDY TABLE: Treating NSAID-Induced Peptic Ulcer Disease	
If you see this...	**Do this...**
NSAID-induced PUD	Stop NSAIDs, treat with H$_2$ blocker or PPI
NSAID-induced PUD, unable to stop NSAID	Treat with PPI
High risk for developing NSAID-induced PUD but needs NSAID treatment*	Initiate prophylaxis with PPI or misoprostol
*High risk is associated with a history of PUD; a history of UGI bleeding; receiving dual antiplatelet therapy or anticoagulation; and 60 years of age or older plus corticosteroid use, dyspepsia, or GERD.	

Initial *H. pylori* therapy includes a PPI and two antibiotics (typically clarithromycin and either amoxicillin or metronidazole) for 2 weeks. If unsuccessful, give a second course of antibiotics that the patient has not already received. The initial treatment of gastric outlet obstruction is nasogastric suction and an IV PPI.

Surgery is reserved for complications of PUD because of the risk of postoperative complications.

STUDY TABLE: Complications of Gastric Surgery	
If you see this...	**Do this...**
Abdominal cramps, nausea, and loose stools 15 minutes after eating followed within 90 minutes by lightheadedness, diaphoresis, and tachycardia	Diagnose dumping syndrome (gastric resection or bypass surgery)
	Treat with small frequent feedings and low-carbohydrate meals
Loose stools and malabsorption	Diagnose blind loop syndrome (gastric bypass)
	Treat with antibiotics and nutritional supplements
Abdominal pain, bloating, difficulty belching	Diagnose gas-bloat syndrome (fundoplication)
	Treat with diet modification; most treatments are untested

Follow-up

Documentation of *H. pylori* eradication is indicated for patients with persistent symptoms, *H. pylori*–associated ulcer, or complicated PUD. Follow-up upper endoscopy for gastric ulcers is indicated if the patient remains symptomatic after treatment, the cause is uncertain, biopsies were not performed during initial endoscopy, or worrisome endoscopic features were noted.

◆ DON'T BE TRICKED

- Duodenal PUD without complications does not require follow-up upper endoscopy.
- Do not order an *H. pylori* antibody assay for eradication testing because antibody titers remain elevated after treatment.

❖ Test Yourself

A 42-year-old man was treated with a PPI, amoxicillin, and clarithromycin for an *H. pylori*–positive duodenal ulcer. He returns 9 weeks after treatment because of recurrent symptoms.

ANSWER: Order a urea breath test. If positive, re-treat with different antibiotics than those prescribed initially.

Gastroparesis

Diagnosis

Consider delayed gastric emptying (gastroparesis) in patients with recurrent nausea, early satiety, bloating, and weight loss. Look for systemic sclerosis, diabetes mellitus, and administration of anticholinergic agents and narcotics. A viral cause is suggested by rapid onset of gastroparesis after a presumed viral infection.

In patients with acute symptoms, upper endoscopy is the initial study to rule out pyloric channel obstruction due to PUD. Patients with chronic symptoms or negative findings on upper endoscopy should have a nuclear medicine solid-phase gastric emptying study.

◆ DON'T BE TRICKED

- Do not order an upper GI barium x-ray to diagnose gastroparesis.

Therapy

Provide nutritional support with liquid supplements or pureed meals. Use IV erythromycin for acute gastroparesis and metoclopramide for chronic gastroparesis. Tardive dyskinesia is a serious complication of metoclopramide therapy.

❖ **Test Yourself**

A 64-year-old woman with a 20-year history of type 2 diabetes mellitus has a 3-year history of postprandial nausea.

ANSWER: The probable diagnosis is diabetic gastroparesis. Order a gastric emptying study.

Celiac Disease

Diagnosis

Celiac disease occurs secondary to ingestion of wheat gluten or related rye and barley proteins in genetically predisposed persons. Characteristic findings are:

- chronic diarrhea or steatorrhea
- bloating, weight loss, and abdominal pain
- pruritic papulovesicular rash on the extensor surfaces (dermatitis herpetiformis; see "Pemphigus Vulgaris and Pemphigoid" in the Dermatology section)
- iron and fat-soluble vitamin deficiencies
- osteoporosis

Not infrequently, celiac disease is misdiagnosed as IBS and may cause isolated elevation of serum ALT levels. Diagnostic tests include an IgA anti–tissue transglutaminase or IgA antiendomysial antibody assay. An association between celiac disease and IgA deficiency can lead to false-negative tests. In patients with IgA deficiency, assays for IgG anti–tissue transglutaminase, IgG antiendomysial antibodies, or IgG antigliadin antibodies are necessary. Definitive diagnosis requires small bowel biopsy or presence of dermatitis herpetiformis.

Be aware that type 1 diabetes and autoimmune thyroid disease occur more commonly in patients with celiac disease. Patients with celiac disease and thyroiditis can have problems absorbing thyroid hormone. Small bowel lymphoma is more common in patients with celiac disease. Measure bone mineral density in all patients with newly diagnosed celiac disease.

◆ **DON'T BE TRICKED**

- **Do not select empiric treatment with a gluten-free diet because it may result in false-negative serologic test results with subsequent testing.**

Therapy

Select a gluten-free diet for treatment of celiac disease or dermatitis. All patients, regardless of symptoms, are treated to prevent intestinal lymphoma, including patients with isolated dermatitis herpetiformis. Patients with osteomalacia should also receive supplemental vitamin D and calcium. The effectiveness of diet therapy is determined by remeasuring IgA antigliadin or IgA anti–tissue transglutaminase antibody titers or repeating small bowel biopsies. Nonadherence is the most common reason for failure of a gluten-free diet. Adherent patients with recurrent malabsorption should be evaluated for intestinal lymphoma.

Malabsorption

Diagnosis

Patients with chronic diarrhea, especially those who report an oily residue in their stool, should be evaluated for possible fat malabsorption. The four most common disorders causing malabsorption are celiac disease, small bowel bacterial overgrowth, short-bowel syndrome, and pancreatic insufficiency.

STUDY TABLE: Chronic Diarrhea and Malabsorption Syndromes	
If you see this...	**Do this...**
History of IBS and iron deficiency anemia	Diagnose celiac disease.
	Obtain IgA anti–tissue transglutaminase or IgA antiendomysial antibody assays.
	Order a gluten-free diet.
Chronic pancreatitis, hyperglycemia, history of pancreatic resection, CF	Diagnose pancreatic insufficiency.
	Obtain tests for excess fecal fat, x-rays for pancreatic calcifications, and consider pancreatic function tests.
	Treat with pancreatic enzyme replacement therapy.
Previous surgery, small bowel diverticulosis, dysmotility (systemic sclerosis or diabetes mellitus)	Diagnose bacterial overgrowth.
	Order empiric trial of antibiotics or hydrogen breath test.
Resection of >200 cm of distal small bowel	Diagnose short-bowel syndrome.
	Replace nutrient and electrolyte deficiencies.
History of resection of <100 cm of distal ileum, now with nonfatty diarrhea	Diagnose short-bowel syndrome with bile acid enteropathy.
	Order empiric trial of cholestyramine.
Arthralgia; fever; neurologic, ocular, or cardiac disease	Diagnose Whipple disease.
	Select small bowel biopsy and polymerase chain reaction for *Tropheryma whippelii*.
	Order antibiotics for 12 months.
Travel to India or Puerto Rico, malabsorption, weight loss, malaise, folate or vitamin B$_{12}$ deficiency, and steatorrhea	Diagnose tropical sprue.
	Order a small bowel biopsy.
	Treat with a sulfonamide or tetracycline and folic acid.
Prolonged traveler's diarrhea, diarrhea after a camping trip, or outbreak in a day-care center	Diagnose giardiasis.
	Identify *Giardia* parasites or *Giardia* antigen in the stool.
	Treat with metronidazole.

◆ DON'T BE TRICKED

- Do not use cholestyramine if ileal resection is >100 cm (will worsen bile salt deficiency and steatorrhea).

❖ Test Yourself

A 54-year-old woman has a 4-month history of diarrhea and weight loss. Laboratory studies show hypocalcemia, microcytic anemia, and an increased prothrombin time.

ANSWER: The probable diagnosis is celiac disease. Order an IgA anti–tissue transglutaminase antibody assay and, if positive, follow with a small bowel biopsy.

Acute Pancreatitis

Diagnosis

Patients with acute pancreatitis usually have the sudden onset of epigastric pain, often radiating to the back, accompanied by nausea, vomiting, fever, and tachycardia. The causes of acute pancreatitis in the United States include:

- gallstone biliary obstruction and alcohol (most common)
- sulfonamides, estrogens, didanosine, valproic acid, thiazide diuretics, and furosemide
- hypertriglyceridemia (>1000 mg/dL)
- ERCP

- CF (young people with pancreatitis)
- hypercalcemia
- pancreas divisum

The serum amylase and lipase levels are elevated in 75% to 90% of patients. If elevated more than three times normal, the specificity for pancreatitis increases. Mildly increased amylase values can be caused by kidney disease, intestinal ischemia, appendicitis, and parotitis. All patients require abdominal ultrasonography to evaluate the biliary tract for obstruction. A CT scan of the abdomen is also indicated if the pancreatitis is severe, lasts longer than 48 hours, or complications are suspected. Severe pancreatitis is associated with hemoconcentration as suggested by elevated hematocrit, creatinine, and BUN. Pancreatic pseudocysts are the most common complication of acute pancreatitis. Repeated episodes of acute pancreatitis may result in chronic pancreatitis.

◆ DON'T BE TRICKED

- **Uncomplicated pancreatitis is not typically associated with rebound abdominal tenderness, absent bowel sounds, high fever, or melena. When these findings are present, consider abscess, pseudocyst, or necrotizing pancreatitis.**

Therapy

In addition to supportive therapy with vigorous IV hydration and pain relief, look for indications for the following treatments:

- bowel rest, IV fluids, and narcotics for mild pancreatitis
- enteral jejunal feedings (preferred) or TPN for moderate to severe pancreatitis
- antibiotics for cholangitis, infected pancreatic necrosis, and infected pseudocysts
- prophylactic antibiotics (imipenem) for pancreatic necrosis (controversial treatment)
- ERCP for cholangitis or severe biliary pancreatitis
- surgery or endoscopic intervention for cholelithiasis, infected pancreatic necrosis, pancreatic abscess, or a pancreatic pseudocyst that does not respond to medical therapy

◆ DON'T BE TRICKED

- **Nutritional support is not beneficial for patients with mild disease.**
- **Do not select antibiotics for interstitial (nonnecrotizing) pancreatitis without evidence of infection.**

❖ Test Yourself

A 71-year-old woman is hospitalized with gallstone pancreatitis. On the sixth day, she has increased pain, fever, and leukocytosis. A CT scan of the abdomen with contrast shows hypodense, nonenhancing areas involving 50% of the pancreas.

ANSWER: The diagnosis is pancreatic necrosis. Arrange a surgical consultation.

Chronic Pancreatitis

Diagnosis

Chronic pancreatitis is an inflammatory disorder characterized by irreversible morphologic changes such as strictures, calculi, and dilatation of the pancreatic duct associated with pain and loss of pancreatic endocrine and exocrine functions. Chronic alcohol abuse is the most common cause in industrialized countries. Patients may report exacerbations of pain following alcohol ingestion or have a history of steatorrhea and diabetes mellitus. Select an imaging study (abdominal CT is most sensitive) to document pancreatic calcifications, which are diagnostic of chronic pancreatitis. Young adults with chronic pancreatitis require genetic testing for CF.

Autoimmune pancreatitis is a type of chronic pancreatitis characterized by:

- hypergammaglobulinemia (specifically IgG4)
- diffuse pancreatic enlargement and/or a mass lesion in the pancreas (mimicking cancer)
- an irregular main pancreatic duct

◆ DON'T BE TRICKED

- **Normal amylase and lipase levels do not rule out chronic pancreatitis.**

Therapy

Treatment of chronic pancreatitis is directed at controlling pain and alleviating the manifestations of diabetes mellitus, malabsorption, and steatorrhea. Administer pancreatic enzymes as initial therapy for malabsorption. If enzyme supplements do not control diarrhea, begin antidiarrheal agents. Select corticosteroids for autoimmune pancreatitis. Surgical or endoscopic decompression is indicated for patients with pancreatic ductal strictures.

Differentiating Cholestatic and Hepatocellular Diseases

Key Considerations

Hepatocellular injury primarily results in elevated AST and ALT values, usually >500 units/L.

- Virus- or drug-induced acute hepatitis usually causes serum aminotransferase elevations >1000 units/L (ALT > AST) and serum total bilirubin levels >15 mg/dL.
- ALT values >5000 units/L are usually due to acetaminophen hepatotoxicity or ischemic hepatitis.
- An AST/ALT ratio >2.0 is highly suggestive of alcoholic hepatitis.
- An AST/ALT ratio >1.0 may suggest cirrhosis in patients chronic viral hepatitis.
- Abnormal PT and serum albumin values imply severe hepatocellular dysfunction.
- AST and ALT elevations in chronic hepatitis are less marked than elevations in acute hepatitis.
- Minimal ALT and AST elevations in a patient with obesity, hyperlipidemia, and hypertension suggest NALD.

Cholestatic liver diseases primarily cause elevated serum bilirubin and alkaline phosphatase values with proportionally lesser elevations of aminotransferase levels. Cholestatic diseases affect microscopic ducts, large bile ducts, or both. Overproduction (hemolysis) or impaired uptake (Gilbert disease) of bilirubin is characterized by >80% indirect (unconjugated) bilirubin, whereas hepatocyte dysfunction or impaired bile flow (obstruction) is characterized by >20% direct (conjugated) bilirubin.

◆ DON'T BE TRICKED

- **Extensive testing is not required to establish the diagnosis of Gilbert disease; verify normal aminotransferase levels and absence of hemolysis with normal hemoglobin and reticulocyte count.**

Gallstones, Acute Cholecystitis, and Cholangitis

Diagnosis

Biliary pain is the most common cause of upper abdominal pain among patients aged >50 years. Look for specific syndromes and mimics of biliary disease.

STUDY TABLE: Biliary Disease Syndromes and Mimics

If you see this...	Diagnose this...
Epigastric and RUQ pain; bilirubin <4 mg/dL; AST, ALT may be minimally elevated	Acute cholecystitis
Biliary colic, cholecystitis, or pancreatitis and no gallstones or bile duct dilation on imaging studies	Biliary crystals (sludge)
RUQ pain, fever, jaundice or these findings plus shock and mental status changes; bilirubin >4 mg/dL; AST and ALT >1000 units/L	Acute cholangitis
Critically ill, febrile, or septic patient (abdominal pain; Murphy sign may be absent)	Acute acalculous cholecystitis
Midepigastric pain radiating to the back, nausea, vomiting, elevated amylase and lipase	Acute pancreatitis
Recent significant alcohol intake; RUQ pain, fever, jaundice, AST 2-3 times greater than ALT; bilirubin >4 mg/dL	Acute alcoholic hepatitis
RUQ pain, pelvic adnexal tenderness, leukocytosis; cervical smear showing gonococci	Fitz-Hugh–Curtis syndrome (gonococcal or chlamydial perihepatitis)
Impacted gallstone in cystic duct, jaundice, and dilated common bile duct caused by extrinsic compression	Mirizzi syndrome
Biliary colic or cholecystitis with small-bowel obstruction and air in biliary tree	Cholecystenteric fistula (gallstone ileus)
RUQ pain, diarrhea, and obstructive jaundice in advanced HIV	AIDS cholangiopathy (*Cryptosporidium* infection)

Select ultrasonography as the initial imaging modality. Dilatation of the cystic or biliary duct indicates an obstructing stone. In patients with cholecystitis, ultrasonography will show pericholecystic fluid and a thickened gallbladder wall. If ultrasonography is nondiagnostic, select cholescintigraphy (e.g., HIDA scan). Nonvisualization of the gallbladder suggests cystic duct obstruction and cholecystitis. If bile duct stones are suspected, select one of the following:

- magnetic resonance cholangiography
- endoscopic ultrasonography
- ERCP

◆ DON'T BE TRICKED

- **HIDA scans can be falsely positive in patients with intrinsic liver disease and elevated serum bilirubin levels.**

Therapy

Patients with symptoms lasting less than 4 to 6 hours, no fever, and no leukocytosis have biliary colic. Treat with NSAIDs to decrease the risk of progression to acute cholecystitis.

Broad-spectrum antibiotics are indicated for acute cholecystitis (pain, fever, and leukocytosis) and signs of complications. Appropriate antibiotic regimens include:

- ampicillin, gentamicin, and metronidazole
- ceftazidime and metronidazole
- monotherapy with piperacillin-tazobactam, ampicillin-sulbactam, or ticarcillin-clavulanic acid

Whether single, double, or triple antibiotic coverage is most effective has not reached consensus. Patients with acute cholecystitis require surgery within 24 to 48 hours.

Select broad-spectrum antibiotics (a fluoroquinolone) and ERCP drainage for acute cholangitis.

◆ DON'T BE TRICKED

- **Surgery is not indicated for asymptomatic gallstones.**
- **Surgery is not indicated for acute cholangitis because surgical procedures are associated with increased mortality.**

❖ **Test Yourself**

A 27-year-old woman is evaluated because of cholecystitis. The serum direct bilirubin level is 5.8 mg/dL. Abdominal ultrasonography shows gallbladder stones. The intrahepatic ducts are dilated. The distal common bile duct is not dilated, and no stones are seen.

ANSWER: The diagnosis is Mirizzi syndrome.

Hepatitis A

Prevention

Hepatitis A vaccine is indicated for travelers to endemic areas, injection drug users, men who have sex with men, and patients with chronic liver disease and clotting factor disorders. Immunization or immune globulin should be given within 2 weeks to household, sexual, and day-care contacts of patients with hepatitis A or persons who ate foods contaminated with HAV. Immune globulin should be administered to travelers leaving for endemic areas in <2 weeks who did not receive hepatitis A vaccine.

Diagnosis

HAV is transmitted by the fecal-oral route and spreads primarily by close personal contact with a person infected with HAV. It is associated with abrupt onset of fatigue, anorexia, malaise, nausea, vomiting, and jaundice. Laboratory findings include marked elevations of serum aminotransferases (usually >1000 units/L). Approximately 50% of patients with HAV have no identifiable source for their infection. Patients with unexplained acute hepatitis or acute liver failure should be tested for IgM anti-HAV. Hepatitis A is not a cause of chronic hepatitis.

Hepatitis B

Prevention

Hepatitis B vaccine plus HBIG is indicated for postexposure prophylaxis after needle-stick injury and for sexual and household contacts of patients with HBV. (See "Immunizations" in the General Internal Medicine section for a comprehensive list of persons who should receive routine vaccinations.)

Diagnosis

HBV is transmitted parenterally by exposure to the blood or body fluids of an infected person, including through:

- injection-drug use
- sexual contact with an infected person
- transmission by an infected mother to her infant during delivery

About 30% to 40% of patients with acute hepatitis B have no identifiable risk factors. Symptoms of acute hepatitis B are similar to those of acute hepatitis A. It is not uncommon for persons to have anicteric or subclinical acute infection. Characteristic findings are unexplained increases in serum aminotransferase (AST/ALT) levels; acute liver failure may occur. Hepatitis B is a cause of chronic hepatitis (an inflammatory process that persists >6 months), can progress to cirrhosis, and is a risk for hepatocellular carcinoma. The presence of HBeAg and HBV DNA are markers of active viral replication.

◆ **DON'T BE TRICKED**
- **Chronic hepatitis B may present as membranous glomerulonephritis, polyarteritis nodosa, or cryoglobulinemia.**

STUDY TABLE: Serologic Diagnosis of Hepatitis B Infection					
Serologic Study	Acute Hepatitis B	Inactive Carriers	Chronic Hepatitis B	Previous Exposure	Previous Vaccination
HBsAg	Positive	Positive	Positive	Negative	Negative
Anti-HBs	Negative	Negative	Negative	Positive	Positive
Anti-HBc	Positive (IgM)	Positive	Positive (IgG)	Positive (IgG)	Negative
HBV DNA	Positive	Negative	Positive	Negative	Negative
HBeAg	Positive	Negative	Positive or negative	Negative	Negative
Anti-HBe	Positive or negative	Positive	Positive or negative	Positive or negative	Negative

Therapy

Consider treating patients with chronic hepatitis B infection and the following findings:

- HBeAg positive, HBV DNA >20,000 units/mL, ALT >2 × upper limit of normal (ULN), and no cirrhosis
- HBeAg positive, compensated cirrhosis, and HBV DNA >2000 units/mL
- HBeAg positive, decompensated cirrhosis, and detectable HBV DNA
- HBeAg negative, ALT >2 × ULN, and HBV DNA >2000 units/mL

Six therapies are approved for chronic hepatitis B: subcutaneous interferon (standard and pegylated) and oral lamivudine, adefovir, entecavir, telbivudine, and tenofovir. The advantages of interferon are its limited duration of therapy, the lack of resistance, and the high response rate. Interferon is contraindicated in patients with advanced liver disease or decompensated cirrhosis; in such patients the oral agents are used. In patients coinfected with HIV and who have not yet been treated for either disease, emtricitabine-tenofovir is typically used as part of the HAART therapy.

◆ DON'T BE TRICKED

- **Interferon alfa should not be used in patients with active autoimmune disorders, severe cytopenias, decompensated cirrhosis, or major depression.**

Because 10% of patients taking interferon alfa develop hypothyroidism, check the thyroid status at follow-up visits. Patients with chronic hepatitis B are at high risk for the development of hepatocellular carcinoma even in the absence of cirrhosis. Surveillance with ultrasonography every 6 to 12 months is advised.

❖ Test Yourself

A 55-year-old woman has a 6-month history of fatigue and malaise. She is taking paroxetine for depression. The serum ALT is 109 units/L. HBsAg, HBeAg, and HBV DNA are positive, and anti-HBV is negative.

ANSWER: The diagnosis is chronic hepatitis B. Begin lamivudine; do not select interferon alfa.

Hepatitis C

Diagnosis

HCV is transmitted parenterally and is the most prevalent bloodborne infection in the United States. HCV usually manifests as chronic liver disease because the acute infection is usually asymptomatic. Test for HCV in patients with chronic liver disease, as well as patients with vasculitis, cryoglobulinemia, glomerulonephritis, and porphyria cutanea tarda. Other high-risk groups include injection drug users, recipients of blood transfusions before 1992, and those with HIV or a sexually transmitted disease. Measurement of anti-HCV is the initial diagnostic study. If positive, test for HCV RNA to determine the presence of active infection. Chronic HCV infection can cause cirrhosis and is a risk factor for hepatocellular carcinoma.

◆ DON'T BE TRICKED

- Because normal aminotransferase levels occur in up to 40% of patients with chronic HCV, normal levels cannot exclude a diagnosis of HCV.

Therapy

Standard treatment for patients with chronic hepatitis C genotypes 2, 3, and 4 is pegylated interferon alfa plus ribavirin. Patients with genotype 1 should be treated using a three-drug regimen using a new protease inhibitor (boceprevir or telaprevir) in combination with pegylated interferon alfa plus ribavirin. The protease inhibitors are approved for treatment of patients with genotype 1 only. The ideal candidate for therapy is the patient with detectable virus, some indication of hepatic inflammation (elevated liver tests or inflammation on the biopsy), and no contraindication to therapy (decompensated cirrhosis, active major depression, pregnancy, previous organ transplant, underlying autoimmune conditions, significant comorbidities).

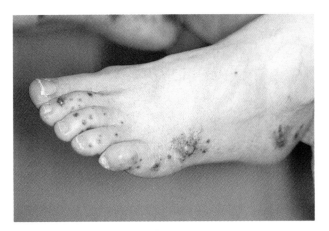

Leukocytoclastic Vasculitis: Palpable purpura consistent with HCV-associated leukocytoclastic vasculitis.

❖ Test Yourself

A 45-year-old male injection drug user has a 3-month history of recurrent purpuric lesions on his legs. Skin biopsy shows leukocytoclastic vasculitis. HBsAg is negative.

ANSWER: The probable diagnosis is HCV. Order anti-HCV testing. If positive, test for cryoglobulins and HCV RNA.

Hemochromatosis

Diagnosis

Hereditary hemochromatosis is an autosomal-recessive disorder characterized by increased intestinal absorption of iron and iron deposition in multiple organs, including the liver, pancreas, heart, joints, thyroid gland, and hypothalamus. Classic manifestations include cirrhosis, diabetes mellitus, erectile dysfunction, and skin hyperpigmentation.

These findings are now uncommon because of earlier detection of the disease. The most common symptoms are fatigue, impotence, destructive arthropathy of the second and third MCP joints characterized by distinctive hook-like osteophytes, and osteoarthritis involving unusual joints, such as the shoulders, ankles, and elbows.

HFE gene testing is indicated when the fasting serum transferrin saturation is >45%. Other disease states that elevate the iron saturation include alcohol use, HCV infection, fatty liver disease, and neoplasms. C282Y/C282Y homozygous or C282Y/H63D compound heterozygous *HFE* genotypes are diagnostic of hemochromatosis. Select liver biopsy in patients with:

- confirmed hemochromatosis and abnormal liver enzymes to determine severity of liver disease
- negative *HFE* genotype but elevated serum transferrin saturation and serum ferritin level >1000 ng/mL to establish a diagnosis

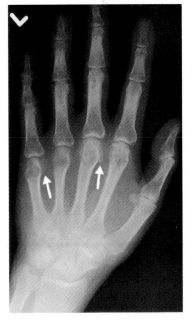

Hemochromatosis: These hook-like osteophytes are characteristic of hemochromatosis.

◆ **DON'T BE TRICKED**

- A nondiagnostic *HFE* genotype does not rule out a diagnosis of hemochromatosis.

Therapy

The treatment of choice is phlebotomy to achieve a target serum ferritin level of <50 ng/mL. In patients with cirrhosis or bridging fibrosis, screen for hepatocellular carcinoma with serum α-fetoprotein levels and ultrasonography of the liver every 6 months.

❖ **Test Yourself**

A 68-year-old man has increasing pain in the second and third MCP joints of both hands. Medical history is significant for type 2 diabetes mellitus and HF.

ANSWER: The probable diagnosis is hemochromatosis; order transferrin saturation and serum ferritin measurement.

Autoimmune Hepatitis

Diagnosis

Autoimmune hepatitis is an inflammatory condition of the liver of unknown cause. It primarily develops in women 20 to 40 years of age who have acute hepatitis or who are asymptomatic but have abnormal liver chemistry test results. As many as 50% of patients with autoimmune hepatitis have a concomitant autoimmune disease such as thyroiditis, ulcerative colitis, or synovitis. Other findings include a serum IgG level that is elevated ≥1.5 times normal, positive ANA and anti–smooth muscle antibody titers, positive p-ANCA, or anti-LKM I antibody ≥1:40. Liver biopsy establishes the diagnosis.

◆ **DON'T BE TRICKED**

- A high serum total protein and low serum albumin level suggest an elevated serum gamma globulin level and may be the only clue to hypergammaglobulinemia.

Therapy

Patients who have active inflammation on liver biopsy specimen or are symptomatic should be considered for treatment with corticosteroids and azathioprine.

Primary Biliary Cirrhosis

Diagnosis

Primary biliary cirrhosis is a chronic progressive autoimmune cholestatic liver disease that occurs predominantly in women between 40 and 60 years of age. Characteristic findings are pruritus, fatigue, weight loss, hyperpigmentation, and xanthomas. Approximately 50% of patients are asymptomatic. The diagnostic triad associated with primary biliary cirrhosis includes:

- a cholestatic liver profile
- positive antimitochondrial antibody titer
- compatible histologic findings on liver biopsy

Other autoimmune diseases are frequently present, and metabolic bone disease, hypercholesterolemia, and fat-soluble vitamin deficiencies are common.

Biliary ultrasonography is required to exclude extrahepatic bile duct obstruction.

Therapy

Ursodeoxycholic acid is the primary therapeutic agent. Vitamin deficiency is uncommon unless the patient has significant jaundice. Select a bisphosphonate for patients with osteoporosis.

Primary Sclerosing Cholangitis

Diagnosis

Primary sclerosing cholangitis is a chronic cholestatic liver disease of unknown cause that is characterized by progressive bile duct destruction and biliary cirrhosis. As many as 80% of patients have an inflammatory bowel disease (most often ulcerative colitis). Characteristic findings are:

- pruritus or jaundice
- elevated serum alkaline phosphatase level
- elevated total bilirubin level
- modestly elevated AST and ALT levels

Abdominal ultrasonography is the initial diagnostic study; if intrahepatic biliary dilation is seen, select MRCP or ERCP to establish the diagnosis (look for the "string of beads" pattern). Patients with primary sclerosing cholangitis are at risk for developing cholangiocarcinoma as well as gallbladder carcinoma and colon cancer (when associated with inflammatory bowel disease). Select annual screening for hepatocellular carcinoma and colon cancer (colonoscopy). No consensus has been reached regarding screening for cholangiocarcinoma and gallbladder cancer.

◆ DON'T BE TRICKED

- Do not confuse primary sclerosing cholangitis with AIDS cholangiopathy (CD4 cell count <100/microliter) due to CMV or *Cryptosporidium* infection.

STUDY TABLE: Differentiating Primary Biliary Cirrhosis and Primary Sclerosing Cholangitis		
	Primary Biliary Cirrhosis	**Primary Sclerosing Cholangitis**
Demographic	Women aged 40-60 years	Men aged 20-30 years
Symptoms/findings	Fatigue, pruritus, weight loss, hyperpigmentation, xanthomas	Pruritus, jaundice
Associated conditions	Other autoimmune disease	Inflammatory bowel disease
Look for...	Positive antimitochondrial antibody titer	"String of beads" on MRCP or ERCP
Therapy	Ursodeoxycholic acid	Endoscopic therapy for extrahepatic dominant strictures

Therapy

Pruritus can be treated with cholestyramine; otherwise, patients with a dominant biliary stricture, pruritus, and jaundice may benefit from endoscopic bile duct dilatation/stenting. Liver transplantation is associated with improved quality of life and survival.

❖ Test Yourself

A 45-year-old man with a 15-year history of ulcerative colitis develops fatigue and pruritus. Serum alkaline phosphatase level is 750 units/L, AST is 48 units/L, ALT is 60 units/L, and total bilirubin is 2.0 mg/dL.

ANSWER: The probable diagnosis is primary sclerosing cholangitis. Schedule ultrasonography followed by MRCP or ERCP.

Alcoholic Hepatitis

Diagnosis

Alcoholic hepatitis is a complication of chronic, daily, heavy use of alcohol for more than 8 years. Acute alcoholic binges can cause fatty liver. The clinical presentation of patients with alcoholic hepatitis ranges from being asymptomatic to development of jaundice, fever, and findings consistent with portal hypertension. Patients with alcoholic hepatitis have AST and ALT measurements <300 to 500 units/L, with an AST/ALT ratio ≥2.0.

Judge the severity of alcoholic hepatitis by using one or more of the following criteria:

- Maddrey Discriminant Function (MDF) score ≥32
- MELD score ≥18
- Glasgow Alcoholic Hepatitis Score (GAHS) ≥9
- presence of encephalopathy and ascites

Therapy

Corticosteroids and pentoxifylline are indicated for patients with an MDF score ≥32, MELD score ≥18, GAHS ≥9, or encephalopathy and ascites.

◆ DON'T BE TRICKED

- **Do not use corticosteroids in patients with alcoholic hepatitis associated with GI bleeding, infection, pancreatitis, or kidney disease.**

❖ Test Yourself

A 46-year-old man has fever and RUQ abdominal pain. He drinks six cans of beer daily. Physical examination discloses ascites. Serum AST is 260 units/L and ALT is 80 units/L. The ascitic fluid leukocyte count is <100/microliter.

ANSWER: The diagnosis is alcoholic hepatitis.

Nonalcoholic Steatohepatitis

Diagnosis

NAFLD refers to a spectrum of histologic changes in the liver initiated by steatosis in the absence of excessive alcohol consumption. NASH is a subset of NAFLD in which steatosis causes oxidative stress, leading to cell death and necroinflammatory hepatic changes.

NASH occurs most often in patients with obesity, diabetes mellitus, and hyperlipidemia and those who have had bypass operations for obesity and have been receiving TPN and high-protein diets. Certain medications (e.g., tamoxifen, estrogen, amiodarone, and corticosteroids) are also associated with the development of NASH.

Ultrasonography shows a hyperechoic pattern consistent with fatty infiltration of the liver, and CT scans reveal low-density hepatic parenchyma. AST/ALT ratio is typically <1 early in disease.

◆ DON'T BE TRICKED

- **Only liver biopsy (not ultrasonography) can confirm or exclude the diagnosis of NASH.**

Therapy

Therapy involves weight reduction of >15% in overweight and obese patients and strict control of diabetes mellitus and hyperlipidemia. Causative medications should be discontinued.

◆ DON'T BE TRICKED

- **Patients with fatty liver disease and elevated aminotransferase levels can be treated with statin therapy.**

❖ Test Yourself

A 38-year-old woman with type 2 diabetes mellitus develops abnormal liver chemistry test results. She is obese. She does not use alcohol excessively. Serum AST is 134 units/L and ALT is 147 units/L. Abdominal ultrasonography shows increased echogenicity of the liver.

ANSWER: The diagnosis is probable NASH. Schedule liver biopsy.

Acute Liver Injury and Acute Liver Failure

Diagnosis

Acute liver injury is associated with a sudden increase in serum AST and ALT levels in a patient without a history of liver disease. Acute liver failure refers to acute hepatic injury complicated by encephalopathy and coagulopathy in patients without previous cirrhosis. The most common causes are acetaminophen hepatotoxicity, idiosyncratic drug reactions, HAV, HBV, and hepatic ischemia.

STUDY TABLE: Differential Diagnosis of Acute Liver Failure		
If you see this...	**Look for this...**	**And choose this...**
Sudden elevation of serum AST and ALT levels up to 20 × normal associated with depression or alcoholism	Acetaminophen overdose, which is the most common cause of acute liver failure Acute liver failure is usually due to acetaminophen ingestion >4 g but can occur with lower doses in patients with alcoholism	Measure serum acetaminophen level and use nomogram to determine if N-acetylcysteine is indicated
Outbreaks of acute liver failure associated with foods such as raspberries and scallions	Acute HAV infection	Order serologic studies for HAV
Episode of hypotension	In hospitalized patients, acute elevation of AST to >1000 units/L is most commonly due to hepatic hypoxia	Review hospital course
Acute elevation of liver enzymes in a young patient and hemolysis, Kayser-Fleischer rings, history of psychiatric disorders, and/or athetoid movements	Wilson disease	Order measurement of serum copper and ceruloplasmin levels and urine copper excretion
Pregnancy, preeclampsia or eclampsia, hemolysis, elevated liver enzymes, and low platelets (thrombocytopenia) in third trimester	HELLP syndrome	Schedule urgent delivery
Pregnancy, preeclampsia, eclampsia, thrombocytopenia, and coagulation abnormalities in third trimester	AFLP May be impossible to distinguish from HELLP syndrome, but presence of hypoglycemia or encephalopathy is suggestive of AFLP	Schedule urgent delivery
Mushroom ingestion	*Amanita* poisoning	Obtain history

The cause of acute liver failure is usually determined by a history of toxin or drug exposure, history of ischemic injury, serology for viral or autoimmune hepatitis, tests for copper overload, or ultrasound for vascular clot. The role of liver biopsy is determined on a case by case basis in consultation with a specialist. Select head CT in patients with altered mental status to rule out intracranial hemorrhage.

Therapy

For patients with acute liver failure, choose:

- chelation with D-penicillamine or trientine for Wilson disease
- *N*-acetylcysteine for confirmed or suspected acetaminophen poisoning
- arteriovenous hemofiltration, with or without dialysis, to support kidney function
- FFP to reduce INR in patients with active bleeding or before diagnostic or therapeutic interventions
- lactulose for any degree of encephalopathy
- liver transplantation in the presence of encephalopathy and coagulopathy

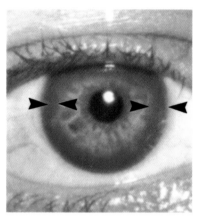

Kayser-Fleischer Ring: A Kayser-Fleischer ring in the cornea is bracketed with arrows.

◆ DON'T BE TRICKED

- **Administer mannitol for elevated intracranial pressure; do not use corticosteroids.**

❖ Test Yourself

A 24-year-old man has a 1-week history of nausea, jaundice, fatigue, and recent confusion. He is lethargic and unable to recite his telephone number. The INR is 2.3, serum AST is 940 units/L, and total bilirubin is 12.6 mg/dL. HBsAg and IgM anti-HBc are both positive.

ANSWER: The diagnosis is acute liver failure secondary to acute hepatitis B infection. Schedule liver transplantation.

Cirrhosis

Diagnosis

Cirrhosis is a pathologic state of the liver characterized histologically by extensive fibrosis and regenerative nodules. Presenting symptoms are related to hepatocyte dysfunction (jaundice, coagulopathy, and edema) or symptoms due to increased portal venous pressure (ascites, bleeding esophageal varices, hepatic encephalopathy, or hypersplenism). Select the following options for care of patients with cirrhosis:

- upper endoscopy for all new patients to screen for varices
- paracentesis for newly discovered ascites and calculation of the SAAG to diagnose the cause of ascites
- paracentesis with ascitic fluid granulocyte count and culture for any change in mental status or clinical condition to diagnose SBP
- vaccination of nonimmune patients against HAV and HBV
- periodic screening for hepatocellular carcinoma with ultrasonography and serum α-fetoprotein

STUDY TABLE: Evaluation of Ascites		
Ascitic Fluid Protein	**SAAG >1.1**	**SAAG <1.1**
<2.5 g/dL	Cirrhosis	Nephrotic syndrome
>2.5 g/dL	Right-sided HF, Budd-Chiari syndrome	Malignancy, tuberculosis

Ascitic fluid granulocyte count >250/microliter confirms SBP.

Diagnose hepatopulmonary syndrome in patients with dyspnea, hypoxemia, and cirrhosis, as well as an increased alveolar-arterial oxygen gradient while breathing ambient air. Patients may exhibit platypnea (increased dyspnea sitting up and decreased dyspnea lying flat). The diagnosis of hepatopulmonary syndrome is confirmed by contrast-enhanced transthoracic echocardiography with agitated saline administration.

Diagnose hepatorenal syndrome in patients with oliguric kidney failure, portal hypertension, ascites, and previous normal renal tubular function. Vigorous diuretic therapy, paracentesis without volume expansion, NSAID use, infections including SBP, and GI bleeding may precipitate hepatorenal syndrome; urine sodium concentration is <10 meq/L (10 mmol/L).

Lack of improvement of kidney failure following withdrawal of diuretics and administration of 1 to 1.5 L of normal saline also suggests hepatorenal syndrome. Kidney replacement therapy is indicated for volume overload or severe electrolyte abnormalities. Albumin and combination therapy with midodrine and octreotide or norepinephrine alone may improve arterial blood flow. Almost all patients with hepatorenal syndrome will require liver transplantation.

Diagnose hepatic encephalopathy when the decrease in the level of consciousness of patients with severe liver disease is reversible. Its sudden development requires evaluation for bleeding, SBP, and electrolyte disorders.

Therapy

STUDY TABLE: Therapy for Cirrhosis	
Indications	**Treatment**
Primary prophylaxis of variceal bleeding	First choice: propranolol or nadolol (must be nonselective β-blockers)
	Second choice: endoscopic band ligation if β-blocker not tolerated or contraindicated
Active variceal bleeding	First choice: octreotide with endoscopic band ligation and prophylactic antibiotics (as indicated below)
	Second choice: TIPS or shunt surgery if endoscopic therapy is unsuccessful
Ascites not responding to low-sodium diet	Spironolactone with or without furosemide
Diuretic-refractory ascites	Serial large-volume paracentesis (with albumin if >5 L) or TIPS
Prevention of SBP in hospitalized patients with cirrhosis and ascitic fluid protein <1.0 g/dL, variceal bleeding, or previous history of SBP	Fluoroquinolones chronically if history of SBP
	Fluoroquinolones while hospitalized if fluid protein <1 g/dL
	Fluoroquinolones for 7 days if active bleeding
SBP	Cefotaxime and albumin infusion
Acute hepatic encephalopathy	Correct precipitating factors, lactulose; add rifaximin if unresponsive
Prevention of hepatic encephalopathy	Lactulose

The primary complication of TIPS is portosystemic encephalopathy. Liver transplantation is the definitive treatment for patients with ESLD and complications such as variceal bleeding, ascites, hepatic encephalopathy, or hepatorenal or hepatopulmonary syndromes.

◆ DON'T BE TRICKED

- Do not select prophylactic protein restriction to prevent hepatic encephalopathy.
- Do not select neomycin to treat hepatic encephalopathy because of the significant adverse effects of this drug.

❖ Test Yourself

A 55-year-old man with alcoholic cirrhosis is hospitalized with fever and abdominal pain. Paracentesis is performed. The ascitic fluid granulocyte count is 650/microliter and the albumin is <1.0 g/dL.

ANSWER: The diagnosis is SBP. Begin IV cefotaxime and albumin. Do not wait for results of Gram stain or cultures before beginning therapy.

Liver Disease Associated with Pregnancy

Diagnosis

STUDY TABLE: Causes of Jaundice During Pregnancy	
Timing	Causes
First and second trimesters	Viral hepatitis (most common), followed by drugs and gallstones
Third trimester	Intrahepatic cholestasis of pregnancy, gallstones, AFLP, and HELLP syndrome

The onset of intrahepatic cholestasis of pregnancy is typically heralded by the development of intense pruritus, which may precede laboratory abnormalities. Abdominal pain is uncommon. Other characteristic findings are markedly elevated serum bilirubin and alkaline phosphatase levels and AST and ALT levels <200 units/L. Patients do not have hemolysis, thrombocytopenia, DIC, evidence of liver failure, or encephalopathy.

Characteristic findings of AFLP are nausea and abdominal pain, elevated AST and ALT levels, and increased PT. The platelet count may be decreased with or without other signs of DIC. About 50% of patients have preeclampsia (hypertension and proteinuria) or eclampsia (preeclampsia plus seizure or coma). Increased hepatic echogenicity is seen on ultrasonography.

The HELLP syndrome is associated with preeclampsia or eclampsia. HELLP syndrome differs from AFLP in that HELLP syndrome is more closely associated with microangiopathic hemolytic anemia and AFLP with more coagulation abnormalities.

Therapy

- Ursodeoxycholic acid is the treatment of choice for intrahepatic cholestasis of pregnancy. Early delivery should be scheduled at the first signs of fetal distress.
- AFLP typically resolves rapidly after delivery of the infant.
- Treatment of HELLP syndrome is delivery of the infant.

Irritable Bowel Syndrome

Diagnosis

The American College of Gastroenterology task force on IBS has recommended a simple definition: abdominal pain associated with altered bowel habits (change in stool form or frequency) over a period of at least 3 months. Other symptoms include straining, urgency, a feeling of incomplete evacuation, passing mucus, and bloating.

Diagnostic studies for most patients with typical symptoms and no alarm features are limited to a history and physical examination, CBC, testing of stool for occult blood, and possibly flexible sigmoidoscopy. Patients with IBS with diarrhea should have serologic tests for celiac disease. Patients older than 50 years of age or with severe or refractory symptoms require colonoscopy.

◆ DON'T BE TRICKED

- "Red flags" atypical of IBS requiring further evaluation include significant weight loss, nocturnal bowel movements, blood in the stool, recent antibiotic use, fever, and symptom onset in patients >50 years of age.

Therapy

Management of IBS focuses on controlling symptoms rather than on cure. Dietary fiber supplements may help decrease constipation. Antispasmodic agents (dicyclomine, hyoscyamine) are first-line treatments for pain. Tricyclic antidepressants may be used for resistant pain, and paroxetine may improve the quality of life in patients with severe IBS and associated psychological stress.

◆ **DON'T BE TRICKED**

- Alosetron should not be used to treat IBS because of the risk of ischemic colitis.

Inflammatory Bowel Disease

Diagnosis

Inflammatory bowel disease comprises a group of related conditions characterized by idiopathic inflammation of the GI tract. The two most common inflammatory bowel disorders are Crohn disease and ulcerative colitis, both of which cause macroscopic inflammation. Microscopic colitis is the least common inflammatory bowel disease and does not cause significant macroscopic abnormalities. Although several features may differentiate Crohn disease from ulcerative colitis, overlap is significant.

STUDY TABLE: Differentiating Ulcerative Colitis from Crohn Disease	
Ulcerative Colitis	**Crohn Disease**
Crypt abscesses and mucosal inflammation (continuous) from rectum through colon	Linear ulcerations with "skip" areas of inflammation involving entire GI tract and transmural involvement
Diarrhea (prominent), hematochezia, weight loss, and fever	Abdominal pain (prominent), diarrhea, inflammatory masses, fever, weight loss, intestinal strictures and fistula (to skin, bladder, vagina, or enteric-enteric)
ASCA in 10% of patients	ASCA in 60% of patients
p-ANCA in 75% of patients	p-ANCA in 10% of patients
Smoking alleviates symptoms	Smoking is a risk factor for disease

Extraintestinal manifestations can occur in both conditions, including arthritis, episcleritis or uveitis, erythema nodosum, pyoderma gangrenosum, and primary sclerosing cholangitis. Stool studies are indicated for *Shigella*, *Salmonella*, *Campylobacter*, *Escherichia coli* O157:H7, ova and parasites, and *Clostridium difficile* toxin. Colonoscopy and biopsy confirm the diagnosis.

Microscopic colitis is characterized by chronic diarrhea without abdominal pain or weight loss. Colonoscopy with biopsies is required for diagnosis. The colonic mucosa appears normal on gross examination. Microscopic colitis is further classified into collagenous colitis or lymphocytic colitis based on histology.

◆ **DON'T BE TRICKED**

- Do not do a barium enema examination in patients with moderate to severe ulcerative colitis because this procedure may precipitate toxic megacolon.
- In patients with Crohn disease and cystitis, consider the possibility of enterovesical fistula.

Therapy

Treatment of Crohn disease and ulcerative colitis is divided into active and maintenance strategies. Specific treatment choices depend on the type, extent, and severity of the disease.

STUDY TABLE: Treatment of Ulcerative Colitis	
Indications	**Principal Therapy**
Mild disease: <4 bowel movements daily; occasional blood in stool; and normal vital signs, hemoglobin, and ESR	5-ASA agents: mesalamine or sulfasalazine (not effective for small bowel disease)
Moderate disease: Intermediate, between mild and severe	Prednisone for remission induction Maintenance therapy with either a 5-ASA agent or 6-MP or azathioprine
Severe disease: >6 bowel movements daily, bleeding, fever, pulse >90/min, ESR >30 mm/h, anemia	IV corticosteroids followed by cyclosporine or infliximab if no response Surgery for refractory disease

STUDY TABLE: Treatment of Crohn Disease	
Indications	**Principal Therapy**
Mild to moderate disease: No fever or abdominal tenderness, <10% weight loss	5-ASA agent as initial therapy for small- or large-bowel disease
	Budesonide for ileal or right colonic disease
Moderate to severe disease: Fever, >10% weight loss, anemia, abdominal pain, and nausea or vomiting	Prednisone for remission induction
	6-MP, azathioprine, or methotrexate for maintenance
	Infliximab or adalimumab for refractory disease
Severe to fulminant disease: Despite oral corticosteroids, high fever, cachexia, vomiting, rebound tenderness, obstruction, or abscess	IV corticosteroids for remission
	Infliximab or adalimumab in corticosteroid-refractory disease
	Surgical intervention with colectomy if patient is extremely toxic or does not benefit from medications
Fistula	Infliximab or adalimumab

Microscopic colitis is best treated with supportive treatment with antidiarrheal agents such as loperamide or bismuth subsalicylate; diphenoxylate may be effective for mild cases. Otherwise, budesonide has the best documented efficacy. Stop NSAIDs, which may contribute to symptoms.

Beginning 8 years after diagnosis, surveillance colonoscopy for colon cancer is needed every 1 to 2 years for patients with ulcerative colitis or Crohn disease involving most of the colon. If dysplasia is found, proctocolectomy is required.

❖ **Test Yourself**

An 18-year-old man has a 3-month history of five or more bowel movements daily, fever, and abdominal pain. Vital signs are stable. Colonoscopy shows ulcerative colitis.

ANSWER: Begin prednisone for remission and oral sulfasalazine for maintenance.

Diverticular Disease

Diagnosis

Diverticular disorders of the colon include diverticulosis, diverticular bleeding, and diverticulitis.

Diverticulosis refers to an asymptomatic herniation (diverticulum) of the intestinal wall.

Diverticulitis is an inflammatory response following microperforation of a diverticulum and is characterized by left lower quadrant abdominal pain and fever. Signs of complications include a tender palpable mass (abscess), fistula, obstruction, and ileus. A CT of the abdomen is indicated for diagnosis and guidance of therapy. A colonoscopy is performed following recovery to rule out cancer.

Diverticular bleeding occurs following rupture of an artery that has penetrated a diverticulum, is typically painless, and usually stops without therapy.

◆ **DON'T BE TRICKED**

- Avoid colonoscopy in the setting of acute diverticulitis, because air insufflation may increase the risk for perforation.

Therapy

For stable patients with diverticulitis, select a clear-liquid diet and a 7- to 10-day course of antibiotics, such as ciprofloxacin and metronidazole. Hospitalize patients if they are unable to maintain oral intake. If fever and pain persist for several days, select a CT to exclude an abscess that may require drainage. After recovering from acute diverticulitis, 30% of patients will have recurrent episodes. After a second episode, the risk of subsequent attacks increases to 50%, and surgical resection of the affected colon is indicated. After the patient has recovered, follow-up colonoscopy is needed to exclude colon cancer.

Mesenteric Ischemia and Ischemic Colitis

Diagnosis

The two most common GI ischemic disorders are mesenteric ischemia and ischemic colitis.

STUDY TABLE: Differential Diagnosis of GI Ischemic Syndromes			
Problem	**Cause**	**Symptoms**	**Diagnosis**
Acute mesenteric ischemia	Emboli (most common), arterial or venous thrombosis, vasoconstriction, rarely vasculitis	Poorly localized severe abdominal pain, often out of proportion to physical findings; peritoneal signs signify infarction	Selective mesenteric angiography
Chronic mesenteric ischemia	Mesenteric atherosclerosis	Postprandial abdominal pain and weight loss	Conventional or MRA
Ischemic colitis	Atherosclerosis, low-flow states, or drugs (digitalis)	Left lower quadrant abdominal pain and self-limited bloody diarrhea	Colonoscopy: patchy segmental ulcerations

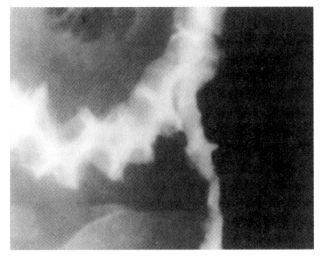

Ischemic Colitis: Thumbprinting (submucosal hemorrhage and edema) is shown in the transverse colon on this barium x-ray.

Therapy

STUDY TABLE: Therapy for Mesenteric Ischemia and Ischemic Colitis	
Condition	**Therapy**
Acute mesenteric ischemia with peritoneal signs	Urgent laparotomy
Acute mesenteric ischemia without peritoneal signs	Surgical embolectomy
	Intra-arterial thrombolysis is an alternative treatment if initiated within 12 hours
Chronic mesenteric ischemia	Surgical reconstruction or angioplasty with stenting
Ischemic colitis	Supportive care with IV fluids and bowel rest

Acute Diarrhea

Diagnosis

STUDY TABLE: Foodborne Diarrhea	
When Symptoms Develop...	**Make this Diagnosis...**
6 hours after ingestion	*Staphylococcus aureus* or *Bacillus cereus*
8-14 hours after ingestion	*Clostridium perfringens*
>14 hours after ingestion	Viral or enterotoxigenic or enterohemorrhagic *Escherichia coli*

Ten percent of patients with enterohemorrhagic *E. coli* O157:H7 (EHEC) colitis develop HUS or TTP. *Yersinia enterocolitica* colitis can mimic appendicitis or Crohn disease. Cryptosporidiosis develops most often in patients with AIDS, but outbreaks also occur in immunocompetent patients and cause a self-limited secretory diarrhea.

Therapy

Supportive care with oral hydration and antidiarrheal medications is sufficient for most patients with acute diarrhea. Antibiotic treatment is reserved for patients with diarrhea lasting >7 days or with symptoms of fever, abdominal pain, or hematochezia. Diarrhea due to parasites (*Giardia lamblia* or *Entamoeba histolytica*) requires therapy with metronidazole.

◆ DON'T BE TRICKED

- Do not choose antibiotics for EHEC colitis.
- Do not choose loperamide or diphenoxylate for acute diarrhea with fever or blood in the stool. Both agents are associated with HUS in EHEC colitis and toxic megacolon in *C. difficile* infection.

Traveler's Diarrhea

Diagnosis

Traveler's diarrhea is the most common illness to affect visitors to developing countries and is most often due to enterotoxigenic *E. coli*. Other pathogens include:

- *Salmonella typhi* and other *Salmonella* species
- *Shigella* species
- *Vibrio* species (including *V. cholerae*)
- *Campylobacter*

Shipboard epidemics of viral gastroenteritis are caused by caliciviruses (Norwalk virus and others). Evaluation (CBC, stool culture, and Gram stain) is needed only for patients with severe disease, prolonged diarrhea, or diarrhea that does not respond to empiric antibiotics. If symptoms last longer than 7 days, consider parasitic causes and antibiotic-related diarrhea.

Therapy

Supportive care includes oral rehydration therapy and a normal diet. Patient-initiated empiric antibiotic therapy (a fluoroquinolone) should be started if fever develops or diarrhea is severe. Loperamide or bismuth subsalicylate can be used as an adjunct to antibiotic therapy.

◆ DON'T BE TRICKED

- Antimotility agents are not appropriate for patients with suspected shigellosis or dysentery (blood in the stool).

❖ **Test Yourself**

A 25-year-old woman is planning a 4-week trip to the Yucatan Peninsula in Mexico and requests advice about how to treat traveler's diarrhea.

ANSWER: Prescribe loperamide and a fluoroquinolone antibiotic.

C. difficile Antibiotic-Associated Diarrhea

Diagnosis

C. difficile is the most common cause of acute care hospital-acquired diarrhea. Presentation varies from frequent watery stools and abdominal cramping to fever, cramps, leukocytosis, and fecal leukocytes. *C. difficile* antibiotic-associated diarrhea may occur following antibiotic administration in the preceding 2 months, tube feedings, chemotherapy, prolonged hospital stay, PPI use, and recent GI surgery. Order an ELISA of the stool for *C. difficile* toxins A and B. Select flexible sigmoidoscopy to establish the diagnosis and rule out ischemic colitis or inflammatory bowel disease when an urgent diagnosis is needed.

◆ DON'T BE TRICKED
- **Severe *C. difficile*–associated diarrhea also occurs in peripartum women and healthy community-dwelling individuals without a history of antibiotic use, recent hospitalization, or other risk factors.**

Therapy

Discontinue the causative antibiotic, and begin metronidazole for 10 to 14 days. Metronidazole is used in patients with mild disease and absent or minimal systemic symptoms. Reserve oral vancomycin for patients with severe disease, metronidazole intolerance, or those who are pregnant. Recheck diagnostic studies after each relapse to confirm that *C. difficile* is still causing the diarrhea, and treat the first relapse with a second course of the original antibiotic (assuming similar severity of disease). Total colectomy is required for fulminant colitis with perforation or toxic megacolon.

◆ DON'T BE TRICKED
- **Do not use antimotility agents, because their use is associated with toxic megacolon.**
- **Hand disinfection products containing alcohol do not eradicate *C. difficile* spores; handwashing with soap is mandatory in the care of patients with *C. difficile* colitis.**

❖ **Test Yourself**

A 38-year-old man is diagnosed with *C. difficile* colitis 8 days after beginning therapy for pyelonephritis. He is treated with metronidazole but has a relapse 7 days after discontinuing therapy.

ANSWER: The probable diagnosis is recurrent *C. difficile* infection. Confirm the diagnosis with stool studies and re-treat with metronidazole.

Amebiasis

Diagnosis

Intestinal amebiasis is caused by the protozoan *Entamoeba histolytica*. Most infections are asymptomatic, but dysentery and liver abscess can occur. Characteristic findings are fever, diffuse abdominal pain, and profuse, bloody diarrhea, most often in travelers to developing countries. Amebiasis is diagnosed by either stool examination or ELISA for *E. histolytica* antigens in stool.

Therapy

Metronidazole is the drug of choice for amebic colitis and amebic liver abscess.

Chronic Diarrhea

Diagnosis

Chronic diarrhea is arbitrarily defined as lasting longer than 4 weeks and is often due to noninfectious causes. Medications are often overlooked as a cause of chronic diarrhea. Stool electrolytes (sodium and potassium) can be measured in liquid stool to calculate the fecal osmotic gap, which helps to differentiate osmotic from secretory diarrhea: the gap is calculated as $290 - 2 \times [Na + K]$; an osmotic gap <50 mosm/kg (50 mmol/kg) is consistent with secretory diarrhea; a gap >125 mosm/kg (125 mmol/kg) suggests an osmotic diarrhea. Stool osmolarity <250 mosm/kg (250 mmol/kg) suggests factitious diarrhea associated with chronic laxative abuse. Osmotic diarrhea is most commonly caused by lactase deficiency. Osmotic diarrhea is associated with eating, responds to fasting, and typically is not nocturnal. Secretory diarrhea is characterized by large-volume, watery, nocturnal bowel movements and is unchanged by fasting (see also Celiac Disease.)

STUDY TABLE: Differential Diagnosis of Chronic Diarrhea	
If you see this...	**Diagnose or do this...**
Bloating, abdominal discomfort relieved by a bowel movement, no weight loss or alarm features	IBS; test for celiac disease
Diarrhea mainly in women aged 45-60 years, unrelated to food intake (nocturnal diarrhea), normal colonoscopy	Microscopic colitis; stop NSAIDs, biopsy
Use of artificial sweeteners or fructose	Carbohydrate intolerance; attempt dietary exclusion or hydrogen breath test
Nocturnal diarrhea and diabetes mellitus or systemic sclerosis	Small bowel bacterial overgrowth; empiric antibiotic trial
Coexistent pulmonary diseases and/or recurrent *Giardia* infection	Common variable immunodeficiency; obtain measurement of immunoglobulins
Somatization or other psychiatric syndromes, history of laxative use	Self-induced diarrhea; obtain tests for stool pH, sodium, potassium, and magnesium
Severe secretory diarrhea and flushing	Carcinoid syndrome; obtain test for 24-hour urinary excretion of 5-HIAA

❖ **Test Yourself**

A 36-year-old woman has watery diarrhea that is not nocturnal. She has six to seven high-volume bowel movements daily, and her symptoms improve with fasting. Fecal leukocytes and stool culture are negative. Stool sodium is 70 meq/L, and stool potassium is 10 meq/L.

ANSWER: The diagnosis is osmotic diarrhea.

A 55-year-old woman who takes daily NSAIDs for osteoarthritis has watery diarrhea without weight loss. Colonoscopy is normal.

ANSWER: The diagnosis is likely microscopic colitis.

Upper GI Bleeding

Diagnosis

Peptic ulcer disease caused by *H. pylori* infection or NSAID use is the most common cause of nonvariceal upper GI bleeding. Characteristic findings are hematemesis, melena, or (infrequently) bright-red blood per rectum or a high serum BUN/creatinine ratio.

STUDY TABLE: Differential Diagnosis of Upper GI Bleeding	
If you see this...	**Diagnose this...**
Dyspepsia, *H. pylori* infection, NSAID use, anticoagulation, severe medical illness	Gastric or duodenal ulcer
Stigmata of chronic liver disease, evidence of portal hypertension or risk factors for cirrhosis (alcohol use, viral hepatitis)	Variceal bleeding
History of heavy alcohol use and retching before hematemesis, hematemesis following weight lifting, or young woman with bulimia	Mallory-Weiss tear
Heartburn, regurgitation, and dysphagia; usually small-volume or occult bleeding	Esophagitis
Progressive dysphagia, weight loss, early satiety, or abdominal pain; usually small-volume or occult bleeding	Esophageal or gastric cancer
NSAID use, heavy alcohol intake, severe medical illness; usually small-volume or occult bleeding	Gastroduodenal erosions

After the patient is stabilized, upper endoscopy is required to document the source of bleeding. If endoscopy shows an ulcer, test for *H. pylori* infection.

◆ DON'T BE TRICKED

- Do not order a barium x-ray because this will interfere with subsequent endoscopy or other studies.

Therapy

Administer volume replacement with IV crystalloid solution, FFP, and vitamin K if the INR is >2 or platelet infusion if the platelet count is <40,000/microliter. Start a PPI in all patients before upper endoscopy. Continue the PPI only if an ulcer is found to be the source of bleeding. Upper endoscopy should be performed within the first 24 hours of admission and emergently for patients with rapid bleeding or with suspected ESLD and variceal hemorrhage. Patients with actively bleeding ulcers, visible vessels, or sentinel clots require endoscopic coagulation with injection, and those with varices need endoscopic band ligation. Interventional radiology or surgery should be considered in patients who continue to bleed despite endoscopic therapy or who have multiple rebleeding episodes, large ulcers along the lesser curvature of the stomach or posterior wall of the duodenum, or aortoenteric fistulae. Stable patients with low-risk lesions (clean-based ulcers, Mallory-Weiss tears) and low risk for rebleeding can be discharged home after a short (12 hours) period of observation; otherwise, monitoring in the hospital is indicated.

◆ DON'T BE TRICKED

- The hemoglobin concentration and hematocrit level are unreliable indicators of volume and should not be used to determine the need for volume replacement.
- H_2-receptor antagonists are not beneficial in managing upper GI bleeding.

Lower GI Bleeding

Diagnosis

Acute, painless lower GI bleeding in older adult patients is usually due to colonic diverticula or angiodysplasia. Ten percent of rapid rectal bleeding has an upper GI source.

STUDY TABLE: Differential Diagnosis of Lower GI Bleeding	
If you see this...	**Diagnose this...**
Painless, self-limited, massive hematochezia	Diverticular bleeding (most common overall cause)
Chronic blood loss or acute painless hematochezia in an older adult patient	Angiodysplasia
Stool positive for occult blood in a usually asymptomatic patient	Colonic polyp or cancer
Risk factors for atherosclerosis and evidence of vascular disease in an older adult patient; typically with abdominal pain	Ischemic colitis
History of bloody diarrhea, tenesmus, abdominal pain, fever	Inflammatory bowel disease
Painless hematochezia in a young patient and normal upper endoscopy and colonoscopy	Meckel diverticulum

Therapy

If the patient is hemodynamically unstable, resuscitate the patient. Although most episodes of lower GI bleeding resolve spontaneously, it is important to establish the cause of the bleeding. Colonoscopy is recommended within the first 48 hours of admission, and endoscopic therapy is used to control continued bleeding. If colonoscopy does not identify a discrete lesion or endoscopic therapy does not control the bleeding, radiologic evaluation or surgery may be indicated. The two primary types of radiologic evaluation are technetium-99m (^{99m}Tc) pertechnetate red blood cell scanning and angiography. Red blood cell scanning is more sensitive than angiography and is often the first radiologic test performed. Angiography cannot detect the bleeding site if the bleeding rate is less than 1 mL/min; however, the advantage of angiography as a primary modality is its ability to provide selective embolization.

Bleeding of Obscure Origin

Diagnosis

Obscure GI bleeding is recurrent blood loss without an identified source of bleeding despite upper endoscopy and colonoscopy. Patients may present with either melena or hematochezia or positive FOBT. The first step is to repeat upper endoscopy and/or colonoscopy, which is diagnostic in approximately 40% of cases.

If the site of bleeding is still not identified, nuclear medicine tagged-erythrocyte study, angiography, wireless capsule endoscopy, or push enteroscopy are other options. Wireless capsule endoscopy can evaluate the entire small bowel. It is the test of choice following negative repeat upper endoscopy/colonoscopy in patients with obscure bleeding.

◆ DON'T BE TRICKED

- Do not order small bowel radiography as a first-line study in the evaluation of obscure GI bleeding.

General Internal Medicine

Biostatistics

Sensitivity, Specificity, Predictive Values, and ROC Curves

- Sensitivity = (all true-positive test results) / (true-positive and false-negative test results). Remember SNout: Sensitive test that is Negative rules OUT disease.
- Specificity = (all true-negative results) / (true-negative and false-positive results). Remember SPin: Specific test that is Positive rules IN disease.
- PPV = (true-positive test results) / (all positive test results). PPV answers the question, "Given a positive test result, what is the probability the patient has the disease?"
- NPV = (true-negative test results) / (all negative test results). NPV answers the question, "Given a negative test result, what is the probability the patient does not have the disease?"

A ROC curve is a graph of the sensitivity vs. (1 − specificity). In medicine, a ROC analysis provides tools to select tests with optimal performance characteristics. The cut-point with the best combined sensitivity and specificity will be closest to the upper left corner. The test with the greatest overall accuracy will have the largest area under the ROC graph.

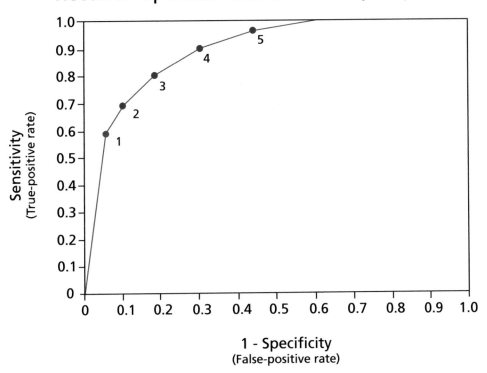

Receiver Operating Characteristic Curve: ROC curve showing sensitivity (true-positive rate) vs. (1 − specificity) (false-positive rate).

◆ DON'T BE TRICKED

- As the prevalence of a condition increases, the PPV increases and the NPV decreases.
- Changes in prevalence do not alter the sensitivity or specificity.

Likelihood Ratios

The LR is a measurement of the odds of having a disease independent of the disease prevalence. You must first assess the patient's pretest probability of having a disease before applying the LR of the test/finding to calculate the posttest probability.

- Positive LR = (sensitivity) / (1 − specificity); negative LR = (1 − sensitivity) / (specificity).
- Positive LR answers the question, "How much more likely is a person to have the disease given a positive test result?"
- LRs of 2, 5, and 10 increase the probability of disease by approximately 15%, 30%, and 45%, respectively.
- LRs of 0.5, 0.2, and 0.1 decrease the probability of disease by approximately 15%, 30%, and 45%, respectively.

STUDY TABLE: Study Designs

Type	Characteristics
Cross-section	The presence of the presumed risk factor and presence of the outcome are measured at the same time in a population.
Retrospective (case control)	Subjects are divided into groups based on the presence or absence of the outcome of interest, and then the frequency of risk factors in each group is compared.
Prospective (cohort)	Subjects are divided into groups based on the presence or absence of the presumed risk factor and followed for a period of time. At the end of the study, the frequency of the outcome is compared.
Randomized controlled trial	Subjects are randomly divided into groups. One group receives the intervention (patients and researchers may be blinded to treatment) and followed forward in time. At the end of the study, the frequency of the outcome is compared. This study design reduces the effect of unmeasured (confounding) variables that may influence outcomes of a study.
Systematic review	Usually, multiple small clinical trials using similar randomization techniques and interventions are combined into one large analysis to address very precise clinical questions. The results may be analyzed using the technique of meta-analysis.

Confidence Interval

CI provides boundaries within which exists a high probability (95% by convention) of finding the "true" value. For example, if the measured mean difference between two groups is 2.4, and the 95% CI is 1.9-3.0, the probability that the true value lies between 1.9 and 3.0 is 95%. When used in association with RR, if the CI includes the number 1, there is no risk or benefit; the outcomes for the control and experimental groups are the same.

Risk Estimates

In clinical trials, measurements of treatment and outcome are reported to quantitate effectiveness of the intervention. The most basic measurement is AR, defined as the rate of an outcome (death, MI, hospitalization) compared with all patients who received the intervention, a/(a+b), or who did not receive the outcome (the control group), c/(c+d). The ARR is simply the difference in AR of patients who received the intervention and those who did not, [a/(a+b)] − [c/(c+d)]. RR is a ratio of the two, [a/(a+b)]/[c/(c+d)].

STUDY TABLE: Risk Estimates

| Treatment | Outcome | |
	Positive	Negative
Yes	a	b
No	c	d

- RR >1 suggests the treatment was harmful.
- RR <1 suggests the treatment was effective.

- RR = 1 means no association with either risk or protection.

An OR estimates the odds of having or not having a particular outcome. When comparing therapeutic outcomes, in most cases OR can be substituted for RR as an equivalent measurement.

AR, RR, and OR are estimates of the cumulative risk over time, usually defined as at the end of the study.

Hazard Ratio

A hazard ratio (HR) is a type of RR and calculates the risk of an outcome in a group exposed to a risk compared with a control group not exposed to the risk. The difference between an HR and RR is that an HR calculates the risk of an event occurring at a particular instantaneous point in time, whereas the RR calculates the cumulative risk of an event occurring over the entire duration of the study period.

Number Needed to Treat and Number Needed to Harm

Number needed to treat (NNT) calculates how many people with a condition require treatment before one person benefits from treatment, NNT = 1/ARR. The number needed to harm (NNH) calculates the number of people with a condition that require treatment before one person experiences harm from the treatment. In this calculation, the denominator is the absolute difference of bad outcomes associated with placebo treatments compared with bad outcomes associated with active treatments.

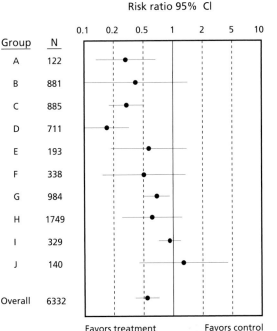

Standard Meta-Analysis: This figure shows a standard meta-analysis plot of the RR ratio for the risk of an outcome comparing an active treatment to placebo or another active treatment. The dots show the point estimates for the RR of each study and the pooled point estimate, and the horizontal lines show the CIs. N is the number of subjects in each study. As a standard convention, an RR of less than 1 denotes a reduction of the event that is being studied compared with the control group or other active treatment. Note that the smaller the study, the larger the CI. Finally, although one study does not favor the intervention (J) and some CIs overlap 1 (B, E, F, H), suggesting no reduction in risk, overall this analysis suggests the intervention is associated with a reduction in risk.

Type I and Type II Errors in Clinical Research

A type I error is incorrectly concluding a statistically significant difference exists between the experimental and control groups. If the study's P value is <0.5, then a <5% chance exists that a type I error has occurred. A type II error is incorrectly concluding no difference exists between the experimental and control groups. Studies with small numbers of subjects may not have the statistical "power" to detect true differences between groups and may commit type II errors.

❖ **Test Yourself**

A 19-year-old woman with right lower quadrant abdominal pain and fever has an estimated pretest probability of acute appendicitis of 50%. An appendiceal CT scan shows inflammation and a thickened appendiceal wall. This finding is associated with an LR of 13.3 for acute appendicitis. What is the posttest likelihood of acute appendicitis?

ANSWER: >95%.

The mortality rate after cardiogenic shock managed with standard care is 72%, but the rate for patients receiving a new medication is 67%. How many patients with cardiogenic shock must be treated with the new medication to save one life?

ANSWER: The NNT is [1/(0.72 − 0.67)] = 1/0.05 = 20.

Smoking Cessation

Therapy

Smoking cessation reduces all-cause mortality by up to 50%. The Five A's and the 5 R's are two motivational interviewing techniques to use when counseling for behavior change.

STUDY TABLE: Behavioral Interventions for Smoking Cessation	
Five A's	**Five R's**
Ask about tobacco use.	Encourage patient to think of **R**elevance of quitting smoking to their lives.
Advise to quit.	Assist patient in identifying the **R**isks of smoking.
Assess willingness to quit.	Assist the patient in identifying the **R**ewards of smoking cessation.
Assist in attempt to quit.	Discuss with the patient **R**oadblocks or barriers to attempting cessation.
Arrange follow-up.	**R**epeat the motivational intervention at all visits.

STUDY TABLE: Pharmacologic Therapies for Smoking Cessation	
Agent	**Notes**
Nicotine gum, patch, spray, inhaler, lozenges	Increases smoking cessation 1.5 times more than control. Avoid with recent MI, arrhythmia, and unstable angina.
Bupropion	Increases smoking cessation rates about 2 times more than control. Avoid with seizure disorder and eating disorder. May be associated with suicidal ideation. Safety in pregnancy is unclear.
Varenicline	Increases smoking cessation rates about 3.5 times more than control and almost 2 times more than bupropion. Associated with suicidal ideation and increased risk of cardiovascular events.

◆ DON'T BE TRICKED

- SSRIs show no significant benefit for smoking cessation.

Screening and Prevention

Key Considerations

STUDY TABLE: Routine Adult Immunizations	
Vaccine	**Recommendation**
Hepatitis A	Occupational (travelers to endemic areas or food handlers)
	Chronic liver disease
	Men who have sex with men
	Users of illicit drugs
	Safety of vaccine during pregnancy uncertain
Hepatitis B	Same populations as hepatitis A
	All children up to 18 years
	End-stage kidney disease
	Safe in pregnancy
HPV	Male and female patients aged 9-26 years regardless of sexual activity, presence of genital warts, or previous positive HPV infection
	Not indicated in pregnant women

(Continued on next page)

STUDY TABLE: Routine Adult Immunizations (*continued*)

Vaccine	Recommendation
Influenza	All adults wishing to reduce their likelihood of influenza infection (including pregnant women)
	Inactivated vaccine appropriate for all except persons allergic to eggs or to those with a history of Guillain-Barré syndrome
	Intranasal live vaccine limited to nonpregnant patients aged <50 years
	Intranasal live vaccine is contraindicated if patient has close contact with immunosuppressed persons (home, work) as well as patients with chronic metabolic diseases, diabetes mellitus, kidney dysfunction, hemoglobinopathies, or immunosuppression
Meningococcal	Travelers, college dormitory residents
	Safety during pregnancy unknown
MMR (mumps, measles, rubella)	Adults born after 1956 without proof of immunity
	Contraindicated during pregnancy
Pneumococcal	All adults aged ≥65 years
	Residents of long-term care facilities
	Adults with risk factors (asthma, cardiovascular disease, COPD, diabetes mellitus, chronic liver disease, chronic kidney disease, nephrotic syndrome, functional/anatomic asplenia, immunosuppressive conditions, chemotherapy)
	Patients who smoke cigarettes
	One-time revaccination for patients aged >65 years if vaccinated more than 5 years ago and were age <65 years at the time of primary vaccination as well as for adults with risk factors
	Safety of vaccine during pregnancy unknown
Tdap	All adults who have not completed primary series
	Single dose of Tdap for patients aged 19-64 years regardless of scheduled Td booster (may administer in place of Td booster if patient is due)
	Any wound if primary series not completed or status unknown
	Dirty wound if primary series completed >5 years previously
	Booster every 10 years
Varicella	Persons aged >13 years without previous chickenpox infection
	Contraindicated in immunocompromised patients
	Contraindicated during pregnancy
Zoster vaccine	Persons aged >60 years regardless of previous episode of zoster (do not measure antibodies)
	Contraindicated in immunocompromised patients
	Contraindicated during pregnancy

Travel Immunizations

Routine vaccines are recommended for a patient whose vaccines are not up to date, including influenza, pneumococcal, varicella (chickenpox), MMR, and Tdap booster. Select the following vaccinations when appropriate:

- polio, hepatitis A and/or immune globulin, and typhoid for travelers to all developing countries
- yellow fever for travelers to Africa and South America
- meningococcal for travelers to sub-Saharan Africa
- rabies for extended-stay travelers or those who will have difficulty accessing postexposure treatment in endemic areas, including Asia, Africa, and South and Central America

◆ DON'T BE TRICKED

- **For pregnant women, do not select live vaccines, including MMR, intranasal influenza, yellow fever, varicella, and zoster vaccines.**

❖ **Test Yourself**

An 18-year-old woman has completed her primary vaccination series for HPV, Tdap, polio, MMR, and varicella. What vaccination is needed before she travels through Western Europe?

ANSWER: She needs the hepatitis B vaccination.

STUDY TABLE: USPSTF-Recommended Screening
Recommendations for General Population
Height and weight (periodically)
Blood pressure (every 2 years)
Problem drinking
Depression
Diabetes mellitus (if blood pressure >135/80 mm Hg)
Total and HDL cholesterol (every 5 years for men aged ≥35 years, women aged ≥45 years who are at increased cardiovascular risk, others with cardiovascular risk factors)
Colorectal cancer screening (average-risk men and women aged ≥50 years)
Mammogram ± clinical breast examination (every 1-2 years for women aged ≥50 years)
Pap test (at least every 3 years starting at age 21 until age 65 years). The USPSTF suggests combination Pap smear and HPV testing every 5 years for women aged 30 years or older who wish to increase the interval of screening.
Chlamydia (sexually active women aged ≤24 years and older at-risk women)
Bone mineral density test (women aged ≥65 years and women aged <65 years whose fracture risk is equal to or greater than that of a 65-year-old white woman who has no additional risk factors for fracture using the WHO FRAX algorithm)
AAA screening (one-time screening for men aged 65-75 years who ever smoked)

Obesity

Diagnosis

STUDY TABLE: Obesity Definitions	
Diagnosis	**BMI**
Overweight	25-29.9
Obese	
Class I	30-34.9
Class II	35-39.9
Class III	≥40

Screen patients diagnosed with obesity for evidence of secondary diseases. In the occasional patient in whom a secondary cause of obesity is found, the most common causes are hypothyroidism, Cushing syndrome, and polycystic ovary syndrome.

Therapy

Discontinue nonessential medications associated with weight gain. Behavioral therapies, including dietary and exercise interventions, are effective approaches. Both low-carbohydrate and low-fat diets work in the short term. Exercise is helpful as an adjunct to diet change but not as monotherapy. Drug treatment is offered if a 5% threshold in weight loss has not been reached by the end of 3 months of therapy. Orlistat inhibits pancreatic lipases and alters fat digestion. Major side effects include cramping, flatus, oily stool, and fecal incontinence. Treatment is associated with an average weight reduction of 2.9 kg; reduced incidence of diabetes; and better blood pressure, lipid levels, and glycemic control. Locaserin is a selective serotonin receptor agonist that induces the feeling of early satiety. Its use is associated with an average weight loss of 5.8 kg and improvement in glycemic control. The combination medication phentermine, a stimulant/appetite suppressant, and topiramate, an anticonvulsant with a weight-loss effect, has been approved for pharmacological treatment of obesity. Locaserin and phentermine-topiramate are indicated for use in adult patients with a BMI ≥30 or ≥27 with ≥1 obesity-related comorbidity.

Bariatric surgery is considered for patients with a BMI >40 and also for BMI >35 with serious obesity-related comorbidities (severe sleep apnea, diabetes, severe joint disease). Bariatric surgery is associated with a 29% reduction in mortality.

STUDY TABLE: Bariatric Surgery Complications	
Surgery	**Complications**
Banding procedures	Intractable nausea and vomiting
	Marginal ulcers, stomal obstruction
	Severe GERD
	Pulmonary embolism
Gastric bypass	Stomal stenosis
	Cholelithiasis
	Deficiencies of vitamin B$_{12}$, iron, calcium, folic acid, 25-hydroxyvitamin D, magnesium, copper, zinc, vitamin A, other B-complex vitamins, and vitamin C
	Pulmonary embolism

❖ **Test Yourself**

A 41-year-old woman is evaluated for persistent nausea and vomiting after laparoscopic gastric bypass surgery 6 weeks ago for morbid obesity.

ANSWER: Select upper endoscopy to diagnose stomal stenosis or marginal ulcer.

Involuntary Weight Loss

Diagnosis

Causes of involuntary weight loss vary according to age (malignancy is most common in the young) and venue (depression, medications, dehydration, and issues related to dementia are most common in extended care facilities). Other causes include:

- endocrine disorders (especially thyroid disorders and diabetes)
- late-stage HF or COPD
- tuberculosis
- HIV disease
- medications

Weight loss is commonly associated with depression and dementia. Socioeconomic and functional problems, such as difficulty obtaining food, lack of financial resources, and social isolation, cause or exacerbate weight loss. Initial diagnostic testing is limited to basic studies unless the history and physical examination suggest a specific cause. In patients with GI symptoms or abnormalities in blood counts or liver tests, obtain an upper GI series, abdominal ultrasonography, abdominal CT, or esophagogastroduodenoscopy, as appropriate.

◆ **DON'T BE TRICKED**

- **Imaging of the thorax and abdomen with CT or MRI in the absence of supporting history, physical examination, or laboratory findings is not helpful.**

Therapy

Treat the specific underlying disorder. The proven benefit of oral nutritional supplementation for weight loss is limited, but nutritional supplementation may be useful when access to calories is an issue because of functional impairments. Appetite stimulants have been shown to promote weight gain, but a survival benefit has never been demonstrated. In some trials, patients who received such agents have experienced increased mortality.

STUDY TABLE: Selected Nutritional Deficiencies	
Finding	**Deficiency**
Hair loss, brittle hair	Biotin, protein, vitamin B_{12}, folate
Coiled, corkscrew hair	Vitamins A and C
Skin desquamation	Riboflavin
Petechiae, perifollicular hemorrhage	Vitamin C
Ecchymosis	Vitamins C and K
Skin pigmentation, cracking, and crusting	Niacin
Acro-orificial dermatitis (erythematous, vesiculobullous, and pustular)	Zinc
Angular stomatitis and cheilosis	Vitamin B complex, iron, and protein
Glossitis	Niacin, folate, and vitamin B_{12}
Ophthalmoplegia and foot drop	Thiamine
Paresthesia	Thiamine, vitamin B_{12}, and biotin
Depressed vibratory and position senses	Vitamin B_{12}
Memory disturbance	Vitamin B_{12}
Wernicke-Korsakoff syndrome	Severe thiamine deficiency

Pressure Ulcers

Diagnosis

Pressure ulcers are ischemic soft tissue injuries resulting from pressure, usually over bony prominences. The external appearance of a pressure ulcer may underestimate the extent of injury.

Therapy

STUDY TABLE: Pressure Ulcer Staging and Therapy	
Ulcer Stage	**Therapy**
Stage 1: The skin is intact with nonblanchable redness	For all ulcer stages: positioning and support to minimize tissue pressure
Stage 2: Shallow ulcer with a red-pink wound bed or serum-filled blister	Occlusive or semipermeable dressing that will maintain a moist wound environment
Stage 3: Subcutaneous fat may be visible	Pain control, correction of nutritional deficiencies (supplements, tube feeding, or hyperalimentation if necessary), debridement, topical or systemic antibiotics
Stage 4: Exposed bone, tendon, or muscle	Same as Stage 3

Dressings should maintain a moist wound environment and manage exudates. Use systemic antibiotics when cellulitis is present; consider the possibility of underlying osteomyelitis. Debridement of eschars and nonviable tissue may be needed. Air-fluidized beds improve healing compared with other pressure-relief devices.

◆ DON'T BE TRICKED

- Hyperbaric oxygen therapy is not effective in the treatment of pressure ulcers.

Hypertension

Diagnosis

The Seventh Report of the Joint National Committee on Prevention, Detection, Evaluation and Treatment of High Blood Pressure (JNC 7) guidelines remain the current U.S. standard for the evaluation, classification, and management of hypertension; as of publication, the eighth report reflecting current research data is in progress.

Classification of hypertension is based on an average of two or more readings obtained at two or more visits.

Consider white coat hypertension in patients that meet the following criteria:

- ≥3 office blood pressure measurements >140/90 mm Hg
- ≥2 measurements <140/90 mm Hg in nonoffice settings
- no evidence of end-organ damage

Ambulatory blood pressure measurement is the gold standard for diagnosing white coat hypertension.

Masked hypertension is defined as elevated blood pressure detected by ambulatory blood pressure measurement but with normal office blood pressure measurement. Masked hypertension is associated with an increased risk of sustained hypertension and increased cardiovascular mortality.

Most patients with established hypertension have essential hypertension. Consider secondary hypertension in patients who have atypical clinical features (early onset, absent family history, hypokalemia, evidence of kidney disease) or have resistant hypertension (not at target goal despite the use of three antihypertensive agents, including a diuretic).

STUDY TABLE: Selected Secondary Causes of Hypertension	
Condition	**Notes**
Drug induced	NSAIDs, amphetamines/cocaine, sympathomimetics, oral contraceptives, corticosteroids
Chronic kidney disease	Elevated BUN, serum creatinine, and potassium; most patients present at an earlier stage with minimal signs and symptoms
Renovascular disease (atherosclerotic and fibromuscular)	Onset of hypertension at young age, especially in women (fibromuscular); atherosclerotic disease often associated with cigarette smoking, flash pulmonary edema, CAD, flank bruits, advanced retinopathy, increased creatinine (usually with bilateral renovascular disease), and increased creatinine after treatment with an ACE inhibitor or ARB; notable for hypokalemia and elevated renin and aldosterone levels
Aortic coarctation	Headache, cold feet, leg pain, reduced or absent femoral pulse, delay in femoral pulse compared with radial pulse, murmur heard between scapulae, figure 3 sign and rib notching on chest x-ray
Primary hyperaldosteronism	Muscle cramping, nocturia, thirst; physical examination normal; hypokalemia and elevated aldosterone to plasma renin activity ratio
Cushing syndrome	Weight gain, menstrual irregularity, hirsutism; truncal obesity, abdominal striae; hypokalemia, metabolic alkalosis
Pheochromocytoma	Sweating, heart racing, pounding headache; pallor; tachycardia; hypertension may be episodic with intervals of normal blood pressure; increased urine or plasma catecholamines or metanephrine

Drug Therapy

Therapeutic lifestyle changes are initiated before or concomitant with drug therapy. Treat stage 1 uncomplicated hypertension (SBP 140-159 mm Hg or DBP 90-99 mm Hg) with a single preferred agent with patients in whom lifestyle modification fails:

- thiazide diuretic

- ACE inhibitor or ARB
- calcium channel blocker

◆ DON'T BE TRICKED

- **Do not select a β-blocker for initial monotherapy unless a compelling indication is present (concomitant HF or angina).**

Add a second drug from a different class if a patient has a partial response to otherwise well-tolerated monotherapy. If a diuretic was not the first choice, use it as the second agent.

Treat stage 2 hypertension (SBP ≥160 mm Hg or DBP ≥100 mm Hg) with two-drug combination therapy that includes a diuretic and either:

- an ACE inhibitor or an ARB
- a β-blocker
- a calcium channel blocker

Treat older patients (≥80 years) if SBP ≥150 mm Hg.

STUDY TABLE: Antihypertensive Drugs at a Glance		
Class of Drug	**Compelling Indications**	**Contraindications**
Diuretics	HF; advanced age; systolic hypertension	Gout
β-Blockers	Angina; HF; post-MI; tachyarrhythmias; migraine	Asthma or bronchospastic COPD; heart block
		Pregnancy; fetal growth restriction
ACE inhibitors	HF; LV dysfunction; post-MI; diabetic nephropathy; proteinuria	Pregnancy; bilateral renal artery stenosis; hyperkalemia
ARBs	ACE inhibitor cough; diabetic nephropathy; HF	Pregnancy; bilateral renal artery stenosis; hyperkalemia
Calcium antagonists	Cyclosporine-induced hypertension; angina, CHD	Heart block (verapamil, diltiazem)
α-Blockers	Prostatic hyperplasia	Orthostatic hypotension

◆ DON'T BE TRICKED

- **With an ACE inhibitor or ARB, an increase in serum creatinine by up to 33% is acceptable and not a reason to discontinue therapy.**
- **Thiazide diuretics are not effective in patients with kidney disease (GFR <30 mL/min/1.73 m²); select a loop diuretic.**

Hypertensive Urgency

The treatment of hypertensive urgency (blood pressure >180/120 mm Hg in the absence of symptoms or progressive target-organ damage) differs if the patient has previously treated hypertension or untreated hypertension.

In patients with preexisting treated hypertension:

- restart the medication(s) in nonadherent patients
- in adherent patients, either increase the dose of the medication(s) or add an additional agent

In patients with previously untreated hypertension:

- consider oral furosemide or small doses of clonidine or captopril and observe for several hours for a blood pressure drop of 20-30 mm Hg (not to normal blood pressure)
- begin a long-acting agent, discharge home with follow-up in 2 to 3 days

Hypertensive Emergency

Hospitalize a patient with hypertensive emergency (blood pressure ≥180/120 mm Hg and symptoms or evidence of end organ damage, including:

- chest pain (aortic dissection, MI)
- encephalopathy (changes in the level of consciousness)
- focal neurologic deficits (stroke)
- retinopathy (retinal hemorrhages, papilledema)
- acute kidney injury

The mean arterial pressure should be lowered by no more than 25% in the first hour of treatment and subsequently decreased to a systolic level of 160 mm Hg and a diastolic level between 100 and 110 mm Hg in the next 2 to 6 hours. Preferred therapies include IV hydralazine, nitroprusside, nitroglycerin, β-blockers (labetalol, metoprolol, esmolol), calcium channel blockers (nicardipine), and ACE inhibitors.

◆ DON'T BE TRICKED

- **Do not select sublingual nifedipine for either hypertensive urgency or emergency.**

❖ Test Yourself

A 35-year-old woman is evaluated for persistent fatigue and resistant hypertension. Serum potassium is 3.3 meq/L (3.3 mmol/L).

ANSWER: The diagnosis is primary aldosteronism. Measure the plasma renin activity to aldosterone ratio.

Syncope

Diagnosis

An uncomplicated faint (vasovagal or neurocardiogenic syncope) is common and can be diagnosed by the history and absence of any suggestion of heart disease from the physical examination and ECG. Look for the 3 P's:

- posture (prolonged standing)
- provoking factors (blood draw, pain, emotion)
- prodromal symptoms (sweating, nausea, feeling warm)

Patients with uncomplicated faint can be discharged home without additional evaluation.

A history of heart disease, significant cardiac risk factors, or exertional syncope suggests structural cardiac disease or arrhythmias as the cause of syncope. Causes of exertional syncope include AS, HCM, mitral stenosis, and pulmonary hypertension (especially due to acute PE). Patients with suspected cardiac causes of syncope should be admitted to the hospital. Syncope caused by arrhythmias occurs without presyncopal symptoms and irrespective of patient position.

STUDY TABLE: Causes of Syncope	
If you see this...	**Diagnose this...**
A prodrome of nausea, diaphoresis, and pallor	Uncomplicated faint (vasovagal or neurocardiogenic syncope)
Preceding pressure on the carotid sinus (tight collar, sudden turning of head)	Carotid sinus hypersensitivity
Association with specific activities (urination, cough, swallowing, defecation)	Situational syncope (neurocardiogenic)
Upon assuming an upright position	Orthostatic hypotension caused by hypovolemia, pharmacologic agents, or autonomic nervous system disorders (e.g., parkinsonism, diabetes)
Brainstem neurologic signs and symptoms	Posterior circulation vascular disease; consider subclavian steal syndrome if preceded by upper extremity exercise
Witnessed "seizure"	Syncope can cause tonic-clonic jerking of extremities; primary seizure is unlikely if findings of diaphoresis or nausea before the event, a brief episode of unconsciousness, and immediate postsyncopal orientation are present
Related to exercise or associated with angina	Obstruction to left ventricular outflow: AS, HCM, PE, and pulmonary hypertension
Syncope with sudden loss of consciousness without prodrome	Arrhythmia, sinoatrial and AV node dysfunction (ischemic heart disease and associated with use of β-blockers, calcium channel blockers, and antiarrhythmic drugs)
Syncope following a meal	Postprandial syncope, often in older adult patients

Consider the appropriate indications for the following diagnostic tests:

- ECG: Done in all cases. The finding of an arrhythmia and conduction block may establish the diagnosis, but a normal ECG does not rule out a cardiac etiology.
- Echocardiography: Obtain if structural heart disease is suspected.
- Ambulatory ECG recording: Indicated if cardiac arrhythmia is suspected or the cause is unclear. The choice of the recording device is determined by the frequency of the patient's symptoms (See Cardiovascular Medicine, Arrhythmia Recording).
- Stress testing: Indicated for patients with exercise-associated syncope or those with significant risks for ischemic heart disease.
- Carotid sinus massage: For suspected carotid sinus syncope or for unexplained syncope in those aged >60 years.
- Tilt-table testing: Reserved for presumed neurocardiogenic syncope only if it is recurrent or represents high risk for injury and to assess whether it is associated with asystole.
- Electrophysiologic testing: Rarely helpful and almost always the incorrect answer.

◆ DON'T BE TRICKED

- Do not order carotid vascular studies to diagnose cause of syncope.
- Do not order brain imaging, cardiac enzymes, or EEG to evaluate syncope.

Therapy

Treatment of structural cardiac disease and arrhythmias is covered in the Cardiovascular Medicine section. For hypovolemia or orthostatic syncope, eliminate α- and β-blockers and anticholinergic agents, if possible. Increase fluid and sodium intake and consider compression stockings. As a last resort, add mineralocorticoids and α-adrenergic receptor agonists. For recurrent neurocardiogenic syncope, choose β-blockers.

❖ Test Yourself

An 18-year-old woman fainted while standing in line to purchase concert tickets. She felt "woozy" and became pale and sweaty before fainting. Friends observed jerking motions of her face and fingers.

ANSWER: Diagnose neurocardiogenic syncope (uncomplicated faint).

Falls

Prevention

The number of falls increases with the number of risk factors. Risk factor reduction has been shown to reduce falls. Medications are the most readily modifiable risk factor. Psychotropic agents lead the list of implicated drugs.

Diagnosis

Look for risk factors, including loose rugs, poor lighting, lack of hand rails, four or more medications, visual acuity <20/60, cataracts, and SBP <110 mm Hg. Remember to perform the "Timed Up and Go" test. Ask the patient to rise from a chair without using his or her arms, walk 10 feet, turn around, and return to the chair. Completion of the test in >10 seconds indicates increased risk for falls, with >14 seconds associated with high risk; aggressive fall prevention interventions should be implemented in these patients.

Therapy

Discontinue contributing medications. Multidisciplinary treatment programs that include assessment for risk factors (medications, sensory deficits), physical therapy, and risk factor modification are the most effective nonpharmacologic interventions for older patients. Vitamin D supplementation reduces the frequency of falls in older patients who are vitamin D deficient.

◆ DON'T BE TRICKED

- Hip protectors in older people who fall are ineffective in preventing hip fractures.

❖ Test Yourself

An 80-year-old woman presents after a mechanical fall at home. Her medications are calcium, clonazepam, amlodipine, levothyroxine, and pantoprazole.

ANSWER: Discontinue clonazepam. Start vitamin D and risk factor modification.

Chronic Cough

Diagnosis

Chronic cough lasts ≥8 weeks. UACS (previously called postnasal drip), asthma, and GERD are responsible for approximately 90% of cases of chronic cough but are responsible for 99% of cases of chronic cough in patients who are nonsmokers, have a normal chest x-ray, and are not taking an ACE inhibitor.

All patients should undergo chest x-ray. Smoking cessation and discontinuation of ACE inhibitors is indicated for 4 weeks before additional evaluation.

STUDY TABLE: Causes and Therapy of Chronic Cough

If you see this...	Diagnose this...	Choose this...
Postnasal drainage, frequent throat clearing, nasal discharge, cobblestone appearance of the oropharyngeal mucosa, or mucus dripping down the oropharynx	UACS	Antihistamine-decongestant combination or intranasal corticosteroid (for allergic rhinitis).
Asthma, cough with exercise or exposure to cold	Cough-variant asthma	Methacholine challenge if diagnosis is uncertain. Standard asthma therapy; may take 6 weeks to respond.
GERD symptoms (GERD may be silent)	GERD-related cough	Empiric PPI therapy without testing; may take 3 months to respond.
Taking ACE inhibitor	ACE-inhibitor cough	Stop ACE inhibitor, substitute ARB. Takes approximately 1 month to respond.
Voluminous sputum production with purulent exacerbations	Bronchiectasis	CT to show thickened bronchial walls in a tramline pattern. Treat with chest physiotherapy and treat acute exacerbations with antibiotics.
Normal chest x-ray findings, normal spirometry, and negative methacholine challenge test	Possible nonasthmatic eosinophilic bronchitis	Sputum induction or bronchial wash for eosinophils. Treat with inhaled corticosteroids, avoidance of sensitizer.
Paroxysm of cough with gagging and vomiting	Pertussis	Nasopharyngeal culture for *Bordetella pertussis*. Treat with a macrolide antibiotic.

Pharyngitis

Diagnosis

Use the 4-point Centor criteria to stratify adult patients according to risk of group A streptococcal pharyngitis:

- fever: subjective
- absence of cough
- tender anterior cervical lymphadenopathy
- tonsillar exudates

Patients with 0 or 1 criterion should neither be tested nor treated with antibiotics. Evaluate adults with 2 or 3 criteria with a confirmatory test (rapid antigen detection test [RADT] or culture, but not both) and treat based on results. Follow-up testing of negative tests with a throat culture is not recommended. Treat patients without testing who have 4 criteria.

Fusobacterium necrophorum infection should be considered in adolescents and young adults with a negative RADT and an unusually prolonged and severe pharyngitis. *F. necrophorum* is the causative agent of Lemierre syndrome, septic thrombophlebitis of the internal jugular vein resulting in metastatic pulmonary infections.

Drug Therapy

Select oral penicillin for 10 days. Choose a macrolide for patients allergic to penicillin. *F. necrophorum* is treated with ampicillin-sulbactam.

Sinusitis

Diagnosis

Acute bacterial sinusitis is defined as lasting 7 or more days and involving any one of the following factors:

- purulent nasal discharge
- maxillary tooth or facial pain, especially unilateral
- unilateral maxillary sinus tenderness
- worsening symptoms after initial improvement

Imaging, including CT, should be considered in patients with AIDS or in other immunocompromised patients to evaluate for fungal infection or other atypical infections but is not otherwise indicated.

Complications of acute sinusitis are unusual but deadly. Patients with cavernous sinus thrombosis have fever, nausea, vomiting, headache, orbital edema, or cranial nerve involvement. Other complications include brain abscess, bacterial meningitis, and osteomyelitis.

◆ **DON'T BE TRICKED**

- **Do not select any imaging tests for immunocompetent patients with acute sinusitis.**
- **Do not treat sinusitis with antibiotics unless high fever or symptoms suggesting complicated illness have lasted ≥7 days.**

Drug Therapy

The first-line choice for suspected bacterial sinusitis is amoxicillin-clavulanate. Doxycycline is recommended for patients allergic to penicillin.

Hearing Loss

Diagnosis

The Weber and Rinne tests help distinguish conductive from sensorineural hearing loss.

STUDY TABLE: Conductive and Sensorineural Hearing Loss			
Condition	**Weber Test Result**	**Rinne Test Result**	**Differential Diagnoses**
Conductive hearing loss	Lateralizes to the bad ear	Bone conduction > air conduction	Cerumen impaction, otitis media, otosclerosis, perforated tympanic membrane
Sensorineural hearing loss	Lateralizes to the good ear	As loud or louder in the bad ear	Meniere disease, acoustic neuroma, sudden sensorineural hearing loss

In patients with a conductive hearing loss, a nonmobile tympanic membrane may indicate fluid or a mass in the middle ear or retraction from negative middle ear pressure.

Select audiography for all patients with unexplained hearing loss. For patients with progressive asymmetric sensorineural hearing loss, select MRI or CT to evaluate for acoustic neuroma.

Sudden sensorineural hearing loss occurs acutely, usually within 12 hours of onset, and is unilateral in 90% of cases. It has many etiologies, including viral, vascular, autoimmune, and most commonly idiopathic.

Therapy

Treat otitis or cerumen impaction if present. Select urgent referral to ENT specialist for sudden, unexplained hearing loss. Treatment with corticosteroids is controversial but frequently provided.

A 35-year-old previously healthy man has had difficulty hearing in his right ear since last night. He has rhinorrhea and nasal congestion. His external auditory canals and tympanic membranes are normal; a 512-Hz tuning fork is placed on his forehead, and he hears the tone louder in his left ear than in his right ear.

ANSWER: Choose sudden sensorineural hearing loss and emergent ENT referral.

External Otitis

Diagnosis

Patients with typical external otitis present with otalgia, ear discharge, pruritus, and conductive hearing loss. Be aware of the several other varieties of external otitis:

- Malignant external otitis is characterized by systemic toxicity and evidence of infection spread beyond the ear canal (mastoid bone, cellulitis) and is typically found in patients with diabetes or who are immunocompromised. Most commonly caused by *Pseudomonas aeruginosa*.

- Ramsay Hunt syndrome is caused by varicella-zoster viral infection and characterized by facial nerve paralysis, sensorineural hearing loss, and vesicular lesions on and in the ear canal.

- Acute myringitis is characterized by hemorrhagic bullae on the lateral surface of the tympanic membrane secondary to viral or *Mycoplasma* infection.

Drug Therapy

Select combination antibiotic and corticosteroid drops for typical external otitis, systemic antipseudomonal antibiotics for malignant external otitis, and antiviral agents for Ramsay Hunt syndrome.

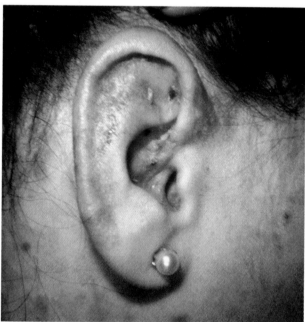

Ramsay Hunt Syndrome: Vesicular lesions on and in the ear canal characteristic of the Ramsay Hunt syndrome caused by varicella-zoster virus infection.

A 70-year-old man with type 2 diabetes mellitus has had a severe left earache since yesterday. He has a fever and tachycardia, and his left external ear canal is swollen. Moist white debris and granulation tissue are visible.

ANSWER: Diagnose malignant external otitis and select IV ciprofloxacin.

Red Eye

Diagnosis

The primary causes of red eye include viral and bacterial conjunctivitis, subconjunctival hemorrhage, allergic conjunctivitis, eyelid abnormalities, episcleritis and scleritis, acute angle-closure glaucoma, uveitis, and keratitis. Of these, the most common is conjunctivitis, primarily viral. Red eye consists of categories of entities with or without ocular pain and/or visual loss. The combination of red eye, ocular pain, and visual loss warrants emergent referral to an ophthalmologist. Select Snellen visual acuity testing for all patients.

STUDY TABLE: Causes and Treatment of Red Eye

If you see this...	Diagnose this...	Do this...
Unilateral then bilateral purulent discharge without pain or visual disturbance	Bacterial conjunctivitis	Topical fluoroquinolones or bacitracin-polymyxin
Conjunctivitis associated with herpes zoster rash	Herpes zoster conjunctivitis	Emergency ophthalmology referral
Acute hyperpurulent discharge in a sexually active adult	*Neisseria gonorrhoeae* conjunctivitis	Topical and systemic antibiotics and emergency ophthalmology referral
Giant papillary conjunctivitis with itching and watery discharge, preauricular lymphadenopathy	Chlamydial conjunctivitis	Oral treatment with tetracycline, erythromycin, or doxycycline
Unilateral then bilateral conjunctivitis with morning crusting of the eye and daytime watery or mucoid discharge	Viral conjunctivitis	Supportive care
Itching and tearing of the eyes, nasal congestion	Allergic conjunctivitis	Topical vasoconstrictors, NSAIDs, ocular antihistamines, cromolyn
Pain, photophobia, inflammation confined to corneal limbus, corneal irregularity, edema	Iridocyclitis or keratitis	Consider associated seronegative spondyloarthropathies, sarcoidosis, and herpes zoster; emergency ophthalmology referral
Unilateral deep ocular pain, nausea, vomiting, fixed nonreactive pupil, shallow anterior chamber	Acute angle-closure glaucoma	Emergency ophthalmology referral
Severe ocular pain that worsens with eye movement and light exposure; a raised hyperemic lesion that may be localized or diffuse and obscures the underlying vasculature.	Scleritis	Commonly associated with collagen vascular and rheumatoid diseases; emergency ophthalmology referral
Nonpainful red, flat, superficial lesion that allows visualization of the underlying vasculature	Episcleritis	Self-limited; no treatment required
Red eye associated with scales and crusts around the eyelashes or dandruff-like skin changes and greasy scales around the eyelashes	Blepharitis	*Staphylococcus* (crusting) or seborrheic dermatitis (greasy scales, dandruff); warm compresses, washing with mild detergent, topical antibiotics

◆ DON'T BE TRICKED

- Do not treat a red eye with topical corticosteroids.

Bacterial Conjunctivitis: The conjunctiva is diffusely erythematous with mucopurulent discharge consistent with bacterial conjunctivitis. Image courtesy of Linda Lippa, MD, University of California, Irvine.

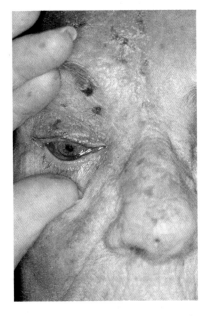

Herpes Zoster: Herpes zoster infection involving the forehead, and top of the head and eye, with evident hyperemic conjunctivitis, is shown. Corneal ulceration, episcleritis, and lid droop can occur.

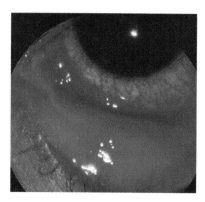

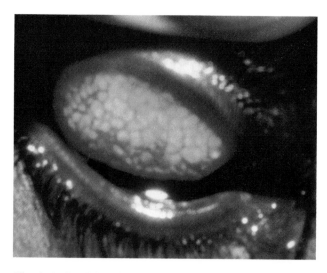

Viral Conjunctivitis: Acute adenovirus conjunctivitis is characterized by diffuse injection of the palpebral and bulbar conjunctivae and pseudomembrane formation involving the palpebral conjunctiva. Image courtesy of Linda Lippa, MD, University of California, Irvine.

Allergic Conjunctivitis: Allergic conjunctivitis with prominent cobblestoning of the palpebral conjunctiva is shown. Image courtesy of Linda Lippa, MD, University of California, Irvine.

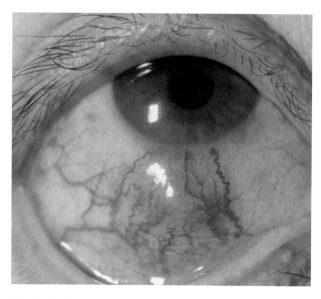

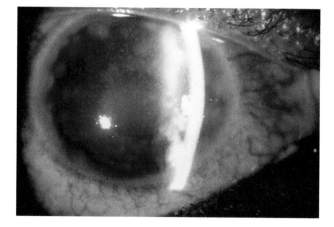

Episcleritis: The nontender, prominent, superficial dilated blood vessels of episcleritis are shown. Image courtesy of Linda Lippa, MD, University of California, Irvine.

Iritis: Intense ciliary flush around the corneal-scleral junction and an irregularly shaped pupil characteristic of iritis are shown. Image courtesy of Linda Lippa, MD, University of California, Irvine.

❖ Test Yourself

A 39-year-old man has bilateral red eyes and pain for 2 days. He has arthritis and chronic low-back pain. Visual acuity is 20/40 bilaterally. Eyes are intensely injected, with prominent circumcorneal erythema.

ANSWER: Diagnose acute iritis associated with ankylosing spondylitis and select emergent referral to an ophthalmologist.

Chronic Fatigue

Diagnosis

Chronic fatigue is disabling and lasts more than 6 months. The core clinical features of this syndrome are physical and mental fatigue exacerbated by physical and mental effort. These are subjective phenomena and are often less evident on objective testing. The common medical diagnoses characterized by chronic fatigue can be established though a standard history, physical examination, and basic laboratory studies. Specialized studies are not needed.

Chronic fatigue is defined as fatigue lasting more than a month that impairs the ability to perform desired activities; it may be caused by a number of medical conditions and generally improves with treatment of the underlying cause.

Chronic fatigue syndrome (CFS) is a distinct entity defined as persistent or relapsing fatigue for at least 6 months that is disabling and medically unexplained. Associated symptoms may include memory impairment, sore throat, myalgia, arthralgia, headaches, unrefreshing sleep, and postexertional malaise lasting >24 hours. Extensive diagnostic evaluation is not needed in patients with typical symptoms and with normal physical examination and basic laboratory study results.

Therapy

Chronic fatigue typically improves with treatment of the underlying medical cause.

Establishing goals of therapy and managing patient expectations are key treatment components of CFS. Focus treatment on minimizing the impact of fatigue through nonpharmacological interventions (cognitive-behavioral therapy and graded exercise), which are beneficial in improving, but not curing, symptoms. No specific class of medication has been shown to be effective in CFS.

Benign Prostatic Hyperplasia

Diagnosis

BPH leads to irritative symptoms (urinary urgency, frequency, and nocturia) and obstructive symptoms (decreased urinary stream, intermittency, incomplete emptying, and straining). BPH is diagnosed primarily by medical history and digital rectal examination. Urinalysis is recommended to identify other causes of lower urinary tract symptoms. When a diagnosis of BPH has been established, the American Urological Association Symptom Index quantifies symptom severity and guides treatment decisions.

Therapy

For most patients, conservative treatment is sufficient (reduce fluid intake, stop contributing medications [diuretics, anticholinergics]). The two major BPH drug classes include:

- α-adrenergic blockers (terazosin, tamsulosin, doxazosin, alfuzosin, and prazosin)
- 5-α reductase inhibitors (finasteride, dutasteride)

α-Adrenergic blockers are superior to 5-α reductase inhibitors. α-Adrenergic blockers plus finasteride are more effective than either drug alone but are associated with increased adverse effects. Transurethral resection of the prostate (TURP) is indicated in patients with severe urinary symptoms, urinary retention, persistent hematuria, recurrent urinary tract infections, or renal insufficiency clearly attributable to BPH.

Acute Prostatitis

Diagnosis

Symptoms of acute prostatitis include fevers, chills, dysuria, pelvic pain, cloudy urine, obstructive symptoms, and blood in the semen. Some men may present in septic shock. The diagnosis is established by finding a tender prostate on physical examination and a positive urine culture.

Therapy

Begin empiric antibiotics that cover gram-negative organisms (trimethoprim-sulfamethoxazole, fluoroquinolone) for 4 to 6 weeks. For patients who appear toxic, hospitalize and add gentamicin to a fluoroquinolone.

Male Sexual Dysfunction

Diagnosis

Endocrine abnormalities, medications, and medical conditions account for most cases. Testosterone deficiency, hyperprolactinemia, diabetes, and thyroid disorders can cause erectile dysfunction. Testosterone deficiency can also decrease libido. Rapid onset of sexual dysfunction suggests psychogenic causes or medication effects, whereas a more gradual onset suggests the presence of medical illnesses. Decreased libido suggests hormonal deficiencies, psychogenic causes, or medication effects. Look for:

- vascular, neurogenic, and endocrine (assess for signs of hypogonadism) disorders
- perineal, pelvic, or nervous system trauma and radiation or surgery to the pelvis or retroperitoneum
- interpersonal relationship problems and affective disorders
- antihypertensive, antidepressant, anticonvulsant, or antiandrogen and NSAID use
- alcohol, tobacco, cocaine, opiate, and marijuana use

Routine laboratory studies include measurement of total serum testosterone, prolactin, and thyroid levels. If total testosterone levels are in the low-normal range, measure bioavailable (free) testosterone. Measurement of serum FSH and LH levels can determine whether a low testosterone level indicates primary (high gonadotropin levels) or secondary (low or normal gonadotropin levels) hypogonadism. Suspect androgen steroid abuse in patients with infertility, muscular hypertrophy, testicular atrophy, and acne; laboratory data show suppressed LH and FSH levels.

Premature ejaculation is the inability to control ejaculation. Most patients have no underlying physical abnormalities.

Therapy

Treat any identified underlying cause. For treatment of erectile dysfunction, select the following strategies in this order:

- oral sildenafil, vardenafil, or tadalafil (contraindicated in men who receive nitrate therapy in any form and men with a history of nonarteritic anterior ischemic optic neuropathy)
- intraurethral alprostadil (contraindicated in men with history of priapism)
- intracavernous alprostadil (contraindicated in men with history of priapism or severe coagulopathy)

Treatment of premature ejaculation:

- Nondrug therapy includes the "pause and squeeze" technique.
- SSRIs are first-line therapy and clomipramine is second-line therapy.

❖ **Test Yourself**

A 72-year-old man cannot maintain an erection. He has diabetes mellitus, peripheral vascular disease, and CAD with stable angina, for which he takes aspirin, atenolol, isosorbide dinitrate, and glipizide.

ANSWER: Begin intraurethral or intracavernous alprostadil.

Acute Scrotal Pain

Diagnosis

Patients with testicular torsion have severe acute pain and may have nausea and vomiting. Absence of the cremasteric reflex on the affected side is nearly 99% sensitive for torsion. The testis is usually high within the scrotum and may lie transversely. Doppler flow ultrasonography demonstrates diminished blood flow to the affected testicle.

Epididymitis causes pain localizing to the posterior and superior aspects of the testicle. Pain onset is subacute and may be accompanied by dysuria, pyuria, and fever. The scrotum may be edematous and erythematous. Orchitis is usually caused by viral infection (mumps) or extension of a bacterial infection from epididymitis or urinary tract infection. The testicle is diffusely tender. In both epididymitis and orchitis, ultrasonography demonstrates normal or increased blood flow to the testicle and epididymis.

Therapy

Treatment of testicular torsion is immediate surgical exploration and reduction. In men younger than 35 years with epididymitis, treat for gonorrhea and chlamydial disease. In men older than 35 years, treat with an oral fluoroquinolone.

Medical Ethics and Professionalism

Patient Privacy

With the advent of the HIPAA regulations, patients must have control over who has access to their personal health information, especially with regard to family members. The preservation of confidentiality is not absolute. Safeguarding the individual or public from harm or honoring the law prevails over protecting confidentiality.

❖ **Test Yourself**

A 78-year-old man is admitted with GI bleeding. Colonoscopy reveals metastatic colon cancer. His daughter wishes to know the results of the colonoscopy.

ANSWER: The information cannot be released unless approved by the patient.

Advanced Planning

Advance care planning allows a competent adult patient to designate a surrogate decision maker and includes living wills and durable powers of attorney for health care. It can include conversations documented in the medical record. Advance directives only become operative when the patient loses the capacity for decision making. When no advance directive exists and a patient's values and preferences are unknown or unclear, decisions should be based on a patient's best interests, whenever possible, as interpreted by a guardian or by a person with "loving knowledge" of the patient.

Decision-Making Capacity

The physician must assess the patient's decision-making abilities to decide whether a surrogate decision maker should be enlisted. To make their own decisions, patients need a set of values and goals, the ability to communicate and understand information, and the ability to reason and deliberate about options. The core components of decisional capacity are (1) understanding the situation at hand, (2) understanding the risks and benefits of the decision being made, and (3) being able to communicate a decision. Minors who are not living independently of their parents, not married, or not in the armed forces cannot legally make their own decisions.

Understand the difference between decision-making capacity and competence. Any physician can determine if a patient has decision-making capacity. "Competence" is a legal term; only the courts can determine competence. If a patient is incapable of medical decision making, a surrogate decision maker is identified. Surrogates can use one of two standards for decision making:

- Substituted judgment standard: The surrogate makes the decision that he or she believes the patient would have made.
- Best interests standard: The surrogate selects the medical treatment that he or she personally feels is best for the patient.

❖ Test Yourself

An 82-year-old woman is hospitalized for the fourth time in 12 months. She lives alone and is unable to take her medications properly. She cannot articulate a plan to manage her disease.

ANSWER: Seek guardianship, because the patient cannot describe realistic plans for living home alone.

Withholding or Withdrawing Treatment

Withdrawing treatment is reasonable if, from the patient's perspective, the expected benefits of treatment no longer outweigh its burdens. Do-not-resuscitate orders must be documented in the medical record, along with notes and orders that describe the affirmative goals of continued care and how they will be met. Patients who have do-not-resuscitate orders are still eligible to receive other therapeutic life-prolonging or palliative measures.

Physicians are not obligated to administer interventions that are physiologically futile. Physicians may also disagree with a patient's legitimate choice of care if it violates their ethical principles. If consensus about treatment cannot be reached, options include transfer of the patient to another physician and review by a hospital ethics committee. Administration of nutrients and fluids by artificial means is a life-prolonging measure, guided by the same principles for decision making that are applied to other treatments.

Disclosing Medical Errors

When patients are injured as a consequence of medical care, whether or not error is involved, they should be informed promptly about what has occurred. An apology should be given if it was due to error or system failure. Data does not support concerns that disclosure of an error promotes litigation.

The Impaired Physician

Physicians are ethically—and in some states, legally—bound to protect patients from impaired colleagues by reporting such physicians to appropriate authorities, including chiefs of service, chiefs of staff, institutional committees, or state medical boards.

Conflict of Interest

A conflict of interest exists when physicians' primary duty to their patients conflicts or appears to conflict with a secondary interest, which may consist of another important professional responsibility, a contractual obligation, or personal gain. Physicians are obligated to avoid significant conflicts of interest whenever possible. For less serious or unavoidable conflicts of interest, disclosure is appropriate. Even small gifts may affect clinical judgment and heighten the perception (or the reality) of a conflict of interest. The acceptance of gifts, hospitality, trips, and subsidies of all types from those in the health care industry is strongly discouraged.

Patient Safety

Diagnostic Errors

Analyses of clinicians' heuristics seek to understand common shortcuts in reasoning and how these shortcuts can lead to diagnostic errors.

STUDY TABLE: Reasoning Errors	
Heuristic	**Definition**
Availability	Clinician has encountered a similar presentation and jumps to the conclusion that the current diagnosis must be the same as the previous
Anchoring	Clinician accepts at face value a previous diagnosis made by another clinician
Blind obedience	Acceptance of a diagnosis or plan made by another of higher authority
Premature closure	Full differential diagnosis is not considered

Error Analysis

A *root-cause analysis* is a group exercise used to determine the contributors to an adverse event. Often, a fishbone pattern is used to illustrate causation, beginning with a problem or error at the fish's head. Working back down the spine, the team is asked repetitively, "And what contributed to this?" This continues until as many prime factors as possible are identified. An average of 6 system-related or cognitive factors contribute to medical error in a single case. This is conceptualized as the "Swiss cheese" model of error, in that there must be a breakdown of several layers in a system to actually cause an injury.

Quality Improvement

A common methodology to improve quality is the Plan-Do-Study-Act (PDSA) cycle. The clinician might *plan* a test of quality improvement, *do* the test by trying the new protocol on a limited number of patients, *study* the results, and *act* by refining the protocol based on what was learned and planning the next test.

Patient Handoffs

The best practice for handoff includes person-to-person communication, providing an opportunity to ask and respond to questions, and providing information that is accurate and concise (including name, location, history, diagnoses, severity of illness, medication and problem lists, status, recent procedures, a "to do" list that has "if/then" statements, and contingency plans).

Hematology

Aplastic Anemia, Pure Red Cell Aplasia, and Paroxysmal Nocturnal Hemoglobinuria

Diagnosis

Aplastic anemia is a disorder in which the stem cells are severely diminished, resulting in hypocellular bone marrow and pancytopenia. All cell lines can be involved. No cause is identified in 50% of patients. Identifiable causes include toxins, ionizing radiation, drugs, nutritional deficiencies, and infections. Some patients have an associated thymoma or an autoimmune disorder. Patients with aplastic anemia are at increased risk of developing acute leukemia and myelodysplastic syndrome.

Some patients with aplastic anemia may have underlying PNH, which results from a genetic mutation of membrane proteins that ameliorate complement-mediated destruction of erythrocytes. PNH is characterized by:

- chronic hemolytic anemia
- iron deficiency through urinary losses
- venous thrombosis (including abdominal venous thrombosis)
- pancytopenia

PNH is diagnosed by documenting lack of expression of CD55 and CD59 on erythrocytes with flow cytometry.

Acquired chronic pure red cell aplasia is characterized by the absence or a marked decrease of erythrocyte production with normal leukocyte and platelet counts. It may occur along with other autoimmune diseases and with thymomas. Bone marrow shows profound erythroid hypoplasia. Flow cytometry shows a monoclonal CD57-positive T-cell population. Parvovirus B19 infection in patients with AIDS can also cause chronic pure red cell aplasia and a transient aplastic crisis in sickle cell disease.

The basic evaluation of aplastic anemia includes:

- a bone marrow aspirate and biopsy (hypocellular with increased fat content)
- cytogenetic analysis to exclude other bone marrow disorders (e.g., myelodysplastic syndrome)
- PNH screen
- B12 and folate levels, liver chemistry tests, hepatitis serologies, and HIV testing
- CT of the chest to rule out an associated thymoma

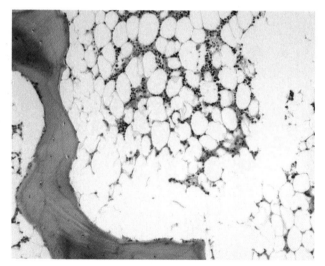

Aplastic Anemia: The bone marrow is profoundly hypocellular, with the marrow space composed mostly of fat cells and marrow stroma.

Therapy

Initial treatment of aplastic anemia involves withdrawal of any potentially causative agents. If a thymoma is found, surgical excision can be curative. HSCT is first-line therapy for young patients (<40 years of age) with an HLA-matched sibling donor and severe or very severe acquired aplastic anemia. Immunosuppressive therapy with antithymocyte globulin and cyclosporine is effective in abating transfusion requirements in up to 80% of patients with aplastic anemia.

Treatment of PNH in the absence of hemolysis is generally not indicated. In symptomatic patients, eculizumab reduces intravascular hemolysis, hemoglobinuria, and the need for transfusion. Allogeneic stem cell transplantation can lead to long-term survival. Prophylactic anticoagulation and supplementation with iron and folic acid are indicated in all patients.

Patients with pure red cell aplasia are treated with transfusion support and immunosuppressive drugs. Thymectomy is indicated for thymoma. IV immune globulin is indicated for patients with AIDS with chronic parvovirus B19 infection.

Normocytic Anemia

Diagnosis

Normocytic anemia is associated with a normal MCV of 80 to 100 fL. The reticulocyte count can help differentiate the cause. An appropriately increased reticulocyte count (>100,000/microliter) almost always reflects either erythrocyte loss (bleeding or hemolysis) or response to appropriate therapy (iron, folate, or cobalamin). A lower than expected reticulocyte count indicates underproduction anemia, including any of the following:

- deficient erythropoietin
- nutritional deficiencies (iron, folate, cobalamin)
- hypometabolism (hypothyroidism, testosterone deficiency)
- inflammatory block
- a primary hematopoietic disorder (red cell aplasia or myelodysplasia)

The most frequent cause of normocytic anemia is inflammatory anemia. Iron deficiency and inflammatory anemia are often confused. Both disorders are associated with a decreased serum iron concentration; however, iron deficiency is more likely in a patient with an elevated serum TIBC and a transferrin saturation (serum iron transferrin) of <10%. A serum ferritin level >100 ng/mL rules out iron deficiency, even in patients with inflammation. Inflammatory anemia is usually not severe and rarely requires therapy.

STUDY TABLE: Differentiating Iron Deficiency and Inflammatory Anemia		
Test	**Iron Deficiency Anemia**	**Inflammatory Anemia**
Serum iron	Low	Low
Ferritin	Low	High
TIBC	High	Low
Transferrin saturation	Low	Low/Normal

Recommended diagnostic studies:

- FOBT for all patients (33% of patients with iron deficiency have a normal MCV)
- peripheral blood smear to detect spherocytes, fragmented erythrocytes (schistocytes), or blister cells associated with hemolysis
- direct antiglobulin (Coombs) test if spherocytes are found on a peripheral blood smear
- hemoglobin electrophoresis if target or sickle cells are found on a peripheral blood smear
- lead level if basophilic stippling is found on a peripheral blood smear
- bone marrow aspiration and biopsy if leukopenia, thrombocytopenia, myelocytes, or nucleated erythrocytes (in normocytic, microcytic, and macrocytic anemias) are found on peripheral smear
- bone marrow aspiration and biopsy if lymphadenopathy or splenomegaly are present

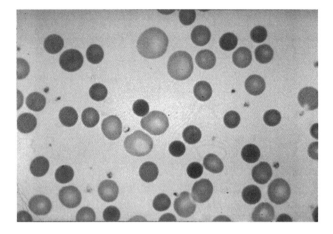

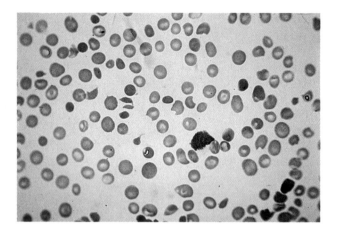

Spherocytes: This peripheral blood smear shows small erythrocytes with loss of usual central pallor. Consider acquired immune hemolytic anemia and hereditary spherocytosis.

Erythrocyte Fragmentation: The erythrocytes show marked anisocytosis and poikilocytosis with prominent fragmentation. Consider disseminated intravascular coagulation, thrombotic thrombocytopenic purpura, mechanical heart valve, or malignant hypertension.

Microcytic Anemia

Diagnosis

Microcytic anemia is associated with an MCV of <80 fL. The most common cause of microcytic anemia is iron deficiency, usually related to menstrual or GI blood loss or malabsorption syndromes (celiac disease). Hypochromia (decreased MCHC) is the first morphologic sign of iron deficiency, followed by microcytosis (decreased MCV). As hemoglobin levels decline, erythrocytes become heterogeneous in size (anisocytosis) and shape (poikilocytosis). An elevated platelet count (usually not >1 million/microliter) is found in early disease. Serum ferritin levels are the most useful test in the diagnosis of iron deficiency. However, because ferritin is an acute-phase reactant, it has less diagnostic value in patients with infection or inflammatory disorders. Virtually all patients with serum ferritin levels <10 to 15 ng/mL are iron deficient. Signs and symptoms of iron deficiency include restless legs syndrome, hair loss, and spoon nails (koilonychia). Other causes of microcytic anemia include:

- inflammatory disorders
- lead intoxication
- thalassemia

Patients with microcytic anemia since childhood should be evaluated for thalassemia trait, other hemoglobinopathies (thalassemia, hemoglobin SC disease), or ineffective erythropoiesis (hemoglobin H disease, and hereditary sideroblastic anemia).

Recommended diagnostic studies:

- serum iron and ferritin levels and TIBC in most patients
- hemoglobin electrophoresis if splenomegaly or bone remodeling are present
- colonoscopy if positive fecal occult blood test or iron deficiency is present
- upper endoscopy if colonoscopy is negative (also, if hereditary hemorrhagic telangiectasia is suspected)

Therapy

Oral iron for 6 months is the standard treatment for iron deficiency. Parenteral iron preparations are indicated only for patients who cannot tolerate or absorb oral iron.

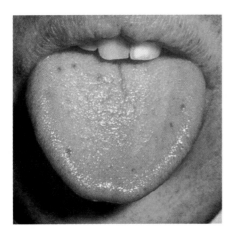

Hereditary Hemorrhagic Telangiectasia: Hereditary hemorrhagic telangiectasia can be associated with mucocutaneous telangiectasias that occur on the face, lips, tongue, buccal mucosa, fingertips, and dorsum of the hand and are associated with GI bleeding in up to one third of patients.

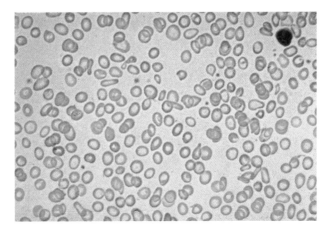

Microcytic Anemia: The erythrocytes show hypochromia, anisocytosis, and poikilocytosis. Erythrocytes in thalassemia have less variability in size and shape, and target cells are seen.

❖ **Test Yourself**

A 20-year-old woman with iron deficiency anemia does not respond to oral iron therapy. Review of systems is remarkable for IBS.

ANSWER: Test for celiac disease.

Macrocytic Anemia

Diagnosis

Macrocytic anemia is associated with an MCV of >100 fL. Macro-ovalocytes suggest megaloblastic maturation of erythrocytes. Hypersegmented neutrophils may also be present. Etiologies include:

- folate and/or cobalamin deficiencies
- drugs affecting folate metabolism and/or DNA synthesis (alcohol, zidovudine, methotrexate)
- acquired idiopathic causes of megaloblastic maturation such as the myelodysplastic syndromes

Anemia associated with an MCV >115 fL is almost always due to megaloblastic disorders. Because megaloblastic causes of anemia affect trilineage hematopoiesis, leukopenia and thrombocytopenia may accompany anemia.

If serum vitamin B_{12} levels are borderline low (200-300 pg/mL), measure serum methylmalonic acid and homocysteine levels. Elevated levels confirm vitamin B_{12} deficiency; elevated homocysteine and normal methylmalonic acid levels are associated with folate deficiency.

Macrocytic anemia may be caused by nonmegaloblastic disorders.

- Large target cells (MCV 105-110 fL) and echinocytes (spur cells with multiple undulating spiny erythrocyte membrane projections) signify membrane changes associated with liver disease.

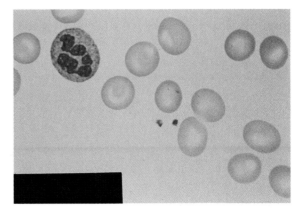

Hypersegmented Polymorphonuclear Cell: The erythrocytes are large ovalocytes, and a single PMN cell has more than 5 nuclear lobes. Consider vitamin B_{12} or folate deficiency (megaloblastic anemia).

- Diminished splenic function (hyposplenism or asplenia) yields large target cells, acanthocytes (erythrocytes with only a few rather than many spiny membrane projections), Howell-Jolly bodies, and variable numbers of nucleated erythrocytes.
- Reticulocytosis (e.g., secondary to hemolysis) can also increase the MCV.

Therapy

Treat vitamin B_{12} deficiency due to pernicious anemia with oral vitamin B_{12}, 1000 to 2000 micrograms/d. Malabsorption syndromes require parenteral vitamin B_{12}.

◆ **DON'T BE TRICKED**

- **Vitamin B_{12} deficiency can present with neurologic symptoms in the absence of anemia or macrocytosis.**

Hemolytic Anemia

Diagnosis

Characteristic findings are anemia; splenomegaly; elevated reticulocyte count, LDH, and indirect bilirubin; and decreased haptoglobin. The MCV is frequently elevated (due to reticulocytosis). When laboratory tests suggest hemolytic anemia, consider:

- cause by type (spherocytic or nonspherocytic)
- site (intramedullary or extramedullary)
- if extramedullary, intravascular or extravascular
- mechanism (immune-mediated or non–immune-mediated)
- intrinsic vs. extrinsic to the erythrocyte

For example, spherocytic hemolytic anemia implicates a membrane defect, either acquired as in warm autoimmune hemolytic anemia or congenital as in hereditary spherocytosis. Nonspherocytic hemolytic anemias include bite cell hemolysis (as in oxidant stress due to G6PD deficiency) and fragmentation hemolysis (as in thrombotic microangiopathies).

Intramedullary hemolysis occurs in various disorders associated with ineffective erythropoiesis, including thalassemia. Extramedullary hemolysis may be extravascular (as in hemolysis mediated by the spleen) or intravascular (as in hemolysis associated with cold agglutinin disease or thrombotic microangiopathies).

Immune-mediated hemolysis is identified by a positive Coombs test, a direct antiglobulin test that detects IgG or complement on the erythrocyte surface. Hemolytic disorders "intrinsic" to the erythrocyte include membrane defects, enzymopathies, and hemoglobinopathies. In all cases, examining the peripheral blood smear is central to identifying erythrocyte morphologies that implicate certain hemolytic mechanisms.

STUDY TABLE: Peripheral Blood Smear Findings in Hemolytic Anemia	
Finding	**Diagnosis**
Schistocytes and thrombocytopenia	TTP-HUS, DIC, HELLP
Schistocytes in a patient with a prosthetic heart valve	Valve leak
Erythrocyte agglutination	Cold agglutinin hemolysis (*Mycoplasma* infection, lymphoproliferative diseases, chronic lymphoid leukemia)
Spherocytes	Autoimmune hemolytic anemia or hereditary spherocytosis
Target cells	Thalassemia, other hemoglobinopathy, or liver disease
Sickle cells	Sickle cell anemia
Bite cells	G6PD deficiency (suggested by eccentrically located hemoglobin confined to one side of the cell)

STUDY TABLE: Tests for Hemolytic Anemia

Test	Condition
Coombs test	Warm-antibody autoimmune hemolytic anemia
Osmotic fragility	Hereditary spherocytosis
Cold agglutinin measurement	Cold agglutinin autoimmune hemolytic anemia
Hemoglobin electrophoresis	Thalassemia or other hemoglobinopathy
G6PD activity measurement	Normal enzyme concentration after a hemolytic episode (test 2-3 months after event to detect deficiency)
Flow cytometry for CD55 and CD59 proteins	Paroxysmal nocturnal hemoglobinuria

Therapy

- Warm-antibody and cold agglutinin autoimmune hemolytic anemia: Initial therapy is corticosteroids. If corticosteroids are ineffective, select splenectomy. Alternative agents are azathioprine, cyclophosphamide, cyclosporine, IV immune globulin, rituximab, or danazol for patients unresponsive to corticosteroids or splenectomy.
- TTP: Treat with emergent plasma exchange.
- Chronic hemolytic anemia: Treat with folic acid supplements.
- Severe anemia in critically ill patients: Select transfusion even if fully matched erythrocytes are not available.
- Hereditary spherocytosis and transfusion-dependent thalassemias: Splenectomy is first-line therapy.
- Severe thalassemia: Stem cell transplantation is standard therapy.
- Severe paroxysmal nocturnal hemoglobinuria: Stem cell transplantation is standard therapy.

◆ DON'T BE TRICKED

- **All patients with hemolytic anemia need daily folic acid.**
- **All patients with sickle cell anemia or other hemolytic anemias need pneumococcal, *Haemophilus influenzae* type B, influenza, and meningococcal vaccinations before splenectomy.**
- **A personal or family history of anemia, jaundice, splenomegaly, or gallstones suggests hereditary spherocytosis.**
- **Do not check the G6PD activity level during an acute hemolytic episode because it can be falsely normal.**

❖ Test Yourself

A previously healthy 28-year-old woman has weakness and a palpable spleen. Hemoglobin concentration is 7.2 g/dL and the reticulocyte count is 9.8%. Peripheral blood smear shows occasional spherocytes.

ANSWER: The probable diagnosis is hemolytic anemia. A Coombs test is indicated.

Sickle Cell Disease

Diagnosis

Hemoglobin S results from a single-base substitution of the β gene. The sickle cell syndromes can be diagnosed by hemoglobin electrophoresis. Most clinical findings in sickle cell disease are related to vaso-occlusion from deformed sickled erythrocytes. Characteristic findings include elevated reticulocyte, platelet, and leukocyte counts and sickle cells on a peripheral blood smear. Aplastic and hyperhemolytic crises are common and may be due to coexisting infection, especially parvovirus B19 infection. Several complications of sickle cell disease mimic other diseases. Keep the following diagnostic points in mind:

ACS vs. pneumonia, fat embolism, and pulmonary embolism:

- ACS is usually characterized by diffuse pulmonary infiltrates.

- Pneumonia is usually a localized infiltration.

- Fat embolism presents with chest pain, fever, dyspnea, hypoxia, thrombocytopenia, and multiorgan failure and may be associated with fat bodies in bronchial washings or sputum.

- Presence of lower extremity thrombophlebitis may help differentiate pulmonary embolism from ACS, but pulmonary arteriography may be needed.

Cholecystitis vs. hepatic crisis:

- Chronic hemolysis may result in gallstones and acute cholecystitis.

- Fever, right upper quadrant pain, and elevated aminotransferase levels may also be due to ischemic hepatic crisis; abdominal ultrasonography can differentiate between the two.

Sickle cell anemia vs. aplastic crisis and hyperhemolysis:

- Anemia that decreases by ≥2 g/dL during a painful crisis could be due to aplastic crisis or hyperhemolysis.

- Aplastic crisis could be due to parvovirus B19 infection or cytotoxic drugs or be idiopathic.

- Hyperhemolysis could be due to infection (*Mycoplasma*), transfusion reaction, or coexistent G6PD deficiency.

- The reticulocyte count is decreased with aplastic crisis and increased with hyperhemolysis.

- Bilirubin, LDH, and aminotransferase levels are elevated in hyperhemolysis but normal or at baseline in aplastic crisis.

Sickle cell pain crisis vs. appendicitis:

- Abdominal pain, fever, and leukocytosis may suggest appendicitis.

- A high LDH level and normal bowel sounds support sickle cell pain syndrome.

STUDY TABLE: Long-Term Complications of Sickle Cell Disease	
If you see this...	**Think this...**
Chronic pain involving hips and shoulders	Osteonecrosis (avascular necrosis)
Cerebrovascular accidents	Ischemic infarction in children and hemorrhage in adults
Exertional dyspnea	HF or pulmonary hypertension
Infection with encapsulated organisms	Functional asplenia
Liver disease	Viral hepatitis, iron overload from transfusions, or ischemic-induced hepatic crisis
Impotence	Prolonged or repeated episodes of priapism
Proteinuria	CKD
Isosthenuria (inability to concentrate urine)	CKD
Decreased visual acuity	Retinopathy

Therapy

Vaccinate all patients against pneumococcus, meningococcus, *H. influenzae* type B, hepatitis B, and influenza. Hydroxyurea is beneficial for patients with more than two pain crises each year or for those with ACS. Exchange transfusion is indicated for patients with an acute stroke, fat embolism, or ACS. Patients with a history of ischemic stroke require prophylactic exchange transfusion. Erythropoietin is used for patients with severe anemia, low reticulocyte counts, and chronic kidney disease. Vaso-occlusive crisis is managed with hydration, supplemental oxygen if the patient is hypoxic, treatment of any precipitating event, and opioids. Iron overload due to multiple transfusions may require chelation therapy.

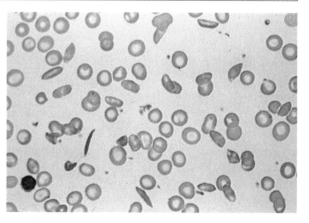

Sickle Cells: Erythrocyte anisocytosis and poikilocytosis involving several sickle cells.

◆ DON'T BE TRICKED

- Hydroxyurea is contraindicated in pregnancy and kidney failure.
- Do not use meperidine to treat painful crises because the accumulation of the metabolite normeperidine can lead to seizures.
- Transfusion target is hemoglobin <10 g/dL to avoid hyperviscosity.

❖ Test Yourself

A 32-year-old woman with sickle cell disease has a low-grade fever and exertional dyspnea. Hemoglobin concentration is 4.2 g/dL, and the reticulocyte count is 0.2%.

ANSWER: Diagnose aplastic crisis due to parvovirus B19 infection.

Thalassemia

Diagnosis

Hemoglobin is a tetrameric molecule. The two α-globin chains and two β-globin chains are linked to heme (iron and protoporphyrin) and reversibly bind one molecule of oxygen. The thalassemic syndromes result from defects in synthesis of the α or β chains and lead to ineffective erythropoiesis and hemolysis. Patients with α-thalassemia or β-thalassemia have microcytosis and target cells on the peripheral blood smear, may have splenomegaly, and may develop pigmented gallstones.

STUDY TABLE: α-Thalassemia		
Gene Deletion	**Clinical Syndrome**	**Treatment**
$(-\alpha/\alpha\alpha)$ [single-gene deletion]	Silent carrier state that is clinically normal	None
$(--/\alpha\alpha$ or $-\alpha/-\alpha)$ [two-gene deletion]	α-Thalassemia trait; mild microcytic anemia; normal or elevated erythrocyte count; normal hemoglobin electrophoresis	None
$(--/-\alpha)$ [three-gene deletion]	Hemoglobin H (β_4); severe anemia and early death	Intermittent transfusion
$(--/--)$ [four-gene deletion]	Hemoglobin Bart's; hydrops fetalis; fetal death	In utero transfusion

β-Thalassemia is most common among persons from the Mediterranean, Southeast Asia, India, and Pakistan. β-Thalassemia results from several abnormalities in the β-gene complex. Decreased β-chain synthesis leads to impaired production of hemoglobin A ($\alpha_2\beta_2$) and resultant increased synthesis of hemoglobin A2 ($\alpha_2\delta_2$) and/or hemoglobin F ($\alpha_2\gamma_2$).

STUDY TABLE: β-Thalassemia		
Condition	**Characteristics**	**Treatment**
β-thalassemia major (Cooley anemia)	No effective production or severely limited production of β globin	Transfusion, iron chelation; consider splenectomy and HSCT
β-thalassemia minor (β-thalassemia trait)	A single β-gene leading to reduced β globin production	None
β-thalassemia intermedia	Intermediate severity, such as in those who are compound heterozygotes of two thalassemic variants	Intermittent transfusion, iron chelation

β-Thalassemia trait and α-thalassemia trait are most commonly confused with iron deficiency anemia.

STUDY TABLE: Iron Deficiency Anemia and β-Thalassemia Trait		
Iron Deficiency Anemia	**α-Thalassemia Trait**	**β-Thalassemia Trait**
Low serum ferritin level	Normal serum ferritin level	Normal serum ferritin level
Low erythrocyte count	Normal or high erythrocyte count	Normal or high erythrocyte count
High RDW	Normal RDW	Normal RDW
Normal hemoglobin electrophoresis	Normal hemoglobin electrophoresis	Elevated hemoglobin A_2 and fetal hemoglobin

◆ DON'T BE TRICKED

- β-Thalassemia can be associated with iron overload even in the absence of transfusion therapy.

Therapy

Treatment of β-thalassemia varies with the type of disease. β-Thalassemia minor requires no therapy. β-Thalassemia major requires early-onset, lifelong transfusion therapy. Iron chelation therapy may be indicated if serum ferritin concentrations exceed 1000 ng/mL. Allogeneic stem cell transplantation is indicated for severe β-thalassemia.

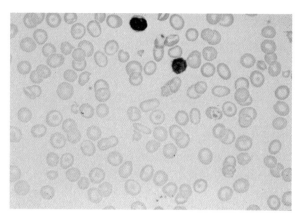

Thalassemia: Microcytosis, hypochromia, and target cells consistent with thalassemia.

❖ Test Yourself

An asymptomatic 18-year-old man has a hemoglobin concentration of 13.0 g/dL, an MCV of 64 fL, and a reticulocyte count of 4.0%.

ANSWER: The probable diagnosis is β-thalassemia or α-thalassemia trait. Order serum ferritin measurement and hemoglobin electrophoresis.

Thrombocytopenia

Diagnosis

Look for decreased platelet production or accelerated destruction. Disorders associated with decreased bone marrow production often affect other cell lines, causing additional cytopenias. Common causes include:

- toxins (alcohol)
- idiosyncratic drug reactions
- metastatic cancer
- infections
- vitamin B_{12} or folic acid deficiency
- acute leukemia
- dysmyelopoietic syndrome
- aplastic anemia

Accelerated destruction occurs in patients with hypersplenism or DIC. Other causes of accelerated platelet destruction include ITP, HIT, and TTP-HUS.

Thrombocytopenia in ITP occurs when antibodies targeting platelet antigens mediate accelerated destruction. The characteristic finding in ITP is isolated thrombocytopenia in a patient without other apparent causes for the reduced platelets. Antibodies arise in three distinct clinical settings: drug induced, disease associated, and idiopathic. Drug-induced ITP is most often linked to quinine or quinidine. Discontinuation of the offending drug should result in platelet recovery. Common disease associations include HIV, SLE, and lymphoproliferative malignancy. A peripheral blood smear shows reduced numbers of platelets and large platelets and normal erythroid and myeloid cells. A bone marrow biopsy/aspiration is usually not necessary to make the diagnosis but should be done for abnormalities in two cell lines, in most older patients with new-onset ITP, or if the peripheral blood smear is abnormal.

◆ DON'T BE TRICKED

- Anemia does not exclude a diagnosis of ITP if the anemia can be explained by bleeding.

- Measurement of platelet-associated antibody is not helpful because the test lacks both sensitivity and specificity.

STUDY TABLE: Thrombocytopenia Associations	
If you see this...	**Think this...**
Schistocytes	DIC, TTP-HUS, HELLP
Platelet clumps	Pseudothrombocytopenia caused by EDTA-dependent agglutinins leads to falsely decreased platelet counts. Repeat count using a citrated or a heparinized tube.
Teardrop (erythrocyte) cells, disorders in two cell lines	Myelodysplastic syndrome
Anemia, leukopenia, and lymphocytosis	Aplastic anemia
Pancytopenia, macrocytosis, macro-ovalocytes, hypersegmented neutrophils	Vitamin B_{12} or folate deficiencies
Thrombocytopenia following heparin administration or thrombocytopenia and thrombosis	HIT
Thrombocytopenia 5 to 10 days after blood transfusion	Posttransfusion purpura

Therapy

At the time of diagnosis, initiate therapy when the platelet count is <30,000/microliter or with evidence of bleeding. Corticosteroids are first-line therapy for ITP. IV immune globulin or anti-D immunoglobulin in persons who are RhD-positive is indicated for corticosteroid-resistant ITP or for management of severe bleeding although the response is typically transient. Reserve splenectomy or rituximab for patients who are unresponsive to drug therapy or who relapse after corticosteroids are tapered. Use of a thrombopoiesis-stimulating agent (romiplostim, eltrombopag) may be attempted in refractory cases.

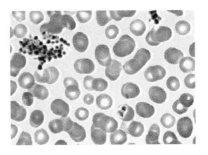

Pseudothrombocytopenia: Platelet clumps on peripheral blood smear associated with pseudothrombocytopenia.

Thrombocytopenia in Pregnancy

Diagnosis

The most common cause of a decreased platelet count in a pregnant woman is gestational thrombocytopenia (incidental thrombocytopenia of pregnancy).

STUDY TABLE: Thrombocytopenia During Pregnancy	
Disorder	**Characteristic**
Gestational thrombocytopenia	Benign thrombocytopenia typically >70,000/µL; second or third trimester; no treatment needed.
Preeclampsia	Hypertension and proteinuria and thrombocytopenia developing at >20 weeks' gestation; treatment is delivery.
HELLP syndrome	Microangiopathic hemolytic anemia; AST >70 units/L, platelet count <100,000/µL developing at >20 weeks' gestation; treatment is delivery.
TTP-HUS	See TTP-HUS section. Develops at >20 weeks' gestation; not affected by pregnancy termination.
ITP	May present before or early in pregnancy. Treatment same as for nonpregnant patients.
DIC	In setting of obstetric emergency, elevated levels of fibrin degradation products and/or D-dimers, decreased fibrinogen level, possible prolongation of the PT and aPTT, and thrombocytopenia.
µL = microliter.	

Thrombotic Thrombocytopenic Purpura–Hemolytic Uremic Syndrome

Diagnosis

Patients with TTP-HUS develop consumptive thrombocytopenia and microangiopathic hemolytic anemia from platelet thrombi that form throughout the microvasculature. Fever, kidney disease, and fluctuating neurologic abnormalities also occur but are seldom all present during earlier phases of the illness.

Laboratory studies show fragmented erythrocytes on peripheral blood smear and elevated serum bilirubin and LDH levels. Patients with TTP have been found to have unusually large multimers of vWF in their plasma and also have ADAMTS13 (vWF-cleaving protease) deficiency. TTP can also occur by other mechanisms in patients with cancer, in transplant recipients, and following administration of chemotherapeutic agents and other drugs (quinine, clopidogrel, cyclosporine). TTP and HUS are difficult to differentiate and are sometimes considered as an overlap syndrome. *Escherichia coli* O157:H7 or *Shigella* infections are more common in patients with HUS than in the general population. Infection leads to the development of abdominal pain and watery diarrhea 1 to 2 days after toxin exposure, followed by bloody diarrhea. As many as 20% of patients with infection-related bloody diarrhea progress to HUS microangiopathic hemolytic anemia and acute kidney injury, generally within 6 days after diarrhea onset.

◆ DON'T BE TRICKED

- Do not order ADAMTS13 activity and inhibitor level to make the diagnosis of TTP because of its poor sensitivity and specificity.

Therapy

TTP caused by immune-mediated drug hypersensitivity requires immediate discontinuation of the causative drug. Treat TTP with plasma exchange. Corticosteroids are usually an add-on to plasma exchange in patients with idiopathic TTP (not related to drugs, cancer, or associated with severe bloody diarrhea) or in those for whom plasma exchange fails. Use rituximab and splenectomy in cases of relapsed/refractory disease. Treat HUS with plasma exchange; it may also require dialysis.

◆ DON'T BE TRICKED

- Do not order platelet transfusion in TTP-HUS because it can exacerbate the microvascular occlusion.
- PT, aPTT, D-dimer, and fibrinogen levels are normal in TTP-HUS and abnormal in DIC.

HIT and HITT

Diagnosis

The characteristic findings of HIT and HITT are a platelet decrease of >50% in a patient taking heparin or a thromboembolic event 5 to 10 days after starting heparin. A syndrome of delayed-onset HIT may develop up to 3 weeks after discontinuing heparin. Patients with recent exposure to heparin may experience the onset of HIT more rapidly after re-exposure to heparin. The SRA is considered the gold standard for diagnosis, but a negative SRA does not exclude HIT. Alternatively, the presence of anti-PF4/heparin antibodies may confirm the diagnosis but is associated with many false-positive test results. Often, therapy must be instituted before assays are back.

Therapy

Heparin must be discontinued. Use a nonheparin anticoagulant (lepirudin, argatroban, or danaparoid) to stabilize the patient; use bivalirudin for those undergoing acute cardiac interventions.

◆ DON'T BE TRICKED

- Lepirudin is contraindicated in patients with kidney disease; argatroban is contraindicated in patients with hepatic dysfunction.
- For HIT or HITT, warfarin or LMWH cannot be substituted for UFH.

❖ Test Yourself

A 75-year-old man who has been hospitalized multiple times for ischemic heart disease is admitted with increasing chest pain. The morning after admission, he has a painful, cold left lower leg. The platelet count is 30,000/microliter.

ANSWER: The diagnosis is HITT. Stop heparin and begin lepirudin, argatroban, or danaparoid.

Approach to Bleeding Disorders

Diagnosis

Bleeding disorders are characterized by defects in primary and secondary hemostasis. Primary hemostasis involves the formation of a platelet plug at the site of vascular disruption. Secondary hemostasis is initiated by the exposure of tissue factor at the site of vascular damage and initiation of the coagulation cascade. A mucocutaneous bleeding pattern (epistaxis, gingival bleeding, easy bruising, and menorrhagia) is the hallmark of primary hemostasis failure. Secondary hemostasis failure is characterized by bleeding into muscles and joints as well as delayed bleeding. Excessive bleeding after childbirth, surgery, or trauma can occur in either category.

Select PT and the aPTT to screen for factor deficiencies and factor inhibitors. Factor levels <35% are needed to prolong the PT and aPTT. A mixing study differentiates factor deficiency from factor inhibitor by mixing patient plasma with normal plasma. Bleeding time identifies platelet disorders and vessel-wall integrity; the commercially available Platelet Function Analyzer-100 (PFA-100) also assesses platelet function. Thrombin time tests the conversion of fibrinogen to fibrin. Fibrinogen, fibrinogen degradation products, and D-dimer are used to identify excessive fibrinolysis.

Common Acquired Bleeding Disorders

Diagnosis

Liver disease: Hepatic dysfunction may be associated with bleeding disorders. Characteristic findings of hepatic dysfunction bleeding disorders are pathologic thrombosis, fibrinolysis, or both. The PT is initially prolonged, followed by prolongation of the aPTT. Dysfibrinogenemia eventually occurs.

Vitamin K deficiency: Patients with liver disease and a prolonged PT require oral or subcutaneous vitamin K. Active bleeding because of vitamin K deficiency is treated with FFP.

Factor inhibitors: Bleeding mimics hemophilia A and B. A factor inhibitor is diagnosed with a mixing study that fails to correct the coagulation abnormality.

DIC: Characteristic findings are thrombocytopenia, prolonged PT and aPTT, decreased serum fibrinogen level, and elevated serum D-dimer. Schistocytes are seen on a peripheral blood smear.

Approach to excessive warfarin administration depends on the presence of bleeding and INR value.

- INR <5 without bleeding: Hold the next dose of warfarin and/or the maintenance dose.
- INR 5-9 without bleeding: Temporarily stop warfarin and add a small dose of oral vitamin K.
- Significant bleeding: Stop warfarin and administer IV vitamin K and FFP.
- Urgent situations (intracranial bleeding): recombinant human factor VIIa or prothrombin complex concentrate.

STUDY TABLE: Causes of Common Coagulation Abnormality Patterns	
Laboratory Findings	**Cause**
Increased PT and aPTT	Clotting factor deficiency (multiple factor deficiency or single deficiency from common pathway)
	Warfarin (mainly PT)
Increased PT and normal aPTT	Factor VII deficiency
Normal PT and increased aPTT that corrects with mixing studies	Factor deficiency (VIII, IX, XI, or XII)
	Factor XII deficiency if no evidence of bleeding
	UFH
Increased aPTT (normal PT) that does not correct with mixing studies	Circulating anticoagulant (inhibitor)

Hemophilia

Diagnosis

Factor VIII (hemophilia A) and factor IX (hemophilia B) deficiencies are X-linked disorders with clinical manifestations seen almost exclusively in men and should be considered in patients with a personal or family history of spontaneous, excessive posttraumatic, or unexpected surgical bleeding. Mild hemophilia can be missed until adulthood.

The PT is normal and the aPTT is abnormal in hemophilia A and B. A factor deficiency is confirmed by a mixing study using the patient's plasma and normal plasma. The results of a mixing study will normalize in a patient with a factor deficiency but will remain abnormal if an inhibitor is present. Factor XI deficiency is rare and is most prevalent in persons of Ashkenazi Jewish descent. Affected patients typically do not have excessive bleeding; they have a prolonged aPTT but normal PT, thrombin time, and bleeding time. Inherited factor XII deficiency is also rare and usually does not cause excessive bleeding; it is associated with a prolonged aPTT.

Therapy

Transfusions and factor VIII or factor IX replacement are indicated for patients with hemophilia A or B, respectively, and life-threatening or severe bleeding. Patients with mild hemophilia A should be given desmopressin for acute bleeding or before undergoing minimally invasive procedures (dental procedures). Prophylactic factor replacement has been proven to reduce the incidence of arthropathy in patients with severe hemophilia.

❖ **Test Yourself**

A 57-year-old man has a left-sided ecchymosis. The hemoglobin concentration is 8.0 g/dL, platelet count is 220,000/microliter, PT is 12 seconds, and aPTT is 67 seconds. The abnormal aPTT does not correct with a mixing study.

ANSWER: The diagnosis is acquired factor VIII inhibitor.

von Willebrand Disease

Diagnosis

The most common inherited bleeding disorder is vWD, an autosomal dominant disorder. Clinically, patients have mild-to-moderate bleeding evidenced by nosebleeds, heavy menstrual flow, gingival bleeding, easy bruising, and bleeding associated with surgery or trauma. vWF adheres platelets to injured vessels and acts as a carrier for factor VIII. Secondary hemostatic dysfunction can occur because of concomitantly low factor VIII levels in vWD. This distinction is important for treatment purposes.

Diagnostic testing includes a prolonged bleeding time and a normal or prolonged aPTT. Definitive diagnosis is based on the vWF antigen level, vWF activity assay, factor VIII level, and a multimer study used to diagnose subtypes of vWD.

Therapy

Select DDAVP for mild to moderate bleeding or before minor invasive procedures (dental procedures). Intermediate-purity factor VIII concentrates, which contain vWF, can also be given.

◆ DON'T BE TRICKED

- **Do not use cryoprecipitate to treat vWD because of its increased transfusion infection risk.**

❖ Test Yourself

A 33-year-old man is evaluated for continued bleeding following a tooth extraction. His mother has easy bruising, and his sister required a transfusion following the birth of her first child. The hemoglobin concentration is 13.0 g/dL, and the platelet count is 210,000/microliter.

ANSWER: The probable diagnosis is vWD. Order an aPTT and bleeding time as an initial screening.

Transfusion Medicine

Treatment Parameters

Erythrocytes, platelets, plasma, cryoprecipitates, and (rarely) whole blood may be used for transfusion. Each unit of packed red blood cells results in an increase of hemoglobin of 1 g/dL. Each unit of platelets transfused results in a 20,000 to 30,000/microliter increase in platelets. An inadequate platelet increment after platelet transfusion may point to conditions that cause increased platelet consumption, such as fever and sepsis, or may indicate the development of antibodies to antigens expressed on platelets. FFP is used to replace coagulation factors. Cryoprecipitates (factor VIII, fibrinogen, vWF) are an adjunct to FFP replacement therapy and are used mainly for their fibrinogen content in patients with DIC.

In emergencies:

- Group O erythrocytes can be transfused to anyone.
- Group AB plasma and platelets can be transfused to anyone.
- Rh-positive patients can safely receive either D-positive or D-negative blood, but Rh-negative patients must receive D-negative blood and platelets.

Transfusion Reactions

An acute hemolytic transfusion reaction results from ABO incompatibility. Characteristic findings are fever, chills, flank and abdominal pain, dyspnea, hypotension, and tachycardia, as well as red plasma and urine and the presence of free hemoglobin in the plasma. A Coombs test is positive. The transfusion must be stopped and blood bank notified. Measures must be initiated to maintain urine output.

A delayed hemolytic transfusion reaction is due to delayed emergence of an alloantibody that causes rapid extravascular clearance of transfused erythrocytes 1 to 3 days after transfusion. Characteristic findings are an unexplained drop in hemoglobin concentration, elevated serum bilirubin and LDH levels, increased reticulocyte count, decreased haptoglobin concentration, and the presence of a new alloantibody.

Posttransfusion purpura is associated with thrombocytopenia that occurs ≥1 week after a transfusion. This reaction is most common in women who become sensitized to HPA-1a after pregnancy or an earlier transfusion. A subsequent transfusion may then cause immune-mediated thrombocytopenia. The diagnosis is made by an assay showing antibodies to HPA-1a. Treatment is IV immune globulin.

A febrile nonhemolytic transfusion reaction occurs at the end of or after a transfusion and is caused by donor leukocyte cytokines or recipient alloantibodies directed against donor leukocytes. The transfusion is stopped, a hemolytic transfusion reaction is ruled out, and antipyretic agents and corticosteroids are given. Cytokine reactions can be prevented if leukocyte reduction is performed before storage rather than during transfusion, whereas leukocyte antibody reactions are prevented by either bedside leukocyte filtration or prestorage leukoreduction.

Transfusion-related acute lung injury (TRALI) is a rare, severe reaction caused by donor antileukocyte antibodies reacting with recipient leukocytes and causing leukocyte aggregation in the pulmonary capillary bed, usually occurring during or within 6 hours of a transfusion. Characteristic findings are hypoxemia, noncardiogenic pulmonary edema, and ARDS. The transfusion is stopped, respiratory support is provided, and vasopressors are given for hypotension.

An allergic transfusion reaction occurs when donor plasma constituents react with a recipient's IgE on mast cells. Characteristic findings are rash, hives, wheezing, and mucosal edema. Treatment includes antihistamines and corticosteroids.

Transfusion-associated GVHD is a rare but fatal complication in which donor lymphocytes engraft in an immunocompromised recipient and cause reactions that affect the bone marrow, skin, liver, and GI tract. Patients at risk include those undergoing chemotherapy, recipients of blood components from first-degree relatives, and premature infants. Transfusion-associated GVHD is prevented by gamma irradiation of cellular blood components in at-risk populations.

STUDY TABLE: Threshold Values for Prophylactic Transfusion	
Condition	**Threshold to Transfuse**
Platelet transfusion; no other risk factors for bleeding	10,000/µL
Platelet transfusion for pulmonary hemorrhage or intracranial bleeding	40,000-50,000/µL
Hemoglobin for most patients	7.0 g/dL
Hemoglobin for patients with acute MI	10.0 g/dL
µL = microliter.	

Thrombophilia

Screening asymptomatic patients for thrombophilia is not recommended.

Diagnosis

Thrombophilia, which increases the risk of thrombosis, is associated with risk factors that may be congenital or acquired, permanent or transient. In patients with an established initial episode of venous thrombosis, no consensus exists regarding whom to test for the inherited thrombophilias, because findings are unlikely to alter intensity or duration of anticoagulation. The risk of recurrent thrombosis is high in patients with idiopathic DVT regardless of whether an inherited thrombophilic disorder is present. Testing might be considered in patients who are strongly thrombophilic:

- first episode of idiopathic DVT before age 50 years
- history of recurrent DVT
- first-degree relative with a history of idiopathic thrombosis before age 50 years

Factor V Leiden and prothrombin gene mutations are by far the most common defects. Other causes include hyperhomocysteinemia, protein C, protein S, and antithrombin deficiencies. Factor V Leiden mutation is the most common hereditary thrombophilia in white populations. The factor V Leiden mutation is tested by screening for resistance to activated protein C with a clotting assay and then confirming positive results by genetic analysis. A molecular genetic test is used to diagnose the prothrombin G20210A mutation. Testing should not be done in the setting of an acute thrombotic event but rather weeks or months after it has occurred and when anticoagulant therapy has been discontinued, because active thrombosis and anticoagulation may alter the level of some proteins.

The antiphospholipid syndrome is the most common acquired thrombophilia. The antiphospholipid antibody is actually an antibody to a protein bound to a phospholipid identified as β_2-glycoprotein 1. There is also a strong correlation between this syndrome and pregnancy loss. The presence of a lupus anticoagulant is suggested by a prolonged aPTT. If the aPTT is prolonged, a mixing study is done. If a lupus anticoagulant is present, mixing the patient's plasma with normal plasma will not correct the prolonged aPTT. The presence of anticardiolipin antibodies is determined by IgG and IgM ELISA. Any positive result should be confirmed later to rule out transient abnormalities from viral infection.

STUDY TABLE: Diagnosis of Antiphospholipid Syndrome	
Clinical Criteria	**Laboratory Criteria**
Presence of at least 1 of the following: vascular thrombosis pregnancy morbidity (fetal death, spontaneous abortion, premature delivery)	Presence of at least 1 of the following: lupus anticoagulant anticardiolipin antibody anti-β_2-glycoprotein 1 antibody

Skin necrosis has been reported within the first days of receiving large doses of warfarin because of rapid depletion of protein C and the development of a hypercoagulable state.

◆ DON'T BE TRICKED

- **Do not test patients for antithrombin, protein C, or protein S deficiency during an acute VTE.**
- **Tests for deficiencies of antithrombin, protein C, and protein S and the presence of a lupus anticoagulant should not be done less than 2 weeks after the completion of anticoagulation.**

Therapy

The treatment of patients with an inherited thrombophilia and DVT is generally the same as for those patients without an inherited thrombophilia. For individuals with antiphospholipid syndrome and a thromboembolic event, long-term oral anticoagulant therapy is indicated.

❖ Test Yourself

A 23-year-old woman with a history of two miscarriages develops a VTE. Before beginning heparin, the aPTT is found to be prolonged.

ANSWER: The probable diagnosis is a lupus anticoagulant. A mixing study is indicated.

Multiple Myeloma

Diagnosis

Plasma cell dyscrasias consist of abnormal clonal proliferation of immunoglobulin-secreting differentiated B-lymphoid cells and plasma cells. Multiple myeloma is the most common malignant plasma cell dyscrasia. Other plasma cell dyscrasias include monoclonal gammopathy of undetermined significance (MGUS), Waldenström macroglobulinemia, and light-chain–associated amyloidosis (AL amyloidosis). Characteristic findings for multiple myeloma include:

- anemia (with rouleaux formation)
- kidney disease
- hypercalcemia
- vertebral compression fractures, osteoporosis, osteopenia, and lytic bone lesions
- (rarely) hyperviscosity syndrome (IgM monoclonal gammopathy: blurred vision, fatigue, mucosal bleeding, HF, headache, and altered mentation)

Diagnostic studies include serum and urine protein electrophoresis, measurement of serum quantitative immunoglobulins with immunofixation, 24-hour urine protein electrophoresis with immunofixation, radiographic bone survey including the long bones, and a bone marrow biopsy. Laboratory findings show an M protein spike on serum or urine protein electrophoresis and a low to nonexistent anion gap.

STUDY TABLE: Diagnosis of Multiple Myeloma and MGUS	
Multiple Myeloma/MGUS	**Findings**
Multiple myeloma	1. Serum or urine monoclonal protein
	2. Bone marrow clonal plasma cells or plasmacytoma
	3. End-organ damage related to plasma cells (e.g., hypercalcemia, kidney injury, lytic bone lesions, anemia)
MGUS	Serum monoclonal protein <3 g
	Bone marrow clonal plasma cells <10%
	No end-organ damage

Evaluate for amyloidosis if hepatomegaly is present. Amyloidosis is also associated with macroglossia, HF, and kidney failure with large kidneys. Confirmation of AL amyloidosis requires detection of a plasma cell dyscrasia by serum and urine immunofixation electrophoresis, serum free light-chain assay, and immunohistochemistry studies of the bone marrow biopsy or fat pad aspiration.

Therapy

Strive to achieve a complete response with early use of dose-intensive chemotherapy with autologous stem cell transplantation for patients <75 years of age. The preferred pretransplant induction chemotherapeutic regimen is combination therapy with dexamethasone plus lenalidomide or thalidomide.

Patients who are not transplant candidates are treated with melphalan and prednisone, because this regimen compares favorably with other multidrug combinations. Bortezomib can be used alone or in combination as initial therapy or for relapsed myeloma.

Supportive care includes:

- plasmapheresis for patients with hyperviscosity syndrome
- corticosteroids and radiation therapy to treat spinal cord compression
- radiation therapy or surgery for pathologic fractures or symptomatic local disease
- pamidronate or zoledronate to reduce the risk of a skeletal event
- erythropoietin to help improve anemia and quality of life
- prophylactic immunizations for pneumonia and influenza (mandatory)
- immunoglobulin infusion to benefit patients with recurrent bacterial infections
- varicella-zoster vaccine for patients receiving bortezomib

◆ DON'T BE TRICKED
- **Do not treat MGUS or asymptomatic myeloma.**
- **Do not use melphalan induction therapy for candidates for stem cell transplantation.**

Chronic Myeloid Leukemia

Diagnosis

The myeloproliferative disorders are a group of clonal stem cell disorders characterized by aberrant regulation of proliferation that results in excess production of myeloid elements in the bone marrow. These include essential thrombocythemia and disorders of erythrocytes (polycythemia vera), fibroblasts (myelofibrosis), and granulocytes (chronic myeloid leukemia). CML is a clonal hematopoietic stem cell disorder characterized by myeloid proliferation associated with a (9;22) (q34;q11) translocation, the Philadelphia chromosome. Patients usually present in the chronic phase and may do well for years. CML may transform into acute leukemia (myeloid in two thirds of patients, lymphoid in one third of patients). The transformation may be recognized as an accelerated phase or as blast crisis.

Characteristic findings in asymptomatic patients are splenomegaly, an elevated leukocyte count, and increased number of granulocytic cells in all phases of development on the peripheral blood smear. Very immature cells or blasts represent 1% to 5% of the granulocytes, with increasing numbers of promyelocytes, myelocytes, and metamyelocytes. When blasts represent more than 10% of the leukocytes, accelerated (10%-20%) or blast phase (>20%) should be considered.

The diagnosis is confirmed by cytogenetic study of the bone marrow aspirate showing a t(9:22) chromosomal abnormality or the presence of the novel *bcr-abl* gene produced by the translocation.

Therapy

STUDY TABLE: Therapy for CML	
Treatment	**Goal**
Hydroxyurea	Palliative, only to alleviate leukocytosis and splenomegaly
Imatinib mesylate, dasatinib, and nilotinib	Disease control with lifelong treatment; eradicating the Philadelphia chromosome and achieving molecular remission in patients with chronic-phase CML
Allogeneic HSCT	Potential cure for younger patients with stable chronic disease and in some patients with accelerated disease or blast crisis

Use platelet transfusion for patients with bleeding or a platelet count <10,000/microliter. Select splenectomy for patients with advanced disease who no longer respond to imatinib mesylate and have painful splenomegaly, thrombocytopenia, and a high transfusion requirement.

❖ **Test Yourself**

An asymptomatic 54-year-old man has an enlarged spleen. The hemoglobin concentration is 13.0 g/dL, platelet count is 470,000/microliter, and leukocyte count is 170,000/microliter, with mostly segmented and band neutrophils and circulating metamyelocytes and myelocytes.

ANSWER: The probable diagnosis is CML. Order cytogenetic analysis of bone marrow cells.

Essential Thrombocythemia

Diagnosis

Essential thrombocythemia, the most common myeloproliferative disorder, occurs in middle-aged and older adults and is characterized by thrombotic and hemorrhagic complications. It is a stem cell disorder marked by a predominant increase in megakaryocytes and platelet counts greater than 600,000/microliter. Symptoms include:

- vasomotor disturbances such as erythromelalgia (red and painful hands or feet with warmth and swelling)
- livedo reticularis
- headache
- vision symptoms
- arterial or venous thromboses

Splenomegaly (up to 50%) may be present. The *JAK2* mutation is found in about half of cases and may help distinguish essential thrombocythemia from secondary thrombocythemia due to bleeding, iron deficiency, chronic inflammatory diseases, and cancer.

Therapy

The platelet count must be lowered quickly in patients with life-threatening symptoms, such as a TIA, stroke, MI, or GI bleeding. Platelet apheresis along with cytoreductive therapy with hydroxyurea is indicated for these patients. For patients with less urgent symptoms, myelosuppression is instituted with lower doses of hydroxyurea, anagrelide, or interferon alfa plus low-dose aspirin. Erythromelalgia responds to low-dose aspirin. Asymptomatic patients can be followed with observation alone or with observation plus low-dose aspirin.

◆ DON'T BE TRICKED

- **Asymptomatic patients <60 years of age without a history of thrombosis and a platelet count <1.5 million/microliter do not require therapy.**

❖ Test Yourself

A 67-year-old man is evaluated because of red and warm painful feet and a platelet count of 975,000/microliter.

ANSWER: The diagnosis is essential thrombocythemia. Prescribe hydroxyurea. Low-dose aspirin can be used to treat the erythromelalgia.

Polycythemia Vera

Diagnosis

PV is characterized by an increased red blood cell mass and may be accompanied by a mild elevation in leukocyte and platelet counts. Characteristic findings are thrombosis or bleeding, facial plethora, erythromelalgia, pruritus exacerbated by hot water (bathing), and splenomegaly. Serious complications may include TIA, MI or stroke, DVT, and Budd-Chiari syndrome.

Repeatedly elevated hematocrit values >60% for men and >56% for women, the presence of *JAK2* V617F mutation in the absence of secondary causes of erythrocytosis, and the presence of splenomegaly establish the diagnosis. A *JAK2* mutation is detected in 95% of patients and can aid in distinguishing PV from secondary causes of erythrocytosis. Low erythropoietin values are highly specific for PV, whereas values above normal suggest secondary erythrocytosis. Bone marrow biopsy will show hypercellularity.

Causes of secondary polycythemia include hypoxemia (most common), volume contraction due to diuretics, use of androgens, and secretion of erythropoietin by kidney or liver carcinoma.

Therapy

Therapeutic phlebotomy should be instituted with the goal of lowering the hematocrit level to <42% in women and <45% in men. Low-dose aspirin is indicated unless the patient has symptoms of easy bruising and an acquired platelet disorder. Hyperuricemia is treated with allopurinol, and patients with pruritus are given antihistamines. Hydroxyurea in addition to phlebotomy is often the treatment of choice for patients at high risk for thrombosis (e.g., >60 years, previous thrombosis).

◆ DON'T BE TRICKED

- **Do not prescribe high-dose aspirin, which may cause increased bleeding.**

❖ Test Yourself

A 67-year-old man has intolerable pruritus. He does not smoke and takes no medications. The hematocrit value is 60%, and he has splenomegaly.

ANSWER: The probable diagnosis is PV. Order PCR for *JAK2* mutation and measure erythropoietin level.

Myelofibrosis with Myeloid Metaplasia

Diagnosis

Myelofibrosis with myeloid metaplasia causes clonal proliferation of abnormal hematopoietic stem cells that release fibrosis-promoting cytokines in the bone marrow. The disorder is characterized by splenomegaly, normocytic anemia, circulating erythroblasts and myeloid precursors, giant platelets, teardrop cells, and bone marrow fibrosis. Splenomegaly and hepatomegaly result from extramedullary hematopoiesis, and patients can develop portal hypertension. Death commonly results from bone marrow failure, transformation to acute leukemia, or portal hypertension complications.

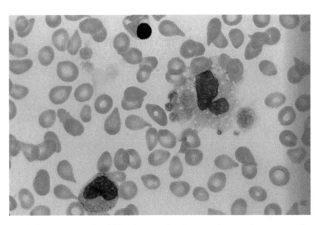

Myelofibrosis: Peripheral blood smear showing tear drop erythrocytes, nucleated erythrocytes, and giant platelets characteristic of myelofibrosis.

Therapy

Therapy is usually supportive. Allogeneic stem cell transplantation is indicated for patients <60 years of age.

◆ **DON'T BE TRICKED**

- Splenectomy is contraindicated because it is associated with hemorrhagic and thrombotic complications, increased risk of progression to leukemia, and no impact on survival.

Myelodysplastic Syndromes

Diagnosis

MDS are clonal disorders of the hematopoietic stem cells that occur predominantly in patients older than 50 years and are characterized by ineffective hematopoiesis and peripheral cytopenias; bone marrow findings show a hypercellular marrow with dyserythropoiesis. Look for cytopenia in at least 2 of 3 cell lines (anemia, leukopenia, thrombocytopenia) and morphologic abnormalities of erythrocytes (macrocytosis with nucleated erythrocytes and teardrop cells). Half of patients may present only with anemia and an elevated MCV. MDS are acquired or secondary to previous radiation or chemotherapy. Detection of clonal abnormalities commonly involving chromosomes 3, 5, 7, 8, and 17 supports the diagnosis. Look for the 5q– syndrome, a subtype of MDS that has a specific therapy. The differential diagnosis includes vitamin B$_{12}$ and folate deficiency, alcohol- or drug-induced cytopenias, and myeloproliferative syndromes. Most patients eventually progress to leukemic syndromes or die of complications of bone marrow failure.

Therapy

Observation is indicated for asymptomatic patients at low risk. The standard of care for symptomatic patients comprises supportive care with cytokines (erythropoietin and granulocyte colony-stimulating factor), erythrocyte and platelet transfusions, and treatment of infections. Use lenalidomide for the specific treatment of 5q-syndrome, because more than two thirds of patients with this syndrome will respond. Select allogeneic stem cell transplantation for young patients who have an HLA-matched sibling donor.

Chronic Lymphocytic Leukemia

Diagnosis

CLL is the most common leukemia encountered in adults. Patients may be asymptomatic or have nonspecific symptoms of fever, night sweats, weight loss, fatigue, or malaise. Splenomegaly and lymphadenopathy may be present.

The key to diagnosis is the recognition of an increased leukocyte count because of increased numbers of mature lymphocytes and "smudge" cells (lymphocytes that appear flattened or distorted) on peripheral smear. The diagnosis of CLL is confirmed by an absolute increase in mature lymphocytes (>5000/microliter). Immunophenotyping by flow cytometry is necessary and will show a mature B-cell lymphocyte phenotype with expression of CD19 and CD20 along with expression of a T-lymphocyte antigen, CD5. Patients may also have autoimmune hemolytic anemia and/or ITP.

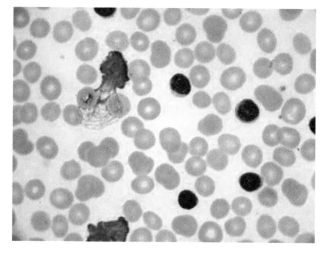

CLL "Smudge Cell": Peripheral blood smear showing a "smudge cell," which is a lymphocyte that appears flattened or distorted that is characteristic of CLL.

Staging of CLL requires clinical assessment for lymphadenopathy and enlargement of the liver and spleen. This is complemented by CT scans of the chest and abdomen to confirm the extent of lymphadenopathy. Because of the association between warm autoimmune hemolytic anemia and CLL, a direct Coombs test is obtained in anemic patients and when spherocytes are observed on the peripheral blood smear.

Transformed CLL is an aggressive relapse with B symptoms (fever, night sweats, loss of >10% of body weight), massive lymphadenopathy, and hepatosplenomegaly (Richter transformation). Restaging is required for patients with transformed CLL.

Therapy

Therapy is reserved for symptomatic patients; typically patients with advanced-stage disease, high tumor burden, severe disease-related B symptoms, or repeated infections.

STUDY TABLE: Drug Treatment for CLL	
Indication	**Treatment**
Early-stage disease	No treatment
Stage III/IV disease	Young patients: Fludarabine plus cyclophosphamide and rituximab
	Older patients: Chlorambucil single agent (well tolerated for symptom control)
Relapse >1 year after initial remission	Repeat initial therapy

Radiation therapy is used to treat localized painful or massive lymphadenopathy. Splenectomy is indicated for persistent cytopenia or symptoms related to splenomegaly. Consider hematopoietic stem cell transplantation for eligible patients with persistent relapsing or refractory disease or those with histologic transformation.

Hairy Cell Leukemia

Diagnosis

Hairy cell leukemia affects older and usually male patients and is characterized by splenomegaly, leukopenia or pancytopenia, and bone marrow infiltration by atypical lymphoid cells with cytoplasmic projections ("hairy cells"). The bone marrow is usually fibrotic and is not easily aspirated, and cells express CD11$^+$ and CD103$^+$ on flow cytometry.

Therapy

Treat with the purine analog cladribine.

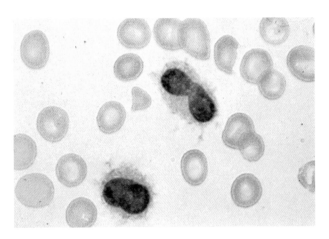

Hairy Cell Leukemia: Atypical lymphocytes with cytoplasmic projections characteristic of hairy cell leukemia.

Acute Lymphoblastic Leukemia/Lymphoma

Diagnosis

ALL is an extremely aggressive disease of precursor T or B cells. The usual presenting clinical features include rapidly rising blast cells in the blood and bone marrow, bulky lymphadenopathy (especially in the mediastinum), a younger age at onset, and cytopenia secondary to bone marrow involvement. Up to 30% of patients with ALL have CNS involvement.

Therapy

Induction therapy involves intensive combination chemotherapy often followed by allogeneic stem cell transplantation consolidation. CNS prophylaxis (intrathecal chemotherapy with or without radiation) and irradiation of bulky tumor masses are also indicated.

Acute Myeloid Leukemia

Diagnosis

AML is a malignant clonal proliferation of myeloid cells that do not fully mature. AML can appear de novo; arise after exposure to radiation, benzene, or chemotherapy; or occur as a result of transformation of a myeloproliferative disorder, such as CML or polycythemia vera. Myelodysplastic syndromes may transform into AML.

AML presents with fatigue, pallor, and easy bleeding. Of all the leukemias, AML will most likely involve significant thrombocytopenia with bleeding, bruising, petechiae, and infection. Patients with AML do not develop lymphadenopathy or hepatosplenomegaly; if present, these findings suggest an alternative or concomitant diagnosis. When the leukocyte count is very high, patients may present with leukostasis syndrome characterized by tissue hypoxia because of reduced blood flow.

The diagnosis of AML is suggested by:

- an elevated leukocyte count
- anemia

- thrombocytopenia
- blasts on the peripheral blood smear

Gingival hypertrophy and leukemia cutis (violaceous, nontender cutaneous plaques) are commonly encountered. Pathognomonic Auer rods may be seen on a peripheral blood smear. The diagnosis is confirmed by bone marrow aspiration and biopsy showing >20% blasts. Typical myeloblasts demonstrate antigens found on immature cells such as CD34 (stem cell marker) and HLA-DR, as well as antigens more specific for granulocytic maturation such as CD33 and CD13. Cytogenetic studies are crucial, because three typical abnormalities carry a good prognosis: t(8;21), t(15:17), and inv(16) or t(16;16). Loss or deletion of chromosome 7 and more complex cytogenetic abnormalities have a poor prognosis. The morphology of the bone marrow cells combined with immunophenotype and cytogenetic studies are used to further classify AML according to the WHO or FAB classification systems.

Acute promyelocytic leukemia is a special case marked by the t(15;17) translocation, which disturbs a retinoic acid receptor. Patients with acute promyelocytic leukemia have significant bleeding because of fibrinolysis and DIC.

Tumor lysis syndrome may develop in treated patients and causes a release of intracellular metabolites (uric acid, potassium, and phosphorus).

Therapy

Platelet transfusion is indicated for patients with hemorrhage or a platelet count <10,000/microliter. Only filtered and irradiated blood products should be used.

Drug therapy and indications are as follows:

- vigorous hydration and allopurinol or rasburicase before chemotherapy to prevent the tumor lysis syndrome
- hemodialysis for acute kidney failure related to tumor lysis syndrome
- cytarabine and an anthracycline (daunorubicin or idarubicin) to induce higher remission rates
- ATRA for acute promyelocytic leukemia
- gemtuzumab ozogamicin to induce remission in relapsed older adult patients with CD33+ AML
- leukapheresis for leukostasis syndrome (usually WBC >50,000/microliter); symptoms include CNS manifestations, hypoxia, and diffuse infiltrates on chest radiograph
- allogeneic and autologous stem cell transplantation for first relapse or second complete remission

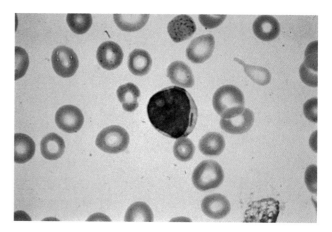

Auer Rod: This myeloblast has a large nucleus, displaced nuclear chromatin, azurophile cytoplasmic granules, and a rod-shaped inclusion (Auer rod), findings associated with AML.

Patients taking ATRA are at risk for developing retinoic acid syndrome. Characteristic findings are fever, pulmonary infiltrates, hypoxemia, and, occasionally, hyperleukocytosis. Treatment is dexamethasone.

Infectious Disease

Fever

Diagnosis

The major causes of fever are infections, neoplasms, and noninfectious inflammatory diseases. Most outpatients with fever have a viral illness that will resolve within 2 weeks. Fevers in hospitalized patients should prompt considerations of the following infectious sources:

- intravascular catheters (bacteremia)
- urinary catheters (UTIs)
- nasogastric tubes (sinusitis)
- recent foreign-body insertions (infected joint replacements, vascular grafts, pacemakers)
- blood transfusions (febrile transfusion reactions)
- decubitus ulcers
- venous thromboembolism

Drug-induced fever can occur at any time but usually appears days to weeks after initiation of a new drug. Associated features may include rash, urticaria, liver or kidney dysfunction, and mucosal ulceration. Laboratory value abnormalities may include elevated serum aminotransferases, leukocytosis or leukopenia, and eosinophilia. Look especially for use of anticonvulsants (phenytoin, carbamazepine), antibiotics (β-lactams, sulfonamides, nitrofurantoin), and allopurinol.

Fever of unknown origin is characterized by a temperature >38.3 °C (100.9 °F) for at least 3 weeks that remains undiagnosed after three outpatient visits or 1 week of inpatient evaluation. The most common cause of a fever of unknown origin is a common illness presenting in an atypical manner. The most common infectious causes of fever of unknown origin are tuberculosis, infective endocarditis, and abdominal or pelvic abscesses.

❖ **Test Yourself**

A 22-year-old woman begins taking phenytoin after undergoing a craniotomy for a subdural hematoma. Twelve days later, she develops a temperature of 38.3 °C (100.9 °F) and a generalized erythematous rash. The leukocyte count is 12,800/microliter with eosinophilia, serum AST level is 66 units/L, and ALT level is 72 units/L.

ANSWER: Select DRESS, also known as hypersensitivity syndrome.

Sepsis

Diagnosis

Sepsis is a documented or presumed infection with some of the clinical and laboratory features of the SIRS.

STUDY TABLE: SIRS, Sepsis, Severe Sepsis, and Septic Shock

Syndrome	Definition
SIRS	Two or more of the following:
	Temperature >38.0 °C (100.4 °F) or <36.0 °C (96.8 °F)
	Heart rate >90/min
	Respiration rate >20/min or arterial P_{CO_2} <32 mm Hg
	Leukocyte count >12,000/μL or <4000/μL with 10% bands (in absence of other known cause of this condition)
Sepsis	Presence of a known or suspected infection (documented positive cultures are not required) and ≥2 criteria for SIRS
Severe sepsis	Organ dysfunction, hypoperfusion, or hypotension. Hypoperfusion and hypotension abnormalities may include, but are not limited to, lactic acidosis, oliguria, or an acute alteration in mental status.
Septic shock	Sepsis-induced hypotension and perfusion abnormalities develop despite adequate fluid resuscitation.

μL = microliter.

Know the differential diagnosis of shock syndromes and their associated hemodynamic parameters (see also Pulmonary Artery Catheterization table in Pulmonary and Critical Care Medicine).

STUDY TABLE: Shock Syndromes

Condition	Characteristics
Cardiogenic shock	Low cardiac output, elevated PCWP, and high SVR
Hypovolemic shock	Low cardiac output, low PCWP, and high SVR
Obstructive shock	Low cardiac output, low PCWP, high SVR. Consider cardiac tamponade, pulmonary embolism, and tension pneumothorax.
Anaphylactic shock	High cardiac output, normal PCWP, and low SVR. Rash, urticaria, angioedema, and wheezing/stridor.
Septic shock	High cardiac output (early) that can become depressed (late) and low SVR. Fever and leukocytosis.

PCWP = pulmonary capillary wedge pressure; SVR = systemic vascular resistance.

Therapy

Early goal-directed therapy refers to the concept of early restoration of hemodynamic stability during the first 6 hours of hospitalization. The goals of treatment are:

- identify, remove, or treat source of infection
- CVP of 8-12 mm Hg
- mean arterial pressure (MAP) >65 mm Hg ([(2 × diastolic) + systolic] / 3)
- urine output >0.5 mL/kg/h
- central venous oxygen saturation (SvcO2) >70%

To achieve these goals:

- give crystalloid or colloid aggressively (500-1000 mL) until the CVP goal is obtained
- if CVP goal is met but MAP remains <65 mm Hg, choose vasoactive agents (norepinephrine or dopamine)
- if CVP and MAP goals are met but SvcO2 is <70%, select transfusion if the hematocrit is <30%, or add inotropic agents (dopamine or dobutamine) if the hematocrit is ≥30%

If the source of infection is unknown, choose empiric broad-spectrum antibiotics based on specific parameters:

- for community-acquired infections, choose monotherapy with a third-generation cephalosporin or a carbapenem (consider addition of vancomycin based on local bacterial resistance patterns)
- for healthcare-associated infections (or for patients who are immunosuppressed or have recently received antibiotics), choose vancomycin, an antipseudomonal β-lactam, and a fluoroquinolone or an aminoglycoside
- for toxic shock syndrome, select carbapenem or penicillin with a β-lactamase inhibitor plus clindamycin

Remember indications for other therapy, including:

- low tidal volume mechanical ventilation (6 mL/kg) and plateau pressures ≤30 cm H2O for ARDS
- maintenance of blood glucose <200 mg/dL

- low-dose corticosteroids for 100 hours to reduce short-term mortality and ICU stay in patients with blood pressure <90 mm Hg despite fluids and vasopressors

◆ DON'T BE TRICKED

- **Do not routinely choose pulmonary artery catheterization in patients with sepsis.**
- **High-dose corticosteroids provide no survival advantage for patients in septic shock and may cause harm.**
- **Do not select epinephrine for vasoconstrictor therapy.**

Toxic Shock Syndrome

Diagnosis

Toxic shock syndrome is characterized by fever, vomiting, diarrhea, hypotension, and a rash. Exfoliation (peeling) of the skin occurs several days after the onset of the infection.

Staphylococcus aureus and group A β-hemolytic streptococci are the usual causative microorganisms. The syndrome is caused by bacterial exotoxins that act as superantigens.

Look for:

- menstruation history and tampon use
- abscess, nasal packings, and gauze-packed wounds
- fever >38.9 °C (102.0 °F) and hypotension (systolic blood pressure <90 mm Hg)
- diffuse sunburn-type rash or erythema
- multisystem organ failure: kidney, liver, GI tract, ARDS, coagulopathy

Therapy

Remove sources of infection and toxin production. Select aggressive IV fluid resuscitation (up to 10-20 L/d). Start broad-spectrum antibiotics initially with a carbapenem or penicillin with a β-lactamase inhibitor plus clindamycin; narrow to clindamycin plus nafcillin when the susceptible organism is identified. IV immune globulin may be helpful.

◆ DON'T BE TRICKED

- **Do not select corticosteroids to treat toxic shock syndrome.**

❖ Test Yourself

A 25-year-old man has three episodes of epistaxis that are stopped by packing his nares with petrolatum-covered cotton balls. The next day, he is confused, his temperature is 39.0 °C (102.2 °F), and blood pressure is 90/82 mm Hg. Erythema of his face, shoulders, and palms is present. The nasal packing is still in place.

ANSWER: Diagnose toxic shock syndrome, remove the nasal packing, and begin antibiotics.

Catheter-Associated UTIs

Prevention

CAUTIs can be prevented by using a urinary catheter only when indicated and removing it as soon as possible. For patients who require long-term catheter drainage of the bladder, intermittent catheter drainage reduces the risk of infection. Maintain a closed catheter system at all times, and keep the catheter bag below the level of the bladder.

Diagnosis

Typical signs and symptoms of UTI may not be present in a catheterized patient. Obtain urine cultures in patients with symptoms attributable to the urinary tract or in patients with altered mental status or fever.

Therapy

If a CAUTI is suspected, management includes catheter removal and urine culture. In general, cefotaxime, ceftriaxone, ciprofloxacin, or levofloxacin is used for suspected gram-negative infection and vancomycin for suspected staphylococcal or enterococcal infection.

◆ DON'T BE TRICKED

- **In patients with a urinary catheter, do not obtain routine urinalysis or cultures and do not treat asymptomatic bacteriuria.**
- **Don't treat asymptomatic candiduria with antifungal therapy; do remove the catheter.**

Hospital-Acquired and Ventilator-Associated Pneumonia

Prevention

HAP is defined as occurring ≥48 hours after admission. Ventilator-associated pneumonia (VAP), a subset of HAP, is defined as occurring >48 hours after endotracheal intubation.

Procedures to reduce VAP include:

- following weaning protocols for timely extubation
- keeping the head of the bed elevated >30 degrees
- avoiding nasal intubation and nasogastric tubes
- using chlorhexidine mouth rinse and subglottic suction catheters

Diagnosis

The diagnosis of HAP is based on a new or progressive radiographic infiltrate plus clinical signs of pneumonia (fever, purulent sputum, leukocytosis, hypoxemia).

Therapy

Antibiotic selection is based on the risk for multi–drug-resistant organisms (MDRO). Risk factors for MDRO are current hospitalization ≥5 days, admission from a health care–related facility, recent antibiotic therapy, and immunosuppression. Choose ceftriaxone or levofloxacin for patients with no MDRO risk factors. If MDRO risk factors are present, select broad-spectrum coverage for both gram-positive and gram-negative organisms, including MRSA (vancomycin) and *Pseudomonas aeruginosa* (e.g., cefepime, ceftriaxone). Narrow the empiric therapy based on culture results.

◆ DON'T BE TRICKED

- **Do not delay empiric antibiotic therapy to perform diagnostic studies.**

❖ Test Yourself

A 78-year-old woman was admitted from a skilled nursing facility for treatment of a hip fracture. Two days after admission, she develops a temperature of 38.3 °C (100.9 °F) and a cough. A chest radiograph shows a new left lower lobe infiltrate.

ANSWER: Diagnose HAP and prescribe vancomycin and ceftriaxone.

Clostridium difficile Antibiotic-Associated Diarrhea

Diagnosis

C. difficile antibiotic-associated colitis is produced by two toxins, A and B. Risk factors include use of antibiotics, enemas, intestinal stimulants, and chemotherapeutic agents that alter the colonic flora.

Patients with known or suspected illness should be placed under contact isolation.

Therapy

Discontinue the offending antibiotic. Metronidazole is given orally for mild to moderate *C. difficile* infection and intravenously for those who cannot receive enteral treatment. A first recurrence is treated in the same way as the initial episode, based on disease severity. Vancomycin is reserved for severe disease (leukocytosis, acute kidney injury, hypoalbuminemia). Patients with very severe disease associated with delayed colonic transit may benefit from the addition of IV metronidazole. Consult a surgeon for consideration of colectomy in patients with severe sepsis due to *C. difficile* antibiotic-associated diarrhea. See also *C. difficile* Antibiotic-Associated Diarrhea in the Gastroenterology chapter.

◆ DON'T BE TRICKED

- **Absence of diarrhea does not exclude *C. difficile* antibiotic-associated diarrhea; severe disease can present with colonic ileus.**

Catheter-Related Intravascular Infections

Prevention

The primary risk factor for a catheter-related intravascular infection is the presence of a central venous catheter. Use of IV catheters should be reserved for patients with a proven need, and the catheter should be removed as soon as clinically possible.

STUDY TABLE: Prevention Strategies for Catheter-Related Intravascular Infections	
Choose...	**Do not choose...**
Maximum sterile barrier precautions and chlorhexidine for skin decontamination during catheter insertion	Femoral artery insertion
Antibiotic-coated catheters and dressings	Routine replacement of central venous catheters
Catheter-care teams	Routine dressing changes

Diagnosis

Consider catheter-related infection in any patient with fever and a central venous catheter. Purulence and cellulitis around the catheter site are specific, but not sensitive, for catheter-related infection. Begin the evaluation of suspected infection by culturing the catheter tip.

- If the tip is culture positive and associated with fever or a positive peripheral blood culture, the diagnosis is catheter-related infection.
- If the catheter blood culture is positive at least 2 hours earlier than the peripheral blood culture, a catheter-related infection is likely.

- A negative central blood culture has a good negative predictive value. However, a positive central or peripheral blood culture alone requires clinical interpretation.

Therapy

Remove the catheter in the following situations:

- tunnel or pocket infection
- sepsis
- metastatic infection (septic thrombosis, endocarditis, or osteomyelitis)
- *S. aureus* or gram-negative bacteremia
- fungemia

STUDY TABLE: Catheter-Related Infections		
Condition	**Characteristics**	**Treatment**
Catheter colonization	Positive catheter culture alone without signs or symptoms of infection	No treatment required
Exit-site infection	Positive culture of exudate from catheter site	7 days of antibiotic therapy
Tunnel infection	Erythema, induration, or tenderness along the subcutaneous tunnel	7-21 days of antibiotic therapy and catheter removal
Catheter-related bloodstream infection	Growth of the same organism from cultures of the blood and the catheter	Antibiotic therapy and possible catheter removal required
Complicated catheter infection	Associated endocarditis, septic thrombophlebitis, or metastatic infection	4-6 weeks of antibiotic therapy and catheter removal

Select vancomycin as empiric antibiotic therapy for gram-positive infections; then narrow to oxacillin or nafcillin if methicillin-susceptible *S. aureus* or -sensitive coagulase-negative staphylococcal infection is confirmed. In neutropenic or septic patients, empiric therapy should provide coverage for gram-negative infections, including *Pseudomonas*. Narrow antibiotic selection based on culture and susceptibility results. Treat for 5 to 7 days if blood culture is negative. In otherwise uncomplicated cases, treat for 10 to 14 days after the first negative blood culture is obtained.

Special circumstances:

- if blood culture is positive for *S. aureus*, obtain a TEE
- if TEE is negative for endocarditis, treat for 2 weeks; if TEE is positive for endocarditis, treat for at least 4 weeks
- select fluconazole for candidemia in the absence of sepsis
- select amphotericin B or an echinocandin for severely ill candidemic patients, those with persistent fungemia despite fluconazole, and those with infections caused by *Candida tropicalis* or *Candida krusei*

◆ DON'T BE TRICKED

- **A normal TTE does not exclude endocarditis in the setting of *S. aureus* bacteremia.**
- **Catheter removal is not required for transient coagulase-negative staphylococcal bacteremia.**

Smallpox and Varicella

Diagnosis

The last reported case of smallpox worldwide occurred in 1977. It remains a concern because of the threat of bioterrorism and the need to distinguish smallpox from similar diseases.

To diagnose smallpox, look for:

- fever >38.5 °C (101.3 °F), fatigue, and headache and backaches
- rash beginning 2 to 3 days after onset of fever
- rash beginning on the face, proximal arms, and legs and then spreading to the chest and distal extremities, including the palms and soles
- rash in the same stage at any one time, in any one location of the body (all papules, all vesicles, all pustules, or all crusts)

To diagnose varicella (chickenpox), look for:

- generally mild prodrome of fever and constitutional symptoms in children and adolescents, occurring simultaneously with rash
- rash beginning on the trunk, then spreading to the face and extremities
- rash in different stages (mix of papules, vesicles, pustules, and crusts) at any one time

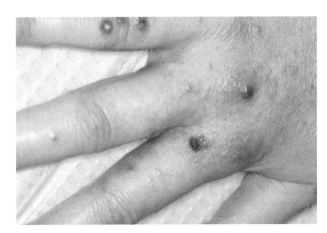

Varicella Infection: Characteristic varicella infection with rash at different stages of development (vesicles, papules, pustules, and crusts) in one region of the body.

Infective Endocarditis

Prevention

Provide prophylaxis for IE only in patients with the highest risk, including:

- prosthetic heart valves or valve repair with prosthetic material
- previous endocarditis
- congenital heart disease
- unrepaired cyanotic congenital heart disease
- palliative shunts and conduits
- prosthetic valve
- repair with prosthetic material or device for the first 6 months after intervention
- valve disease in heart transplant recipients

Prophylaxis is only indicated for the highest risk procedures:

- dental procedures that involve mucosal bleeding
- procedures that involve incision or biopsy of the respiratory mucosa
- procedures in patients with ongoing GI or GU tract infection
- procedures on infected skin, skin structures, or musculoskeletal tissue
- surgery to place prosthetic heart valves or prosthetic intravascular or intracardiac materials

Most patients requiring prophylaxis will be undergoing dental procedures, and the indicated antibiotic is oral amoxicillin 30 to 60 minutes before the procedure. If the patient is allergic to penicillin, select cephalexin, azithromycin, clarithromycin, or clindamycin.

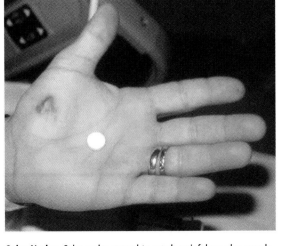

Osler Nodes: Osler nodes are red to purple painful papules, papulopustules, or nodules found in the pulp of fingers or occasionally hands and feet and seen in cases of IE.

Diagnosis

Risk factors for IE include injection drug use and the factors listed above. Fever, malaise, and fatigue are sensitive but nonspecific symptoms associated with IE. Suggestive physical examination findings include:

- new cardiac murmur
- new-onset HF
- conduction abnormalities on ECG (suggests perivalvular abscess)
- focal neurologic signs (septic emboli)
- splenomegaly
- petechiae, splinter hemorrhages
- Osler nodes (violaceous, circumscribed, painful nodules found in the pulp of the fingers and toes)
- Janeway lesions (painless, erythematous, macular lesions found on the soles and palms)
- Roth spots (hemorrhagic lesions of the retina)
- leukocytosis, anemia, and hematuria
- multiple bilateral small nodules on chest x-ray (septic emboli)

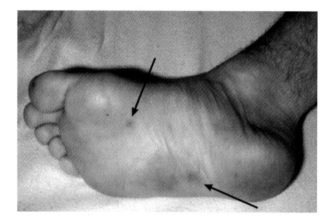

Janeway Lesions: Janeway lesions are macular, erythematous, nontender microabscesses in the dermis of the palms and soles caused by septic emboli that are considered pathognomonic for IE.

Select a transthoracic echocardiogram (TTE) for all patients with bacteremia. In patients with high clinical suspicion of IE but normal TTE, obtain a TEE, particularly in the setting of *S. aureus* bacteremia. TEE is the test of choice to identify a paravalvular abscess.

Apply the "modified for easy memory" Duke Criteria (below) to diagnose endocarditis. Diagnose endocarditis in patients with two major criteria or one major and three minor criteria.

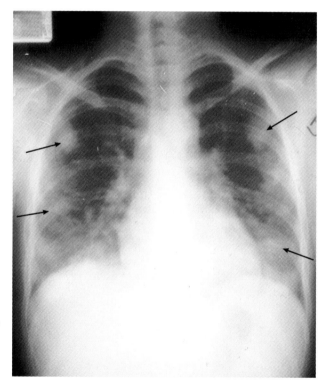

Septic Pulmonary Emboli: Septic pulmonary emboli are characterized by multifocal, patchy, and otherwise ill-defined infiltrates; cavitation may occur.

STUDY TABLE: Diagnosing Endocarditis	
Major Duke Criteria	**Minor Duke Criteria**
Positive blood culture for endocarditis × 2	Predisposing heart condition or injection drug use
Positive echocardiogram	Fever
New valvular regurgitation	Embolic vascular phenomena
	Immunologic phenomena (glomerulonephritis or rheumatoid factor)
	Positive blood culture not meeting major criteria

The HACEK organisms (*Haemophilus aphrophilus*; *Actino-bacillus actinomycetemcomitans*; *Cardiobacterium hominis*; *Eikenella corrodens*; and *Kingella kingae*), previously associated with "culture-negative" endocarditis are now easily isolated when incubated for at least 5 days.

◆ DON'T BE TRICKED

- Don't give antimicrobial prophylaxis to patients with mitral valve prolapse or other low-risk valvular abnormalities.
- The most common reason for negative or slow-growing cultures in endocarditis is antibiotic treatment before culture.
- Look for colon cancer in patients with *Streptococcus bovis* or *Clostridium septicum* endocarditis.

Therapy

Patients with valvular dysfunction and acute HF require surgery. Other indications for surgery include persistent bacteremia (≥3 days) on antibiotic therapy, relapse after prolonged

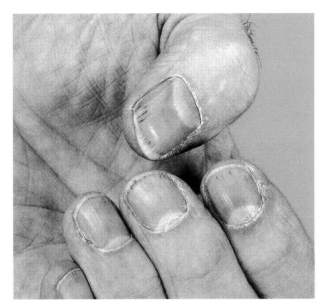

Splinter Hemorrhages: Fingernails with splinter hemorrhages, which are nonblanching, linear, reddish-brown lesions found under the nail bed, are shown.

antibiotic therapy for prosthetic valve endocarditis, and *S. aureus*-related prosthetic valve endocarditis. Valve repair is preferred over replacement to reduce the risk of prosthetic infection.

Patients with suspected IE and good cardiovascular function do not require empiric treatment before culture results. In decompensated patients, start empiric antibiotics immediately after blood cultures are obtained.

STUDY TABLE: Empiric therapy for IE	
Condition	**Therapy**
Community-acquired native valve IE	Vancomycin or ampicillin-sulbactam plus gentamicin
Nosocomial-associated IE	Vancomycin, gentamicin, rifampin, and an antipseudomonal β-lactam
Prosthetic valve IE	Vancomycin, gentamicin, and rifampin

Narrow antibiotic selection after bacterial susceptibilities are known. Continue treatment for 4 to 6 weeks except in uncomplicated right-sided native valve endocarditis due to methicillin-susceptible *S. aureus*, which can be treated for 2 weeks with a combination of nafcillin and gentamicin.

◆ DON'T BE TRICKED

- Oral antibiotics are not recommended for treatment of IE.

Epstein-Barr Virus

Diagnosis

EBV is a herpesvirus spread by intimate contact. EBV is the primary agent of infectious mononucleosis and is associated with the development of B-cell lymphoma, T-cell lymphoma, Hodgkin lymphoma, and nasopharyngeal carcinoma. Another EBV manifestation is oral hairy leukoplakia that characteristically affects the lateral portions of the tongue as white corrugated painless plaques. Oral hairy leukoplakia is highly specific for HIV infection.

Typical symptoms in patients with acute infectious mononucleosis include:

- severe fatigue, headache, and sore throat
- fever associated with posterior cervical lymphadenopathy
- splenomegaly
- atypical lymphocytosis

Consider EBV infection in all patients with aseptic meningitis or encephalitis, hepatitis, hemolytic anemia, and thrombocytopenia.

◆ DON'T BE TRICKED

- **The morbilliform rash appearing in patients with infectious mononucleosis following the administration of ampicillin is not an allergic reaction; patients can subsequently use ampicillin without rash recurrence.**

Select a Monospot test (heterophile antibody test), which is specific but not very sensitive early in disease. If the Monospot test is negative, repeat in 2 weeks or select EBV serology. Infectious mononucleosis syndrome can also be caused by CMV or HIV infection; it is often not possible to make a clinical diagnosis and serologic testing is necessary.

STUDY TABLE: Epstein-Barr Virus Serology	
Condition	**Antibody**
Acute primary infection	Elevated VCA IgM, VCA IgG, and EA IgG
	Low or undetectable EBNA-1 IgG
Past infection	Undetectable VCA IgM and EA IgG
	Elevated VCA IgG and EBNA-1 IgG
EA = early antigen; EBNA = Epstein-Barr nuclear antigen; VCA = viral capsid antigen.	

Therapy

Supportive care is typically sufficient. Select corticosteroids only if airway obstruction or other life-threatening condition such as hemolytic anemia is present.

◆ DON'T BE TRICKED

- **Do not prescribe antiviral drugs for treatment of infectious mononucleosis.**

❖ Test Yourself

An 18-year-old female soccer player has malaise, anorexia, and a sore throat for 3 days. She has exudative pharyngitis, tender anterior and posterior cervical lymph nodes, and fullness in her left upper abdominal quadrant. Leukocyte count is 8500/microliter with moderate atypical lymphocytes.

ANSWER: The patient has infectious mononucleosis and should avoid contact sports because of the risk of splenic rupture in the setting of splenomegaly.

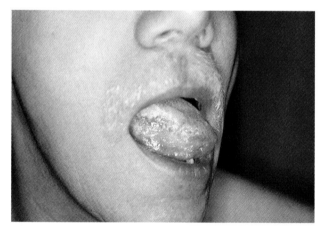

Oral Hairy Leukoplakia: A patient with HIV with oral hairy leukoplakia, white corrugated painless plaques on the lateral tongue, is shown.

Influenza Virus

Prevention

See Screening and Prevention in the General Internal Medicine section. For institutional outbreaks, vaccinate staff members and residents not already immunized and give chemoprophylaxis with zanamivir or oseltamivir for at least 2 weeks following immunization.

◆ DON'T BE TRICKED

- Do not administer live attenuated influenza vaccine to persons who have close contact with immunocompromised patients.

Diagnosis

During November through April, look for acute onset of high fever, headache, fatigue, nonproductive cough, sore throat, nasal congestion, rhinorrhea, and myalgia. Use diagnostic testing in patients for whom results would influence management (e.g., initiating antiviral treatment, performing other diagnostic testing, or inpatient infection control measures).

Therapy

Treat all hospitalized patients with confirmed infection and outpatients at high risk for severe disease. Select zanamivir or oseltamivir, both of which are active against influenza A and B.

Risk factors for severe disease:

- immunosuppression (highest risk)
- chronic pulmonary disease (highest risk)
- age >64 years
- pregnancy (or delivery within 2 weeks)
- American Indian race
- diabetes
- significant cardiovascular, kidney, liver, or hematologic disease

◆ DON'T BE TRICKED

- Do not administer amantadine or rimantadine to prevent or treat influenza virus because of the high rate of resistance.
- Zanamivir (inhaled) has been associated with rare bronchospasm and is contraindicated in patients with pulmonary or cardiovascular disease.

❖ Test Yourself

A 68-year-old woman with diabetes is admitted to the hospital in November with the acute onset of fever, chills, nonproductive cough, and fatigue. Her 6-year-old granddaughter has had similar symptoms for 3 days.

ANSWER: Diagnose probable influenza and start oseltamivir immediately.

Community-Acquired Pneumonia

Diagnosis

Streptococcus pneumoniae is the most common identified bacterial cause of CAP in patients of all ages. CAP due to *Moraxella* and *Haemophilus* species occurs mainly in patients with chronic pulmonary disease. CAP caused by *Legionella pneumophila* requires contact with an environmental source, rather than with an infected person. Atypical microorganisms that cause CAP include *Mycoplasma pneumoniae* and *Chlamydophila pneumoniae*. Pneumonia due to atypical microorganisms is more common in persons 20 to 40 years of age.

Look for poor dentition and aspiration risk (anaerobic pneumonia) owing to GI or neurologic disease, episodes of altered consciousness (e.g., alcohol use), injection drug use (*S. aureus* pneumonia), and antibiotic therapy during the past 3 months. Pay attention to travel and occupational history.

Severity of illness scores such as the CURB-65 criteria (Confusion, Uremia, Respiratory rate, low Blood pressure, and age ≥65 years) may help predict a complicated course. Scoring 1 point for each positive criterion, patients with a score of 0 to 1 can be managed as outpatients, those with a score of 2 should be admitted to a hospital ward, and those with a score of 3 or higher often require ICU care. Also consider hospitalization for patients who do not respond to outpatient therapy or have decompensated comorbid illness, complex social needs, or require IV antibiotics or oxygenation.

Fever and a chest x-ray demonstrating one or more focal pulmonary infiltrates are diagnostic of pneumonia. Sputum culture is not helpful in the diagnosis of CAP. Blood cultures are specific but not sensitive in the identification of causative organisms. A positive urine antigen test for *L. pneumophila* is also diagnostic, but this test is only available for *L. pneumophila* serogroup 1. A similar test is available for pneumococcal pneumonia.

STUDY TABLE: Risks of Community-Acquired Pneumonia	
Modifying Factor Putting Patient at Risk	**Pathogen**
Residence in a nursing home; underlying cardiopulmonary disease; multiple medical comorbidities; recent antibiotic therapy	Enteric gram-negative bacteria
Structural lung disease (bronchiectasis); corticosteroid therapy (prednisone >10 mg/d); broad-spectrum antibiotic therapy for >7 days in the past month; malnutrition	*P. aeruginosa*
Influenza epidemic in the community	Influenza virus, *S. pneumoniae*, *S. aureus*, *Haemophilus influenzae*
COPD; smoking history	*S. pneumoniae*, *H. influenzae*, *Moraxella catarrhalis*, *P. aeruginosa*, *Legionella* species, *C. pneumoniae*
Poor dental hygiene; aspiration; presence of a lung abscess	Oral anaerobes
Animal exposure	Farm animals (*Coxiella burnetii*); birds (*Chlamydia psittaci*, *Cryptococcus*, *Histoplasma*); bat or bird droppings (*Histoplasma*)
Travel or residence in southwestern United States	*Coccidioides* species, *Hantavirus*
Travel or residence in Southeast and East Asia	*Burkholderia pseudomallei* (melioidosis)

◆ DON'T BE TRICKED

- Edentulous patients do not get anaerobic pneumonias.
- The presence of cavities with air-fluid levels suggests abscess formation (staphylococci, anaerobes, or gram-negative bacilli), whereas the presence of cavities without air-fluid levels suggests tuberculosis or fungal infection.

Therapy

STUDY TABLE: Empiric Therapy for CAP	
Patient Characteristics	**Therapy**
Outpatient, no comorbidities	Azithromycin, clarithromycin, or doxycycline
Outpatient, comorbid medical condition, and/or recent antibiotic use	β-lactam (cefuroxime, cefpodoxime, amoxicillin-clavulanate) and a macrolide or doxycycline; or monotherapy with an antipneumococcal fluoroquinolone (levofloxacin, gatifloxacin, or moxifloxacin)
Inpatient, general medicine ward	IV antipneumococcal fluoroquinolone or β-lactam and a macrolide or doxycycline. Consider risk factors for *Pseudomonas* infection, and add coverage if appropriate
ICU, no risk factors for *P. aeruginosa*	β-lactam plus a macrolide or antipneumococcal fluoroquinolone.
ICU, risk factor(s) for *P. aeruginosa* (cardiopulmonary disease, corticosteroid use), or gram-negative rods on sputum Gram stain	Combination therapy with an antipseudomonal β-lactam (piperacillin-tazobactam, cefepime, imipenem, or meropenem) plus a fluoroquinolone
ICU with or without risk factors for *P. aeruginosa* and community-acquired MRSA is suspected	Add vancomycin or linezolid

◆ DON'T BE TRICKED

- Do not select the same class of antibiotics that patients have received in the past 3 months.

Change to oral antibiotic therapy when patients have improved symptoms, have no fever on two occasions 8 hours apart, and are able to take oral medications. Follow these general rules for duration of antibiotic therapy:

- Give antibiotics for ≤7 days if clinical response is good, no fever for 48 to 72 hours, and no sign of extrapulmonary infection.
- Treat severe infections, empyema, lung abscess, meningitis, or documented infection with pathogens such as *P. aeruginosa* or *S. aureus* for ≥10 days.
- Treat bacteremic *S. aureus* pneumonia for 4 to 6 weeks and obtain TEE to rule out endocarditis.
- Treat uncomplicated bacteremic pneumococcal pneumonia for 7 to 10 days.

Tuberculosis

Screening

Select TST using PPD for all patients at high risk of exposure to TB, including:

- those with close contact to a person known or suspected to have TB
- recent immigrants from countries with a high prevalence of TB (Asia, Africa, Latin America, Eastern Europe, and Russia)
- health care workers who care for clients at high risk
- medically underserved, low-income populations
- injection drug users
- persons who have been incarcerated
- those with a medical condition that increases the risk of active TB, including HIV

Another screening option is the IGRAs, which are more specific than TST for the diagnosis of active and latent TB infection (LTBI) and may be used for the same indications as TST; although more expensive, IGRAs are increasingly being used in place of the TST.

◆ DON'T BE TRICKED

- **TST is not contraindicated for persons who received the BCG vaccine.**
- **Interpret a positive TST in a patient with a history of BCG vaccination the same as in a person without a history of this vaccination.**
- **Neither TST nor IGRA can distinguish latent from active infection.**

Diagnosis

Know the different TST threshold measurements for TB infection.

STUDY TABLE: Interpretation of Tuberculin Skin Test Results		
Criteria for Tuberculin Positivity by Risk Group		
≥5 mm Induration	**≥10 mm Induration**	**≥15 mm Induration**
Persons who are HIV positive	Recent (<5 yr) arrivals from high-prevalence countries	All others with no risk factors for TB
Recent contacts of persons with active TB	Injection drug users	
Persons with fibrotic changes on chest x-ray consistent with old TB	Residents or employees of high-risk congregate settings: prisons and jails, nursing homes and other long-term facilities for older adults, hospitals and other health care facilities, residential facilities for patients with AIDS, homeless shelters	
Patients with organ transplants and other immunosuppressive conditions (receiving the equivalent of ≥15 mg/d of prednisone for >4 weeks)	Mycobacteriology laboratory personnel; persons with clinical conditions that put them at high risk for active disease; children aged <4 years or those exposed to adults in high-risk categories	

LTBI is defined by a positive tuberculin skin test or IGRA in the absence of any systemic manifestation of active infection and a normal chest radiograph. Active TB infection is characterized by constitutional or pulmonary signs or symptoms that are often insidious and include:

- cough >3 weeks, chest pain, and hemoptysis
- fever, chills, and night sweats
- easy fatigability
- weight loss and anorexia

Obtain acid-fast bacilli smears and cultures, chest x-ray, and TST (or IGRA) in patients with suspected active TB. A false-negative skin test may occur in anergic patients and in up to 25% of patients with active TB. Sputum or tissue culture is the gold standard for diagnosis, but results may be delayed for weeks. Acid-fast bacillus stains are rapid, but neither sensitive nor specific. Nucleic acid amplification (NAA) tests of sputum may be used to exclude TB in patients with false-positive sputum results (nontuberculous mycobacteria) or to confirm the disease in some patients with false-negative smears. Select drug susceptibility testing on all culture isolates. In persons not already known to be HIV positive, test for HIV infection.

Chest x-ray abnormalities include the following patterns:

- reactivation TB: infiltrates in the apical-posterior segments of the upper lung and superior segments of the lower lobe
- primary progressive TB: hilar lymphadenopathy or infiltrates in any part of the lung
- cavitary TB: cavities without air-fluid levels; may be associated with either primary progressive or reactivation TB
- immunocompromised patients: atypical or absent radiologic findings are common
- miliary TB: characteristic "millet seed" appearance (uniform reticulonodular infiltrate)

CT scans may identify abnormalities not yet visible on chest x-ray.

◆ DON'T BE TRICKED

- **For suspected pleural TB, select pleural biopsies when pleural fluid analysis does not establish the diagnosis.**

Therapy

Exclude active TB before starting treatment for latent TB. Select isoniazid for 9 months as the preferred LTBI therapy. For active TB, select isoniazid, rifampin, pyrazinamide, and ethambutol (or streptomycin) initially for 2 months (induction phase) followed by isoniazid and rifampin for an additional 7 months.

◆ DON'T BE TRICKED

- **Do not treat latent TB with rifampin and pyrazinamide.**
- **Never add a single drug to a failing TB regimen.**

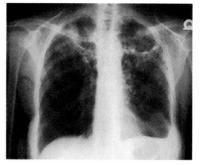

Reactivation Tuberculosis: Reactivation tuberculosis with infiltrate and cavity in right upper lobe.

❖ Test Yourself

A 40-year-old asymptomatic female hospital employee has a 10-mm TST reaction following routine screening. The employee was born in India and has lived in the United States for 10 years. She was vaccinated with BCG as a child. Her chest x-ray is normal.

ANSWER: Treat with isoniazid for 9 months.

Pneumocystis jirovecii Pneumonia

Prevention

Select prophylaxis (usually with trimethoprim-sulfamethoxazole) for patients with HIV infection and a CD4 cell count <200/microliter. In patients treated with HIV antiretroviral medications, discontinue prophylaxis in patients who maintain a CD4 cell count >200/microliter for 3 months.

Diagnosis

In patients infected with HIV, *Pneumocystis jirovecii* pneumonia is gradual in onset and characterized by nonproductive cough and progressive dyspnea. Other findings may include:

- fever, chills, night sweats, and weight loss
- tachypnea and crackles on lung examination
- chest x-ray that may show consolidation or diffuse infiltrates

The diagnosis is established by silver stain examination of induced sputum or a bronchoscopic sample showing characteristic cysts.

◆ DON'T BE TRICKED

- **The most common cause of a pneumothorax in a patient with AIDS is *P. jirovecii* pneumonia.**
- **The chest x-ray may be normal in some patients with HIV and *P. jirovecii* pneumonia.**
- ***P. jirovecii* pneumonia can occur in patients not infected with HIV, typically in association with immunosuppressant drug therapy.**

STUDY TABLE: Classification of *Pneumocystis jirovecii* Pneumonia	
ABG Findings (Ambient Air)	**Classification**
A-a <35 mm Hg and Po_2 >70 mm Hg	Mild
A-a 35-45 mm Hg and Po_2 >70 mm Hg	Moderate
A-a >45 mm Hg and Po_2 <70 mm Hg	Severe
A-a = alveolar-arterial oxygen gradient.	

Therapy

Select 3 weeks of therapy with:

- oral trimethoprim-sulfamethoxazole for mild to moderate pneumonia
- IV trimethoprim-sulfamethoxazole for moderate to severe pneumonia
- corticosteroids within 72 hours for A-a ≥35 mm Hg or arterial Po_2 <70 mm Hg
- IV pentamidine or IV clindamycin plus oral primaquine for patients with sulfa allergy

❖ Test Yourself

A 45-year-old man with HIV and a CD4 count of 100/microliter presents with 3 weeks of dry cough and progressive dyspnea on exertion, now present at rest. On examination, his temperature is 38.3 °C (100.9 °F) and Po_2 is 67 mm Hg on ambient air. His chest x-ray shows diffuse bilateral infiltrates.

ANSWER: Initiate empiric treatment with IV trimethoprim-sulfamethoxazole and corticosteroids for presumed *P. jirovecii* pneumonia; begin diagnostic evaluation.

Anthrax

Diagnosis

Three types of anthrax occur in humans: cutaneous, GI, and inhalational. Cutaneous anthrax is the most common type of anthrax in the United States. Look for anthrax risk factors, including:

- travel to the Middle East, Africa, South America, or Asia
- exposure to wool, hides, or animal hair from endemic countries
- bioterrorism

Select cutaneous anthrax if the patient has an enlarging, painless ulcer with black eschar surrounded by edema or large gram-positive bacilli on Gram stain. Look for inhalational anthrax if the patient has dyspnea, fever, chest pain, and a widened mediastinum on chest x-ray or CT scan.

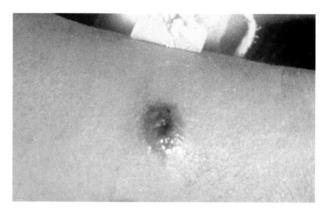

Cutaneous Anthrax: The primary lesion of cutaneous anthrax is a painless, pruritic papule. As the lesion matures, a painless ulcer covered by the characteristic black eschar surrounded by nonpitting edema develops.

Therapy

To prevent inhalational anthrax, select postexposure vaccination and ciprofloxacin for 60 days. Select oral ciprofloxacin for cutaneous anthrax and IV ciprofloxacin and two additional antibiotics for inhalational anthrax, anthrax meningitis, and severe cutaneous disease (involving the head, neck).

❖ **Test Yourself**

A 57-year-old male government clerk has 3 days of malaise, fever, cough, and headache. Temperature is 39.0 °C (102.2 °F), and lung crackles are heard bilaterally. A chest x-ray shows scattered pulmonary infiltrates and a widened mediastinum.

ANSWER: Select inhalational anthrax and IV ciprofloxacin and two other antibiotics.

Botulism

Diagnosis

The *Clostridium botulinum* neurotoxin inhibits acetylcholine release at ganglia and neuromuscular junctions, causing bulbar palsy and symmetric flaccid paralysis beginning 12-72 hours after exposure. Remember the "Five D's" of botulism:

- Diplopia
- Dysphonia
- Dysarthria
- Dysphagia
- Descending paralysis (starting with facial muscles)

Therapy

Ventilatory capacity must be monitored (often in the ICU), and respiratory support may be required. In patients with wound botulism, the wounds should be débrided. A trivalent (types A, B, C) equine serum antitoxin is available from the CDC and should be administered as early as possible to prevent progression, as it cannot reverse existing paralysis.

Rocky Mountain Spotted Fever

Diagnosis

RMSF is a tick-borne rickettsial infection. In the United States, RMSF is most prevalent in the southeastern and south central states. Look for a history of tick bite and recent travel to an endemic area; febrile illness in spring and summer months; and nonspecific symptoms such as nausea, myalgia, dyspnea, cough, and headache. Also look for a macular rash starting on the ankles and wrists; lesions spread centripetally and become petechial. Thrombocytopenia and elevated aminotransferase levels are characteristic. Select indirect fluorescent antibody assay to make the diagnosis.

Therapy

Select doxycycline. In patients who are pregnant, choose chloramphenicol.

Leptospirosis

Diagnosis

Leptospirosis is a zoonosis caused by the spirochete *Leptospira interrogans*. Most clinical cases occur in the tropics (Hawaii in the United States). Patients typically become infected following exposure to animal urine or contaminated water or soil. Most patients present with the abrupt onset of fever, rigors, myalgias, and headache; kidney failure, uveitis, respiratory failure, myocarditis and rhabdomyolysis can occur. A key physical sign is conjunctival suffusion, infrequently found in other infectious disease. The diagnosis is usually made by serologic confirmation.

Therapy

Most cases are self-limited, but doxycycline and penicillin may be helpful in severe disease or shortening the duration of mild disease.

Malaria and Babesiosis

Prevention

Select chloroquine for travelers to areas where chloroquine-resistant *Plasmodium falciparum* has not been reported. Select mefloquine, atovaquone-proguanil, or doxycycline for travelers to:

- Thailand
- Myanmar
- Cambodia
- Vietnam

Diagnosis

Most infections are caused by *P. falciparum* or *Plasmodium vivax*, and most deaths are due to *P. falciparum*. Fever develops with the release of merozoites from ruptured, infected erythrocytes. Look for:

- cyclical paroxysms of rigors
- fever, drenching sweats

- travel history and inadequate antimalarial prophylaxis
- jaundice
- splenomegaly
- coma, seizure

Select thick and thin peripheral blood smears to diagnose malaria. Parasitemia levels >2% are most consistent with *P. falciparum* infection.

Babesiosis is a tick-borne malaria-like illness endemic to the northeast coast of the United States. Symptomatic babesiosis can result in severe hemolytic anemia, jaundice, kidney failure, and death. A Wright- or Giemsa-stained peripheral blood smear will show intraerythrocytic parasites in ring, or more rarely, tetrad formations (Maltese cross shaped). Consider PCR for *Babesia* DNA in cases of low parasitemia.

◆ DON'T BE TRICKED

- **Any traveler who has returned from a malaria-endemic area in the past year and has an undiagnosed febrile illness should undergo malaria evaluation.**

Therapy

Use chloroquine for malaria acquired where chloroquine resistance has not been reported. Choose quinine, doxycycline, mefloquine, atovaquone-proguanil, or artemether-lumefantrine for malaria acquired where chloroquine-resistant parasites are present.

Treat babesiosis with quinine and clindamycin or with atovaquone and azithromycin.

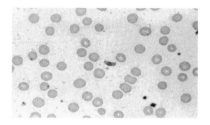

***Plasmodium falciparum* Infection:** In the center of the peripheral blood smear is a banana-shaped gametocyte diagnostic of *P. falciparum* infection.

Ehrlichiosis and Anaplasmosis

Diagnosis

Ehrlichia chaffeensis and *Anaplasma phagocytophilum* are rickettsia-like organisms that infect leukocytes. *E. chaffeensis* causes human monocytic ehrlichiosis (HME) and *A. phagocytophilum* causes human granulocytic anaplasmosis (HGA). Ehrlichiosis and anaplasmosis are spread by ticks.

The clinical syndromes of HME and HGA are very similar:

- fever, headache, and myalgia
- nonspecific trunk rash in up to 40% of patients with HME
- multiorgan failure and a mortality rate of 3%
- fever of unknown origin (symptoms can persist for months)
- leukopenia and thrombocytopenia
- presence of morulae (clumps of organisms in the cytoplasm of the appropriate leukocyte)

Convalescent serologic testing is the most commonly used diagnostic test.

Treatment

IV or oral doxycycline is the treatment of choice for HME and HGA.

Osteomyelitis

Diagnosis

Microorganisms can reach the bone by contiguous spread from adjacent soft tissue or joints, hematogenous seeding, or direct inoculation as a result of surgery or trauma. Adults with osteomyelitis usually have nonspecific pain around the involved site without systemic features. A draining sinus tract may be present over the area of involved bone. Look for purulent, serous, or serosanguineous discharge or foot ulcer with exposed bone or positive "probe to bone" test. Additional clues include diabetes mellitus, previous surgery, rheumatoid arthritis, peripheral vascular disease, injection drug use, and long-term IV catheter placement. Patients who have undergone total joint arthroplasty and have had joint pain since surgery are more likely to have a prosthetic joint infection compared with pain-free patients.

STUDY TABLE: Categorization and Characterization of Osteomyelitis

Category	Characteristics
Acute hematogenous osteomyelitis	Infection of intervertebral disc space and two adjacent vertebrae
Contiguous osteomyelitis	Patients >50 years old with diabetes mellitus or peripheral vascular disease and a foot ulcer
Following dog or cat bite	*Pasteurella multocida* may cause contiguous-focus osteomyelitis after dog or cat bites
Following foot puncture wound	*Pseudomonas* is frequently isolated following puncture wounds through the rubber sole of a shoe.
Sternal osteomyelitis	Wound healing complications, unstable sternum, and fever after thoracic surgery
Clavicular osteomyelitis	Pain, cellulitis, or drainage after subclavian vein catheterization
Sternoclavicular joint osteomyelitis	Pain and fever in an injection-drug user
Sickle cell disease	Bone infarcts and bone marrow thrombosis predispose to osteomyelitis most commonly caused by *Salmonella* species and *S. aureus*.

MRI is the imaging procedure of choice for patients with suspected osteomyelitis. Half of patients with acute hematogenous osteomyelitis will have positive blood cultures, but cultures are less likely to be positive with contiguous osteomyelitis. Microbiologic diagnosis with bone culture is preferred and is best performed by surgical sampling or by needle aspiration under radiographic guidance. In stable chronic osteomyelitis, antimicrobial therapy is withheld until deep bone cultures have been obtained.

◆ DON'T BE TRICKED

- Normal ESR and CRP values do not rule out osteomyelitis.
- Do not select sinus tract and wound drainage cultures.

Therapy

In patients with suspected diabetic foot osteomyelitis who are not ill and in whom no evidence of extensive concurrent soft tissue infection or cellulitis exists, withhold antibiotics before obtaining a bone biopsy to increase the diagnostic yield. In these patients, therapy is guided by the culture results. In patients requiring immediate empiric therapy, multiple antibiotic regimens are acceptable:

- piperacillin-tazobactam
- ampicillin-sulbactam
- ticarcillin-clavulanic acid
- a third- or fourth-generation cephalosporin combined with metronidazole

Vancomycin, linezolid, or daptomycin may be added to any of these regimens in patients in whom concern or proof of MRSA exists or in ill patients for whom no cultures are available to guide therapy. Diabetic foot osteomyelitis is treated for at least 4 to 6 weeks. Also choose surgery to débride devitalized bone and remove all foreign bodies. In patients with poor arterial vascular supply, also choose revascularization.

The most common organism found in vertebral osteomyelitis is *S. aureus* (including MRSA); coagulase-negative staphylococci are also common. Patients with imaging studies suggestive of vertebral osteomyelitis but negative blood cultures should undergo a CT-guided percutaneous needle biopsy. Empiric antibiotic treatment may be given if an etiologic agent is not identified to guide specific therapy. Vancomycin plus an antipseudomonal third- or fourth-generation cephalosporin (ceftazidime or cefepime, respectively) or an extended-spectrum β-lactam antibiotic are appropriate choices.

Also consider:

- hyperbaric oxygen as an adjunctive therapy in posttraumatic or chronic osteomyelitis
- removal of orthopedic hardware for most patients with orthopedic implant–associated osteomyelitis
- a prolonged course (3-6 months) of fluoroquinolone and rifampin therapy when implant removal is not possible

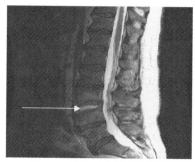

Hematogenous Osteomyelitis: MRI shows moderate destruction of the inferior L3 and superior L4 vertebral bodies compatible with osteomyelitis. Moderate narrowing of the thecal sac is seen at this level due to retropulsion of an enhancing bony fragment.

◆ **DON'T BE TRICKED**

- **Surgery is not needed for uncomplicated hematogenous vertebral osteomyelitis.**

❖ **Test Yourself**

A 60-year-old previously healthy man has nonradiating pain in his lower thoracic spine that began 10 days ago. Six weeks ago, he was unable to urinate and required an indwelling urinary catheter. Temperature is 37.9 °C (100.2 °F). Point tenderness of the lower thoracic spine is present.

ANSWER: Choose probable acute hematogenous osteomyelitis of the vertebral spine with cord compression secondary to vertebral collapse or epidural abscess formation. Select surgical consultation.

Cystitis

Prevention

Screen for asymptomatic bacteriuria only in patients who are pregnant or are about to undergo an invasive urologic procedure.

Select treatment for asymptomatic bacteriuria only in:

- pregnant women
- patients who are about to have an invasive urologic procedure

Diagnosis

A UTI in an individual with an indwelling urinary catheter, neurogenic bladder, kidney stones, obstruction, immunosuppression, pregnancy, kidney disease, or diabetes mellitus is defined as complicated and may predispose to treatment failure or require modified approaches to management because of infection with antibiotic-resistant microorganisms. These patients require a urine culture.

Symptomatic cystitis is associated with:

- dysuria, frequency, urgency

- hematuria
- suprapubic pain

Obtain a urinalysis in most women to help confirm the diagnosis of cystitis. The physical examination and urinalysis can be omitted for healthy women with acute cystitis if no complicating factors are present. When the diagnosis is not clear, the urine dipstick for leukocyte esterase and/or nitrite is an acceptable screening tool. Obtain a culture for suspected cystitis only if:

- an unusual or antimicrobial-resistant microorganism is suspected (in a patient recently infected with an organism other than *Escherichia coli* or who recently received antimicrobial therapy)
- the patient is pregnant
- the episode represents a relapse or treatment failure

◆ DON'T BE TRICKED
- **Do not select routine urinary tract imaging to evaluate UTI.**

Therapy

For women with symptoms of uncomplicated cystitis, prescribing antibiotics over the telephone without seeing the patients or obtaining a urinalysis is acceptable. For empiric treatment of nonpregnant women with uncomplicated cystitis, select 3 days of oral trimethoprim-sulfamethoxazole, 5 days of oral nitrofurantoin, or a single 3-g oral dose of fosfomycin. In patients at high risk for complicated UTI, obtain a urine culture and initiate treatment empirically for 7 to 14 days with a fluoroquinolone.

Choose 7 days of empiric therapy for pregnant women with amoxicillin-clavulanate, nitrofurantoin, cefpodoxime, or cefixime. Obtain a urine culture after treatment.

For recurrent uncomplicated UTIs, select one or more of the following:

- postcoital antibiotic prophylaxis, particularly if UTIs are temporally associated with coitus
- continuous antibiotic prophylaxis, particularly if UTIs are not associated with coitus or use of spermicide-based contraception
- self-initiated therapy for frequent recurrent episodes not associated with coitus

◆ DON'T BE TRICKED
- **Do not schedule a routine follow-up urinalysis or culture for nonpregnant women with uncomplicated cystitis after treatment.**
- **Old age is not an indicator of a complicated UTI in the absence of other indicators.**

Pyelonephritis

Diagnosis

Pyelonephritis is associated with the abrupt onset of fever, chills, sweats, nausea, vomiting, diarrhea, and flank or abdominal pain. Urinary frequency and dysuria may precede pyelonephritis. Hypotension and septic shock may occur. Look for risk factors including obstruction, kidney stones, neurogenic bladder, and indwelling catheters.

Bacteriuria and pyuria are the gold standard for the diagnosis of pyelonephritis if they are associated with a suggestive history and physical findings. Gram stain of the urine sediment is particularly useful when selecting empiric antibiotic therapy. Obtain urine cultures for all patients and blood cultures for clinically ill patients. Imaging studies are indicated only for patients in whom an alternative diagnosis or a urologic complication is suspected.

Therapy

For patients with uncomplicated infection who are able to tolerate oral therapy, select an oral fluoroquinolone. Use an IV fluoroquinolone if nausea and vomiting precludes use of oral medications. Treat uncomplicated infection for 7 to 14 days.

Choose broad-spectrum antibiotic coverage with an extended-spectrum β-lactam or a carbapenem in the following settings:

- suspected infection with resistant organisms
- recent antibiotic use
- urinary obstruction
- immunosuppression

Patients admitted from a long-term care facility should also receive empiric coverage for vancomycin-resistant *Enterococcus* and fluoroquinolone-resistant gram-negative rods.

Obtain ultrasonography or CT for persistent fever or continuing symptoms after 72 hours of antibiotics to evaluate for complications of pyelonephritis (e.g., perinephric abscess). CT and MRI should be considered in patients with persistent or relapsing pyelonephritis despite a negative ultrasound.

◆ DON'T BE TRICKED

- Do not use ampicillin, nitrofurantoin, trimethoprim-sulfamethoxazole, or first-generation cephalosporins to treat pyelonephritis.

Neisseria gonorrhoeae Infection

Diagnosis

Neisseria gonorrhoeae infection should be suspected in men with purulent or mucopurulent urethral discharge and in women with mucopurulent cervicitis. Gonorrhea and *Chlamydia trachomatis* infection are also common causes of epididymitis in sexually active men aged <35 years, proctitis in persons who engage in anal receptive intercourse, and pharyngitis in persons who engage in oral sex. Infection at any site, most notably infection of the pharynx and rectum, may be asymptomatic, allowing for unrecognized sexual transmission. Disseminated gonococcal infection is manifested by:

- presentation during or shortly after menstruation in women
- sparse peripheral necrotic pustules
- monoarthritis or oligoarthritis (knees, hips, and wrists)
- tendon sheath inflammation

Consider terminal component complement deficiency as a possible cause of recurrent disseminated gonococcal infection.

STUDY TABLE: Diagnostic Studies for Gonorrhea	
Condition	**Best Test**
Male urethritis	Gram stain
Proctitis or pharyngitis	Culture (not Gram stain)
Cervicitis	DNA probe or nucleic acid amplification of discharge and urine (not Gram stain)
Arthritis	Joint fluid culture
Disseminated infection	Blood culture

◆ DON'T BE TRICKED

- Do not forget to test for chlamydia, syphilis, and HIV infection in patients with gonorrhea.

Therapy

Treat presumed chlamydial infection with azithromycin or doxycycline. Because of high coinfection rates of chlamydia with gonorrheal infections, treat uncomplicated mucosal infections (cervicitis, urethritis, and proctitis) due to gonorrhea with ceftriaxone (or other suitable third-generation cephalosporins) and azithromycin or doxycycline. In sexually active men <35 years of age, treat epididymitis with ceftriaxone and azithromycin or doxycycline for 10 days. Treat disseminated gonorrheal infection with a 7- to 14-day course of ceftriaxone.

◆ **DON'T BE TRICKED**

* **Do not select fluoroquinolones to treat gonorrhea because of antibiotic resistance.**

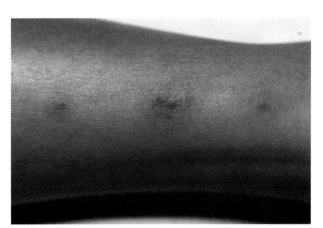

Gonorrhea: Several necrotic pustules and surrounding erythema on the leg associated with disseminated gonorrhea infection.

Syphilis

Diagnosis

The primary lesion in patients with syphilis is an ulcer (chancre) that develops approximately 3 weeks after inoculation. The ulcer has a clean appearance with heaped-up borders, is usually painless, and resolves spontaneously.

Secondary syphilis develops 2 to 8 weeks after the appearance of the primary chancre and is characterized by widespread hematogenous dissemination involving most often the skin, liver, and lymph nodes. Secondary syphilis resolves spontaneously.

To diagnose secondary syphilis, look for:

* fever and any type of rash (except vesicles), often with palmar or plantar involvement
* nontender generalized lymphadenopathy
* headache, cranial nerve abnormalities, altered mental status, or stiff neck
* mucous patches (a slightly elevated oval erosive lesion with surrounding inflammation) and condylomata lata lesions (grey to white, raised, wart-like lesions on moist surfaces)

Manifestations of late (tertiary) syphilis may occur years after initial infection. Tertiary syphilis may cause:

* meningitis and subarachnoid arteritis (a cause of stroke in a young patient)
* aortitis
* general paresis and tabes dorsalis
* gumma in any organ

Obtain a specimen for darkfield or direct fluorescent antibody testing of the chancre, erosions, or condylomata lata. The rapid plasma reagin or VDRL tests are 100% sensitive for secondary syphilis. A negative test rules out secondary syphilis. If either test is positive, choose the FTA-ABS test and *Treponema pallidum* particle agglutination (TPPA) assay as confirmatory tests. Nontreponemal tests should decrease in titer and may become negative after treatment (but will rise again in the setting of reinfection);

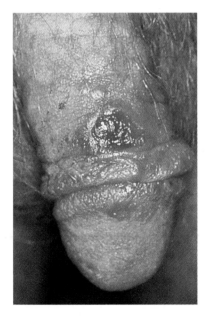

Syphilis: Primary chancre of syphilis characterized by a clean-based, nonpainful genital ulcer.

the FTA-ABS and microhemagglutination assay for *T. pallidum* antibodies (MHA-TP) will remain positive indefinitely. Test all patients for HIV infection.

Perform a CSF examination for patients with primary or secondary syphilis and the presence of any neurologic sign or symptom or for any HIV-infected patient with any stage of syphilis. Diagnose neurosyphilis when any one of the following are present: CSF lymphocytes >5/microliter, elevated CSF protein, and positive CSF VDRL test.

STUDY TABLE: Differential Diagnosis of Genital Ulcers	
Disease	**Characteristics**
Herpes (HSV type 1 or 2)	Multiple 1- to 2-mm tender vesicles or erosions and tender lymphadenopathy
Syphilis (*T. pallidum*)	Single 0.5- to 1.0-cm painless indurated ulcers and nontender bilateral inguinal lymphadenopathy
Chancroid (*Haemophilus ducreyi*)	Ragged, purulent, painful ulcers with tender lymphadenopathy
Lymphogranuloma venereum (*C. trachomatis*)	Single 0.2- to 1.0-cm ulcer, sometimes painful, with tender unilateral lymphadenopathy, which may suppurate
Fixed drug eruptions (NSAIDs, phenobarbital, antibiotics)	Single or multiple blisters or erosions, 1-3 cm, frequently on the glans penis

Therapy

The preferred therapy for syphilis at all stages is parenteral penicillin, which is the only acceptable therapy for pregnant patients. Treat primary or secondary syphilis with one dose of IM benzathine penicillin. Latent syphilis or tertiary nonneurosyphilis is treated with three weekly doses of IM benzathine penicillin. Doxycycline and tetracycline are alternatives for penicillin-allergic nonpregnant patients. Failure of nontreponemal serologic test results to decrease fourfold in the 6 to 12 months after treatment indicates treatment failure or reacquisition. Treat neurosyphilis with continuous penicillin infusion or IM benzathine penicillin every 4 hours for 10 to 14 days.

Secondary Syphilis: Pink to reddish-brown macules and papules on the palms, characteristic of secondary syphilis.

◆ DON'T BE TRICKED

- **Pregnant patients who are allergic to penicillin must be desensitized and treated with penicillin.**

- **The Jarisch-Herxheimer reaction is an acute febrile illness occurring within 24 hours of treatment for any stage of syphilis and is not an allergic reaction to penicillin.**

Herpes Simplex Virus Infection

Diagnosis

Inoculation of HSV at mucosal surfaces or skin sites results in the sudden appearance of multiple vesicular lesions on an inflamed, erythematous base. Primary infection may also be associated with systemic symptoms, such as fever and malaise. After primary infection resolves, the virus lives in a latent state in nerve cell bodies in ganglion neurons and can reactivate.

Several herpetic syndromes are possible in the adult.

STUDY TABLE: Selected Herpes Simplex Virus Syndromes	
Manifestation	**Description**
Oral	First-episode infections are most commonly gingivostomatitis and pharyngitis, whereas herpes labialis is the most frequent sign of reactivation disease
Herpetic whitlow	HSV infection of the finger often mistaken for bacterial infection
Genital herpes	Multiple painful vesicular or ulcerative lesions on penis or vulva that are most often caused by HSV-2
Keratitis	Punctate or branching epithelial keratitis
Encephalitis	Rapid onset of fever, headache, seizures, focal neurologic signs, and impaired consciousness
Hepatitis	Rare complication of either HSV-1 or HSV-2 that is most common in immunosuppressed patients (corticosteroid use, HIV infection, cancer, myelodysplastic syndromes, and pregnancy)
Associated HIV infection	Infection can occur anywhere and often presents as extensive oral or perianal ulcers (not vesicles) or as esophagitis, colitis, chorioretinitis, acute retinal necrosis, tracheobronchitis, and pneumonia
Bell palsy	HSV is implicated in Bell palsy syndrome

The diagnosis of cutaneous and genital disease can often be made on clinical grounds, but culture or direct fluorescent antibody testing and polymerase chain reaction (PCR) testing are useful when the diagnosis is unclear.

◆ DON'T BE TRICKED

- **A positive HSV-2 antibody test indicates only previous infection and is not a clinically useful diagnostic test.**

Therapy

For the first episode of genital herpes, treat with acyclovir, famciclovir, or valacyclovir for 7 to 10 days. Treat recurrent disease for 3 to 5 days. Treatment decreases duration of symptoms and reduces viral shedding. Suppressive therapy may be necessary to decrease the frequency of recurrences.

Treat primary episodes of oral HSV infection the same as genital lesions. Recurrent disease is generally not treated. Suppressive therapy can be considered for frequent recurrences, particularly in immunosuppressed patients.

Treat primary herpes keratoconjunctivitis with topical trifluorothymidine, vidarabine, or acyclovir. Ophthalmology referral is mandatory.

Use IV acyclovir to treat suspected or confirmed herpes encephalitis. Corticosteroids may be beneficial for Bell palsy with severe facial paralysis. The role of antiviral therapy is unclear.

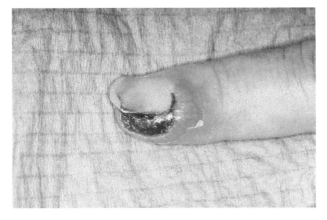

Herpetic Whitlow: Herpetic whitlow involving the lateral aspect of the index finger.

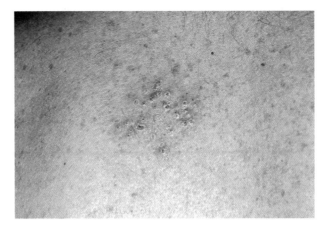

Cutaneous HSV Infection: Grouped vesicles on the skin characteristic of cutaneous HSV infection.

◆ DON'T BE TRICKED

- Do not treat herpetic keratitis with topical corticosteroid drops.

HIV Infection

Screening

Routinely screen all Americans aged 13 to 64 years for HIV infection. One-time testing is reasonable in persons at low risk, but persons engaged in high-risk behavior should be tested annually.

Diagnosis

Suspect primary HIV infection (initial acute HIV infection) if a febrile illness occurs within several weeks of a potential HIV exposure. Additional symptoms may include fatigue, lymphadenopathy, pharyngitis, rash, and/or headache. During the "window period" before seroconversion, the diagnosis of primary infection is confirmed with an HIV RNA viral load or viral antigen (p24 antigen) determination. The HIV RNA viral load is 100% sensitive for diagnosis in the window period, but only 97% specific (false-positives do occur). High viral loads (>50,000) are the rule for patients with acute HIV.

Test for HIV in any patient with signs or symptoms of immunologic dysfunction, weight loss, generalized lymphadenopathy, fever and night sweats of more than 2 weeks' duration, or severe aphthous ulcers.

Certain diagnoses warrant HIV testing:

- severe or treatment-refractory HSV infection
- oral thrush or esophageal candidiasis
- *P. jirovecii* pneumonitis
- cryptococcal meningitis
- disseminated mycobacterial infection
- CMV retinitis or GI disease
- toxoplasmosis
- severe seborrheic dermatitis or new or severe psoriasis
- recurrent herpes zoster infections

Obtain a highly sensitive ELISA (blood, oral secretions, or urine, or rapid tests) as the initial test. All positive results require confirmatory Western blot analysis.

The HIV RNA viral load is the most reliable marker for predicting the long-term risk of progression to AIDS or death. The CD4 cell count is the most reliable marker for the current risk of opportunistic complications.

AIDS is diagnosed in an HIV-infected person if the CD4 cell count is <200/microliter or if an AIDS-defining illness is present.

Therapy

Select combination ART for accidental needle-stick exposure to HIV-contaminated blood and when the HIV status of needle-stick exposure is unknown.

Consider initiating therapy in all patients motivated to start life-long medication, regardless of CD4 count. Select combination ART (three or more agents) for all patients with:

- CD4 count <350/microliter or <500/microliter who are motivated to be treated

- HIV nephropathy, regardless of CD4 count
- hepatitis B coinfection requiring treatment, regardless of CD4 count
- pregnant women, regardless of CD4 count

Preferred initial combination therapy in nonpregnant, treatment-naïve patients combines two nucleoside reverse transcriptase inhibitors (NRTIs) and a non-nucleoside reverse transcriptase inhibitor (NNRTI). The NRTIs tenofovir and emtricitabine are generally well tolerated and form the "backbone" of most initial regimens. Alternative regimens use two NRTIs plus a protease inhibitor or integrase inhibitor (raltegravir). Give protease inhibitors with a small dose of ritonavir, which is used as a "booster" of pharmacologic levels for the other protease inhibitor.

Do resistance testing on all patients before starting ART. Check the viral load 4 weeks after ART is initiated or changed. The goal of ART is a viral load of <50 copies/mL. A slow gradual increase in viral load may signal the presence of drug resistance.

As immune function recovers after successful ART therapy, the IRIS may occur in one of two ways:

- a preexisting subclinical infection is "unmasked" by immune system recovery
- a previously treated infection may "paradoxically" recur because of the presence of persistent antigens

The most important therapy for IRIS is treatment of the underlying infection. Corticosteroids and/or NSAIDs are sometimes added to decrease the inflammatory response.

◆ DON'T BE TRICKED

- **A therapy answer should include three or more drugs to be correct.**
- **A sudden spike in viral load does not indicate resistance; rather, it suggests the patient stopped therapy.**
- **Do not use efavirenz in women who are or may become pregnant.**
- **Do not stop ART in the setting of IRIS.**

STUDY TABLE: Common ART Side Effects	
NRTIs	**Side Effects**
Zidovudine	Anemia, neutropenia, and myopathy
Didanosine	Peripheral neuropathy and pancreatitis
Stavudine	Peripheral neuropathy, lactic acidosis, and fat atrophy
Abacavir	Hypersensitivity reaction (with or without rash)
NNRTIs	**Side Effects**
Nevirapine	Rash (including Stevens-Johnson syndrome) and hepatotoxicity
Efavirenz	Mood or psychiatric alterations, vivid dreams, or hallucinations
Tenofovir	Kidney dysfunction
Protease Inhibitors	**Side Effects**
Saquinavir, ritonavir, nelfinavir, and tipranavir	Hyperlipidemia, pancreatitis, fat distribution, and insulin resistance
Indinavir	Same as for other protease inhibitors, plus kidney stones, kidney insufficiency, and elevated indirect bilirubin
Atazanavir	Increased indirect bilirubin

STUDY TABLE: Prophylaxis for Patients with HIV Infection		
Preventable Condition	**When**	**Agent**
P. jirovecii pneumonitis	CD4 cell count <200/μL	Trimethoprim-sulfamethoxazole
Toxoplasmosis	CD4 cell count <100/μL and positive IgG for toxoplasmosis	Trimethoprim-sulfamethoxazole
Mycobacterium avium complex infection	CD4 cell count <50/μL	Azithromycin
Active or latent TB	TST ≥5 mm induration	See TB section in this chapter
Influenza	Annual vaccination for all HIV-infected patients	Killed influenza vaccine
Pneumococcal pneumonia	Vaccination every 5 to 10 years for all HIV-infected patients	Pneumococcal vaccine
Hepatitis A and B	One-time vaccination	Hepatitis A and B vaccine
μL = microliter.		

Discontinue *P. jirovecii*, toxoplasmosis, and *M. avium* complex prophylaxis when ART therapy produces CD4 cell counts >200/microliter and a negative viral load for at least 3 months.

❖ **Test Yourself**

A 29-year-old man with recently diagnosed pulmonary TB is found to have late-stage HIV infection. Three-drug ART and four-drug TB therapy is initiated, and he quickly improves. Four weeks later, he develops recurrent fever and neck pain and swelling. He has bilateral tender cervical lymphadenopathy.

ANSWER: Select IRIS. Continue ART and antituberculous drugs.

Toxoplasmosis

Diagnosis

Toxoplasmosis is caused by an intracellular protozoan parasite, *Toxoplasma gondii*. Immunocompetent persons with primary infection are usually asymptomatic, but latent infection can persist, and reactivation of the infection is a risk if the person becomes immunocompromised. Look for:

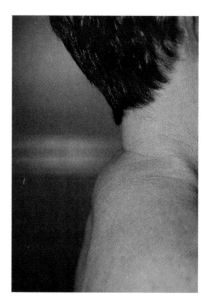

Protease Inhibitor Fat Dystrophy: Increase in subcutaneous fat at back of neck, creating a "buffalo hump" in a patient with HIV taking a protease inhibitor.

- encephalitis, chorioretinitis, or pneumonitis in immunocompromised patients
- any focal neurologic syndrome, acute or subacute
- mononucleosis-like syndrome

Select IgM and IgG serologic testing in patients with suspected toxoplasmosis and brain MRI or head CT for neurologic signs and symptoms. Typical findings on imaging include multiple ring-enhancing lesions.

STUDY TABLE: Differential Diagnosis of Cerebral Toxoplasmosis in Immunocompromised Patients	
Diagnosis	**Characteristics**
Lymphoma (primary CNS, B-cell lymphoma)	Often a solitary lesion is located in the periventricular or periependymal area or in the corpus callosum.
	Neither clinical nor neuroradiologic findings reliably distinguish lymphoma from toxoplasmosis. Brain biopsy is diagnostic.
Progressive multifocal leukoencephalopathy	Dementia is often the presenting symptom.
	PCR of CSF can show JC virus. Brain biopsy is diagnostic.
Cryptococcus neoformans	Headache, fever, and altered mental status are present.
	CSF culture for *Cryptococcus* or cryptococcal antigen tests on CSF and serum are diagnostic. Elevated CSF opening pressure is characteristic.
Mycobacterium tuberculosis	Basilar meningitis with cranial nerve abnormalities.
	CD4 cell count is usually >300/L. Culture and PCR of CSF are diagnostic.
Cytomegalovirus	Diffuse encephalitis and fever are characteristic.
	CD4 cell counts are <50/μL. CSF PCR is positive, and brain biopsy is diagnostic.
Neurosyphilis	Atypical and accelerated neurosyphilis is seen in HIV infection. Positive serum VDRL test, FTA-ABS, and MHA-TP.
μL = microliter.	

Therapy

Select empiric treatment with sulfadiazine, pyrimethamine, and folic acid in patients with multiple ring-enhancing lesions, positive *T. gondii* serologic test results (IgG), and immune suppression (CD4 cell count <200/microliter). Treat patients with persistent immunosuppression indefinitely. Biopsy lesions that fail to respond to 2 weeks of empiric therapy.

Candida Infections

Diagnosis

Mucocutaneous candidiasis may present as an erythematous intertriginous rash with satellite lesions. Oral candidiasis appears as adherent, painless white plaques on the tongue and buccal mucosa. Local invasion is most apparent in the esophagus and tends to occur in persons with reduced cell-mediated immunity or severe neutropenia. Risk factors for invasive candidiasis include:

- exposure to broad-spectrum antibiotics
- presence of central venous catheters
- parenteral nutrition
- immunosuppression, particularly neutropenia
- kidney failure
- prolonged ICU stay

Diagnosis is made by positive culture from the blood or a normally sterile body fluid or site.

◆ DON'T BE TRICKED

- *Candida* in a blood culture should never be considered a contaminant.

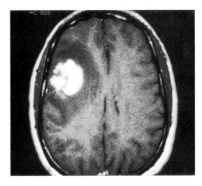

Intracerebral Toxoplasmosis: MRI showing a single ring-enhancing brain lesion associated with edema consistent with toxoplasmosis. Most patients with AIDS with cerebral toxoplasmosis have multiple ring-enhancing brain lesions.

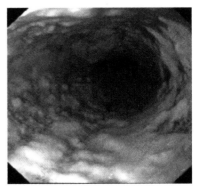

Esophageal *Candida*: White mucosal plaque-like lesions consistent with *Candida* seen on upper endoscopy.

Therapy

Treatment of *Candida* infections seems equally effective whether triazoles or echinocandins and amphotericin derivatives are used. Administration of amphotericin derivatives appears to be declining because other drugs are better tolerated and less expensive. Caspofungin, micafungin, and anidulafungin have been shown to be effective for treatment of *Candida* esophagitis.

Fluconazole is effective in preventing *Candida* infections in neutropenic oncology patients, but it has limited effectiveness for preventing other fungal infections.

◆ DON'T BE TRICKED

- Treatment is not indicated for *Candida* in the sputum of patients receiving mechanical ventilation. *Candida* pneumonia is very rare.
- Do not treat asymptomatic candiduria except in neutropenic patients or those undergoing invasive urologic procedures.

Aspergillosis

Diagnosis

STUDY TABLE: Pulmonary Aspergillosis Syndromes	
Condition	Characteristics
Allergic bronchopulmonary aspergillosis	Usually occurs in the setting of asthma or CF. Other findings are a positive skin test, elevated IgE, and eosinophilia. Presents as difficult-to-control asthma and recurrent pulmonary infiltrates.
Aspergilloma (fungus ball)	Occurs in preexisting pulmonary cavities or cysts, or in areas of devitalized lung. Symptoms are cough, hemoptysis, dyspnea, weight loss, fever, and chest pain.
Invasive sinopulmonary aspergillosis	Occurs in immunocompromised hosts. CT scan may show the "halo sign", a target lesion with a necrotic center and surrounding ground-glass attenuation (hemorrhage).

Neutropenic oncology patients and organ transplant recipients are at increased risk for developing *Aspergillus* infections. An effective noninvasive diagnostic test is not available. Blood cultures are rarely positive. The gold standard diagnostic test for *Aspergillus* infection is obtaining cultures from deep-body specimens. The serum galactomannan enzyme assay can support the diagnosis in the right clinical setting, and it can be followed serially to assess response to therapy.

Therapy

Voriconazole is a reasonable first-line treatment in patients with documented or suspected invasive aspergillosis. Treat allergic bronchopulmonary aspergillosis with oral corticosteroids.

Cryptococcal Infection

Diagnosis

The least-severe cryptococcal syndrome is characterized by lung involvement without dissemination. Disseminated disease may include bacteremia and meningitis and occurs in patients with HIV infection and organ transplant recipients.

Cryptococcal meningitis is the most common form of meningitis in patients with AIDS, who typically present with symptoms such as headache, irritability, and nausea. Most patients have a CD4 cell count of less than 100/microliter. The diagnosis is based on detection of cryptococcal antigen in the CSF or culture of *C. neoformans* in the CSF. The opening CSF pressure is typically elevated.

Therapy

Choose fluconazole for primary cutaneous infection without dissemination or for isolated mild pulmonary disease. For extrapulmonary disease, select amphotericin B plus flucytosine. Management of elevated intracranial pressure via serial therapeutic lumbar punctures is an essential part of treatment of CNS cryptococcosis.

Endemic Mycosis

STUDY TABLE: Differentiation of Endemic Mycoses		
Infection	**Geographic Distribution**	**What to Look For**
Blastomycosis (*Blastomyces dermatitidis*)	Midwestern, southeastern, and south central United States (Mississippi, Missouri, and Ohio river valleys)	Symptom onset 4-6 weeks after exposure
		Consider in patients with primary skin lesion or concurrent pulmonary and skin findings
		Consider in patients with acute pneumonia or subacute lung disease (e.g., TB, malignancy)
Coccidiomycosis (*Coccidioides* species)	Southern Arizona, south central California, southwestern New Mexico, west Texas	Symptom onset 1-3 weeks after exposure
		Consider in patients with pulmonary symptoms and erythema nodosum or erythema multiforme
		Consider in patients with pulmonary symptoms and prolonged constitutional symptoms (fever, fatigue)
Histoplasmosis (*Histoplasma capsulatum*)	Midwestern states in the Ohio and Mississippi valley regions	Symptom onset 2-3 weeks after exposure
		Consider in patients with complex pulmonary disease (nodular, cavitary, lymphadenopathy)
		Consider patients being evaluated for sarcoidosis, TB, or malignancy

Posttransplantation Infections

Diagnosis

Within the first 4 postoperative weeks, the most common infections in transplant recipients are the same as those that develop postoperatively in patients who have undergone non–transplant-related surgery:

- bacterial wound infection
- *C. difficile*–associated diarrhea
- central line–associated bloodstream infection
- CAUTI
- and health care–related pneumonia

CMV frequently occurs after the first month of transplantation, occurring most often in the setting of a CMV-negative transplant recipient with an organ from a CMV-positive donor. CMV is associated with:

- an increased risk for renal graft failure
- GI perforations and significant bleeding
- CMV-related pneumonia and respiratory failure
- EBV, polyomavirus BK, polyomavirus JC, and hepatitis B and C reactivation

Kidney transplant patients with polyomavirus BK infection may develop nephropathy, organ rejection, or ureteral strictures. HSCT recipients may develop hemorrhagic cystitis.

- Polyomavirus JC virus may cause progressive multifocal leukoencephalopathy.
- EBV infection is found in almost all patients with posttransplantation lymphoproliferative disease.

Therapy

Prophylaxis with ganciclovir, valganciclovir, or high-dose acyclovir is appropriate for transplant recipients at risk for or with known CMV infection. Patients receiving adequate anti-CMV prophylaxis have a lower incidence of polyomavirus BK and EBV reactivation. The only known effective treatment for polyomavirus JC infection is to reverse immunosuppressive therapy.

❖ **Test Yourself**

A 63-year-old woman is evaluated for fever and hypotension 4 days after kidney-pancreas transplantation surgery. She has erythema and tenderness around the surgical wound.

ANSWER: Select staphylococcal wound infection as the most likely cause of an early infection in a transplant patient.

Nephrology

Glomerular Filtration Rate

Because the serum creatinine concentration can be an inaccurate marker of the GFR, the Cockcroft-Gault and Modification of Diet in Renal Disease (MDRD) study equations are recommended as an alternative method of estimating kidney function in patients with stages 3 to 5 chronic kidney disease (CKD).

Conditions that decrease kidney perfusion, such as dehydration or HF, are associated with increased reabsorption of BUN in the proximal tubules and a disproportionate increase in the BUN-creatinine ratio, typically to 20:1 or higher.

◆ DON'T BE TRICKED

- A reduction or loss of muscle mass due to advanced age, liver failure, or malnutrition may cause a disproportionately low serum creatinine concentration, which results in overestimation of the GFR.
- The Cockcroft-Gault and MDRD do not accurately estimate kidney function in healthy persons, pregnant women, or patients with acute kidney injury.

Urinalysis

Proteinuria

Albumin is the only protein that is detected on dipstick urinalysis, and dipstick technology only detects albumin excretion >300 to 500 mg/24 h. A spot urine albumin-creatinine ratio is recommended to detect microalbuminuria (defined as 30-300 mg/g, corresponding to 30-300 mg/24 h), and either a spot urine albumin-creatinine or protein-creatinine ratio can be used to measure proteinuria (abnormal protein-creatinine ratio defined as >0.2 mg/mg).

Proteinuria is a marker of renal parenchymal and glomerular disease and an independent predictor of progressive kidney disease, cardiovascular disease, and peripheral vascular disease.

◆ DON'T BE TRICKED

- Dipstick urinalysis does not detect immunoglobulin light chains associated with multiple myeloma.
- Positional (orthostatic) proteinuria, a benign cause of isolated proteinuria, is diagnosed by obtaining split daytime (standing) and nighttime (supine) urine collections.

Hematuria

Hematuria is classified as glomerular and extraglomerular. Erythrocyte casts and dysmorphic erythrocytes (red blood cells with "Mickey Mouse" ears) in the urine indicate glomerular disease. Coexisting proteinuria supports glomerular causes of hematuria, even in the absence of casts.

Hematuria with preserved erythrocyte morphology in the urine, often without proteinuria or casts, is consistent with extra-glomerular bleeding (GU cancer, kidney stones, trauma, infection, and medications) and requires additional diagnostic studies to locate the extraglomerular source.

Consider the following sequenced evaluation of extraglomerular bleeding:

- urine culture to exclude infection, and if normal...
- noncontrast helical CT to detect calculi and cancer, and if normal...
- urine cytology, then stop evaluation if normal and patient is at low risk for malignancy (age <50 years, no other risk factors), otherwise...
- cystoscopy for patients with positive urine cytology, aged >50 years, or if risk factors for malignancy are present (cigarette smoking, analgesic abuse, benzene exposure, or voiding abnormalities)

◆ DON'T BE TRICKED

- **Evaluate hematuria even in patients taking anticoagulants.**
- **Patients with hemolysis and rhabdomyolysis test positive for blood on dipstick urinalysis in the absence of intact erythrocytes on urine microscopy.**

Leukocytes and Other Formed Elements

Leukocytes in the urine may be caused by glomerular or tubulointerstitial inflammation, infection, or an allergic reaction.

Remember:

- Sterile pyuria (pyuria and a negative urine culture) suggests *Mycobacterium tuberculosis*, interstitial cystitis, or interstitial nephritis.
- Eosinophiluria suggests acute interstitial nephritis, postinfectious glomerulonephritis, atheroembolic disease of the kidney, septic emboli, or small-vessel vasculitis.

Urine lipids and fat are almost always associated with heavy proteinuria or the nephrotic syndrome. These may appear as free lipid droplets, round or oval fat bodies, or fatty casts.

Casts are cylindrical aggregates of Tamm-Horsfall mucoprotein that trap the intraluminal contents and appear in the urine.

Different types of casts are associated with specific disorders:

- Erythrocyte casts indicate glomerular disease.
- Leukocyte casts indicate inflammation or infection of the renal parenchyma.
- Broad, muddy brown casts are associated with acute tubular necrosis.

Approach to Acid-Base Problem Solving

Answer these four questions when solving acid-base problems:

1. What is the primary disturbance?
2. Is compensation appropriate?
3. What is the anion gap?
4. Does the change in the anion gap equal the change in the serum bicarbonate concentration (a value called the delta-delta)?

When diagnosing a primary acid-base disorder, remember that:

- Acidemia is defined as a pH <7.38. Metabolic acidosis = [HCO_3] <24 meq/L and respiratory acidosis = arterial P_{CO_2} >40 mm Hg.
- Alkalemia is defined as a pH >7.42. Metabolic alkalosis = [HCO_3] >24 meq/L and respiratory alkalosis = arterial P_{CO_2} <40 mm Hg.

STUDY TABLE: Compensatory Response to a Primary Acid-Base Disturbance

Condition	Expected Compensation	Interpretation
Metabolic acidosis	Acute: Δ arterial $P_{CO_2} = (1.5)[HCO_3^-] + 8 \pm 2$	Failure of the arterial P_{CO_2} to decrease to expected value = complicating respiratory acidosis
	Chronic: Δ arterial $P_{CO_2} = [HCO_3^-] + 15$	Excessive decrease of the arterial P_{CO_2} = complicating respiratory alkalosis
Respiratory acidosis	Acute: 1 meq/L $\uparrow$ in $[HCO_3^-]$ for each 10 mm Hg $\uparrow$ in arterial P_{CO_2}	Failure of the $[HCO_3^-]$ to increase to the expected value = complicating metabolic acidosis
	Chronic: 3.5 meq/L $\uparrow$ in $[HCO_3^-]$ for each 10 mm Hg $\uparrow$ in arterial P_{CO_2}	Excessive increase in $[HCO_3^-]$ = complicating metabolic alkalosis
Metabolic alkalosis	0.7 meq/L $\uparrow$ in arterial $[HCO_3^-]$ for each 1 mm Hg $\uparrow$ in P_{CO_2}	This response is limited by hypoxemia
Respiratory alkalosis	Acute: 2 meq/L $\downarrow$ in $[HCO_3^-]$ for each 10 mm Hg $\downarrow$ in arterial P_{CO_2}	Failure of the $[HCO_3^-]$ to decrease to the expected value = complicating metabolic alkalosis
	Chronic: 4 meq/L $\downarrow$ in $[HCO_3^-]$ for each 10 mm Hg $\downarrow$ in arterial P_{CO_2}	Excessive decrease in $[HCO_3^-]$ = complicating metabolic acidosis

Anion Gap

The normal anion gap is 12 ± 2 meq/L; anion gap = $[Na^+] - ([Cl^-] + [HCO_3^-])$.

Always calculate the anion gap, regardless of the metabolic disturbance.

- When the primary disturbance is a metabolic acidosis, the anion gap differentiates increased anion gap from normal anion gap acidosis.
- When the primary disturbance is not a metabolic acidosis, the anion gap helps detect a "hidden" anion gap metabolic acidosis.
- An anion gap (<4 meq/L) suggests multiple myeloma or hypoalbuminemia.

Common causes of anion gap acidosis include:

- DKA
- CKD
- lactic acidosis (usually due to tissue hypoperfusion)
- aspirin toxicity
- alcoholic ketosis
- methanol and ethylene glycol poisoning

Common causes of normal anion gap metabolic acidosis include:

- GI HCO_3^- loss (diarrhea)
- kidney HCO_3^- loss (ileal bladder, proximal renal tubular acidosis)
- reduced kidney H^+ secretion (distal renal tubular acidosis, type IV renal tubular acidosis)
- Fanconi syndrome (phosphaturia, glucosuria, uricosuria, aminoaciduria)
- carbonic anhydrase inhibitor use

Urine Anion Gap

The UAG is defined as (urine $[Na^+]$ + urine $[K^+]$) – urine $[Cl^-]$. The UAG is normally between 30 to 50 meq/L (30 to 50 mmol/L). Metabolic acidosis of extrarenal origin is usually suggested by the clinical circumstances but in uncertain cases is suggested by a large negative UAG. The UAG is positive in patients with metabolic acidosis caused by distal (type 1) renal tubular acidosis, hypoaldosteronism (including type 4 renal tubular acidosis), and CKD.

Delta–Delta

In anion gap acidosis, the expected ratio between the change in anion gap and the change in plasma $[HCO_3]$ concentration (Δ anion gap/Δ $[HCO_3]$) is 1 to 2.

- If (Δ anion gap/Δ $[HCO_3]$) is <1, consider concurrent normal–anion gap acidosis.
- If (Δ anion gap/Δ $[HCO_3]$) is >2, consider concurrent metabolic alkalosis.

Metabolic alkalosis is often caused by upper GI loss of hydrogen chloride or by kidney loss of hydrogen chloride during diuretic therapy and is maintained by extracellular fluid volume contraction, chloride depletion, hypokalemia, or elevated aldosterone activity.

Test your understanding:

- Problem #1: pH, 7.31; arterial Pco_2, 10 mm Hg; sodium, 127 meq/L; chloride, 99 meq/L; bicarbonate, 5 meq/L.
- Problem #2: pH, 7.20; arterial Pco_2, 23 mm Hg; sodium, 134 meq/L; chloride, 80 meq/L; bicarbonate, 8 meq/L.

Answers:

- Mixed anion gap and normal–anion gap metabolic acidosis and respiratory alkalosis
- Mixed anion gap metabolic acidosis and metabolic alkalosis

Alcohol Poisoning

Diagnosis

Determine the presence of an osmolal gap, which is the difference between measured and calculated osmolality. The calculated plasma osmolality = $2 \times$ serum $[Na^+]$ + $[BUN]/2.8$ + blood $[glucose]/18$; sodium concentration is measured as meq/L, and BUN and glucose concentration are measured as mg/dL.

The normal osmolal gap is 10 mosm/kg H_2O. If a larger gap exists, consider alcohol poisoning as the source of unmeasured osmoles. Ethanol is the most common cause of alcohol poisoning.

STUDY TABLE: Clues for Ingestion of Specific Types of Alcohol	
Clues	**Alcohol Type**
Somnolence or coma and normal acid-base homeostasis	Isopropyl alcohol
Severe anion gap metabolic acidosis and acute visual symptoms or severe abdominal pain	Methanol (pancreatitis and retinal toxicity)
Severe anion gap metabolic acidosis and acute kidney injury	Ethylene glycol (metabolizes to glyoxylate and oxalic acid, which may cause calcium oxalate nephrolithiasis and acute kidney injury)
Anion gap metabolic acidosis and ketoacidosis	Ethanol

Therapy

Treat mild isopropyl alcohol poisoning with IV fluids and gastric lavage. Severe isopropyl alcohol poisoning (hypotension and shock) requires hemodialysis. Treat methanol and ethylene glycol poisoning with fomepizole and hemodialysis. Treat alcoholic ketoacidosis with IV normal saline and glucose.

Calcium Oxalate Crystals: Characteristic envelope-shaped calcium oxalate dihydrate crystals.

Hyponatremia

Diagnosis

The first step in assessing hyponatremia is to classify it as either hyperosmolar or hypo-osmolar. Patients with hyponatremia and hyperosmolality have pseudohyponatremia. In these patients, look for the presence of an osmotically active substance that is confined to the extracellular fluid. Conditions associated with pseudohyponatremia include hyperlipidemia, hyperproteinemia, and hyperglycemia. Irrigating solutions containing sorbitol and exogenous solutes such as mannitol can also cause pseudohyponatremia.

If the patient has hypo-osmolar hyponatremia, further classify the hyponatremia based on the patient's volume status.

STUDY TABLE: Evaluating Hypo-osmolar Hyponatremia		
Volume Status	**Laboratory Studies**	**Differential Diagnosis**
Hypovolemia (hypotension, tachycardia)	Spot urine sodium <10 meq/L BUN/creatinine >20:1 Urine osmolality >450 mosm/L	GI or kidney fluid losses, dehydration, adrenal insufficiency
Hypervolemia (edema, ascites)	Spot urine sodium <10 meq/L BUN/creatinine >20:1 Urine osmolality >450 mosm/L	HF, cirrhosis, kidney failure
Euvolemia (normal volume)	Spot urine sodium >20 meq/L BUN/creatinine <20:1 Urine osmolality usually >300 mosm/L	SIADH, hypothyroidism
Euvolemia (normal volume)	Spot urine sodium >20 meq/L BUN/creatinine <20:1 Urine osmolality 50-100 mosm/L	Compulsive water drinking

SIADH = syndrome of inappropriate antidiuretic hormone secretion.

Causes of SIADH include malignancy (small cell lung cancer); intracranial pathology; and pulmonary diseases, especially those that increase intrathoracic pressure and decrease venous return to the heart. Many medications can cause SIADH, including thiazides, SSRIs, tricyclic antidepressants, narcotics, phenothiazines, and carbamazepine.

Cerebral salt wasting syndrome causes hypo-osmolar hyponatremia and laboratory parameters exactly like that of SIADH. However, cerebral salt wasting syndrome is associated with hypovolemia, hypotension, and a neurosurgical procedure or subarachnoid hemorrhage within the previous 10 days.

◆ DON'T BE TRICKED

- Do not miss adrenal insufficiency as a cause of hypo-osmolar hyponatremia.

Therapy

IV volume replacement with normal saline is indicated for hyponatremia due to volume depletion, including hyponatremia from thiazide diuretics and cerebral salt wasting syndrome. For hypo-osmolar hyponatremia associated with neurologic symptoms, choose 3% hypertonic saline infusion and furosemide to correct the serum sodium to 120 meq/L. Central pontine myelinolysis (osmotic demyelination syndrome) may occur if hyponatremia is corrected too rapidly. Fluid restriction is used initially for asymptomatic outpatients with SIADH. Demeclocycline can also be used for outpatients who do not respond to fluid restriction. The IV V_1 and V_2 receptor antagonist conivaptan and the oral V_2 receptor antagonist tolvaptan (vaptans) are approved for treatment of euvolemic and hypervolemic hyponatremia. Therapy must be initiated in the hospital and is very expensive. No data to date show the vaptans are associated with improved patient outcomes compared with conventional therapy.

◆ DON'T BE TRICKED

- Do not correct the serum sodium faster than 0.5 meq/h (about 12 meq over 24 hours).

- **Vaptan agents should not be used to treat hypovolemic hyponatremia.**

❖ Test Yourself

A 53-year-old man has a 3-week history of increasing weakness and anorexia. On physical examination, blood pressure is 130/70 mm Hg, and pulse rate is 80/min without orthostatic changes. Laboratory studies: BUN, 12 mg/dL; serum creatinine, 0.8 mg/dL; serum sodium, 123 meq/L; potassium, 3.4 meq/L; chloride, 91 meq/L; bicarbonate, 22 meq/L; and urine sodium, 110 meq/L.

ANSWER: The diagnosis is SIADH. Select fluid restriction.

Hypernatremia

Diagnosis

Hypernatremia is serum sodium >145 meq/L. Severe hypernatremia indicates a defective thirst mechanism, inadequate access to water (older patients in nursing homes), a kidney concentrating defect (DI, most commonly due to lithium), and/or impaired pituitary secretion of ADH. Most commonly, hypernatremia is due to loss of hypotonic fluids (GI, kidney, skin) with inadequate water replacement.

Therapy

Therapy is directed at sodium chloride replacement, free water replacement, and correction of the underlying problem leading to hypotonic fluid loss. The water deficit is calculated as TBW − (desired [Na$^+$]/current [Na$^+$] × TBW), where TBW = 0.5 × weight (kg) in women or 0.6 × weight (kg) in men.

In volume depletion, fluid resuscitation with normal saline should precede correction of the water deficit with hypotonic fluids. Correct at a rate no greater than 1 meq/L/h with a goal of 50% correction at 24 to 36 hours and complete correction in 3 to 7 days. Neurogenic (central) DI is treated with intranasal desmopressin.

Hyperkalemia

Diagnosis

Hyperkalemia occurs as a result of shifts in potassium from the intracellular compartment to the extracellular fluid or (rarely) through total body potassium excess.

The most common causes of hyperkalemia include:

- hyporeninemic hypoaldosteronism
- acute and chronic kidney failure
- low urine flow states
- medications (ACE inhibitors, ARBs, potassium-sparing diuretics, pentamidine, trimethoprim-sulfamethoxazole, and cyclosporine)
- potassium shifts (rhabdomyolysis, hemolysis, hyperosmolality, insulin deficiency, β-adrenergic blockade, and metabolic acidosis)

Characteristic findings are ventricular arrhythmias and peaked T waves, flattened P waves, and a widened QRS on ECG.

Pseudohyperkalemia is an in vitro phenomenon caused by the mechanical release of potassium from cells during phlebotomy or specimen processing or in the setting of marked leukocytosis and thrombocytosis. Measure the plasma potassium concentration to confirm the diagnosis of pseudohyperkalemia.

◆ DON'T BE TRICKED

- Significant hyperkalemia associated with a normal ECG suggests pseudohyperkalemia.

Therapy

If hyperkalemia is associated with ECG changes or arrhythmias, begin IV calcium gluconate to stabilize the myocardium and shift potassium inside the cells with insulin and glucose or inhaled β-adrenergic agonists and by removing potassium from the body with oral cation exchange resins, loop diuretics (particularly if volume is overloaded), and dietary potassium restriction. Hemodialysis is often needed to correct life-threatening hyperkalemia but is never the "first step" because of the time delay in initiating dialysis.

◆ DON'T BE TRICKED

- Absolute levels of potassium cannot reliably determine if a life-threatening condition exists. Only ECG can assess the effect of hyperkalemia on the cardiac membrane.

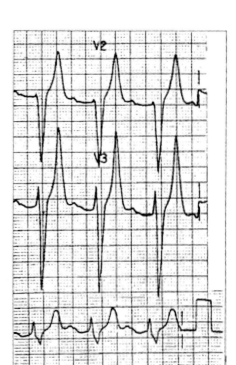

Characteristics of Hyperkalemia: ECG showing flattened P waves; prolonged PR interval; widened QRS; and tall, peaked T waves characteristic of hyperkalemia.

Hypokalemia

Diagnosis

Hypokalemia occurs through shifting potassium from extracellular fluid to intracellular fluid or through total body potassium depletion via urinary or GI losses. The most common causes of hypokalemia are vomiting and diarrhea (urine [Cl⁻] <20 meq/L) and use of diuretics (elevated urine [Cl⁻]).

Rare causes include:

- primary aldosteronism (hypertension, urine [Cl⁻] >40 meq/L, low plasma renin activity, and elevated aldosterone level)
- Bartter syndrome (normal blood pressure, hypokalemia, metabolic alkalosis, and elevated renin and aldosterone levels)
- Gitelman syndrome (hypokalemia and hypomagnesemia)
- inhaled β₂-agonists (may lead to hypokalemia in certain clinical settings)

Characteristic findings of hypokalemia include ileus, muscle cramps, rhabdomyolysis, and hypomagnesemia. ECGs may show U waves and flat or inverted T waves.

Therapy

For severe hypokalemia, IV potassium chloride is indicated. Total body potassium deficits are typically large (200-300 meq for a serum potassium concentration of 3 meq/L). Hypomagnesemia should be corrected, if present.

Hypomagnesemia

Diagnosis

The most common causes of hypomagnesemia include:

- GI losses (diarrhea, steatorrhea, intestinal bypass, pancreatitis)
- kidney losses (loop and thiazide diuretics, alcohol-induced)
- medications (cisplatin, aminoglycosides, amphotericin B, cyclosporine)
- hungry bone syndrome following parathyroidectomy

If no cause is clinically apparent, GI and kidney losses can be differentiated by measuring the 24-hour urine magnesium excretion. Hypomagnesemia is often associated with hypokalemia because of urine potassium wasting. Hypomagnesemia is also associated with hypocalcemia because of lower PTH secretion and end-organ resistance to PTH. If hypomagnesemia is suspected, look for neuromuscular irritability, hypocalcemia, and hypokalemia.

◆ DON'T BE TRICKED

- **Correction of hypokalemia and hypocalcemia is difficult unless magnesium depletion is also corrected.**

Therapy

Administer oral slow-release magnesium and IV magnesium sulfate to achieve a serum magnesium level >1 mg/dL.

❖ Test Yourself

A 30-year-old woman with Crohn disease has an ileostomy. For the past week, she has noted increased ostomy output, weakness, and paresthesias. Laboratory studies show serum sodium, 129 meq/L; potassium, 2.9 meq/L; bicarbonate, 18 meq/L; calcium, 5.5 mg/dL; and phosphorus, 1.3 mg/dL. After treatment with isotonic saline plus potassium chloride and sodium bicarbonate, the bicarbonate concentration is 22 meq/L. However, the serum potassium level is still 2.9 meq/L, and the serum calcium level is 5.3 mg/dL.

ANSWER: The diagnosis is hypomagnesemia. Begin IV magnesium replacement.

Hypophosphatemia

Diagnosis

Phosphate is primarily excreted through the kidneys and is reabsorbed mainly in the proximal tubule. The primary hormonal factors regulating phosphorus balance are PTH (which decreases phosphorus reabsorption and promotes kidney phosphate excretion) and calcitriol (which stimulates phosphate absorption in the gut). Characteristic findings in severe hypophosphatemia are HF, muscle weakness, rhabdomyolysis, hemolytic anemia, and metabolic encephalopathy.

Common causes:

- refeeding after starvation
- insulin administration for severe hyperglycemia
- hungry bone syndrome following parathyroidectomy
- respiratory alkalosis
- chronic diarrhea
- chronic alcoholism
- hyperparathyroidism
- vitamin D deficiency

Elevated urine excretion of phosphorus differentiates between kidney phosphate wasting and hypophosphatemia caused by ionic shifts or intestinal malabsorption.

Therapy

In asymptomatic patients, administer oral phosphorus replacement as a sodium or potassium salt. Parenteral therapy with either of these agents is indicated for symptomatic patients or those whose phosphorus level is <1 mg/dL.

Acute Kidney Injury

Prevention

In patients at high risk requiring imaging with contrast, use the smallest possible dose of a low-osmolar or iso-osmolar contrast agent, and treat with isotonic saline or bicarbonate before and immediately after the procedure. *N*-acetylcysteine may also be beneficial.

Diagnosis

AKI is defined as an abrupt elevation in the serum creatinine concentration or a decrease in urine output. The etiology may be secondary to decreased perfusion from prerenal causes, ischemic renal parenchymal disease, toxins, tubular obstruction, immunologic events or allergic reactions, or postrenal obstruction of urine outflow. Aminoglycosides constitute the most common cause of medication-induced AKI.

AKI is divided into oliguric (≤400 mL/24 h) and nonoliguric (>400 mL/24 h) forms. The lower the urine output, the worse the prognosis. Prerenal and postrenal causes must be distinguished from intrinsic renal parenchymal disease because they are often rapidly reversible.

Diagnostic studies include:

- urinalysis for protein, erythrocytes, leukocytes, and casts
- kidney ultrasonography to assess obstruction and kidney size
- peripheral blood smear for schistocytes (HUS, TTP, malignant hypertension, scleroderma renal crisis)
- serum aminotransferase levels in patients with evidence of chronic liver disease
- FE_{Na} to help differentiate prerenal azotemia from ATN. $FE_{Na} = ([\text{Urine Na}]/[\text{Serum Na}] \times 100\%) / ([\text{Urine creatinine}]/[\text{Serum creatinine}])$

Interpretation of the FE_{Na} in patients with oliguria:

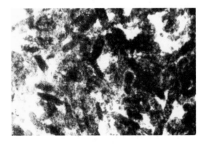

Muddy Brown Granular Casts: Muddy brown granular casts consistent with kidney injury secondary to tubular necrosis.

- If >1%, consider ATN or AIN. Urinalysis will help define the underlying pathology (AIN is associated with leukocytes and leukocyte casts, occasionally with eosinophils).
- If <1% (or spot urine sodium is <10 meq/L) and urinalysis is benign, consider prerenal azotemia.
- If <1% (or spot urine sodium is <10 meq/L) and urinalysis shows erythrocytes, dysmorphic erythrocytes, and erythrocyte casts or proteinuria, consider glomerulonephritis.

STUDY TABLE: Differential Diagnosis of Acute Kidney Injury

When You See This...	Think of...	And Select...
Minimal proteinuria, no hematuria or pyuria; presence of broad, muddy brown casts	ATN	FE_{Na} and/or spot urine sodium
Erythrocytes, erythrocyte casts, or dysmorphic erythrocytes	Glomerulonephritis	As appropriate: Titers for ANA, anti-dsDNA antibodies, and antistreptolysin O antibodies and C3, C4, and CH_{50}; hepatitis and HIV serologies and cryoglobulins; p-ANCA/c-ANCA and anti-GBM antibodies
Pyuria	Pyelonephritis, AIN	Culture urine Examine medication list
Eosinophilia, eosinophiluria, and rash	AIN, cholesterol emboli	Examine medication list Look for previous vascular procedure (angiography)
Livedo reticularis (violaceous reticular rash)	Cholesterol emboli	Look for previous vascular procedure (angiography) Consider vasculitis
Hypercalcemia and anemia	Multiple myeloma	Serum and urine protein electrophoresis, quantitative immunoglobulins
Nephrotic syndrome, urine protein >300 mg/dL	Diabetes mellitus, renal vein thrombosis	Plasma glucose Renal vein Doppler study
Obstruction on kidney ultrasound	BPH, nephrolithiasis, obstructing malignant mass, retroperitoneal fibrosis	Residual bladder volume, noncontrast CT or MRI
Complete anuria	Renal cortical necrosis	Kidney ultrasonography
Large kidneys on ultrasound	Amyloidosis, diabetes (early), HIV nephropathy	Serum protein electrophoresis, HIV serologic studies, plasma glucose
Kidney failure following colonoscopy	Phosphate-containing enemas (acute calcium phosphate crystal deposition in the kidneys)	Supportive care (fluids, stop ACE inhibitors, ARBs, NSAIDs)
Recent abdominal surgery, hemorrhage or acute pancreatitis	Abdominal compartment syndrome	Intravesicular pressure >20 mm Hg
Peripheral blood smear schistocytes, thrombocytopenia	Thrombotic microangiopathy (HUS/TTP, DIC, scleroderma renal crisis)	As indicated, CBC, coagulation parameters
Urine dipstick positive for blood, no erythrocytes on urinalysis	Hemolysis, rhabdomyolysis	Serum CK, serum haptoglobin, reticulocyte count, peripheral blood smear
AKI associated with acute leukemia or lymphoma or its treatment	Tumor lysis syndrome	Uric acid, phosphorus, potassium (all elevated)

Therapy

Begin IV normal saline for patients with volume depletion, and IV albumin for those with cirrhosis and intravascular volume depletion. Stop ACE inhibitors, diuretics, cyclosporine, and NSAIDs.

Select dialysis for:

- refractory hyperkalemia, acidemia, or volume overload
- signs or symptoms of uremia (altered mentation, asterixis, pericardial friction rub, vomiting)
- prolonged AKI (duration greater than several days)

For urinary obstruction, choose a catheter to relieve bladder outlet obstruction. If the obstruction is above the bladder, select retrograde or antegrade nephrostomies.

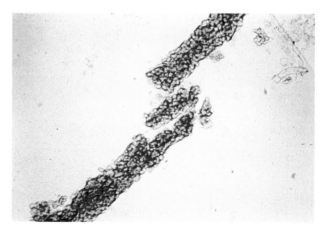

Glomerulonephritis: Erythrocyte casts consistent with glomerulonephritis.

◆ **DON'T BE TRICKED**

- Do not withhold dialysis until BUN, creatinine, or both reach "threshold" values.

STUDY TABLE: Acute Kidney Injury Treatment Protocol	
Indication	**Treatment**
Severe acidemia (pH <7.20)	IV bicarbonate or hemodialysis
Severe hypertension	Vasodilators, β-blockers, calcium channel blockers
Rapidly progressive glomerulonephritis, granulomatosis with polyangiitis (also known as Wegener granulomatosis), and severe IgA nephropathy	Cyclophosphamide, corticosteroids
Scleroderma renal crisis	ACE inhibitor, regardless of serum creatinine level
Hydronephrosis on ultrasound	Bladder catheter or nephrostomy tube
Abdominal compartment syndrome	Surgical decompression

◆ **DON'T BE TRICKED**

- Do not select routine loop diuretics (without evidence of volume overload), dopamine, or mannitol to treat acute kidney injury.

Chronic Kidney Disease

Prevention

To prevent or slow progression of CKD, aggressively manage causative diseases and avoid kidney toxins (contrast agents, NSAIDs). Treatment goals for patients with diabetes mellitus include a target hemoglobin A_{1c} of <7% and blood pressure of <140/90 mm Hg (or <130/80 mm Hg if diabetic nephropathy is present). Target blood pressure for patients with >1 g proteinuria is <130/80 mm Hg. Avoid gadolinium-enhanced MRI, because the risk of nephrogenic systemic fibrosis increases progressively with decreasing GFR and is greatest in patients receiving dialysis.

Diagnosis

CKD, characterized by an alteration in kidney function or structure for ≥3 months, occurs most often in patients with diabetes and hypertension. Characteristic findings of uremia are asterixis, loss of appetite, nausea, vomiting, and a pericardial rub.

Differential diagnosis of CKD:

- Diabetic kidney disease: Look for early microalbuminuria (spot albumin-creatinine ratio, 30-300 mg/g), followed by overt proteinuria, declining GFR, and a bland urine sediment. The presence of retinopathy strongly suggests coexisting diabetic nephropathy.
- Glomerular disease: Look for glomerular hematuria, proteinuria, and hypertension, often with other systemic manifestations (lupus nephritis and postinfectious glomerulonephritis). If nephrotic syndrome is present, look for focal segmental glomerulosclerosis, membranous nephropathy, minimal change disease, and amyloidosis. Kidney biopsy is often needed to make a specific diagnosis and guide therapy.
- Tubulointerstitial disease: Look for proteinuria, glycosuria, concentrating defect, sterile pyuria, and leukocyte

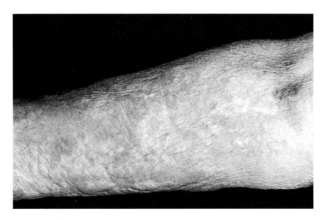

Nephrogenic Systemic Fibrosis: The patient has nephrogenic systemic fibrosis associated with an erythematous plaque, edema, and peau d'orange appearance. Image courtesy of Mark A. Perazella, MD, FACP.

casts, as well as papillary necrosis on ultrasound. Consider analgesic nephropathy (medication use, papillary necrosis), infection (TB, legionnaires disease, leptospirosis), allergic drug reaction (eosinophilia, eosinophiluria), autoimmune disorder (SLE, sarcoidosis, Sjögren syndrome), and lead nephropathy (occupational exposure).

- Vascular disease: Look for hematuria, proteinuria, and associated systemic illness. Vasculitis often presents with rapidly progressive glomerulonephritis and palpable purpura (leukocytoclastic vasculitis).

- After transplantation: CKD in the kidney transplant recipient may be caused by chronic allograft nephropathy, drug toxicity (cyclosporine), polyomavirus BK infection, or recurrence of disease.

- Structural disease (polycystic kidney disease): Look for hypertension, hematuria, palpable kidneys (advanced disease), family history of CKD.

◆ DON'T BE TRICKED

- If the kidneys are markedly scarred and small (<9 cm), do not select aggressive diagnostic or therapeutic measures.

Therapy

Begin restriction of sodium, potassium, and phosphorus. Drug therapy is based on specific findings.

STUDY TABLE: Drug Therapy for CKD	
If You See This...	**Select...**
Hypertension	An ACE inhibitor or ARB; use a loop diuretic rather than a thiazide for GFR <30 mL/min/1.73m²
Serum protein-creatinine ratio ≥200 mg/mg	Titrate ACE inhibitor and ARB to achieve minimal proteinuria even if patient is normotensive
Hemoglobin A$_{1c}$ >7%	More intensive intervention to maintain hemoglobin A$_{1c}$ <7%
Anemia	Erythropoietin to maintain hemoglobin levels of 10-11 g/dL and iron to maintain iron stores (always check iron levels before starting erythropoietin)
Hypocalcemia, hyperphosphatemia	Phosphate binders (calcium acetate, calcium carbonate, sevelamer) to maintain [PO$_4$] between 3.5-5.5 mg/dL; cinacalcet, a calcimimetic, is approved for treatment of secondary hyperparathyroidism in dialysis patients
Metabolic acidosis	Alkali therapy to maintain [HCO$_3$] between 20-26 meq/L
Lipids	Statin therapy to reduce LDL cholesterol <100 mg/dL
Vitamin D deficiency	Calcitriol (or vitamin D analogues)

Remember these guidelines when treating calcium and phosphorus disorders:

- Use calcium carbonate and calcium gluconate to maintain the serum phosphorus level between 2.7 and 4.6 mg/dL.

- If serum phosphorus levels remain elevated or a patient cannot tolerate calcium-containing binders (hypercalcemia or constipation), use phosphate binders (such as sevelamer).

- Use calcitriol or vitamin D analogs to suppress elevated PTH levels in stage 3 and stage 4 CKD.

- Cinacalcet is used in patients receiving dialysis therapy who do not respond to therapy with vitamin D analogues, calcium supplements, and phosphate binders.

Remember these points regarding kidney replacement therapy:

- Kidney transplantation is associated with superior quality of life and is less expensive compared with long-term dialysis.

- All patients with end-stage kidney disease are considered candidates for kidney transplantation unless they have systemic malignancy, chronic infection, severe cardiovascular disease, or neuropsychiatric disorders.

- Transplantation is particularly beneficial in young patients and those with diabetes mellitus.

For patients receiving hemodialysis, arteriovenous fistula creation is indicated when the serum creatinine level increases to near 4 mg/dL or the GFR decreases to <30 mL/min/1.73 m². Peritoneal dialysis catheters are placed approximately 1 month before therapy is initiated.

◆ **DON'T BE TRICKED**

- **Do not use aluminum-containing antacids because of the risk of aluminum toxicity.**
- **Do not use magnesium-containing antacids in patients with end-stage kidney disease.**

❖ Test Yourself

A 55-year-old woman with chronic lower back pain and chronic polyuria and nocturia is found to have CKD. Urinalysis shows no protein or erythrocytes, 5-10 leukocytes/hpf, and no casts. Urine culture shows no growth. Kidney ultrasound shows only papillary necrosis.

ANSWER: The diagnosis is tubulointerstitial disease, secondary to analgesic abuse.

Nephrotic Syndrome

Diagnosis

Nephrotic syndrome is defined by proteinuria (>3.5 g/24 h), hypoalbuminemia, and edema. Other findings may include hyperlipidemia with lipiduria ("Maltese cross" fat droplets in urine seen with polarized light microscopy). Massive proteinuria results in loss of anticoagulant proteins C and S and places the patient at risk for venous thromboembolism.

Many systemic conditions, medications, and recreational drugs may cause nephrotic syndrome, including:

- diabetes mellitus, SLE, multiple myeloma, and amyloidosis (particularly in older patients)
- group A streptococcal pharyngitis or cellulitis, HBV and HCV infection, HIV infection, syphilis
- colon, breast, and lung cancer or lymphoma
- NSAIDs, penicillamine, gold, interferon alfa, pamidronate
- heroin, cocaine

Diagnostic studies:

- fasting plasma glucose (diabetes)
- ANA (SLE)
- serum and urine protein electrophoreses and immunoelectrophoreses (multiple myeloma and amyloidosis)
- HBsAg, HCV antibodies (chronic hepatitis infection)
- HIV screening (HIV causes a collapsing focal segmental glomerulosclerosis)
- age- and sex-appropriate screening for malignancy (solid organ cancer-associated membranous glomerulonephritis)
- kidney ultrasonography to detect structural abnormalities of the kidneys, including cystic diseases and reflux nephropathy

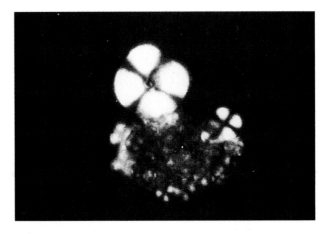

Fat Droplet: Typical "Maltese cross" appearance of a fat droplet under polarized light microscopy commonly found in the nephrotic syndrome.

In adults with idiopathic nephrotic syndrome, membranous nephropathy is most common in white Americans; focal segmental glomerulosclerosis is most common in black Americans. Minimal change disease is the most steroid-sensitive glomerular disease.

Renal vein thrombosis, DVT, and PE may complicate the nephrotic syndrome, especially if it is associated with membranous glomerulonephritis. Renal vein thrombosis may worsen proteinuria and kidney injury. Thromboembolic disorders require systemic anticoagulation therapy.

Therapy

Choose drug therapy based on the following:

- intensive therapy to optimize glycemic control for diabetes mellitus
- an ACE inhibitor or an ARB for proteinuria with stable kidney function
- a statin for hyperlipidemia
- a loop diuretic for edema
- a loop diuretic combined with albumin infusion or the addition of spironolactone for severe hypoalbuminemia

In adults with nephrotic syndrome, obtain a kidney biopsy before beginning corticosteroids or other immunosuppressive therapy. Hemodialysis, peritoneal dialysis, or kidney transplantation is indicated for patients with nephrotic syndrome and advanced CKD (GFR <30 mL/min/1.73 m^2).

Nephritic Syndrome

Diagnosis

Nephritic syndrome is characterized by:

- hypertension
- edema
- oliguria
- azotemia
- hematuria

The urine sediment may reveal hematuria with or without proteinuria (may include nephrotic-range proteinuria) and may contain erythrocytes, pigmented casts, and cellular debris. Rapidly progressive glomerulonephritis is characterized by an increase in creatinine over days to weeks, associated with a ≥50% loss of kidney function.

Glomerulonephritis

Diagnosis

Damage to the glomerular epithelial cells (podocytes) or the GBM alters the permeability of the capillary wall and results in proteinuria. Rupture of the capillary wall or proliferation of the resident mesangial cells of the glomerulus causes hematuria. Inflammatory infiltrations into the glomerulus may cause areas of necrosis and crescent formation that invade and sometimes replace Bowman's space.

STUDY TABLE: Causes of Acute Glomerulonephritis

Disease Type	Clinical Features
Acute poststreptococcal glomerulonephritis	Hematuria occurs 1-3 weeks after sore throat.
	Serum complement levels are low, and anti-DNAse B assay is positive.
	Kidney biopsy shows crescents, subepithelial deposits (humps), and mesangial deposits on electron microscopy.
IgA nephropathy	Hematuria occurs 1-2 days after a sore throat.
	Clinical manifestations range from asymptomatic microscopic hematuria to acute or chronic kidney failure.
	IgA deposits are present on the immunofluorescence staining of the kidney biopsy.
Idiopathic membranoproliferative glomerulonephritis (MPGN)	Hypocomplementemia, thickened capillary loops on light microscopy, and immune deposits are seen on electron microscopy.
Secondary MPGN	MPGN is seen in the setting of a chronic infection (HCV, syphilis, endocarditis, HIV), systemic disease (diabetes mellitus, RA), drugs (NSAIDs, penicillamine), and solid tumors (breast, colon, lung, kidney).
ANCA-associated glomerulonephritis (prototype is granulomatosis with polyangiitis [Wegener granulomatosis])	Nasal congestion, ulceration, chronic sinusitis, and/or pulmonary (often nodular) infiltrates are found.
	Pathologic findings include a proliferative glomerulonephritis in the setting of positive c-ANCA or p-ANCA.
Anti-GBM antibody disease (Goodpasture disease)	Glomerulonephritis and pulmonary hemorrhage are present.
	Linear staining of the GBM seen on immunofluorescence microscopy.
Cryoglobulinemia	Palpable purpura, arthritis, neuropathy, and digital ischemia are present.
	Low complement levels and cryoglobulins are present in the serum or on kidney biopsy specimens.
	Can be associated with HCV.

Diagnostic studies:

- blood or throat cultures, antistreptolysin O antibodies, and anti-DNAse antibodies; if positive, consider poststreptococcal glomerulonephritis
- serum complement levels (C3, C4, CH$_{50}$); if low, consider postinfectious glomerulonephritis, lupus nephritis, cryoglobulinemic nephritis (HCV), IE, and MPGN
- serologic tests for HBV and HCV
- ANA and anti-dsDNA antibodies for SLE
- mixed cryoglobulins for cryoglobulinemic glomerulonephritis (HCV) or MPGN
- p-ANCA, c-ANCA, and anti-GBM antibodies for vasculitis (granulomatosis with polyangiitis [Wegener granulomatosis] and Goodpasture syndrome)
- chest x-ray to detect granulomas (granulomatosis with polyangiitis [Wegener granulomatosis]) or pulmonary hemorrhage (Goodpasture syndrome)

Confirm the diagnosis of acute glomerulonephritis by kidney biopsy if other diagnostic studies are nonspecific.

Therapy

Manage the symptoms of acute glomerulonephritis, including edema (prescribe a loop diuretic) and hypertension.

◆ DON'T BE TRICKED

- **Do not prescribe ACE inhibitors and ARBs early in the course of glomerulonephritis because they may worsen the GFR.**

Treat the underlying cause of acute glomerulonephritis:

- appropriate antibiotics for postinfectious glomerulonephritis

- corticosteroids, cyclophosphamide, or mycophenolate mofetil, alone or in combination, for autoimmune-mediated glomerulonephritis (SLE, ANCA vasculitis, anti-GBM antibody disease, cryoglobulinemic glomerulonephritis)

- corticosteroids or mycophenolate mofetil for progressive IgA nephropathy

- corticosteroids for MPGN

- pegylated interferon alfa-2a and ribavirin therapy for MPGN and HCV

- prednisolone, interferon alfa, and lamivudine therapy for HBV-associated polyarteritis nodosa

- plasmapheresis for anti-GBM antibody disease

❖ **Test Yourself**

A 42-year-old woman's serum creatinine level has increased from 1 mg/dL to 2.3 mg/dL during the past year. On physical examination, blood pressure is 160/98 mm Hg. She has hepatosplenomegaly and a purpuric rash on her lower extremities. Serum total CH_{50} is reduced. Urinalysis shows erythrocyte casts and 3+ protein.

ANSWER: The diagnosis is hypocomplementemic glomerulonephritis with vasculitis (palpable purpura). Obtain measurements of serum cryoglobulins and serologic studies for HCV.

Pulmonary-Renal Syndromes

Diagnosis

The combination of acute glomerulonephritis and pulmonary hemorrhage defines the pulmonary-renal syndrome. The most common causes of the pulmonary-renal syndrome are granulomatosis with polyangiitis (Wegener granulomatosis), anti-GBM antibody disease (Goodpasture syndrome), and SLE.

◆ **DON'T BE TRICKED**

- **Nearly 95% of patients with granulomatosis with polyangiitis have sinus disease. The absence of sinus disease rules out this disorder.**

STUDY TABLE: Differential Diagnosis of Pulmonary-Renal Syndrome		
If you see this...	**Think this...**	**Choose this...**
Pulmonary infiltrates or nodules, sinusitis, nasal ulcers, saddle nose deformity, or glomerulonephritis	Granulomatosis with polyangiitis (Wegener granulomatosis)	c-ANCA, p-ANCA, and antiproteinase-3 (anti-PR3)
Glomerulonephritis and alveolar hemorrhage	Anti-GBM antibody disease (Goodpasture disease)	Anti-GBM antibodies; immunofluorescence microscopy revealing linear staining of IgG lining the GBM
Pulmonary hemorrhage, nephritis, arthralgia, serositis, rash, anemia, thrombocytopenia, leukopenia	SLE	Anti-dsDNA or anti-Sm antibodies
Bacterial endocarditis or cryoglobulinemia	Immune complex–mediated disorders	Serum cryoglobulins and blood cultures

Therapy

Plasmapheresis, corticosteroids, and cyclophosphamide are indicated for patients with anti-GBM antibody disease. Corticosteroids and cyclophosphamide are used to treat granulomatosis with polyangiitis (Wegener granulomatosis) and SLE with glomerulonephritis and alveolar hemorrhage.

Renal-Dermal Syndromes

Watch for glomerulonephritis and dermal inflammation, including palpable purpura, necrosis, ulcers, and nodules. These renal-dermal syndromes include:

- SLE
- Henoch-Schönlein purpura
- ANCA-associated vasculitis
- cryoglobulinemia

Polyarteritis nodosa is characterized by necrotizing inflammation of the medium-sized or small arteries without glomerulonephritis. The kidneys, skin, joints, muscles, nerves, and GI tract are commonly involved, usually in some combination. Biopsy of affected tissues makes the diagnosis.

Renal Tubular Acidosis

Diagnosis

Normal anion gap metabolic acidosis is associated with all three types of RTA.

STUDY TABLE: Differential Diagnosis of Renal Tubular Acidosis		
Diagnosis	**Metabolic Findings**	**Associated Findings**
Distal (classic or type 1) RTA	Normal anion gap acidosis, hypokalemia, positive UAG, urine pH >5.5 (in the setting of systemic acidosis), serum $[HCO_3] \cong 10$ meq/L	Nephrolithiasis and nephrocalcinosis, autoimmune disorders (SLE, Sjögren syndrome), amphotericin B use, urinary obstruction
Proximal (type 2) RTA	Normal anion gap metabolic acidosis, normal UAG, hypokalemia, urine pH <5.5, serum $[HCO_3] \cong 16\text{-}18$ meq/L	Glycosuria, phosphaturia, uricosuria, aminoaciduria, and tubular proteinuria (Fanconi syndrome)
Type 4 RTA	Normal anion gap metabolic acidosis, hyperkalemia, positive UAG, urine pH <5.5	Diabetes mellitus, urinary tract obstruction

Therapy

In proximal RTA, correction of acidemia in patients with bicarbonate therapy is often not possible. The addition of a thiazide diuretic may help by inducing volume depletion, lowering the GFR and thereby decreasing the filtered load of bicarbonate. The addition of a potassium-sparing diuretic may limit the degree of kidney potassium wasting.

In distal RTA, administration of bicarbonate usually corrects the metabolic acidosis. The potassium deficit should be corrected before correcting the acidemia.

In type 4 RTA, the primary goal of therapy is to correct the hyperkalemia, which will treat the acid-base disturbance. These patients may develop severe hyperkalemia following treatment with ACE inhibitors or ARBs.

❖ **Test Yourself**

A 31-year-old woman with inflammatory bowel disease passes a kidney stone. Serum sodium is 142 meq/L, potassium is 2.9 meq/L, chloride is 112 meq/L, and bicarbonate is 20 meq/L. Urine pH is 6.5.

ANSWER: The diagnosis is distal RTA.

Nephrolithiasis

Diagnosis

Kidney stones are predominantly composed of calcium but may be formed by other substrates such as uric acid, struvite, or cystine.

Important risk factors for stone formation include:

- insufficient fluid intake
- increased dietary sodium and protein intake
- hypercalciuria, hyperuricemia, hyperoxaluria
- low urine citrate levels (citrate inhibits crystal formation)
- primary hyperparathyroidism with hypercalciuria
- metabolic syndrome and type 2 diabetes mellitus
- recurrent UTIs with urease-splitting organisms such as *Klebsiella* and *Proteus* (struvite stones)

Patients with suspected nephrolithiasis should be asked about:

- a personal or family history of stone disease
- polycystic kidney disease, medullary sponge kidney, distal renal tubular acidosis
- high-risk medical illness (Crohn disease, ileostomy)
- high-risk medications (indinavir, acetazolamide)
- diets with increased protein (Atkins diet)
- repeated UTIs, high urine pH, and staghorn calculi (*Proteus* infections)

The classic symptoms of nephrolithiasis are acute flank pain and hematuria. Urinalysis reveals blood, and the urine sediment has intact, nondysmorphic erythrocytes. Initial laboratory studies include urinalysis and measurement of serum electrolytes, calcium, phosphorus, and uric acid. Plain radiography of the abdomen can be done initially (but select ultrasonography for pregnant women). If the plain x-ray is nondiagnostic, order a noncontrast helical CT, the gold standard for diagnosis. Straining and analyzing the urine for stone collection is necessary to definitively establish the stone type.

◆ DON'T BE TRICKED

- **The absence of erythrocytes on urinalysis does not rule out nephrolithiasis.**

Therapy

Therapy varies according to the specific findings. Kidney stones <5 mm in diameter typically pass spontaneously. Stones >10 mm often require invasive measures.

Acute treatment:

- IV saline solution for acute nephrolithiasis only if extracellular fluid volume depletion is present
- nifedipine and corticosteroids or tamsulosin for distal ureteral stones <10 to 15 mm in diameter (corticosteroids reduce ureteral edema to facilitate stone passage; nifedipine and tamsulosin induce ureteral dilatation and relaxation)
- parenteral ketorolac for acute renal colic
- shock wave lithotripsy

Chronic treatment:

- Calcium stones and hypercalciuria: thiazide diuretics; potassium citrate supplements; increased water intake; dietary calcium 800 to 1200 mg/d (do not restrict); and reduced animal protein, salt, oxalate, and total calories
- Calcium stones and hyperuricosuria: allopurinol

- Uric acid stones and hyperuricosuria: allopurinol and reduced animal protein intake
- Large struvite stones: percutaneous nephrostolithotomy and long-term prophylactic antibiotics

◆ **DON'T BE TRICKED**

- Asymptomatic kidney stones found on imaging studies do not require urgent stone removal.
- Do not select a low-calcium diet for patients with kidney stones. Calcium restriction does not prevent stones and may actually increase stone formation and contribute to bone demineralization.

❖ **Test Yourself**

A 35-year-old woman is evaluated in the emergency department for right flank pain and hematuria. She has a long history of Crohn disease and has had multiple operations to remove portions of her ileum and colon.

ANSWER: The probable diagnosis is calcium oxalate stones secondary to increased oxalate absorption in the GI tract and subsequent hyperoxaluria.

Autosomal-Dominant Polycystic Kidney Disease

Diagnosis

Polycystic kidney disease is characterized by multiple epithelial-lined kidney cysts scattered throughout both kidneys. ADPKD is caused by a mutation on chromosome 16 (*PKD1*). Early clinical manifestations of ADPKD include back and flank pain, hematuria, kidney stones, hypertension, UTIs, and stroke. ADPKD is associated with cerebral aneurysms and hepatic cysts. Kidney ultrasonography is the diagnostic test of choice. The number of kidney cysts seen on ultrasound required to establish a diagnosis varies based on the patient's age, PKD genotype, and whether a family history of ADPKD is present. Complications of ADPKD include progressive renal insufficiency, infected renal cysts (flank pain and fever accompanied by a bland urinalysis and a negative urine culture), and hemorrhage into a cyst.

◆ **DON'T BE TRICKED**

- Routine screening for intracranial aneurysms is not justified.

STUDY TABLE: Kidney Cystic Diseases to Remember	
Disease	**Characteristics**
Acquired kidney cystic disease	Associated with long-standing kidney insufficiency and increased risk for renal cell carcinoma, usually papillary
von Hippel-Lindau disease	Associated with solid tumors
	Extrarenal manifestations, including retinal or CNS hemangioblastomas, pheochromocytomas, pancreatic cysts, and epididymal cystadenoma

Therapy

Prescribe an ACE inhibitor or ARB for hypertension and normal or near-normal kidney function (target blood pressure is <130/80 mm Hg). Infected cysts are treated empirically with a fluoroquinolone or trimethoprim-sulfamethoxazole. Hemorrhage into a cyst is treated with bed rest and increased fluid intake. Patients may require nephrectomy for severe abdominal pain due to cyst hemorrhage and cyst infection unresponsive to medical treatment.

Neurology

Ischemic Stroke and Transient Ischemic Attack

Prevention

Begin warfarin in most patients with atrial fibrillation (AF; see Cardiovascular Medicine, Atrial Fibrillation). Start aspirin therapy in patients with nonvalvular AF who are at low risk of stroke and meet the following criteria:

- patients <75 years of age
- normal blood pressure
- normal LV function
- no previous transient ischemic attack (TIA) or stroke
- no diabetes mellitus

◆ DON'T BE TRICKED

- **The classification of type of AF (paroxysmal, persistent, or permanent) does not affect the decision to anticoagulate.**

Diagnosis

Stroke is a sudden focal neurologic deficit caused by either ischemia (85%) or hemorrhage (15%). Ischemic stroke may be further characterized by the etiologic mechanism (large-artery atherosclerosis, cardioembolic, small-vessel disease). Hemorrhagic stroke is classified as either subarachnoid (5%) or intracerebral (intraparenchymal) (10%).

TIA is a transient focal neurologic deficit resulting from ischemia rather than infarction. TIAs are classically defined as lasting <24 hours, although some experts advocate for a duration of <1 hour and no evidence of infarction on imaging.

All patients with stroke or TIA require emergent head CT without contrast to rule out intracranial hemorrhage.

STUDY TABLE: Cerebrovascular Territories and Syndromes	
Artery	**Major Clinical Features**
Anterior cerebral artery	Contralateral leg weakness
Middle cerebral artery	Contralateral face and arm weakness greater than leg weakness; sensory loss, visual field cut, aphasia, or neglect (depending on side)
Posterior cerebral artery	Contralateral visual field cut
Deep/"lacunar"	Contralateral motor or sensory deficit without cortical signs (aphasia, apraxia, neglect, and loss of higher cognitive functions), clumsy hand–dysarthria syndrome, and ataxic hemiparesis
Basilar artery	Oculomotor deficits and/or ataxia with "crossed" sensory/motor deficits. Crossed signs include sensory or motor deficit on one side of the face and the opposite side of the body
Vertebral artery	Lower cranial nerve deficits (vertigo, nystagmus, dysphagia, dysarthria, and tongue or palate deviation) and/or ataxia with crossed sensory deficits

Obtain an ECG and vascular studies early in the initial stroke. In most patients, this may include echocardiography, carotid artery ultrasonography, and MRA or CTA of the head and neck. Routine testing for antiphospholipid antibodies is probably not warranted.

Patients with TIA have an elevated risk of subsequent stroke, particularly in the next 48 hours.

◆ **DON'T BE TRICKED**

- Hospitalize all patients with acute TIA or stroke for urgent evaluation.
- Consider vertebral-basilar stroke in elderly persons with persistent vertigo.

Therapy

Select intubation and mechanical ventilation for patients with a decreased level of consciousness.

Administer recombinant tissue plasminogen activator (rtPA) to all patients with ischemic stroke within 3 hours of stroke onset (if unknown onset, then within 3 hours of the last time the patient was seen to be well). rtPA may be administered up to 4.5 hours after onset in selected patients who do not possess any of the following exclusionary criteria:

- age >80 years
- severe stroke
- diabetes mellitus with a previous infarct
- anticoagulant use

Additional exclusionary criteria for thrombolysis include:

- history of ICH
- ischemic stroke or head trauma during the previous 3 months
- GI or GU bleeding during the previous 3 weeks
- major surgery or trauma during the previous 14 days
- arterial puncture at noncompressible site within 7 days
- heparin therapy within the previous 48 hours with elevated aPTT
- glucose <50mg/dL or >400 mg/dL; INR >1.7; platelet count <100,000/microliter
- systolic blood pressure >185 mm Hg and diastolic pressure >110 mm Hg
- seizure at stroke onset

In patients with suspicion of a thrombolysis-induced intracranial hemorrhage, stop ongoing infusion of rtPA and evaluate with another CT.

Additional therapy in patients with stroke:

- Treat temperature >38.0 °C with acetaminophen.
- Treat blood glucose >150 mg/dL with insulin.
- Administer normal saline to maintain euvolemia.
- Allow for permissive hypertension (see following).
- Give aspirin, 325 mg, unless thrombolysis is planned.
- Start DVT prophylaxis within 48 hours.

Do not begin antihypertensive treatment unless:

- systolic blood pressure is >220 mm Hg, diastolic pressure is >120 mm Hg, or mean arterial pressure >140 mm Hg
- thrombolytic therapy is planned (target <185/110 mm Hg)
- acute coronary syndrome or aortic dissection is present

If the patient is eligible for thrombolysis, blood pressure must be lowered and stabilized to <185 mm Hg systolic and <110 mm Hg diastolic and maintained below these levels for at least 24 hours after therapy. Preferred antihypertensive agents include IV labetalol and IV nicardipine infusion.

A swallowing assessment is recommended for patients who have experienced strokes before they start to eat or drink. Select early stroke rehabilitation to improve clinical outcomes.

STUDY TABLE: Secondary Prevention of Stroke	
Intervention	**Indication**
Antiplatelet therapy	Begin 24 hours after giving thrombolytic agents. Aspirin plus dipyridamole is superior to aspirin alone. Clopidogrel is equivalent to aspirin and is used when aspirin is contraindicated.
Anticoagulation therapy	After 48 hours, treat high-risk cardioembolic etiologies of stroke and TIA with warfarin, including in patients with AF, left atrial appendage thrombus, LV thrombus, and dilated cardiomyopathy with reduced EF.
Endarterectomy	Endarterectomy is recommended within 2 weeks after a nondisabling stroke or TIA if ipsilateral carotid stenosis is >70% provided the patient is likely to live 5 years. For ipsilateral moderate (50%-69%) carotid artery stenosis, carotid endarterectomy is also usually recommended, depending on patient-specific factors (such as age, sex, comorbidities, and severity of initial symptoms).
Statins	Begin statin therapy for all patients regardless of cholesterol level.
Hypertension	Maintain blood pressure <140/90 mm Hg after recovery from the acute event.

◆ DON'T BE TRICKED

- The 3- to 4.5-hour window for rtPA treatment begins at the onset of symptoms. If stroke occurred during sleep, onset is defined as the last time the patient was awake and behaving normally.

- If the patient is unable to report the time of onset and there are no witnesses to the onset, rtPA treatment is contraindicated.

- Do not select heparin for most patients with ischemic stroke.

- Do not select anticonvulsant medications after stroke unless the patient has had a seizure.

- Do not combine aspirin and clopidogrel for the secondary prevention of stroke.

- Do not close patent foramen ovale for secondary stroke prevention.

- Do not select carotid endarterectomy for carotid artery stenosis <50%.

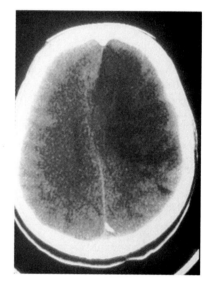

Ischemic Stroke: CT scan of the brain without contrast shows a large wedge-shaped hypodensity with mass effect 24 hours after onset of symptoms.

Subarachnoid Hemorrhage

Prevention

Patients with small (<7 mm) unruptured aneurysms can be followed with MRI; those with larger aneurysms should consider surgery. The risk of rupture increases with size and location of the aneurysm in the posterior circulation.

Diagnosis

Spontaneous SAH most commonly results from the rupture of saccular ("berry") aneurysms of the circle of Willis. SAH less commonly results from rupture of an AVM, arterial dissection, coagulopathy, and cocaine abuse. Most patients present to the emergency department with sudden onset of the "worst headache of my life" or severe neck pain. However, up to 40% of patients with SAH experience a "sentinel hemorrhage" characterized as severe headache during the previous 2 to 3 weeks. Common findings include meningism. Subhyaloid hemorrhage may be seen on funduscopy. Focal neurologic deficits occur from aneurysms that compress a cranial nerve, bleed into brain parenchyma, or cause focal ischemia due to vasospasm.

Noncontrast CT establishes the diagnosis of SAH in >90% of patients. Blood in the subarachnoid space is very dense and looks white. Early conventional cerebral angiography identifies the aneurysm and determines management. Other causes of abrupt severe headache include arterial dissection and venous sinus thrombosis, both of which may be detected with vascular imaging; pituitary apoplexy; hypertensive emergency; and ICH.

- If the CT scan is normal, always select CSF examination to look for erythrocytes or xanthochromia.
- If angiography is negative, order a repeat study 4 to 6 weeks later.

Therapy

The three main neurologic complications for a patient with a SAH are rebleeding, delayed brain ischemia from vasospasm, and hydrocephalus. Treat ruptured aneurysms with surgical clipping or coiling within 48 to 72 hours. Prescribe nimodipine for 21 days to prevent post-SAH vasospasm and stroke. Any change in mental status should prompt emergency CT to evaluate for repeat bleeding and for signs of hydrocephalus, which is treated with ventricular drainage.

❖ **Test Yourself**

A 44-year-old woman comes to the emergency department reporting "the worst headache of my life." She has meningism but no focal neurologic findings. CT scan is normal.

ANSWER: The diagnosis is SAH. Select CSF examination.

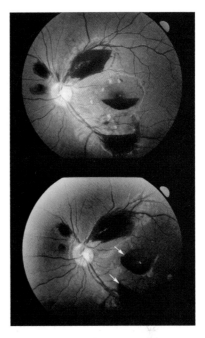

Subhyaloid Hemorrhage: Bleeding under the vitreous membrane (subhyaloid hemorrhage) is a finding associated with subarachnoid hemorrhage.

Intracerebral Hemorrhage

Diagnosis

The most common risk factor for ICH is hypertension (common in patients with hemorrhage in the basal ganglia, thalamus, and cerebellum). Other risk factors include amyloid angiopathy (primarily in older adult patients with lobar hemorrhage), vascular malformations, coagulopathy, and use of cocaine or alcohol.

ICH, with symptoms similar to those of ischemic stroke, cannot be reliably distinguished by clinical criteria alone. CT without contrast establishes the diagnosis. Cerebral angiography is indicated for patients <45 years of age with ICH related to cocaine use (which is associated with a high incidence of vascular anomalies).

Therapy

Identify and reverse anticoagulation. Mannitol, barbiturate coma, and hyperventilation may be used to reduce intracranial pressure. IV nitroprusside, nicardipine, or labetalol is indicated to maintain systolic blood pressure between 140 and 160 mm Hg (mean arterial blood pressure between 70 and 130 mm Hg). Intraventricular hemorrhage requires prompt ventricular drainage to reduce intracranial pressure. Cerebellar hemorrhages require posterior fossa decompression.

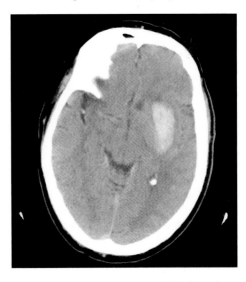

Intracerebral Hemorrhage: CT scan of the brain shows a brightly enhancing hemorrhage in the left basal ganglia.

◆ **DON'T BE TRICKED**

- **Treatment with IV factor VIIa limits early enlargement of hemorrhage volume but does not improve function or survival.**
- **Corticosteroids are not recommended for intracranial hemorrhage.**

Dementia

Diagnosis

Dementia is an acquired chronic impairment of memory and other aspects of intellect that impedes daily functioning. Mild cognitive impairment describes cognitive decline greater than expected for age but without interference with daily functioning. The rate of progression of mild cognitive impairment to dementia is 10% per year. Alzheimer disease is the most prevalent dementia; however, non-Alzheimer dementia constitutes one third of cases of dementia.

Characteristic findings of Alzheimer disease are memory loss, getting lost, difficulty finding words, and difficulty with dressing, grooming, and doing housework.

A score <24 on the Folstein Mini–Mental State Examination is compatible with dementia.

Usual but unproved laboratory studies include a CBC, a comprehensive metabolic profile, TSH and vitamin B_{12} levels, and screening tests for syphilis. Routinely obtain brain imaging with CT or MRI. Screen all patients for depression. Consider lumbar puncture and CSF examination in patients:

- with delirium
- at risk for carcinomatous meningitis
- at high risk for CNS infections
- with rapidly progressive disease
- with positive syphilis serology

Abrupt cognitive, behavioral, and neurologic deterioration in patients with dementia commonly results from infection (e.g., urinary tract infection, pneumonia) or medication errors.

STUDY TABLE: Differential Diagnosis of Memory Dysfunction	
When you see this...	**Choose this...**
Acute onset, fluctuating course, inattention, disorganized thinking, and altered consciousness	Delirium
Evidence of objective memory impairment in the absence of other cognitive deficits and intact activities of daily living	Mild cognitive impairment
Gradual memory loss, aphasia, apraxia, agnosia, inattention, delusional thinking, decrease in executive function, and left-right confusion	Alzheimer disease
Stepwise deterioration, multiple infarcts on neuroimaging	Vascular dementia
Mild parkinsonism, delusions, and visual hallucinations	Dementia with Lewy bodies
Prominent personality changes, behavioral disturbances including disinhibition and impulsivity, diminished frontal and/or temporal lobes on MRI, onset before age 60 years	Frontotemporal dementia
Clinical triad of dementia, shuffling gait, and urinary incontinence	Normal-pressure hydrocephalus
Axial rigidity, bradykinesia, retropulsion, and vertical gaze palsy (key finding)	Progressive supranuclear palsy
Choreoathetosis and dementia, autosomal dominant pattern of inheritance	Huntington disease
Prominent myoclonus, characteristic EEG pattern of triphasic sharp waves, CSF protein 14-3-3, rapidly progressive onset at early age	Creutzfeldt-Jakob disease

◆ DON'T BE TRICKED

- Do not order apolipoprotein E genotyping in patients with suspected Alzheimer disease.

Therapy

Choose cholinesterase inhibitors (donepezil, rivastigmine, and galantamine) to slow intellectual decline in patients with mild to moderate Alzheimer disease. Cholinesterase inhibitors can have prominent cholinergic side effects, including diarrhea, nausea and vomiting, bradycardia, syncope, and heart block. Memantine delays cognitive decline in patients with moderate to advanced Alzheimer disease (Mini–Mental State Examination score of 3 to 14). Memantine may be used alone or in combination with a cholinesterase inhibitor. No agents have received FDA approval for the treatment of dementia-related psychosis, but atypical antipsychotic agents, such as quetiapine, are widely used in patients with parkinsonism because they are less likely to cause or exacerbate extrapyramidal syndromes. All antipsychotic agents are associated with an increased risk of death in patients with dementia; most deaths are related to infection (e.g., pneumonia). Treat depression with SSRIs. Manage atherosclerotic risk factors and use aspirin in patients with vascular dementia. Perform CSF drainage for normal-pressure hydrocephalus.

◆ **DON'T BE TRICKED**

- Do not prescribe high-dose vitamin E to slow the progression of Alzheimer disease.
- Do not select amitriptyline or imipramine for depression, because they can exacerbate confusion.

Delirium

Diagnosis

Diagnosis of delirium is based on the Confusion Assessment Method diagnostic algorithm, which provides greater accuracy than laboratory tests, imaging studies, or other tests. Choose delirium if the first two points and either point 3 or 4 are present.

1. acute onset and fluctuating course
2. inattention
3. disorganized thinking
4. altered level of consciousness

Look for triggers of delirium, particularly medications known to cause delirium and polypharmacy. Pay particular attention to sedative-hypnotics, barbiturates, alcohol, antidepressants, anticholinergics, opioid analgesics, antipsychotics, anticonvulsants, antihistamines, and antiparkinsonian agents. Also consider fluid and electrolyte abnormalities, uncontrolled pain, hypoxemia, anemia, infections, immobility, visual and hearing impairment, sleep cycle disruption, and catheters and other "tethers" (IV lines, ECG leads, and restraints).

◆ **DON'T BE TRICKED**

- Brain imaging is usually not helpful in diagnosing delirium unless there is a history of falls or evidence of focal neurologic impairment.

Therapy

Treat or eliminate precipitating factors. Achieve behavior control with environmental or social measures rather than pharmacologic or physical restraints. Choose haloperidol or risperidone for agitated delirium only in life-threatening circumstances (such as in the ICU) or when behavioral measures are ineffective.

◆ **DON'T BE TRICKED**

- Always select behavioral interventions first and order a "sitter" instead of using restraints or drugs.
- All atypical antipsychotics (aripiprazole, clozapine, olanzapine, quetiapine, risperidone, and ziprasidone) and older antipsychotics (haloperidol) are associated with an increased risk of mortality in patients with dementia and psychosis or behavioral disturbances.

Myelopathy

Diagnosis

Spinal cord dysfunction, or myelopathy, can occur because of a lesion arising within the spinal cord or extrinsic compression of the spinal cord. Myelopathy typically presents as motor or sensory dysfunction of the limbs and trunk at or below the site of a lesion. Typical patterns include symmetric or asymmetric spastic paraparesis (associated with a cervical or thoracic lesion) or quadriparesis (associated with a cervical lesion). Some patients note a sensory level below which they perceive numbness or neuropathic discomfort (burning, prickling, or a tight band-like sensation around the limb or trunk). Examination findings include paraparesis or quadriparesis accompanied by spasticity, hyperreflexia, and extensor plantar responses; a truncal sensory level detected with pinprick examination; impaired vibratory and proprioceptive sensation; and abnormal gait. Causes of noncompressive myelopathy include inflammatory or demyelinating lesions, spinal cord infarction, and vitamin B_{12} or copper deficiency.

STUDY TABLE: Selected Causes of Myelopathy

Cause	Features
Multiple sclerosis	See MS in the following section
Neuromyelitis optica (NMO; Devic disease)	Recurrent episodes of myelitis and optic neuritis without the brain lesions typical of MS; NMO-IgG autoantibody may be present
Idiopathic transverse myelitis	Subacute onset of weakness, sensory changes, and bowel/bladder dysfunction, typically after a viral infection
Vitamin B_{12} deficiency	Paresthesias, lower-extremity weakness, and gait instability. Findings may include paraparesis, vibration and position sense loss, and sensory ataxia. Anemia may be absent
Copper deficiency	Mimics vitamin B_{12} deficiency. May develop secondary to malabsorption after bariatric surgery or from excessive zinc ingestion
Infarction of the spinal cord	Acute onset, findings correspond to the territory of the anterior spinal artery. Weakness and pinprick sensation loss below the level of the infarction but sparing vibration and position sense

Select MRI of the spine to exclude spinal cord compression in all patients with clinical suspicion of spinal cord disorder. Lumbar puncture may be beneficial in patients with suspected inflammatory or demyelinating spinal cord lesions.

◆ DON'T BE TRICKED

- Do not exclude vitamin B_{12} deficiency in patients with normal or borderline serum measurements. Check methylmalonic acid and homocysteine measurements to confirm the diagnosis.

Therapy

Treatment of acute compressive myelopathy is urgent surgery. Epidural metastasis may also respond to corticosteroids or radiation. There is no treatment for spinal cord infarction. For treatment of demyelinating diseases, see the next section on MS. Treat vitamin B_{12} and copper deficiencies with supplementation. Direct treatment of inflammatory and infectious myelopathy at the underlying disorder. Treat transverse myelitis with IV methylprednisolone, and consider plasmapheresis or cyclophosphamide if transverse myelitis is corticosteroid refractory.

Multiple Sclerosis

Diagnosis

MS is characterized by episodes of dysfunction due to demyelinating lesions (plaques) in different areas of the CNS (brain, brain stem, or spinal cord) at different times. Clinical course follows one of three patterns: relapsing-remitting, secondary progressive, or primary progressive disease. Relapsing-remitting MS is characterized by clinical episodes of neurologic dysfunction, typically lasting weeks before improving, that may in some patients lead to the accumulation of disability. About

50% of patients with relapsing-remitting disease develop secondary progressive disease, characterized by the disappearance of evidence of clinical relapses and by progressive disability.

Characteristic findings of MS include sensory loss or paresthesias (especially elicited by neck flexion), internuclear ophthalmoplegia (failure of adduction of the affected eye), optic neuritis, ataxia, hyperreflexia, spasticity, and heat sensitivity that causes worsening fatigue or neurologic symptoms.

Order MRI of the brain and spinal cord; ovoid white matter lesions in a patient with appropriate findings is consistent with MS. Imaging will also exclude a compressive lesion. CSF may contain oligoclonal IgG bands or an elevated IgG index. CSF analysis is not necessary but can be helpful when the diagnosis remains questionable.

Therapy

IV methylprednisolone followed by oral corticosteroids speeds recovery from acute exacerbations, most effectively in acute optic neuritis. Treat fever and look for underlying infection before beginning corticosteroids, because fever worsens symptoms of MS (pseudorelapse) and treatment of the underlying trigger will improve symptoms.

After the first attack of a clinically isolated syndrome (optic neuritis, spinal cord syndrome, or brain stem–cerebellar syndrome), prescribe interferon-β or glatiramer acetate if imaging suggests MS. Prescribe interferon-β or glatiramer acetate for confirmed relapsing-remitting MS. Natalizumab and mitoxantrone are used for interferon- and glatiramer-refractory disease but have potential for serious side effects (risk of progressive multifocal leukoencephalopathy and cardiotoxicity, respectively). MS relapses that have no or minimal impact on function may simply be observed. If functional status (vision, strength, balance, or coordination) is impaired, IV methylprednisolone will speed recovery but does not alter the ultimate degree of recovery.

Encourage regular physical activity or physical therapy to maintain musculature and minimize disability.

Encourage smoking cessation because of the threefold increase in the risk of secondary progression associated with cigarette smoking.

◆ DON'T BE TRICKED

- Interferon agents are contraindicated in patients with liver disease or depression.

❖ Test Yourself

A 25-year-old woman has a 2-week episode of new-onset gait ataxia, nystagmus, and dysarthria. Two years ago, she had optic neuritis. An MRI of the brain now shows brain lesions consistent with MS.

ANSWER: The diagnosis is relapsing-remitting MS. Choose IV methylprednisolone and interferon-β.

Multiple Sclerosis Lesions: Fluid-attenuated inversion recovery MRI shows MS lesions in the paraventricular white matter bilaterally.

Amyotrophic Lateral Sclerosis

Diagnosis

Motoneuron diseases consist of an acquired group of degenerative disorders involving cortical motoneurons in the frontal lobe (primary lateral sclerosis), anterior horn cells in the spinal cord (progressive muscular atrophy), and cortical motoneurons and anterior horn cells (ALS). Characteristic features include progressive painless weakness, clonus, spasticity, fasciculations, an extensor plantar response, and preserved reflexes or hyperreflexia.

Muscle weakness in patients with ALS usually begins distally and asymmetrically, although 20% of patients have bulbar-onset ALS with difficulty speaking and swallowing. All patients with suspected ALS should undergo EMG to test for muscle degeneration and MRI of the appropriate anatomic areas to diagnose treatable neurologic disorders that may mimic

ALS. Pulmonary function tests and overnight pulse oximetry studies can establish the presence of respiratory insufficiency. Patients with bulbar signs or symptoms require evaluation of swallowing function.

◆ DON'T BE TRICKED

- Findings not typical for ALS include predominant sensory symptoms or pain, cognitive impairment, and ocular muscle weakness.
- Fasciculations in the absence of associated muscle atrophy or weakness are not due to ALS.
- Weakness in the absence of fasciculations is not due to ALS.

Therapy

Riluzole may increase survival by about 3 months. Begin noninvasive ventilatory support for patients with respiratory insufficiency. Placement of a percutaneous endoscopic gastrostomy (PEG) tube is indicated when weight loss or swallowing difficulty occurs.

Parkinson Disease

Diagnosis

Parkinsonism is a generic term referring to any cause of parkinsonian symptoms and signs. Parkinson disease, a distinct clinicopathologic entity caused by the degeneration of dopaminergic neurons in the substantia nigra of the midbrain, is characterized by at least two of the following conditions: bradykinesia, rigidity, resting tremor, postural reflex abnormality, and gait freezing. Patients with parkinsonism are at increased fall risk and may present for evaluation of frequent falls.

Neurologic signs and symptoms are asymmetric at onset. Clinical improvement usually occurs after administration of levodopa and/or a dopamine agonist. In advanced disease, look for evidence of autonomic dysfunction, such as orthostatic hypotension, urinary frequency and urgency, constipation, and diarrhea. Seborrheic dermatitis is a well-recognized Parkinson disease cutaneous association.

Brain imaging may be obtained to exclude other disease processes such as vascular disease, hydrocephalus, and other degenerative diseases that may mimic Parkinson disease.

◆ DON'T BE TRICKED

- Early symmetric symptoms or signs, early falls, rapid progression, poor or waning response to levodopa, dementia, early autonomic failure, and ataxia suggest a diagnosis other than Parkinson disease.

STUDY TABLE: Differential Diagnosis of Parkinson Disease	
Disease	**Considerations**
Multiple system atrophy (Shy-Drager syndrome)	Severe orthostatic hypotension and ataxia. MRI showing "necrosis" of the putamen and cerebellar atrophy
Progressive supranuclear palsy	Unexplained falls (typically backward), inability to move eyes vertically, and parkinsonian features
Dementia with Lewy bodies	Dementia, parkinsonism, and hallucinations
Medication-induced parkinsonism	Antiemetics (prochlorperazine, metoclopramide), antipsychotics (haloperidol), reserpine, lithium, and methyldopa

Therapy

Levodopa is the most effective medication used in the treatment of Parkinson disease but is associated with motor fluctuations, such as dyskinesias and a "wearing-off" effect, which refers to enhanced parkinsonian symptoms due to ineffective dopamine therapy. These motor fluctuations develop at a rate of 10% annually in patients older than 60 years but seem to develop more rapidly and are more severe in younger patients. Therefore, most clinicians will initiate therapy with a dopamine agonist (pramipexole, ropinirole) in patients younger than 65 years. At some point, however, all patients will require the addition of levodopa therapy. Levodopa is the drug of choice in older patients. Levodopa is administered in conjunction with carbidopa, which prevents the peripheral conversion of levodopa to dopamine. Side effects of dopamine agonists include sedation and increase in compulsive behaviors such as gambling, shopping, and hypersexuality.

Increasing the dose or frequency of levodopa is indicated to treat the symptoms of wearing off. The surgical procedure of choice is deep-brain stimulation of the subthalamic nucleus, which may decrease the effects of wearing off and help patients decrease medication dosages.

◆ DON'T BE TRICKED

- Begin drug therapy when symptoms begin to interfere with function.
- Avoid cabergoline and bromocriptine, because they are associated with valvular heart disease.

❖ Test Yourself

A 68-year-old woman has a 2-year history of falls and imbalance. She has a staring facial expression and impaired upward gaze.

ANSWER: The diagnosis is supranuclear palsy.

Hyperkinetic Movement Disorders

Diagnosis

Hyperkinetic movement disorders include tremors (rhythmic oscillation), dystonia (sustained contraction of opposing muscles, resulting in repetitive movements or abnormal posture), myoclonus (abrupt jerking movements of the extremities), and chorea.

STUDY TABLE: Hyperkinetic Movement Disorders		
Condition	**Key Manifestations**	**Therapy**
Essential tremor	Bilateral postural tremor, as when the hands are outstretched, or kinetic, as during writing; improves with alcohol	Propranolol or primidone
Huntington disease	Abnormal involuntary movements, progressive dementia, and psychiatric manifestations	Symptomatic only
	Autosomal dominant	
Drug-induced dystonia	Can be caused by neuroleptics, antiemetics, and serotoninergic medications	Stop the offending drug
		IV diphenhydramine, benztropine, or biperiden
Cervical dystonia (torticollis)	Cervical muscle contractions resulting in abnormal posture of the head and neck	Botulinum toxin or anticholinergic medications
Restless legs syndrome	Restlessness or unpleasant sensations in the legs that are caused by rest and relieved by walking or stretching	Treat iron deficiency anemia
		Choose ropinirole or pramipexole
Periodic limb movement disorder	Repetitive jerky movements primarily involving the legs and occurring with sleep	As above
	Highly associated with restless legs syndrome	

◆ DON'T BE TRICKED

- Rigidity and resting tremor are not features of essential tremor.

Migraine Headache

Diagnosis

More than 90% of headaches are primary headaches, including migraine, tension-type headaches, and cluster headaches. Secondary headache disorders include acute sinusitis, SAH, meningitis, encephalitis, brain tumor, and benign intracranial hypertension. Migraine is the most common headache in clinical practice and is frequently missed or misdiagnosed as another type of headache (tension-type or sinus headache). Approximately 20% of patients with migraine experience aura during or within the hour before the headache. An aura may manifest as visual loss, hallucinations, flashing lights, numbness, tingling, weakness, or confusion. Use the POUND mnemonic to diagnose migraine:

- Pulsatile quality
- One-day's duration (between 4 and 72 hours)
- Unilateral in location
- Nausea or vomiting
- Disabling intensity (patient goes to bed)

Three or more features are 90% predictive of migraine headache. Rule out medication overuse headache ("rebound"). Patients with this finding must be weaned off headache medications.

◆ DON'T BE TRICKED

- **Ninety percent of patients with "sinus headache" have migraine headache that will respond to triptan medications.**
- **Neuroimaging is indicated only for atypical headache features or for headaches that do not meet the strict definition of migraine.**

Carotid artery dissection may present as a migraine mimic or stroke. It characteristically develops after head or neck trauma but may occur spontaneously with ipsilateral throbbing neck, head, or orbital pain with possible Horner syndrome. Neurologic findings may include contralateral numbness or weakness or ipsilateral monocular visual symptoms. MRA of the carotid arteries and carotid duplex ultrasonography are the diagnostic tests of choice.

STUDY TABLE: Differential Diagnosis of Headaches	
Disease	**Considerations**
Tension-type headache	30 minutes to 7 days
	Typically bilateral location
	Pressure or tight quality
	Does not prohibit activity
	Not associated with nausea
	Treat acute headache with NSAIDs
	A tricyclic antidepressant may be needed for prophylaxis
Cluster headache	20-60 minutes, several times per day
	Repeating over weeks, then disappearing for months or years
	Unilateral tearing and nasal congestion or rhinorrhea
	Pain usually periorbital
	Treat with a triptan for acute headache, corticosteroids to break cycle of headaches, and verapamil for long-term prevention. Oxygen therapy may be helpful
Trigeminal neuralgia	Brief paroxysms of unilateral lancinating pain in the V_2 or V_3 distribution of the trigeminal nerve, often triggered by light touch of affected area
	Obtain an MRI to exclude intracranial lesions and MS
	Select carbamazepine for treatment
Frontal sinusitis	Usually worse when lying down; associated with nasal congestion; tenderness over affected sinus
	Treat with decongestants; use antibiotics only if severe systemic symptoms or duration >7 days
Medication overuse headache (rebound headache)	Chronic headache that occurs at least 15 days per month
	Related to frequent use of headache medications, including triptans, narcotics, caffeine, and NSAIDs
	Must withdraw all pain medications
Chronic daily headache	Headache disorders that occur daily or near daily and last 4 or more hours; the most common diagnoses are chronic tension headache, rebound headache, and chronic (transformed) migraine
	Identify and treat underlying depression, anxiety, panic disorder, and sleep disturbance

Therapy

Migraine treatment is categorized as acute, prophylactic, and rescue. Acetaminophen, NSAIDs, or aspirin is the first-line treatment for acute mild-to-moderate migraine. A triptan may be used for severe acute migraine or poor response to first-line treatment. Choose codeine, hydrocodone, or oxycodone as rescue medications if no relief occurs within 1 hour of triptan administration. Metoclopramide is effective for migraine-associated nausea and enhances the efficacy of the abortive medication.

Choose prophylaxis when migraines occur more than 2 times per week or more than 8 times per month. Evidence-based migraine prophylaxis (in nonpregnant patients) includes topiramate, valproic acid, amitriptyline, metoprolol, propranolol, and timolol. Women ≥35 years of age who have migraine without aura and women of any age who have migraine with aura should not use combined (estrogen-progestin) oral contraceptives because of increased risk of stroke.

◆ DON'T BE TRICKED

- Do not choose oral medications for patients with nausea and vomiting.
- Triptans are contraindicated in the presence of CAD.
- Do not use acute therapies more than 2 to 3 days per week to avoid medication overuse (rebound) headaches.

❖ Test Yourself

A 39-year-old woman has chronic headaches that occur daily and do not respond to analgesics. Medications are zolmitriptan, naproxen, acetaminophen with codeine, and amitriptyline.

ANSWER: The diagnosis is chronic daily headache from medication overuse. Taper all medications.

Epilepsy

Diagnosis

Epilepsy is a collection of brain disorders characterized by two or more unprovoked seizures. Partial or localization-related seizures result from an electrical discharge that originates in a focal region of the brain. Primary generalized seizures are caused by an electrical discharge that involves all areas of the brain simultaneously. The electrical discharge in secondarily generalized seizures is focal in onset but rapidly spreads to involve the entire cerebral cortex.

STUDY TABLE: Seizure Classifications	
Seizure Type	**Characteristics**
Simple partial seizure	Normal consciousness and awareness
	Single neurologic modality (sensory, motor, olfactory, visual, gustatory) involving a single region of the body, such as the hand or arm
Complex partial seizure	Conscious but unresponsive or staring
	Automatism (lip smacking, swallowing, or manipulating objects)
	Postictal confusion
Primary generalized seizure	Loss of consciousness at onset
	No prodromal symptoms
	Whole-body stiffening (tonic seizures) or jerking (clonic seizures)
	Brief, lightning-like jerks (myoclonic seizures) of the arms

Order an EEG, although a normal EEG does not rule out a seizure. Laboratory evaluation should include a CBC, electrolyte and glucose levels, and a toxicology screen. All patients with a seizure should have a brain MRI (or head CT), unless evidence from the history and EEG is convincing for a primary generalized seizure disorder or if an unrelated contraindication to MRI exists (such as a pacemaker or aneurysm clip). CSF examination should also be done if the patient has fever, altered mental status after the seizure, or severe headache. The initial evaluation should be directed at determining an underlying cause for the seizure before diagnosing a primary seizure disorder.

Status epilepticus is characterized by continuous seizure for 30 minutes. Complications include fever, hemodynamic instability, acidosis, rhabdomyolysis, and pulmonary edema and are associated with a mortality rate of approximately 20%. Thiamine and glucose can be administered if alcohol abuse is suspected or the cause of the status epilepticus is unknown. Emergent head imaging can also be useful in the absence of a known underlying cause but should not delay treatment.

◆ DON'T BE TRICKED

Avoid misdiagnosis:

- Syncope: Look for sweating and nausea, brief loss of consciousness, occasional tonic-clonic jerking, and recovery without confusion.
- Pseudoseizure (nonepileptic seizure): Look for long duration (10-30 minutes), asynchronous movement of arms or legs, and "stopping and going" of the seizure.
- Absence seizure: Do not choose this in an adult.

Therapy

For most adults who have had a first seizure, the risk for a second event is 30% to 60%. Patients with an abnormal EEG and a remote symptomatic cause (head trauma, previous stroke) have the highest risk. After a second seizure, the risk for recurrence increases to 80% to 90%. Starting anticonvulsant therapy after two or more unprovoked seizures is appropriate. Choose single-agent therapy and increase the dosage until seizures are controlled or the patient develops adverse medication effects. If unsuccessful, discontinue the first drug, and initiate a second drug as a single agent. Although serum drug level monitoring may be helpful, targeting a clinical response is more important than achieving a specific serum level. Addition of new medications that alter the metabolism of anticonvulsants may result in loss of seizure control.

Antiepileptic medication may be effectively withdrawn in many patients who have been seizure free for 2 to 5 years. Predictors of relapse include:

- an abnormal EEG before or during medication withdrawal
- an abnormal neurologic examination
- mental retardation
- frequent seizures before achieving remission

◆ DON'T BE TRICKED

- Primary prophylaxis with antiepileptic drugs is not indicated for a new stroke or tumor.
- Patients with juvenile myoclonic epilepsy require lifelong medication.

STUDY TABLE: Treating Seizures	
Seizure Type	**Treatment**
Partial onset seizures (simple or complex)	First choice: carbamazepine or lamotrigine
Primary generalized seizures (tonic-clonic or myoclonic)	First choice: valproic acid or lamotrigine

Surgery is the only treatment that may cure epilepsy. The most common surgical procedure is resection of mesial temporal lobe sclerotic lesions associated with partial seizures. The vagus nerve stimulator is appropriate for patients with medically refractory epilepsy who are not candidates for epilepsy surgery.

The most common cause of status epilepticus is a low antiepileptic drug blood level. An IV benzodiazepine (lorazepam), followed by phenytoin or the patient's maintenance drug, should be administered after 5 minutes of continuous seizing.

Antiepileptic medications raise the risk of congenital malformation. Most women will require continued drug therapy during pregnancy. The goal is to reduce the medication to the greatest extent and still maintain seizure control. Low-dose monotherapy is preferred. When possible, valproic acid should be discontinued (pregnancy risk category D drug).

❖ **Test Yourself**

A 33-year-old woman has "spells" during which she is conscious but unresponsive and unaware of her environment. She has repetitive hand movements that last approximately 1 minute followed by several minutes of mild confusion.

ANSWER: The diagnosis is partial complex seizure. Begin carbamazepine.

Peripheral Neuropathy

Diagnosis

Patients with neuropathy may present with pain, paresthesias, weakness, or autonomic dysfunction. Neuropathies are classified by anatomic distribution and etiology.

Mononeuropathies, isolated disorders affecting a single peripheral nerve, are most frequently caused by nerve entrapment or compression (carpal tunnel syndrome).

Mononeuropathy multiplex involves multiple noncontiguous peripheral nerves, either simultaneously or sequentially. This is often the result of a systemic disease (vasculitis or sarcoidosis).

Polyneuropathy refers to a diffuse, generalized, and usually symmetric peripheral neuropathy. Polyneuropathy is often a manifestation of systemic disease or exposure to a toxin or medication.

In all neuropathies, EMG can be helpful to characterize the type (axonal or demyelinating), severity, and distribution of the disease. Other useful tests include vitamin B_{12} level, serum protein electrophoresis, ESR, and plasma glucose level.

STUDY TABLE: Diagnosing and Managing Peripheral Neuropathy		
If you see this...	**Think this...**	**And choose this...**
Sensory loss over palmar surface of first three digits and weakness with thumb abduction and opposition	Median neuropathy (carpal tunnel syndrome)	Wrist splints or corticosteroid injections for mild disease; surgical release if severe
Numbness of the fourth and fifth fingers and weakness of interosseous muscles	Ulnar neuropathy	Elbow splinting or elbow pads; surgical release if severe
Pain, tingling, and numbness in great toe and along medial foot	Tarsal tunnel syndrome	Local corticosteroid injection; decompression surgery if severe
Upper and lower face weakness	Bell palsy most likely caused by HSV infection	Prednisone if within 72 hours of onset
Multiple, noncontiguous nerve deficits (mononeuritis multiplex)	Consider vasculitis (especially if painful), lymphoma, amyloidosis, sarcoidosis, Lyme disease, HIV, leprosy, and diabetes	Treat underlying disorder
Distal and symmetric (stocking-glove) paresthesias or pain	Axonal polyneuropathies; diabetes and alcohol are the most common etiologies; other causes include arsenic exposure, Charcot-Marie-Tooth disease, vitamin B_{12} deficiency, paraproteinemia, paraneoplastic disease, antineoplastic drugs, uremia, and hypothyroidism	Treat underlying disorder; treat pain and dysesthesias symptomatically with tricyclic antidepressants, gabapentin, pregabalin, or duloxetine
Severe unilateral leg pain, numbness, proximal weakness, atrophy, and weight loss	Diabetic lumbosacral radiculoplexus neuropathy (diabetic amyotrophy)	Treat diabetes
Acute, ascending, areflexic paralysis and paresthesias often preceded by GI illness or URI; CSF shows elevated protein and a normal cell count	Guillain-Barré syndrome	Plasma exchange and IV immune globulin
Progressive proximal motor and sensory neuropathy that evolves over months	Chronic inflammatory demyelinating polyneuropathy	Prednisone, plasma exchange, and IV immune globulin
Flaccid paralysis and distal sensory loss, cranial nerves spared; often associated with sepsis and organ failure	Critical illness polyneuropathy	Supportive
Progressive proximal weakness and diminished tendon reflexes that improve with repetitive movement of affected muscles	Eaton-Lambert syndrome	Search for and treat underlying malignancy

Therapy

Treatment of axonal polyneuropathies is centered on removal of the toxic agent (alcohol) or improvement of the underlying metabolic condition (diabetes, vitamin B_{12} deficiency).

◆ **DON'T BE TRICKED**
- **Do not treat Bell palsy with antiviral drugs.**

❖ **Test Yourself**

A 37-year-old woman has difficulty going up stairs. She had diarrhea and low-grade fever 2 weeks ago. Physical examination shows weakness of both lower extremities and diminished deep tendon reflexes.

ANSWER: The diagnosis is Guillain-Barré syndrome. Begin plasma exchange and IV immune globulin.

Myasthenia Gravis

Diagnosis

MG is an autoimmune disease caused by antibodies directed against the acetylcholine receptor, which results in impaired neuromuscular transmission. Characteristic findings of MG include:

- ptosis or diplopia
- muscle weakness, including dysphagia and dyspnea
- positive anti–acetylcholine receptor antibody titer (although a negative titer does not rule out MG)
- normal deep tendon reflexes and sensation

Symptoms are worsened by fatigue, exertion, increased body temperature, stress, and intercurrent infections. Single-fiber EMG can also establish the diagnosis. Serum TSH levels should be measured because of the association of MG with autoimmune thyroid disorders. Perform CT of the chest to detect thymoma.

Include botulism and Eaton-Lambert myasthenic syndrome in the differential diagnosis. Botulism starts with cranial nerve involvement, including diplopia, dysphagia, and sluggish or nonreactive pupils, whereas the pupils are normal in MG.

Eaton-Lambert myasthenic syndrome involves progressive proximal weakness and diminished tendon reflexes that improve with repetitive movement of affected muscles and is caused by antibodies to voltage-gated calcium channels. Fifty to sixty percent of patients with this syndrome have an undetected malignancy, typically small cell lung cancer.

Therapy

Pyridostigmine is the initial therapy. Reduce the dosage if increased salivation, respiratory secretions, sweating, or bradycardia develops. Patients with more severe symptoms may benefit from immunosuppressive therapy with agents such as prednisone, cyclosporine, azathioprine, and mycophenolate mofetil. If vital capacity decreases to <15 mL/kg, intubate the patient and begin plasmapheresis. Thymectomy is indicated if a thymoma is found on CT or MRI.

Vertigo

Diagnosis

Vertigo is a sensation of rotation or movement, representing vestibular dysfunction in most cases.

Peripheral causes of vertigo:

- Benign positional vertigo is typically induced by positional change, such as looking up or rolling over in bed. Attacks lasting 10 to 30 seconds occur multiple times per day.
- Vestibular neuritis (labyrinthitis) is acute, severe, and characterized by nausea, vomiting, and imbalance. Symptoms last for hours. Residual symptoms last for days.
- Meniere disease is characterized by repeated episodes of tinnitus, fluctuating hearing loss, and severe vertigo accompanied eventually by a progressive sensorineural hearing loss.

Central causes of vertigo:

- Vertebrobasilar insufficiency involves multiple brain stem findings, including facial weakness, diplopia, dysarthria, and vertigo.
- Acoustic neuroma is associated with dizziness, but cochlear symptoms (tinnitus and hearing loss) often predominate.
- Cerebellar hemorrhage causes instability, diplopia, and lethargy.
- MS induces relapsing and remitting neurologic abnormalities, such as optic neuritis.

The Dix-Hallpike maneuver (Nylen-Barany maneuver) helps differentiate types of vertigo:

- Peripheral causes of vertigo are confirmed if nystagmus begins in 3 to 40 seconds, stops within 30 seconds, and decreases with repetition (fatigability). Horizontal and rotary nystagmus is most common.
- Central causes of vertigo are confirmed if nystagmus develops immediately, does not stop rapidly, and does not decrease with repeated testing (no fatigability). Vertical nystagmus is more common.

Obtain an audiogram for all patients with hearing loss, ear fullness, or tinnitus. Meniere disease is associated with a fluctuating, low-frequency hearing loss. Asymmetric hearing loss suggests retrocochlear pathology (acoustic neuroma, meningioma) and is evaluated with an MRI of the internal auditory canal (and brain if other cranial nerves are involved).

Therapy

STUDY TABLE: Management of Selected Causes of Vertigo/Dizziness	
Diagnosis	**Treatment**
Vestibular neuritis (labyrinthitis)	Corticosteroids to facilitate resolution; meclizine for symptom control; vestibular rehabilitation program
Benign positional vertigo	Reassurance and follow-up (gradually resolves in most patients); habituation exercises; canalith repositioning (Epley) maneuver
Meniere disease	Meclizine for symptoms; salt restriction, diuretics if frequent recurrences; surgery for refractory cases

❖ **Test Yourself**

A 55-year-old man has brief episodes of vertigo when moving his head. He develops delayed onset and fatigable horizontal nystagmus during Dix-Hallpike testing.

ANSWER: The diagnosis is positional vertigo. Select the canalith repositioning (Epley) maneuver.

Viral Encephalitis

Diagnosis

Encephalitis is almost always caused by viral infections such as enterovirus and HSV. However, in up to 60% of patients, the specific etiologic agent is not identified. For viral encephalitis, look for:

- acute onset
- febrile illness associated with headache

- altered level of consciousness
- focal neurologic signs

The clinical presentation is similar to that of meningitis, although meningitis is not characterized by focal neurologic signs. HSV is the most common cause of nonepidemic sporadic focal encephalitis in the United States. In HSV infection, MRI of the head shows temporal lobe enhancement, and CSF shows lymphocytic pleocytosis, erythrocytes, and an elevated protein level. The diagnosis is confirmed by finding HSV in the CSF on PCR testing.

West Nile virus encephalitis is an epidemic mosquito-borne infection that often causes subclinical disease but can result in severe encephalitis, particularly in older adults. The most common manifestations are encephalitis, meningitis, reduced level of consciousness, flaccid paralysis, and fever. IgM antibodies in the CSF confirm the diagnosis.

Therapy

In HSV encephalitis, beginning acyclovir without waiting for test results reduces mortality. No specific treatment is available for West Nile virus encephalitis.

◆ DON'T BE TRICKED

- **Brain biopsy is reserved for patients who do not respond to acyclovir.**

❖ Test Yourself

A 58-year-old man is evaluated after a seizure. He has a 1-week history of headache, fever, and confusion. MRI shows a hyperintense lesion in the inferior medial temporal lobe, and CSF examination reveals lymphocytic pleocytosis (100 leukocytes/microliter), 350 erythrocytes/microliter, a protein level of 80 mg/dL, and a normal glucose level.

ANSWER: The diagnosis is HSV encephalitis. Begin acyclovir.

Meningitis

Prevention

College freshmen living in dormitories, travelers to endemic areas, and asplenic patients should receive the meningococcal vaccine.

Diagnosis

- Characteristic findings are fever, nuchal rigidity, and change in mental status. The clinical presentations of viral and bacterial meningitis are similar. CSF examination is used to differentiate bacterial from other types of meningitis.
- *Streptococcus pneumoniae* is the most common etiologic agent of bacterial meningitis and may occur in patients with other foci of infection (otitis media or endocarditis) or after head trauma with leakage of CSF.
- *Neisseria meningitidis* is the second most common etiologic agent of bacterial meningitis in the United States, occurring primarily in children and young adults. Patients with deficiencies in the terminal complement components (C5-C9) are predisposed to repeated infection.
- Meningitis caused by *Listeria monocytogenes* is associated with extremes of age (neonates and persons >50 years), alcoholism, malignancy, immunosuppression, diabetes mellitus, hepatic failure, kidney failure, iron overload, collagen vascular disorders, and HIV infection.

STUDY TABLE: CSF Examination for Diagnosis of Meningitis

CSF Finding	Bacterial	Viral	Tuberculous	Cryptococcal
Leukocyte count (cells/µL)	>1000 (neutrophils)	<500	<300 (lymphocytes)	<500 (lymphocytes)
Glucose (mg/dL)	<40	>40	<40	<40
Protein (mg/dL)	>100	<300	<300	>100

µL = microliter.

The latex agglutination test is used to detect bacterial antigens if CSF findings are compatible with bacterial meningitis but the Gram stain is negative.

Therapy

STUDY TABLE: Empiric Antibiotic Therapy for Suspected Bacterial Meningitis

If you see this...	Choose this...
Age <50 years	Vancomycin + third-generation cephalosporin (cefotaxime or ceftriaxone) ± ampicillin
Age ≥50 years	Vancomycin + third-generation cephalosporin (cefotaxime or ceftriaxone) + ampicillin
Basilar skull fracture	Vancomycin + third-generation cephalosporin (cefotaxime or ceftriaxone)
Post-neurosurgery or CSF shunt	Vancomycin + ceftazidime OR cefepime OR meropenem

For adults with known or suspected pneumococcal meningitis, choose dexamethasone shortly before or at the same time as the first antibiotic dose.

◆ DON'T BE TRICKED

- In suspected bacterial meningitis, do not delay antibiotic therapy by waiting for CT and CSF results.
- If Gram stain shows gram-positive diplococci, do not treat with cefotaxime alone. Add vancomycin to cover penicillin-resistant pneumococci.

Metastatic Brain Tumors

Diagnosis

Parenchymal metastases usually present as multiple, ring-enhancing, centrally necrotic lesions. These lesions have a proclivity for the junction between the gray and white matter and are typically associated with significant surrounding edema and mass effect. Characteristic findings are headache, mental status changes, focal neurologic deficits, and seizure. If a metastatic brain tumor is the first indication of malignancy, evaluate the patient for lung cancer, breast cancer, and melanoma.

Lymphoma and leukemia cause leptomeningeal metastases and may present with headache or spinal pain, cranial nerve or spinal radicular pain, weakness, and mental status changes. Communicating hydrocephalus may be present. Leptomeningeal tumors are characterized on MRI by a diffuse or patchy enhancement of the surface of the brain and spinal cord or roots. When a leptomeningeal tumor is suspected in a patient with a negative MRI, obtain CSF examination to look for elevated protein and reduced glucose levels and positive cytologic findings.

◆ DON'T BE TRICKED

- MRI is required for all patients with systemic cancer and new neurologic findings.
- In patients with active, biopsy-proven systemic malignancy and multiple enhancing brain lesions, brain biopsy is not indicated.

Therapy

Corticosteroids are a first-line treatment for parenchymal and leptomeningeal tumors. Chemotherapy (methotrexate and cytarabine) is the initial therapy for patients with leptomeningeal metastases from leukemia and lymphoma. Palliative whole-brain radiation therapy is indicated for multiple parenchymal metastases from a known primary solid tumor. Surgical resection followed by whole-brain radiation is appropriate for a solitary metastasis and limited systemic tumor.

◆ DON'T BE TRICKED

- Chemotherapy is not indicated for parenchymal brain metastases from most solid tumors.

❖ Test Yourself

A 60-year-old woman with a history of adenocarcinoma of the lung has a 3-week history of diplopia, dysphagia, and foot drop. CT scan of the head shows only enlargement of the entire ventricular system.

ANSWER: The diagnosis is probable leptomeningeal metastases.

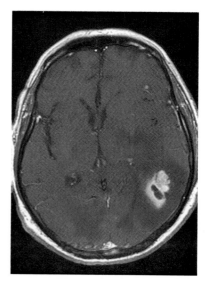

Parietal Lobe Nodule: Axial postcontrast T1-weighted MRI showing an enhancing nodule in the left parietal lobe with surrounding edema and mass effect.

Meningioma

Diagnosis

Meningiomas are usually benign in histology and behavior. These tumors are also typically asymptomatic and small and may be discovered incidentally during neuroimaging for unrelated symptoms. Symptomatic patients typically have progressive headache and focal neurologic lesions. CT scan of the head will show a partially calcified, homogeneously enhancing extra-axial mass adherent to the dura and an enhancing dural "tail."

Therapy

Surgical resection is the treatment of choice for symptomatic meningiomas or enlarging meningiomas. Observation is appropriate for small, asymptomatic meningiomas.

◆ DON'T BE TRICKED

- Chemotherapy has no established role in patients with meningioma.

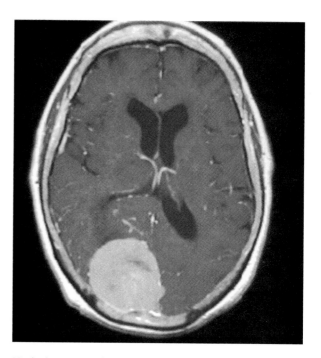

Meningioma: Coronal MRI with contrast shows meningioma with the enhancing dural "tail" inferior to the tumor's dural attachment.

Coma

Diagnosis

Coma is a state of unarousable unresponsiveness. It can be caused by diffuse insults to the cerebral hemispheres, damage to the reticular activating system, or a combination of hemispheric and brain stem dysfunction. Unilateral hemispheric lesions do not result in coma unless edema and mass effect cause compression of the reticular activating system. Coma can be caused by a variety of structural lesions and toxic, metabolic, and infectious causes.

Patients in a vegetative state are unaware of self and the environment and show no purposeful responses to stimuli. They continue to have sleep-wake cycles and brain stem function.

The three cardinal findings of brain death are coma, absence of brain stem reflexes, and apnea.

STUDY TABLE: Key Points in the Evaluation of Coma	
Finding	**Consider**
Coma without focal signs, fever, or meningism	Hypoxia or a metabolic cause, toxic reaction, drug-induced state, infection, or postictal state
Coma without focal signs but with meningism	Meningitis, meningoencephalitis, or SAH
Coma with focal signs	Stroke, hemorrhage, tumor, or abscess
Quadriplegic, mute, but preserved vertical eye movements	"Locked-in" state caused by a pontine infarction or hemorrhage

Focal findings or any unexplained coma is an indication for emergent imaging of the brain to exclude hemorrhage or mass lesion. CT can typically be obtained more rapidly than MRI and is the appropriate test in emergency situations. Lumbar puncture is indicated when meningitis or SAH is suspected but neuroimaging is normal. Emergent EEG can exclude nonconvulsive status epilepticus.

◆ DON'T BE TRICKED

- **Respiratory drive and motor posturing signs are incompatible with a diagnosis of brain death.**

Therapy

Attend to airway, breathing, and circulation first. All patients with unexplained coma should be urgently treated with thiamine and glucose (unless rapid finger stick rules out hypoglycemia). Give naloxone if an opiate overdose is suspected and flumazenil if a benzodiazepine overdose is being considered.

Oncology

Breast Cancer

Prevention and Screening

See Women's Health chapter.

Diagnosis

Characteristic findings include:

- a breast mass
- asymmetry of the breast
- nipple inversion
- edema and thickening of the skin (peau d'orange)
- an axillary or supraclavicular mass

Schedule mammography (and ultrasonography as needed) in women with any new breast symptoms or abnormal findings on physical examination. In premenopausal women, following the abnormality through one menstrual cycle instead of scheduling immediate imaging is reasonable. Schedule biopsy for suspicious lesions noted during physical examination or screening mammography. Any fluid discharge from the nipple requires a cytopathologic examination. If histopathologic studies confirm invasive breast cancer, determine estrogen/progesterone (ER/PR) receptor and *HER2/neu* status. The two factors that are most prognostic are tumor size and axillary lymph node status.

◆ DON'T BE TRICKED

- **A normal mammogram or ultrasonogram does not rule out breast cancer.**
- **A breast lump should always be biopsied, even if a mammogram is normal.**
- **Bone scan, CT scan, or tumor marker tests are not routine studies for diagnosing in situ or invasive breast cancer.**

Therapy

Mastectomy and lumpectomy (breast conservation surgery) followed by radiation therapy represent equivalent therapeutic options with comparable survival in most women with breast cancer. Lumpectomy and radiation is appropriate for patients with focal disease (tumor <5 cm) or ductal carcinoma in situ. Choose mastectomy for patients with very large tumors or contraindications to radiation therapy (previous irradiation). Perform axillary lymph node dissection only if sentinel node biopsy is positive.

Prescribe a 5-year course of adjuvant tamoxifen for premenopausal women and aromatase inhibitors (anastrozole, letrozole, exemestane) for postmenopausal women with ER/PR receptor–positive tumors following lumpectomy and radiation therapy.

Radiation therapy is also indicated after mastectomy in patients with close surgical margins, dermal invasion, or four or more positive lymph nodes.

The decision to use systemic chemotherapy is based on the risk of recurrent disease. Involvement of the axillary lymph nodes remains the most powerful prognostic factor for recurrence. In general, patients with tumors >1 cm or patients with lymph node involvement should receive adjuvant chemotherapy.

For patients with *HER2*-positive breast cancer, a monoclonal antibody, trastuzumab, is used as adjuvant therapy. Patients should undergo evaluation of left ventricular function before trastuzumab treatment.

Treat ER/PR receptor–positive patients with only bone or small-volume visceral disease with endocrine therapy alone. For those with lytic bone disease, bisphosphonate therapy reduces pain, pathologic fractures, and the need for radiation therapy.

◆ DON'T BE TRICKED

- **Aromatase inhibitors are contraindicated in premenopausal women.**
- **Do not select mastectomy in patients with metastatic disease unless required for local cancer control.**

Various systemic hormonal and chemotherapeutic regimens have been developed for treatment of breast cancer.

STUDY TABLE: Breast Cancer Drug Treatment	
Indications	**Treatment**
ER/PR receptor–positive cancer	Tamoxifen
	Aromatase inhibitor (postmenopausal women only)
Most patients with invasive breast cancer	Adjuvant chemotherapy
Locally advanced disease (inflammatory breast cancer or matted axillary lymphadenopathy)	Chemotherapy followed by surgery and radiation therapy
ER/PR receptor–positive cancer with either bone or asymptomatic small-volume visceral metastases	Serial endocrine therapies, including tamoxifen, aromatase inhibitors, fulvestrant, and megestrol acetate
ER/PR receptor–negative metastatic cancer or endocrine resistant cancer	Sequential single-agent or combination chemotherapy
Lytic bone disease	Bisphosphonates (pamidronate, zoledronate) or denosumab and/or radiation therapy for painful lesions
HER2-positive cancer	Trastuzumab with or without chemotherapy

Osteonecrosis of the jaw is a rare but serious complication of bisphosphonate therapy, particularly in patients with dental disease or dental procedures.

◆ DON'T BE TRICKED

- **Do not give trastuzumab concurrently with anthracycline agents (to avoid the occurrence of HF).**
- **Do not order routine follow-up blood tests or imaging studies in the absence of specific symptoms.**

❖ Test Yourself

A 50-year-old premenopausal woman has a 1.5-cm moderately differentiated breast cancer. The lesion is completely excised (lumpectomy), and the surgical margins are negative. Three axillary lymph nodes are positive. The tumor is negative for ER/PR receptors and is highly positive for *HER2/neu*.

ANSWER: Select postoperative radiation therapy, chemotherapy, and trastuzumab but not tamoxifen or aromatase inhibitors.

Cervical Cancer

Prevention and Screening

See Women's Health chapter.

Diagnosis

Abnormal vaginal bleeding is the most common clinical presentation (postmenopausal, postcoital, and intermenstrual). Associated pain and abnormal discharge are usually signs of advanced disease.

Punch biopsy of obvious lesions or colposcopy-directed biopsy is usually required for diagnosis.

Therapy

Early (stage IA1) cancers may be treated with loop electrosurgical excision procedure or cervical conization to preserve childbearing; patients who have finished childbearing may undergo hysterectomy without lymph node dissection. Radiation therapy and cisplatin chemotherapy are used for patients with stage II, III, or IV disease. Treat metastatic disease with local radiation (for local control) or chemotherapy.

Endometrial Cancer

Diagnosis

Characteristic findings include irregular vaginal bleeding after age 40 years or in perimenopausal women, persistent pink or brown vaginal discharge, postmenopausal bleeding, and a Pap smear defined as atypical glandular cells of undetermined significance or containing endometrial cells. The diagnosis is made by endometrial biopsy.

Therapy

Surgical resection of the uterus, cervix, and adnexa is first-line treatment, and radiation therapy and/or chemotherapy may be added for higher-risk disease. Radiation therapy alone is an alternative for high-risk surgical patients.

Imaging is not more effective than a physical examination for diagnosing recurrent endometrial cancer.

◆ DON'T BE TRICKED

- **Do not screen for endometrial cancer; screening does not reduce mortality.**

Ovarian Cancer

Prevention

Oophorectomy after childbearing or at age 35 years can be offered to women with *BRCA1/BRCA2* genetic mutations or two or more first-degree relatives with ovarian cancer.

Screening

Screening women at average risk for ovarian cancer is not indicated. Screening with serum CA-125, pelvic examination, and transvaginal ultrasonography is a reasonable but unproven strategy for women at high risk (e.g., ovarian cancer in a first- or second-degree family member, family member with ovarian cancer at age <50 years).

Diagnosis

Patients may have a family history of breast, ovarian, or colon cancer. Characteristic findings are abdominal swelling, ascites, and pain as well as abnormal vaginal bleeding and dyspareunia. A pelvic mass or nodularity may be present in the cul-de-sac. Ovarian cancer is staged by exploratory laparotomy.

◆ **DON'T BE TRICKED**

- If ovarian cancer is suspected, schedule only CA-125 testing and pelvic or transvaginal ultrasonography. Do not order an extensive staging evaluation; surgery is the primary staging modality.
- Women with peritoneal carcinomatosis of unknown primary site have ovarian cancer until proven otherwise.

Therapy

Surgery is indicated to remove the ovaries and any evidence of grossly visible disease within the abdomen. Most patients with stage IA and IB disease with grade 1 (well-differentiated) histology do not receive adjuvant chemotherapy. Patients with stage IA or IB disease with either high-grade (grade 3) or clear-cell tumor histology and all patients with stage IC to IV disease are treated with adjuvant platinum-based chemotherapy. Intraperitoneal chemotherapy shows a survival benefit in patients with small amounts of residual disease confined to the peritoneal cavity following surgery. Patients with relapsed ovarian cancer who are being considered for surgery may experience enhanced survival if they undergo comprehensive secondary surgical cytoreduction.

◆ **DON'T BE TRICKED**

- Do not opt for "second-look surgery" following completion of chemotherapy.

Limit follow-up to physical examination with pelvic examination and serum CA-125 measurement (if initially elevated).

❖ **Test Yourself**

A 60-year-old woman has a 3-month history of increasing abdominal girth, pain, and constipation. Physical examination is normal except for ascites. Pelvic ultrasonography is normal. Laparoscopy shows diffuse peritoneal carcinomatosis.

ANSWER: The diagnosis is adenocarcinoma of unknown primary site. Treat for ovarian cancer.

Prostate Cancer

Prevention

Finasteride reduces the incidence of prostate cancer but not cancer mortality rates.

Screening

In the most recent recommendation statement, the U.S. Preventive Services Task Force (USPSTF) recommends against PSA-based screening for prostate cancer. This recommendation applies to men in the general U.S. population, regardless of age. At the time of publication, these guidelines were classified as "updates in progress" and still under "draft" status.

Diagnosis

Most patients with prostate cancer are asymptomatic at the time of diagnosis. Characteristic findings include:

- a rapidly rising serum prostate-specific antigen (PSA) level
- a nodule or firmness on rectal examination
- obstructive symptoms, although these are more likely associated with BPH

Obtain transrectal ultrasonography–guided prostate biopsy for a significantly elevated or rapidly rising PSA level or a nodule or firmness on digital rectal examination.

Tumors are classified according to their histology using the Gleason score. In the Gleason scoring system, tumors are graded from 1 to 5 based on the degree of glandular differentiation and structural architecture. The composite Gleason score is derived by adding together the two most prevalent differentiation patterns (a primary and a secondary grade). Patients with a Gleason score >7, serum PSA >15 ng/mL, large tumors, or the presence of bone pain require a bone scan and CT of the abdomen and pelvis to evaluate for metastatic disease.

◆ DON'T BE TRICKED

- **Acute urinary retention significantly increases the PSA level regardless of the cause of obstruction.**

Therapy

The National Comprehensive Cancer Network has developed guidelines for the initial treatment of men with prostate cancer based on their risk score and general life expectancy. The three major treatment strategies for localized prostate cancer are surgery, radiation therapy, and observation.

STUDY TABLE: Prostate Cancer Drug Treatment		
Risk	**Life Expectancy**	**Treatment Options**
Low	<10 years	Observation
	>10 years but <20 years	Observation
		Radiation therapy
		Radical prostatectomy
	≥20 years	Radiation therapy
		Radical prostatectomy
Intermediate	<10 years	Observation
		Radiation therapy
		Radical prostatectomy
	≥10 years	Radiation therapy
		Radical prostatectomy
High	<5 years	Observation with hormonal therapy
	≥5 years	Radiation therapy with hormonal therapy
		Radiation therapy alone
		Radical prostatectomy

General rules:

- Radical prostatectomy, with or without pelvic lymph node dissection, is generally considered for patients with disease limited to the prostate who have a life expectancy >10 years.
- Radiation therapy and surgery have similar disease-free survival and are interchangeable.
- Patients with high-risk disease may benefit from 4 to 6 months of androgen deprivation therapy (hormonal therapy) using a gonadotropin-releasing hormone agonist (e.g., leuprolide, goserelin).
- Hormonal therapy is also used for patients with a rising serum PSA level after initial definitive therapy for prostate cancer.
- Hormonal therapy is as effective as bilateral orchiectomy (surgical castration) in treating patients with metastatic disease.

Docetaxel-based therapy improves median overall survival in patients with hormone-refractory metastatic prostate cancer. Bisphosphonates (e.g., zoledronic acid) or denosumab reverse or prevent osteopenia due to hormonal therapy, inhibit tumor-mediated bone resorption, and decrease morbidity from bone fractures or bone pain.

◆ DON'T BE TRICKED

- **Do not use diethylstilbestrol as an antiandrogen.**
- **Surgery or radiation therapy is not indicated for metastatic prostate cancer in the absence of local GU symptoms.**

Testicular Cancer

Diagnosis

Primary testicular cancer, or germ-cell tumor, is the most common solid malignant tumor in men between the ages of 20 and 35 years. Characteristic findings in a young man include a testicular mass, testicular swelling and pain, weight loss, retroperitoneal lymphadenopathy, and metastatic pulmonary lesions.

Diagnostic studies include tissue (inguinal orchiectomy, not needle biopsy) for histopathologic examination; chest x-ray; CT of the abdomen and pelvis; and measurement of the β-hCG and AFP levels. An elevated serum AFP level always indicates the tumor has a nonseminomatous component, whereas hCG may be present in seminomatous or nonseminomatous tumors. Any testicular cancer that has a nonseminomatous component based on histologic examination or the presence of an elevated serum AFP level is considered a nonseminoma and is treated as such.

◆ DON'T BE TRICKED

- **Do not order testicular biopsy.**

Therapy

Semen cryopreservation is common for all men before they undergo therapy for testicular cancer. Inguinal orchiectomy is the initial step in treatment. Additional treatment modalities are determined by tumor histology and clinical stage.

Seminoma

- Low-risk, early-stage seminomas (stage I disease) are usually treated with radiation therapy to the para-aortic lymph nodes or with carboplatin chemotherapy.
- Radiation therapy or cisplatin-based chemotherapy is recommended for patients with intermediate disease (stage IIA or IIB).
- Chemotherapy (cisplatin based) is recommended for advanced disease (stage IIC or III).
- Chemotherapy (cisplatin based) is recommended for nonpulmonary visceral metastases.

Nonseminoma

- Orchiectomy is most commonly followed by retroperitoneal lymph node dissection.
- If metastases are found during retroperitoneal lymph node dissection, chemotherapy (cisplatin based) is usually recommended.
- Patients with elevated serum tumor marker levels postoperatively but without radiographic evidence of disease also receive chemotherapy.

Residual retroperitoneal masses are common after chemotherapy. If tumor markers have normalized, treat with surgical resection of residual masses for nonseminoma (masses may represent a teratoma) and follow up with CT for seminoma.

Patients with either seminoma or nonseminoma require frequent follow-up chest radiography, serum tumor marker assays, and CT of the abdomen and pelvis because of the potential for cure even in patients with recurrent disease.

❖ Test Yourself

A 28-year-old man has weight loss and abdominal pain. Evaluation reveals para-aortic lymphadenopathy. Testicular examination is normal. A lymph node biopsy shows poorly differentiated cancer of unknown primary origin.

ANSWER: Measure the serum AFP and/or β-hCG levels.

Colorectal Cancer

Screening

Colorectal cancer screening is recommended for men and women beginning at age 50 years. The USPSTF does not recommend routine screening in patients 75 to 85 years of age, although considerations in individual patients may support screening. The USPSTF does not recommend screening in patients older than age 85 years.

Acceptable USPSTF screening strategies for persons at average risk for colon cancer include:

- yearly FOBT
- sigmoidoscopy every 5 years combined with FOBT ever 3 years
- colonoscopy every 10 years

More intense screening is recommended for patients at higher risk for colon cancer.

Early screening is recommended for patients with the following familial syndromes:

- Familial adenomatous polyposis, which is an autosomal dominant disorder that requires prophylactic colectomy.
- Gardner syndrome, which is a type of familial adenomatous polyposis with extraintestinal manifestations, including osteomas, duodenal ampullary tumors, thyroid cancers, and medulloblastomas.
- HNPCC or Lynch syndrome, which is an autosomal dominant disorder.

If an inherited colon cancer syndrome is suspected, the patient and family members should be referred for genetic testing.

Screening recommendations and frequency of screening are based on consensus opinion.

STUDY TABLE: Colon Cancer Screening	
Risk Profile	**When to Initiate Screening**
Average risk	Age 50 years (any modality)
First-degree relative with colon cancer	Age 40 years (any modality)
First-degree relative diagnosed with an adenomatous polyp or colon cancer at age ≤50 years	Age 40 years, or 10 years younger than the earliest diagnosis in the family (any modality)
Two first-degree relatives with colon cancer	Age 40 years, or 10 years younger than the earliest diagnosis in the family (colonoscopy every 3-5 years)
HNPCC risk	Colonoscopy every 1-2 years starting at age 20 or 25 years, or 10 years earlier than the age of youngest person in family diagnosed with colon cancer
Familial adenomatous polyposis risk	Age 12 years (annual sigmoidoscopy)
Pancolitis (ulcerative colitis or Crohn disease)	8-10 years after initial diagnosis (colonoscopy)

◆ DON'T BE TRICKED

- **A single positive FOBT finding constitutes a positive screening test and requires follow-up colonoscopy.**
- **The role of CT colonography for screening is not yet defined.**

Different levels of follow-up are recommended for patients discovered to have a colonic polyp on screening colonoscopy.

- Patients with only one or two small (<1 cm) tubular adenomas with only low-grade dysplasia should have their next follow-up colonoscopy in 5 to 10 years.
- Patients with 3 to 10 adenomas, with any adenoma ≥1 cm, with any adenoma with villous features, or with high-grade dysplasia should have their next follow-up colonoscopy in 3 years.
- Patients who have more than 10 adenomas at one examination should be examined again in less than 3 years.

◆ **DON'T BE TRICKED**

- Patients with hyperplastic polyps should be screened according to general population guidelines (i.e., every 10 years).

Diagnosis

Characteristic findings are rectal bleeding or change in bowel habits. Other findings include pelvic pain or tenesmus, weight loss, rectal or abdominal mass, hepatomegaly, and iron deficiency anemia. Patients with obstruction have hypogastric abdominal pain, abdominal distention, nausea, and vomiting. Colonoscopy is the diagnostic procedure of choice.

◆ **DON'T BE TRICKED**

- Do not obtain a serum carcinoembryonic antigen level to screen for or diagnose colon cancer.

Therapy

General rules for colon cancer therapy:

- Confined to colon (stage I) or local invasion (stage II) → resection for cure
- Metastatic to regional lymph nodes (stage III) → resection and adjuvant chemotherapy
- Distant metastases (stage IV) → resection of primary lesion for palliation (if needed) and chemotherapy (Leucovorin, 5-FU, and oxaliplatin [FOLFOX])
- Stage II-III rectal cancer → radiation therapy and FOLFOX before or after surgery

Adjuvant chemotherapy with FOLFOX is associated with improvement in disease-free survival for patients with stage II and stage III disease. Patients with stage II and stage III rectal cancer are treated with preoperative (neoadjuvant) radiation therapy and chemotherapy and postoperative (adjuvant) chemotherapy alone.

In patients with metastatic colorectal cancer and a limited number of metastatic lesions, surgical resection can result in cure in about 25% of cases. In metastatic colorectal cancer, agents include oxaliplatin or irinotecan combined with a fluoropyrimidine. The addition of bevacizumab, an antiangiogenesis monoclonal antibody, further increases the efficacy of chemotherapy. Recommended follow-up includes:

- carcinoembryonic antigen measurement every 3 to 6 months for the first 2 years and then every 6 months for the subsequent 3 years
- colonoscopy 1 year following resection, 3 years later, and then every 5 years
- CT of the chest, abdomen, and pelvis annually for 3 years for patients with perineural invasion or poorly differentiated tumors

◆ **DON'T BE TRICKED**

- In patients with metastatic colon cancer who are not eligible for curative resection, surgery is indicated only for control of bleeding or relief of obstruction.
- Surgery is a potentially curative option in highly selected patients with disease limited to a single organ (liver, lung).

❖ Test Yourself

A 63-year-old man has a 4-month history of increasing fatigue and a nonobstructing colon cancer metastatic to the liver and lungs. His hemoglobin is 12.5 g/dL.

ANSWER: Begin multiagent chemotherapy. Surgery is not indicated.

Hepatocellular Carcinoma

Screening

Patients with cirrhosis and patients with chronic hepatitis B without cirrhosis should be screened with abdominal ultrasonography every 6 months.

Diagnosis

Order a contrast-enhanced CT or MRI of the liver when the abdominal ultrasonogram is abnormal. A serum AFP level >400 ng/mL in a patient with cirrhosis and a liver mass is virtually diagnostic. Because the radiographic findings of hepatocellular carcinoma are fairly characteristic (arterial phase enhancement), biopsy for confirmation is usually not necessary.

STUDY TABLE: Other Hepatic Tumors and Cysts	
Type	**Characteristics**
Cavernous hemangioma	Early peripheral nodular enhancement on contrast CT or MRI, followed by delayed fill-in toward the center of the lesion. No therapy is required.
Hepatic adenoma	Early arterial enhancement with rapid loss of enhancement and return to isointensity with the surrounding liver. Adenomas are typically heterogeneous in appearance because of regions of hemorrhage or necrosis. Patients may have a history of using oral contraceptives. Treat with resection.
Focal nodular hyperplasia	Early arterial enhancement with rapid loss of enhancement in the portal venous phase with return to isointensity with the surrounding liver. Many larger focal nodular hyperplasias have a central stellate scar. No therapy is required.
Metastatic tumors	Single or multiple hypoechoic lesions on ultrasonography that are hypovascular on contrast-enhanced CT scans. Isolated lesions may be amenable to resection.

Therapy

Surgical resection or liver transplantation is first-line therapy. Percutaneous ethanol injection or radiofrequency ablation is used for patients who cannot undergo surgery or liver transplantation. Chemotherapy is used for patients with advanced hepatocellular carcinoma who are not candidates for surgical resection, liver transplantation, or ablative therapy. Sorafenib improves overall survival in patients with advanced/metastatic hepatocellular carcinoma.

❖ Test Yourself

A 60-year-old man with chronic hepatitis C and cirrhosis is found to have a 4-cm liver mass on screening ultrasonography. A CT scan showed the mass enhances on arterial phase.

ANSWER: Select liver transplant.

Gastric Cancer

Diagnosis

Because the signs and symptoms of gastric cancer are often vague and nonspecific, most patients have locally advanced or metastatic disease at diagnosis. The most common symptoms are weight loss, abdominal pain, nausea, anorexia, bleeding, and dysphagia. Findings may include any of the following:

- ascites
- periumbilical nodule (Sister Mary Joseph node)
- left supraclavicular lymphadenopathy (Virchow node)

- enlarged ovary (Krukenberg tumor)
- mass in the cul-de-sac on rectal examination (Blumer shelf)

The initial diagnostic procedure is upper endoscopy. CT scans are used to identify the presence of regional and metastatic disease. Endoscopic ultrasonography is superior to CT in the evaluation of depth of tumor invasion and lymph node involvement and aids in preoperative evaluation.

◆ DON'T BE TRICKED
- **Always obtain upper endoscopy and biopsy in a patient with "achalasia" to rule out gastric cancer.**

Therapy

For patients with localized tumors, undertake surgery with curative intent. Standard adjuvant therapy for gastric cancer is concurrent chemotherapy and radiation therapy. For patients fit enough to receive aggressive therapy, neoadjuvant therapy followed by postoperative adjuvant therapy is a reasonable treatment option. Use antibiotic and PPI therapy for early-stage mucosa-associated lymphoid tissue (MALT) lymphoma of the stomach and evidence of *Helicobacter pylori* infection.

Carcinoid Tumor

Diagnosis

Carcinoid tumors may arise anywhere in the GI tract (75% are in the small intestine) and in the bronchi. These tumors synthesize and release various biologically active compounds. In patients with GI carcinoid tumors, manifestations of the carcinoid syndrome do not occur until hepatic metastases are present. Characteristic findings include:

- episodic cutaneous flushing (often precipitated by alcohol or stress)
- venous telangiectasia
- secretory diarrhea
- bronchospasm
- right-sided cardiac valvular lesions

The initial diagnostic test is the 24-hour urinary excretion of 5-HIAA. Abdominal CT and somatostatin receptor scintigraphy are used for tumor localization.

Therapy

Surgical removal is the primary treatment for localized tumors. For metastatic disease associated with flushing and/or diarrhea, select treatment with octreotide.

◆ DON'T BE TRICKED
- **Endobronchial carcinoid is not associated with carcinoid syndrome.**

Lung Cancer

Screening and Prevention

Smoking cessation is the most effective preventive measure for lung cancer; 90% of lung cancers are smoking-related.

Annual low-dose CT screening in patients with a 30-pack-year history of smoking, including those who quit smoking in the preceding 15 years, has been associated with a decrease in lung cancer and all-cause mortality. National guidelines are undergoing revision, and it is not clear if these findings will be incorporated (issues of design flaws, cost, and radiation exposure) as standard care.

◆ DON'T BE TRICKED

- Do not screen for lung cancer with chest radiography and/or sputum cytology.
- Do not prescribe vitamin A derivatives (β-carotene and retinol) or vitamin E (α-tocopherol) to prevent lung cancer.

Diagnosis

Common symptoms include hemoptysis, pulmonary infections, dyspnea, cough, or chest pain. Patients with small cell lung cancer often present with symptoms of metastatic disease and paraneoplastic syndromes (hyponatremia, Cushing syndrome, hypercalcemia), mechanical effects of tumor (superior vena cava syndrome), or Horner syndrome (ipsilateral ptosis, miosis, enophthalmos, and anhidrosis) from invasion of the paravertebral sympathetic chain.

The most characteristic finding is a mass lesion on chest x-ray. Histologic confirmation is necessary for diagnosis and can be obtained by percutaneous lung biopsy, peripheral lymph node biopsy, pleural fluid cytology, or transbronchial biopsy. Whenever possible, select the biopsy site that will simultaneously diagnose and stage the disease (peripheral lymph node, mediastinal node). Sputum cytology is reserved for patients with poor pulmonary function who cannot tolerate invasive procedures. Treatment and prognosis vary based on whether the patient has non–small cell lung cancer (NSCLC) (adeno-carcinoma, large cell carcinoma, or SCC) or small cell lung cancer (SCLC).

Small Cell Lung Cancer

SCLC is generally viewed as a systemic (metastatic) disease at the time of diagnosis; most patients have obvious extensive disease. Differentiate between limited- and extensive-stage disease on imaging studies. Limited-stage disease is confined to one hemithorax, with hilar and mediastinal lymphadenopathy that can be encompassed within one tolerable radiotherapy portal. Extensive-stage disease consists of any disease that exceeds those boundaries, including malignant pleural effusion. SCLC characteristically produces peptide hormones, which can cause endocrine syndromes, such as hyponatremia from the syndrome of inappropriate antidiuretic hormone secretion (SIADH) and hypercortisolism through secretion of ACTH. Neurologic symptoms, such as the Lambert-Eaton syndrome, cortical cerebellar degeneration, limbic encephalitis, and peripheral neuropathy, may also occur in patients with lung cancer, but they are relatively rare.

Non–Small Cell Lung Cancer

In staging NSCLC, the task is to identify metastatic disease, which eliminates surgery as a therapeutic option. Perform a staging evaluation with chest and upper abdominal CT plus a PET scan to assess for lymphadenopathy.

Measurement of the CBC and serum calcium, alkaline phosphatase, and aminotransferase levels can detect more advanced disease. A bone scan is indicated only if bone pain or elevated serum calcium or alkaline phosphatase levels are present. A brain MRI is indicated only in the presence of neurologic signs or symptoms.

◆ DON'T BE TRICKED

- Do not order routine bone scans or CT of the head in patients without bone or neurologic symptoms.
- If a patient has a lung mass and hypercalcemia, choose SCC as the likely cause.

Therapy

STUDY TABLE: Treatment of Small Cell Lung Cancer	
If you see this...	**Select this...**
Limited-stage disease	Concurrent chemotherapy and radiation therapy
Extensive-stage disease	Chemotherapy
Complete or partial response to therapy (both limited and extensive stages)	Add prophylactic cranial irradiation
Symptomatic brain metastases	Whole-brain radiation therapy
Bone metastases	IV pamidronate or zoledronate, radiotherapy to the involved sites, surgical stabilization

STUDY TABLE: Treatment of Non–Small Cell Lung Cancer	
If you see this...	**Select this...**
Stage I disease (tumor ≤3 cm with no lymphadenopathy or metastases) or stage II disease (hilar lymphadenopathy or tumor invading chest wall)	Surgical resection for cure followed by adjuvant chemotherapy
Stage IIIA disease (involving mediastinum or contralateral mediastinal lymph nodes)	Surgery followed by chemoradiation or chemoradiation alone
Metastatic cancer	Chemotherapy
Malignant pleural or pericardial effusion	Chemotherapy
Solitary brain metastasis	Surgical excision and postoperative whole-brain radiation therapy

Use corticosteroids and radiation therapy for patients with brain metastases. Select thoracic irradiation for pulmonary airway obstruction, superior vena cava syndrome, and spinal cord metastases (following surgical decompression). Radiation therapy relieves pain, particularly bone pain, visceral pain secondary to capsular distention, or pain due to nerve compression. Treat symptomatic pleural effusions with thoracentesis and pleurodesis to obliterate the pleural space, if necessary.

◆ DON'T BE TRICKED

- Do not treat patients with stage I, II, or IV NSCLC or patients with malignant pleural or pericardial effusions (stage IIIB) with adjuvant radiation therapy.
- Do not treat patients who have NSCLC with poor performance status (extreme fatigue or weakness, weight loss >10%, severe symptoms) with chemotherapy, regardless of stage.
- Patients with extensive-stage SCLC and poor performance status because of tumor burden should be offered chemotherapy because it can significantly improve symptoms and increase survival.

❖ Test Yourself

A 51-year-old man presents with facial plethora, neck vein distention, shortness of breath, and a hilar mass.

ANSWER: The diagnosis is superior vena cava syndrome. Establish the diagnosis with appropriate imaging and tissue diagnosis.

Pancreatic Cancer

Diagnosis

Approximately 95% of the primary tumors are located in the exocrine pancreas, of which more than 50% occur in the head and 20% in the body or tail. Diffuse involvement of the pancreas is found in the remaining cases. Symptoms are influenced by tumor site and extent and may include:

- upper abdominal discomfort and lumbar back pain
- anorexia and weight loss
- obstructive jaundice
- marked weight loss
- vascular thromboses (Trousseau syndrome)

Physical examination findings may include a palpable gallbladder and jaundice. If a helical CT scan of the abdomen is inconclusive, schedule endoscopic ultrasonography. All patients require biopsy of a pancreatic mass with histologic or cytologic studies.

Look for the following characteristics:

- Stage I → tumor limited to the pancreas
- Stage II → tumor extending into the duodenum, bile duct, or peripancreatic tissues
- Stage III → regional lymph node involvement
- Stage IV → tumor extending directly into the stomach, spleen, colon, or adjacent large vessels or the presence of metastatic disease

◆ DON'T BE TRICKED

- **Serum tumor markers are not used to diagnose pancreatic cancer.**
- **Autoimmune pancreatitis can be mistaken for pancreatic cancer; look for elevated serum levels of IgG4 and biopsy the pancreas.**

Therapy

Surgical resection is appropriate for patients with resectable pancreatic cancer. For patients with locally advanced but unresectable disease, treatment is controversial. Choices include:

- radiation therapy alone
- 5-FU plus radiation therapy
- single-agent chemotherapy (usually gemcitabine)

Gemcitabine alone is typically recommended for metastatic cancer.

Palliative measures to alleviate pain in patients with unresectable or metastatic disease include optimization of analgesic medications, radiation therapy, chemical splanchnicectomy, or celiac nerve blocks. Palliation of biliary obstruction may be achieved with:

- surgical biliary bypass
- percutaneous radiologic biliary stent placement
- endoscopic biliary stent placement

Renal Cell Carcinoma

Diagnosis

Characteristic findings are abdominal or flank pain, hematuria, lower extremity edema, acute varicocele, erythrocytosis, fever, and hypercalcemia. Liver chemistry tests may be abnormal and revert to normal after removal of the tumor. The diagnosis is established by CT scan of the abdomen and pelvis and chest x-ray. A bone scan is indicated for patients with bone pain or an elevated serum alkaline phosphatase level

Therapy

Manage early-stage localized renal cancer surgically by either partial or radical nephrectomy. Use radiation therapy to control pain, bleeding, and symptomatic CNS or bone involvement. Treatment of advanced or metastatic disease is evolving and may include targeted therapy with agents such as sunitinib, sorafenib, pazopanib, and temsirolimus or high-dose interleukin-2. Zoledronate decreases skeletal complications and delays progression of bone lesions.

❖ **Test Yourself**

A 48-year-old man has progressive, severe headaches. Physical examination is normal. Hemoglobin is 20.2 g/dL and urinalysis shows 30 to 50 erythrocytes/hpf. A chest x-ray shows multiple bilateral noncalcified nodules measuring 1 to 2 cm.

ANSWER: The probable diagnosis is renal cell carcinoma. Select an abdominal CT.

Thyroid Cancer

Diagnosis

The four main types of thyroid cancer are papillary (75%), follicular (15%), medullary (5%), and anaplastic (5%). Characteristic findings are rapid nodule growth, a very firm nodule with fixation to adjacent structures, vocal cord paralysis, and enlarged regional lymph nodes. Consider multiple endocrine neoplasia (MEN) type 2A or 2B and associated medullary thyroid cancer in a patient with:

- headache, sweating, palpitations, and hypertension (pheochromocytoma)
- kidney stones and hypercalcemia (hyperparathyroidism)
- marfanoid habitus and ganglioneuromas on the tongue, lips, and eyelids (MEN type 2B)
- elevated serum calcitonin level (nearly 100% sensitive and specific for medullary thyroid cancer)

FNAB is the diagnostic study for thyroid nodules >1 cm. The aspirate should be analyzed for the *BRAF* gene mutation when the diagnosis is indeterminate. The *BRAF* gene mutation is specific for papillary carcinoma and more aggressive forms of thyroid cancer. Inherited forms of medullary thyroid cancer are associated with germ-line mutations in the *RET* proto-oncogene. Screen family members for disease when a patient presents with a new diagnosis of medullary thyroid cancer.

Therapy

Treat papillary thyroid cancer and follicular thyroid cancer with total thyroidectomy followed by radioiodine therapy in most cases. Medullary thyroid cancer is treated with total thyroidectomy and varying degrees of neck dissection to remove involved lymph nodes.

◆ **DON'T BE TRICKED**
- **Radioiodine is not taken up by C cells and is not a treatment option for medullary thyroid cancer.**
- **Chemotherapy does not prolong or improve the quality of life for patients with metastatic thyroid carcinoma.**

❖ **Test Yourself**

A 37-year-old woman has a 2-cm right-sided thyroid nodule that is firm, nontender, and moves when she swallows. Serum TSH is 1.8 microunits/mL, and serum calcium is 11.8 mg/dL.

ANSWER: The probable diagnosis is medullary thyroid cancer. Order a serum calcitonin measurement.

Hodgkin Lymphoma

Diagnosis

Hodgkin lymphoma comprises 10% of all newly diagnosed lymphoid neoplasms and represents a B-cell malignancy with immunoglobulin gene rearrangements. Hodgkin lymphoma is divided into two subgroups: classic Hodgkin lymphoma and lymphocyte-predominant Hodgkin lymphoma. Reed-Sternberg cells are characteristic of classic Hodgkin lymphoma.

Disease spread is commonly contiguous, usually emanating from a cervical lymph node. Characteristic findings include:

- unexplained cervical, supraclavicular, or mediastinal lymphadenopathy associated with pruritus
- fever
- night sweats
- unexplained weight loss
- anterior mediastinal mass on chest x-ray
- pain after ingestion of alcohol (specific but not sensitive finding)
- eosinophilia

All patients require an excisional biopsy of an entire accessible lymph node (not needle or core biopsy) plus CT of the chest, abdomen, and pelvis and whole-body PET scan. Bone marrow biopsy is required for patients with B symptoms (fever, night sweats, and weight loss) and clinical stage III or stage IV disease.

Therapy

STUDY TABLE: Ann Arbor Staging System of Hodgkin Lymphoma	
Stage	**Description**
Stage I	Involvement of a single lymph node region (I) or a single extralymphatic organ or site (I_E).
Stage II	Involvement of ≥2 lymph node regions on the same side of the diaphragm alone or limited involvement of contiguous extralymphatic organ or tissue (II_E).
Stage III	Involvement of lymph node regions on both sides of the diaphragm, which may include the spleen (III_S), or limited involvement of contiguous extralymphatic organ or site (III_E), or both (III_{ES}).
Stage IV	Multiple or disseminated foci of involvement of ≥1 extralymphatic organs or tissues, with or without lymphatic involvement.

All cases are subclassified to indicate the absence (A) or presence (B) of fever, night sweats, or weight loss. The subscript "$_E$" refers to extranodal contiguous extension. The subscript "$_S$" refers to spleen involvement.

STUDY TABLE: Prognostic Groupings of Hodgkin Lymphoma	
Prognosis	**Description**
Early favorable	Stage IA or IIA, no extranodal sites, ESR <50 mm/h, size <10 cm, <3 lymph node groups
Early unfavorable	Stage IA, IB, IIA, or IIB, ESR ≥50 mm/h, size ≥10 cm, ≥3 lymph node groups
Advanced stage	Stage III, IV, or IIB plus size ≥10 cm

Treatment of classic Hodgkin lymphoma:

- Treat patients with early-stage disease (IA and IIA) with a short course of chemotherapy (e.g., ABVD) and irradiation to involved lymph node sites.
- Patients with bulky stage I or II disease or B symptoms should receive a full course of chemotherapy (ABVD) followed by radiation therapy to initially bulky areas.
- Typically treat patients with higher-stage disease with chemotherapy (ABVD).

Treatment of lymphocyte-predominant variant of Hodgkin lymphoma:

- Preferentially treat patients with an early-stage disease with involved-field or regional radiation. A watch-and-wait approach is appropriate for patients who cannot tolerate radiation.
- The treatment of choice for patients with B symptoms or more disseminated disease is the same as that used in treating those with classic Hodgkin lymphoma.

Refer all patients <70 years of age with recurrent disease for evaluation for stem cell transplantation. Sperm cryopreservation is an option before therapy for men who wish to preserve fertility.

Evaluate for secondary cancers (breast, lung, skin) and myelodysplastic syndrome. For women, begin annual mammography and MRI at age 40 years or 8 years following radiation therapy.

◆ DON'T BE TRICKED

- **Evaluate all patients with chest pain after radiation therapy for CAD, regardless of age.**

Non-Hodgkin Lymphoma

Diagnosis

Patients with indolent lymphoma/leukemia most commonly have very slowly advancing lymphadenopathy or lymphocytosis, often without other symptoms. The most common indolent lymphomas are follicular lymphoma and chronic lymphocytic leukemia/small lymphocytic lymphoma. Long periods of stability or even spontaneous disease regression may occur. Most patients with more advanced indolent lymphoma have widespread lymphadenopathy and bone marrow and hepatosplenic involvement. Indolent lymphoma/leukemia is not considered curable in advanced stages.

Patients with aggressive lymphoma/leukemia have rapidly progressive, symptomatic disease, often initially localized to one organ or compartment (such as the bone marrow). The most common types of aggressive lymphoma are diffuse large B-cell lymphoma, high-grade lymphomas (including Burkitt and Burkitt-like lymphoma), and lymphoblastic lymphoma. These disease entities are curable with administration of aggressive chemotherapeutic regimens and sometimes with adjunctive radiation therapy, even in advanced stages.

Patients <40 years of age usually have aggressive lymphoma/leukemia, whereas older patients have indolent or aggressive forms. Unexplained fever, night sweats, and weight loss (B symptoms) plus fatigue and localized pain are common in more aggressive lymphomas. Physical examination findings include lymphadenopathy, masses, and hepatosplenomegaly. Evaluation focuses on:

- histologic type of the tumor
- extent of disease
- performance status

◆ DON'T BE TRICKED

- **The most critical study in the evaluation of non-Hodgkin lymphoma is the histopathologic evaluation of an intact lymph node. Do not select needle or core biopsy.**

Common complications include:

- spinal cord compression
- pericardial tamponade
- hypercalcemia
- superior or inferior vena cava syndrome
- hyperuricemia, tumor lysis syndrome
- autoimmune hemolytic anemia
- thrombocytopenic purpura

Therapy

Follicular lymphoma is the most common indolent lymphoma. Patients with early-stage disease (stages IA and IIA) often are treated with radiation therapy. Patients with disseminated disease need systemic treatment when the decision is made to abandon watchful waiting. The decision to initiate treatment is based on the presence of symptoms, threat to vital organ function, issues over appearance because of enlarged lymph nodes, and patient preference. Systemic therapy may include rituximab alone or added to combination chemotherapy.

MALT lymphoma often is associated with *H. pylori* infection. A combination of antibiotics, including metronidazole, amoxicillin, or clarithromycin with PPI therapy, is used to eradicate the *H. pylori* infection and is associated with up to an 80% complete response for localized gastric lymphoma.

Diffuse large cell lymphoma is treated with cyclophosphamide, doxorubicin, vincristine, and prednisone (CHOP) with rituximab; radiation may be included. Patients with advanced high-risk disease may be treated with high-dose chemotherapy with autologous stem cell rescue.

Patients with lymphoblastic lymphoma receive the same treatment regimens as those administered to patients with acute lymphocytic leukemia. Patients with Burkitt lymphoma receive a brief, high-intensity chemotherapy regimen, also with CNS treatment.

Carcinoma of Unknown Primary Origin

Diagnosis

Metastatic CUP accounts for as many as 3% to 5% of patients with solid tumors. Diagnostic testing in patients with CUP focuses on the head and neck, rectum, prostate, testicles, ovaries, and breasts.

A tumor biopsy is indicated. At minimum, perform CT, CBC, urinalysis, and FOBT. Additional tests, including serum PSA measurement, breast MRI or mammography, and ER/PR receptor assays should be performed depending on the clinical scenario. Perform fine-needle aspiration or core biopsy when patients present with a neck mass to determine histologic cell type. Diagnosis generally falls into one of three categories:

- epithelial tumors, such as SCC, adenocarcinoma, or anaplastic tumors
- lymphoma
- melanoma

Perform upper-airway panendoscopy (laryngoscopy, bronchoscopy, and esophagoscopy) and dedicated CT of the head and neck as part of the diagnostic evaluation of a neck mass. Consider a diagnosis of breast cancer in women whose only site of disease is unilateral axillary lymph nodes.

Ovarian cancer should be strongly considered in women presenting with a combination of peritoneal carcinomatosis and malignant ascites with histologic evidence of carcinoma. Consider occult extragonadal germ cell tumors in young adults, especially young men, who present with midline tumors of the mediastinum or retroperitoneum.

◆ DON'T BE TRICKED
- Do not select routine radiographic contrast studies of the GI tract.

STUDY TABLE: Tests for Carcinoma of Unknown Primary Origin	
Indication	**Test**
All patients	Chest radiography and abdominal/pelvic CT
Women	Mammography
Women with cancer in axillary lymph nodes but nondiagnostic mammogram	Breast MRI
All patients with enlarged cervical lymph nodes	CT (or PET scan or PET/CT) of the head and neck plus upper-airway panendoscopy

Therapy

STUDY TABLE: Treating Carcinoma of Unknown Primary Origin	
Indication	**Treatment**
SCC and poorly differentiated carcinoma in mid or high cervical lymph nodes	Surgery and radiation therapy (same as for head and neck cancer)
Isolated axillary lymph node involvement in women	Surgery, radiation therapy, and adjuvant treatment (same as for breast cancer)
Peritoneal carcinomatosis and serous/papillary histologic findings in women	Chemotherapy with platinum agent and paclitaxel (same as ovarian cancer)
Midline mediastinal or retroperitoneal mass and poorly differentiated carcinoma histology in men ≤50 years of age	Platinum-containing regimen suitable for germ cell tumors
Patients not in above subgroups	Systemic chemotherapy

❖ **Test Yourself**

A 45-year-old woman has an axillary lymph node that is positive for adenocarcinoma. Bilateral mammogram, breast MRI, and CT scans of the chest and abdomen are normal. She has never smoked.

ANSWER: The diagnosis is adenocarcinoma of unknown primary origin. Treat as if she had breast cancer.

Cancers of Infectious Origin

Key Considerations

STUDY TABLE: Malignancies with Infectious Causes	
Cancer	**Associated Infection**
Cervical and anal cancers	HPV
	Increased incidence in HIV infection
	Risk proportional to number of sexual partners
Kaposi sarcoma	Human herpesvirus 8
	Primarily in younger HIV-infected men who have sex with men
	May be mistaken for bacillary angiomatosis (bartonellosis)
Hodgkin lymphoma	Epstein-Barr virus
Burkitt lymphoma	EBV t(8;14)-positive
	Increased incidence in HIV infection (AIDS-defining cancer)
	Presents as oral and nasopharyngeal cancer in China and Southeast Asia and as posttransplantation lymphoma in immunosuppressed patients
MALT lymphoma	*H. pylori*
	Usually involves the GI tract, particularly the stomach
	Treat early disease with antibiotics and PPIs (localized radiation therapy for *H. pylori*–negative disease)
Hepatocellular carcinoma	Cirrhosis and hepatitis B infection are the most important risk factors
Non-Hodgkin lymphoma	Increased incidence in HIV infection (AIDS-defining cancer)
Head and neck (nasopharynx)	Epstein-Barr virus
Head and neck (oropharynx)	HPV

Febrile Neutropenia

Diagnosis

Characteristic findings are a single episode of fever ≥38.3 °C (101.0 °F) or sustained temperature ≥38.0 °C (100.4 °F) for >1 hour in a patient with an absolute neutrophil count <500/microliter or <1000/microliter with an expected nadir of <500/microliter. A common infection associated with neutropenia is typhlitis (necrotizing enterocolitis), which should be suspected in patients with even minimal right lower quadrant abdominal pain and infections caused by encapsulated organisms (*Streptococcus pneumoniae*, *Neisseria meningitidis*, and *Haemophilus influenzae* in asplenic patients), gram-positive organisms, or fungal pathogens. Patients with possible typhlitis require a CT scan of the abdomen.

Be alert for nodular patchy pulmonary infiltrates and angioinvasive aspergillosis in patients with leukemia who are using prolonged antibiotic therapy. Biopsy is required for diagnosis, and aggressive antifungal treatment is required for cure.

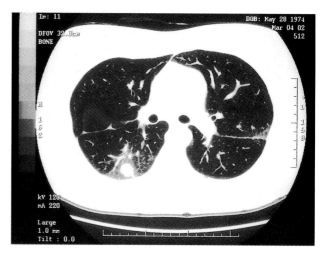

Invasive Aspergillosis: CT scan showing a dense infiltrate surrounded by a ground glass–appearing halo ("halo sign") suggestive, but not diagnostic, of invasive aspergillosis.

◆ DON'T BE TRICKED

- Select CSF testing only if the suspicion of infection is high and the risk of bleeding is low.
- Do not select CT of the chest if a chest x-ray is normal.

Therapy

Begin an empiric trial of broad-spectrum antibiotics. Common choices include a single agent with an antipseudomonal β-lactam agent (e.g., cefepime, meropenem, imipenem, piperacillin-tazobactam). An aminoglycoside, fluoroquinolone, and/or vancomycin may be added to meet special circumstances or when antimicrobial resistance is suspected or proven. If an infectious source is identified, continue therapy for the standard duration and site of that infection and until fever and neutropenia resolve.

STUDY TABLE: Treatment of Febrile Neutropenia	
If you see this...	**Choose this...**
Patient with high risk for gram-positive infection (intravascular devices, soft tissue infection)	Add vancomycin and discontinue in 3 days if not supported by a positive culture result.
Unexplained hypotension or septic shock	Add vancomycin.
Fever for 5 additional days and continued neutropenia with empiric antibiotics	Add antifungal therapy. Itraconazole is equivalent to amphotericin B.
Positive cultures are now negative, signs of infection are gone, and neutrophil count is >500/μL	Continue antibiotic coverage for at least 7 more days.
Cultures were never positive, no source of infection identified, temperature normal for 48 hours, and neutrophil count is >500/μL	Stop empiric antibiotics now.
Cultures were never positive, no source of infection identified, temperature normal, and neutrophil count is <500/μL	Continue same antibiotic regimen until neutrophil count is >500/μL.
μL = microliter.	

◆ DON'T BE TRICKED

- Do not begin routine antiviral therapy unless clinical or laboratory evidence of viral infection is seen.
- Do not select colony-stimulating factors for routine use in patients with febrile neutropenia.

❖ Test Yourself

A 73-year-old man with acute myeloid leukemia develops febrile neutropenia on the eighth day of chemotherapy. Ceftazidime is begun, but after 5 days of therapy he remains febrile and neutropenic. Blood cultures are negative, and he has no localizing signs of infection.

ANSWER: Add amphotericin B or itraconazole.

Cancer Emergencies

Hypercalcemia

Characteristic findings are elevated serum calcium, low parathyroid hormone, low or normal phosphorus, and low or normal 1,25-dihydroxyvitamin D_3 levels. All patients require immediate volume repletion with normal saline. Use bisphosphonates such as pamidronate and zoledronate. Add corticosteroids in steroid-sensitive malignancies such as myeloma and lymphoma.

Hyponatremia

Initially treat asymptomatic or mildly symptomatic patients with the syndrome of inappropriate antidiuretic hormone secretion (SIADH) with fluid restriction (500-1000 mL/d). Give 3% sodium chloride and furosemide to symptomatic patients with altered mental status or other neurologic findings to raise the serum sodium concentration to 120 meq/L. An alternative treatment in hospitalized patients is use of the antidiuretic hormone receptor antagonist conivaptan (very expensive, with no evidence of improved outcomes). Do not exceed a correction rate of 1 to 2 meq/L/h.

Deep Venous Thrombosis

Begin long-term LMWH for initial treatment and secondary prevention of thromboembolic disease in patients with underlying cancer. Use an inferior vena cava filter if anticoagulation is contraindicated.

◆ **DON'T BE TRICKED**

- **In patients with hypercalcemia, do not use furosemide with saline infusion until volume status is restored.**
- **In patients with active cancer, do not treat venous thromboembolism with warfarin.**

Spinal Cord Compression

Characteristic findings include:

- localized spinal or radicular pain
- sensory loss (especially perineal)
- muscle weakness
- change in bowel or bladder function
- autonomic dysfunction

The diagnosis is established by gadolinium-enhanced MRI of the entire spine.

◆ **DON'T BE TRICKED**

- **Do not order plain x-rays or bone scans to diagnose spinal cord compression.**

Therapy

Treat immediately with corticosteroids and decompressive surgery followed by radiation therapy. Systemic chemotherapy is useful in patients with highly chemosensitive tumors such as lymphoma or breast cancer. Prescribe opioid therapy as needed for pain.

Superior Vena Cava Syndrome

Characteristic findings are shortness of breath, cough, facial edema, plethora, swollen arms, neck vein distention, stridor (tracheal obstruction), and prominent collateral veins on the anterior chest wall.

STUDY TABLE: Interventions for Superior Vena Cava Syndrome	
Situation	**Response**
Superior vena cava syndrome	Biopsy tissue external to obstructing mass
If biopsy is unsuccessful	Mediastinoscopy or thoracotomy
Syndrome due to previously untreated SCLC, lymphoma, or germ cell tumor	Chemotherapy
Syndrome due to previously treated SCLC, lymphoma, germ cell tumor, or chemosensitive malignancies	Radiation therapy alone or in combination with chemotherapy

Pericardial Tamponade

Characteristic findings are:

- dyspnea, orthopnea, and clear lungs
- jugular venous distention and hepatic engorgement
- sinus tachycardia, hypotension, narrow pulse pressure, distant heart sounds, and pulsus paradoxus

See Pericardial Tamponade and Constriction in Cardiovascular Medicine. Life-threatening hemodynamic compromise is treated with immediate drainage of fluid via pericardiocentesis or pericardiotomy.

Tumor Lysis Syndrome

Tumor lysis syndrome is the result of rapid breakdown of malignant cells, resulting in dangerous increases in serum uric acid, potassium, and phosphate concentrations. Symptoms may include:

- nausea, vomiting, and diarrhea
- lethargy
- HF
- seizures, tetany, and syncope
- sudden death

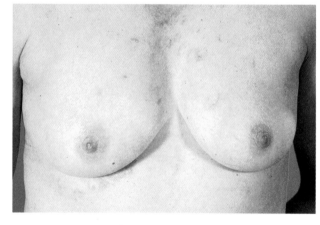

Superior Vena Cava Syndrome: The sudden appearance of dilated veins on the chest of this patient heralded the onset of the superior vena cava syndrome.

Typically, tumor lysis syndrome occurs within 1 to 5 days of treatment and develops most commonly in patients with hematologic malignancies or other rapidly dividing tumors, such as acute leukemia and high-grade lymphoma. Risk factors include bulky disease, a high leukocyte count, high pretreatment levels of lactate dehydrogenase or uric acid, compromised kidney function, and use of nephrotoxic agents.

Tumor lysis syndrome is prevented and managed by aggressive hydration and use of allopurinol or rasburicase. IV rasburicase is indicated for patients at high risk for tumor lysis syndrome or when rapid reduction of uric acid levels is indicated (e.g., emergently administered chemotherapy). Hyperkalemia is also aggressively treated. If acute kidney failure develops, hemodialysis may be indicated.

Effects of Cancer Therapy

STUDY TABLE: Short- and Long-Term Effects of Cancer Therapy	
Category	**Potential Complications**
Cardiac	Doxorubicin: dose-related HF
	Trastuzumab: non–dose-related HF
	Mediastinal radiation: myocardial, valvular, pericardial fibrosis, and premature CAD.
Pulmonary	Bleomycin: pulmonary toxicity, most commonly bleomycin-induced pneumonitis
	Radiation: radiation-induced pneumonitis
Reproductive	Chemotherapy: premature ovarian failure
	Chemotherapy: male infertility
	Tamoxifen: endometrial cancer, venous thromboembolic disease
Endocrine	Radiation therapy to head and neck: hypothyroidism
Musculoskeletal	Aromatase inhibitors: osteoporosis
	Leuprolide, goserelin, castration: osteoporosis
Cancer	Mantle radiation: breast, lung, and esophageal cancer
	Chemotherapy (breast cancer): myelodysplastic syndrome and acute leukemia

❖ **Test yourself**

A 44-year-old man is evaluated for cough and dyspnea 2 weeks after he completed his ABVD therapy for Hodgkin lymphoma. The chest x-ray shows bilateral interstitial infiltrates.

ANSWER: Bleomycin-induced lung injury.

Palliative Care

Key Considerations

STUDY TABLE: Symptomatic End-of-Life Care	
Condition	**Recommendations**
Medical support	Medicare hospice benefit eligibility requires documentation by physicians that a patient is terminally ill with a likely survival of 6 months or less. For patients surviving longer, hospice eligibility must be re-evaluated at least every 60 days.
Dyspnea	Treat underlying cause if possible. Oxygen is not helpful in the absence of hypoxemia. Systemic opioids are useful for treating cancer-associated dyspnea, HF, and COPD.
Cachexia	Megestrol acetate improves appetite and weight gain but lacks demonstrated benefit for increasing quality of life or survival.
Anxiety	Benzodiazepines can help reduce anxiety in a palliative care setting.
Depression	Psychostimulants such as methylphenidate, dextroamphetamine, or pemoline may produce benefits within days, rather than in weeks required with conventional antidepressants.
Pain	See Cancer Pain following

Cancer Pain

Drug Therapy

Follow these five steps to answer Board Examination questions about pain control:

1. Use acetaminophen, aspirin, or NSAIDs for mild to moderate pain.

2. If pain persists or increases, add a low-dose or low-potency opioid (e.g., codeine, oxycodone).

3. Increase opioid potency (e.g., morphine) or add higher doses for persistent or moderate to severe pain at onset.

4. Add adjuvant agents at any step (tricyclic antidepressants, anticonvulsants).

5. Prescribe around-the-clock analgesics for persistent, chronic pain rather than as needed.

NSAIDS and acetaminophen have an analgesic efficacy ceiling that cannot be exceeded. The following are ceiling doses when analgesics are combined:

- acetaminophen, 4 g/d
- ibuprofen, 2400 mg/d
- naproxen, 1250 mg/d
- aspirin, 4000 mg/d

Opioids do not have an analgesic efficacy ceiling and can be titrated upward as needed, until limiting side effects appear. Common side effects of opioids include constipation, sedation, nausea, and itching (not from an allergy). Except for constipation, tolerance develops to each side effect. Constipation is prevented with a stimulant laxative and a stool softener. Pruritus is managed with antihistamines.

Use around-the-clock, long-acting opioids for baseline pain control and fast-onset, short-acting preparations (morphine) for breakthrough pain. Titrate the total analgesic dose by adding the amount of short-acting opioids used in the past 24 hours to the chronic opioid dose to establish the new long-acting daily opioid dose. Begin IV patient-controlled analgesia for hospitalized patients when oral analgesics are not possible or are no longer effective.

◆ DON'T BE TRICKED

- **Do not select meperidine (even in biliary disease).**
- **Naloxone does not reverse CNS toxicity caused by normeperidine and may actually increase neuroexcitability.**

STUDY TABLE: Adjuvant Therapy for Pain Control	
When you see this...	**Choose this...**
Neuropathic pain	Tricyclic antidepressants, anticonvulsants, oral local anesthetics, or topical analgesics
A need for anti-inflammatory effects, mood elevation, and improved appetite, especially in patients with cancer pain	Corticosteroids
Patients with known osteolytic bone lesions	IV bisphosphonate (pamidronate, zoledronate)

Do not confuse tolerance and physical dependence with addiction. Tolerance is defined as the need for increasing amounts of drug to achieve the same analgesic effect and occurs in most patients. Physical dependence is a physiologic state manifested by opioid withdrawal symptoms when opioids are discontinued abruptly or when opioid antagonists are administered. Addiction involves abnormal behavior, such as a person obsessed with the acquisition and use of a drug despite adverse social, psychosocial, or physical consequences.

Psychiatry

Alcohol Abuse

Screening

Ask all patients about their level of alcohol consumption and follow up with screening tests as appropriate. Patients with AUDIT-C scores >6 or a CAGE questionnaire score >1 are candidates for further evaluation. Look for alcoholism in patients with associated conditions, including repeated trauma, hypertension, atrial fibrillation, HF, pancreatitis, alcoholic hepatitis, and cirrhosis. Laboratory clues such as an elevated MCV, γ-glutamyltransferase level, and AST-ALT ratio >2 are suggestive but not diagnostic.

Diagnosis

STUDY TABLE: Categories and Patterns of Alcohol Use	
Categories	**Patterns**
At-risk drinking	Men: >14 drinks per week or >4 drinks per occasion
	Women: >7 drinks per week or >3 drinks per occasion
Alcohol abuse	One or more of the following in 1 year: Inability to fulfill major role obligations, use in hazardous situations, legal problems, social or interpersonal problems
Alcohol dependence	Three or more of the following in 1 year: tolerance, withdrawal, and overwhelming involvement in acquisition and use despite adverse social, psychosocial, or physical consequences; activities given up because of alcohol; drinking more or longer than intended; persistent desire to cut down

In patients undergoing alcohol withdrawal, look for:

- tremor, anxiety, diaphoresis, and palpitations 6 to 36 hours after the last drink
- visual, auditory, and tactile hallucinations 12 to 48 hours after the last drink
- generalized tonic-clonic seizure within 2 days after the last drink
- delirium tremens (hallucinations, delirium, agitation, fever, palpitations, and hypertension) 48 to 96 hours after the last drink

◆ DON'T BE TRICKED

- **Multiple seizures (more than one) are not consistent with alcohol withdrawal syndrome and should prompt an evaluation for another disorder.**
- **Alcoholic hallucinosis does not cause clouding of the sensorium.**

Therapy

For management of alcohol abuse and dependence, the U.S. Preventive Services Task Force recommends referral for specialty treatment. For alcohol misuse, brief behavioral counseling (such as the five A's and the five R's, listed in the following tables) may be useful. Use naltrexone to prevent relapse of alcohol abuse and dependence and in patients who are actively drinking. Naltrexone is contraindicated in patients receiving or withdrawing from any opioid and in those with liver failure or hepatitis. Acamprosate enhances abstinence but is contraindicated in kidney insufficiency. Disulfiram leads to the accumulation of acetaldehyde if alcohol is consumed, resulting in flushing, headache, emesis, and the need to avoid all additional alcohol-containing items.

STUDY TABLE: "Five A's" Framework for Brief Counseling	
Assess	Ask about behavioral health risks, such as smoking, substance use, diet, exercise. Assess beliefs, behaviors, knowledge, motivation, and past experience.
Advise	Give clear, specific, well-timed, and personalized behavior change advice. Advise in a noncoercive, nonjudgmental manner that respects readiness for change and patient autonomy.
Agree	Collaboratively select appropriate goals and methods based on the patient's interest and willingness to change. For those with multiple risks, agree on what to tackle first.
Assist	Aid the patient in achieving agreed-upon goals with use of social/environmental supports and adjunctive medical treatments when appropriate (including pharmacotherapy).
Arrange	Schedule follow-up (in person or by phone) to provide ongoing support and to adjust the plan as needed, including referral for more specialized interventions.

STUDY TABLE: "Five R's" of Counseling	
Relevance	Encourage the patient to discuss why quitting is personally relevant. Motivation is greatest if behavior has relevance to disease risk, family, or social situation.
Risks	Ask the patient to identify negative consequences of the behavior.
Rewards	Ask the patient to identify potential benefits of stopping the behavior.
Roadblocks	Ask the patient to identify barriers or impediments to quitting. Note elements of treatment that could address the barriers.
Repetition	Repeat the motivational intervention at subsequent office visits.

Hospitalize patients with moderate to severe alcohol withdrawal or another compelling need for hospitalization.

Benzodiazepines are indicated for:

- patients with previous alcohol-related seizures or delirium tremens
- significant withdrawal symptoms
- severe or long-standing alcohol dependence
- a history of multiple detoxification attempts
- pregnant patients
- patients with acute medical or surgical illnesses

Use a symptom-triggered regimen to treat alcohol withdrawal. Administer a long-acting benzodiazepine on a fixed schedule for a patient who has a history of experiencing a seizure when withdrawing from alcohol (even if the patient is currently asymptomatic). Adjunctive therapy with β-blockers and clonidine may help if control of tachycardia and hypertension is needed.

◆ DON'T BE TRICKED

- **Give thiamine replacement before administering glucose.**
- **Do not prescribe antipsychotic medications because these agents lower the seizure threshold.**
- **No evidence supports that continuous infusion therapy with short-acting benzodiazepines provides better outcomes than oral therapy for acute alcohol withdrawal.**
- **Not all heavy drinkers who stop abruptly experience withdrawal, and treatment with benzodiazepines is not always needed.**
- **Standing orders for benzodiazepines for alcohol withdrawal in patients with cirrhosis can precipitate hepatic encephalopathy.**

❖ Test Yourself

A 36-year-old man with a history of heavy alcohol use is evaluated within 24 hours of his last drink. Blood pressure is 172/98 mm Hg, and pulse rate is 120/min. He is tremulous and having visual hallucinations.

ANSWER: The diagnosis is alcohol withdrawal syndrome. Hospitalize the patient, and treat him with benzodiazepines using a symptom-triggered protocol.

Eating Disorders

Diagnosis

Anorexia nervosa consists of two types:

- restricting, in which patients restrict intake (anorexia nervosa)
- binge eating/purging, in which patients binge and purge to control weight (bulimia nervosa)

Diagnostic criteria for the restricting type of anorexia consist of refusal to maintain weight within 15% of normal level, fear of weight gain, distorted body image, and amenorrhea or lack of onset of menstruation. The medical complications include anemia, osteopenia, hypotension, and arrhythmias. During the first few weeks of eating, patients are at risk for the refeeding syndrome, which can include cardiac arrest and delirium caused by exacerbation of hypophosphatemia and hypokalemia.

Diagnostic criteria for bulimia nervosa are episodes of binging with loss of control occurring minimally 2 times per week for 3 months, followed by purging (vomiting, diuretic or laxative abuse), fasting, or excessive exercise. Patients usually have normal weight. The medical complications can involve acid-induced dental disease, esophageal tears, and electrolyte derangements (low chloride and potassium). Laboratory clues include metabolic alkalosis.

Therapy

For anorexia nervosa, daily supplementation with calcium and vitamin D is used to treat osteopenia. Cognitive behavioral therapy is considered first-line treatment. Psychotropic drugs have minimal efficacy in underweight patients with anorexia.

Patients with bulimia respond to cognitive behavioral therapy, and antidepressants (fluoxetine or imipramine) and nutritional rehabilitation are effective adjunctive therapy.

◆ DON'T BE TRICKED

- Do not choose bupropion for eating disorders because of the increased incidence of tonic-clonic seizures.

❖ Test Yourself

A 24-year-old woman has reflux esophagitis, recurrent sore throat, and a dry cough. She exercises regularly and is "always dieting" because of her "weight problem." BMI is 25.3. On physical examination, the posterior pharynx and soft palate are injected without exudate. The tooth enamel is eroded.

ANSWER: The diagnosis is bulimia nervosa. Begin cognitive behavioral therapy and fluoxetine.

Depression

Screening

Routine screening is recommended for all adults, including postpartum women and the elderly, utilizing the two-question model:

- "Over the past 2 weeks, have you felt down, depressed, hopeless?"
- "Over the past 2 weeks, have you felt little interest or pleasure in doing things?"

Diagnosis

Patients commonly present with physical symptoms, reporting on average seven somatic symptoms. Four categories of depression are relevant to internal medicine:

- major depression

- minor depression (also known as subthreshold depression)
- bipolar disorder
- dysthymia

STUDY TABLE: Diagnosing Depression		
Diagnosis	**Symptom Criteria (following)**	**Duration**
Major depression	≥5 symptoms including either depressed mood or anhedonia	≥2 weeks
Minor depression	2-4 symptoms	≥2 weeks
Dysthymia	≥2 symptoms	≥2 years

Symptom criteria:

- depressed mood
- loss of interest in daily activities
- weight loss or gain
- insomnia or hypersomnia
- psychomotor agitation or retardation
- fatigue
- feelings of worthlessness or guilt
- diminished ability to concentrate
- recurrent thoughts of death or suicide

Refer patients with a suicide plan or psychotic features to a psychiatrist, and hospitalize any patient (even against the patient's wishes) who is in imminent danger of harming himself or herself or others.

◆ DON'T BE TRICKED

- **Be alert for increased suicide risk associated with initiation of drug therapy for depression.**
- **Select bipolar disorder if depression is accompanied by previous or current manic symptoms.**

Mimics of depression:

- Situational adjustment reaction with depressed mood: depression with a clear precipitant. Usually resolves without medication following resolution of the acute stressor.
- Bipolar disorder: one or more manic or mixed manic and depressive episodes, usually accompanied by major depressive disorder.
- Seasonal affective disorder: a subtype of major depression, with onset during fall or winter and seasonal remission. Responds to phototherapy and SSRIs.
- Grief reaction: transient major depression may be present, but sadness without complete depression is more common. Pervasive and generalized guilt and persistent vegetative signs and symptoms are not consistent with normal grief. Loss of self-esteem is a symptom of depression rather than grief.
- Premenstrual dysphoric disorder (PMDD): characterized by the cyclical recurrence of five or more symptoms of depression, anxiety, and emotional lability that have their onset within 1 week before menstruation and resolution within 1 week after menstruation.
- Medical conditions: consider substance abuse, hypothyroidism, Cushing syndrome, Parkinson disease, and medications (interferon, β-blockers, corticosteroids). Routine laboratory testing for these conditions is not warranted unless suggested by history and physical examination findings.

Therapy

Begin psychotherapy, pharmacologic therapy, or both for mild to moderate major depression. Dysthymia responds only to pharmacologic therapy. Combine psychotherapy and antidepressants for severe depression. Any second-generation antidepressant medication can be used to treat major depressive disorder or dysthymic disorder. Guide selection of an anti-depressant by differences in side-effect profiles and personal or family history of response to a specific agent. Commonly tested benefits and side-effect profiles include:

- sertraline is safe for patients with cardiovascular disease
- bupropion has fewer effects on sexual function and weight gain
- mirtazapine causes sedation and weight gain (useful for patients with weight loss)
- venlafaxine can cause nausea and increased blood pressure

For patients in whom treatment with a single SSRI is unsuccessful, response does not differ whether patients receive a different SSRI, a non-SSRI antidepressant, a combination of two antidepressants, augmentation with lithium, or cognitive therapy. Therefore, in nonresponding patients, modify treatment (increase dose, switch, or add another drug) if the patient does not have ≥50% reduction in symptom score to pharmacotherapy within 6 to 8 weeks.

STUDY TABLE: Managing Antidepressant Therapy	
Indications	**Therapy**
First episode of depression	Initiate treatment and continue at the dosage required to achieve remission for an additional 4 to 9 months.
First recurrence of depression	Increase maintenance treatment to one to two times the inter-episode interval (for example, choose 18 to 36 months if the second episode occurs 18 months after the first episode).
Three or more recurrences of depression, recurrence within 1 year of successful treatment, or suicide attempt	Select lifetime maintenance therapy

Be alert for serotonin syndrome in patients taking SSRIs, particularly with concurrent use of monoamine oxidase inhibitors (MAOIs), St. John's wort, trazodone, dextromethorphan, linezolid, and buspirone. Mild symptoms include nausea, vomiting, flushing, and diaphoresis. Severe symptoms include hyperreflexia, myoclonus, muscular rigidity, and hyperthermia.

St. John's wort may be used as an alternative treatment for mild to moderate depression but may cause drug interactions (with digoxin, theophylline, simvastatin, warfarin, and SSRIs) and may decrease the serum levels of protease inhibitors and non-nucleoside reverse transcriptase inhibitors.

Bipolar Disorder

Diagnosis

Bipolar disorder features episodes of depression as well as periods of mania or hypomania. Manic findings include elevated, expansive, or irritable mood; hypersexuality; spending sprees; grandiosity; decreased need for sleep; and disruption of social or occupational functioning. Mimics of bipolar disorder include thyrotoxicosis, partial-complex seizures, SLE, and corticosteroid side effects.

Therapy

Lithium is the most effective mood stabilizer, but long-term therapy carries significant side effects, including kidney insufficiency, hypothyroidism, and DI. Anticonvulsants and second-generation antipsychotics are alternative first-line treatments. Monotherapy with SSRIs can unmask mania in patients with untreated bipolar disorder.

❖ **Test Yourself**

A 27-year-old woman requests thyroid medication to make her "stronger" because she wants to run for the senatorial position for the state of California. She is sleeping 2 to 3 hours per night and has not been eating. She spends her time writing her political action plan and shopping and has exceeded the limit on her credit card.

ANSWER: The diagnosis is mania.

Generalized Anxiety Disorder

Diagnosis

Generalized anxiety disorder, panic disorder, and posttraumatic stress disorder (PTSD) are the most common anxiety disorders occurring in primary care patients. Generalized anxiety disorder is characterized by pervasive and excessive anxiety about a variety of events or activities, restlessness, difficulty concentrating, irritability, functional impairment, and sleep disturbance. Patients commonly have a comorbid psychiatric disorder.

Medical mimics of generalized anxiety and panic disorders include hyperthyroidism (goiter, eye findings, and tremor), hypoglycemia, carcinoid syndrome (flushing, asthma, and diarrhea), cardiac arrhythmia, pheochromocytoma (elevated blood pressure, tachycardia), and substance abuse (amphetamines, cocaine, caffeine, nicotine, and alcohol).

Therapy

Cognitive behavioral therapy, with or without pharmacologic therapy, is first-line treatment for generalized anxiety disorder. SSRIs and SNRIs are effective. Benzodiazepines are acceptable for short-term use while titrating antidepressant doses, but dependence and tolerance complicate long-term use and benzodiazepines should be avoided in patients with a history of substance abuse.

Panic Disorder

Diagnosis

Diagnose panic attacks when 4 or more of the following are present:

- palpitations, sweating, and shortness of breath
- fear of dying
- chest pain
- nausea or abdominal distress
- unsteadiness, lightheadedness, faintness, paresthesias
- self-detached feeling

Panic disorder involves recurrent, unexpected attacks and persistent worry about future attacks.

Therapy

Cognitive behavioral therapy and SSRIs are first-line treatment. Long-acting benzodiazepines can be used as short-term therapy for disabling disorders until first-line treatments become effective. Avoid alprazolam.

◆ DON'T BE TRICKED

- **Do not prescribe benzodiazepines as first-line, long-term treatment for panic disorder.**

Posttraumatic Stress Disorder

Diagnosis

Indicators suggesting PTSD include 1) history of exposure to trauma, 2) persistent re-experiencing of the traumatic event, 3) avoidance of stimuli associated with the trauma, 4) and increased arousal. Assess for coexisting psychiatric disorders and domestic abuse.

Therapy

Cognitive behavioral therapy is the treatment of choice for PTSD. Sertraline and paroxetine are FDA-approved, adjuvant treatments. Benzodiazepines have not been shown to be effective.

◆ **DON'T BE TRICKED**
  • **Do not prescribe benzodiazepines for PTSD.**

Social Anxiety Disorder

Diagnosis

Diagnostic criteria for social anxiety disorder include severe fear of social or performance situations resulting in symptoms such as blushing, dyspnea, palpitations, and emotional distress. Anxiety may be generalized or specific to a single activity.

Therapy

Treat social anxiety disorder with cognitive behavioral therapy and SSRIs. Consider offering a β-blocker for nongeneralized social anxiety disorder (e.g., public speaking).

Obsessive-Compulsive Disorder

Diagnosis

Obsessions are defined as persistent ideas, thoughts, impulses, or images experienced as intrusive and inappropriate and associated with significant anxiety or distress.

Compulsions are repetitive behaviors (handwashing, checking, and ordering) or mental acts (counting or repeating words silently) performed to try to decrease the anxiety or stress associated with the obsessions. The person must recognize the obsessions or compulsions are excessive or unreasonable.

Therapy

Obsessive-compulsive disorder is treated with cognitive behavioral therapy and often with an SSRI.

Borderline Personality Disorder

Diagnosis

Characteristic findings are unstable interpersonal relationships, mood swings, impulsive self-destructive behaviors (sexual promiscuity), and recurrent suicidal, self-mutilating, or self-damaging behaviors. Also watch for difficulty controlling anger.

Therapy

Obtain psychiatric referral, and begin SSRIs for mood- and anxiety-related symptoms.

A 28-year-old woman is hospitalized because of an acetaminophen overdose. She is tearful and says her boyfriend is going to leave her. She bitterly complains about the unbearable night nurse and contrasts her day nurse and you, who have been so wonderful.

ANSWER: The diagnosis is borderline personality disorder.

Schizophrenia

Diagnosis

The following usually begin in mid to late adolescence:

- unusual perceptual experiences
- false beliefs
- illogical thoughts
- disorganized speech, such as frequent derailment or incoherence
- grossly disorganized or catatonic behavior
- negative symptoms, such as affective flattening, alogia (concrete replies to questions and restricted spontaneous speech), or avolition (inability to initiate and persist in goal-directed activities)

Mimics of schizophrenia include Huntington disease, Wilson disease, temporal lobe epilepsy, heavy metal poisoning, Wernicke-Korsakoff syndrome, HIV infection, syphilis, and herpes encephalitis.

Therapy

Begin a second-generation antipsychotic agent (olanzapine, risperidone, quetiapine, aripiprazole).

Somatoform Disorders

Diagnosis

Somatoform disorders are defined by the presence of physical symptoms in patients who have no demonstrable organic disease to explain the symptoms. Somatoform disorders include conversion disorder, hypochondriasis, pain disorder, body dysmorphic disorder, somatization disorder, factitious disorders, and malingering.

Somatization disorder is the most frequently encountered and is characterized by multiple unexplained physical symptoms for at least 6 months, along with symptom-related social or occupational impairment. Patients attribute their symptoms to an undiagnosed disorder despite multiple negative evaluations and are often not reassured despite repeated evaluations.

Therapy

The principles of therapy for patients with somatization disorder include regular office appointments with one physician. The patient should be reassured that life-threatening conditions have been ruled out and should be given a plausible explanation for the symptoms. Among all treatments, cognitive behavioral therapy has the broadest evidence of benefit across a number of somatoform disorders.

◆ **DON'T BE TRICKED**
- Choose malingering if a patient adopts a physical symptom for the purpose of gain.
- Choose factitious disorder if a patient adopts symptoms to remain in the sick role.

Autism Spectrum Disorders

Diagnosis

Autism is defined as impairment in social interaction and communication, and repetitive patterns of behavior, interests, or activities plus delay in communication, social interaction, or play with onset before 3 years of age.

Asperger disorder is defined as impairment in social interaction and communication with repetitive behaviors and without language or cognitive delay.

Therapy

Autism spectrum disorders are treated with a combination of behavioral therapy and environmental modifications.

Attention-Deficit/Hyperactivity Disorder

Diagnosis

ADHD usually first manifests in childhood and is characterized by inattention, hyperactivity, and impulsivity with functional impairment in at least two settings (home, work, school). ADHD is more prevalent in patients with mood disorders and substance abuse.

Therapy

Treat ADHD with stimulants (e.g., amphetamine or methylphenidate) but beware of the potential for abuse and use with caution in patients with hypertension or cardiovascular disease. Atomoxetine is an SNRI approved for treatment of ADHD in adults. Cognitive behavioral therapy may be used as an adjunctive therapy.

Pulmonary and Critical Care Medicine

Pulmonary Function Tests

Indications

The four pulmonary function tests commonly used to measure static lung function are spirometry, flow-volume loops, lung volumes, and D_{LCO}.

Pulmonary function testing is indicated for patients with unexplained pulmonary symptoms, abnormal pulmonary findings (abnormal chest radiograph, hypoxemia, crackles), monitoring known pulmonary disease, and preoperative assessment for lung resection.

Key Tests and Patterns

Spirometry is used to diagnose airflow obstruction such as asthma, COPD, and bronchiectasis.

- FEV_1/FVC <0.7 indicates airflow obstruction.
- A ≥12% increase in either FEV_1 or FVC and an increase ≥200 mL from baseline in either parameter with bronchodilator therapy indicates reversible airway obstruction.
- Equal reductions in FEV_1 and FVC suggest restrictive lung disease.

Flow-volume loops can help localize anatomic sites of airway obstruction. Refer to the "Flow-Volume Loops" figures and consider the following factors:

- A "scooped-out" pattern with a decreased slope on the expiratory curve that does not improve with bronchodilation indicates COPD (Figure A).
- A "scooped-out" pattern with a decreased slope on the expiratory curve that improves with bronchodilation indicates reversible obstructive airway disease (asthma) (Figure B).
- "Flattening" in both inspiratory and expiratory curves and decreased airflow indicate fixed obstruction outside the chest (tracheal stenosis) (Figure C).
- Following attainment of peak flow, the flow rate declines linearly and proportionally to volume, producing a relatively straight slope characteristic of a normal flow-volume loop (Figure D).

Lung volumes aid in confirming findings on spirometry.

- Total lung capacity <80% indicates restrictive lung disease (fibrosis, scoliosis).
- Decreased vital capacity with increased residual volume indicates airflow obstruction.

D_{LCO} evaluates gas transport across the alveolar-capillary membrane.

- D_{LCO} is reduced in patients with emphysema, pulmonary fibrosis, and bronchiectasis.
- When spirometry and lung volumes are normal, low D_{LCO} suggests pulmonary vascular disease and high D_{LCO} suggests pulmonary hemorrhage, left-to-right shunt, and polycythemia.

◆ DON'T BE TRICKED

- **In patients with low lung volumes, a normal D_{LCO} suggests an extrapulmonary cause.**

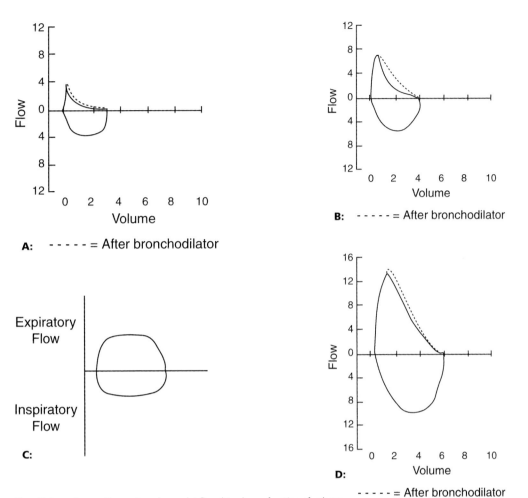

A: - - - - - = After bronchodilator

B: - - - - - = After bronchodilator

C:

D: - - - - - = After bronchodilator

Flow-Volume Loops: Flow-volume loops plot flow (L/sec) as a function of volume.

STUDY TABLE: Understanding Important Pulmonary Tests	
Tests	**Considerations**
Pulse oximetry	Measures percentage of oxyhemoglobin either at rest or during exercise
	Oxygen desaturation with exercise is a sensitive but not specific indicator of gas exchange abnormalities (COPD, pulmonary fibrosis)
Methacholine challenge test	A normal test effectively rules out asthma
Cardiopulmonary exercise testing	Is performed for unexplained dyspnea, symptoms disproportionate to the measured pulmonary function abnormality, and other exercise-related symptoms, such as exercise-induced bronchospasm

◆ DON'T BE TRICKED

- Pulse oximetry is normal in patients with carbon monoxide and cyanide poisoning.
- Pulse oximetry may be falsely low in patients with tissue underperfusion.

Asthma

Diagnosis

The onset of asthma usually occurs during childhood but may begin at any age. Most patients with asthma are atopic; however, some patients, particularly those with adult-onset asthma, have no clear allergic basis for their disease. The cardinal features of asthma are reversible airway obstruction, inflammation, and airway hyperresponsiveness.

Characteristic findings are wheezing and dyspnea; consider any cough that is nocturnal, seasonal, or related to a workplace or activity as possible asthma. Look for nasal polyps and aspirin sensitivity.

Diagnostic studies include spirometry before and after bronchodilator administration. In patients with atypical features, perform pulmonary function tests to determine lack of airflow reversibility, restrictive patterns, and significantly reduced vital capacity and FEV_1 that suggest other diseases.

Bronchoprovocation testing with methacholine or histamine is indicated for patients with a suggestive clinical history for asthma but normal spirometry. Bronchoprovocation testing with exercise is indicated to diagnose exercise-induced asthma in patients who have dyspnea following exercise but normal spirometry.

◆ DON'T BE TRICKED

- **Normal spirometry does not rule out asthma.**
- **A normal bronchoprovocation test rules out asthma; a positive test does not rule it in.**
- **Wheezing does not equal asthma; consider HF, COPD, vocal cord dysfunction, and upper airway obstruction.**

STUDY TABLE: Differential Diagnosis of Asthma

Disease	Characteristics
Chronic eosinophilic pneumonia	Chest radiograph shows "photographic-negative" pulmonary edema (peripheral pulmonary edema). Clinical findings: striking peripheral blood eosinophilia, fever, and weight loss in a long-term smoker.
	Diagnose by bronchoscopy with biopsy or bronchoalveolar lavage showing a high eosinophil count.
Allergic bronchopulmonary aspergillosis	Asthma manifests with eosinophilia, markedly high serum IgE levels, and intermittent pulmonary infiltrates.
	Diagnose with positive skin test for *Aspergillus* and IgG and IgE antibodies to *Aspergillus*.
	This is often overlooked until onset of more advanced disease, including fixed obstruction and bronchiectasis. Look for a patient with brown sputum.
Churg-Strauss syndrome	Upper airway and sinus disease precedes difficult-to-treat asthma. Look for flares associated with use of leukotriene inhibitors and corticosteroid tapers.
	Serum p-ANCA may be elevated.
	Hallmark diagnostic finding is eosinophilic tissue infiltrates.

Consider alternative diagnoses when asthma is difficult to control. Additional studies in these cases may include chest x-ray and echocardiography. Obtaining flow-volume loops and direct visualization of the larynx during an acute episode may be helpful in diagnosing tracheal obstruction and vocal cord dysfunction. Asthma is an extraesophageal manifestation of GERD.

Therapy

If asthma is difficult to control, discontinue β-blockers (including ophthalmologic agents). If β-blockers must be continued, use selective β-blockers (metoprolol, atenolol). Also stop aspirin and NSAIDs if the patient is sensitive to these drugs.

Asthma must be classified correctly to select proper therapy. Severity is based on the worst feature present.

STUDY TABLE: Step Classification of Asthma

Step Classification	Symptoms	Nocturnal Symptoms
Step 1: Intermittent	Symptoms ≤2 per week	≤2 per month
		Asymptomatic and normal PEF between exacerbations
Step 2: Mild persistent	Symptoms >2 per week but <1 per day	>2 per month
Step 3: Moderate persistent	Need for daily use of short-acting β-agonist	≥1 per week
		Acute exacerbations ≥2 per week
Step 4: Severe persistent	Continual symptoms that limit physical activity	Frequent

- Step 1, intermittent: Select a short-acting β-agonist, as needed.
- Step 2, mild persistent: Add a low-dose inhaled corticosteroid.
- Step 3, moderate persistent: Add one of the following: (1) preferred treatment is low to medium doses of an inhaled corticosteroid and a long-acting β-agonist (salmeterol or formoterol); (2) medium doses of an inhaled corticosteroid; or (3) low to medium doses of an inhaled corticosteroid and a single long-term controller medication (leukotriene modifier or theophylline).
- Step 4, severe persistent: Add high doses of an inhaled corticosteroid plus a long-acting bronchodilator and possibly oral corticosteroids.

Allergy immunotherapy may be helpful in carefully selected patients but the individual response is difficult to predict. Peak flow meters can be used at home for serial measurement of lung function and to assess the relationship of lung function to symptoms. For all patients, remember annual influenza vaccination and instruction about proper inhaler technique. Evaluate for thrush, hoarseness, and osteopenia caused by inhaled corticosteroids. Consider calcium and vitamin D supplements for patients at risk for osteopenia due to chronic corticosteroid use, and schedule early screening with DEXA.

◆ DON'T BE TRICKED

- **Do not administer theophylline with fluoroquinolones or macrolides (may result in theophylline toxicity).**
- **Do not use long-acting β-agonists as single agents in asthma (increased mortality rate).**

Treatment of exercise-induced asthma:

- For infrequent symptoms, treat with albuterol, cromolyn sodium, or nedocromil 15 to 30 minutes before exercise.
- For symptoms more than twice weekly, treat with montelukast/zafirlukast, or use the step algorithm in the Step Classification of Asthma Study Table shown earlier.

Treatment of asthma in pregnancy:

- Control GERD.
- Step-care therapy for chronic asthma is the same for pregnant and nonpregnant patients.
- Early addition of corticosteroids is indicated for rapid reversal of airway obstruction during an exacerbation.

Treatment of severe asthma exacerbation in the emergency department:

- Administer repeated doses of albuterol by continuous flow nebulizer or metered-dose inhaler with a spacer.
- Early IV corticosteroids should be given when inhaled albuterol is ineffective.
- Inhaled ipratropium may be helpful.
- IV magnesium sulfate may be helpful for patients who have life-threatening exacerbations.
- Helium-oxygen (heliox) may be helpful but is not standard therapy.
- Hospitalize patients who do not respond well after 4 to 6 hours.
- Patients discharged home should be given oral corticosteroids, inhaled corticosteroids, an asthma action plan, and follow-up instructions.

◆ DON'T BE TRICKED

- **A normal arterial P_{CO_2} in a patient with severe symptomatic asthma indicates impending respiratory failure.**

❖ Test Yourself

A 35-year-old woman with asthma has daily coughing and shortness of breath. She uses triamcinolone, 4 puffs BID, and albuterol, 2 puffs BID as needed. Her sleep is disturbed nightly by coughing. The chest examination shows soft bilateral expiratory wheezing. PEF is 60% of predicted.

ANSWER: The diagnosis is severe persistent asthma. Add a long-acting bronchodilator. The short-term addition of an oral corticosteroid to the inhaled corticosteroid and a long-acting bronchodilator would also be correct.

Occupational Asthma and Reactive Airways Dysfunction Syndrome

Diagnosis

Characteristic findings of occupational asthma include:

- onset of asthma after entering the workplace
- workplace exposure to an agent known to incite occupational asthma
- work-related changes in FEV_1 or PEF
- a positive response to a specific inhalation challenge test (the "gold standard" for diagnosis, but not always necessary)

Reactive airways dysfunction syndrome (RADS), or irritant-induced asthma, typically occurs after a single exposure to high concentrations of nonspecific irritants (chlorine gas, bleach, ammonia). Patients present with cough, wheezing, chest tightness, and shortness of breath within 24 to 48 hours of exposure. Symptoms do not improve away from work, and spirometry shows obstruction. The symptoms may persist for many years.

Therapy

The patient should not return to the workplace or the site of the irritant. Inhaled corticosteroids are recommended for all patients with anything more than mild occupational asthma. Reactive airways dysfunction syndrome is treated like asthma and often requires inhaled corticosteroids.

❖ **Test Yourself**

A previously healthy 45-year-old man has a cough of 6 months' duration. He is a lifelong nonsmoker and works as an automobile spray painter. Physical examination discloses a few expiratory wheezes. FEV_1 is 0.65 and FEV_1/FVC ratio is 65% of predicted, and a 22% improvement occurs after bronchodilator administration.

ANSWER: Obtain spirometry or measure PEF before and after work (or during vacation) to confirm the diagnosis of occupational asthma.

Chronic Obstructive Pulmonary Disease

Screening

Screening asymptomatic patients for COPD is not recommended. No studies report improved outcomes for treating asymptomatic individuals with airflow obstruction.

Diagnosis

COPD is a heterogeneous disorder that includes emphysema, chronic bronchitis, obliterative bronchiolitis, and asthmatic bronchitis. Patients typically present with cough, sputum production, dyspnea, and decreased exercise tolerance and energy level. The features most predictive of COPD in a symptomatic patient are:

- >40-pack-year smoking history

or the combination of:

- smoking history
- wheezing on auscultation
- self-reported wheezing

Look for signs of hyperinflation, including barrel chest, hyperresonant percussion note, distant breath sounds, and prolonged expiratory time. Pursed-lips breathing, paradoxical chest or abdominal wall movements, and use of accessory muscles of respiration are all signs of severe airflow limitation. Diagnose COPD when postbronchodilator spirometry shows an FEV_1/FVC ratio <0.70 associated with symptoms of chronic bronchitis, emphysema, or both. Test for AAT deficiency in the following situations:

- age ≤45 years
- no risk factors for COPD (smoking, occupational dust exposure)
- family history of AAT deficiency
- presence of basilar lung predominance of emphysema on imaging studies, unexplained liver disease, or necrotizing panniculitis

Spirometry should be obtained to diagnose airflow obstruction in patients with respiratory symptoms.

STUDY TABLE: Mimics of COPD	
Disease	**Characteristics**
Bronchiectasis	Often secondary to an inciting event, such as childhood pneumonia or tuberculosis; may be associated with foreign body, CF, immotile ciliary syndrome, and aspergillosis
	Large-volume sputum production with purulent exacerbations
	Chest radiograph showing "tram lines"
	Diagnose with HRCT
Cystic fibrosis	Positive sweat chloride test result (onset usually at birth but may not present until adulthood in rare patients)
Adult bronchiolitis	Found in current or former smokers; may be idiopathic or associated with other diseases such as rheumatoid arthritis; poorly responsive to bronchodilators; responds to smoking cessation and corticosteroids
Bronchiolitis obliterans	Presents with flulike illness and often mistaken for community-acquired pneumonia; consider in patients after lung transplant
Upper airway obstruction	Stridor, which may be both inspiratory and expiratory
	Flow-volume loop shows expiratory or inspiratory plateau, or both

Therapy

Strong evidenced-based recommendations:

- For symptomatic patients with COPD and FEV_1 <60% of predicted, monotherapy using either long-acting inhaled anticholinergics or long-acting inhaled β-agonists is recommended.
- For symptomatic patients with an FEV_1 <50% of predicted, pulmonary rehabilitation is recommended.
- For patients with COPD who have severe resting hypoxemia (arterial Po_2 <55 mm Hg or O_2 saturation <88%), continuous oxygen therapy is recommended.

Weaker evidence-based recommendations:

- For stable patients with COPD with respiratory symptoms and FEV_1 between 60% and 80% of predicted, treatment with inhaled bronchodilators may be used.
- For symptomatic patients with stable COPD and FEV_1 >60% of predicted, combination inhaled therapies (long-acting inhaled anticholinergics, long-acting inhaled-agonists, or inhaled corticosteroids) may be considered.
- For symptomatic or exercise-limited patients with an FEV_1 >50% of predicted, pulmonary rehabilitation may be considered.

Additional indications to consider long-term oxygen therapy:

- arterial blood Po_2 is 55 to 60 mm Hg with signs of tissue hypoxia (polycythemia, pulmonary hypertension, right-sided HF)
- exercise arterial blood Po_2 is ≤55 mm Hg or O_2 is saturation ≤88%

Antibiotics, corticosteroids, oxygen supplementation, and noninvasive ventilation are indicated for exacerbations of COPD defined by increased sputum production, purulent sputum, and worsening dyspnea. Consider:

- tetracycline or trimethoprim-sulfamethoxazole for mild exacerbations
- β-lactam/β-lactamase inhibitor, extended-spectrum macrolides, second- or third-generation cephalosporins, or a fluoroquinolone for moderate or severe exacerbations
- corticosteroids continued for 2 weeks after initiation
- short-acting bronchodilators (albuterol, ipratropium, or both)
- noninvasive ventilation (unless patient is obtunded, vomiting, or has excessive secretions)

All patients with COPD require smoking cessation (to slow loss of lung function), annual influenza vaccination, and pneumococcal vaccination. Pulmonary rehabilitation will improve quality of life (but not survival) in patients with severe COPD. Augmentation therapy with IV human AAT is indicated for patients with homozygous AAT deficiency. Lung volume reduction surgery should be considered for patients with upper lobe emphysema (homogeneous disease) and low baseline exercise capacity to improve mortality, exercise capacity, and quality of life.

◆ DON'T BE TRICKED

- **Do not use short-acting and long-acting anticholinergic agents together.**
- **Do not consider lung volume reduction surgery for patients with an FEV_1 ≤20% of predicted.**
- **Clubbing is not a feature of COPD and suggests bronchiectasis, right-to-left cardiac shunts, or malignancy.**

Cystic Fibrosis

Diagnosis

Chronic airway inflammation and bacterial infection characterize CF-related pulmonary disease. Most adults with CF present with pulmonary disease. Characteristic findings are recurrent or persistent respiratory infections with *Pseudomonas aeruginosa* or *Burkholderia cepacia*, bronchiectasis or hyperinflation, chronic sinusitis and nasal polyps, clubbing, steatorrhea, inability to gain weight, infertility, diabetes, and chronic or recurrent pancreatitis. The diagnosis is confirmed by a sweat chloride test.

◆ DON'T BE TRICKED

- **In patients with CF and acute abdominal pain, consider intestinal intussusception.**

Therapy

All patients should receive pneumococcal polysaccharide and influenza vaccines.

Select:

- antipseudomonal antibiotics for acute pulmonary exacerbations
- aerosolized tobramycin for suppression of chronic pulmonary infections
- aerosolized recombinant human DNase or hypertonic saline for persistent airway secretions
- inhaled bronchodilators and corticosteroids for airway obstruction
- chest physiotherapy
- pancreatic enzyme replacement and fat soluble vitamin supplementation if indicated

Choose evaluation for transplantation for patients with advanced lung or liver disease.

❖ Test Yourself

A 34-year-old woman has had frequent episodes of bronchitis and three episodes of pneumonia in the past 5 years. Between episodes, she has a persistent cough producing yellow sputum. She also has been treated for multiple episodes of sinusitis. The patient is a lifelong nonsmoker. BMI is 18. The thorax is hyperresonant to percussion and has diminished air movement bilaterally. Digital clubbing is present.

ANSWER: The probable diagnosis is CF. Choose a sweat chloride test.

Pleurisy and Pleural Effusion

Diagnosis

Pleural fluid is characterized as transudative or exudative. Transudates form when hydrostatic pressures favor fluid formation exceeding clearance, whereas exudates form by means of increased vascular permeability. Serum and pleural fluid protein and LDH measurements are used to classify the type of pleural effusion with 99% accuracy.

STUDY TABLE: Laboratory Tests for Identifying a Pleural Effusion as an Exudate	
Test	**Interpretation**
1. Pleural fluid protein	>3 g/dL
2. Pleural fluid protein–serum protein ratio	>0.5
3. Pleural fluid LDH	>200 units/L (or >2/3 the upper limit of normal)
4. Pleural fluid LDH–serum LDH ratio	>0.6

If conditions 2 and 3 are not both met, the fluid is almost always a transudate. However, treatment (diuretics for HF), a dual diagnosis (HF and a concomitant parapneumonic effusion), or some specific diagnoses (e.g., chylothorax) can result in discordant exudates (an exudate by either the protein or LDH criterion but a transudate by the other criteria).

STUDY TABLE: Common Causes of Transudative and Exudative Pleural Effusions	
Transudative Pleural Effusions	**Exudative Pleural Effusions**
Increased hydrostatic pressure (HF, constrictive pericarditis, superior vena cava obstruction)	Infection
Decreased oncotic pressure (hypoalbuminemia, nephrotic syndrome, cirrhosis, malnutrition)	Neoplasm
	Collagen vascular diseases
	Pulmonary infarction
	Hemothorax

Key points:

- Almost all exudates have a total nucleated cell count >1000/microliter.
- Cell counts >10,000/microliter with a predominance of neutrophils occur most commonly in uncomplicated parapneumonic effusions, acute pancreatitis, and subdiaphragmatic abscesses.
- Cell counts >50,000/microliter suggest a complicated parapneumonic effusion or empyema.
- Chronic exudates with a mononuclear cell predominance and cell counts <5000/microliter are typical of tuberculosis and malignancy.
- Serum triglyceride concentration >110 mg/dL suggests a chylothorax.
- Pleural fluid hematocrit >50% of the peripheral hematocrit is diagnostic of a hemothorax.
- Elevated pleural fluid amylase suggests acute pancreatitis, pancreaticopleural fistula, or esophageal perforation.

The only effusions that usually require chest tube insertion are complicated parapneumonic effusions, empyema, and malignancy. Insert a chest tube if the pleural fluid pH is <7.20 or has other characteristics of an empyema, such as glucose <50% of plasma glucose, LDH >1000 units/L, or a positive Gram stain or culture. Drainage of malignant effusions can

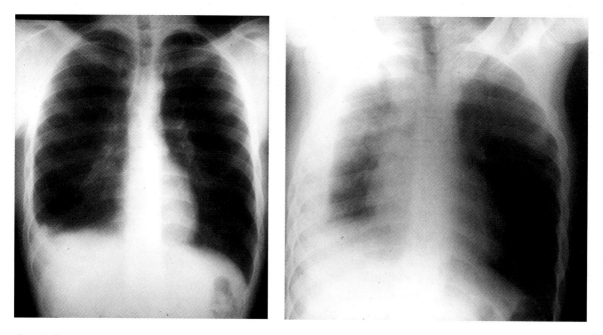

Pleural Effusion: Chest radiograph showing a right-sided pleural effusion (*left panel*) that layers out along the right thorax in the right lateral decubitus view (*right panel*).

be accomplished either by placing an indwelling catheter as an outpatient or performing pleurodesis (typically an inpatient procedure) using a chemical agent.

◆ DON'T BE TRICKED

- Always obtain thoracentesis for effusions associated with pneumonia.
- Pleural effusions associated with nephrotic syndrome are common, but PE should be excluded in such patients because PE and renal vein thrombosis often occur in patients with nephrotic syndrome.
- Consider lymphangiomyomatosis when chylothorax is diagnosed in a premenopausal woman.

❖ Test Yourself

A 65-year-old woman has a 2-week history of shortness of breath. A chest radiograph shows a large right-sided pleural effusion. Serum LDH is 190 units/L and total protein is 6.0 g/dL. Thoracentesis is performed; pleural fluid protein is 2.8 g/dL and pleural fluid LDH is 110 units/L.

ANSWER: The diagnosis is a transudative pleural effusion.

Pneumothorax

Diagnosis

Characteristic symptoms are chest pain and dyspnea. Spontaneous pneumothorax is considered to be primary when the lung is overtly normal. Tall men who smoke are at risk. Other risk factors include cocaine use and Marfan syndrome. Subpleural blebs and bullae are commonly detected on CT scan and predispose to primary pneumothorax.

Secondary pneumothorax is associated with lung disease, most commonly COPD. Consider lymphangioleiomyomatosis in premenopausal women presenting with a spontaneous pneumothorax and lung disease, *Pneumocystis jiroveci* pneumonia in patients with HIV disease, or interstitial lung disease (Langerhans cell histiocytosis). Tension pneumothorax is suggested by falling blood pressure and oxygen saturation, tracheal deviation, and no breath sounds in one hemithorax.

Obtain an upright chest radiograph in patients with dyspnea, pleurisy, or both, even if the physical examination is normal.

◆ DON'T BE TRICKED

- Do not wait for chest radiograph results before treating suspected tension pneumothorax with needle decompression.

Therapy

Treatment depends on the type of pneumothorax:

- observation and oxygen in asymptomatic patients with a small pneumothorax (rim of air <2 cm on chest radiograph)
- release of pressure with a large needle for tension pneumothorax
- simple aspiration for symptomatic primary spontaneous pneumothorax of any size
- chest tube if the secondary pneumothorax measures >3 cm
- pleurodesis for a first secondary spontaneous pneumothorax
- ipsilateral thoracoscopy for a second primary spontaneous pneumothorax

◆ DON'T BE TRICKED

- Patients with a primary spontaneous pneumothorax that resolves with aspiration may be discharged, but hospitalize patients with a secondary spontaneous pneumothorax.

Insomnia

Diagnosis

Insomnia includes problems of sleep initiation, sleep maintenance, early morning waking, or nonrestorative and poor-quality sleep. Acute insomnia is ≤1 week in length, short-term insomnia lasts from 1 week to 3 months, and chronic insomnia lasts >3 months. Insomnia may be associated with shift work and an irregular sleep schedule, obesity, "crowded pharynx," and restless legs syndrome. Obtain polysomnography for suspected sleep apnea or periodic limb movement disorder.

STUDY TABLE: Differential Diagnosis of Insomnia and Daytime Sleepiness	
Condition	**Characteristics**
Restless legs syndrome	An uncomfortable or restless feeling in the legs most prominent at night and at rest, associated with an urge to move and alleviated by movement
	Look for iron deficiency
	Associated with periodic limb movement disorder in most patients
Periodic limb movement disorder	Repetitive stereotypic leg movement during sleep and during quiet wakefulness
Central sleep apnea syndrome	Repetitive pauses in breathing during sleep without upper airway occlusion
	Associated history of HF or CNS disease
Obstructive sleep apnea syndrome	Upper airway obstruction during inspiration in sleep
	History of snoring, witnessed pauses in respiration, large shirt collar size, and daytime sleepiness
Shift-work sleep disorder	History of insomnia associated with shift work
	Permanent night shifts
Sleep deprivation	Six hours or less of sleep is associated with daytime sleepiness and performance deficits
Narcolepsy	Daytime sleepiness with cataplexy, hypnagogic hallucinations, and sleep paralysis, frequently coexisting with other sleep disorders

Therapy

Advise patients about good sleep hygiene practices, including regular bedtimes and waking times; spending no more than 8 hours in bed; and avoiding caffeine, nicotine, and alcohol. A γ-aminobutyric acid agonist (estazolam, flurazepam, quazepam, temazepam, triazolam, zolpidem) is used to treat acute or short-term insomnia. Restless legs syndrome is treated with dopaminergic agents (pramipexole or ropinirole) or with levodopa-carbidopa. Prescribe supplemental iron for patients with restless legs syndrome when the serum ferritin level is <50 ng/mL. Treatments for narcolepsy include modafinil, methylphenidate, or an amphetamine. These stimulants may cause serious cardiovascular and psychiatric side effects.

◆ DON'T BE TRICKED

- Do not select antidepressants for insomnia unless the patient is depressed.
- Do not select an antihistamine for insomnia.

Obstructive Sleep Apnea

Diagnosis

An obstructive apnea is defined as the absence of airflow for at least 10 seconds despite persistence of respiratory effort. The severity of obstructive sleep apnea (OSA) can be classified based on the apnea-hypopnea index (AHI, number of apneas plus hypopneas per hour of sleep) as:

- mild (AHI 5-15)
- moderate (AHI 16-30)
- severe (AHI >30)

Characteristic findings of OSA include snoring, apnea, excessive daytime sleepiness, and obesity (determined by either BMI or neck circumference >17 in) and an enlarged and elongated soft palate (crowded pharynx).

Patients with untreated OSA have a greater likelihood of developing CAD, acute MI during sleep, systemic and pulmonary arterial hypertension, HF, recurrent atrial fibrillation, stroke, insulin resistance, mood disorders, and parasomnias.

Diagnose OSA in patients with an AHI of >5/h during a sleep study.

◆ DON'T BE TRICKED

- Do not confuse obesity-hypoventilation syndrome with sleep apnea. Obesity-hypoventilation syndrome is usually associated with COPD and always with elevated arterial P_{CO_2} levels when awake.
- Obesity-hypoventilation syndrome may coexist with sleep apnea.

Therapy

Educate patients about lifestyle changes, including losing weight, avoiding alcohol and sedatives before bedtime, and sleeping in the lateral position. CPAP is the treatment of choice. CPAP functions as a pneumatic splint to prevent narrowing of the nasopharyngeal airway. CPAP therapy has been shown to improve quality of life, cognitive function, and symptoms of daytime sleepiness.

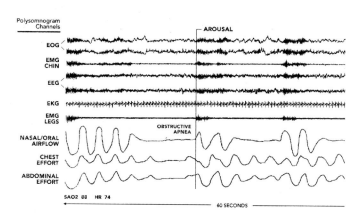

Obstructive Sleep Apnea: This polysomnogram shows obstructive apneas, indicated by the absence of flow and ongoing abdominal and rib cage effort that is terminated with evidence of an electroencephalographic arousal.

Bilevel positive airway pressure therapy, in which inspiratory and expiratory pressures can be adjusted separately, may be useful in patients who do not tolerate CPAP, have concurrent central sleep apneas, or have persistent oxygen desaturation because of hypoventilation despite CPAP therapy. CPAP may help patients with daytime hypercapnia due to related obesity-hypoventilation syndrome. Therapy may be required for up to 4 weeks before arterial blood gases improve.

◆ DON'T BE TRICKED

- Supplemental oxygen is not recommended as a primary therapy for OSA.

Solitary Pulmonary Nodule

Diagnosis

A solitary pulmonary nodule is a lesion of the lung parenchyma measuring ≤3 cm in diameter that is not associated with other lesions or lymphadenopathy and is not invading other structures. Approximately 35% of solitary nodules are bronchogenic carcinomas. The probability of malignancy varies from 10% to 70% among various patient populations but can be crudely estimated from the smoking history, age of the patient, size of the lesion, and whether or not a history of malignancy is noted.

Malignant nodules tend to have:

- spiculated margins
- little or no calcification
- intermediate doubling times (between 30 and 500 days)

STUDY TABLE: Diagnostic Tests for a Pulmonary Nodule	
Test	**Considerations**
Comparison with previous chest radiograph	Stability over time helps rule out malignancy
Contrast-enhanced CT	Most useful imaging method
Fiberoptic bronchoscopy	Provides sufficient information in only 30% of lesions
Percutaneous transthoracic needle aspiration biopsy	Has a higher yield of malignant lesions but is not always diagnostic
PET scan	Positive in >90% of malignant solitary nodules >1 cm in diameter

◆ DON'T BE TRICKED

- PET scans may be falsely negative in alveolar cell carcinoma or lesions <1 cm in diameter and falsely positive in various inflammatory lesions.
- A nonspecific negative result from fiberoptic bronchoscopy or transthoracic needle aspiration biopsy does not reliably exclude the presence of a malignant growth.

Therapy

STUDY TABLE: Recommendations for Pulmonary Nodule Evaluation Based on Risk		
Nodule Size (mm)	**Low-Risk Initial Follow-up[a]**	**High-Risk Initial Follow-up[b]**
<4	None	12 months
4-6	12 months	6-12 months
6-8	6-12 months	3-6 months
>8	Consider contrast CT , PET scan, or biopsy around 3, 9, and 24 months	Consider contrast CT , PET scan, or biopsy around 3, 9, and 24 months

[a]Never-smoker or no other risk factors
[b]Current or former smoker, asbestos or radon exposure, or family history of lung cancer
Modified with permission from MacMahon H, Austin JH, Gamsu G, et al; Fleischner Society. Guidelines for management of small pulmonary nodules detected on CT scans: a statement from the Fleischner Society. Radiology. 2005;237(2):395-400. [PMID: 16244247] Copyright 2005, Radiological Society of North America.

Hemoptysis

Diagnosis

Bronchitis, bronchogenic carcinoma, and bronchiectasis are the most common causes of hemoptysis, and diagnosis can be further narrowed by considering patient risk factors.

Common causes of hemoptysis:

- acute bronchitis (acute cough syndrome in an otherwise healthy patient with no other risk factors)
- lung cancer (older adult, smoking history)
- bronchiectasis (chronic history of cough, voluminous sputum production, and "tram lines" on chest radiograph)
- aspergilloma (fungus ball in lung cavity as shown in the Infectious Disease chapter; patient may have disease that causes pulmonary cavities or have allergic bronchopulmonary aspergillosis)
- tuberculosis (fever, night sweats, weight loss, prison stay, HIV, immigrant status)
- PE and infarction (pleural-based triangular opacity with a rounded apex [Hampton hump] or area of hyperlucency [Westermark sign] on chest radiograph)
- pulmonary-renal hemorrhage syndrome (hematuria and kidney disease)
- mitral stenosis (opening snap and rumbling diastolic murmur)
- HIV (bacterial infections, tuberculosis, and Kaposi sarcoma)

◆ DON'T BE TRICKED
- Confirm a patient has hemoptysis rather than epistaxis or GI bleeding; then check the platelet count and coagulation parameters.

STUDY TABLE: Diagnostic Tests for Hemoptysis	
Test	**Considerations**
Chest x-ray	Crucial initial study, but normal findings do not exclude lung cancer
Fiberoptic bronchoscopy	For patients at high risk for lung cancer, even if chest radiograph is normal
Chest CT	Alternative test when fiberoptic bronchoscopy is contraindicated or when bleeding persists despite normal bronchoscopic findings

Therapy

The cause of death from massive hemoptysis is almost always asphyxiation from airway obstruction. Management includes airway protection. If the bleeding site can be localized to one lung, position the patient with the bleeding lung dependent. Intubation and mechanical ventilation are required when adequate gas exchange is threatened. Angiography can localize and treat bronchial artery lesions.

Pulmonary Arteriovenous Malformation

Diagnosis

Pulmonary AVMs consist of abnormal communications between pulmonary arteries and veins. They are included in the differential diagnosis of hypoxemia, pulmonary nodules, and hemoptysis. The following suggest a pulmonary AVM:

- hemoptysis
- mucocutaneous telangiectasias
- evidence of right to left pulmonary shunts (hypoxemia, polycythemia, clubbing, cyanosis, stroke, brain abscess)

Chest CT is the initial diagnostic test.

Therapy

Symptomatic or large pulmonary AVMs (>2 cm) are treated with either embolo-therapy or surgery.

❖ Test Yourself

A 46-year-old man is evaluated for a transient ischemic attack. Telangiectasias are present on the lips. The lungs are clear, and cardiovascular and neurovascular examinations are normal. Laboratory evaluation reveals polycythemia and an arterial Po_2 of 68 mm Hg. Chest radiograph shows a 2-cm solitary pulmonary nodule.

ANSWER: The diagnosis is pulmonary AVM.

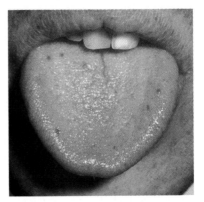

Telangiectasia: Telangiectasia on the tongue in a patient with hereditary hemorrhagic telangiectasia.

Sarcoidosis

Diagnosis

Sarcoidosis is a multisystem granulomatous inflammatory disease of unknown cause. The most common presenting manifestations involve the lymphatic and pulmonary systems, along with the eyes and skin. The presenting symptoms tend to be more widely distributed and more severe in black patients, whereas an abnormal chest radiograph in an otherwise asymptomatic patient is more common in whites.

Characteristic findings include:

- fever, weight loss, and night sweats
- dry cough and dyspnea
- eye pain or burning and photosensitivity
- erythema nodosum (EN)
- violaceous or erythematous indurated papules, plaques, or nodules of the central face (lupus pernio); often associated with pulmonary disease
- a variety of papular, nodular, and plaque-like cutaneous lesions
- lymphadenopathy and hepatosplenomegaly
- asymmetric joint swelling
- Löfgren syndrome (fever, bilateral hilar lymphadenopathy, EN, and often ankle arthritis)
- uveoparotid fever (Heerfordt syndrome, featuring anterior uveitis, parotid gland enlargement, facial palsy, and fever)
- hypercalcemia (extrarenal production of calcitriol by granuloma cells)
- bilateral hilar lymphadenopathy, often with other enlarged mediastinal lymph nodes
- lymphadenopathy and lung parenchymal disease on chest radiograph

A definite diagnosis requires a compatible clinical picture, pathologic demonstration of noncaseating granulomas, and the exclusion of alternative explanations for the abnormalities (known causes of granulomatous inflammation such as infection). A likely diagnosis can be made without histologic studies in a patient with clinical manifestations and typical chest radiography features.

Diagnostic studies include:

- fiberoptic bronchoscopy with transbronchial biopsy and bronchoalveolar lavage for interstitial lung disease
- serum parathyroid hormone (low) level for patients with hypercalcemia/hypercalciuria
- MRI for neurosarcoidosis
- biopsy of suspicious skin lesions
- slit-lamp examination for all patients

- electrocardiography to rule out heart block or other cardiac abnormalities in all patients
- pulmonary function testing (sarcoidosis may cause obstruction, restriction, or both)

◆ DON'T BE TRICKED

- **Always rule out tuberculosis and fungal infections by ordering appropriate stains on tissue biopsy.**
- **Exposure to beryllium (often found in workers in light bulb or semiconductor factories) may cause a sarcoidosis-like clinical syndrome.**
- **Don't select a serum angiotensin-converting enzyme level. It won't confirm the diagnosis or help in managing sarcoidosis.**

Therapy

Topical corticosteroids are prescribed for skin lesions or anterior uveitis, and inhaled corticosteroids are used for nasal polyps or cough. Oral corticosteroids are indicated for progressive or symptomatic pulmonary sarcoidosis, hypercalcemia, or cardiac, ophthalmologic, or neurologic sarcoid. Patients with corticosteroid-refractory disease are treated with immunosuppressive, cytotoxic, and antimalarial agents. Löfgren syndrome has a very high rate (80%) of spontaneous remission and resolution. Lung transplantation is recommended for patients with severe pulmonary compromise despite appropriate medical therapy.

◆ DON'T BE TRICKED

- **Do not treat asymptomatic sarcoidosis.**

❖ Test Yourself

A 66-year-old man is hospitalized because of azotemia and hypercalcemia. Laboratory studies show a normal serum parathyroid hormone level and an elevated 1,25-dihydroxyvitamin D_3 level. A chest radiograph shows an interstitial infiltrate and an enlarged left paratracheal lymph node.

ANSWER: The probable diagnosis is sarcoidosis. Choose transbronchial lung biopsy.

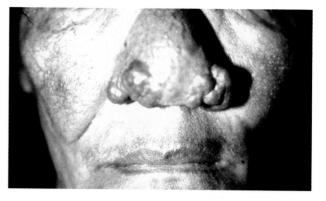

Waxy Papular Lesions: Waxy papular lesions on the nose consistent with sarcoidosis. Image courtesy of Dr. David Crosby.

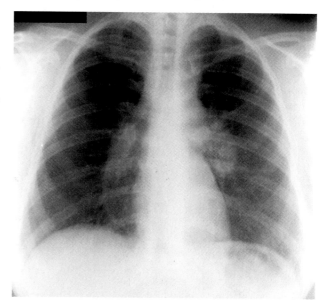

Sarcoidosis: The x-ray shows bilateral hilar lymphadenopathy characteristic of sarcoidosis. Sarcoidosis can be associated with interstitial lung disease.

Idiopathic Pulmonary Fibrosis

Diagnosis

Idiopathic pulmonary fibrosis, the most common of the idiopathic interstitial pneumonias, is a fibrosing interstitial pneumonia. Characteristic findings are the gradual onset of a nonproductive cough and dyspnea over approximately 3 months. Physical examination findings include:

- normal temperature
- bibasilar crackles ("dry," end-inspiratory, and "Velcro-like" in quality)
- late-phase cor pulmonale
- clubbing (25% of patients)

Chest radiograph shows peripheral reticular opacities and honeycomb changes at the lung bases. HRCT scan reveals sub-pleural cystic changes and traction bronchiectasis. A restrictive pattern is found on pulmonary function tests.

Serum ANA, rheumatoid factor, c-ANCA, and p-ANCA levels are negative or low. Video-assisted thoracoscopic lung biopsy is indicated for patients with atypical presentations.

Diagnosis is based on clinical and radiographic findings, absence of exposure to substances or drugs that can cause interstitial lung disease, and negative evaluation for rheumatologic disease.

STUDY TABLE: Mimics of Idiopathic Pulmonary Fibrosis	
Disease	**Characteristics**
Collagen vascular diseases (systemic lupus erythematosus, systemic sclerosis, rheumatoid arthritis)	Joint pain, musculoskeletal pain, fever, photosensitivity, Raynaud phenomenon, pleuritis, dry eyes, dry mouth, pulmonary hypertension, and positive serologic studies
Granulomatosis with polyangiitis (Wegener granulomatosis), Goodpasture syndrome	Hemoptysis and kidney insufficiency
	Positive ANCA or anti-GBM antibodies
Hypersensitivity pneumonitis:	Exposure to known antigen with positive precipitating antibodies
Farmer lung (thermophilic *Actinomyces* in hay/grain)	HRCT shows centrilobular nodules, middle- and upper-lung predominance, and absence of honeycombing
Bird fancier lung	Severe cases respond to corticosteroids
Hot tub lung (nontuberculosis mycobacteria)	Immunocompetent patients: avoidance rather than antibiotics is treatment of choice
Drug-induced diffuse parenchymal lung disease	Onset related to the use of a drug, with a clinical response following stopping the drug or administering corticosteroids
	Examples: busulfan, bleomycin, methotrexate, nitrofurantoin, sulfasalazine, phenytoin, procainamide, gold salts, and amiodarone
Sarcoidosis	Bilateral hilar lymphadenopathy with or without peripheral lymphadenopathy, liver involvement, uveitis, skin nodules or plaques, or arthritis
	Laboratory tests may show hypercalcemia
Chronic eosinophilic pneumonia	Asthma, peripheral blood eosinophilia, and chest radiograph showing "photographic-negative" pulmonary edema (peripheral pulmonary edema)
	Treatment with oral corticosteroids
Langerhans cell histiocytosis (eosinophilic granuloma, histiocytosis X)	Young male cigarette smokers with recurrent pneumothorax
	HRCT shows stellate nodules and thin-walled, upper-zone pulmonary cystic lesions
	Treatment is smoking cessation
Idiopathic BOOP or COP	Preceding flu-like illness; patients initially treated for "pneumonia"
	Waxing and waning peripheral pulmonary infiltrates
	Chest radiograph shows patchy air-space consolidation in the periphery of the lung and often in the lower lung zones
	May respond to corticosteroids
Desquamative interstitial pneumonia or respiratory bronchiolitis interstitial lung disease	Affects smokers in their 40s or 50s
	HRCT shows diffuse "ground-glass" appearance with little fibrosis
	Treatment is smoking cessation
Acute interstitial pneumonia	Fulminant respiratory failure and early death
	May present similarly to ARDS
	Treatment is supportive; role of corticosteroids is unclear
Pulmonary alveolar proteinosis	Slower onset than ARDS (over 2-12 months) with progressive course
	Characteristic "crazy paving" pattern on HRCT
	An opaque or milky fluid on bronchoalveolar lavage
	Treatment is bronchoalveolar lavage
Occupational pneumoconiosis	History of exposure (coal dust, particulates, sandblasting)

Therapy

No medical therapy can alter the natural history of idiopathic pulmonary fibrosis. Lung transplantation may improve survival and quality of life. Immunosuppressive therapies (corticosteroids and cytotoxic agents) are the conventional approach to medical treatment, but only a few patients respond and therapy does not improve survival. Oxygen therapy is indicated for patients with hypoxemia.

Asbestos-Associated Lung Diseases

Diagnosis

The most important risk factor for development of asbestos-related lung disease is the cumulative exposure to the asbestos fiber. Occupations with the greatest exposure include those in the construction industry, the automotive servicing industry, and the shipbuilding and repair industry. The latent period for development of asbestosis and mesothelioma is 10 to 15 years. Cigarette smoking increases the risk of mesothelioma.

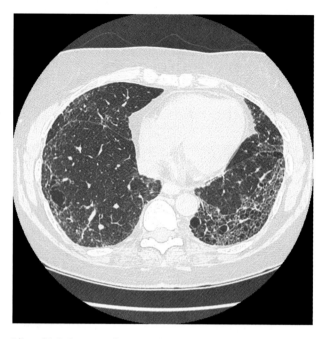

Idiopathic Pulmonary Fibrosis: High-resolution, thin-section chest CT scan showing extensive parenchymal involvement with fibrotic and honeycomb changes compatible with idiopathic pulmonary fibrosis.

STUDY TABLE: Asbestos-Related Lung Syndromes	
Condition	**Characteristics**
Pleural plaques (localized, often partially calcified)	Often incidental finding; usually bilateral; most common manifestation of asbestos exposure. Monitor patients for development of intrathoracic disease.
Diffuse pleural thickening	Extensive pleural thickening extends into the visceral pleura and obliterates the costophrenic angles. May cause hypercapnic respiratory failure secondary to impairment of ventilation.
Rounded atelectasis	Presents as single or multiple masses due to infolding of thickened visceral pleura with collapse of the adjacent peripheral lung. The classic radiographic finding is a "comet tail" on chest CT scan extending from the hilum toward the base of the lung and then sweeping into the inferior pole of the lesion. Can cause ventilatory failure.
Benign pleural effusion	Exudative hemorrhagic effusion. May be painful.
Mesothelioma	Suggested by weight loss, fever, cough, dyspnea, chest pain, unilateral pleural abnormalities, and pleural effusion. Tissue diagnosis required.
Asbestosis	Manifests with bilateral interstitial fibrosis of the lung parenchyma, bibasilar inspiratory crackles, clubbing, restrictive physiology, and low D_{LCO}.
Lung cancer	Most cases occur in patients with asbestosis, but a diagnosis of asbestosis is not necessary to attribute lung cancer to asbestos exposure.

Therapy

Surgery is indicated for patients with localized mesothelioma, and radiation therapy is used to prevent recurrences. Most patients with mesothelioma are treated symptomatically by controlling pleural effusions with thoracentesis. Newly diagnosed patients who are not candidates for surgery are treated with combination chemotherapy.

Mountain Sickness

Diagnosis

Mountain sickness most often develops with travel above 1900 m (6300 ft). Characteristic findings are headache, insomnia, anorexia, nausea, vomiting, ataxia, and disturbed consciousness. Patients may report previous episodes of acute mountain sickness. Related syndromes are HAPE and HACE.

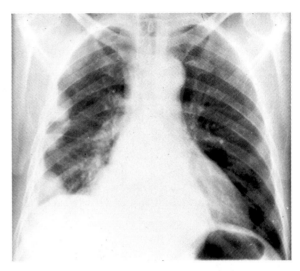

Mesothelioma: Frontal chest x-ray showing multiple pleural-based nodular infiltrates at the right chest wall and pleural thickening consistent with mesothelioma.

Therapy

Use acetazolamide to prevent acute mountain sickness. Management of both HAPE and HACE is immediate evacuation to a lower altitude and administration of supplemental oxygen and/or hyperbaric therapy. Prescribe furosemide and nifedipine or sildenafil for HAPE and dexamethasone for HACE.

Chronic Hypercapnic Respiratory Failure

Diagnosis

Chronic hypercapnic respiratory failure occurs most often in patients with COPD, neuromuscular disease (myasthenia gravis, amyotrophic lateral sclerosis, multiple sclerosis), chest wall skeletal disorders (kyphoscoliosis), and obesity. Obtain measurement of maximal inspiratory and expiratory pressures to diagnose neuromuscular disease. If results are normal or near normal, disorders of ventilatory control are more likely. Patients with respiratory muscle weakness, obesity-hypoventilation syndrome, and disorders of ventilatory control first hypoventilate during rapid eye movement sleep. Schedule polysomnography if nocturnal hypoventilation is suspected (daytime sleepiness, nocturnal awakenings, morning headaches).

Therapy

Most patients (except patients with COPD) have improved outcomes after noninvasive nocturnal ventilation.

❖ **Test Yourself**

A 36-year-old man with myotonic dystrophy awakens at night gasping for air and experiences increasing fatigue. Cardiopulmonary examination is normal. Neurologic examination shows 4+/5 strength in all muscle groups.

ANSWER: The probable diagnosis is nocturnal hypercapnic respiratory failure. Select polysomnography.

Acute Respiratory Distress Syndrome

Diagnosis

ARDS is a syndrome of hypoxemic respiratory failure due to alveolar damage and the leakage of fluid across the alveolar-capillary barrier (noncardiogenic pulmonary edema).

Diagnose ARDS when:

- onset is acute; 48 to 72 hours
- arterial blood Po_2/Fio_2 ratio is ≤300 mm Hg
- bilateral alveolar infiltrates are present on chest radiograph
- no evidence of left-sided HF is present
- a risk factor for ARDS is present

Mild ARDS is defined as arterial Po_2/Fio_2 of 200 to ≤300 mm Hg; moderate ARDS as 100 to ≤200 mm Hg; and severe ARDS as ≤100 mm Hg.

Precipitating causes of ARDS include pulmonary infection, hemorrhagic shock, pancreatitis, trauma, transfusions, and sepsis. Hemodynamic measurements by pulmonary artery catheterization are sometimes necessary to exclude cardiogenic pulmonary edema when clinical examination and bedside echocardiography are indeterminant. A pulmonary capillary wedge pressure ≥18 mm Hg favors cardiogenic pulmonary edema.

STUDY TABLE: Differential Diagnoses of Abnormal Pulmonary Artery Catheterization Pressure Readings	
Elevated RV Systolic Pressure (>25 mm Hg)	**Elevated RV Diastolic Pressure (>12 mm Hg)**
Pulmonary hypertension	RV failure
Pulmonic stenosis	RV ischemia and infarction
PE	Restrictive cardiomyopathy
	Cardiac tamponade
Elevated Pulmonary Arterial Pressures (SBP >25 mm Hg, DBP >15 mm Hg)	**Normal Mean Pulmonary Artery Wedge Pressure (9 mm Hg)**
Left HF	Estimates LV end-diastolic pressure in the absence of obstruction to flow between the left atrium and left ventricle
Primary lung disease	
Mitral valve disease	
PE	
Hypoxemia	
Pulmonary arterial hypertension	
Left to right shunts	

STUDY TABLE: Mimics of ARDS	
Disease	**Characteristics**
Cardiogenic pulmonary edema	History of cardiac disease, enlarged heart, S3, chest radiograph showing an enlarged cardiac silhouette, pleural effusions, and Kerley B lines
	Rapid improvement with diuresis or afterload reduction
Diffuse alveolar hemorrhage	Kidney disease or other evidence of vasculitis present
	Associated with stem cell transplantation
	Hemosiderin-laden macrophages in bronchoalveolar lavage fluid
Acute eosinophilic pneumonia	Cough, fever, pleuritic chest pain, and myalgia; may be precipitated by initiation of smoking
	>15% eosinophils in bronchoalveolar lavage fluid
Acute PE	Occurs acutely, occasionally accompanied by severe hypoxemia that may be resistant to oxygen and by hypotension requiring vasopressors, mimicking ARDS with sepsis
	Patients typically have risk factors for acute PE and may not have common precipitating causes of ARDS
Hypersensitivity pneumonitis	Typically slower onset than ARDS (over weeks) with progressive course; however, may present in an advanced stage, mimicking ARDS
	Positive exposure history (farmers, bird fanciers, hot tub exposure)
BOOP or COP	May be precipitated by viral syndrome
	Slower onset than ARDS (>2 weeks) with progressive course; however, may present in an advanced stage, mimicking ARDS
Acute interstitial pneumonia	May be impossible to distinguish
	Absence of typical inciting factors for ARDS
	May respond to corticosteroid administration

Therapy

Optimal mechanical ventilation includes lung-protective ventilation using volume-controlled ventilation with a tidal volume of 6 mL/kg of ideal body weight, plateau (end-inspiratory) pressure <30 cm H_2O (even if this results in "permissive" hypercapnia and acidosis), and the least amount of PEEP needed to achieve 88% oxyhemoglobin saturation on an F_{IO_2} of 60%. Maintain the CVP <4 mm Hg or the pulmonary artery occlusion pressure <8 mm Hg.

◆ DON'T BE TRICKED

- Using higher levels of PEEP does not offer an advantage compared with lower PEEP levels in improving outcomes.
- Corticosteroids are not indicated for the acute treatment of ARDS.

❖ Test Yourself

A 55-year-old woman with acute pancreatitis has increasingly severe shortness of breath for 12 hours. She has no history of cardiac disease. Pulse rate is 116/min, respiration rate is 40/min, and arterial O_2 saturation is 86% (on supplemental oxygen). Diffuse bilateral crackles are heard. Chest radiograph shows diffuse airspace disease. She is intubated and mechanically ventilated. On an F_{IO_2} of 1.0, her arterial P_{O_2} is 150 mm Hg.

ANSWER: The diagnosis is ARDS. Choose a tidal volume of 6 mL/kg of ideal body weight.

Preoperative Pulmonary Assessment

Common Considerations

Postoperative pulmonary complications are as common as cardiac complications and equally important clinically in terms of mortality, morbidity, and length of hospital stay.

Variables associated with respiratory failure:

- type of surgery: abdominal aortic aneurysm repair, thoracic surgery, upper abdominal surgery, vascular surgery, neck surgery, neurosurgery

- emergency surgery
- advanced age
- functional status: totally dependent, partially dependent, or independent
- history of COPD
- BUN >30 mg/dL

Therapy

Patients with COPD should continue β-agonists, anticholinergic agents, and corticosteroids until immediately before surgery and resume as soon as possible postoperatively, especially if they are at high risk for postoperative pulmonary complications. Selective nasogastric decompression is indicated after abdominal surgery in patients with nausea, vomiting, or abdominal distention, and incentive spirometry and deep-breathing exercises prevent postoperative pulmonary complications. At least 2 months of preoperative smoking cessation reduces postoperative pulmonary risk.

◆ DON'T BE TRICKED

- **Preoperative spirometry should not be used routinely to predict risk for postoperative pulmonary complications.**

Noninvasive Positive-Pressure Ventilation

Indications

Noninvasive positive-pressure ventilation (NPPV) is the use of positive-pressure ventilation without the need for an invasive airway. NPPV may be used as the ventilatory mode of first choice in four conditions:

- COPD exacerbations (not stable COPD)
- cardiogenic pulmonary edema
- acute respiratory failure in immunosuppressed patients
- prevention of recurrent respiratory failure in recently extubated patients

The most common contraindications to NPPV include:

- respiratory arrest
- arterial blood pH <7.10
- medical instability
- inability to protect airway and/or excessive secretions
- uncooperative or agitated patient

Improvements in blood gas values and clinical condition should occur within 2 hours of starting NPPV. If not, intubation should be considered to avoid undue delay and prevent respiratory arrest.

Mechanical Ventilation

Indications

Patients may require mechanical ventilatory support for impaired oxygenation (low arterial P_{O_2}) or impaired alveolar ventilation (increased arterial P_{CO_2}). In general, if a patient cannot maintain an arterial P_{O_2} >60 mm Hg or an O_2 saturation >90% despite supplemental oxygen of 60% or higher, initiating mechanical ventilation is usually appropriate, regardless of the arterial P_{CO_2}.

Management

In volume-targeted ventilation, set tidal volume first.

- Tidal volumes are based on the patient's weight.
- The recommended range is 5 to 10 mL/kg of ideal body weight.
- Tidal volumes that are too high can result in barotrauma, respiratory alkalosis, and decreased cardiac output.
- Tidal volumes that are too low can result in atelectasis, hypoxemia, and hypoventilation.

Set respiratory rate:

- The respiratory rate is usually started at 8 to 14/min if the patient is otherwise clinically stable.
- A respiratory rate that is too high can result in respiratory alkalosis and air trapping (auto-PEEP).
- A respiratory rate that is too low can result in hypoventilation, acidosis, hypoxemia, and patient discomfort.

Set oxygen flow to maintain arterial P_{O_2} >60 mm Hg.

Be alert for auto-PEEP:

- In the presence of increased airway resistance, a high demand for ventilation, or a short expiratory time, air flow may still occur at end exhalation, resulting in positive pressure in the alveoli at end exhalation.
- Suspect auto-PEEP if the flow tracing on the ventilator shows continuous expiratory flow until the start of inspiratory flow.

Common causes of auto-PEEP include COPD or acute asthma, an endotracheal tube that is too narrow, long ventilator tubing, ARDS (increased flow resistance), and a high minute ventilation (>12-15 L/min). Characteristic findings are wheezing and marked expiratory prolongation, drop in blood pressure, and patient restlessness. Strategies to minimize auto-PEEP:

- Treat airway obstruction (e.g., bronchodilators in COPD or asthma).
- Decrease the respiratory rate or tidal volume.
- Increase the peak inspiratory flow rate.
- Prolong the expiratory phase.
- Allow permissive hypercapnia (best option for patients with ARDS).
- Sedate or paralyze the patient.

STUDY TABLE: Ventilator Management			
If you would like to...	**...the intermediate step is...**	**... make the ventilator do this by:**	**Notes:**
Improve respiratory acidosis	↓ Arterial P_{CO_2}	Increasing respiratory rate Increasing tidal volume: in volume control mode, directly choose the tidal volume; in pressure control modes, increase the inspiratory support pressure to increase tidal volume.	Watch for auto-PEEP at high respiratory rates, which can cause hypotension by reducing preload. Don't be tricked: If the patient has ARDS, respiratory acidosis should generally be tolerated rather than raising the tidal volume >6 mL/kg.
Improve respiratory alkalosis	↑ Arterial P_{CO_2}	Decreasing respiratory rate Decreasing tidal volume	If the patient is breathing faster than the set ventilator rate, this strategy won't work. Determine why respiratory alkalosis is present (sepsis, PE, liver disease, pain).
Improve tissue oxygenation	↑ O_2 saturation, arterial P_{O_2}	Increasing F_{IO_2} Increasing PEEP	Occasionally, increasing PEEP will lower cardiac output by reducing preload. This can worsen oxygen delivery to tissues. If no contraindications, attempt to increase preload with IV fluids.

Difficult ventilation or complications of mechanical ventilation due to changes in airway resistance may first be manifested by an increase in the peak inspiratory pressure alone, resulting from:

- bronchospasm
- secretions in airways, endotracheal tube, or ventilator tubing
- obstructing mucus plug
- agitation with dyssynchrony with the ventilator

Difficult ventilation resulting from a change in lung compliance will be manifested by an increase in both peak inspiratory pressure and plateau pressure, resulting from:

- right mainstem intubation
- pneumothorax
- worsening airspace disease (ARDS, pneumonia, pulmonary edema)

Prescribe H_2-receptor antagonists or PPIs to decrease the risk of stress gastric ulcers in patients receiving mechanical ventilation. Placing intubated patients in a semirecumbent position and selective decontamination of the oropharynx (using topical gentamicin, colistin, or vancomycin) reduces the risk of ventilator-associated pneumonia.

When a patient can maintain an arterial O_2 saturation >90% on FIO_2 ≤0.5, PEEP <5 cm H_2O, and pH >7.30, it is reasonable to consider extubation. Paired daily spontaneous awakening trials (withdrawal of sedatives) with daily spontaneous breathing trials result in a reduction in mechanical ventilation time, ICU and hospital length of stay, and 1-year mortality rates.

◆ DON'T BE TRICKED

- **Do not select synchronized intermittent mandatory ventilation as a weaning mode, because studies have demonstrated it actually takes longer to liberate patients from the ventilator.**

❖ Test Yourself

A 73-year-old woman who weighs 56 kg (123 lb) is admitted to the ICU with an exacerbation of severe COPD. Intubation and mechanical ventilation are required: FIO_2 of 0.4, tidal volume of 700 mL, and respiration rate of 16/min. Thirty minutes later, her blood pressure has dropped to 82/60 mm Hg. She is restless and has diffuse wheezing with prolonged expiration.

ANSWER: The diagnosis is auto-PEEP. Treat the airway obstruction or lower the tidal volume or respiration rate.

Venous Thromboembolic Disease

Prevention

Minor surgery in mobile patients and fully mobile medical patients does not require prophylaxis. Most general surgical patients require low-dose subcutaneous UFH (two or three times daily), LMWH, or fondaparinux. LMWH, fondaparinux, or warfarin may be required for patients who are undergoing hip or knee arthroplastic surgery, hip fracture surgery, or major trauma or spinal cord surgery. The benefit/risk ratio for medical patients is less clear. In hospitalized medical patients, including patients with acute stroke, heparin prophylaxis is associated with a significant reduction in PE and in increase in all bleeding events and no effect on mortality or symptomatic DVT. In most patients, the reduction in PE outweighs the harm of increased bleeding. The benefit is less clear in patients with acute stroke.

In patients with kidney impairment, LMWH dosing must be adjusted (GFR <30 mL/min/1.73 m²) and fondaparinux is contraindicated.

LMWH is also preferred for patients undergoing general surgery for malignancy and those with a coagulation factor inhibitor deficiency state. Moderate- to high-risk surgical patients who are at high risk for bleeding should receive mechanical prophylaxis with intermittent pneumatic compression.

Diagnosis

The probability of DVT is categorized as low, intermediate, or high based on a scoring index. Each of the following is scored as 1 point:

- active cancer
- paralysis or recent plaster cast
- recent immobilization or major surgery
- tenderness along the deep veins
- swelling of the entire leg
- >3-cm difference in calf circumference compared with the other leg
- pitting edema
- collateral superficial veins
- clinical suspicion of a likely alternative diagnosis earns −2 points

The pretest probability of DVT is considered high in patients with scores of ≥3, moderate in patients with scores of 1 to 2, and low in patients with scores of ≤0.

STUDY TABLE: Probability and Evaluation of PE		
Probability	**Criteria**	**Evaluation**
Low probability (unlikely)	1. Symptoms incompatible with PE or compatible symptoms (see following high-probability section) that can be explained by an alternative process, such as pneumonia, pneumothorax, or pulmonary edema 2. No radiograph or ECG abnormalities compatible with PE or presence of findings that can be explained by an alternative diagnosis 3. Absence of risk factors for venous thromboembolism	Order D-dimer. If negative, no further evaluation is indicated.
Intermediate probability (possible/probable)	1. Symptoms compatible with PE, but no associated radiographic or ECG findings 2. Constellation of findings not consistent with low or high clinical probability	Order either V/Q scan or CT study. Normal test excludes diagnosis. If test is indeterminate, obtain Doppler ultrasonography of legs; if negative, no further evaluation or therapy.
High probability (very likely)	1. Symptoms compatible with PE (sudden-onset dyspnea, pleuritic chest pain, tachypnea, or syncope), not otherwise explained 2. Radiographic or ECG findings compatible with PE, or widened alveolar-arterial oxygen gradient, not otherwise explained 3. Presence of risk factors for VTE	Begin therapy first. Perform imaging study next. If negative, perform Doppler ultrasonography of legs.

V/Q scans with matched or small defects or CT scans that do not show intraluminal filling defects are considered nondiagnostic. If the clinical suspicion for PE remains strong or the patient is unstable, nondiagnostic scans (including "negative" CT scans) should be followed with pulmonary angiography.

◆ DON'T BE TRICKED

- Normal pulse oximetry or arterial P_{O_2} does not rule out PE.
- A normal D-dimer does not exclude DVT or PE in a patient with high probability.

Therapy

Therapeutic options:

- UFH or LMWH
- warfarin overlapping 4 to 5 days with heparin (two INR measurements in therapeutic range 24 hours apart)
- warfarin dose adjustment to achieve an INR of 2 to 3
- recombinant hirudin (lepirudin) and the L-arginine derivative argatroban for HIT
- LMWH for secondary prevention of VTE in patients with active cancer
- IV- or catheter-directed thrombolysis for massive iliofemoral DVT associated with risk of limb loss
- IV thrombolytic therapy for shock or cardiac arrest
- IV thrombolytic therapy for confirmed PE associated with hypotension in patient with no contraindications
- embolectomy for massive PE and shock when anticoagulation or thrombolytic therapy is unsuccessful or contraindicated
- IVC filter for unstable PE in patients with strong contraindications to anticoagulation

Patients should wear graduated compression stockings following the diagnosis of DVT to reduce the risk for postthrombotic syndrome.

◆ DON'T BE TRICKED

- **Adjust LMWH dosing for very obese patients or patients with kidney disease.**
- **IV thrombolytic therapy for PE does not improve overall survival rate.**

Follow-up

STUDY TABLE: Duration of Anticoagulation Therapy after PE	
Number of Episodes	**Duration**
First episode with reversible risk factors (immobilization, surgery, trauma, or estrogen use)	As long as risk factor is present or 3-6 months
First episode of idiopathic thromboembolism	3 months minimum, with consideration of lifelong therapy
Recurrent episodes of idiopathic thromboembolism or antiphospholipid antibody syndrome	Indefinite

Some studies suggest that patients with unprovoked PE who have elevated serum D-dimer levels several weeks after anticoagulation therapy has been stopped (regardless of the duration of therapy) have a higher risk of recurrence and may benefit from prolonged anticoagulation.

❖ Test Yourself

A 53-year-old man has sudden-onset dyspnea that developed 1 hour ago, 47 hours after total hip arthroplasty. Temperature is 38.5 °C (101.3 °F), blood pressure is 156/92 mm Hg, pulse rate is 110/min, and respiration rate is 24/min. Cardiopulmonary examination is normal. Arterial O_2 saturation is 87% measured by pulse oximetry (breathing oxygen at 3 L/min by nasal cannula).

ANSWER: The diagnosis is high-probability PE. Begin treatment and order a V/Q scan or CTA.

Pulmonary Hypertension

Screening

Patients with systemic sclerosis (scleroderma) should be screened with TTE. Also screen the following patients: liver transplantation candidates with portal hypertension, first-degree relatives of patients with familial pulmonary arterial hypertension, and patients with congenital heart disease with systemic-to-pulmonary shunts.

Diagnosis

Pulmonary arterial hypertension is a general term for disorders that directly narrow the lumen of small pulmonary arteries and arterioles, raising pulmonary vascular resistance and pulmonary artery pressure. Characteristic findings include:

- unexplained dyspnea
- decreased exercise tolerance
- syncope and near-syncope
- chest pain
- lower extremity edema

Other findings may include an RV heave, right-sided S_3, increased P_2, and a murmur of tricuspid regurgitation. Ask about the use of fenfluramine, amphetamines, and cocaine and the presence of Raynaud phenomenon (suggesting SLE and systemic sclerosis). In some patients following an acute PE, thromboemboli within the pulmonary arteries become remodeled into large occlusive scars, causing chronic thromboembolic pulmonary hypertension (CTEPH).

Echocardiography is the initial study. A systolic pulmonary artery pressure >40 mm Hg is suggestive of pulmonary hypertension. Bubble contrast echocardiography or TEE is indicated to evaluate for intracardiac shunts (e.g., ASD). Right heart catheterization confirms the diagnosis and quantifies the degree of pulmonary hypertension. Additional recommended tests to rule out other causes of pulmonary hypertension include pulmonary function tests, polysomnography if clinically indicated, and serologic tests for HIV infection or connective tissue disease. If the diagnosis is confirmed, order a vasoreactivity test using acute vasodilating agents (inhaled nitric oxide, IV adenosine, or IV prostacyclin [epoprostenol]) with a right heart catheter in place.

◆ DON'T BE TRICKED

- Do not select an HRCT scan to diagnose CTEPH. A V/Q scan is superior.

Therapy

Always begin warfarin if no contraindications exist. Oxygen therapy is indicated for O_2 saturation ≤90%. Prescribe calcium channel blockers for patients who achieve a significant reduction in mean pulmonary artery pressure (10-40 mm Hg) associated with no change or an increase in cardiac output with a vasoreactivity test. Patients who do not respond to calcium channel blockers and are categorized as NYHA class III or IV are candidates for endothelin receptor antagonists, sildenafil, treprostinil, inhaled iloprost, or prostacyclin (epoprostenol). Heart-lung transplantation is indicated for NYHA class III or IV patients who do not respond to medical therapy.

◆ DON'T BE TRICKED

- Do not select calcium channel blockers if pulmonary artery pressure is not decreased with a vasoreactivity test.

Organophosphate Poisoning

Diagnosis

Characteristic findings include:

- pesticide exposure (often found in farmers)
- SLUDGE (Salivation, Lacrimation, Urination, Diarrhea, GI upset, Emesis)
- DUMBELS (Diarrhea, Urination, Miosis, Bronchospasm, Emesis, Lacrimation, Salivation)

Diagnostic studies include serum and erythrocyte acetylcholinesterase levels, pulse oximetry, and ECG or telemetry.

◆ **DON'T BE TRICKED**

- Do not wait for test results to start treating patients with severe poisoning.

Therapy

Patients with severe poisoning require external decontamination and ventilatory support. Begin atropine; titrate the dose to minimize dyspnea, airway resistance, and bronchial secretions. The main signs of atropine toxicity are fever and delirium. If these develop, discontinue atropine, at least temporarily. Add pralidoxime for patients with CNS toxicity and benzodiazepines (diazepam, lorazepam) for those with convulsions.

Follow-up

Monitor serial serum acetylcholinesterase levels to confirm a trend toward normal.

Carbon Monoxide Poisoning

Diagnosis

Characteristic findings are unexplained flulike symptoms, frontal headache, lightheadedness, difficulty concentrating, confusion, delirium, coma, dyspnea, nausea, and chest pain that are often associated with use of a grill or burning heat source indoors. Order arterial blood gas studies and serum carboxyhemoglobin measurement for all patients with neurologic changes, dyspnea, chest pain, or smoke exposure. A carboxyhemoglobin level >25% in any patient is diagnostic of severe acute carbon monoxide poisoning.

◆ **DON'T BE TRICKED**

- Pulse oximetry data are unreliable because the oximeter is unable to differentiate carboxyhemoglobin from oxyhemoglobin.

Therapy

Normobaric oxygen therapy is the treatment of choice. Hyperbaric oxygen therapy is indicated for patients with severe carbon monoxide poisoning (characterized by loss of consciousness and persistent neurologic deficits), pregnant patients, or patients with evidence of cardiac ischemia.

❖ **Test Yourself**

A 39-year-old man is found unconscious by his family. He had not been seen since late the previous evening. The outside temperature has been below freezing overnight. He is unresponsive and deeply cyanotic. The patient is intubated and ventilated with 100% oxygen. Although the O_2 saturation is 100%, he remains comatose.

ANSWER: The diagnosis is carbon monoxide poisoning. Measure the carboxyhemoglobin level.

Poisoning with Therapeutic Agents

Key Considerations

STUDY TABLE: Poisoning with Common Therapeutic Agents		
Toxin	**Clinical Syndrome**	**Antidote/Intervention**
Acetaminophen	Hepatotoxicity	*N*-acetylcysteine
Amphetamines	Sympathomimetic	Benzodiazepines
Benzodiazepines	Sedative/hypnotic	Flumazenil
β-Adrenergic blockers	Bradycardia, hypotension	Glucagon, calcium chloride, pacing
Calcium channel blockers	Bradycardia, hypotension	Calcium, glucagon, pacing
Digoxin	Dysrhythmias	Digoxin-immune Fab
Heparin	Bleeding diathesis	Protamine sulfate
Narcotics	Narcotic effects	Naloxone, nalmefene
Salicylates	Metabolic acidosis/respiratory alkalosis	Urine alkalinization, hemodialysis
Tricyclic antidepressants	Anticholinergic effects	Blood alkalinization, α-agonist

Hyperthermia

Diagnosis

Heat stroke is characterized by body temperatures >40.0 °C (104.0 °F). Such temperatures are life threatening. Signs of heat stroke include absence of sweating and warm, dry skin. At temperatures >40.5 °C (105.0 °F), findings include loss of consciousness, muscle rigidity, seizures, rhabdomyolysis with kidney failure, DIC, and ARDS.

Malignant hyperthermia is an inherited skeletal muscle disorder precipitated by exposure to halothane, isoflurane, enflurane, desflurane, sevoflurane, succinylcholine, or decamethonium.

The neuroleptic malignant syndrome is caused by an idiosyncratic reaction to neuroleptic tranquilizers (dopamine D_2-receptor antagonists) and some antipsychotic drugs (haloperidol, fluphenazine). It may occur in patients who have abruptly discontinued L-dopa. Patients with malignant hyperthermia and neuroleptic malignant syndrome have symptoms similar to those of heat stroke as well as muscle rigidity.

Like the neuroleptic malignant syndrome, the serotonin syndrome presents with high fever, muscle rigidity, and cognitive changes. Findings unique to the serotonin syndrome are shivering, hyperreflexia, myoclonus, and ataxia. The serotonin syndrome is caused by the use of SSRIs and often the addition of a second drug that increases serotonin release or further blocks its uptake or metabolism.

Therapy

Heat stroke treatment includes cooling blankets, cold IV fluids, and oxygen. Patients with severe heat stroke require cold gastric and peritoneal lavage. Benzodiazepines decrease excessive shivering during treatment. Treatment for malignant hyperthermia and neuroleptic malignant syndrome includes stopping the offending agent, general supportive measures as for heat stroke, and dantrolene.

❖ Test Yourself

A 45-year-old woman undergoes open cholecystectomy. At the conclusion of the operative procedure, her temperature has abruptly increased to 39.2 °C (102.5 °F).

ANSWER: Diagnose malignant hyperthermia due to anesthesia. Begin dantrolene.

Nutritional Support During Critical Illness

Diagnosis

Malnutrition impairs wound healing and immunologic function and increases the risk for infection and death. Patients in the ICU generally require 25 to 30 nonprotein kcal/kg/d and 1.0 to 1.5 protein kcal/kg/d. A serum prealbumin level <5 mg/dL indicates severe protein and calorie malnutrition.

Therapy

Oral or enteral feeding is preferred. If aspiration is a risk, place a feeding tube in the small intestine. Continuous enteral feeding decreases the risk of aspiration. Metoclopramide can be given to improve gastric motility. Administer total parenteral nutrition through a central venous catheter. Complications include electrolyte abnormalities, hyperglycemia, and elevated serum aminotransferase levels. Total parenteral nutrition is associated with GI mucosal atrophy and translocation of gut bacteria into the bloodstream, which predisposes patients to infection.

Critical Illness Neuropathy

Diagnosis

Critical illness neuropathy is typically recognized when a patient is unable to be weaned from mechanical ventilation or when severe, generalized weakness of the extremities develops during or after recovery from a critical illness. A clinical evaluation and EMG are required to exclude other disorders. The specific EMG finding in critical illness neuropathy is an axonal sensorimotor peripheral neuropathy.

Therapy

Stop corticosteroids and neuromuscular junction–blocking agents because they may play a role in pathogenesis. Treatment is supportive and includes ongoing physical and occupational therapy.

Rheumatology

Septic Arthritis

Diagnosis

Septic arthritis should be considered in any patient who presents with:

- sudden onset of monoarthritis
- acute worsening of chronic joint disease
- previously painless joint prosthesis that is now painful
- radiographic loosening or migration of a cemented prosthetic device

The risk for infection is increased in persons with previously damaged joints (e.g., patients with rheumatoid arthritis), in older adults, and in immunosuppressed patients. In patients with underlying rheumatologic disorders, a sudden joint flare that is not accompanied by other features of the preexisting disorder and is unresponsive to usual therapy suggests a diagnosis of infectious arthritis.

The hallmark of a septic joint is pain on passive range of motion in the absence of trauma, and an infected joint typically appears swollen and warm with overlying erythema.

Gonococcal arthritis is the most common form of bacterial arthritis in young sexually active persons in the United States. This condition manifests as either a purulent arthritis or a syndrome of disseminated gonococcemia. The arthritis usually involves one or two joints sequentially, most commonly the knees, wrists, ankles, or elbows. Disseminated gonococcemia is characterized by a prodrome of tenosynovitis, polyarthralgia, and cutaneous lesions that progress from papules or macules to pustules and usually are sterile on culture. Fever and rigors are common. Most patients with purulent gonococcal arthritis do not have systemic features or cutaneous involvement; therefore, gonococcal arthritis should be considered in all sexually active patients. Blood cultures for *Neisseria gonorrhoeae* are positive in 50% of infected patients. Obtaining culture specimens from the pharynx, genitals, and rectum in addition to synovial fluid cultures increases the diagnostic yield.

Other less common causes of septic arthritis:

- Gram-negative infections are more common in older, immunosuppressed, and postoperative patients and those with IV catheters.
- Tuberculous arthritis typically is indolent, does not cause systemic features, and is not associated with positive TST; synovial fluid is usually inflammatory with a predominance of polymorphonuclear cells and a negative Gram stain.
- Fungal arthritis typically manifests as subacute monoarthritis in patients with a systemic fungal infection.

STUDY TABLE: Synovial Fluid Characteristics				
Characteristic	Normal	Group I[a] (Noninflammatory)	Group II[b] (Inflammatory)	Group III[c] (Septic)
Leukocytes/µL	200	200-2000	2000-100,000	>50,000 (usually >100,000)
Polymorphonuclear cells (%)	<25	<25	>50	>75

µL = microliter.
[a] Examples: osteoarthritis, osteonecrosis, hemochromatosis, sickle cell disease.
[b] Examples: crystalline arthritis, rheumatoid arthritis, spondyloarthropathy, SLE.
[c] Infectious arthritis, including staphylococcal, gonococcal, and tuberculous.

A synovial fluid leukocyte count >50,000/microliter is specific for infectious or crystalline arthropathy.

◆ DON'T BE TRICKED

- Always select arthrocentesis with Gram stain, polarized microscopy for crystals, cell count, and differential for all acutely swollen, painful joints.
- Septic arthritis can develop in patients with gout or pseudogout, and the presence of crystals in synovial fluid does not exclude a concomitant infection.
- More than 40% of patients with nongonococcal septic arthritis present without fever.
- X-rays are not helpful in the early diagnosis of acute native joint infection.

Therapy

Begin immediate empiric antibiotic therapy even if culture results are pending or negative.

STUDY TABLE: Empiric and Definitive Antibiotic Treatment for Septic Native Joint Arthritis			
Gram Stain Results	**Likely or Identified Pathogen**	**First-Line Therapy**	**Second-Line Therapy**
Gram-positive cocci	*Staphylococcus aureus,* other staphylococcal species	Ceftriaxone	Cefazolin or nafcillin
	If MRSA is a concern (risk factors or known MRSA carrier)	Vancomycin or linezolid	Teicoplanin
Gram-negative cocci	*N. gonorrhoeae*	Ceftriaxone	Fluoroquinolones
Gram-negative bacilli	Enteric gram-negative bacilli	Ceftriaxone or cefotaxime	Fluoroquinolones
	Pseudomonas aeruginosa	Ceftazidime (plus gentamicin if proven)	Carbapenems, cefepime, piperacillin-tazobactam, fluoroquinolones
Gram stain unavailable	At risk for *N. gonorrhoeae* infection	Ceftriaxone or cefotaxime	
	No risk for *N. gonorrhoeae*; *S. aureus* or gram-negative bacilli are likely	Vancomycin plus ceftazidime	Vancomycin plus quinolone

Use needle aspiration to drain reaccumulated purulent joint fluid. If this procedure fails or is too difficult to complete, perform arthroscopy/arthrotomy drainage. Manage infected prosthetic joints with surgery plus antibiotics, usually for 6 weeks.

◆ DON'T BE TRICKED

- Suspect tubercular septic arthritis if the appropriate empiric antimicrobial therapy is unsuccessful.

❖ Test Yourself

A 28-year-old woman has a 9-day history of arthritis, fever, and chills followed by pain and swelling of the second and third metacarpophalangeal joints. As swelling resolves, the right wrist becomes inflamed. As the wrist improves, the right knee becomes inflamed. She also has a 5-mm vesicle surrounded by red skin on the forearm.

ANSWER: The diagnosis is disseminated gonorrhea. Prescribe ceftriaxone and doxycycline for empiric treatment of chlamydia.

Lyme Disease

Prevention

The risk of Lyme disease following a tick bite is low. Watchful waiting is preferred to giving a prophylactic antibiotic.

Diagnosis

Lyme disease has three stages (early, disseminated, and late) based on the time that has elapsed after exposure. The clinical presentation differs for each stage of the disease.

STUDY TABLE: Common Manifestations of Lyme Disease by Stage		
Stage	**Findings**	**Management**
Acute, localized	Within 30 days of exposure: erythema migrans, fever, fatigue, headache, arthralgia, myalgia	Treat without serologic confirmation.
Acute, disseminated	Weeks to months after exposure: multiple erythema migrans lesions, heart conduction block, cranial neuropathy, radiculoneuropathy, lymphocytic meningitis, acute attacks of monoarticular or oligoarticular arthritis	Treat if ELISA is positive. Obtain Western blot if ELISA is indeterminate.
Late	Months to years after exposure: attacks of monoarticular or oligoarticular arthritis and/or chronic monoarthritis or oligoarthritis, peripheral neuropathy, or encephalomyelitis	Treat if ELISA is positive. Obtain Western blot if ELISA is indeterminate.

ELISA = enzyme-linked immunosorbent assay.

◆ DON'T BE TRICKED

- Serologic test results are often negative in acute localized Lyme disease.

Therapy

In patients with erythema migrans and early disease, begin doxycycline, amoxicillin, or cefuroxime without laboratory confirmation of *Borrelia burgdorferi*. Manage late carditis or neurologic disease with ceftriaxone, and manage arthritis and facial nerve palsy with doxycycline.

◆ DON'T BE TRICKED

- Do not confuse late Lyme disease with "chronic Lyme disease" or post–Lyme disease syndrome.
- Do not treat "chronic Lyme disease" (post–Lyme disease syndrome) with antibiotics.
- Do not rely on serologic test results to decide on the adequacy of treatment.
- Do not prescribe doxycycline for pregnant women.

Erythema Migrans: A large erythematous ring characterizes erythema migrans and early Lyme disease.

Osteoarthritis

Diagnosis

Age is the most important risk factor for developing primary OA in women and men. Additional risk factors include genetics, obesity, and trauma-induced mechanical joint instability. OA most often affects the lower cervical and lumbar spine; hips; knees; DIP, PIP, and first carpometacarpal joints.

Characteristic findings include:

- morning joint stiffness lasting <30 minutes
- gelling (brief stiffness after inactivity)
- crepitus

- tenderness along the joint line
- reduced joint motion
- bony enlargement (including Heberden and Bouchard nodes)
- involvement of the first carpometacarpal joint results in "squaring" at the base of the thumb

Two important variants are erosive OA of the hand and DISH.

Erosive inflammatory OA is characterized by pain and palpable swelling of the soft tissue in the PIP and DIP joints. This condition also may be associated with disease flares during which these joints become more swollen and painful.

DISH is an often asymptomatic form of OA that causes significant radiographic changes similar to those associated with degenerative spondylosis or ankylosing spondylitis. X-rays of the spine in patients with DISH reveal flowing ossification that develops along the anterolateral aspect of the vertebral bodies, particularly the anterior longitudinal ligament. However, neither disk-space narrowing nor syndesmophytes are visible in this setting, as they are in lumbar spondylosis or ankylosing spondylitis, respectively.

Secondary OA results from previous joint injury or metabolic diseases such as hemochromatosis. Consider metabolic causes when OA develops in atypical joints (e.g., MCP joints, shoulder, wrist).

Be alert for an acutely painful calf mimicking a DVT, which represents a ruptured Baker cyst (herniation of fluid-filled synovium of the posterior knee) or ruptured gastrocnemius muscle.

No pathognomonic laboratory tests are available for OA. An x-ray is not helpful in the diagnosis of symptomatic hand OA (clinical examination is more specific) but is the "gold standard" for hip and knee OA. X-rays show joint-space narrowing, subchondral sclerosis, and osteophytes. Synovial fluid is usually noninflammatory, with a leukocyte count <2000/microliter. Ultrasonography is useful in the diagnosis of Baker cyst.

◆ DON'T BE TRICKED

Typical OA radiographic changes do not exclude other diagnoses. Be alert for:

- **septic arthritis superimposed on OA**
- **trochanteric and anserine bursitis causing hip and knee pain**
- **de Quervain tenosynovitis mimicking carpometacarpal OA**
- **hemochromatosis, particularly if involving the second and third metacarpophalangeal joints**
- **gout or CPPD deposition disease**

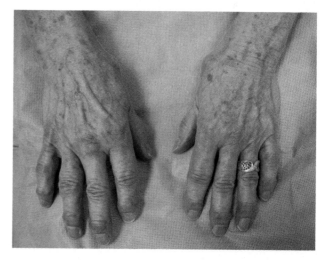

Hand Photograph, Osteoarthritis: Bony enlargement of the DIP joints and squaring of the first carpometacarpal joint characteristic of osteoarthritis.

Therapy

Medical therapy includes:

- acetaminophen as first-line therapy for hip and knee OA
- NSAIDs in patients who do not respond to acetaminophen or as initial therapy for severe pain
- tramadol if NSAIDs are contraindicated or ineffective
- intra-articular corticosteroids for acute exacerbations of knee OA
- intra-articular hyaluronan injection, which has comparable efficacy to NSAID therapy for knee OA
- glucosamine sulfate, although data for its use are conflicting

Patients with hip and knee OA benefit from weight loss; patients with knee OA benefit from quadriceps-strengthening exercises. Joint arthroplasty of the hip or knee is indicated for pain that does not respond to nonsurgical treatment, especially when lifestyle or activities of daily living are affected.

◆ DON'T BE TRICKED

- **Patients with signs of inflammation should not undergo intra-articular corticosteroid therapy until synovial fluid analysis excludes infection.**
- **Do not select arthroscopic lavage, debridement, or closed lavage for knee OA.**

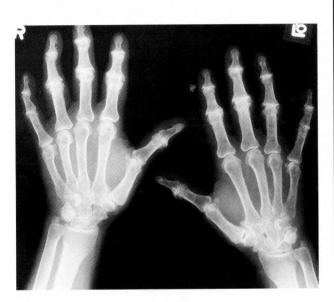

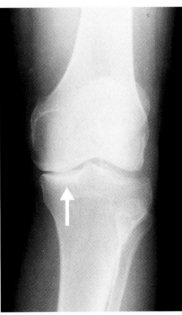

Hand X-ray, Osteoarthritis: Joint-space narrowing, sclerosis, and osteophyte formation are shown. Prominent involvement of the PIP and DIP joints indicates osteoarthritis.

Knee X-ray, Osteoarthritis: Medial compartment joint space-narrowing and subchondral sclerosis consistent with osteoarthritis are shown.

Rheumatoid Arthritis

Diagnosis

RA is a symmetric inflammatory polyarthritis that primarily involves the small joints of the hands and feet. Characteristic findings include:

- morning stiffness lasting >1 hour
- seven classic sites of symmetric joint pain (PIP, MCP, wrist, elbow, knee, ankle, and MTP joints)
- synovitis characterized by soft-tissue swelling or effusion
- subcutaneous nodules over bony prominences or extensor surfaces

Laboratory findings include:

- positive rheumatoid factor (sensitivity 80%; specificity 87%)
- elevated ESR or CRP level
- normocytic anemia
- positive anti-CCP antibody assay (sensitivity 76%; specificity 96%)

An x-ray can reveal periarticular osteopenia, erosions, and symmetric joint-space narrowing. MRI and ultrasonography are more sensitive for detecting early RA.

◆ DON'T BE TRICKED

- Negative rheumatoid factor does not exclude RA; anti-CCP antibody assay may be positive.
- A positive rheumatoid factor alone is not diagnostic of RA.
- Not all symmetric arthritis is RA.

STUDY TABLE: Rheumatoid Arthritis Mimics	
If you see symmetric arthritis and...	**Diagnose this...**
Skin rash and leukopenia	SLE
Psoriasis or pitted nails	Psoriatic arthritis
Daycare worker or mother of small children	Parvovirus B19 infection (usually self-limited; 1 to 3 months)
2nd and/or 3rd MCP and PIP joint arthritis	Hemochromatosis
Raynaud phenomenon and sclerodactyly	Systemic sclerosis
Proximal muscle weakness	Polymyositis or dermatomyositis
Recent immunizations	Post–rubella immunization arthritis

RA extra-articular manifestations:

- arm paresthesias and hyperreflexia → C1-C2 subluxation (increased risk of cord compression with tracheal intubation)
- cough, fever, pulmonary infiltrates → BOOP
- foot drop or wrist drop → mononeuritis multiplex (vasculitis)
- hoarseness → cricoarytenoid involvement
- multiple basilar pulmonary nodules → Caplan syndrome
- dry eyes and/or mouth → Sjögren syndrome
- pleural effusion with low plasma glucose (<30 mg/dL) → rheumatoid pleuritis
- pulmonary fibrosis → rheumatoid interstitial lung disease
- skin ulcers, peripheral neuropathy → rheumatoid vasculitis
- splenomegaly and granulocytopenia → Felty syndrome
- red, painful eye → scleritis
- HF → rheumatoid disease or anti-TNF therapy

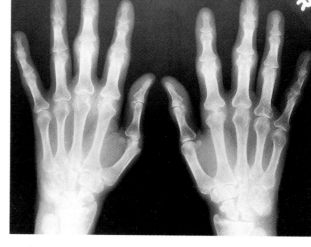

Hand X-ray, Rheumatoid Arthritis: Carpal, metacarpal, and PIP joints show periarticular osteopenia, joint-space narrowing, and marginal erosions, all characteristic of rheumatoid arthritis.

Other complications include increased risk of CAD and osteoporosis.

Therapy

Early treatment with one or more DMARDs is essential. Choose NSAIDs and low-dose oral and intra-articular corticosteroids for quick symptomatic relief, but recognize these agents do not alter the course of the disease.

Monotherapy with hydroxychloroquine or sulfasalazine or combination therapy with these agents is indicated to manage early, mild, and nonerosive disease.

In the absence of contraindications, methotrexate with or without the addition of another DMARD should be instituted immediately in patients with erosive disease.

In some patients, combination therapy with hydroxychloroquine, sulfasalazine, and methotrexate has been shown to be more effective than monotherapy with methotrexate or sulfasalazine plus hydroxychloroquine.

Initiate biologic therapy when adequate disease control is not achieved with oral DMARDs. The initial biologic therapy should be a TNF-α inhibitor:

- add a TNF-α inhibitor to baseline methotrexate therapy
- screen for TB before starting therapy
- treat for latent TB if TST is positive before beginning any biologic therapy
- perform periodic TST screening while the patient continues to receive biologic therapy

Common toxicities of TNF-α inhibitor therapy include pancytopenia, positive ANA formation associated with lupus-like syndromes, and demyelinating disorders. Combination therapy with multiple biologic therapies is not recommended.

Indications for surgical intervention include intractable pain or severe functional disability from joint destruction. Patients may also require surgical repair of ruptured tendons.

All patients taking corticosteroids require osteoporosis screening and serum calcium and vitamin D level measurement. If osteopenia or osteoporosis is diagnosed, prescribe a bisphosphonate. Annual influenza vaccination is indicated for all patients using immunosuppressants, and pneumococcal vaccination is indicated before beginning treatment with methotrexate, leflunomide, or a biologic agent.

The most common cause of death in patients with RA is CAD. Begin aggressive coronary risk factor reduction in all patients. Also, begin adjuvant physical and occupational therapy.

◆ DON'T BE TRICKED

- **Hydroxychloroquine and sulfasalazine can be used during pregnancy.**

❖ Test Yourself

A 46-year-old man has a 3-month history of swelling of the PIP and MCP joints and 90 minutes of morning stiffness. Rheumatoid factor is negative.

ANSWER: The probable diagnosis is RA. Select anti-CCP antibody assay.

Sjögren Syndrome

Diagnosis

Sjögren syndrome is an autoimmune disease characterized by keratoconjunctivitis sicca and xerostomia. Salivary gland enlargement occurs in nearly half of patients during the course of the disease and is most obvious in the parotid glands. This condition may occur as a primary disease process or may be associated with another autoimmune disease, most commonly rheumatoid arthritis. A cardinal feature of Sjögren syndrome is the presence of antibodies to Ro/SSA and La/SSB.

A positive ANA, RF, and hypergammaglobulinemia are also frequently found. Diagnosis is established by biopsy of a labial minor salivary gland. Patients with Sjögren syndrome are up to 44 times more likely than the general population to have a B-cell lymphoma. Careful follow-up is therefore required.

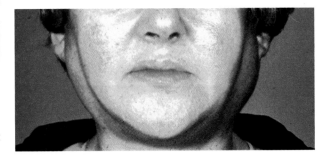

Parotid Gland Enlargement: Bilateral parotid gland enlargement in a patient with Sjögren syndrome.

Therapy

Treatment is symptomatic. Choose artificial tear replacement and artificial saliva and mouth lubricants. Systemic immunosuppressive therapy is indicated only in patients with severe systemic manifestations.

Spondyloarthritis

Key Considerations

Spondyloarthritis comprises several systemic inflammatory joint disorders that share distinct clinical, radiographic, and genetic features. These disorders are:

- psoriatic arthritis
- reactive arthritis (formerly Reiter syndrome)
- ankylosing spondylitis
- IBD-associated arthritis

Characteristics include:

- inflammatory spine and sacroiliac disease
- asymmetric inflammation in four or fewer peripheral joints (typically large joints)
- inflammation at the sites of ligament and tendon insertion (enthesitis)
- the presence of HLA-B27
- extra-articular conditions, such as uveitis, colitis, urethritis, aortitis, and psoriasis

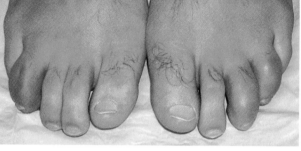

Dactylitis: Diffuse swelling of the left third and fourth toes and right fourth toe characteristic of dactylitis.

Psoriatic Arthritis

Characteristic findings are classic psoriasis (thick silvery scale on a well-demarcated red patch) and nail pitting in a patient with joint pain and stiffness. Skin involvement commonly precedes joint inflammation, although 15% of patients first develop joint inflammation.

Patterns of joint involvement are various. Approximately 40% of patients present with symmetric oligoarthritis of the large joints of the lower extremities, and 25% of these patients develop small-joint polyarthritis, similar to RA. Spinal involvement occurs in almost 50% of patients with psoriatic arthritis. A sausage-shaped finger or toe (dactylitis) may be found and the DIP joints are often involved, which helps distinguishes psoriatic arthritis from RA.

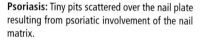

Psoriasis: Tiny pits scattered over the nail plate resulting from psoriatic involvement of the nail matrix.

Patients with psoriatic arthritis tend to be seronegative for rheumatoid factor, but at least 15% are seropositive, as are a similar percentage of patients with uncomplicated psoriasis. Serum uric acid levels may be elevated in patients with psoriatic arthritis because of rapid turnover of skin cells. X-rays may show a "pencil-in-the-cup" appearance of one or more involved joints. Other radiographic findings include syndesmophytes and sacroiliitis of the axial skeleton.

◆ DON'T BE TRICKED

- **No relationship exists between the extent of skin and joint disease in patients with psoriatic arthritis.**
- **Do not make a diagnosis of gout based solely on joint pain and elevated serum uric acid levels.**

Use NSAIDs for mild joint inflammation and minimal skin involvement; prescribe methotrexate for severe skin and erosive peripheral joint disease. A TNF-α inhibitor is indicated for methotrexate-resistant peripheral disease and may be indicated as first-line treatment for patients with axial involvement and for those with dactylitis or enthesitis that does not respond to NSAIDs and locally injected corticosteroids. NSAIDs, antimalarial drugs, and (withdrawal from) oral corticosteroids may exacerbate psoriasis.

Reactive Arthritis

Reactive arthritis is an acute aseptic inflammatory arthritis that occurs 1 to 3 weeks after an infectious event originating in the GU or GI tract. A high prevalence of HIV infection is found in patients with symptoms of reactive arthritis.

Characteristic findings include:

Keratoderma Blennorrhagicum: A papular and pustular rash of the palms and soles is associated with reactive arthritis. Image courtesy of David Crosby, MD.

- acute asymmetric oligoarthritis (usually in weight-bearing joints)
- dactylitis
- mouth ulcers
- inflammatory eye conditions

Patients may also have keratoderma blennorrhagicum (a psoriasis-like skin lesion on the palms and soles) or circinate balanitis (shallow, moist, serpiginous ulcers with raised borders on the glans penis).

Diagnostic studies include throat culture for *Streptococcus*, urogenital culture for *Chlamydia*, and serologic studies for *Salmonella*, *Yersinia*, *Campylobacter*, *Neisseria*, and HIV. Obtain urinalysis for protein, blood, and leukocytes.

If the causative organism can be isolated (β-hemolytic streptococci, *N. gonorrhoeae*, *Chlamydia*), begin specific antibiotics. If infection is ruled out, treat with an intra-articular corticosteroid injection in the acutely inflamed joint. If arthritis persists for longer than 3 to 5 months, begin DMARDs. Sulfasalazine is a common first-line choice.

◆ DON'T BE TRICKED

- **The classic triad of arthritis, conjunctivitis, and urethritis (or cervicitis) is found in only one third of patients with reactive arthritis.**
- **Do not prescribe chronic antibiotic therapy for patients with reactive arthritis.**

❖ Test Yourself

A 33-year-old man has a 3-month history of left shoulder and right ankle pain and a left inflamed second toe. He had 4 days of bloody diarrhea 3 months ago.

ANSWER: The diagnosis is reactive arthritis, consistent with an enteric infection.

Ankylosing Spondylitis

Ankylosing spondylitis primarily affects the spine and sacroiliac joints. It also may involve the shoulders and hips, although the small peripheral joints are not affected. Ankylosing spondylitis occurs most often in patients <40 years of age and presents as chronic low back pain. Characteristic findings are pain and stiffness that worsen at night and are relieved with physical activity or heat.

Physical examination findings include:

- decreased hyperextension, forward flexion, lateral flexion, and axial rotation
- diminished chest expansion
- asymmetric peripheral arthritis involving the large joints
- painful heels (enthesitis)

X-rays show subchondral bony sclerosis, vertebral body squaring, and bony ankylosis ("bamboo spine"). When radiographic findings are equivocal or absent, MRI can detect the early changes of sacroiliitis. HLA-B27 testing is neither sensitive nor specific for ankylosing spondylitis and does not distinguish ankylosing spondylitis from other spondyloarthropathies.

Extra-articular manifestations include acute anterior uveitis (most common), aortic valvular regurgitation and cardiac conduction defects, apical pulmonary fibrosis and cavitation, and cauda equina syndrome.

A patient with ankylosing spondylitis with increased pain and mobility of the neck following a minor accident may have a fracture and requires an urgent CT of the cervical spine.

◆ DON'T BE TRICKED

- **Ankylosing spondylitis occurs in both men and women.**

NSAIDs, not aspirin, are the mainstay of management. Use corticosteroid injections for recalcitrant enthesitis and persistent synovitis. Prescribe sulfasalazine for patients with primarily peripheral arthritis and a TNF-α inhibitor for primarily axial disease. Calcium and vitamin D supplements and exercise to retain good posture, spinal mobility, and chest expansion are beneficial. Begin a bisphosphonate if osteopenia or osteoporosis is present.

◆ DON'T BE TRICKED

- **Do not prescribe traditional DMARDs for patients with axial disease because they are ineffective. Select a TNF-α inhibitor.**

❖ Test Yourself

A 40-year-old man has increasing neck pain after a fall from the second rung of a ladder 5 days ago. He has a long history of stiffness and pain in the neck and lower back and loss of lumbar spine flexion.

ANSWER: The probable diagnosis is ankylosing spondylitis with an acute cervical fracture. Select neck immobilization and emergent CT.

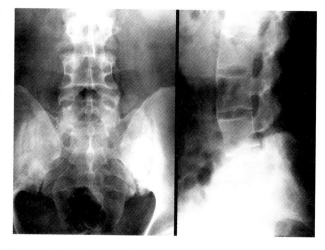

X-rays, Ankylosing Spondylitis: Sclerosis and erosions of sacroiliac joints and bridging of the intervertebral disks by syndesmophytes are characteristic of ankylosing spondylitis.

IBD-Associated Arthritis

Inflammatory arthritis can complicate Crohn disease and ulcerative colitis. Up to 20% of patients with IBD develop a peripheral arthritis, which manifests as either a polyarticular arthritis resembling RA or an asymmetric oligoarthritis predominantly of the lower extremities resembling reactive arthritis. The course of arthritis often fluctuates with the activity of the underlying bowel involvement. Another 20% of patients have spinal involvement ranging from asymptomatic sacroiliac disease to a clinical presentation identical to that of ankylosing spondylitis. Unlike peripheral arthritis, the progression of spinal involvement is independent of the course of the bowel disease.

The therapies that benefit intestinal disease also have efficacy in the treatment of the associated peripheral joint and extra-articular manifestations. These therapies include corticosteroids, sulfasalazine, azathioprine, methotrexate, infliximab, and adalimumab.

◆ DON'T BE TRICKED

- **Etanercept has not shown efficacy in treating IBD.**

Gout

Diagnosis

Gout is caused by the inflammatory reaction to monosodium urate crystal deposition in synovial tissue, bursae, and tendon sheaths. Gout is often precipitated by use of diuretics. Gout progresses through three stages:

- asymptomatic hyperuricemia, which may last several decades
- acute intermittent gout
- chronic tophaceous gout, which usually develops only after years of acute intermittent episodes

Monosodium urate crystals (needle-shaped, negatively birefringent crystals) in the joint fluid and uric acid tophi are diagnostic. Other characteristic findings of acute intermittent gout include monoarticular arthritis (typically of the first MTP or tarsal joints), self-limited acute attacks, and hyperuricemia. If disease presents classically at the first MTP joint (podagra), synovial fluid analysis is not required to make the diagnosis.

With time, attacks of gout may become more frequent and involve more joints. Patients may progress to have a chronic, smoldering arthritis. Tophi are yellowish nodular deposits of monosodium urate, sometimes with surrounding erythema, that develop on extensor surfaces of the extremities, on finger pads, and along tendons. Transplantation-associated gout is associated with the use of calcineurin antagonists (cyclosporine).

X-rays show bone erosions with overhanging edges. The synovial fluid leukocyte count ranges from 2000 to 75,000/microliter. Monosodium urate crystals may be visible on joint aspiration when an acute flare is not occurring.

◆ DON'T BE TRICKED

- **An elevated uric acid level alone is not diagnostic of gout.**
- **A normal uric acid level at the time of an acute attack does not rule out gout.**
- **Leukocyte counts higher than 50,000/microliter should raise suspicion for a concurrent bacterial joint infection, even when monosodium urate crystals have been identified.**

Therapy

Dietary purine restriction, weight loss, and discontinuation of alcohol may help to decrease uric acid levels in patients with mild hyperuricemia and symptomatic gout. Medications that raise serum uric acid levels, such as thiazide diuretics and low-dose salicylates, should be discontinued.

For an acute gouty flare, NSAIDs are first-line therapy. Use oral corticosteroids when NSAIDs are unsafe (in older adult or postoperative patients, patients requiring anticoagulation, and those with chronic kidney disease or peptic ulcer disease). Prescribe intra-articular corticosteroids for a single joint if other interventions are ineffective or contraindicated.

Patients with 2 or more attacks each year or with the presence of tophi or kidney stones require allopurinol to achieve a serum uric acid level <6 mg/dL. More than 50% of patients require allopurinol, >300 mg/d, to reach this target serum uric acid level. Doses must be adjusted (lowered) for patients with kidney impairment. When starting allopurinol, also begin low-dose colchicine to prevent acute gout; colchicine can be discontinued when the uric acid level stabilizes. Febuxostat is useful if patients cannot tolerate allopurinol and in patients with chronic kidney disease.

Patients with kidney disease, especially those concomitantly taking hydrochlorothiazide, who are treated with allopurinol have an increased risk for a rare but potentially fatal hypersensitivity syndrome characterized by severe dermatitis, fever, eosinophilia, hepatic necrosis, and acute nephritis.

◆ DON'T BE TRICKED

- **Do not select NSAIDs for patients with gout who also have chronic kidney disease or peptic ulcer disease.**

- Do not use allopurinol and azathioprine together, because azathioprine is metabolized through xanthine oxidase, which is inhibited by allopurinol.
- Do not begin allopurinol during an acute attack of gout; wait 1 or 2 weeks.
- Do not use uricosuric therapy (e.g., probenecid) in patients with a low estimated GFR who are at risk for nephrolithiasis or chronic kidney disease.
- Do not prescribe colchicine for patients with kidney failure.

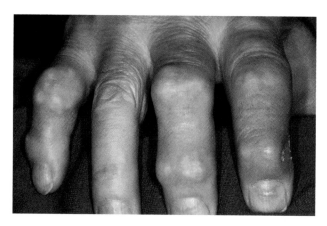

Chronic Tophaceous Gout: Swollen interphalangeal joints and multiple tophi characteristic of chronic tophaceous gout.

❖ **Test Yourself**

A 78-year-old man has a 6-hour history of an acutely painful and swollen left first MTP joint. Two days ago, he had an MI. His serum creatinine level is 1.7 mg/dL.

ANSWER: The diagnosis is gout. Aspirate the joint, and treat with an intra-articular corticosteroid after infection is excluded.

Calcium Pyrophosphate Deposition Disease

Diagnosis

CPDD is caused by crystallization of calcium pyrophosphate dihydrate (CPPD) crystals in articular tissues. CPDD has varied presentations with symptoms that may suggest other diagnoses.

Characteristic findings in acute pseudogout syndrome include:

- inflammation localized to one joint, affecting the knee, wrist, shoulder, or ankle
- acute onset of several painful joints following trauma or surgery

Characteristic findings in chronic pseudogout syndrome include:

- asymmetric involvement of the shoulders, wrists, MCP joints, or knees
- swelling and deformity of joints and morning stiffness

Characteristic findings in asymptomatic chondrocalcinosis include calcification of the:

- triangular fibrocartilage of the wrist joint (space between the carpal bones and distal ulna)
- menisci of the knee joint (appearing as a line in the cartilage)
- symphysis pubis

CPDD may be associated with underlying metabolic disorders. Screen patients with CPDD who are <50 years of age for:

- hemochromatosis
- hyperparathyroidism
- hypothyroidism
- gout

The definitive diagnosis of CPDD requires both the presence of positively birefringent, rhomboid-shaped crystals and typical cartilage or joint capsule calcification on x-ray.

◆ DON'T BE TRICKED

- The absence of chondrocalcinosis on x-ray does not rule out CPDD.

Therapy

NSAIDs are appropriate as initial therapy for most patients. Prescribe colchicine for patients with any variant of CPPD deposition disease that does not respond to NSAIDs. Intra-articular corticosteroids are indicated for acute pain after infection is ruled out. This is always the correct treatment for a patient with a noninfectious inflammatory monoarticular arthritis who cannot take NSAIDs because of an elevated serum creatinine level.

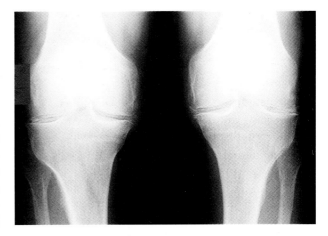

X-ray of Knees, Chondrocalcinosis: Linear calcifications of the meniscus and articular cartilage are characteristic of CPDD.

Hypertrophic Osteoarthropathy

Diagnosis

Hypertrophic osteoarthropathy causes a proliferation of skin and osseous tissue at the distal parts of the extremities. Characteristic findings are digital clubbing, painful periostosis of long bones, synovial effusions, and new periosteal bone formation. Pain is generally alleviated by elevating the affected limbs. Associated disorders include lung cancer, chronic pulmonary infections, and right-to-left cardiac shunts.

❖ Test Yourself

A 64-year-old man has a 1-month history of bilateral ankle pain. Elevating his feet alleviates the discomfort. On physical examination, his lower legs are warm. Pitting edema begins 6 cm above the malleoli; this area is very tender to palpation. An x-ray shows new periosteal bone formation of the tibia above the ankle joints.

ANSWER: The probable diagnosis is hypertrophic osteoarthropathy. Order a chest x-ray to determine the cause.

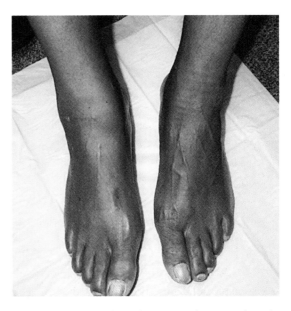

Hypertrophic Osteoarthropathy: Hypertrophic osteoarthropathy in this patient is characterized by clubbing of the toes (particularly the great toes), ankle effusions, and lower extremity edema.

Systemic Lupus Erythematosus

Diagnosis

SLE is a chronic multisystem autoimmune disease with immune complex deposition of unknown cause. Diagnosis is established based on characteristic clinical features and laboratory studies. Diagnose SLE when any four of the following are present:

- positive ANA
- malar ("butterfly") rash that spares the nasolabial folds and areas beneath the nose and lower lip
- discoid rash characterized by erythematous, raised patches with keratotic scaling and follicular plugging
- photosensitivity

- oral ulcers
- arthritis (oligoarticular or polyarticular, or asymmetric or symmetric); joint pain is frequently the presenting symptom
- serositis (pleural, pericardial, abdominal)
- kidney disorder (new-onset hypertension, proteinuria with or without hematuria)
- neurologic disorder (peripheral neuropathy, mononeuritis multiplex, cranial neuritis, transverse myelitis, aseptic meningitis, stroke, encephalitis, psychosis, seizures)
- hematologic disorder (autoimmune hemolytic anemia, leukopenia, lymphopenia, thrombocytopenia)
- immunologic disorder (antiphospholipid antibody syndrome [venous and arterial thrombosis, recurrent fetal loss])

◆ DON'T BE TRICKED

- **Do not diagnose SLE in a patient with a positive ANA and facial rash that involves the nasolabial folds; consider rosacea instead.**

The ANA assay is sensitive but not specific for diagnosing SLE. Assays for anti-dsDNA and anti-Sm antibodies are highly specific. Anti-dsDNA antibodies correlate with disease activity.

Activation of the complement pathway, manifested by depressed serum C3 and C4 levels, often accompanies major flares of SLE.

Additional manifestations:

- livedo reticularis (anticardiolipin antibodies and thrombophilia)
- nonbacterial endocarditis
- increased risk of cardiovascular disease, including stroke
- neonatal heart block (high-titer anti-Ro/SSA antibodies)

Drug-induced lupus is most often caused by hydralazine, procainamide, isoniazid, minocycline, or TNF-α inhibitors. Symptoms are usually limited to fever, serositis, and arthritis. ANA assays are positive, but anti-dsDNA and anti-Sm antibody assays are negative. Antihistone antibody assay may be positive.

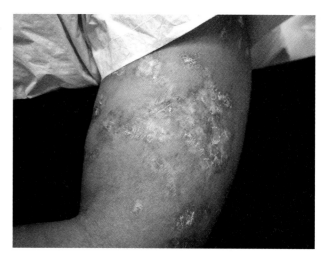

SLE Rash: The discoid rash of lupus erythematosus consists of chronic, slowly progressive, scaly, infiltrative papules and plaques or atrophic red plaques on sun-exposed skin surfaces. Discoid lupus can be present in the absence of any other clinical feature of SLE.

◆ DON'T BE TRICKED

- **Monitoring ANA titers is not warranted because these values do not reflect disease activity.**

Therapy

Cardiovascular disease is the major cause of death in patients with SLE; reduce atherosclerosis risk factors in all patients. Prescribe vitamin D and calcium supplements for all patients and bisphosphonates for those with osteoporosis and osteopenia. Manage arthritis with NSAIDs and hydroxychloroquine. For photosensitive cutaneous lupus, choose sun block, topical corticosteroids, and hydroxychloroquine. Hydroxychloroquine should be initiated and continued indefinitely in most patients to help prevent flares of SLE even in patients with quiescent disease. Patients taking hydroxychloroquine require annual routine ophthalmologic examinations.

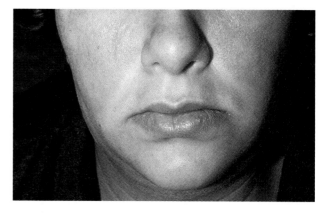

Malar Skin Rash: Bright red, sharply demarcated plaques in a butterfly pattern that spares the nasolabial folds and areas beneath the nose and lower lip are associated with SLE.

Prescribe IV cyclophosphamide (or mycophenolate mofetil) and high-dose corticosteroids for proliferative glomerulonephritis. Manage any life-threatening disease such as lupus pneumonitis, inflammatory CNS disease, or severe cytopenia with high-dose corticosteroids and (usually) cyclophosphamide, azathioprine, or mycophenolate mofetil.

Systemic Sclerosis

Diagnosis

Systemic sclerosis (also known as scleroderma) is a disease of unknown cause characterized by microvascular injury and excessive connective tissue deposition. The presence of typical skin findings and one or more of the following features supports a diagnosis:

- sclerodactyly
- digital pitting
- interstitial lung disease
- Raynaud phenomenon
- pulmonary hypertension
- polyarticular arthritis
- GERD
- Pseudo-obstruction (small bowel)
- malabsorption due to bacterial overgrowth

Systemic sclerosis is classified according to the degree of skin involvement.

STUDY TABLE: Differentiating Diffuse from Limited Cutaneous Systemic Sclerosis		
Findings	**Diffuse Cutaneous Systemic Sclerosis**	**Limited Cutaneous Systemic Sclerosis**
Skin findings	Skin thickening proximal to the elbows and knees. May affect the face.	Skin thickening distal to the elbows and knees; possibly affecting the face
Antibodies	ANA and anti–Scl-70 antibodies	ANA and anticentromere antibodies
Pulmonary disease	Interstitial lung disease	Pulmonary hypertension
Scleroderma renal crisis	Present	Absent
CREST syndrome	Usually absent	Present
CREST = calcinosis, Raynaud phenomenon, esophageal dysmotility, sclerodactyly, and telangiectasia.		

Scleroderma renal crisis is characterized by hypertension, microangiopathy, hemolytic anemia and thrombocytopenia, proteinuria, and nonoliguric kidney failure. In addition, corticosteroid therapy is a risk factor and may be associated with normotensive renal crisis (acute kidney injury in the absence of hypertension).

Patients with systemic sclerosis also may develop an inflammatory, typically nonerosive arthritis.

The primary cause of morbidity and mortality in patients with systemic sclerosis is pulmonary disease. Screening tests include HRCT and pulmonary function tests (including D_{LCO}) for interstitial lung disease and echocardiography for pulmonary hypertension.

Syndromes that can mimic systemic sclerosis:

- Eosinophilic fasciitis: woody induration of the skin, sparing the hands and feet, and peripheral blood eosinophilia. Full-thickness skin biopsy establishes the diagnosis.
- Mixed connective tissue disease: inflammatory myopathy, SLE features, arthritis, and scleroderma overlap with positive anti-RNP antibodies.
- Idiopathic pulmonary fibrosis: restrictive lung disease but no Raynaud phenomenon, GI symptoms, or skin changes. Serologic tests for scleroderma-specific antibodies are negative.

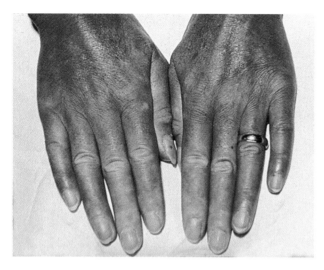

Sclerodactyly: Thickening and induration of the skin over the fingers and wrists is characteristic of scleroderma.

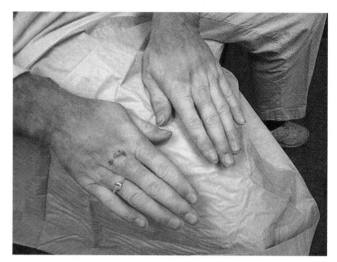

Raynaud Phenomenon: Areas of vasospastic skin blanching seen in a patient with Raynaud phenomenon.

Therapy

Therapies are for organ-specific manifestations; no overall disease-modifying therapy is available.

Use nifedipine, amlodipine, felodipine, sildenafil, and nitroglycerin paste to manage Raynaud phenomenon. Prescribe PPIs for GERD and promotility agents for gastric and intestinal dysmotility. Prescribe ACE inhibitors for scleroderma renal crisis regardless of the serum creatinine level and continue even in the setting of kidney failure. Bacterial overgrowth manifests as diarrhea and is managed with broad-spectrum antibiotics. Manage arthritis similarly to RA.

◆ DON'T BE TRICKED

- **Scleroderma is not managed with corticosteroids.**

❖ Test Yourself

A 59-year-old woman has accelerated hypertension and chronic kidney disease. She has a history of Raynaud phenomenon. Blood pressure is 160/122 mm Hg. Her fingers appear tapered with very smooth skin and ulcers on the fingertips. Serum creatinine level is 5.4 mg/dL.

ANSWER: The patient is in scleroderma renal crisis. Prescribe an ACE inhibitor.

Idiopathic Inflammatory Myopathies

Diagnosis

The idiopathic inflammatory myopathies are heterogeneous immune-mediated disorders; the major types are polymyositis, dermatomyositis, and inclusion body myositis.

The characteristic finding in polymyositis and dermatomyositis is the gradual onset of painless proximal muscle, pharyngeal, and respiratory muscle weakness. Photosensitivity rashes are commonly associated with dermatomyositis. The presence of Gottron papules (scaly, purplish papules and plaques over the metacarpal and interphalangeal joints) and heliotrope rash (edematous lilac discoloration of periorbital tissue) is virtually diagnostic of dermatomyositis. "Mechanic's hands" (scaly, rough, dry, cracked horizontal lines on the palmar and lateral aspects of the fingers) may occur in either polymyositis or dermatomyositis.

ANA is present in 80% of patients with polymyositis or dermatomyositis. Anti–Jo-1 antibodies are found in 20% of patients with myositis and are associated with an antisynthetase syndrome characterized by:

- interstitial lung disease
- inflammatory polyarthritis
- fever
- Raynaud phenomenon
- increased risk of premature death

Diagnostic tests for inflammatory myositis include measurement of serum CK levels and EMG. Muscle biopsy is the definitive study. MRI of the proximal musculature, particularly the thighs, may assess the degree of muscle inflammation and damage and may be helpful when other diagnostic studies are equivocal or to identify the most promising biopsy site.

The onset of symptoms in inclusion body myositis is insidious and involves proximal and distal muscles, frequently with an asymmetric distribution. Quadriceps, wrist, and finger flexor muscle weakness is common. ANA is found in <20% of patients with inclusion body myositis.

Certain medications (corticosteroids, statins) or alcohol may also cause a toxic myopathy.

◆ DON'T BE TRICKED

- **Serum aspartate and alanine aminotransferase levels may be elevated in myositis, mimicking liver disease.**
- **Muscle pain in patients with an inflammatory myopathy is atypical and, if present, is generally mild.**

STUDY TABLE: Mimics of Polymyositis	
If you see this...	**Diagnose this...**
Muscle fasciculations	Amyotrophic lateral sclerosis
Oculomotor weakness with ptosis	Myasthenia gravis
Proximal muscle tenderness	Polymyalgia rheumatica
Muscle atrophy, hyporeflexia	Peripheral neuropathy
Goiter, delayed reflexes, weight gain	Hypothyroidism
Treatment with a statin	Statin myopathy

If myositis is unresponsive to treatment, consider a diagnosis of inclusion body myositis. When two or more connective tissue diseases are present, diagnose an overlap syndrome. When two or more connective tissue diseases are associated with high titers of anti-RNP antibodies, diagnose mixed connective tissue disease.

The association between malignancy and the inflammatory myopathies is well established. The types of malignancies correlate with those that develop in an age-matched population, except that ovarian cancer is more common. No guidelines exist for the evaluation of malignancy in patients with inflammatory myositis. Minimally, follow such patients with sex- and age-appropriate cancer screening.

Therapy

High-dose oral corticosteroid therapy is first-line treatment for polymyositis and dermatomyositis. Adding methotrexate and/or azathioprine may be indicated if disease is refractory to high-dose corticosteroid therapy or if patients develop intolerable corticosteroid-related side effects. Use IV immune globulin in patients with refractory disease. Hydroxychloroquine may help to treat cutaneous manifestations of dermatomyositis. Baseline bone mineral density testing is indicated in patients who undergo long-term high-dose corticosteroid therapy. Begin

Heliotrope Rash: Heliotrope rash on edematous eyelids characteristic of dermatomyositis.

prophylactic therapy for osteoporosis with calcium and vitamin D supplementation and bisphosphonates.

◆ **DON'T BE TRICKED**

- Suspect corticosteroid-induced myopathy in patients with continued or new-onset worsening of proximal muscle weakness despite normalization of muscle enzyme levels.
- CK elevation may occur several years before clinical manifestations of hypothyroidism. Always check TSH levels when evaluating myopathy.

❖ **Test Yourself**

A 34-year-old man has a 3-month history of pain and swelling of his hands, wrists, and ankles. He also has difficulty climbing stairs and reaching over his head; this weakness is not associated with pain.

ANSWER: The diagnosis is an overlap syndrome with elements of polymyositis and arthritis. Select an anti-RNP antibody assay.

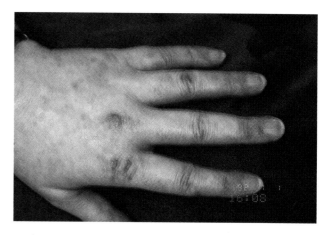

Gottron Papules: Red patches and plaques over the knuckles (Gottron papules) characteristic of dermatomyositis.

Vasculitis

Diagnosis

Vasculitis is an inflammation of blood vessels that causes stenosis, obstruction, or attenuation with subsequent tissue ischemia, aneurysms, or hemorrhage. This condition may be secondary to an underlying process or occur as a primary disease of unknown cause. Primary vasculitides may be categorized based on the size of the blood vessel that is predominantly involved, the pattern of organ involvement, and the histopathology.

Large-vessel vasculitis:

- Giant cell arteritis → older adults with headaches, scalp tenderness, jaw claudication, and visual symptoms. Obtain an ESR (>40 mm/h) and temporal artery biopsy.
- Polymyalgia rheumatica → older adults with aching and morning stiffness in the proximal muscles of the shoulder and hip girdle; may also develop in patients with giant cell arteritis or as a primary condition. Obtain an ESR (>40 mm/h).
- Takayasu arteritis → young women with arm/leg claudication, pulse deficits, vascular bruits, and asymmetric blood pressure readings. Obtain aortography.

Medium-vessel vasculitis:

- Polyarteritis nodosa → nonglomerular kidney disease, hypertension, mononeuritis multiplex, and skin lesions. Obtain hepatitis B serologic studies, biopsy of involved tissue (usually skin or testicle), and mesenteric angiography (aneurysms and stenoses).
- Thromboangiitis obliterans → distal-extremity ischemia associated with tobacco smoking. Obtain angiography to exclude atherosclerosis.

Small-vessel vasculitis:

- Granulomatosis with polyangiitis (also known as Wegener granulomatosis) → recurrent middle ear infections, destructive rhinitis or sinusitis, pulmonary infiltrates/cavities/hemoptysis, and glomerulonephritis. Obtain c-ANCA and antiproteinase-3 antibody assays; biopsy often required to make diagnosis.

- Churg-Strauss syndrome → asthma, eosinophilia, and pulmonary infiltrates/hemoptysis. Obtain p-ANCA and anti-myeloperoxidase antibody assays and biopsy.
- Microscopic polyangiitis→ pulmonary infiltrates/hemoptysis, glomerulonephritis. Obtain p-ANCA and antimyelo-peroxidase antibody assays and biopsy.
- Henoch-Schönlein purpura → palpable purpura, joint, and gut involvement and glomerulonephritis. Obtain skin biopsy (IgA immune complex deposition).
- Leukocytoclastic vasculitis → palpable purpura (lower legs), recent viral infection, or diagnosis of malignancy. Obtain skin biopsy.
- Cryoglobulinemic vasculitis → skin lesions (red macules, palpable purpura, nodules, or ulcers), glomerulonephritis, and elevated serum aminotransferase levels. Obtain serum cryoglobulins and hepatitis C serologic studies.
- Behçet syndrome → oral and genital ulcers; uveitis; and nonerosive, asymmetric oligoarthritis. This is a clinical diagnosis.
- Cogan syndrome → keratitis and acute hearing loss (clinical diagnosis).

Therapy

STUDY TABLE: Treatment of Vasculitis

Disease	Treatment
Takayasu arteritis	Prednisone
Giant cell arteritis	Prednisone; treat immediately and obtain biopsy in <2 weeks
Polymyalgia rheumatica	Low-dose prednisone
Granulomatosis with polyangiitis	Prednisone and cyclophosphamide
Microscopic polyangiitis	Prednisone and cyclophosphamide
Polyarteritis nodosa	Prednisone; lamivudine for concomitant hepatitis B virus infection
Churg-Strauss syndrome	Prednisone; cyclophosphamide added for severe, multiorgan disease
HCV-associated cryoglobulinemic vasculitis	Interferon alfa and ribavirin for underlying HCV infection
Leukocytoclastic vasculitis	NSAIDs, antihistamines, colchicine, or dapsone; if drug-associated, withdraw offending drug
Henoch-Schönlein purpura	Typically self-limited; corticosteroids for severe glomerulonephritis

❖ **Test Yourself**

A 72-year-old woman has had a headache for the past 8 days with blurred and double vision that lasted 15 minutes this morning.

ANSWER: The diagnosis is giant cell arteritis. Select immediate prednisone, and arrange for temporal artery biopsy.

A 32-year-old woman has a 6-month history of fever, myalgia, arthralgia, and weight loss. She is of Korean descent. Two days ago, she developed achy pain in her arms when working with her arms above her head.

ANSWER: The diagnosis is Takayasu arteritis. When ethnicity is identified, it is an essential key to the diagnosis.

Relapsing Polychondritis

Diagnosis

Relapsing polychondritis is a systemic inflammatory connective tissue disease characterized by inflammation and destruction of cartilaginous structures. Auricular pain and swelling are the most common presenting features. Characteristic findings are red, hot, painful ears; respiratory stridor caused by tracheal collapse; and saddle nose deformity. Relapsing polychondritis is often a clinical diagnosis, and biopsy of affected cartilage is confirmatory. Saddle nose deformity can also occur in syphilis and granulomatosis with polyangiitis.

Therapy

Corticosteroids are indicated for acute flares and NSAIDs for chronic disease management.

Regional Pain Syndromes

Elbow

Olecranon bursitis is inflammation of a bursa that lies in the posterior aspect of the elbow and presents as a fluid-filled mass. This condition can result from repetitive trauma, infection, or systemic inflammatory conditions. Olecranon bursitis does not cause restriction or pain with range of motion of the elbow.

Aspirate a bursa to analyze fluid for crystals and infection. NSAIDs and rest (if noninfectious) are first-line treatments.

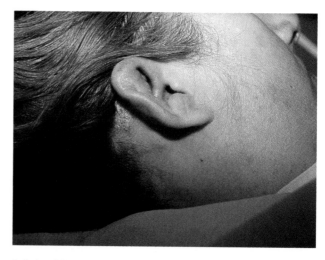

Polychondritis: Recurrent episodes of polychondritis involving the ear can permanently alter the structure of cartilage, resulting in a "cauliflower" appearance.

Epicondylitis involves inflammation or pain at the extensor radii tendon that inserts on the lateral or medial epicondyle of the humerus. Lateral epicondylitis ("tennis elbow") is caused by repetitive overuse that involves pronation and supination with the wrist flexed. Treatment involves immobilization of the elbow with a sling and anti-inflammatory medications.

Back

The initial evaluation of patients with low back pain should focus on whether a systemic disease is causing the pain and whether neurologic deficits require prompt surgical evaluation. Look for the "red flags" for low back pain suggesting a need for early imaging and intervention that are related to malignancy, spinal infection, fracture, and cauda equina syndrome. The symptoms of cauda equina syndrome include urinary retention or incontinence, diminished perineal sensation, and bilateral motor deficits. Perform diagnostic imaging and testing for patients with low back pain when severe or progressive neurologic deficits are present or when serious underlying conditions are suspected on the basis of history and physical examination.

Look for a herniated disk when acute back pain radiates down the leg and is associated with:

- positive straight leg raising
- weakness of the ankle and great toe dorsiflexion (L5)
- loss of ankle reflexes (S1) and sensory loss in the feet
- less commonly, loss of knee reflex (L4)

Spinal stenosis usually occurs in older adults and is characterized by neurogenic claudication—radiating back pain and lower extremity numbness—that is exacerbated by walking and spinal extension but improved by sitting and leaning forward. A wide-based gait and abnormal Romberg test are highly specific for spinal stenosis. MRI establishes the diagnosis.

Most patients with acute back pain, even those with sciatica, can be treated conservatively, and most are substantially improved within 1 to 3 months. Patients with sciatica assigned to early surgery and those assigned to conservative treatment have similar 1-year outcomes. Patients with spinal stenosis treated surgically have greater improvement in pain and function at 2 years compared with patients treated nonsurgically.

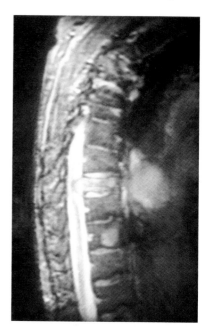

Collapsed Vertebral Body: Unenhanced T2-weighted MRI of the thoracic spine shows collapse of the vertebral body and compression of the spinal cord from posteriorly displaced bony fragments in a patient with metastatic breast cancer.

Neoplastic epidural spinal cord compression, including the cauda equina syndrome, is a surgical emergency. Begin management by administering dexamethasone and obtaining immediate MRI of the entire spine.

◆ **DON'T BE TRICKED**
- **Do not perform back imaging in the absence of "red flags."**
- **Select normal activities as tolerated for mechanical back pain and sciatica. Do not select prolonged bed rest or inactivity.**
- **Exercise is not beneficial for patients with acute low back pain.**

Knee

The most common cause of knee pain in patients aged <45 years, especially women, is the patellofemoral pain syndrome. The pain is peripatellar and exacerbated by overuse (running), descending stairs, or prolonged sitting. Diagnosis is confirmed by firmly compressing the patella against the femur and moving it up and down along the groove of the femur, reproducing pain. The condition is self-limited. Minimizing high-impact activity, performing quadriceps strengthening exercises, and treatment with NSAIDs improve symptoms.

Prepatellar bursitis is associated with anterior knee pain and swelling anterior to the patella and is often caused by trauma or repetitive kneeling. Always perform a joint aspiration to rule out infection if warmth and erythema are present. The anserine bursa, which is located medially about 6 cm below the joint line, can cause knee pain that is worse with activity and at night. Anserine bursitis is common in patients with osteoarthritis. In general, bursitis treatment includes:

- rest
- ice
- NSAIDs
- local corticosteroid injection for persistent symptoms

Iliotibial band syndrome is a common cause of knife-like lateral knee pain that occurs with vigorous flexion-extension activities of the knee (running). Treat with rest and stretching exercises.

Trauma may result in a fracture or ligament tear, which produces a noticeable "popping" sensation in 50% of patients. Typically, a large effusion collects rapidly. Check for stability of major ligaments by stressing the ligament; normal knees will have minimal give. Meniscal tears present with pain, locking, and clicking. Tenderness usually localizes to the joint line on the affected side, and tibial rotation as the leg is extended. No physical examination maneuver reliably rules in or rules out the diagnosis.

Hip

Look for trochanteric bursitis, characterized by lateral point tenderness and full range of motion except for abduction. Manage with local corticosteroid injection and stretching exercises. Consider osteonecrosis of the hip (continuous groin, thigh, and buttock pain) in patients who have SLE or sickle cell disease or who are taking or have ever taken corticosteroids. Diagnose osteonecrosis with hip MRI. Treatment of osteonecrosis is hip replacement. Consider bone metastases to the hip in patients with a history of cancer. Most patients with chronic hip pain have degenerative arthritis associated with other large-joint arthritis symptoms.

◆ **DON'T BE TRICKED**
- **True hip joint pain usually presents as groin pain.**
- **Do not select plain hip radiography to diagnose osteonecrosis.**

Ankle

Look for any petechiae or ecchymoses around the joint (suggesting bleeding in the region of a torn ligament) and any swelling or obvious deformity. A normal gait rules out fracture or severe sprain. Look for Achilles tendon rupture (a snapping sound followed by posterior ankle pain and inability to plantar flex) in older men who are taking a fluoroquinolone antibiotic.

◆ **DON'T BE TRICKED**

- **Select ankle radiography following trauma only if the patient cannot bear weight or if bone pain is localized to the lateral or medial malleolus, base of the fifth metatarsal, or the navicular bone.**

Foot

Plantar fasciitis, the most common cause of inferior heel pain, is characterized by pain that worsens with walking, especially with the first steps in the morning or after resting, in addition to localized tenderness along the plantar fascia or the calcaneal insertion site. Manage with stretching exercises.

Symptoms of a Morton neuroma include pain, numbness, and tingling in the forefoot, aggravated by walking on hard surfaces and wearing tight or high-heeled shoes. Compressing the forefoot reproduces the symptoms. Initial therapy includes wearing wider shoes and arch support.

◆ **DON'T BE TRICKED**

- **Do not order heel radiography for plantar fasciitis.**

Hand

de Quervain tenosynovitis is characterized by a positive Finkelstein test, in which the patient folds fingers over thumb to make a fist, and the examiner rotates the hand, stretching the tendon, which produces pain. Consider carpal tunnel syndrome, characterized by pain and paresthesias, particularly at night, localized to the thumb, first two fingers, and the radial half of the ring finger. Keep in mind secondary causes of carpal tunnel syndrome, such as hypothyroidism, diabetes mellitus, pregnancy, and RA of the wrist. Splinting at night plus NSAIDs is first-line therapy for carpal tunnel syndrome before surgical intervention. Carpal tunnel release surgery is indicated for severe carpal tunnel syndrome (by clinical or EMG evidence) and has an excellent outcome in more than 90% of patients.

Shoulder

Patients with rotator cuff tendinitis and subacromial bursitis typically have gradually worsening pain, especially with overhead activity that limits range of motion. The pain is worse at night and may extend down the arm but rarely below the elbow. Consider the following:

- Pain without weakness is consistent with tendinitis.
- Pain with weakness is consistent with a tendon tear.
- Severe pain and frank weakness (inability to maintain the arm at 90 degrees of abduction) suggest complete rupture of the rotator cuff tendon.

MRI is the most sensitive and specific imaging modality for complete or partial rotator cuff tears, although ultrasonography is more cost effective.

Look for:

- impingement syndrome when lateral deltoid pain is aggravated by reaching
- frozen shoulder when an impingement pain pattern is accompanied by stiffness and loss of active and passive external rotation or abduction
- rotator cuff tear when pain is associated with weakness and loss of active external rotation or abduction but intact passive motion
- anterior shoulder pain (acromioclavicular joint, glenohumeral joint, or long head of the biceps)

Acromioclavicular joint pain is localized to the distal end of the clavicle. Glenohumeral joint pain is aggravated by any movement. Pain due to biceps tendinitis is aggravated by lifting and wrist supination.

Rupture of the biceps tendon is often associated with a traumatic event or may be spontaneous. Physical examination findings include a visible or palpable mass near the elbow or mid arm ("Popeye the Sailor arm") and ecchymosis.

Initial therapy for rotator cuff tendinitis includes a trial of an NSAID and rest for 2 weeks. If no improvement occurs within 4 to 6 weeks, physical therapy, subacromial corticosteroid injection, or (rarely) surgery may help. Refer if 6 weeks of conservative therapy produces no response.

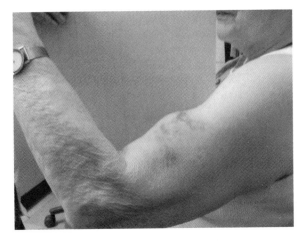

Biceps Tendon Rupture: Biceps tendon rupture showing a visible mass at the mid arm with associated ecchymoses.

◆ DON'T BE TRICKED

- Constant shoulder pain with normal shoulder examination suggests referred pain (e.g., Pancoast tumor) or neuropathic pain (e.g., cervical spine radiculopathy).

Fibromyalgia

Diagnostic criteria for fibromyalgia include the presence of widespread pain (above and below the waist) for at least 3 months. Also look for:

- fatigue
- difficulty sleeping
- subjective sensations of swelling
- dizziness
- cognitive difficulties

Nonpharmacologic therapy such as regular aerobic exercise and cognitive behavioral therapy is the cornerstone of treatment for fibromyalgia and should be initiated in all affected patients. Centrally acting medications and graded exercise are the first-line treatments of fibromyalgia. Medications that have demonstrated efficacy include tricyclic antidepressants and SSRIs. Pregabalin, milnacipran, and duloxetine are approved by the FDA for treating fibromyalgia.

◆ DON'T BE TRICKED

- Do not diagnose fibromyalgia in the presence of red flags such as fever, anemia, weight loss, and synovitis.
- Avoid opioids in the treatment of fibromyalgia.

Complex Regional Pain Syndrome

Diagnosis

Complex regional pain syndrome is characterized by pain, swelling, limited range of motion, vasomotor instability, skin changes, and patchy bone demineralization of the extremities. It typically follows an injury, surgery, MI, or stroke. Look for onset of pain after injury, persistence of pain, and at least two associated symptoms or signs, including:

- neuropathic pain (allodynia, hyperalgesia, hyperpathia)
- autonomic dysfunction of the affected extremity (edema, color changes, sweating)
- swelling

- dystrophy (hair loss, skin thinning, ulcers)
- movement disorder (difficulty initiating movement, dystonia, tremor, weakness)

No tests are needed for the diagnosis but usually are required to exclude underlying pathology. The finding of abnormal bone metabolism and osteoporosis by bone scan, bone densitometry, MRI, or plain radiography supports the diagnosis.

Therapy

Physical therapy is essential to preserve joint mobility and prevent contractures and osteoporosis. Corticosteroids may abort the syndrome if started soon after symptom development. Early sympathetic blockade is effective. Gabapentin and tricyclic antidepressants are adjuvants for pain control. Bisphosphonates are effective treatment for pain even in the absence of osteoporosis.

Familial Mediterranean Fever

Diagnosis

FMF occurs most often in persons from the Eastern Mediterranean basin. Characteristic findings are recurrent, self-limited attacks of fever, serositis (abdominal or pleuritic pain), arthritis, and rashes that last 3 to 4 days. Laboratory findings include an elevated ESR and serum CRP concentration, positive serum amyloid A (AA) protein, proteinuria, and the Mediterranean fever (*MEFV*) gene.

Therapy

Begin colchicine for confirmed or suspected FMF to prevent symptomatic attacks and development of AA amyloidosis.

❖ **Test Yourself**

A 23-year-old woman has episodic fever and abdominal pain every 1 to 2 months, lasting 2 to 3 days per episode. She is well between episodes. She is of Ashkenazi Jewish descent. Physical examination and imaging studies are normal.
ANSWER: The diagnosis is FMF.

Adult-Onset Still Disease

Diagnosis

The clinical features of adult-onset Still disease (AOSD) include a quotidian fever in which the temperature usually spikes once daily and then returns to subnormal; fatigue, malaise, arthralgia, and myalgia; proteinuria and serositis; and evanescent pink rash. Joint manifestations include an intense but typically nonerosive inflammatory arthritis. Ferritin levels are elevated in AOSD, and serum levels >2500 ng/mL are highly specific for this condition and reflect disease activity.

Therapy

NSAIDs are generally used as first-line agents in management, but corticosteroids may be helpful in patients whose disease is refractory to NSAIDs. In patients with refractory disease, therapy with methotrexate, a TNF-α inhibitor, or the interleukin-1 receptor antagonist anakinra may be helpful.

Serologic Studies in Rheumatologic Disorders

STUDY TABLE: Serologic Studies/Associations

Test	Association (does not establish diagnosis)
Anticentromere pattern of ANA	CREST syndrome/limited cutaneous systemic sclerosis
Anti-dsDNA antibody	SLE
Anti–smooth muscle antibody	Autoimmune hepatitis
Anti-La/SSB antibody	Sjögren syndrome, neonatal SLE
Anti-RNP antibody	Mixed connective tissue disease
Anti–Scl-70 antibody	Scleroderma/diffuse cutaneous systemic sclerosis
Antihistone antibody	Drug-induced SLE
Anti-Ro/SSA antibody	Sjögren syndrome, neonatal heart block, subacute cutaneous lupus
c-ANCA	Granulomatosis with polyangiitis
p-ANCA	Churg-Strauss syndrome and microscopic polyangiitis
Anti-Jo-1 antibody	Polymyositis
Anti-CCP antibody	RA

CREST = calcinosis, Raynaud phenomenon, esophageal dysmotility, sclerodactyly, and telangiectasia.

Women's Health

Breast Cancer

Prevention

Consider tamoxifen for women between 35 and 60 years of age with a 5-year breast cancer risk ≥1.66% based on the Gail model. The risk of endometrial cancer and thromboembolic disease increases in postmenopausal women treated with tamoxifen. Raloxifene carries a lesser risk but is slightly less effective in breast cancer prevention. Bilateral prophylactic mastectomy is offered to women with any of the following characteristics:

- a family history of multiple relatives with premenopausal or bilateral breast cancer
- the *BRCA1* or *BRCA2* gene mutation
- the *p53* gene mutation (Li-Fraumeni syndrome)

To decrease the risk of ovarian and breast cancer, prophylactic oophorectomy can be offered to women who have tested positive for a *BRCA1* or *BRCA2* gene mutation after they have completed childbearing.

◆ DON'T BE TRICKED

- Testing for the breast cancer susceptibility gene (*BRCA*) is recommended only for women whose family history suggests increased risk for mutations in the *BRCA1* or *BRCA2* gene (first-degree relative, or two second-degree relatives on the same side of the family, with breast or ovarian cancer).

Screening

Annual screening mammography should begin at age 40 to 50 years. No consensus exists regarding an upper age limit for discontinuing screening mammography.

Cervical Cancer

Prevention

A vaccine against high-risk HPV has been approved for males and females aged 9 to 26 years and should ideally be administered before onset of sexual activity. The presence of previous HPV disease is not a contraindication to primary vaccination.

Screening

The USPSTF recommends cervical cancer screening in women aged 21 to 65 years with cytology (Pap test) every 3 years. The screening interval can be increased to every 5 years in women aged 30 to 65 years by combining cytology and HPV testing. The USPSTF recommends against routine screening in women younger than 21 years, older than 65 years (provided normal results were obtained on previous screenings and patient is not otherwise at high risk), and in women who have had a hysterectomy.

- If the cytology results are negative but high-risk HPV DNA testing is positive, both tests should be repeated at 6 to 12 months.
- If HPV DNA test remains persistently positive, refer for colposcopy.

- If the cytology result is atypical squamous cells of undetermined significance (ASUS), test for HPV infection (alternatively, repeat Pap test at 6 and 12 months and refer for colposcopy if results are grade ASUS or higher).
- If the cytology is positive for high-grade squamous intraepithelial lesions, squamous cell cancer (SCC), or atypical glandular cells, refer for colposcopy regardless of HPV results.

◆ **DON'T BE TRICKED**

- **HPV vaccine does not protect against all HPV infections and does not treat existing HPV.**
- **HPV vaccine can be given to patients who are HIV positive and otherwise immunosuppressed.**

Vaginitis and Cervicitis

Screening

Screen all sexually active women age ≤25 years and all women age >25 years with risk factors for *Chlamydia* infection.

Diagnosis

Vaginitis is characterized by vaginal irritation, pruritus, pain, or unusual discharge. The three most common infectious causes of acute vaginitis are bacterial vaginosis, vulvovaginal candidiasis, and *Trichomonas.* Trichomoniasis is the only cause of vaginitis that is sexually transmitted. Noninfectious causes include allergic reactions to vaginal contraceptives or other products, such as douches, tampons, or soap; coitus-induced friction; or postmenopausal atrophy.

STUDY TABLE: Diagnosis of Vaginitis	
Test	**Characteristics**
Physical examination	Bacterial vaginosis: Thin, white discharge with "fishy" odor but without irritation or pain
	Candidiasis: External and internal erythema with itching and irritation; nonodorous, white, curd-like discharge
	Trichomoniasis: Frothy, yellow discharge; erythema of the vagina and cervix ("strawberry cervix")
Vaginal pH (normal <4.5)	Bacterial vaginosis and trichomoniasis: >4.5
	Candidiasis: <4.5
"Whiff" test	Bacterial vaginosis: "Fishy" odor after adding KOH
Microscopic examination of vaginal fluid	Bacterial vaginosis: Squamous epithelial cells covered with bacteria that obscure edges ("clue cells")
	Candidiasis: Budding yeast and pseudohyphae
	Trichomoniasis: Motile trichomonads

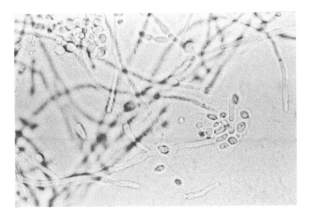

Candida albicans: A KOH wet mount shows budding yeast and pseudohyphae, indicating *Candida albicans*.

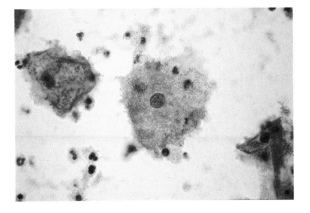

Clue Cell: An epithelial cell with borders that are studded by bacteria (clue cell) indicates bacterial vaginosis.

Cervicitis may be asymptomatic or symptomatic. When present, symptoms include vaginal discharge, postcoital bleeding, dysuria, and dyspareunia. The presence of endocervical mucopus defines cervicitis. Easily induced endocervical bleeding also may occur. Cervical motion tenderness suggests pelvic inflammatory disease. Cervicitis can be caused by *Chlamydia*, *Neisseria gonorrhoeae*, and *Trichomonas*. Definitive diagnosis of *Neisseria* and *Chlamydia* can be made by nucleic acid amplification test performed on vaginal or urine specimens (see also Infectious Diseases, *Neisseria gonorrhoeae* Infection).

Therapy

STUDY TABLE: Treating Vaginitis, *Chlamydia* Infection, and Gonorrhea	
If the diagnosis is...	**Treat with...**
Vaginal candidiasis	Topical imidazole (e.g., clotrimazole, miconazole)
	Single dose of fluconazole (contraindicated during pregnancy); less effective in complicated conditions (e.g., diabetes, HIV infection)
Recurrent vaginal candidiasis	Weekly oral fluconazole for 6 months (correct any underlying precipitating factor, such as uncontrolled hyperglycemia)
Bacterial vaginosis	Oral or topical metronidazole
Trichomoniasis	Oral metronidazole (also for male partner)
Urogenital, rectal, and pharyngeal gonorrhea	Ceftriaxone (safe during pregnancy) or cefixime (also for male partner)
	Treat for *Chlamydia* as well (see below)
Urogenital, rectal, and pharyngeal gonorrhea and penicillin allergy	Single dose of azithromycin
Chlamydia infection	Doxycycline for 7 days or a single dose of azithromycin (preferred therapy in pregnancy); also treat male partner

◆ DON'T BE TRICKED

- Because vaginal yeast is found in 10% to 20% of healthy women, the identification of *Candida* species in patients without symptoms does not require treatment.
- *Lactobacillus* oral or vaginal tablets taken after antibiotic therapy do not prevent the occurrence of candidiasis.

❖ Test Yourself

A 21-year-old woman has a vaginal discharge and odor. Pelvic examination shows a thin, white homogeneous vaginal discharge with a normal cervix and normal vaginal mucosa. Wet mount is negative for *Trichomonas* and *Candida*. Vaginal pH is 6.0.

ANSWER: The diagnosis is bacterial vaginosis.

Genital Herpes

Diagnosis

Genital herpes (HSV infection) lesions typically begin as vesicles that ulcerate and become quite painful. The initial infection is often the most severe and can be accompanied by local lymphadenopathy and systemic symptoms. Recurrences, typically less severe, are usually subclinical but nonetheless infectious. Viral shedding can occur for 2 to 3 weeks after lesions appear, and asymptomatic viral shedding can occur in patients even in the absence of recent lesions. Patients with late-stage HIV infection are prone to developing frequent recurrences and chronic mucocutaneous ulceration (not typical vesicles).

The diagnosis of genital herpes is often suspected clinically but should be confirmed by viral culture, HSV antigen detection, or PCR of HSV DNA.

Also test for syphilis and HIV. HSV increases rates of HIV transmission.

Be alert for two additional illnesses linked to HSV recurrences: benign recurrent lymphocytic meningitis (Mollaret meningitis) and recurrent erythema multiforme.

- Do not select the Tzanck test (showing multinucleated giant cells) to diagnose HSV infection; the test is neither specific nor sensitive.

Therapy

Prescribe oral acyclovir, valacyclovir, or famciclovir. Increase doses of antiviral agents for patients with AIDS who do not respond to standard doses. Order resistance testing for patients who do not respond to high-dose therapy. Patient-initiated therapy is appropriate for infrequent recurrences. Chronic suppressive therapy is indicated for frequent recurrences ($\geq$6 per year) in nonimmunosuppressed patients; attempt to wean from medication after 1 year.

- Topical acyclovir is not effective for treating genital herpes.
- A positive HSV-2 antibody test indicates only previous infection and may be negative in primary infection.

Pelvic Inflammatory Disease

Diagnosis

PID is a polymicrobial infection of the endometrium, fallopian tubes, and ovaries that is diagnosed by the presence of abdominal discomfort, uterine or adnexal tenderness, or cervical motion tenderness. Other criteria include:

- temperature >38.3 °C (101.0 °F)
- cervical or vaginal mucopurulent discharge
- leukocytes in vaginal secretions
- documentation of gonorrhea or *Chlamydia* infection

PID most often occurs within 7 days of the onset of menses. Gonorrhea and *Chlamydia* are the primary causes of PID, but studies also implicate "bacterial vaginosis" organisms. Order PCR to diagnose *N. gonorrhoeae* and *Chlamydia trachomatis*. All sexually active women should have a pregnancy test to rule out ectopic pregnancy. Measure serum aminotransferase levels in patients with right upper quadrant abdominal pain (gonorrhea or *Chlamydia* perihepatitis). Complications include infertility, ectopic pregnancy, and chronic pelvic pain.

Therapy

Outpatient treatment is as effective as inpatient treatment for women with mild-to-moderate PID. Acceptable treatment regimens include single parenteral doses of ceftriaxone, cefotaxime, or ceftizoxime plus doxycycline with or without metronidazole for 14 days.

Choose hospitalization for the following scenarios:

- uncertain diagnosis
- no clinical improvement after 48 to 72 hours of antibiotic treatment
- inability to tolerate oral antibiotics
- severe illness with nausea, vomiting, or high fever
- suspected pelvic abscess
- pregnancy
- nonadherence to outpatient therapy

Inpatients are treated with parenteral cefoxitin or cefotetan and doxycycline. If the patient is nonresponsive to antibiotics in 48 to 72 hours, choose ultrasonography for evaluation of possible tubo-ovarian abscess.

◆ DON'T BE TRICKED

- Because of increasing rates of *N. gonorrhoeae* fluoroquinolone resistance, do not select fluoroquinolones for empiric treatment of PID.

Primary Amenorrhea

Diagnosis

Primary amenorrhea is the failure of menstruation (never occurred). Approximately 50% of primary amenorrhea is caused by chromosomal disorders.

STUDY TABLE: Most Common Causes of Primary Amenorrhea	
Diagnosis	**Characteristics**
Turner syndrome	45 XO karyotype
	Lack of secondary sexual characteristics, growth retardation, webbed neck, and frequent skeletal abnormalities
Hypothalamic/pituitary disorders	Functional (stress, excessive exercise, weight loss), developmental defects of cranial midline structures, tumors, or infiltrative disorders (sarcoidosis)
Androgen-resistance syndromes	XY karyotype
	Absence of or minimal pubic and axillary hair, a shallow vagina, and often a labial mass (testes)
Polycystic ovary syndrome	Most commonly associated with secondary amenorrhea but can cause primary amenorrhea. See "Polycystic Ovary Syndrome"

Primary ovarian failure is diagnosed by an elevated FSH level. If the FSH is low or normal, obtain prolactin and thyroid-stimulating hormone (TSH) levels.

Secondary Amenorrhea

Diagnosis

Look for absence of menstruation for three cycle intervals or 6 consecutive months in women with previous menstrual flow. All women with secondary amenorrhea should be tested for pregnancy, the most common etiology. Premature ovarian failure may result from:

- surgical oophorectomy
- chemotherapy
- radiation
- autoimmune destruction of ovarian tissue

Primary ovarian failure is diagnosed by an elevated FSH. Vaginal bleeding will not occur after a progesterone challenge because estrogen levels are low. But bleeding will occur after estrogen priming followed by a progesterone challenge, demonstrating the integrity of the uterine lining and outflow tract.

When amenorrhea is associated with a low or inappropriately normal FSH level, consider PCOS, hypothalamic amenorrhea, androgen or prolactin excess, and hypothyroidism.

STUDY TABLE: Secondary Amenorrhea		
Diagnosis	**Characteristics**	**Evaluation**
PCOS	Ovulatory dysfunction, evidence of hyperandrogenism and polycystic ovaries on ultrasonography See "Polycystic Ovary Syndrome"	Mild elevation in testosterone and DHEAS (not needed for diagnosis)
Hyperprolactinemia	May be associated with galactorrhea Related to medications (tricyclic antidepressants, phenothiazines, and metoclopramide) and tumors that secrete prolactin or compress the pituitary stalk, history of cranial radiotherapy	First rule out hypothyroidism. If TSH is normal and serum prolactin level >100 ng/mL, obtain brain MRI to diagnose tumor
Hypothalamic amenorrhea	Most commonly functional (related to stress, weight loss, excessive exercise)	Low or normal LH level, and low estradiol level
Hypothyroidism	Causes secondary increase in serum prolactin levels	High TSH
Adrenal tumor	Signs of hyperandrogenism and virilization, usually acute onset and severe	Decreased LH and FSH, increased or normal estradiol, and increased testosterone and DHEAS levels
Sheehan syndrome (postpartum pituitary necrosis)	History of difficult delivery (blood loss, hypotension) and inability to breastfeed	Varying levels of panhypopituitarism
Asherman syndrome (uterine synechiae)	History of previous dilatation and curettage amenorrhea due to fibrous uterine scarring	Normal LH and estradiol levels; no response to estrogen and progesterone challenge

Therapy

Treat the underlying disorder. Prevent osteoporosis by choosing estrogen and progesterone replacement until menstruation returns to normal. For suspected functional etiology, choose reduced exercise, improved nutrition, and attention to emotional needs as helpful adjuncts.

Polycystic Ovary Syndrome

Diagnosis

PCOS is the most common etiology of hirsutism with oligomenorrhea. Symptoms normally start at puberty or several years later and are slowly progressive. Diagnosis requires two of the following:

- ovulatory dysfunction (amenorrhea, oligomenorrhea, infertility)
- laboratory or clinical evidence of hyperandrogenism (hirsutism, acne)
- ultrasonographic evidence of polycystic ovaries

Insulin resistance is an important feature of the disorder, as is being overweight/obese. A mild elevation in testosterone and DHEAS levels and an LH/FSH ratio greater than 2:1 are typical.

◆ DON'T BE TRICKED
- **Do not routinely order testosterone or DHEAS testing, because PCOS is a clinical diagnosis and laboratory evaluation is only necessary when androgen-producing neoplasms must be ruled out.**

Therapy

Instruct patients in intensive lifestyle modification to reduce weight, control abdominal obesity, and restore insulin sensitivity. Treatment follows two models:

- If fertility is not desired, first-line treatment of hirsutism is spironolactone and oral contraceptives. Hormonal therapy can be used in combination with mechanical methods to manage hirsutism.

- If fertility is desired, ovulation induction can be brought about with clomiphene citrate. Metformin (not FDA approved for this indication) improves ovulation rates.

❖ **Test Yourself**

A 27-year-old woman has had oligomenorrhea since age 14 years. She also has acanthosis nigricans and hirsutism but no galactorrhea; she is obese. She does not desire pregnancy.

ANSWER: The diagnosis is PCOS. Begin intensive lifestyle modification, oral contraceptives, and spironolactone.

Infertility

Diagnosis

Infertility is defined as the inability to conceive after 1 year of intercourse without contraception. Regular menses is correlated with regular ovulation. If necessary, documenting an LH surge at presumed ovulation and an elevated serum progesterone level 1 week later confirms ovulation. Semen analysis can be performed at any time. The role of hysterosalpingography is not completely defined.

Abnormal Uterine Bleeding

Diagnosis

Bleeding is excessive, scanty, or occurs outside the normal menstrual cycle. Pregnancy must always be considered. Uterine fibroids are the most common cause of menorrhagia. Besides conditions responsible for secondary amenorrhea, disorders listed below may cause abnormal uterine bleeding.

STUDY TABLE: Selected Causes of Abnormal Uterine Bleeding		
Disorder	**Characteristics**	**Evaluation**
Anatomic lesions	Endometrial polyps, uterine fibroids (leiomyomata), and endometrial hyperplasia or carcinoma	Pelvic examination, Pap test, and a bimanual examination
		Ultrasonographic imaging
		Endometrial biopsy if endometrium is 4-5 mm in thickness or is heterogeneous
von Willebrand disease	20% of adolescents with menorrhagia	Bleeding time, aPTT, and functional and quantitative measurement of von Willebrand factor
Kidney failure	Interferes with estrogen clearance	Serum creatinine level
	Associated with abnormalities in platelet function	
Cirrhosis	Reduced ability to metabolize estrogen	Liver chemistry tests
Thyroid disease	Scanty or heavy menstrual bleeding	TSH level

Therapy

Combination oral contraceptives can regularize anovulatory bleeding. In patients who are at risk for endometrial hyperplasia (postmenopausal unopposed estrogen stimulation, PCOS), obtain a biopsy before hormonal manipulation. NSAIDs inhibit endometrial prostaglandins and decrease blood flow. Surgery is indicated when bleeding is excessive and/or unresponsive to medical therapy or when a cervical or endometrial polyp, cancer, or fibroid is present.

Premenstrual Syndrome

Diagnosis

PMS is characterized by physical and behavioral symptoms that occur within 5 days of the onset of menses. The most common symptoms of PMS are abdominal bloating, fatigue, breast tenderness, labile mood, irritability, tension, depressed mood, increased appetite, forgetfulness, and difficulty concentrating. Premenstrual dysphoric disorder (PMDD) is a severe form of PMS characterized by anger, irritability, and internal tension. Patients are asked to record symptoms prospectively for 2 months. If symptoms persist during the follicular phase of the menstrual cycle, choose evaluation for a mood or anxiety disorder.

Therapy

Mild symptoms can be treated with exercise and vitamin B_6 supplementation. Fluoxetine, sertraline, and paroxetine are effective first-line treatments for PMS and PMDD.

Menopause

Diagnosis

When menstruation ceases, an FSH level >30 milliunits/mL is considered diagnostic of menopause, but this finding is not usually needed for diagnosis. Perimenopause is marked by menstrual cycle irregularity, but approximately 30% of women experience the hallmarks of menopause, hot flushes and night sweats, before menstrual changes. Estrogen deficiency can lead to dyspareunia, atrophic vaginitis, dysuria, urgency, and frequency. Menopause is defined as the time following 12 months of amenorrhea.

Vaginal epithelial cells contain less glycogen, resulting in increased vaginal pH and increased growth of *Escherichia coli*. Loss of lactobacilli leaves this pale, thin, friable tissue vulnerable to infection and ulceration.

Therapy

Vaginal moisturizers or lubricants are indicated for urogenital atrophy. Exercise and cessation of cigarette smoking may relieve menopausal symptoms. Use short-term hormone replacement therapy (2 to 3 years) only for patients with intolerable vasomotor symptoms. Gabapentin, serotonin-norepinephrine reuptake inhibitors (SNRIs), or SSRIs are alternatives for reducing hot flushes. Local (topical) estrogen helps relieve dyspareunia and vaginal dryness.

◆ DON'T BE TRICKED

- **Do not prescribe hormone replacement therapy for prevention or relief of urinary incontinence, decreased libido, or cardiovascular risk, which could even increase with this therapy.**
- **Do not select phytoestrogens and black cohosh for the treatment of menopausal symptoms. They are no more effective than placebo.**

Primary Dysmenorrhea

Diagnosis

Patients with a history of menstrual pain that begins within 1 to 2 years of menarche and sometimes worsens over time usually have primary dysmenorrhea, in which no pathologic cause for the menstrual pain exists. An underlying cause for dysmenorrhea is likely in the setting of noncyclic pain, abnormal discharge, dyspareunia, or heavy or irregular bleeding.

Therapy

NSAIDs are an effective first-line therapy. For women who are not trying to conceive, oral contraceptive pills are also effective therapy, as are transcutaneous electrical nerve stimulation and vitamin B_1.

Endometriosis

Diagnosis

Endometriosis is characterized by ectopic endometrial implants, usually in the pelvis, but they can be found anywhere and cause cyclic bleeding: lungs (hemoptysis), CNS (catamenial headache), or rectum (rectal bleeding during menses). It is a common cause of chronic pelvic pain that is worse just before and during menses and is associated with dysmenorrhea. Watch for a history of pelvic infections or primary infertility. Physical examination findings may be normal or may include abdominal masses and tenderness and abnormalities of the cervix, uterus, and adnexa. Also look for abnormalities of uterosacral ligaments on bimanual examination.

The lesions can be visualized by laparoscopy, the gold standard for diagnosis, but it is not required for medical treatment when other causes of pelvic pain have been ruled out. All patients with chronic pelvic pain require a urine pregnancy test and transvaginal ultrasonography. Cervical culture or DNA probe is indicated for patients at risk for *Chlamydia* infection and gonorrhea.

STUDY TABLE: Differential Diagnosis of Pelvic Pain	
If you see this...	**Diagnose this...**
Acute pelvic or abdominal pain, vaginal discharge, and fever	PID, usually caused by *Chlamydia* infection or gonorrhea
Pelvic heaviness, abnormal uterine bleeding, infertility, and enlarged uterus on bimanual examination or ultrasonography	Uterine fibroids
History of sexual abuse and normal physical examination and ultrasonography	Chronic pelvic pain
Adolescents with dysmenorrhea	Primary dysmenorrhea
Urinary frequency, urgency, nocturia, and dysuria	Interstitial cystitis
Suprapubic pain possibly relieved with voiding	
Examination that shows vestibular and suprapubic tenderness	

◆ DON'T BE TRICKED

- Endometriosis does not cause fever or vaginal discharge.

Therapy

NSAIDs are first-line therapy, followed by oral contraceptives (if pregnancy is not desired) when NSAIDs are ineffective. Severe symptoms call for gonadotropin-releasing hormone agonists for pain relief. Surgical ablation or resection of endometrial tissue is recommended for patients who do not respond to conservative measures. However, women with noncyclic pain, migratory pain, and normal pelvic examinations are unlikely to benefit from surgery.

Counseling is important for abused women with chronic pelvic pain syndrome.

Osteoporosis

Screening

DEXA is indicated for all women >65 years of age and in women <65 years with one additional risk factor for osteoporosis:

- Glucocorticoid therapy
- Low body weight
- Current cigarette smoking
- Alcohol use
- Previous fragility fracture
- Family history of hip fracture

In women, the two most important risk factors are increasing age and previous fracture. Screen men and women with risk factors for secondary osteoporosis (corticosteroid use, hyperparathyroidism, androgen deprivation therapy, malabsorption).

◆ **DON'T BE TRICKED**

- **Do not repeat annual DEXA in women with normal DEXA results without risk factors. Although the optimal screening interval is unknown, most experts recommend 3 to 5 years for normal women with no risk factors.**

Diagnosis

Osteoporosis is a silent skeletal disorder characterized by compromised bone strength and an increased predisposition to fractures. A DEXA T-score of −1.0 to −2.4 defines osteopenia. A score of ≤−2.5 defines osteoporosis. Osteoporosis is also diagnosed by a history of fragility fracture.

The most common cause of osteoporosis in women is estrogen deficiency. Secondary causes include:

- hyperthyroidism, hyperparathyroidism, Cushing syndrome
- malabsorption (Crohn disease, intestinal resection, celiac disease)
- rheumatoid arthritis
- medications (excessive thyroid hormone, corticosteroids, phenobarbital, phenytoin, thiazolidinediones)
- multiple myeloma
- chronic kidney disease, chronic liver disease
- vitamin D deficiency

Reasonable tests include: CBC; TSH; calcium, phosphorus, and creatinine levels; liver chemistry tests; ESR; serum 25-hydroxyvitamin D (if vitamin D deficiency is suspected) level; and tissue transglutaminase antibodies (if celiac disease is suspected). In the absence of fractures, primary osteoporosis is associated with no abnormalities on laboratory testing.

Therapy

Encourage all patients to stop smoking, reduce alcohol intake, and begin resistance exercises. Exposure to sunlight is especially important for home-bound persons or nursing-home residents. Recommend calcium intake of 1200 to 1500 mg/d. Recommended vitamin D intake is 400 to 600 units/d for all adults age >50 years or 800 units/d for those at risk for deficiency, including older, chronically ill, home-bound, or institutionalized persons.

Antiresorptive therapy is indicated in patients with osteoporosis or in patients with osteopenia if additional high-risk factors are present, or in any patient with a previous fragility vertebral or hip fracture. The Fracture Risk Assessment Tool (FRAX) estimates the 10-year probability of hip fracture and major osteoporotic fracture. Treatment is cost effective when the 10-year risk of fractures is approximately 2.5% to 5%. Choose the following treatments:

- alendronate, ibandronate, or risedronate as first-line therapy
- raloxifene for patients who cannot tolerate bisphosphonates
- teriparatide (synthetic recombinant human parathyroid hormone 1-34) for severe osteoporosis with fractures
- calcitonin for pain from osteoporotic fractures

Bisphosphonates are taken on an empty stomach, and patients must remain upright for at least 30 minutes. These agents are contraindicated in patients with chronic kidney disease or esophageal disease. IV zoledronate (once yearly) or IV ibandronate (once every 3 months) are alternative dosing options.

No recommended duration of therapy is available. Stopping therapy after 5 years is reasonable in women who have a stable BMI, no history of fracture, and are at low risk for fracture. The duration of the drug holiday is unknown but may be determined by changes in DEXA measurements.

Drugs for osteoporosis have various adverse effects. Oral bisphosphonate therapy may lead to erosive esophagitis, and IV bisphosphonate therapy can lead to osteonecrosis of the jaw in patients with cancer. Raloxifene is associated with thromboembolic disease. Teriparatide is associated with osteosarcoma. Treatment with teriparatide should be limited to 2 years.

◆ DON'T BE TRICKED

- Do not select hormone replacement therapy for osteoporosis.
- Do not combine teriparatide with a bisphosphonate.
- IV bisphosphonates are contraindicated in patients with severe hypocalcemia and chronic kidney disease.
- Raloxifene has not been shown to reduce hip fracture risk.

Follow-up

DEXA should be done 12 to 24 months after beginning therapy for osteoporosis.

❖ Test Yourself

An 82-year-old woman has been taking thyroid hormone since age 31 years. She has lost about 7.6 cm (3.0 in) in height. Serum TSH level is <0.01 microunits/mL (normal 0.5 to 5.0 microunits/mL).

ANSWER: The diagnosis is thyroid hormone–induced osteoporosis. Reduce the thyroid hormone dose and schedule DEXA.

Urinary Incontinence

Diagnosis

Normal bladder filling and emptying require accommodation of increased bladder volumes at a low intravesicular pressure, a bladder outlet that is closed at rest and remains closed during increased abdominal pressure, and the absence of involuntary bladder contractions.

STUDY TABLE: Diagnosis and Treatment of Urinary Incontinence		
If you see this...	**Diagnose this...**	**Choose this...**
Daytime frequency, nocturia, bothersome urgency	Urge incontinence, overactive bladder dysfunction	Bladder training, anticholinergics (oxybutynin, tolterodine)
Involuntary release of urine secondary to effort or exertion (sneezing, coughing, physical exertion)	Stress incontinence	Pelvic floor muscle training for women (Kegel exercises), biofeedback, surgery in recalcitrant cases
Nearly constant dribbling of urine, incomplete emptying of bladder, postvoiding residual urine	Overflow incontinence	Timed urination, intermittent bladder catheterization
Unable to get to bathroom on time because of mental or physical limitations	Functional incontinence	Portable commode, prompted urination, treatment of underlying disorders

Therapy

Begin nondrug therapy in all patients with urinary incontinence regardless of what other interventions may eventually be needed. Evaluate for other reversible factors contributing to symptoms, such as diuretics or poorly controlled diabetes.

- Oxybutynin and tolterodine provide minor relief of urge incontinence but are associated with side effects related to anticholinergic properties.
- Stress incontinence cannot be treated with medications. Topical estrogen helps women with stress incontinence and atrophic vaginitis. Pelvic floor muscle training and biofeedback is also effective for stress incontinence.
- Imipramine (not FDA approved for this indication) may offer some benefit for combined urge and stress incontinence, although anticholinergic side effects are a factor.
- Prompted urination (asking about incontinence, reminding patient to use the toilet, positive feedback for continence and toilet use) is effective for functional incontinence (inability to get to the toilet because mental or physical disability).

◆ DON'T BE TRICKED

- **Do not prescribe systemic estrogen-progestin therapy because it can worsen stress and urge incontinence.**
- **Do not order urodynamic testing because outcomes are no better than those associated with management based on clinical evaluation alone.**

❖ Test Yourself

A 78-year-old woman has urinary urgency, nocturia, and urine loss with coughing and sneezing. Her medical history includes HF and glaucoma.

ANSWER: The diagnosis is combined stress and urge incontinence. Begin pelvic muscle exercises and bladder training techniques. Imipramine is contraindicated because of its anticholinergic effects.

Domestic Violence

Diagnosis

Physical and psychological domestic violence are associated with significant mental and physical health consequences for both male and female victims. Abuse frequently starts or increases during pregnancy.

Characteristic findings:

- exacerbations or poor control of chronic medical conditions
- seeming nonadherence to medications
- abdominal pain
- sleep or appetite disturbances, fatigue, reduced concentration, or chronic pain
- depression, anxiety, acute or posttraumatic stress, somatization, and eating disorders
- suicide attempts and substance abuse
- frequent appointment changes
- STDs, HIV, unplanned pregnancies
- visible bruises or injuries

Assess the risk of homicide, suicide, or serious injury. Inquire about:

- escalating threats or abuse and escalating level of fear
- stalking
- weapons, especially firearms, in the home

- sexual assault and abuse during pregnancy
- recent separation or abuser's awareness of impending separation

Therapy

Initiate safety planning. Determine if the patient wants to leave home, return home, or have the abuser removed from his or her household. Refer the patient to a domestic violence advocate.

Breast Lump

Diagnosis

A dominant breast mass is defined as a lump or suspicious change in the breast texture that is discrete and distinctly different from the rest of the surrounding breast tissue. The differential diagnosis of a dominant breast mass includes cysts, fibroadenomas, fibrocystic changes, fat necrosis, carcinoma in situ, and invasive carcinoma.

STUDY TABLE: Evaluation of Breast Mass

Breast Finding	Diagnostic Testing
Palpable lump or mass and age <30 years	Consider observation to assess resolution within 1 or 2 menstrual cycles.
	If persistent, choose ultrasonography.
	If simple cyst on ultrasound, aspirate and repeat clinical breast examination in 4-6 weeks.
	If complex cyst on ultrasound, perform mammography and fine-needle aspiration or core-needle biopsy.
	If aspirate fluid is bloody or a mass persists following aspiration, choose mammography and biopsy.
	If solid on ultrasonography, choose mammography and obtain tissue diagnosis (fine-needle aspiration, core biopsy, or surgical excision).
Palpable lump or mass and age ≥30 years	Mammography: If BI-RADS category 1-3 (benign or close follow-up recommended), obtain ultrasonography and follow protocol above. If BI-RADS category 4-5 (suspicious or highly suspicious), obtain tissue diagnosis.
Nipple discharge, no mass, any age	Bilateral, milky: Pregnancy test (if negative, choose endocrine evaluation).
	Persistent, spontaneous, unilateral, one duct, or serous/bloody: Cytology is optional; choose mammography and surgical referral for duct exploration.
Skin changes (erythema, peau d'orange, scaling, nipple excoriation, eczema) and age <30 years	Consider mastitis and treat with antibiotics if appropriate and reevaluate in 2 weeks. Otherwise, evaluate as below.
Skin changes (erythema, peau d'orange, scaling, nipple excoriation, eczema) and age ≥30 years	Perform bilateral mammography.
	If normal, obtain skin biopsy.
	If abnormal or indeterminate, obtain needle biopsy or excision (also consider skin punch biopsy).

BI-RADS = Breast Imaging Reporting and Data System.

◆ DON'T BE TRICKED

- Do not stop the evaluation of a breast mass if mammogram is normal. Ultrasonography is followed by aspiration of cysts or biopsy of solid breast masses regardless of mammogram results.

Contraception

Key Considerations

The combination estrogen-progestin OCPs, containing ethinyl estradiol and one of various progestins, are very effective. Use is associated with reduced risks of ovarian cancer and endometrial cancer. Users experience less acne and reduced severity of abnormal uterine bleeding, menstrual blood flow, and anemia.

The risk for VTE is higher in patients who smoke and have thrombophilia, although routine screening for thrombophilia is not recommended. The risks for MI and ischemic stroke are higher in patients with diabetes or hypercholesterolemia. Breast cancer risk is controversial. OCPs are safe in nonsmoking women older than the age of 35 years until menopause.

Other hormonal contraceptives include the topical patch, vaginal ring, progestin-only pill, and medroxyprogesterone acetate injection. A single-rod progestin implant is now available in the United States that provides contraception for 3 years. Progesterone-only contraceptives are alternatives for women who cannot take estrogen because of breastfeeding or estrogen side effects.

Two types of pills are available for emergency contraception. Both must be taken within 5 days of a risked pregnancy. Levonorgestrel is the preferred formulation because it is more efficacious and has the fewest side effects. The second option is a combination of ethinyl estradiol and levonorgestrel.

STUDY TABLE: Nonhormonal Contraceptives	
Method	**Important Notes**
Cervical cap	Protects against pelvic infection and cervical dysplasia
	Alternative to diaphragm for diaphragm-induced, recurrent urinary tract infections
Diaphragm	Protects against pelvic infection and cervical dysplasia
Male condom	As effective as oral contraceptives when used with spermicide
IUD	Contraindicated in women with a history of pelvic infection
Copper IUD	Effective for 10 years
	Can cause bleeding and cramping
Levonorgestrel IUD	Effective for 5 years
	Decreases period-related bleeding and cramping
IUD = intrauterine device.	

◆ DON'T BE TRICKED

- Spermicides do not prevent the spread of STDs and may actually increase the spread of AIDS and should be avoided by women at high risk for HIV.

Gestational Diabetes Mellitus

Screening

GDM is diagnosed during pregnancy. The U.S. Preventive Services Task Force and the Canadian Task Force on Preventive Health Care have determined evidence for or against screening for diabetes during pregnancy is insufficient. The American Diabetes Association (ADA) recommends screening as soon as pregnancy is recognized in patients at high risk, including those with:

- marked obesity
- glycosuria
- history of GDM during previous pregnancies
- family history of diabetes

If screening is undertaken, it involves measurement of the plasma glucose concentration 1 hour after administration of a 50-g oral glucose load. If the 1-hour value is ≥140 mg/dL, a formal oral glucose tolerance test is performed. If it is >200 mg/dL, GDM is diagnosed. The ADA recommends testing not be performed for patients at low risk, who have the following characteristics:

- younger than 25 years
- normal prepregnancy weight
- no family history of diabetes
- not a member of a high-risk ethnic group
- no history of abnormal glucose testing or poor obstetric outcomes

GDM is associated with increased risk of fetal macrosomia, neonatal hypoglycemia, jaundice, polycythemia, and hypocalcemia. Maternal hypertensive disorders and the need for cesarean section are increased. Importantly, women with GDM are also at increased risk for diabetes after pregnancy (approximately 50% within 10 years of delivery). The ADA recommends a repeat oral glucose tolerance test 6 weeks postpartum, with ongoing periodic surveillance.

Abbreviations

5-ASA	5-aminosalicylic acid
5-FU	5-fluorouracil
5-HIAA	5-hydroxyindoleacetic acid
6-MP	6-mercaptopurine
A-a	alveolar-arterial oxygen gradient
AAA	abdominal aortic aneurysm
AAT	α_1-antitrypsin
ABG	arterial blood gas
ABI	ankle-brachial index
ABVD	doxorubicin (Adriamycin), bleomycin, vinblastine, dacarbazine
ACE inhibitor	angiotensin-converting enzyme inhibitor
ACS	acute coronary syndrome; acute chest syndrome
ACTH	adrenocorticotropic hormone
ADHD	attention-deficit/hyperactivity disorder
ADPKD	autosomal dominant polycystic kidney disease
AF	atrial fibrillation
AFLP	acute fatty liver of pregnancy
AFP	α-fetoprotein
AGEP	acute generalized exanthematous pustulosis
AIDS	acquired immunodeficiency syndrome
AIN	acute interstitial nephritis
AKI	acute kidney injury
ALI	acute lung injury
ALL	acute lymphoblastic leukemia/lymphoma
ALS	amyotrophic lateral sclerosis
ALT	alanine aminotransferase
AML	acute myeloid leukemia
ANA	antinuclear antibody
anti-CCP	anti–cyclic citrullinated peptide
anti-dsDNA	anti–double-stranded DNA
anti-HBc	antibodies to hepatitis B core antigen
anti-HBe	antibodies to hepatitis B e antigen
anti-HBs	antibodies to hepatitis B surface antigen
anti-RNP	antiribonucleoprotein
anti-Sm	anti-Smith
AOSD	adult-onset Still disease
aPTT	activated partial thromboplastin time
AR	aortic regurgitation; absolute risk
ARB	angiotensin receptor blocker
ARDS	acute respiratory distress syndrome
ARR	absolute risk reduction
ART	antiretroviral therapy
AS	aortic stenosis
ASCA	anti–*Saccharomyces cerevisiae* antibodies
ASD	atrial septal defect
AST	aspartate aminotransferase
ATN	acute tubular necrosis
ATRA	all-*trans*-retinoic acid
AUDIT	Alcohol Use Disorders Identification Test
AV	atrioventricular
AVM	arteriovenous malformation
BCG	bacille Calmette-Guérin
β-hCG	beta-human chorionic gonadotropin
BID	twice daily
BMI	body mass index
BNP	B-type natriuretic peptide
BOOP	bronchiolitis obliterans organizing pneumonia
BPH	benign prostatic hyperplasia
BUN	blood urea nitrogen
CABG	coronary artery bypass graft surgery
CAD	coronary artery disease
c-ANCA	cytoplasmic antineutrophil cytoplasmic antibody

CAP	community-acquired pneumonia
CAUTI	catheter-associated urinary tract infection
CBC	complete blood count
CF	cystic fibrosis
CFS	chronic fatigue syndrome
CH_{50}	total hemolytic complement
CHD	coronary heart disease
CI	confidence interval
CK	creatine kinase
CKD	chronic kidney disease
CLL	chronic lymphocytic leukemia
CML	chronic myeloid leukemia
CMR	cardiac magnetic resonance (imaging)
CMV	cytomegalovirus
CNS	central nervous system
COP	cryptogenic organizing pneumonia
COPD	chronic obstructive pulmonary disease
CPAP	continuous positive airway pressure
CPDD	calcium pyrophosphate deposition disease
CPPD	calcium pyrophosphate dihydrate
CRP	C-reactive protein
CSF	cerebrospinal fluid
CT	computed tomography
CTA	computed tomography angiography
CTEPH	chronic thromboembolic pulmonary hypertension
CUP	carcinoma of unknown primary
CVI	common variable immunodeficiency
CVP	central venous pressure
DBP	diastolic blood pressure
DDAVP	1-deamino-8-D-arginine vasopressin
DEXA	dual energy x-ray absorptiometry
DHEAS	dehydroepiandrosterone sulfate
DI	diabetes insipidus
DIC	disseminated intravascular coagulation
DIP	distal interphalangeal
DISH	diffuse idiopathic skeletal hyperostosis
DKA	diabetic ketoacidosis
D_{LCO}	diffusing capacity of lung for carbon monoxide
DMARD	disease-modifying antirheumatic drug
DRESS	drug reaction with eosinophilia and systemic symptoms
DVT	deep venous thrombosis
E. coli O157:H7	enterohemorrhagic *Escherichia coli*
EA	early antigen
EBNA	Epstein-Barr nuclear antigen
EBV	Epstein-Barr virus
ECG	electrocardiogram
EDTA	ethylenediaminetetraacetic acid
EEG	electroencephalogram
EF	ejection fraction
EHEC	enterohemorrhagic *Escherichia coli* O157:H7
ELISA	enzyme-linked immunosorbent assay
EMG	electromyography
EN	erythema nodosum
ENT	ear, nose, and throat
ERCP	endoscopic retrograde cholangiopancreatography
ESLD	end-stage liver disease
ESR	erythrocyte sedimentation rate
FAB	French-American-British (classification system)
FE_{Na}	fractional excretion of sodium
FEV_1	forced expiratory volume in 1 second
FFP	fresh frozen plasma
F_{IO_2}	fraction of inspired oxygen

FMF	familial Mediterranean fever
FNAB	fine-needle aspiration biopsy
FOBT	fecal occult blood testing
FSH	follicle-stimulating hormone
FTA-ABS	fluorescent treponemal antibody absorption
FVC	forced vital capacity
G6PD	glucose 6-phosphate dehydrogenase
GAHS	Glasgow Alcoholic Hepatitis Score
GBM	glomerular basement membrane
GDM	gestational diabetes mellitus
GE	gastroesophageal
GERD	gastroesophageal reflux disease
GFR	glomerular filtration rate
GH	growth hormone
GI	gastrointestinal
GU	genitourinary
GVHD	graft-versus-host disease
H_2 receptor blocker	histamine-2 receptor antagonist
HACE	high-altitude cerebral edema
HAE	hereditary angioedema
HAP	hospital-acquired pneumonia
HAPE	high-altitude pulmonary edema
HAV	hepatitis A virus
HBeAg	hepatitis B e antigen
HBIG	hepatitis B immune globulin
HBsAg	hepatitis B surface antigen
HBV	hepatitis B virus
HCM	hypertrophic cardiomyopathy
HCV	hepatitis C virus
HDL	high-density lipoprotein
HELLP	hemolysis, elevated liver enzyme levels, and a low platelet count
HF	heart failure
HGA	human granulocytic anaplasmosis
HIDA	hepatobiliary iminodiacetic acid
HIPAA	Health Insurance Portability and Accountability Act
HIT	heparin-induced thrombocytopenia
HITT	heparin-induced thrombocytopenia with thrombosis
HIV	human immunodeficiency virus
HLA	human leukocyte antigens
HME	human monocytic ehrlichiosis
HNPCC	hereditary nonpolyposis colorectal cancer
HPA	human platelet antigen
HPV	human papillomavirus
HRCT	high-resolution CT
HSCT	hematopoietic stem cell transplantation
HSV	herpes simplex virus
HUS	hemolytic uremic syndrome
IBD	inflammatory bowel disease
IBS	irritable bowel syndrome
ICD	implantable cardioverter defibrillator
ICH	intracerebral hemorrhage
ICU	intensive care unit
IE	infective endocarditis
IGF-I	insulin-like growth factor 1
IgM anti-HAV	IgM antibodies to hepatitis A virus
IGRA	interferon-γ release assays
IM	intramuscular
INR	international normalized ratio
IRIS	immune reconstitution inflammatory syndrome
ITP	immune thrombocytopenic purpura
IV	intravenous
IVC	inferior vena cava
KOH	potassium hydroxide
LAD	left anterior descending (coronary artery)
LBBB	left bundle-branch block
LDH	lactate dehydrogenase
LDL	low-density lipoprotein
LES	lower esophageal sphincter
LH	luteinizing hormone
LHRH	luteinizing hormone-releasing hormone
LKM	liver-kidney microsome
LMWH	low-molecular-weight heparin
LR	likelihood ratio
LTBI	latent tuberculosis infection
LV	left ventricular
LVEF	left ventricular ejection fraction
LVH	left ventricular hypertrophy
LVRS	lung volume reduction surgery
MALT	mucosa-associated lymphoid tissue
MAOIs	monoamine oxidase inhibitors
MAP	mean arterial pressure
MCP	metacarpophalangeal
MCHC	mean corpuscular hemoglobin concentration
MCTD	mixed connective tissue disease
MCV	mean corpuscular volume
MDF	Maddrey Discriminant Function
MDRD	Modification of Diet in Renal Disease
MDS	myelodysplastic syndromes
MELD	Model for End-Stage Liver Disease
MEN	multiple endocrine neoplasia
MET	metabolic equivalent
MG	myasthenia gravis
MGUS	monoclonal gammopathy of undetermined significance
MHA-TP	microhemagglutination assay for *Treponema pallidum* antibodies
MI	myocardial infarction
MIBG	metaiodobenzylguanidine
MICU	medical intensive care unit
MMR	measles, mumps, rubella
MPGN	membranoproliferative glomerulonephritis
MPO	myeloperoxidase
MR	mitral regurgitation
MRA	magnetic resonance angiography
MRCP	magnetic resonance cholangiopancreatography
MRI	magnetic resonance imaging
MRSA	methicillin-resistant *Staphylococcus aureus*
MS	mitral stenosis; multiple sclerosis
MSSA	methicillin-susceptible *Staphylococcus aureus*
MTP	metatarsophalangeal
MVP	mitral valve prolapse
NAFLD	nonalcoholic fatty liver disease
NALD	nonalcoholic liver disease
NASH	nonalcoholic steatohepatitis
NMO	neuromyelitis optica
NNH	number needed to harm
NNRTIs	non-nucleoside reverse transcriptase inhibitors
NNT	number needed to treat
NPH	intermediate-acting insulin or Lente
NPV	negative predictive value
NPPV	noninvasive positive-pressure ventilation
NRTIs	nucleoside reverse transcriptase inhibitors
NSAIDs	nonsteroidal anti-inflammatory drugs
NSCLC	non–small cell lung cancer
NSTEMI	non–ST-segment elevation myocardial infarction
NYHA	New York Heart Association
OA	osteoarthritis
OCP	oral contraceptive pill
OR	odds ratio
OSA	obstructive sleep apnea
PAD	peripheral arterial disease
p-ANCA	perinuclear antineutrophil cytoplasmic antibodies
PCI	percutaneous coronary intervention
PCOS	polycystic ovary syndrome
PCR	polymerase chain reaction
PDE-5	phosphodiesterase type 5
PDSA	Plan-Do-Study-Act
PE	pulmonary embolism
PEEP	positive end-expiratory pressure
PEF	peak expiratory flow
PEG	percutaneous endoscopic gastrostomy

PET	positron emission tomography		STEMI	ST-segment elevation myocardial infarction
PID	pelvic inflammatory disease		STI	sexually transmitted infection
PIP	proximal interphalangeal		SVT	supraventricular tachycardia
PMDD	premenstrual dysphoric disorder		T_3	triiodothyronine
PMN	polymorphonuclear		T_4	free thyroxine
PMS	premenstrual syndrome		TB	tuberculosis
PNH	paroxysmal nocturnal hemoglobinuria		TBW	total body water
PPD	purified protein derivative		Tdap	diphtheria and reduced tetanus toxoids and acellular pertussis vaccine
PPI	proton pump inhibitor			
PPV	positive predictive value		TEE	transesophageal echocardiography
PSA	prostate-specific antigen		TEN	toxic epidermal necrolysis
PT	prothrombin time		TIA	transient ischemic attack
PTH	parathyroid hormone		TIBC	total iron-binding capacity
PTSD	posttraumatic stress disorder		TID	three times daily
PTT	partial thromboplastin time		TIMI	Thrombolysis in Myocardial Infarction (risk score)
PUD	peptic ulcer disease		TIPS	transjugular intrahepatic portosystemic shunt
PV	polycythemia vera		TLC	total lung capacity
PVC	premature ventricular complex		TNF	tumor necrosis factor
QTc	calculated QT		tPA	tissue plasminogen activator
RA	rheumatoid arthritis		TPN	total parenteral nutrition
RADT	rapid antigen detection test		TPPA	*Treponema pallidum* particle agglutination assay
RAST	radioallergosorbent test		TR	tricuspid regurgitation
RBBB	right bundle-branch block		TRALI	transfusion-related acute lung injury
RCRI	Revised Cardiac Risk Index		TSH	thyroid-stimulating hormone
RDW	red cell distribution width		TST	tuberculin skin testing
RF	rheumatic fever		TTE	transthoracic echocardiography
RLS	restless legs syndrome		TTP	thrombotic thrombocytopenic purpura
RMSF	Rocky Mountain spotted fever		TURP	transurethral resection of the prostate
ROC	receiver operating characteristic		UACS	upper airway cough syndrome
RR	relative risk		UAG	urinary anion gap
RTA	renal tubular acidosis		UFH	unfractionated heparin
rtPA	recombinant tissue plasminogen activator		UGI	upper gastrointestinal
RUQ	right upper quadrant		ULN	upper limit of normal
RV	right ventricular		URI	upper respiratory tract infection
SAAG	serum-ascites albumin gradient		UTI	urinary tract infection
SAH	subarachnoid hemorrhage		VAP	ventilator-associated pneumonia
SBP	systolic blood pressure; spontaneous bacterial peritonitis		VCA	viral capsid antigen
			VDRL	Venereal Diseases Research Laboratory
SC	subcutaneous		VF	ventricular fibrillation
SCAR	severe cutaneous adverse reactions		Vo_2	low peak oxygen uptake
SCC	squamous cell carcinoma		V/Q	ventilation/perfusion
SCLC	small cell lung cancer		vs.	versus
SIADH	syndrome of inappropriate antidiuretic hormone secretion		VSD	ventricular septal defect
			VT	ventricular tachycardia
SICU	surgical intensive care unit		VTE	venous thromboembolism
SIRS	systemic inflammatory response syndrome		vWD	von Willebrand disease
SJS	Stevens-Johnson syndrome		vWF	von Willebrand factor
SLE	systemic lupus erythematosus		WHO	World Health Organization
SRA	serotonin release assay		WPW	Wolff-Parkinson-White
SSRI	selective serotonin reuptake inhibitor		x-ray	radiograph